The Foreign Policies of

FRANCE

1944–1968

The Foreign Policies of

FRANCE

1944 – 1968

Guy de Carmoy

Translated by Elaine P. Halperin

The University of Chicago Press

CHICAGO & LONDON

Revised and translated from the French Les Politiques
étrangères de la France, 1944–1966. © *1967 by Editions de la
Table Ronde. Published by La Table Ronde, Paris 7ᵉ
Standard Book Number 226–13991–3
Library of Congress Catalog Card Number: 71–85446
The University of Chicago Press, Chicago 60637
The University of Chicago Press, Ltd., London
English translation © 1970 by The University of Chicago
All rights reserved. Published 1970
Printed in the United States of America*

CONTENTS

v]

III · *Decolonization*

BOOK TWO / THE FIFTH REPUBLIC

I · *Decolonization and Cooperation*

II · *Defense and Alliances*

III · *Europe*

Contents

PREFACE

To WRITE A HISTORY of recent foreign policy is not easy, but I believe it can and should be done. Difficulties arise because the diplomatic archives are closed and the public figures involved in the action, or hoping to plunge back into it, are reticent and concerned about their image.

Nevertheless, the task is feasible. Documentary collections and political yearbooks provide the essential facts. Modern communications media supply speeches, communiqués, and press comments. Scholarly works abound.

The task is certainly necessary. With the progress now being made in the dissemination and democratization of education, foreign policy must not remain an esoteric subject. Many men with administrative or economic responsibilities continue to entertain illusions about the real relationship of power in the international world. They are unable to foresee sudden reversals or assess the importance of certain movements.

Three major trends have altered the realities of international politics during recent decades. The first has to do with the nature of alliances. The multipolar system of the balance of European powers, inherited from the Treaty of Vienna and undermined in 1918, disappeared in 1945. The major nation-states of Europe ceased to be "powers." Only the extra-European continent-states enjoyed the right to be so designated. The world became polarized around the United States and the Soviet Union. Industrial technology, coupled with vastness of territory, population, and investments, fashioned a new hierarchy of states in terms of armaments. Medium-sized nations like France had to align themselves, at least for a while, with one of the two superpowers.

The second trend was decolonization. The principal European states, notably England, had been "colonial powers." The continent-states backed the worldwide movement toward the liberation of peoples. Former colonies acquired the status of sovereign states, but they often exchanged one form of dependence for another. France resisted this movement and waged two wars against decolonization.

The third trend derives from the two preceding ones. Deprived of their possessions or, at any rate, wielding less influence overseas, and exhausted by two domestic wars within the space of two generations, the European states felt the need for some sort of understanding. It was in Western Europe, a zone enjoying the generous protection of the United States, that the movement for European economic and political unity began. A compensatory reaching out for power, or an effort to safeguard a certain kind of civilization, this movement experienced both successes and failures. France shared in it, acting now as a catalyst, now as a brake.

All three trends were fused under the two regimes that prevailed in France from 1944 to 1968. They represent the essence of this book, which is divided into two parts. The first deals with the foreign policy of the Fourth Republic, the second with that of the Fifth.

I have used the plural in the title of the book to emphasize the fact that French foreign policy did not pursue a single objective during the period under consideration. Ever since the Provisional Government of the French Republic, General de Gaulle has followed a path that at times was sinuous but whose general direction has not varied. During his interregnum, the Fourth Republic followed a different path. Such, in any case, is my interpretation of recent French diplomatic history.

My method in presenting this material is quite simple. It consists in describing the facts and contrasting antithetical theses. Accordingly, I cite both protagonists and observers before offering a commentary. I hope in this way to be as objective as possible. At the same time I will not withhold my own convictions.

I would like to express my gratitude to my colleagues at the Paris Institut d'études politiques, Raoul Girardet and Pierre Gerbet. Trained in history, they helped me with their advice while the book was being written. I owe them a great deal.

The Foreign Policies of
F R A N C E

1944-1968

INTRODUCTION

The Domestic Policy of the
Fourth Republic

The Preliminary Phase (1944–1947)

H EAD OF THE PROVISIONAL GOVERNMENT of the French Republic
from June 1944 onward, General de Gaulle included in his cabinet
politicians of the Third Republic who belonged to the old political parties,
notably the Communists. He ruled without an assembly until the Constituent
Assembly elections of October 21, 1945.

The losers in this contest were the traditional Right, because of Vichy,
and the Radicals, because of Munich. The winners were three political parties
of approximately equal strength—the Communists, the Socialists, and the
Catholic Mouvement Républicain Populaire (M.R.P.). Together the Communists and Socialists had an absolute majority—302 of the 586 seats.

Although unanimously elected head of the government, de Gaulle at once
collided with a party system of which he disapproved. He resigned on
January 20, 1946.

Thereupon power was assumed not by a Socialist-Communist Popular
Front but by a tripartite combination comprising Socialists, Communists, and
the M.R.P., and headed by a Socialist president, Félix Gouin.

The three parties did not agree about the constitution. The draft submitted to a referendum on May 5, 1946, established a regime of government
by assembly. The M.R.P., the Radicals, and the Right opposed it. The draft
was rejected by the electorate.

This introduction, specially written for the English-language edition, was inspired
by Jacques Fauvet's book La IVᵉ République (Paris:Arthème Fayard, 1959).

A second Constituent Assembly was elected on June 2, 1946. The Socialists lost ground and the M.R.P. gained. This made it the strongest political party in the Assembly. One of its members, Georges Bidault, became head of the government. A second draft of the constitution was prepared. It retained many of the features of a government by assembly and eliminated the authoritarian regime de Gaulle had advocated in his Bayeux speech on June 16, 1946.

Although violently attacked by de Gaulle, the second draft of the constitution was adopted by the electorate on October 13, 1946. The National Assembly elected on November 10, 1946, showed a further loss for the Socialists and a gain in Communist strength. The M.R.P.'s representation was virtually unchanged.

On January 21, 1947, after Léon Blum's brief premiership, the Assembly chose a Socialist, Paul Ramadier, as the head of the government. Another Socialist Vincent Auriol was elected president of the Republic on January 16.

Under Ramadier, the Assembly's influence on the government increased. The problems facing the nation were both military and economic; the war in Indochina had begun, and inflation had been steadily mounting since the Liberation. A conflict over military appropriations and salary policies arose between the Communist ministers and their colleagues. It ended on May 5, 1947, with the eviction of the Communists from the government.

Meanwhile, the failure of the Moscow Conference on April 24 underscored the split between East and West and the emergence of two antagonistic blocs. One was led by the Soviet Union; the other was headed by the United States. Abandoning de Gaulle's neutralism and his attempts to arbitrate between the two superpowers, France joined the Western camp. Thus ended the first phase of the Fourth Republic, a phase in which France was trying to find herself, as Jacques Fauvet put it.

The Plateau (1947–1952)

The second phase of the Fourth Republic was highlighted by the existence of a twofold opposition consisting of Communists and Gaullists. The other political parties, dedicated to parliamentary rule, became known as the Third Force. The term, however, is imprecise. The groups that composed the Third Force were less well organized and disciplined than the opposition.

Internally, the Third Force had first to contend with a series of strikes. These, backed by the Communists, lasted from June 1947 to December 1948. They were precipitated by a 100 per cent increase in prices, insufficient production, and a decline in the purchasing power of wages.

On the question of the colonies, the Third Force, in refusing in 1947 to negotiate with Ho Chi-minh, had thereby lost the chance of resolving the Indochinese problem peacefully.

[4

In foreign affairs, the M.R.P. and the Socialists worked for European unification.

The ministerial instability persisted. The Ramadier cabinet fell on November 19, 1947, only to be succeeded by the Robert Schuman cabinet, which fell on July 19, 1948. A prolonged crisis ensued with two more cabinets that lasted only a few days, until the investiture on September 11 of the Radical premier, Henri Queuille, a veteran of the Third Republic. Queuille fell on October 6, 1949. Georges Bidault served in his place until June 24, 1950. Another crisis ensued, with a ministry that lasted two days. René Pleven became premier July 13, 1950. He too was overthrown, on February 28, 1951. Finally, Queuille was brought back on March 10, 1951, and remained in office until the end of the legislature's term.

The most constructive move on the part of the Third Force during this period was Robert Schuman's declaration of May 9, 1950, which sealed France's reconciliation with Germany. The Pleven and Queuille cabinets engaged in a delaying action against America's determination to rearm Germany.

The Queuille cabinet managed to have a law passed whose purpose was to strengthen the Third Force political parties at the expense of the Communists and Gaullists. An effort was made to form political alliances that would prevent a division of the next Assembly into three factions—Gaullists, Communists, and the Third Force. No two of these would have been capable of governing.

In the legislative elections of June 17, 1951, the M.R.P. was deserted by half of its supporters. The Socialists continued to lose ground. The Radicals and the Moderates held their own, whereas the Rassemblement du Peuple Français (R.P.F.), led by de Gaulle, obtained 20 per cent of the vote. It was now the second strongest party, surpassed only by the Communists who received 26 per cent of the vote. But in terms of seats the Gaullists and the Communists were effectively penalized by the recently enacted electoral law.

Nevertheless, the new Assembly never managed to muster a consistent Third Force majority. The situation fluctuated according to the question under consideration.

For example, on the issue of aid to private, that is to say, Catholic, schools, the R.P.F. deputies voted with the government whereas the Socialists and two-thirds of the Radicals joined the opposition.

The Communists and the R.P.F. voted against ratification of the treaty creating the European Coal and Steel Community whereas all the Socialist, M.R.P., Radical, and Moderate deputies banded together to form a majority.

The opening of the second legislature was followed by more ministerial instability. René Pleven became premier on August 11, 1951, and again on January 7, 1952. Edgar Faure's cabinet did not last forty days. Antoine Pinay assumed the premiership on March 8, 1952. He was the first Moderate to hold office. Twenty-seven dissident Gaullist deputies supported him; the Socialists were part of the opposition. Pinay inspired confidence by halting inflation temporarily. His ministry was the bridge from the second to the third phase of the Fourth Republic, the period when it foundered.

The Decline (1952–1958)

The final phase of the Fourth Republic was marked by a preponderance of foreign policy problems, and by a steady growth in the role of the Gaullist opposition, which obstructed both European unification and the emancipation of the colonies.

The Treaty of the European Defense Community (E.D.C.), signed on May 27, 1952, was attacked by the opponents of German rearmament and the adversaries of supranational institutions. Paradoxically enough, Premier Pinay was overthrown on December 23, 1952, because the M.R.P. failed to support him. They reproached Pinay for failing to place the treaty before the Assembly. The new premier, René Mayer, was a Radical. The votes of a number of Gaullist deputies made his investiture possible. In order to obtain them, Mayer had to promise that he would add some protocols to the treaty. Nonetheless, the Gaullists soon withdrew their support. Mayer was overthrown on May 21.

The ministerial crisis lasted several weeks. Finally, on June 28, 1953, the premiership was assumed by Joseph Laniel, a Moderate. His cabinet included Gaullist ministers who could oppose the treaty from within the government. Under Laniel, the political and military situation in Indochina deteriorated. The climactic defeat came at DienBienPhu on May 7, 1954. The Laniel cabinet fell on June 12, while the major powers were holding a conference on what to do about Indochina.

For a long time Pierre Mendès-France had been advocating a negotiated peace in Indochina. He took office on June 18, 1954. Because of the large majority that had invested him with the premiership, he could do without the support of the Communists. The antagonism between Mendès-France and Georges Bidault, foreign minister in the Laniel cabinet, was so great that the M.R.P. deputies joined neither the government nor the parliamentary majority. The Geneva accords on an armistice in Indochina were signed on July 31. Immediately afterward, Mendès-France went to Brussels. There he made a vain attempt to persuade France's partners to amend the E.D.C. Treaty. It was rejected by the National Assembly on August 30. The government had taken a firm stand. The "Europeanists" reproached the premier for his ambiguity. On February 3, 1955, in the course of a debate on North Africa, Mendès-France was voted out of office.

The Algerian rebellion broke out on November 1, 1954. For several

[6

years it was to dominate French political life. Mendès-France's successor, Edgar Faure, was also a member of the Radical party. As minister of finance for almost two years, he had managed to keep prices stable. Now, as premier, he devoted all his efforts to a solution of the Moroccan problem. When his ministry failed on November 29, 1956, he invoked a provision of the constitution to dissolve the Assembly.

Guy Mollet and Pierre Mendès-France quickly formed an alliance. They established a "Republican Front" composed of Socialists and Mendès-France Radicals. But they had no real program. The law on political alliances was still in effect, but the discord between the political parties produced proportional representation in many of the provinces. In the legislative elections of January 2, 1957, the Communists and Socialists held their own; the Radicals and Moderates registered slight gains. More than half of the considerable ground lost by the Gaullists was captured by a new political party. It was nationalist and anti-parliamentarian, and comprised discontented peasants, small businessmen, and craftsmen from the poorer districts. These were the "Poujadists" who had taken their name from Pierre Poujade, a shopkeeper from the Massif Central. The Right Center parties lost their majority. The Left Center parties of the "Republican Front" remained a minority. On February 2, 1956, they formed a new cabinet headed by Guy Mollet. Mendès-France, denied the post of foreign minister, refused the portfolio of finance minister, which went to Paul Ramadier.

The implementation of the government's social program, to say nothing of the Algerian war, produced a rise in prices and a deficit in the balance of payments. The monetary reserves were exhausted. The cabinet resigned on May 15, 1957. Its fall was due presumably to the Moderates' criticism of its financial policies but actually to its failure to impose war controls on the economy at a time when the conscripts were being sent to Algeria.

No government, however, could be formed without the Socialists. Maurice Bourgès-Maunoury, a member of the Radical party, succeeded Guy Mollet. He managed, despite heavy Communist and Gaullist opposition, to marshal a majority in support of the Treaty of Rome, which created the Common Market. But he too fell, on September 9, 1957, after urging adoption of the "Loi Cadre," a slightly more liberal statute for Algeria that was soon to become superfluous.

As leader of the Gaullists, Jacques Soustelle had spearheaded the attack against Bourgès-Maunoury. Now he harassed Félix Gaillard, Bourgès-Maunoury's successor and like him a member of the Radical party. Gaillard pushed through an adulterated statute for Algeria and announced the devaluation of the franc—already an accomplished fact. The two last cabinets had only a semblance of power. Algiers controlled Paris. The *colons* and the army were in rebellion against the mother country. The final vestiges of

7]

authority disappeared when Félix Gaillard, defeated on April 15, 1958, by the combined forces of Communists and Moderates, was replaced on May 13, 1958, by a member of the M.R.P., Pierre Pflimlin. On the day of Pflimlin's accession, the plot against the Fourth Republic exploded in Algiers. Members of the National Assembly were afraid that Algerian army parachutists would land in Paris. Charles de Gaulle appeared as the only alternative to a military *putsch*. No one stood up to defend a discredited regime. Pflimlin resigned on May 28. On June 1 the Assembly vested authority in de Gaulle. The Fifth Republic was about to begin.

BOOK ONE

THE
FOURTH
REPUBLIC

I

Defense and Alliances

1

From One Enemy to Another

Peace Aims in Wartime

IN 1939 AN INTRA-EUROPEAN WAR pitted the four principal nation-states against each other—France and England against Germany and Italy. In 1945 a world war pitted Germany and Japan against the two extra-European continent-states—the United States and the Soviet Union. Compared with these powers, England seemed a minor partner and France a supernumerary.

The Provisional Government of the French Republic was not recognized until October 1944. Its army, equipped by America, participated in Europe's campaigns of liberation.

The United States and the Soviet Union were in agreement on war aims: the destruction of the totalitarian regimes in Germany and Japan; the liberation of the occupied territories. But they disagreed on the peace aims.

The United States favored the establishment of a world organization founded on collective security. At the wartime interallied conferences it made an all-out effort on behalf of the drafting of a United Nations Charter. It was not seeking hegemony either in Europe or in the Far East. It resisted Soviet proposals that the two superpowers should divide spheres of influence between them. But Roosevelt believed that "in order to make a friend of Stalin, he would have to show him friendship."

The Soviet Union had every intention of satisfying its national ambitions. To that end it made use of Marxist-Leninist ideology. As early as March 1941, Stalin declared at the Moscow Conference that Eastern Europe must become part of the Russian sphere of influence and that the frontiers of Poland must

13]

be pushed westward at Germany's expense. In December 1943, the Americans and British agreed at Teheran to allow the Russians to keep the territories they had annexed in 1939, under the terms of the Nazi-Soviet Pact: the Baltic states and eastern Poland. In October 1944, they consented at Moscow to the Armistice conventions signed by the Soviet Union with Rumania, Bulgaria, Hungary, and Finland. Two of the conventions provided for cessions of territory (Rumania and Finland), and all the conventions provided for military occupation. An accord between Stalin and Beneš altered Czechoslovakia's frontiers for the benefit of the Soviet Union. Thus, in the midst of war, Russia annexed European territory the size of France with half her population (500,000 square kilometers and 23,000,000 inhabitants). Russia's new frontiers enabled her to dominate all the area conquered by her armies. The Yalta Conference of February 1945 gave the Soviet Union a protectorate over Poland and all of Eastern Europe. The Americans agreed to divide Europe into spheres of influence. Thus, even before Germany's capitulation, Russia achieved most of her peace aims in Europe. Having recovered the territorial power of the tsars, through new frontiers and spheres of influence, she could once again influence the destiny of Europe.

The Status of Germany and Europe

Roosevelt's decision, at Casablanca in 1943, to demand the unconditional surrender of Germany had grave consequences. It strengthened the faltering German army's will to resist and facilitated Soviet conquests by the prolongation of the war. It pitted Americans and Russians against each other in Europe.

In October 1943 the Allies decided at Moscow to occupy all of Germany. In November 1943 they discussed the partition of Germany at Teheran. In October 1944 they agreed at Quebec to create three zones of occupation and to occupy Berlin jointly. At Yalta the partition of Germany was again discussed. On May 8, 1945, Stalin proclaimed that the Soviet Union had no intention of dismembering Germany. On June 5, 1945, the Allied military command announced that there was no longer a central government in Germany and that it would assume supreme command of the country.

At the Potsdam Conference in August 1945 the British and Americans gave *de facto* recognition to the Oder-Neisse line as the border between Germany and Poland; they authorized the transfer of German inhabitants to the west of this line. Each commander-in-chief of the occupying troops assumed supreme authority over the area he controlled. Meanwhile, at meetings in Berlin of the Control Council, the commanders-in-chief made decisions affecting all of Germany; each member could exercise the veto power. Finally, a Council of Foreign Ministers was charged with working out peace treaties for Germany as well as for her former allies and for Austria, which was to be restored to independence.

Germany thus became the stake about which the two superpowers were to negotiate. There was of course latent rivalry in a disarmed, divided, and occupied Europe.

Roosevelt died on April 12, 1945. Edward Stettinius, the American secretary of state, observed in his report to the incoming president of the United States: "Since the Yalta Conference, the Soviet Government has taken a firm and uncompromising position on nearly every major question that has arisen in our relations."[1] On April 4, Averell Harriman, the American ambassador to Moscow, telegraphed that "the Communist Party or its associates everywhere are using economic difficulties in areas under our responsibilities to promote Soviet concepts and policies and to undermine the influence of the Western allies."[2]

As early as May 12, 1945, Churchill expressed his anxiety to Truman: "What will the situation be in one or two years? By then the American and British armies will have disappeared, the French will not be sufficiently organized, whereas Russia might very well decide to keep two or three hundred active divisions." And he added, in alluding to the Russians: "An iron curtain has been lowered on their front. We know nothing about what is happening behind it. It seems highly probable that the rest of the area east of the Lübeck-Trieste-Corfu line will soon be in their hands." Actually, the number of American, British, and Canadian troops in Europe decreased from five million at the time of capitulation to less than one million in 1946, whereas the Soviet Union kept four million men under arms.

The inequality in political strength was just as great. "National front" organizations were set up in Eastern Europe. The Communist Party made short shrift of the old democratic parties. In Western Europe, the Communist Party was represented in the governments of Italy, France, and eight other countries.

The Status of France

The Provisional Government of the French Republic, inaugurated in Paris in August 1944, was formally recognized by the Allies on October 23. Asked to comment on this recognition, General de Gaulle icily remarked at a press conference on October 25: "The French government is satisfied to note that it is being called by its name."[3] What was to be the status of France?

[1] Harry S. Truman, *Memoirs* (New York: Doubleday & Co., 1955), 15.
[2] James Forrestal, *Diaries* (New York: Viking Press, 1951), 39.
[3] Charles de Gaulle, *Mémoires de guerre* (Paris: Plon, 1959), III, 44.

In spite of the 1940 defeat, would she become a great power, consulted about the fate of Germany and the conduct of world affairs? Who would back the demand for rank to which her leader attached so much importance?

There was abundant evidence of the Soviet Union's hostility to the restoration of France. According to Harry Hopkins, at Teheran Stalin "did not consider that France could be trusted with any strategic positions outside her own borders in the postwar period."[4] At the Dumbarton Oaks Conference in August 1944, it was the Anglo-Saxons who insisted on accepting France as one of the five "great powers" in the future United Nations. France was to have a permanent seat on the Security Council, the organ charged with "the principal responsibility for maintaining peace and international security." Again according to Harry Hopkins, at Yalta the British "fought like tigers for France."[5] It was Churchill who, in opposition to Stalin, pleaded with Roosevelt to give France a zone of occupation in Germany and Austria. It was he, too, who asked that she be made a member of the Control Commissions in Berlin and Vienna. At Potsdam, France was invited by the Allies to join the Council of Foreign Ministers that dealt with European questions.

Thus, thanks to the Anglo-Saxons and in spite of the Russians, France recovered her rank. The smallest of the great powers, she had the prerogatives —a voice in the diplomatic concert—although she lacked the means. She was not responsible for the status of Europe but she shared in the decisions that affected it.

General de Gaulle's Foreign Policy

One man dominated the Provisional Government of the French Republic. He was not shackled by Parliament. What line would he follow in foreign affairs? Would he be the spokesman for a mutilated continental Europe in dealing with the extra-European victors and insular England? Would he lean on England, the weakest but the most European of the Big Three? Because of the inequality of the contending forces, England doubtless wanted France restored to a position of influence in Europe. Or would de Gaulle seek Russian support by renewing the reverse alliance of 1892 against Germany?

De Gaulle chose the latter course. On May 7, 1944, he said in Tunis: "Once the enemy has been defeated, the French will want to be a center of direct and practical cooperation in the West and to make a permanent ally of the good and powerful Russia in the East."[6]

[4] Robert Sherwood, *Roosevelt and Hopkins: An Intimate History* (New York: Harper Bros., 1948), 781–82.

[5] Robert Murphy, *Diplomat among Warriors* (New York: Doubleday & Co., 1964), 237.

[6] Charles de Gaulle, *Discours et messages* (Paris: Berger-Levrault, 1946), 440.

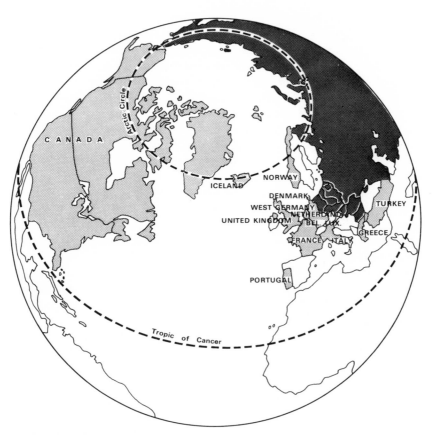

The Atlantic Pact system and
the Warsaw Pact system

In his *Mémoires*, de Gaulle revealed the two reasons for his decision: "Franco-Russian solidarity . . . was nonetheless in harmony with the natural order of things, in view of the German threat and the Anglo-Saxon attempts at hegemony."[7]

His decision becomes clearer when we examine his ideas on the status of Germany and Europe. "No more centralized Reich! In my opinion, this is a necessary condition to prevent the Germans from reverting to their old tendencies." The general spoke in favor of internal autonomy for "each of the states belonging to the Germanic entity"; a special "international status" for the Ruhr; the Saar made into a separate state but joined economically to France. "Thus, the Germanic world, having recovered its diversity and turned toward the West, would lose its potential for war but not its capacity for progress." As for Europe, it "could find equilibrium and peace only by association with Slavs, Germans, Gauls, and Latins. It would doubtless be necessary to take into account the elements of tyranny and desire for conquest that presently existed within the Russian regime." But as soon as Germany was no longer a threat, subordination to Russia would eventually become intolerable to the Eastern nations. "After which, the unity of Europe could be worked out in the form of an organized association of peoples, from Iceland to Istanbul, from Gibraltar to the Urals."[8]

Winston Churchill was the first head of an Allied government to call on de Gaulle. On November 10, 1944, he suggested they examine together the possibility of an Anglo-French alliance. In the course of the discussions, de Gaulle remarked that England did not really want to come to a definite agreement with France on the future of Germany. Furthermore, England shied away from the Near Eastern question. Therefore, he declined to sign a treaty with England. In his opinion, it would not have been based on a common will.

Invited to Moscow, on December 2, the general had a first interview with Marshal Stalin. On the question of Germany's status, Stalin was just as reticent as Churchill. The problems of the Rhine, the Saar, and the Ruhr were to be discussed exclusively in negotiations between the four powers. De Gaulle, on the other hand, was altogether willing to see the eastern frontier of Germany established on the Oder-Neisse line. During de Gaulle's Moscow visit Churchill made a new proposal: a tripartite treaty between Russia, France, and England. De Gaulle rejected it. He felt that "in the face of the German danger, Russia and France should conclude a separate accord because they were more directly and immediately threatened."[9] The Franco-Soviet Pact was signed on December 10. On December 21, explaining "the

[7] De Gaulle, *Mémoires*, III, 54.
[8] *Ibid.*, 46–47.
[9] *Ibid.*, 68.

philosophy of the Franco-Russian alliance" before the Consultative Assembly, de Gaulle asserted: "This pact signifies the desire of Russia and France to collaborate closely in everything that may affect the future of Europe."

In spite of the pact, the future status of Europe was discussed at the Yalta Conference which France did not attend. "I was well aware that it was President Roosevelt who refused to allow France to participate," the general wrote. On January 27, Harry Hopkins was delegated to discuss with de Gaulle the unfortunate relations that existed between the United States and France. The general reminded Hopkins of America's belated intervention in the last two European wars. Concluding the interview, he said: "Frenchmen are under the impression that you no longer consider the greatness of France necessary to the world or to yourselves. . . . If you really want to establish a different basis for relations between America and France it is up to you to do whatever is necessary."[10] On the very day (February 12) that the communiqué on the Yalta Conference was published, de Gaulle received a personal message from Roosevelt inviting him to Algiers. "Roosevelt's invitation seemed ill-timed. . . . I did not feel inclined to confer with the president on the morrow of a conference to which he had refused to invite me. . . . How could I accept a summons from the head of a foreign state to go to a place that was part of our national territory?" Such were the grounds on which de Gaulle based his refusal. He was surprised to learn that it had "aroused considerable feeling in world opinion."[11]

Distrust of England, friendliness toward Russia, tension with the United States—such was the nature, four months after the recognition of the French Republic's Provisional Government, of France's relations with her three allies. In the ensuing months her relations with the "Anglo-Saxons" deteriorated further. As for the Russian alliance, it brought none of the expected rewards.

A dispute arose over an order issued by de Gaulle to General Alphonse Juin to annex small sections of Italian territory. This was contrary to the regulations laid down by the commander-in-chief, General Eisenhower. "While they were discussing it," de Gaulle wrote, "we confronted them with an accomplished fact."[12] Robert Murphy reported that France was not invited to the Potsdam Conference because Truman was outraged over the incident.[13]

On May 31 a more serious quarrel over Syria and Lebanon pitted France against England. The British intervened between France and the states placed under France's mandate. The British sent their ally an ultimatum demanding

[10] *Ibid.*, 81–84.
[11] *Ibid.*, 87–88.
[12] *Ibid.*, 183.
[13] Murphy, *Diplomat among Warriors*, 287.

a cease-fire in Damascus. The French government had already ordered a cease-fire. Was England's move an indication of her desire to weaken de Gaulle politically? The general maintained that it was. In any case, on June 4 he spoke harshly to the British ambassador: "We are not, I acknowledge, in a position to make war upon you at present. But you have outraged France and betrayed the Occident. This cannot be forgotten."[14]

The Consultative Assembly was exceedingly reserved in its support of de Gaulle. "This incident led me to assess the depth of the discord which, contrary to all appearances, separated me from the politicians in regard to our nation's foreign affairs."[15] In the summer of 1945 French public opinion actually favored the conclusion of an Anglo-French pact despite the quarrel over Syria and Lebanon. De Gaulle stood his ground. The day after the Potsdam Conference the general reaffirmed his position on Germany. In a communiqué dated August 10, he stressed his intention of "separating the Rhineland from Germany once and for all." Toward the latter part of August he had an interview with Truman. The American president was not enthusiastic about the proposal to dismember Germany but insisted on the need to feed her. In September, at the London Conference, Georges Bidault presented the French plan for a federal Germany. It was not approved. At a meeting of the Control Commission in Berlin, France vetoed the establishment of a central administration, hoping thereby to achieve the dismemberment of Germany.

In January 1946 General de Gaulle resigned as head of the government.

Rivalry among the Victors

The latent rivalry of the victors was apparent at the Potsdam Conference. Within a short space of time it intensified and widened.

Disputes pitted the United States against the Soviet Union, not only in Europe but in the Far East and throughout the naval and air lanes that linked the eastern Mediterranean to the western shores of the Pacific Ocean—in other words, all around continental Asia.

The unconditional surrender of Japan in August 1945 resulted in a situation similar to the one brought about by Germany's capitulation in May. It created a political void in an area which neither of the two victors could afford to disregard because of its industrial potential and its strategic position. Moreover, the nuclear bombing of Hiroshima highlighted the advent of a new and incomparable weapon which the Americans alone possessed.

The United States and the Soviet Union confronted each other in many parts of the Northern hemisphere. The diplomatic and strategic arena thus

[14] De Gaulle, *Mémoires*, III, 194.
[15] *Ibid.*, 197.

attained planetary dimensions. At the same time, dramatic political changes occurred and power relationships altered.

The two continent-states rose to a position higher than that of the nation-states; the latter had been weakened, some even abolished.

The multipolar system of equilibrium that had prevailed in Europe in 1914, and had persisted to some extent until 1939, tended now to give way throughout the world to a bipolar system. The first system consisted in a "plurality of rival states whose resources, though unequal, did not create a basic disparity." The second was a "configuration of power relations that grouped political units around the two strongest nations."[16]

Russian policy became aggressive and systematic. The Soviets made conquests without waging war in the territories they controlled. They instigated political subversion in these and other territories by disseminating the Marxist-Leninist gospel. In the beginning, American policy was defensive and hesitant. It consisted in combating subversion with economic and military aid. In addition, it aimed at obtaining permission to station American troops at strategic bases. The principle of a free democracy was expounded in an effort to counteract Marxism.

As early as 1945 the Soviet Union became active in the Far East and in the eastern Mediterranean. It occupied Manchuria and North Korea, encouraged guerrilla warfare in Southeast Asia, made territorial demands in Turkey, and participated in the Greek civil war. It also concluded a series of bilateral treaties with the Communist nations of Eastern Europe. These agreements provided for mutual assistance against Germany.

At the Council of Foreign Ministers, at the Control Commission in Berlin, and at the United Nations, the Soviet Union consistently followed a policy of obstructionism based on distrust. American efforts to overcome Russian suspicions were utterly unsuccessful.

In June 1946, at the first meeting of the Control Commission of Atomic Energy at the United Nations, the United States suggested the creation of an international organization for the manufacture and storing of atomic weapons. Known as the Baruch Plan, the proposal was adopted by the majority of the Commission but rejected by the Soviet Union on the ground that it restricted Russian sovereignty. In July 1946, at the Council of Foreign Ministers, the Americans proposed a four-power pact. It would have obliged the United States to guarantee the demilitarization of Germany for twenty-five years. The proposal was rejected. Finally, the Moscow meeting in March 1947 proved a total failure. The Americans and Russians could not agree on reparations, the economic unification of Germany, or the *de jure* recognition of the Oder-Neisse line.

[16] Raymond Aron, *Paix et guerre entre les nations* (Paris: Calmann-Lévy, 1962), 137, 144.

Throughout 1947 the Soviet Union was bent on liquidating the democratic political parties of Rumania, Bulgaria, Hungary, Poland, and Czechoslovakia. Ninety million Europeans were forced to submit to Communist domination.

American reaction to the Russian threat took three forms: the political consolidation of West Germany; the establishment of a barrier in Southern Europe; the erection of a barrier west of the iron curtain.

On September 5, 1946, the American secretary of state, James F. Byrnes, delivered a speech before the forces of occupation and German officialdom. It clearly defined the American reaction to Soviet strategy. Byrnes announced the desire of the United States to enable the German people "to devote their talents and energies, which are considerable, to peaceful activities"; the United States also hoped to give the Germans "the responsibility of managing their own affairs." To this end, Byrnes recommended the creation of a provisional government for all of West Germany. He rejected the idea of separating the Rhineland and the Ruhr from the rest of Germany. Byrnes assured the German people that no decisions were reached at Potsdam in regard to Germany's eastern border. Finally, he promised that the United States would continue to interest itself in the affairs of Europe and that it would maintain its troops in Germany.[17]

The second important American reaction was the congressional decision to give massive aid to Greece and Turkey. On March 12, 1947, President Truman outlined American motives in the following terms: "I believe that it must be the policy of the United States to support free peoples who are resisting attempted subjugation by armed minorities or by outside pressure."

The third reaction had more far-reaching consequences. On June 5, 1947, Secretary of State Marshall launched the idea of a program for European recovery. It was to benefit all of Europe, both Western and Eastern, including the Soviet Union. Stalin rejected the offer of American aid not only for Russia but also for her satellites. The Cominform was created to counter the Marshall Plan. Russia's rejection of American aid resulted in a close entente between the United States and Western Europe.

In 1948 the crystallization of the two rival blocs around the two superpowers became even more pronounced. The Americans, British, and French proceeded to organize economically their three zones of occupation in Germany. They also instituted monetary reform. In the opinion of the Russians, their action spelled separatism. They therefore quit the Control Commission and launched a blockade of West Berlin. The Americans answered the challenge by an air lift. The two rivals, however, showed they were capable of caution. Loath to engage the Russian divisions, the Americans

[17] André Fontaine, *Histoire de la guerre froide* (Paris: Fayard, 1966), 370–71.

did not use force against the blockade. Nor did the Russians employ force against the air lift, for fear of an American thermonuclear bomb.

The system of bipolar equilibrium was thus established.

From the German Threat to the Russian Threat

During the years when Russo-American rivalry was most pronounced and the system of bipolar equilibrium was established, the major obsession of French policy was defense against the German threat. French awareness of the Russian threat was belated and reluctant.

Georges Bidault, de Gaulle's foreign minister and for sixteen months the interpreter of his ideas, functioned in this capacity until July 1948. Although deeply influenced by the nationalist conceptions of his first chief, he gradually developed a more flexible outlook. This was evidenced in his attitude toward Germany and the budding Western Alliance.

The German policy of the Allies was at first inconsistent. "Defeated Germany must be self-sufficient; at the same time she must be deprived of her industrial potential yet pay ample reparations."[18]

As early as 1946, the Americans joined the British in distributing aid to the German population in the Anglo-American zone. The Americans also favored the reduction of reparations, the restoration of German productive capacity, and the repatriation of prisoners of war.

The French wanted to secure economic and strategic advantages. They resorted to delaying tactics on the question of reparations. On December 21, 1946, under the Léon Blum government, the French sought to gain an economic advantage by throwing a tariff cordon around the Saar. They withdrew their demand for the Rhineland, which de Gaulle had put forward. In April 1946, Georges Bidault asked that the Ruhr "be treated as a political entity independent of Germany and placed under international political and economic control." He renewed this demand at the Moscow meeting in April 1947. The Russians, of course, were ready to install themselves in the Ruhr. The British and Americans vetoed this. At the same time they agreed to France's request in regard to the Saar.

The failure of the Moscow Conference marked a reversal in the French diplomatic position. France no longer fluctuated between East and West in her quest for support. Instead, she definitively joined the Western camp.

Two almost concurrent developments in French internal politics facilitated this shift. On May 4, 1947, Ramadier dismissed the Communist members of his ministry. In April, General de Gaulle had created the Rassemblement du

---

[18] Alfred Grosser, *La IVᵉ République et sa politique extérieure* (Paris: Armand Colin, 1961), 208.

Peuple Français (R.P.F.). A centrist political majority—the Third Force—came into being.

Two months before, Georges Bidault had taken the first step toward the creation of a Western alliance. The Franco-British Treaty, negotiated under Blum, was signed in Dunkirk on March 4, 1947. It was directed primarily against Germany. One year later, on March 17, 1948, the treaty establishing the Western European Union was signed in Brussels. The parties were France, England, and the Benelux nations. The assassination of Jan Masaryk in Prague was a tangible proof of the Russian threat. The treaty did not refer to German aggression but merely to the possibility that one of the signatories "might become the object of armed aggression in Europe." On March 4, Georges Bidault discreetly suggested to General Marshall that "collaboration between the old and new continents be tightened in military matters." This was the origin of the Atlantic Pact.

Early in June 1948, the signatories of the Treaty of Brussels and the American secretary of state met in London to discuss possible changes in the status of Germany in connection with the launching of the European recovery program. They recommended the unification of the three Western zones and the preparation of a democratic constitution for Germany. In a statement made on June 9, de Gaulle asked the National Assembly to reject the recommendations contained in the London communiqué: "This would amount to creating a Reich in Frankfurt; little by little, we would give in until we conceded everything." The parliamentary debate was trying. On June 17, a resolution was voted by a slim majority of 297 against 289. It approved the communiqué's recommendations but reaffirmed France's demand that the Ruhr be internationalized and the German industrial potential curtailed.

France attempted to delay the formation of a Western bloc because she was still undecided about what position to take on the German problem.

2

From a Traditional to an Integrated Alliance

Negotiations for an Atlantic Pact

S HORTLY AFTER THE BRUSSELS TREATY was signed, President Truman told Congress: "I am certain that the resolve of the free nations of Europe to protect themselves will be accompanied by an equal resolve on our part to help them do so." The Berlin blockade and the signing of a series of treaties between the Soviet Union and its satellites stimulated the negotiators of the Western camp.

For the Americans, a persistent obstacle was the Monroe Doctrine. On July 11, 1948, Arthur Vandenberg asked the United States Senate to adopt a resolution calling upon the government to pursue "the progressive development of regional and other collective arrangements for individual and collective self-defense in accordance with the purposes, principles, and provisions of the Charter." American isolationism was dead.

The prospective treaty was based on Article 51 of the Charter which invoked the natural right of legitimate defense. As René Mayer, treaty rapporteur to the National Assembly, stated, the treaty sprang from "a very general feeling of insecurity which was the exact opposite of the collective security that the Charter intended to insure."

On the European side, negotiations were conducted by Ernest Bevin for England and Robert Schuman, Bidault's successor, for France. Italy joined the signatories of the Brussels Treaty at the request of France. Denmark and Norway, as well as Iceland and Portugal, naturally followed the British lead. Switzerland and Sweden preserved their traditional neutrality; Ireland did not budge from its wartime isolationism. The Franco regime did not allow

Spain to participate in a coalition of states that advocated democratic principles.

The treaty was made public on March 18. Called the Atlantic Pact, it was signed in Washington on April 4, 1949. It covered the metropolitan territories of the signatory states as well as their occupation forces in Europe. The military and political status of West Germany had to be adapted to the new coalition that would henceforward protect it. The occupation regime was modified by the Washington accords of April 8, 1949. A tripartite High Commission with headquarters in Bonn replaced the quadripartite Control Council in Berlin. It was given the powers hitherto exercised by the occupation authorities.

The Big Three were in agreement regarding the constitutional law enacted on May 8. This statute instituted a federal and parliamentary regime in West Germany. On May 28, 1949, the Big Three also established the International Authority of the Ruhr. This body, which included representatives from the Benelux countries, was to oversee the distribution of coal and steel for the benefit of its six members.

The Debates on Ratification

On July 26 the French National Assembly was asked to vote on the treaty. Of particular interest was the new status of Germany. Ever since March, the French public had been discussing it.

Frenchmen were faced with three basic choices: an American alliance, allegiance to the Soviet Union, or neutralism. Robert Schuman, speaking before the Assembly, summarized the position of the Communist Party: "According to it, France has no choice but isolation or allegiance to the Soviets." He went on to state his own view: "We want neither of these, and the nation approves of our refusal." He reminded his listeners that the Cominform was constituted prior to the Atlantic Pact. He interpreted the October 5, 1947, statement as "a concerted international action with goals that transcend the concerns of domestic politics or the preoccupations of a militant ideology." Schuman concluded: "The establishment of this bloc reveals a desire for isolation as well as systematic antagonism." The Assembly agreed with the minister. The Atlantic Pact was ratified by a vote of 395 to 189 (Communists, Progressists, and a few African and Muslim deputies). There were only fifteen abstentions.

The parliamentarians then speculated about the scope of the American guarantee. Some criticized the lack of "automaticity," others expressed concern that France might be dragged into a war against her will. Schuman remarked that the complaints were contradictory. René Mayer, the treaty rapporteur, reminded the Assembly that each member would be the judge of the measures that mutual assistance might require. This stipulation, he said, was a "compromise . . . between 'automaticity,' which was impossible, and the absence of any commitment whatsoever." Its "full value will be realized only if the permanent organs, established by Article 9, are prepared in advance for the different possibilities—the various and gradual measures which the threat of an armed aggression entails."[1] Moreover, the treaty served to complement the economic aid furnished the European allies under the Marshall Plan and also the American military aid. By these three inter-related measures, the United States was attempting to overcome the feeling of collective insecurity, thus attesting the seriousness of its intentions.

Finally, the status of Germany became the central issue of the debate. Would the requirements of the Alliance lead to the rearmament of yesterday's enemy? This was the opinion of Sirius (*Le Monde*, April 6): "German re-armament is lodged in the Atlantic Pact like an embryo in an egg." Did the government have some foreboding that the Americans were not saying everything that was on their minds for fear of wounding French sensibilities on the eve of ratification? Informed or merely over-cautious, Schuman excluded this possibility. He based his arguments on law. "The question (of allowing Germany to become a member of the Atlantic Pact) cannot be raised. This is not a peace treaty. Germany has no army and may not have one. She has no weapons and will not be allowed to acquire them." The Assembly responded by taking a juridical precaution: the inclusion of new members would be subject not only to the government's consent but also to the enactment of a law by Parliament. Schuman replied: "The German problem has not been solved. We hope to solve it within the framework of peaceful European cooperation." Did the deputies attribute to this remark the importance it deserved? The minister spoke with his usual modesty, but what he said contained all the elements of a great policy.

De Gaulle criticized Germany's status more than the tenor of the pact itself. In a speech in Vincennes on May 22, he denounced "the incredible spectacle of the great German Reich disguised as the champion of European freedom." Edmond Michelet, his spokesman in the Assembly, voted for ratification but advocated a strategy that provided for the defense of the European continent east of the French borders—in other words, in Germany. The strategy was adopted; and it was this that led to German rearmament.

The Treaty

The North Atlantic Treaty consisted of fourteen articles and three pages of text. Its preamble referred to the tie that united both shores of the

---

[1] René Mayer, *Le Pacte de l'Atlantique* (Paris: Presses Universitaires de France [P.U.F.], 1949), 29–30.

Atlantic: a common heritage and civilization of their peoples, "founded on the principles of democracy, individual liberty and the rule of law." By its very sobriety, the declaration expressed the intentions of the signatories.

The goal of collective security was assured by the maintenance and development of "their individual and collective capacity to resist armed attack" (Article 3). "The parties will consult together whenever, in the opinion of any of them, the territorial integrity, political independence or security of any of the parties is threatened" (Article 4).

Article 5 contained the basic stipulation: "The parties agree that an armed attack against one or more of them . . . shall be considered an attack against them all; and consequently they agree that, if such an armed attack occurs, each of them, in exercise of the right of individual or collective self-defense . . . will assist the party or parties so attacked by taking forthwith, individually and in concert with the other parties, such action as it deems necessary, including the use of armed force."

The treaty constituted a commitment by the United States to defend Europe. Formulated in terms identical to those laid down in the Inter-American Treaty of Mutual Assistance of September 2, 1947, it was stronger than the commitments the United States was to incur subsequently in other parts of the world, especially in the Pacific and South-east Asia.[2] It showed that the United States placed the defense of Europe on a par with the defense of the Americas.

Article 6 delimited the geographical scope of the treaty: the territories of the contracting parties, "the islands, vessels or aircraft" north of the Tropic of Cancer. At France's request, the Algerian departments were included in the protective perimeter. The overseas possessions of the signatory nations were left out. The United States was not willing to undertake the defense of its allies' colonial empires.

Article 9 stipulated that a council would be established "to consider matters concerning the implementation of this Treaty." It was also to set up the necessary subsidiary bodies. Article 12 provided that the treaty could be reviewed at the end of ten years upon the request of any one party and after consultation. Article 13 stipulated that "any party may cease to be a party" after the Treaty had been in force for twenty years. All in all, it was a traditional alliance between sovereign states. It respected the fiction of the juridical equality of states, the cornerstone of the United Nations. Decisions were to be reached on the basis of unanimity.

The rivalry between the United States and the Soviet Union was soon to lead the champions of the Atlantic Pact to alter the nature of the Alliance.

---

[2] Raymond Aron, *Paix et guerre entre les nations* (Paris: Calmann-Lévy, 1962) 382.

Rivalry on Two Fronts

The signing of the pact consolidated America's position in Europe. The Russians effected a tactical retreat: the blockade of Berlin ended late in May 1949, and the Greek Communist insurrection ended in October.

Inversely, the definitive Communist victory over the Chinese Nationalists in 1949 undermined the American position in the Far East. In June 1950 the Russians encouraged the army of the North Korean People's Republic to invade South Korea. North Korea was under Russian control, South Korea under American protection. At the head of a world police force, the United States intervened in Korea as the mandatory of the Security Council of the United Nations.

The Korean aggression impelled the Americans to strengthen the Atlantic Alliance. Through a satellite in the Far East, the Russians provoked a secondary conflict. Would they be tempted to start a major conflict in Europe? The threat that hung directly over Western Europe indirectly affected the United States as well. The Council of the North Atlantic Treaty met in New York in September 1950 to blueprint Western strategy and devise ways of implementing it.

Such was the interdependence of the European and Asian theaters of action—of cold war and hot war—in a bipolar system that embraced the entire planet.

Preventive Strategy

The major objective of the Atlantic Alliance was to deter the Soviet Union from using force in Europe.

The mission of the Allied troops could be considered limited in character: to offer enough resistance to a Russian invasion to enable the Americans to intervene with atomic weapons. But the troops could also have a more ambitious goal: to counter any attempt at invasion without resort to atomic arms.

Believing it would be better to protect Europe than to liberate it, the Council decided in favor of a forward-looking strategy. The Atlantic army would have to be capable of halting aggression as far east as possible. This strategy would be carried out with the two types of weapons available to the Alliance: conventional arms, which were unevenly distributed among the member states, and atomic weapons, which the United States alone possessed.

The magnitude of the Atlantic army's task and the distribution of weapons among the members led the Council to seek out new allies and to create an integrated military organization.

It would be impossible to protect Europe as far as possible to the east—meaning German soil—without West Germany's military and political collaboration. In December 1950, at a meeting of the North Atlantic Council

29]

in Brussels, the three occupying powers were asked to seek an appropriate understanding with the German government on such a collaboration. France objected to German rearmament. This produced a crisis within the Alliance. It was also important strategically to bring Greece and Turkey into the Alliance. Both countries were already receiving military aid from the United States. As early as October they had participated in some of the Alliance's undertakings; in February 1952 they became full-fledged members.

The Military Organization (NATO)

In peacetime a very tight military organization was needed to protect a disparate coalition against an enemy that had overwhelming superiority in conventional weapons.

The North Atlantic Treaty Organization (NATO) was a combination of permanent executive bodies constituted under Article 9 of the treaty. All these organs were to be answerable to the North Atlantic Council, made up of representatives of the member states. They were to be created by unanimous decisions of the Council.

At the December 1950 meeting in Brussels, the North Atlantic Council decided to place the organization under the command of an American general. It also came out in favor of an organization that would represent a compromise between the principles of national sovereignty and military integration.

In April 1951 General Dwight Eisenhower, the supreme commander of the Allied forces in Europe, set up headquarters outside Paris. His jurisdiction extended from the North Cape to the Mediterranean, from the Atlantic to the eastern border of Turkey. With the armed forces assigned to him, he established subordinate commands in North, Central, and Southern Europe, and in the Mediterranean. He was assisted by an integrated general staff.

Early in 1952 an international Secretariat was established in Paris. Its head, the secretary-general, was to preside over the North Atlantic Council.

The conventional armed forces of the member states were divided into three categories: (a) those assigned in peacetime to NATO commands; (b) reserves to be assigned to these commands in wartime; (c) forces that were to remain under national control. The armed forces were to be recruited on a national basis. The member states could transfer their NATO troops to other areas, or, for example, to some theater of operations outside the zones covered by the treaty.

Strategic forces, that is, planes carrying atomic bombs, were to remain national; they were not assigned to NATO. In 1949, these consisted of only the American deterrent, whose use would be determined not by the supreme Allied commander in Europe but by the president of the United States.

The Atlantic Alliance was integrated to the extent that it had a common staff and a common infrastructure in peacetime. The purpose was to plan defense strategy. In wartime, the Allied conventional land, sea, and air forces stationed in the treaty zones would be placed under a single command.

As for the strategic force of the United States, it was assigned to air bases that ringed the Soviet Union, in NATO countries and in Third World nations within the range of American bombers.

The Evolution of Power Relationships (1949–1954)

The period 1949–1954 was one of considerable effort in the area of defense. The gross annual military expenditures of the Allies increased from 19 to 56 billion dollars. The United States contributed four times as much as all the European allies combined. In 1954 NATO had approximately twenty full-strength divisions for the defense of the Central European front. They were trained by staff headquarters to collaborate and hold international maneuvers.

At a meeting in Lisbon in 1952, the Atlantic Council had originally planned to station twenty-five to thirty divisions on the Central European front in order to stop a possible Soviet surprise attack without resorting to atomic weapons.

By 1954 both the Americans and the Russians had the A-bomb. The two superpowers were working hard to develop the H-bomb, but the Americans had a one-year lead. The American strategic air force was superior to the Russian in both size and equipment. Its air bases ringed Soviet territory.[3] In 1952 the British exploded their first A-bomb. From then on the British air force, modest though it was, augmented the American.

In 1954 the Americans were still the sole possessors of a deterrent force. In 1953 they formulated the doctrine of massive retaliation. The secretary of state, John Foster Dulles, was the spokesman for this doctrine: he declared that any Soviet aggression in the American sphere of influence would be punished swiftly with atomic weapons. The doctrine aroused anxiety among Europeans. They were now less vulnerable to attack with conventional weapons than they had been in 1950, but they were also far more vulnerable to an atomic attack.

The ratio of military strength, however, had changed in favor of Western Europe, which was no longer totally unarmed. Moreover, Europe was protected by the unequivocal commitment of the United States. The conventional forces that protected Europe in 1954 constituted more than a tripwire to an aggressor. But Europe was not strong enough to dispense with atomic protection.

Germany had no army to contribute to the NATO forces because of

[3] Raymond Aron, *Le grand débat* (Paris: Calmann-Lévy, 1963), 26.

France's objections. French NATO forces had been depleted as a consequence of the war in Indochina.

The ratio of military strength was less favorable in the Far East than in Europe. After a number of battles, the American intervention in Korea halted the Russian advance. An armistice was signed in July 1953. In 1950 the colonial war in Indochina was still a secondary theater in the rivalry between the two blocs, although the Chinese Communists openly supported the Vietnamese. In December 1952 the North Atlantic Council officially acknowledged this fact. In May 1954, after the fall of DienBienPhu, the war was lost despite American financial aid. Indochina was partitioned. North Vietnam fell under the influence of China. South Vietnam sought the protection of the United States.

In 1949 France had played an important part in the conclusion of the Atlantic Pact and consequently in the crystallization of the Western bloc. Her colonial wars, however, weakened the bloc in the Far East; her policy toward Germany, which we shall analyze, hampered the over-all attempt to protect Europe.

3

The European Army and the German National Army

How Should Germany Be Rearmed?

THE MAIN QUESTION had been resolved: Germany was to be rearmed. This was the decision of the Atlantic Council. In a communiqué of September 16, 1950, it declared: "The Council has agreed that Germany shall be enabled to contribute to the establishment of Western European defense."

Two alternatives were envisaged—German participation in an integrated force or the establishment of a German national army. The Council signified its preference. In a communiqué of September 19 it stated: "The ministers unanimously believe that the reconstitution of a German army will not serve the true interests of Germany or of Europe. This view, they feel, is shared by the vast majority of Germans. The ministers have taken note, however, of the sentiment recently expressed in Germany and elsewhere in favor of German participation in an integrated force dedicated to the defense of European freedom." The Atlantic Council took this position at the request of the French government and in view of the recent direction of its diplomacy. France was seeking security through reconciliation with Germany. Such a reconciliation, rather than vain opposition to the recovery of her former enemy, would lay the foundations for a united Europe.

The change in French attitude, which will be analyzed in another chapter, began when on May 9, 1950, Robert Schuman urged that France and Germany should produce jointly two basic commodities—coal and steel. Why should they not cooperate for purposes of defense as well as for the production of heavy industrial goods?

By linking the building of European unity with Atlantic defense, René Pleven hoped to overcome the widespread opposition which the prospect of

German rearmament inevitably aroused in France. He explained his views before the National Assembly. On October 24, 1950, it passed an ambiguous resolution (349 for, 235 against) prohibiting the reconstitution of a German army. Parliament, like the government, was playing for time.

Yet the majority of the Assembly favored the concept of a federated Europe. The Mouvement Républicain Populaire (M.R.P.) and the Socialist Party played the largest role in the decisions of the Assembly.

International negotiations for the conclusion of a treaty to establish the European Defense Community (E.D.C.) were protracted. They were still going on in February 1952 when the Assembly was called upon to discuss the plan. A meeting of the Atlantic Council scheduled for Lisbon impended. The elections of June 17, 1951, had brought 120 R.P.F. (Gaullist) deputies into Parliament. They were avowed opponents of a European army. The position of the M.R.P. and the Socialists was not as strong as it had been in 1950. By a slim majority—327 against 287—the Assembly passed a resolution favoring the plan but containing numerous reservations and conditions. At this point a serious ideological controversy arose in Parliament and in public opinion that was to continue until the treaty was rejected on August 30, 1954.

An analysis of the treaty and an account of the objections that were raised will clarify a debate which is still going on. It centered on how to define and defend Europe.

The European Defense Community Treaty

The treaty was signed in Bonn on May 26, 1952, by France, Germany, Italy, and the Benelux countries. Its purpose was to establish a truly European ministry of defense with an integrated armed force.

The European army consisted of contingents furnished by the member states and subject to common rules in regard to recruitment, organization, and training. The basic unit composed of personnel from one nation was the "group," a division with lighter logistics. The integrated unit was the army corps.

The European army comprised all the land and air forces of the member states, except for those assigned to defend the overseas territories; provision was made for the transfer of troops from one base to another. The armed forces were under the orders of the supreme allied commander in Europe. The E.D.C. was a supranational organ.

The joint executive, or Commissariat, administered the common defense budget; prepared and executed the arms, equipment, and infra-structure programs; conducted scientific and technical research. It was responsible not to a government but to the Assembly of the European Coal and Steel Community (E.C.S.C.) which had been created by a treaty ratified on December 13, 1951.

To complete the edifice, it was necessary to establish between the occupying forces and West Germany "new relationships that would not be those of victors to vanquished, of occupier to occupied; rather they would give the Federal Republic the status of an associate called upon to participate on an equal footing in the construction of Europe." Such, in any case, was the object of the "contractual accords" concluded in Bonn when the treaty was signed. Germany was to recover part of her sovereignty. The Big Three, however, reserved all the rights set forth in the quadripartite agreements of 1945. These had to do with the posting of armed forces in Germany, the status of Berlin, the unification of Germany. All this was done in order eventually to sign a peace treaty with the Soviet Union.

This complicated institutional structure was attempted in the atmosphere that prevailed at the time of the May 9 declaration. On February 9, 1952, Schuman spoke to the French Assembly on the subject. His concluding remarks set the tone: "The European Defense Community is and hopes to be a preliminary step toward a federated or confederated Europe."

To be sure, care should have been taken to establish beforehand a European authority to which the joint European defense ministry would have been responsible. An army that reports to no government, commissioners that assume no responsibility to an elected parliament, lend themselves to criticism. An effort was made to fill this void by having the *ad hoc* Assembly— an emanation of the E.C.S.C.—prepare a plan that would provide political authority.

Such as it was, the plan for a European Defense Community possessed two major advantages. The first was psychological and political. A West Germany associated with the effort to build European unity and integrated with her Western partners, especially France, was far less likely to remain a center of militarism. A national German army could not offer the same long-term guarantees.

The second advantage was military and industrial. NATO's intergovernmental regime had not been able to make substantial progress in the standardization of weapons. With a single military administration that bought supplies in a large market and had a sizable budget, continental Europe could decrease the cost of production and increase the effectiveness of its conventional weapons. With the technical help of the United States, it could also begin to manufacture its own strategic nuclear weapons. Since West Germany was prohibited from manufacturing new arms, they could be made in France.

The Opponents of a European Army

The E.D.C. project had three kinds of political adversaries. The first consisted of all those opposed to German rearmament. The Communists, who were hostile to the Atlantic Pact, were of course in this group. They were joined by those representatives of the non-Communist Left, who still hoped that France would follow a policy of neutrality, or rather of neutralism, in the struggle between East and West. In addition there were some right-wing traditionalists who could not overcome their Germanophobia. Neutralists and traditionalists were both anti-American; in their opinion, the American support for the treaty was an additional reason for opposing it. This opposition was irreducible.

In the second category were Gaullist deputies, both orthodox and dissident; other right-wing traditionalists; neo-Jacobin Radicals, more hostile to the supranationalism of a European army than to the idea of German rearmament. They all criticized the treaty on the ground that it limited French independence. This category was as uncompromising as the first.

The third category comprised deputies left of center, especially the Socialists. They were primarily anxious to secure guarantees against a strong Germany. Germany's potential power was all the more threatening since a considerable part of the French army had been assigned to the Indochinese theater of operations. A number of Socialists insisted on two mutually exclusive conditions before they would sign the treaty—close association with England, and "subjection of the European army to a supranational political authority with limited but real power."

Although business circles were divided, the advocates of protectionism were opposed to the notion of pooling all armaments.

The governments that succeeded one another until the 1954 crisis concentrated on trying to satisfy this third category of critics, the least systematic of the three.

The Debate from 1952 to 1954

Discussions continued unabated within the government, in Parliament, and among the public, at home and abroad.

In March 1952, Antoine Pinay was named premier with the backing of dissident Gaullists. The Socialists joined the opposition. The government declared it would not sign the treaty unless England and other signatories of the Atlantic Pact promised their assistance. On June 5, a few days after the treaty was signed, de Gaulle expressed his categorical opposition: "France, along with vanquished Germany and Italy, will have to pour men, arms, and money pell-mell into a stateless hodgepodge. This degradation is inflicted on her in the name of equality of rights, so that Germany can be said to have no army while she reconstitutes her military force. And of course France, of all the great nations that today have an army, is the only one that loses hers."

For some unknown reason, Schuman never transmitted the signed treaty to Parliament for ratification.

In December 1952, the North Atlantic Council reiterated its approval of the treaty. In January 1953, René Mayer replaced Pinay as premier. A few days before the debate on investiture, de Gaulle, talking to a journalist, Harold King, criticized the treaty. He advocated a European political confederation instead of a supranational organization. The armies of the confederated states must remain national armies. Moreover, England and the United States "have not shown the slightest inclination to give up absolute control of their armed forces." French metropolitan forces and her forces in the overseas territories must constitute an indivisible bloc. To counter this third criticism, and because he needed all the Gaullist votes possible, Mayer promised the Assembly to add protocols to the treaty which "should enable us to maintain the unity and integrity of our army and of the French Union." Georges Bidault replaced Robert Schuman as foreign minister. More nationalist, less European than his predecessor, he was reticent on the subject of a European political community. He obtained the signatures of France's partners to the additional protocols. His efforts, however, did not disarm General de Gaulle. In a press conference of February 25, the general said: "It is clear that this treaty, together with America's present policy, will lead directly to the political and military hegemony of the Reich in Europe." Before the National Council of the R.P.F., he declared on March 1: "With or without protocols, the treaty is entirely unacceptable."

Germany ratified the treaty in May. Should it be submitted to the National Assembly? Keen political observers like Jacques Fauvet thought the treaty would have been ratified in 1952 and even in 1953.[1] René Mayer was overthrown on May 21, 1953, apparently over a question of financial powers but actually because of his foreign policy. Although defeated in the municipal elections, the Gaullist Party did not relent on the E.D.C. André Diethelm, its spokesman, said at the time of the balloting: "We are not dead since we still have the power to destroy."[2]

After a protracted crisis, Joseph Laniel was invested on June 28. For the first time the R.P.F. parliamentarians were part of the government. Georges Bidault remained foreign minister. Laniel concentrated on finding a diplomatic solution to the Indochinese problem. A new factor intervened: the détente in international relations following the death of Stalin in March. The Korean armistice was signed in July. The time was apparently ripe for exploring the possibilities of an entente between East and West. The pressing issues were Germany and Indochina, the first stemming from a latent, the second from an open conflict. Prospects for international conferences in these

[1] Jacques Fauvet, *La IVe République* (Paris: Arthème Fayard, 1959), p. 229.
[2] *Année politique 1953*, 43.

fields, plus internal antagonisms, accounted for the government's delay in presenting the treaty to Parliament for ratification.

In preparation for the impending debate in the National Assembly, the Gaullist opposition clarified its position. Michel Debré, addressing the Senate on October 27, 1953, said there was an alternative to the E.D.C.: Germany's entry into the Atlantic Pact, an organization based on the principle of association, not merger.

On November 12, in a press conference, the general denounced a system that would "turn the German and French armies into stateless armies, into a technocracy." He contended that the United States alliance had become a protectorate of sorts and reminded his listeners that France was still an ally of the Soviet Union: "France must find out whether it is possible to reach an understanding with the Soviet Union."

Within the Assembly the quarrel was bitter. The Moderates, Radicals, and Socialists were seriously divided. Bidault had prepared an excellent speech in favor of the treaty but was unable to deliver it because of illness. It stressed the need to extend the British and American guarantees. The Assembly passed an ambiguous resolution that made no mention of the E.D.C.

Because of the delaying tactics of the French, the treaty, which should have been handled exclusively by the Atlantic bloc, became a bone of contention between the two rival superpowers.

The Americans, long skeptical about the E.D.C., began to champion it when the chances for its acceptance became slim. In their opinion, any arrangement that would help to build European unity was as important as Germany's contribution to collective defense. American pressure for adoption of the treaty was accompanied by the threat of an "agonizing reappraisal"—the expression used by John Foster Dulles at the meeting of the Atlantic Council on December 14, 1953. It described the policy the United States would pursue toward Europe if the treaty were rejected.

The Russians naturally exerted pressure in the opposite sense. The Soviet note of August 15, 1953, pointed out that the E.D.C. would transform West Germany into a satellite of the North Atlantic bloc.

The Berlin Conference of January 1954 discussed the reunification of Germany. The Western nations admitted that a united Germany would be free to decide whether it wished to assume the international obligations previously contracted by the two Germanies. On the other hand, the Soviet Union refused to countenance free elections to decide the question of German reunification.

The conference was a failure. The participants, however, decided to meet again on April 26 to discuss Indochina. The plight of the French army by this time was so desperate that the convention providing for cooperation between the United Kingdom and the E.D.C., signed on April 13, as well as President

Eisenhower's message guaranteeing the E.D.C. (April 16), went almost unnoticed. Yet the message contained an important statement: the United States intended to share "more and more in all information relating to the military use of new arms and techniques."

DienBienPhu fell on May 7. On June 13 the Laniel cabinet fell over disputes about Indochina and the E.D.C. The defeat in Asia intensified nationalist feeling in metropolitan France.

The 1954 Crisis

For several months the three major problems of French foreign policy were debated jointly: defense and alliance, the construction of Europe, and decolonization.

To choose between two methods of defending Western Europe—through a European army or a German national army—was also to choose between a supranational organization and an association of states as the best way to build a united Europe.

For France, the choice between a role in NATO and Europe and a role overseas was closely connected with the option between a liberal and an authoritarian conception of the French Union.

Pierre Mendès-France was invested by the National Assembly on June 18, 1954. He was intent on coming to a decision about these alternatives, which had been left up in the air too long. He attacked Bidault with unusual violence on the question of Indochina, and thus lost the support of the M.R.P. Their defection weakened the government greatly: the M.R.P., more than any other political party, had backed the federal conception of Europe. The rift between the premier and the M.R.P. also jeopardized the treaty at the very moment when a majority of the Socialist deputies, defying the express wishes of their own party, announced they would oppose a federated Europe.

On the question of the E.D.C., Mendès-France said: "France cannot further prolong an ambiguous situation that is hurting the Western alliance." He committed himself to submit detailed proposals to the Assembly before the summer recess. Turning his back on Communist support, he reaffirmed his loyalty to the Atlantic Pact. The government, like the Assembly, comprised both partisans and adversaries of the treaty.

The premier outlined his plans for a compromise. Unlike his predecessors, he tried to win the support of the Gaullists, who were more opposed to supranationalism than to German rearmament,

The protocol proposed as an addition to the treaty, which Mendès-France submitted to the Six in Brussels on August 19, contained several suggestions: an eight-year suspension of all supranationalist clauses; permission to withdraw from the treaty in the event of German reunification or of withdrawal from the Atlantic Pact; integration limited to the armed forces posted in Germany; the retention, however, of the main clauses providing for the integration of armaments. To France's partners, these clauses seemed excessive. The Six were uncompromising on the basic principle of the Treaty, and irritated by the way the French proposal was handled. Shortly afterward, Mendès-France explained the situation to the National Assembly: "I was faced with men . . . who were exasperated . . . by our policies of the last few years. The uncertainty, the hesitation, the delaying tactics, the fact that we had not been able to decide on a move that, according to them, had been initiated by us, the fact that after interminable delays—two, almost three years—France was still irresolute and uncertain—all this was intolerable to them."

The bitter discussion ended in utter discord. Mendès-France went from Brussels to London to see Churchill. A few days later he was to say to the National Assembly—and it expressed his profound conviction: "One axiom of French policy should be never to separate ourselves from Great Britain." After the Churchill interview, Reuter published the following unofficial comment: "Great Britain will probably unite with the United States to obtain from France an accord on some other form of German contribution to defense."

The premier intended to lay before Parliament not the protocol resolution that was rejected at Brussels, but the treaty itself. Would the government commit itself, as Mendès-France had promised on assuming office? The government, thoroughly divided, would have fallen apart. Contrary to the opinion of René Coty, Mendès-France decided that the ministers should abstain in the balloting. He justified his attitude before the Assembly in the following terms: "The government cannot raise the question of confidence on a text that remains a cause of disunity among Frenchmen."

Mendès-France's speech before the principal commissions on August 25 and his speech before the Asesmbly on the 29th were considered by advocates of a European army an indictment of the treaty.

Two of the premier's statements should be singled out. One foreshadowed the near future: "The problem of Germany and her rearmament, should the Assembly again refuse to ratify it, will again be raised." The other was a value judgment of the treaty: "In my opinion, the most obvious advantage of the E.D.C. would be that it will link the German Federal Republic politically with the Western world."

Too many Frenchmen, including the most illustrious, did not realize that this obvious advantage was fundamental. On the eve of the debate, Vincent Auriol and General de Gaulle declared their unalterable opposition to the E.D.C. Edouard Herriot supported a preliminary motion in the Assembly. It was adopted on August 30, 1954, by a vote of 319 against 264, with 41 abstaining. Without any thorough discussion, the treaty was rejected.

The majority included not only the Communists and Progressists (99) and almost all the Gaullists (Social Republicans, 67 out of 73), but also half of the Radicals (34 out of 67), half of the Socialists (55 out of 105), and more than a third of the Moderate Right (44 out of 124). Only the M.R.P. voted as a block for the treaty.

On the German question, the extremist parties succeeded in splitting the center.

Two questions were raised *a posteriori* in regard to the balloting: Did Mendès-France expect his protocol to triumph or was he preparing an alternative solution? Were his Brussels partners wrong to reject the protocol? Mendès-France certainly believed that the treaty was too supranational, too little oriented toward England. But his compromise, in his opinion and in that of many of his Socialist opponents, did contain an important guarantee: the joint execution of the armament programs. Thereafter, he was to attempt in vain to achieve such a guarantee.

Had Spaak and his friends been wrong at the Brussels meeting? An answer to this question depends upon the answer to the first question. If Mendès-France was sincere, he should have been taken at his word; the Center parties would have been won over and the Social Republicans isolated; Germany would have been rearmed and a European federation assured, even if somewhat belatedly.

Germany in NATO

Once the treaty was rejected, the Europeans and Americans sought an alternative. There were two possible solutions. One was envisaged by the American government, the other by certain French circles.

Since France's opposition to German rearmament was practically insurmountable, should not the United States conclude a bilateral military accord with West Germany, which was recognized as a sovereign state? A precedent had already been established: the military accord between the United States and Spain. It was concluded on September 26, 1953, thus completing the European arrangements for NATO. Spain's membership in the Atlantic Pact had raised objections because of the Franco regime. This solution was acceptable for a peripheral state. But it involved serious strategic disadvantages for Germany because she was situated in the heart of Europe where NATO's lines of communications converge and where the eventual adversary will be met.

Nonetheless, Dulles explored this possibility. He went to Bonn and to London in September without stopping in Paris. Adenauer and Eden both persuaded him to drop the idea. But the situation was serious. Mendès-France recalled this before the National Assembly on December 23: "I said that our Allies might consider rearming Germany without us. I did so because in September we came very close to unlimited rearmament, without any control and without our consent." The "agonizing reappraisal" of American foreign policy did not mean that the United States would give up the defense of Europe. Rather, it signified that the Americans would choose some other foothold on the European continent.

The other extreme solution favored by neutralists and certain militant nationalists was an understanding between East and West on the unification and neutralization of Germany. The failure of the Berlin conference in February 1954 did not discourage some of the French parliamentarians; they were afraid that the Soviet Union would refuse to put an end to the war in Indochina as long as there was a chance that the National Assembly might ratify the treaty.

Once the treaty was rejected, might not the Soviet Union make overtures to the Western nations? Might it not become more flexible on the crucial question of free elections for all of Germany? Moscow remained silent. Doubtless the Soviet Union preferred a divided Germany half rearmed by the West to a unified and disarmed Germany entirely Western in orientation. Mendès-France admitted this was true.

With Dulles persuaded and Moscow silent, a middle road—Germany's entry into the Atlantic Pact—was open. Suggested in November 1953 by Michel Debré, doubtless desired by Mendès-France, this solution found a skillful agent in Anthony Eden.

The formula Eden presented would restore the sovereignty of the Federal Republic so that, as a first step, it could become associated with the Brussels Treaty, a purely European body. A second step was affiliation with the Atlantic Pact. The negotiations conducted in London, then in Paris, resulted in the signing, on October 23, of a series of diplomatic covenants known as the Paris Accords.

A protocol referring to ending German occupation, signed by the United States, England, and France on one side, and West Germany on the other, amended the Bonn Convention of May 26, 1952 (annexed to the E.D.C. Treaty), and recognized the Federal Republic's "full authority as a sovereign state in domestic and foreign affairs" except for questions pertaining to Berlin and reunification. In exchange, the Federal Republic consented to the continued stationing on its territory of armed forces of the same nationalities and sizes as heretofore.

Upon the inclusion of both Germany and Italy, the Brussels Treaty was modified and completed. Its structure was strengthened by a Council of Ministers and a parliamentary assembly for the "Western European Union" (W.E.U.). England promised not to withdraw her troops (four divisions) from the Continent if that was the wish of the majority of members of the W.E.U., save in the event of a grave overseas or financial crisis. The maximum contribution of land and air forces was fixed at the level prescribed by the E.D.C. Treaty. Thus, the maximum German contingents (twelve divisions) remained smaller than the French (fourteen divisions). These armed forces were subject to the orders of the supreme commander for Europe of the Atlantic Pact. Germany undertook to refrain from manufacturing atomic, biological or chemical weapons on her own territory. She promised, moreover, not to manufacture certain kinds of matériel without the express permission of the W.E.U.'s Council. A European agency for the control of armaments was to make sure that these prohibitions were respected.

The entry of Germany into the Atlantic Pact was accompanied by a strengthening of the integrated conventional forces assigned to the Supreme Allied Command in Europe. A resolution adopted by the NATO Council empowered it to deploy forces and broadened its logistic powers. Since Germany had no overseas territories to defend, her entire army was placed under NATO command. Moreover, on joining NATO and the W.E.U., the Federal Republic promised "never to resort to force to achieve reunification of Germany."

In view of this commitment, the governments of the United States, France, and the United Kingdom jointly declared that "they regarded the government of the Federal Republic as the only freely and legitimately constituted German government, empowered by this pact to speak in the name of Germany . . . in all international affairs (Article 1); . . . the peaceful creation of a completely free and unified Germany remains a fundamental objective of their policy" (Article 4).

Thus, the restoration of German sovereignty was accompanied by internal and external guarantees against the dangers that might result from the existence of a German national army.

Sovereign Germany could not accept the provisional regime that France had established in the Saar in 1947. It rested on an economic tie with France and on the political division of Germany. The authoritarian control of the first years had become more flexible but the freedom of opinion of the pro-German political parties had not been restored. The Franco-Saar convention of 1953, elaborated in conjunction with the E.D.C. at the insistence of René Mayer, gave rise to criticism that was widespread in Germany but confined to nationalist circles in France. Subsequent Franco-German negotiations had not been completed by August 1954. An accord reached on October 23, 1954, entrusted the conduct of the Saar's foreign relations to a commissioner appointed by the W.E.U., restored freedom of opinion, and provided for a referendum to ratify the European status of the Saar.

The Ratification of the Paris Accords

The National Assembly devoted two sessions to a consideration of German rearmament. The first took place early in October after the London conference; the second, at the end of December, ratified the Paris Accords of October 23, 1954. The debates were dominated by the threat of a direct entente between the United States and possibly England with Germany. But this time the tenor was less passionate. A majority of the parliamentarians had resigned themselves to the obvious necessity of rearming Germany. The earlier enthusiasm of some for a united Europe and the violent feeling of others against restoring Germany's sovereignty yielded to this necessity.

After the premier's comments, the most significant remarks were made by Robert Schuman and Paul Reynaud during the first session, by Jacques Soustelle and Léon Noël during the second.

Mendès-France, alluding to East-West relations, declared that the Soviet government "knows that some German rearmament is inevitable and that, if it wanted to prevent it, it could have done so with the means at its disposal." Schuman said he regretted to see a "coalition of national armies" replace the idea of political integration. The "objective is too limited to attract and hold Germany permanently," Schuman added. Reynaud deplored the fact that European leadership no longer belonged to France but rather to Great Britain, which "would direct from on high, from on very high, a continent in which distrust would reappear."

Jacques Soustelle, speaking for the Social Republicans, said that the Paris Accords constituted a reversal of alliances that benefited Germany and damaged France. His main argument against ratification was the danger that the Franco-Soviet Pact, set forth by the Soviet government in a note of December 16, might be destroyed. Acknowledging that this pact had been made meaningless by the Russians, Soustelle nonetheless insisted that a geographical imperative remained "that transcends questions of regime." He spoke of a "alliance de revers," which tallied with the view expressed by de Gaulle in 1944. Léon Noël said he was afraid that Germany would wield an increasing influence within the Western European Union. He therefore suggested, as de Gaulle had done on November 12, 1953, that the Soviet government be sounded out beforehand on the subject of controlled disarmament.

Mendès-France revealed during the discussion that in September, after the rejection of the E.D.C., the rearmament of Germany had almost been decided upon without the consent of France. He stressed the three features of the Paris Accords which were in his view the most important: the introduction of no more supranationalism than was indispensable for the unification of Europe; the association of England with the Continent; the solution of the problem of the Saar.

The balloting on the question of Germany's entry into NATO took place on December 29, with 287 voting in favor, 256 against, and 76 abstaining. The M.R.P. wanted to limit the impact of Mendès-France's victory; 52 of its 85 members voted against ratification. Most of the Socialists rallied in favor.

The Radicals remained split. As for the Social Republicans, 37 supported ratification, 23 opposed it, and 11 abstained.

Knowing how difficult it would be to persuade the Senate to ratify the Paris Accords, and concerned about Russia's reactions, Mendès-France wrote to Dulles and Churchill on January 5, 1955. He told them that he hoped to set up in May a four-power conference with Russia on the status of Germany and Europe—a suggestion he had made to the United Nations Assembly on November 22, 1954. The Americans reacted violently. "It was reported that . . . Dulles threatened severe reprisals against France and accused Mendès-France of trying to use the half-ratified treaty as a means of 'selling out' to the Russians at a high price."[3] An exchange of letters between Mendès-France and Churchill was made public after an appearance by Antoine Pinay, foreign minister in the Edgar Faure cabinet, before the Senate's Foreign Affairs Commission on March 10, 1955. In his reply of January 12, Churchill, although approving the idea of an international summit meeting, declared that prior ratification of the Paris Accords was a necessary condition for such a meeting. To postpone ratification further would mean that other solutions would have to be found. "I would then be obliged," he added, "to support the so-called 'empty-chair' policy, even though it would entail important military and political changes in the NATO infrastructure." The United States, England, the Commonwealth, and the Federal Republic would be strong enough to guarantee to the Benelux countries and other allies "real and certain security based on a physical and moral capacity to retaliate."[4]

The Mendès-France government fell on February 15, before it had a chance to launch the Senate debate on ratification of the Paris Accords. But such a debate did take place from the 23rd to the 28th of March. Michel Debré, rapporteur for the Foreign Relations Commission, spoke in favor of ratification. He concluded his remarks by saying: "The notion of East and West, with Europe in between, is meaningless today. Two civilizations exist. . . . In the face of a Soviet civilization, there can be no such thing as a European and an American system. But a Western civilization does exist, and we must preserve it." Edgar Faure, the premier, had two things to say on the subject. The first was that "we will not qualify for negotiators with the Eastern powers by quarreling with the Germans or splitting with our Allies." The second was to outline a threefold policy: "(1) To work for the construction of a united Europe; (2) to strengthen Atlantic unity in the political domain; (3) to promote an East-West détente not by asking France to play the role of mediator, for which she has no special fitness, but by arranging for

[3] David Schoenbrunn, *The Three Lives of Charles de Gaulle* (New York: Atheneum, 1966), 214.

[4] *Année politique 1955*, 342, 343, 682.

her intervention as a member of the Atlantic Alliance." The treaty was ratified on March 28 by a vote of 184 to 110.

At the London conference in September 1954, Dulles had promised to advise the president of the United States to keep American troops in Europe. England had already pledged to keep her troops there. On March 5, 1955, President Eisenhower publicly declared that United States forces would remain in Europe as long as their presence seemed necessary.

On May 5, 1955, the German Federal Republic became a member of NATO. On May 7, the Soviet Union denounced the Franco-Soviet Pact. To counterbalance NATO, it organized the Warsaw Pact on May 14. It comprised Russia and her satellite states. East Germany was invited to join the pact on January 27, 1956. The crystallization of the two blocs thus became manifest.

The Effects of the Ideological Controversy

The ideological controversy that split French opinion transcended the vicissitudes of the changing composition of majority governments. It had to do with fundamental problems of political philosophy and geostrategy on which Frenchmen could not agree.

Discussion was pitched at several levels—national, European, Atlantic, and East-West. The real bone of contention was the status of Germany and Europe. Compared to the United States and the Soviet Union, France had only a minor share in the determination of this status, even though her views should have been decisive for geographical and historical reasons.

A question of political philosophy was involved in the future of a nation-state of forty to fifty million inhabitants in a Europe divided into two spheres of influence, American and Soviet. In an age of atomic weapons and continent-states, should a nation-state attempt to recover its sovereignty? Or should several nation-states associate and then federate in order to reconstitute themselves by combining their material and moral resources? During the wars of the first half of the twentieth century, such a solution had obviously proved inadequate. It had merely led to the present state of dependence.

The problem of geostrategy must be considered in terms of promises of mutual assistance and power relationships. Should France seek security in a coalition that would allow her considerable freedom of action? Or should she opt for an "integrated" system that involves a great deal of "automaticity" in the matter of commitments between the European states and between these states and America? To come to grips with this dilemma was to entertain both hope and foreboding about the status of Germany.

The foreign policy of Robert Schuman required France to seek security within the framework of a European system in which West Germany would have an equal place. "The European Defense Community must establish a definitive tie between Germany and the West which will remove the nightmare of reunification. . . . The assumption is that negotiations with the E.D.C. for reunification would be futile, and that negotiation without the E.D.C. would be dangerous";[5] futile with the E.D.C. because the prospects for a unified Europe would lessen the regrets over the destruction of the German fatherland; and dangerous without the E.D.C. because Germany might be tempted to draw closer to the Soviet Union in order to regain her unity. But the creation of a ministry of war that would not be subject to government control was conceivable only as a first step toward a federated Europe. From a psychological point of view, France would be giving the new Germany a vote of confidence.

General de Gaulle's conception was quite different. He wanted France to recover her full sovereignty, especially in her relations with her allies. He did not accept equality of rights for Germany. He advocated a European confederation, with the understanding that the confederated states would retain their national armies. He reminded the public that France was still an ally of the Soviet Union, that she was still seeking an understanding with it. He did not trust Germany.

Thus, Frenchmen imbued with a sense of the past were pitted against those who looked toward the future. The first group thought in terms of national security and traditional alliances, the second in terms of collective security and pre-federalism.

The solution finally adopted consisted of trying, by purely technical means, to establish the desired tie between Germany and the West. "Integration was no longer a political weapon but a military method."[6]

---

[5] Raymond Aron and Robert Lerner, *France Defeats E.D.C.* (Cambridge, Mass.: Massachusetts Institute of Technology, 1956), Part III, p. 16.

[6] *Ibid.*, Part III, p. 8.

4

East–West Détente and
Internal Tensions in the West

The Evolution of Weaponry within the Alliance

THE NATO COMMAND did not have enough divisions in 1954 to repel a Russian attack with conventional weapons. Consequently, it obtained permission from the Atlantic Council to consider the use of tactical atomic weapons. "This decision was reached because the NATO forces were insufficient and atomic weapons were abundant."[1] The American divisions posted in Europe were at once equipped with tactical atomic weapons.

At its December 1957 meeting, held shortly after the Soviet Union launched its first Sputnik, the Atlantic Council decided to stockpile nuclear warheads in Europe and to make some intermediate-range ballistic missiles available to the central command.

Bilateral accords were negotiated between the United States and several European states for stockpiling these weapons. Agreements were also reached on the conditions under which these weapons were to be employed and on the installation of launching platforms for I.R.B.M.'s.

No launching platforms were installed in France because of the criticism expressed by the government and the opposition to the Atlantic Pact.

The Evolution of Strategy

The technical revolution in atomic weapons altered the Alliance's strategy. The global strategy concept formulated in 1956 was that of the

[1] Raoul Girardet, *Problèmes généraux de défense nationale* (Paris: Cours à l'Institut d'Etudes Politiques, 1965), 204.

sword and the shield. The sword symbolized the retaliatory forces whose mission it would eventually be to launch a nuclear counteroffensive to repel aggression. The shield represented the conventional forces charged with the defense of land and sea and the strategic protection of bases. In 1956 the Atlantic Council affirmed "the absolute determination of the Alliance members to use these forces if necessary." This statement of policy, reiterated in 1958, alarmed the Europeans. Unlike the United States, they were vulnerable on land as well as in the air. They were afraid that an exclusively nuclear strategy might lead to the dilemma of total war or capitulation.

However, the doctrine of massive retaliation, formulated in 1954 by the Americans and accepted by NATO in 1958, was then being challenged by the United States. Both the Russians and the Americans had acquired thermonuclear bombs. The British military expert, Liddell Hart, wrote that this tended to nullify the advantage of possessing nuclear arms.[2] The Americans became aware of the vulnerability of their territory during the brief interval when the Russians enjoyed a temporary superiority in intercontinental ballistic missiles. The "all-or-nothing" theory altered and became more measured. A doctrine of graduated response was adopted in 1961. It will be explained in Book Two.

Meanwhile, the danger of massive destruction impelled the two superpowers continually to sound out each other's intentions and to explore the possibility of achieving a general disarmament.

European Détente and Disarmament Negotiations

A détente followed the death of Stalin. East-West negotiations on disarmament, begun in the United Nations in 1946, had been at a virtual standstill since 1948. They were resumed in 1954 by the United Nations Disarmament Commission. Installed in London, its members included the Big Four and Canada.

At the close of 1954 the Commission examined an Anglo-French plan for partial disarmament. Early in 1956 the same countries made suggestions for restricting the use of atomic weapons. A Soviet proposal made at Geneva in July 1955, during a meeting of the heads of government of the four occupying powers, provided for a defensive alliance of the Big Four. It was to be a first step toward abolition of NATO and the Warsaw Pact. The proposal was rejected. In August 1957, a Western plan for total disarmament, to be supervised by the United Nations, was put forward. The production of all fissionable matter was to be controlled and the participants were to refrain from using atomic weapons save for purposes of legitimate defense. The Soviet

[2] Liddell Hart, *Deterrent or Defence* (London: Stevens & Sons, 1960), 8.

Union rejected the plan, but in the autumn it was adopted by the United Nations General Assembly.

In October 1957, Adam Rapacki, Polish foreign minister, made another proposal to the United Nations on behalf of the Eastern bloc. He suggested a partial accord on disarmament. Its main feature was the creation of a denuclearized zone in Central Europe embracing the two Germanies, Poland, and Czechoslovakia. In addition, a Soviet memorandum suggested a non-aggression pact between the members of NATO and the Warsaw Pact. The Rapacki plan was rejected by the West because of space considerations. The range of the I.R.B.M.'s greatly exceeded the denuclearized zone, which comprised only 500 kilometers. Raymond Aron remarked that the Soviet bloc could easily pull back its line of defense for several hundred kilometers but the Atlantic bloc could not do so unless it ceased to be a military organization.[3] On May 3, 1958, the United States rejected the Rapacki plan.

Tension in the Middle East and the Suez Expedition

Although relations between the two blocs were fairly satisfactory in Europe, tensions increased in the Middle East where the Soviet Union tried to wield political and economic influence. In May 1954, Egypt concluded an important commercial agreement with the Soviet Union. Egypt was also liberating itself from British control. An Anglo-Egyptian agreement stipulated that British troops must evacuate the Suez Canal by June 1956.

The Israeli-Arab conflict, which had been quiescent since the Israeli successes in 1949, flared anew when Nasser came to power in Egypt. Iraq became the center of British diplomatic activity in the Middle East as a result of the impending departure of the British from Egypt. At the urging of England, the Bagdad Pact was concluded between Turkey and Iraq in February 1955. England joined the pact in April 1955; Pakistan and Iran followed suit. Although the United States did not become a member, it gave maximum support to the participants.

Nasser made himself the champion of decolonization in the Arab world. He backed the Algerian rebels and opposed the Bagdad Pact. At the same time he solicited funds from the West to improve conditions in Egypt.

On July 19-20, 1956, the United States and England made it plain that they were not willing to contribute to the financing of the Aswan Dam. On July 26 Nasser ordered the nationalization of the Suez Canal. He promised to indemnify the stockholders "after all the assets of the company had been transferred to the Egyptian state."

England and France convoked a conference. It took place in London and

[3] Raymond Aron, *Paix et guerre entre les nations* (Paris: Calmann-Lévy, 1962), 495.

was attended by the representatives of eighteen nations. The Anglo-French plan was to set up an international body to administer the canal; Egypt would be invited to participate but would not be given a preponderant voice. In September 1956 a more flexible American plan was put before Nasser. In conjunction with the United Nations, all the states involved would have a say in the administration of the canal. Nasser rejected the plan. The United Nations Security Council was called upon to arbitrate. By a vote of 11 to 9 it decided that the American plan should serve as a basis for further discussion.

While negotiations were under way, the two premiers, Eden and Mollet, hatched secret plans for a military expedition against Egypt. They did not even inform their foreign ministries.

Their common objective was to keep the canal open to everyone, insure the free flow of oil, block Russian infiltration in the Middle East, and overthrow Nasser. The more specific goal of the French government was to weaken the Algerian rebellion by overthrowing its principal foreign supporter.

Plans for the Anglo-French move were completed by October 16. Apparently unbeknown to the British, France concluded a separate agreement with Israel. On the morning of October 30, Israeli troops invaded the Sinai Peninsula. That evening, Eden and Mollet informed their respective parliaments. To justify their action, they contended that it would serve to separate the Israelis from the Egyptians. In the House of Commons the Labour Party voiced violent opposition. Eden received only 270 favorable votes; 218 opposed him. Hugh Gaitskell prefaced the balloting by the remark: "The Anglo-French decision is a negation of the United Nations." In the French National Assembly, a much larger majority approved the expeditions—368 to 182. The opposition consisted mainly of Communists and Poujadists. Pierre Mendès-France abstained, as did a dozen or so Radicals.

The belligerents had counted on American and Soviet neutrality. The Americans were holding presidential and legislative elections and the Russians were confronted with a worker's uprising in Hungary.

The belligerents were mistaken. The Security Council met on October 30, at the request of the United States. The United Nations General Assembly met on November 4. By a vote of 57, with none dissenting, the Assembly ordered a cease-fire and decided to dispatch an international police force to Egypt.

The Anglo-French expedition did not have the advantage of surprise. An air bombardment of several days preceded the parachutists who were sent in on November 5 and the main landing on November 6.

The military miscalculation was compounded by the political error. On the night of November 5–6, while Soviet troops were crushing the rebellion in Budapest, Marshal Bulganin sent a warning to London and Paris. The tone of the message was ominous: "What would happen if France were attacked by states possessing all the terrible means of modern destruction? . . . The Soviet government is fully determined to resort to force to crush the aggressors and re-establish peace in the Orient."

Domestic opposition in Britain, which included even the Conservatives, together with the objections from the Commonwealth, the United States, and the Soviet Union, obliged Eden to capitulate. Mollet had no choice but to follow his example. In the afternoon of November 6, a cease-fire was announced.

The results of the adventure were the very reverse of what the belligerents had hoped to achieve. The flow of oil was curtailed for several months, Soviet prestige increased, and Nasser's position was fortified. Actually, the Israeli army alone could have penetrated to the very center of Egypt.

Thus it became dramatically plain that France and England could not pursue an autonomous policy in a secondary theater of operations.

The British and French had to withdraw for two very fundamental reasons. One was the fear of a Russian atomic attack that would not be countered by American retaliation. For the first time, Soviet atomic weapons, which were considerable, played a deterrent role in the relations between the two superpowers. Although France and England were included in the Big Five, they were not really first-rate powers, despite England's small atomic force.

The second reason was the fear of losing American goodwill and of under-mining the Atlantic Alliance. Were Eden and Mollet surprised by the attitude of the United States? Probably not. They had been careful to conceal their plans from Dulles. At that time the foreign policy of the United States was resolutely defensive. American diplomacy was based on avoidance of the use of force, in accordance with its commitments to the United Nations. The Anglo-French expedition was unquestionably an act of aggression. Extremely uncompromising on moral issues, the United States "put respect for the law above friendship."[4] It intended to deserve the respect of the Third World, even if in so doing it allowed the Soviet Union to win a victory without fighting for it.

England and France had embarked on the adventure without weighing the matter carefully, because their passions had been aroused. The United States responded by invoking ideals—moral law—and its own passionate anti-colonialist sentiments.

According to Liddell Hart, Great Britain was no longer capable of playing the amoral game of power politics.[5] The same could also be said of

---

[4] *Ibid.,* 468.
[5] Hart, *Deterrent,* 32.

France. Yet neither nation had entirely given up playing the game. Their policies on nuclear weapons were proof of this.

French Nuclear Armaments

In July 1946 the MacMahon Act decreed that the United States must not share its atomic secrets. A few months before, Anglo-American collaboration in nuclear research had been interrupted. Nonetheless, England decided to produce her own atomic bomb. In 1954 Congress amended the MacMahon Act to eliminate secrecy in the peaceful application of atomic energy. Two Anglo-American accords were concluded and approved by Congress in 1955 and 1957 respectively. They authorized limited military collaboration between the two countries.

By 1958 England had a fleet of supersonic bombers capable of transporting thermonuclear bombs; she did not attempt to manufacture ballistic missiles. The limited nature of her strategic weapons gave her additional prestige but no real deterrent power. It was inconceivable that Great Britain would resort to atomic weapons without the consent of the United States.

Created in 1945, the French Commissariat of Atomic Energy was initially concerned with the peaceful utilization of atomic energy. In 1955, Gaston Palewski was the minister in charge of atomic energy in the Edgar Faure cabinet. Convinced that, unlike England, France would not receive American help in manufacturing nuclear armaments, he decided to launch a secret research program on their military use.

In his investiture speech of January 1956, Guy Mollet announced his firm opposition to nuclear armaments for France. Rather, he favored French participation in the European Atomic Energy Community (Euratom).

In its original version, the Euratom draft treaty contained a clause stipulating that no member was to embark on military nuclear research without the consent of at least half of the other Euratom partners. In July 1956, during a debate on Euratom, Guy Mollet officially announced that France was pursuing military research, but he promised that France would refrain from exploding a bomb before 1961. In July 1957, Mollet asked Parliament to ratify the Euratom Treaty, reserving for France the right to proceed with her nuclear military experiments. In the course of the discussion, Maurice Bourgès-Maunoury, minister of national defense, said that France must decide between acquiring nuclear weaponry or abandoning the idea of national defense. The Gaullist deputies voted in favor of ratification. In the second five-year plan of the Commissariat of Atomic Energy, Guy Mollet saw to it that appropriations were included for an isotope separation plant. In 1958 the premier, Félix Gaillard, commenting on the total lack of progress in negotiations for nuclear disarmament, decided to manufacture a plutonium bomb in order to test it in 1960. Although by the end of the Fourth Republic France was not yet a nuclear power, she was trying to become one. She had not yet formulated, however, a doctrine for the use of this projected weapon.

Centrifugal Forces within the Alliance

Between 1954 and 1958, England's nuclear arms and France's atomic research did not hamper the smooth functioning of the Alliance. The centrifugal forces at work in England and especially in France resulted from the overseas responsibilities both countries had undertaken and continued to assume.

The Suez crisis was the most spectacular manifestation of their attitude. But it was not to have in England the same sequel that it had in France. England accepted the fact that she could not defy America. Eden had miscalculated; he was forced to withdraw from the political scene. The "Suez Group" that defended him had very little influence within the Conservative Party.

In February 1957, the British government notified the W.E.U. that it intended to withdraw about one-third of its troops from Germany. Faced with one of its recurrent balance-of-payments crises, it invoked the financial clause of the W.E.U. Treaty. Although to meet the request of its partners it withdrew only one of the four divisions posted to NATO, it maintained all the units assigned to the Mediterranean, Africa, the Arabian peninsula, and the Far East. Thus, the British guarantee for the defense of the Continent, which the negotiators of the Paris Accords had cited as a diplomatic triumph, was proving highly unreliable, little more than two years after it had been secured.

Unlike Eden, Mollet's position was strengthened by the Suez expedition. Public opinion ascribed its failure to a lack of solidarity between the United States and its European allies, perhaps even to collusion of sorts between the United States and the Soviet Union, both of which opposed European colonialism.

The prolongation of the war in Algeria reinforced anti-American sentiment and distrust of the Atlantic Pact. The Algerian affair was a particularly delicate issue for NATO. Algeria was within the perimeter covered by the treaty, but the war was a colonial one. As such it was frowned upon by the United States. Officially, to be sure, Dulles accepted the French thesis that this was a purely internal affair. In June 1957 he clearly stated his noninterventionist position. But in the course of a debate in the United States Senate, John Kennedy declared that the solutions envisaged by France were no longer possible. He went on to say that he favored some form of political independence. Jacques Soustelle, speaking before the National Assembly, replied: "The Western Alliance cannot withstand the loss of Algeria, especially if America appears to be contributing to it."

The impact of the Algerian war on France's position within the Atlantic Alliance was twofold. Successive governments transferred to Algeria the largest possible number of French soldiers posted in both Germany and France and assigned to the Atlantic command in peacetime. By 1958, the French contribution to the integrated forces had been reduced to two divisions. The Gaullist group in Parliament, backed by public opinion, objected to the eventual installation of I.R.B.M. launching platforms in France. In the Senate in November 1957, Michel Debré reproached Christian Pineau, the foreign minister, for having requested (in September) I.R.B.M. launching platforms which France would not be free to use as she saw fit. In December he told the Council of the Republic that the Atlantic Pact was becoming an American tool in the hands of the Anglo-Saxons. By a unanimous vote, the National Assembly adopted a resolution requiring parliamentary approval for the installation of any "military equipment not controlled by the French government." This led Félix Gaillard, in an interview with an American weekly, to say that such approval would depend on the degree of political harmony that existed among NATO member states in areas outside of the perimeter covered by the Atlantic Pact. It would also depend, he added, on the manner in which decisions regarding the use of missiles were reached. In an interview accorded *Carrefour*, Debré stated that France intended to place any nuclear arms she manufactured under an exclusively national command.[6] In the course of a lecture delivered in Lausanne in February 1958, Marshal Juin said: "If France had the atom bomb, her rights would not be questioned." Such was the atmosphere in which negotiations took place for a Franco-American accord on I.R.B.M.'s and their bases. Conversations were interrupted by the fall of the Gaillard government in April after France let it be known that she would conclude the accord only if she were allowed to join the atomic club.

The Suez crisis and the events in Algeria led the Atlantic Council to re-examine the conditions under which the Alliance could function. A three-member committee stated that "NATO must not forget that the influence and the interests of its members are not limited to the zone of the treaty, that events outside this zone can gravely affect their collective interests." Reacting to this statement, the NATO Council arranged for a series of internal political consultations. In doing so, it proceeded on the assumption that any differences between the members that could not be settled among themselves should be submitted to the good offices of NATO.

[6] *Journal de Genève*, Jan. 7, 1958.

The Evolution of the German Problem

Germany's position within NATO was strengthened as a result of the withdrawal of British and French troops from the Continent. By the beginning of 1958 the Federal Republic was contributing seven divisions to NATO's conventional forces, whereas France and England contributed only two and three, respectively.

The Franco-German controversy over the Saar was settled satisfactorily between them, but not on the basis laid down by the Paris Accords. The accords decreed that, pending the conclusion of a peace treaty with Germany, a procedure should be established for the Europeanization of the Saar, which was to enjoy political autonomy while remaining tied to the customs union with France. A Franco-Saar convention of May 3, 1955, modified the earlier 1950 agreement to take into account the stipulations of the Paris Accords. The question of the Saar's European status was put to a referendum and the pro-German political parties were authorized to campaign. Sixty-nine per cent of the voters rejected Europeanization on October 23, 1955. They elected an even larger majority of pro-German deputies to the Saarbruck Parliament. New negotiations between France and Germany resulted in the return of the Saar to Germany. The customs union with France was to continue until January 1, 1960. France obtained the permission of Germany and Luxembourg to build a canal in the Moselle River in order to promote the Lorraine metallurgical industry, and a guarantee for coal supplies from the Saar.

Mindful of their German nationality, the Saarlanders had voted to return to Germany. Anyone could have predicted this. The precedent of the 1930's was repeated. As a member of a political alliance founded on respect for democratic freedom, France could not refuse the inhabitants of the Saar the right to choose their nationality. Fortunately, the inconvenience this occasioned did not affect her reconciliation with Germany.

The eventual reunification of Germany continued to be discussed between East and West. At a meeting in Geneva in July 1955, the four heads of governments, in a directive to their foreign ministries, agreed that "the settlement of the German question and the reunification of Germany on the basis of free elections will be effectuated in accordance with the national interests of the German people and the requirements of European security." The NATO Council, in a communiqué of December 1957, informed the Soviet Union that they endorsed this position.

5

The Atlantic Alliance and France in 1958

Actions and Results

NINE YEARS AFTER SIGNING the Atlantic Pact, Western Europe had not only survived; it had prospered in a climate of peace and freedom. Its territorial status remained unchanged. The liberty and freedom that prevailed in the West attracted a large number of East Germans.

The Atlantic Pact, together with the Marshall Plan, had prevented aggression, contained Russia, and helped to promote a Franco-German reconciliation. It had not, however, obliterated the consequences of the Yalta and Potsdam decisions: the division of Europe and Germany. The gains were largely due to a combination of strategy and diplomacy, armaments and negotiation.

The Atlantic Alliance represented a credible defense; it preserved a satisfactory diplomatic cohesion. Militarily, the Alliance followed the classical rule of unanimity and paid lip service to the doctrine of national sovereignty. Although in principle the member states enjoyed equality, in reality they did not. The preeminence of the United States and the understanding between the European states facilitated the integration of the military staffs as well as that of the infrastructure. NATO'S conventional forces, placed under a single command, were coordinated with America's strategic force.

While NATO strengthened its armaments and adapted its strategy to the technical revolution in the manufacture of bombs and vehicles to deliver them, the United States, France, and England continued to negotiate with the Soviet Union on the two basic problems of disarmament and the status of Germany. Negotiations on military and territorial questions were pursued uninterruptedly, yet no solution was found.

Disarmament, worldwide or partial, was attempted but failed. Peace reigned in an atmosphere dominated by the balance of terror and the fear of destruction.

The Status of Germany

Persistent apprehension and the precarious balance of power induced the two superpowers to respect the German status quo. Both nations felt continuously threatened by the possibility of a technological breakthrough. Whoever dominated all of Germany would dominate Europe. Since Germany was and remained divided, neither of the superpowers could control Europe. West Germany belonged to the Atlantic Pact; NATO troops were posted on her soil. East Germany belonged to the Warsaw Pact; she was occupied by Russian troops.

The Federal Republic enjoyed relatively little national sovereignty despite its recognition by the West and its economic progress.

Three territorial problems remained. The first was Berlin. The city was strategically indefensible, yet its importance to the cause of freedom was immense. Berlin was a source of friction between the two blocs. Any serious change in its status would constitute a *casus belli*.

The second problem was the frontier between East Germany and Poland, the Oder-Neisse line. At the Potsdam Conference the Americans and British had refused to recognize this frontier; thereafter they had not budged from their position. The West Germans demanded a return to the frontiers of 1937, the year which preceded the first annexations effected by the Third Reich. In the event of a rapprochement between East and West Europe— which seemed most unlikely in 1958—the new frontier could hardly be challenged.

Reunification was the third territorial problem. When the German Federal Republic joined the North Atlantic Treaty and signed the Brussels Treaty, it promised "never to resort to force to obtain German reunification." Reunification by negotiation presupposed an agreement between the United States and the Soviet Union. On what basis could such an agreement be reached? The neutralization of a reunified Germany? For the West this was conceivable only if free elections were held in all of Germany. The outcome was certain: rejection of Communism. Would a Germany unified on the basis of democratic elections remain neutral? The Russians doubted it. Thus, the question was tossed back and forth from meeting to meeting, and neither side was convinced by the other's arguments. All things considered, the Russians preferred the rearmament of the two Germanies to a unified Germany oriented toward the West. The Federal Republic maintained its position as a matter of principle but abstained from formulating immediate demands, in the hope of hastening political integration with Western

Europe. Ever since their surrender and the division of their country, most Germans wanted to become part of a larger fatherland, Europe. In 1958 reunification was of no moment. Germans said little about it. They did not believe it would happen in the foreseeable future.

To be sure, if West Germany were rearmed, she might acquire a measure of military sovereignty. But it would be a rather limited one, of course, since she was not allowed to manufacture atomic weapons. At all events, in view of the twenty-five Russian divisions stationed in East Germany, West Germany would not be really sovereign; she lacked the means of self-defense. Only with the aid of the Atlantic Alliance, that is to say, with the assistance of the American guarantee, could West Germany survive. Yet within the Alliance, her position depended upon the attitude of France.

France's German Policy

The French policy toward Germany went through two phases: in the first, it favored partition, in the second, reconciliation. The latter survived the impact of the various methods envisaged for German rearmament.

In 1944, when the Allies recognized the French Provisional Government, General de Gaulle announced his determination to see to it that Germany would be in no position to cause trouble. This, in his view, was the object of the Franco-Soviet Pact. De Gaulle indicated to Stalin that he was altogether in agreement with him on the question of the Oder-Neisse line. He demanded the partition of the Reich, especially the separation of the Ruhr and the left bank of the Rhine from the rest of Germany. The French protectorate over the Saar, which Michel Debré defended until the 1955 referendum, marked the final phase of this policy, which was rejected by the Russians as well as the Americans.

Actually, the rivalry of the two superpowers led to the division of Germany along the line of the Soviet zone, and consequently to the fusion of the three Western zones. This was the situation at the time of France's adherence to the Marshall Plan, when she had to come to terms with the Anglo-American goal: to hasten West Germany's economic recovery, which was inseparable from the recovery of the Western Europe. The Centrist majority that supported Robert Schuman's cabinet in 1948 patterned its political policy on that of England and the United States. A few deputies, who were responsive to de Gaulle's objections, did not go along.

By his proposal of May 9, 1950, Robert Schuman opened the way to Franco-German reconciliation. He suggested the establishment of a European Coal and Steel Community. This was an important step in the right direction. The object was to overcome the rivalry of two nations faced with the virtual collapse of an entire civilization. There was less fear, of course, of reconciliation with a weakened and truncated Germany. But most people thought it was all the more important to tie her, by supranational bonds, to France and the other European states. Parliament ratified the Schuman plan in 1951 against a coalition of Gaullists and Communists.

The policy of reconciliation had scarcely been initiated when it was put to the test by the necessity of rearming Germany in order to strengthen the Atlantic Alliance.

To avoid a revival of the German army, the French government suggested to its allies the creation of a supranational organization patterned on the Coal and Steel Community, the E.D.C. The goal would be the same: to tie Germany solidly to the West. This gave rise to a controversy that centered far more on the federal nature of the institution than on the desirability of a reconciliation with Germany. The Gaullist and Communist opposition naturally tried to play up the danger of a strong Germany. But it was apparent in the course of the debate that the idea of Germany as the hereditary enemy had vanished. The non-Communist opponents feared both military and political integration and the possible consequences of German re-unification. A rearmed West Germany might start a war to reconquer East Germany; a Germany unified through negotiation might seek an under-standing with the Soviet Union. The French nationalists did not see any contradiction in their attitude. The most effective guarantee against these possible dangers was precisely a Western Europe federation. It would give the Germans, who had lost a part of their country, a larger fatherland.

The treaty suggested by France was rejected in the National Assembly by a rather slim majority consisting of Communists, Gaullists, neo-Jacobin Radicals, and those Socialists who believed that England should serve as a counterbalance to Germany in any European organization. France decided to broaden Germany's sovereignty in order not to restrict her own.

The alternative suggested by Mendès-France and adopted by Parliament was identical with that proposed by Debré in 1953: the inclusion of Germany in the North Atlantic and Brussels Treaties and the reconstitution of the German national army. An attempt was made to replace political integration in a pre-federated state with an operational integration of NATO's con-ventional forces—a precarious solution because it represented a contractual obligation. England (which was associated militarily with Europe of the Six within the W.E.U.) no longer constituted the desired counter-balance because, two years after the creation of NATO, she had asked to be relieved of part of her commitment to station British troops on the Continent.

By 1958 Germany had more army divisions assigned to NATO than France and England combined. A resurgence of German nationalism was not apparent, but French nationalism, epitomized by General de Gaulle, had sowed the seed.

The Atlantic Policy of France

When the world became crystallized into a bipolar system, France was destined to become part of the Western bloc. Her liberation by the British and American armies, her geographical position in Western Europe and along the ocean, made this inevitable.

It was not de Gaulle who launched France on this road in 1944. He did not favor such a policy, or perhaps he did not realize how necessary it was. He refused to accept England's offer of an alliance, although this would have been a natural prelude to an alliance with the United States. On the contrary, long before the end of hostilities, de Gaulle deliberately sought and obtained an alliance with the Soviet Union. It was to prove disappointing. Yet it was not the Russians but the Americans and the British who gave back to France the external symbols of sovereignty and the right to participate in the debate on the destiny of Germany and Europe. Led by de Gaulle, France attempted until 1947 to act as the arbiter between East and West.

The eviction of the Communists from the government, the bilateral and then the collective American economic aid through the Marshall Plan, the division of Germany into eastern and western sectors, the almost total military void in Western Europe—all these spurred Georges Bidault to ask the United States for permanent military aid. The Dunkirk Treaty with England in 1947 and the Brussels Treaty with England and the Benelux countries in 1948 were forerunners of the North Atlantic Treaty signed in 1949. France ratified it by a very large majority that included a few Gaullist deputies.

As the initiator of the treaty, France was a loyal partner of the Alliance, save during the period of the Suez expedition. In the early years, Franco-American difficulties arose over the question of German rearmament. Throughout the period under consideration, the process of decolonization gave rise to differences between the two countries.

The reluctance of France to see Germany rearmed and the controversy over the E.D.C. delayed (from 1950 to 1954) the implementation of the NATO Council's decision to allow West Germany to share in joint defense efforts.

Only when Communist China intervened did France benefit from American aid in Indochina. The North Atlantic Council waited until December 1952 to approve France's military action in the Far East.

The war in Algeria produced persistent tension between France and the United States. Algeria was within the perimeter covered by the treaty, but successive French governments maintained that this was a purely internal affair. The Suez expedition, which was primarily designed to overthrow Nasser, who was supporting the Algerian rebels, was undertaken without any prior consultation with the United States. It was ended by the American injunction. A section of French public opinion rebelled against the Americans. Its most convincing spokesmen were the Gaullists. They repeated the criticism that de Gaulle had voiced in 1954 when he charged that the Alliance had become an American protectorate of sorts.

The Gaillard cabinet openly demanded that the geographical limits of the treaty be extended to embrace the worldwide activities of the Western powers. The same request had been made more diffidently by Gaillard's predecessors.

France's participation in the common defense was limited because her army was stationed in foreign theaters. The Paris Accords stipulated that fourteen divisions constituted the maximum France would be expected to contribute to NATO's conventional forces. At that time France was actually contributing only six division because of the war in Indochina. The war in Algeria further reduced to two the number of French divisions assigned to NATO.

Although the French army was very well trained in guerrilla warfare, it was less aware of the need for Atlantic cooperation. Military men could not understand why America did not support their overseas operations, or why aid should be belated when and if it did come. Part of the officer corps were inclined to echo the grievances of their politicians in regard to the Atlantic Pact.

These grievances led the last of the Fourth Republic's governments, pressured by the nationalist faction in Parliament, to postpone the installation on French soil of launching platforms for ballistic missiles. The argument was that France was not free to control the use of these missiles.

Pushed by the Gaullist minister, Gaston Palewski, the Edgar Faure cabinet began to study the problem of acquiring nuclear armaments. Guy Mollet and Félix Gaillard explored the possibility of making France a nuclear power, but failed to specify what her attitude should be regarding the utilization of these new weapons when they became operational. Debré made no secret of the Gaullist point of view on the subject: nuclear weapons must be placed under national control.

Thus, the idea of joint defense and loyalty to the Atlantic Alliance conflicted with the notion of an exclusively national system dictated in part by resentment against the United States. France's Atlantic policy declined as the Fourth Republic lost ground and the Gaullist opposition gained.

The Ratio of Armed Forces within the Alliance

The Atlantic Alliance placed greater reliance on continuing American help than on an increase in Europe's contribution. By 1958 the United States was contributing the lion's share for armaments and finance.

The alliance included conventional forces assigned to NATO and non-integrated strategic forces under national command. Conventional forces totaled forty-five to fifty divisions. Of these, twenty-two were stationed in Central Europe, the most dangerous of all fronts. The United States maintained the equivalent of six divisions in Germany, all of them on a war footing. They comprised approximately one-quarter of all the troops assigned to the Central European front.

Both England and America possessed strategic forces but the nuclear power of the United States was approximately a hundred times greater than that of the British. Moreover, technically and politically, the British force was merely an auxiliary of the American.

The United States lost no occasion to manifest its willingness to contribute to Europe's strategic forces. American divisions posted in Germany were given tactical atomic weapons. Similar arms, under dual control, were supplied to a number of states. Launching platforms for intermediate-range ballistic missiles were installed in England and scheduled for early installation in Italy and Turkey. In every instance, however, nuclear warheads were to remain under American control.

The supreme allied commander in Europe was responsible for coordinating the conventional with the strategic forces. The Atlantic Council determined the use of the conventional forces. The president of the United States controlled the strategic forces.

The Atlantic conventional forces were far less powerful than those of the Soviet Union, not including Russia's satellites. A minimum ratio between offensive and defensive forces had not yet been established. The conventional forces of Western Europe were therefore extremely vulnerable to Soviet attack. This situation led to a greater stockpiling of tactical nuclear weapons in Europe. Both factors gave America a preponderant role within the Alliance.

Europe alone was responsible for the inadequacy of its conventional forces. The considerable effort to rearm that had been made during the years of East-West tension did not continue during the period of détente, although there was great prosperity in Europe. In 1958 the NATO European member states spent 5.1 per cent of their gross national product for military purposes, whereas the United States spent 10.2 per cent.[1] In monetary terms, the United States spent more than three times as much as Europe.

The absence of a European nuclear force was due to political divisions as well as to America's determination not to share its atomic know-how with Europe. In 1954 secrecy in atomic research could have been terminated for

[1] United States Congress (88th, 1st Session), *Foreign Operation Appropriations for 1964, Hearings before the Subcommittee of the Committee on Appropriations*, House of Representatives, part 2, Military Assistance Program, 219.

the sake of a European army. Some of the secrecy was discarded in 1956 in order to aid England. But the inadequacy of England's financial and technical resources made it impossible for her to relieve the United States of the responsibility for European defense, at least in the foreseeable future. An isolated European state lacked the means to pay for complete and effective thermonuclear armaments, especially in view of the technological progress achieved by 1958. The cost could have been met had Europe been federated.

In short, in 1958 Europe's territorial integrity rested on the American guarantee concretely evidenced by the presence of United States troops and atomic weapons on European soil.

It seems surprising that Europe should have failed to assume responsibility for its own atomic defense. "Fairly bursting with prosperity, Western Europe today should be able to maintain several dozen large combat units on a permanent basis. It is unprecedented that a great center of civilization should give up the idea of protecting itself, . . . that some of the richest countries in the world should declare their incapacity, even by collective action, to acquire an army powerful enough to challenge a *fraction* of the Soviet army, operating two to three thousand kilometers from its bases."[2]

Raymond Aron's judgment was a condemnation of Europe's unwillingness to make financial sacrifices for the establishment of an adequate conventional force. Also open to criticism was its unwillingness to make the political sacrifices that would have enabled it to establish a nuclear force. Had it done so, Europe would have been an equal partner within the Atlantic Alliance.

Although all the states of Western Europe, including the neutrals, enjoyed the protection of the United States, military and financial contributions to the common defense were entirely unequal.

The Central European front was the most vulnerable to a nuclear attack because of the density of its population; it was also the most exposed to conventional attacks because of the heavy concentration of Russian troops in East Germany. The conventional forces of the Alliance were concentrated in West Germany: seven German divisions, six American, three British, and two French.

England's decision to acquire atomic arms and to defend certain of her overseas territories, together with France's need to send most of her troops to Algeria, served to strengthen Germany's position within the Alliance. Germany fulfilled the obligations of the Paris Accords with utmost punctuality because her geographical position called for considerable vigilance. Her seven divisions were set up with the help of American instructors.

The two European nations that made the heaviest military contributions,

[2] Raymond Aron, *Paix et guerre entre les nations* (Paris: Calmann-Lévy, 1962), 489.

both absolutely and relatively, were England and France (6.9 per cent of their gross national product in 1958). Germany's rearmament was necessarily very gradual; in 1958 the cost represented only 3 per cent of her gross national product.

The Alliance was less cohesive in 1958 than it had been in 1954. "The Atlantic Pact is more than a traditional alliance within the zone of the two blocs; it is less than that outside of this zone."[3] Hence the internal tensions provoked by colonial conflicts. In 1958, with the end of decolonization, one might have expected these tensions to decrease.

The prestige of the United States was declining: the Sputnik demonstrated that the Soviet Union was leading in the ballistics race.

Although unwilling to increase their military and financial contributions, the European states demanded some measure of autonomy from the Americans. The hegemony of the United States was criticized primarily in France, where a powerful opposition led the attack.

Western Europe had no army of its own; the member states furnished unequal numbers of contingents to the Atlantic army. "For the time being," Raymond Aron wrote, "Europe prefers security amid impotence to anxiety amid the dangers of a restored autonomy."[4]

[3] *Ibid.*, 440.
[4] *Ibid.*, 498.

II

The Construction of Europe

6

An Ancient Dream and a New Opportunity

Several Nations, One Civilization

E UROPE IS NOT a geographical or ethnological phenomenon, but a historical one, steeped in intellectual and moral tradition. Europe exists in the consciousness of Europeans—a collective consciousness. It is common traditions that fashion a civilization.

Europe is also a collection of nations, each differentiated from the others by language, religion, ethnology, size, resources, and ambitions.

This single yet diversified civilization has always been subjected to internal centripetal and centrifugal forces. The dream of a unified Europe is as ancient as the existence of national rivalries.

In the nineteenth century, on the morrow of Napoleon's attempt to unify Europe by force, the conflict between nations and civilizations was latent. Collaboration among the great powers, the search for national unity in Germany and Italy, the colonial expansion of England and France, the carrying out of a political and an industrial revolution—all these offered a vast field for the energies of Europeans who experienced a century of peace—save for a few limited incidents.

In the twentieth century the conflict between nations and civilizations was an open one. It arose at a time when Europe had reached the height of its spiritual influence and material dominance. It was a deadly conflict. For the first time in centuries Europe, as it emerged from the Treaty of Versailles, impoverished, fragmented, isolated, was exposed to foreign pressures: American capitalism in the West, Marxist ideology in the East.

Europe—*Willingly or by Force*

A few philosophers and statesmen were concerned about the excesses of nationalism. "Europe is a danger to itself," Lucien Romier wrote in 1926. "Instead of promoting the idea of civilization, the intellectual movement has for a long time been evolving exclusively around the concepts of state and nation."[1] The pan-European union of Count Coudenhove-Kalergi, created in 1924, aspired to win over an élite to ideals centered on European unification.

To this cause a statesman, Aristide Briand, brought the prestige of his name. On September 5, 1929, he addressed the League of Nations: "I believe that between peoples that are grouped together geographically like the peoples of Europe, some kind of federal bond should exist." Cautious, vague, Briand went on to say that such a federal bond could be beneficial "without affecting the sovereignty of any one nation that might belong to such an association." On May 1, 1930, he sent the interested states a note in the name of France: *Memorandum on a European Organization*. It proposed that there be established, within the framework of the League of Nations, a conference, an assembly of all the European states, a political committee, a permanent executive body, and a secretariat. The plan was received with little enthusiasm despite the fact that is envisaged an association, not a federation. England, in particular, refused to join any European organization other than the League of Nations. Winston Churchill, who held no government post at that time, published an article on the United States of Europe in the *Saturday Evening Post*. Although approving the idea of a federation for the Continent, he rejected it for England because of her Commonwealth: "We are with Europe but not part of it. We are interested in and associated with it but not encompassed by it."[2]

We see then that as early as 1930 the question of European unity was raised—its modality, association or federation—and its territory—the European continent, with or without England.

Briand's death, the worldwide economic crisis, the rise to power of German national socialism—all these overshadowed the first official attempt to unify Europe through persuasion and argument.

Shortly thereafter an attempt was made to unify Europe by force. Hitler maintained that he was a European. But he wanted a unitary, dictatorial Europe, submissive to German hegemony; the supremacy of one nation was to follow armed conflict between nations.

All Europe was to be defeated in this struggle—but not the idea of European unity.

[1] Lucien Romier, *Nation et Civilisation* (Paris: Simon Kra, 1962), 101.
[2] Cited by Roger Massip, "Churchill et l'Europe," *Communautés européennes*, Feb. 1965, 5.

The First Step

Like individuals, collectivities draw closer in times of crises. While Eastern Europe was gradually succumbing to Soviet domination, Western Europe sought American assistance and protection. In this truncated but none the less privileged continent, the peoples preserved their freedom of speech, but the nations no longer controlled their political destinies.

Would the democratic unification of Western Europe enable most of the nations to recover their lost sovereignty?

The first authoritative voice to mention a United States of Europe was that of Winston Churchill. Speaking in Zurich on September 19, 1946, he said: "Why should there not exist a European body that would give a broader sense of patriotism and a common citizenship to the peoples of this powerful continent?" But he added one condition: "The first step in the resurrection of the European family must be the association of France and Germany." He also had one reservation, which he had already expressed in 1930: "Great Britain, the British Empire . . . must be the friend and guarantor of the new Europe"—a friend but not a partner.

The speech was not well received in France. Memories of the war were too fresh. Following de Gaulle's lead, the government demanded the partition of Germany, which Jacques Bainville had advocated earlier.

Meanwhile, the growing tension between the United States and the Soviet Union underscored the split in Europe. After the Moscow Conference of March 1947, the French government made no further demands regarding Germany, save for the Saar.

In these circumstances, Churchill's voice reverberated throughout the Continent. Movements were organized to promote European unity. Politicians from all the democratic parties joined them. They coordinated their efforts so that it was possible by May 1948 to convene a European Congress at the Hague. It was the first manifestation of European political opinion. The congress passed resolutions urging the European nations to sacrifice part of their sovereignty and to establish a Legislative Assembly composed of representatives of the national parliaments.

In March 1948 France signed the Treaty of Brussels. On this occasion, Georges Bidault told the National Assembly: "The time has come to act as quickly and as drastically as possible to organize what remains of Europe."

The French government was committed to building European unity. The Socialists and the M.R.P. were favorable to the idea, as were some Radicals and a section of the Right. The Communists had been part of the opposition since May 1947. They were firmly opposed to unification. De Gaulle, too, was in the opposition camp. He expressed a wish for the resurrection of Europe, "May it be free, may it be unified," but on two conditions: Germany must be partitioned (speech of March 1948 at Compiègne) and France must become strong (speech of October 1947 at Bayonne).

Who Would Be the Federator?

Churchill had tossed the ball. Bidault tossed it back. In 1949 the game of power politics was played both for and against the creation of a cohesive Western European unity.

England had rendered the cause of democracy a great service. One could rely on her political experience. Her industrial potential was unimpaired. It was therefore natural that she should be called upon to take the lead in the movement toward unification. The most prominent statesmen of her Commonwealth, Menzies and Fraser, urged her to undertake the task. The politicians on the Continent were more than willing for her to do so. On May 4, 1948, Ernest Bevin told the House of Commons that the Brussels Treaty "has truly made us part of Europe." The Labour Party, however, objected to the Hague Congress and discouraged its members from attending. Churchill was no longer in power. His voice could no longer influence British public opinion. Moreover, he would have been the first to remind England that she owed allegiance to three political entities. She was the leader of the British Commonwealth of Nations. She was a member of the Anglo-Saxon community of peoples; because of this she enjoyed special relations with the United States. She was one of the principal states of Western Europe. The trials and tribulations of Europe in no way modified this order of priorities.

Responsible for and victim of the recesses of nationalism, Germany, divided and occupied, was not qualified to speak in the name of Western Europe. But because of her federal tradition, Germany was predisposed to accept new political and administrative structures.

It was therefore France—not because she had any special aptitude for the task but rather because there was no other candidate—that was called upon to play a federative role. Her centralist tradition was alien, even hostile, to federal institutions. Her social divisions, the legacy of the oscillations between authoritarian and representative regimes, had become attenuated by up-surges of nationalism, whether of the Jacobin or Maurrasian variety. Poor financial and monetary management decreased the authority of successive governments. Nevertheless, whenever France championed a generous cause, she always found sincere support. This was also true when she embraced the cause of European unity.

The pressures from without intensified those from within. Willy-nilly, the United States became the protector of Western Europe. It believed that a Europe unified through its own political efforts involved less risk than a divided Europe.

But fear of the Soviet Union constituted a more powerful stimulus than American support. The Communist show of force at Prague in February 1948, the Berlin blockade of October, were examples to ponder.

The unification of Europe was therefore closely connected from the very beginning with Atlantic defense.

The Instrument and the Various Stages

The instrument of unification, like the agency of collective defense, was an international organization.

Organizations aimed merely at cooperation derived from a very ancient institution: the international conference. They lent it the quality of permanence. Their powers were limited to administration or supervision.

The organizations whose goals were integration—the trend toward organic union—exercised higher functions in the legislative, executive, or judicial domains through a delegation of sovereignty by the member states.[3]

The first European institution, the Organization for European Economic Cooperation, was created at the urging of the United States. The second was established through the efforts of France: the Council of Europe. Both organizations aimed primarily at cooperation.

The goal of integration made its appearance with the formation of the European Coal and Steel Community which brought together a limited number of states for the purpose of improving one specific sector of the economy. It was an answer to Churchill's wish for Franco-German reconciliation.

The European Coal and Steel Community (E.C.S.C.) was the first supranational organization. It was patterned after the federal conception of the relations between states. The European Defense Community (E.D.C.) was based on the same principle. Its failure led to renewed efforts to create a federal Europe of the Six.

With the establishment of the European Economic Community (E.E.C.) and Euratom, a fresh attempt was made to complete the economic edifice of the Six, of which the E.C.S.C. was but one pillar.

Responsible for the launching and subsequent failure of the E.D.C., France was not the initiator of the Common Market. She was, however, a firm supporter.

Throughout the various stages of European reconstruction, there was always one stumbling block—the status of Germany. The political consolidation and economic recovery of West Germany were the indispensable prerequisites of a unified Europe. Yet French public opinion was divided not only on how to unify Europe but also on the place that West Germany should occupy in it. At every stage the position of the Federal Republic grew stronger while uncertainty about German reunification persisted.

[3] Paul Reuter, *Institutions internationales* (Paris: P.U.F., 1963), 194.

7

From the Marshall Plan to the European Coal and Steel Community

The European Economy on the Morrow of World War II

WHEN WESTERN EUROPE was liberated by Anglo-American troops, it was largely without food supplies or raw materials. It had hardly any tools and limited means of payments. England and the neutral countries—Switzerland, Sweden, and Portugal—were relatively prosperous. Economic life was semi-paralyzed in France, Belgium, the Netherlands, and Italy. In Germany it had come to a virtual standstill.

Western Europe was therefore obliged to import food, coal, and machinery. It had little capacity to export and insufficient gold reserves.

If Europe had been obliged to rely exclusively on its own rseources it would have been faced with the following dilemma: either to reduce imports to a bare minimum, accept a very low standard of living, and postpone the restoration of its productive capacity, or import a great deal more and thus quickly use up its monetary reserves.

What Europe actually did was to import less, borrow from the United States, and use up a part of its reserves.

Despite American loans to England, France, and other nations, in 1947 Western Europe faced a serious payments crisis.

The Marshall Plan

To meet the situation, the United States decided to alter its methods of furnishing aid. Instead of bilateral assistance, which had been given in the form of long-term loans, it decided to give collective aid for a period of four

[74

consecutive years. Aid was in the form of grants, on condition that the nations of Europe were committed to a policy of mutual assistance.

"Our policy," General Marshall told the Harvard graduating class on June 5, 1947, "is directed not against any country or any doctrine but against hunger, poverty, desperation, and chaos. Its purpose should be the revival of a working economy in the world so as to permit the emergence of political and social conditions in which free institutions can exist."

American aid was therefore to benefit all Europe, Western and Eastern, including the Soviet Union. Acceptance of the offer might have led to collaboration between the two superpowers. But Russian distrust precluded this.

The French and British governments asked Molotov to meet with Bidault and Bevin in Paris on June 27. The American offer was turned down by the Soviet Union and consequently by its satellites.

From then on the Marshall Plan performed two roles. It evidenced the solidarity that existed between the United States and Western Europe. And it became a weapon in the ideological struggle between a free society and Communism. A Europe freed from inflationary pressures and capable of developing international trade would cease to be attracted by Marxist-Leninist theories. An American law providing for economic cooperation was approved on April 3, 1948. It established an administration to supervise American aid. Bilateral accords were to be concluded between the United States and each of the European countries receiving aid. The latter were to participate in an institution empowered to administer collective aid and to help formulate a common economic policy.

The policy was to include West Germany, that is, the Anglo-American bizone and the French occupied zone. In February 1948 the Big Three met in London to discuss the economic and also the political status of Germany. The Benelux countries asked to be included and they were invited to join the discussions. An interallied accord was concluded in June. The communiqué that was subsequently published contained a series of recommendations regarding Germany.

France and the New Status of Germany

Discussions between France and her allies centered on the economic status of the Ruhr and the political status of West Germany.

The French government favored internationalization of the Ruhr industries. It had to acquiesce, however, to the creation of the International Authority for the Ruhr charged with supervising the distribution of coal, coke, and steel and with seeing to it that these industries did not become an instrument of aggression.

The June 7 communiqué on Germany's status defined the objective as follows: "To enable the German people . . . ultimately to recover their unity within the framework of a free and democratic government." It was not difficult for the three occupying powers to agree that a Constituent Assembly should be convoked and that the constitution should be ratified by the German people.

The French preferred a very loose federation between the German states or *Länder* whereas the Americans favored strong centralization. Agreement was reached on a federal constitution that would protect the rights of the various states yet provide for a central authority strong enough to guarantee individual rights and freedom. Thus, as the communiqué stated, the Germans would be "free to have, prior to the time when they could take over all governmental responsibility, political organizations and institutions enabling them to assume at once those governmental responsibilities that were consistent with the minimal requirements of occupation and control."

The publication of the communiqué brought a violent reaction from de Gaulle. In a lengthy statement, he analyzed the London recommendations, commented on them, and concluded with a bitter condemnation.

According to him, West Germany would probably develop into a totalitarian Reich. Thus, German unity of sorts might be achieved around Prussia, leaving France with only flimsy guarantees. Alluding to "the Germanies"—a conception of Jacques Bainville and Charles Maurras—he described them as "German states, each with its own institutions, personality, and sovereignty. They could form a federation of their own and become part of a European group in which they would find the proper framework and means for their development." His opinion was categorical: since his resignation, French diplomacy had been no more than "a series of retreats that finally constituted a surrender." It followed, of course, that "France cannot and must not accept the 'recommendations' of this strange communiqué from London."

Le Monde commented that the victors could not impose on the German people a political organization that was repulsive to them. It expressed surprise at the prophecy that East Germany would impose her system on West Germany: "This is like acknowledging the superiority of the Soviet system, as if we have no faith in American help and efforts, or in Western Europe's attempts to become unified and to integrate Germany." In conclusion, and without beating about the bush, *Le Monde* stated apropos of French policy: "A mixture of churlishness, blindness, and false grandeur will not bring us success."[1]

The Council of Ministers approved the London accords negotiated by Bidault. It decided to submit them to the National Assembly in order to obtain a vote on foreign policy. The government was supported by the

[1] *Le Monde*, June 10, 1948.

Socialists, the M.R.P., and the non-Gaullist Radicals. But it encountered the combined opposition of the Communists, the Gaullists, and most of the Moderates. "Let's raise ourselves to the level of Europe!" Paul Reynaud exclaimed. He carried with him a dozen rightist deputies. The premier, Robert Schuman, intervened to support Bidault: "Our real guarantee is interallied solidarity." The government won by a slim majority—300 to 286.

The balloting of June 17, 1948, was important for more than one reason. First of all, a year after the Communists had joined the opposition, it underscored the new French policy toward Germany. France was now tending toward a political and economic rapprochement with democratic Germany. In spite of its reservations, the resolution endorsed the London recommendations. Furthermore, the vote highlighted the nature of the political alignments for or against this policy. The Center parties favored European reconstruction. The Communists, the Gaullists, and the old nationalist Right were hostile to it. This coalition of extremist parties was to influence the outcome of several important votes on foreign policy during the ephemeral life of the Fourth Republic.

A few weeks later, the National Assembly was called upon to ratify the Convention of European Economic Cooperation. It thus established the European body envisaged by the Marshall Plan (whose functions will be analyzed in the following section). Ratification of the bilateral Franco-American accord was voted on July 7 by 336 to 183 (Communists and their sympathizers), a number of Gaullists (following Edmond Michelet's lead) abstaining; many Moderates also abstained.

The Organization for European Economic Cooperation

The Convention was signed in Paris on April 16, 1948. It created the Organization for European Economic Cooperation comprising sixteen countries of Western Europe. Initially, West Germany was represented by the commanders-in-chief of the American, French, and British zones. She became a full-fledged member in 1949. Spain was excluded because of her political regime. The geographical proximity of Russia prevented Finland from joining. Yugoslavia was prohibited from belonging because of her ideological kinship with the Soviet Union. The O.E.E.C. therefore embraced those European countries which shortly afterward were to sign the North Atlantic Treaty, as well as the neutrals: Switzerland, Sweden, Austria, and Ireland.

The new organization was a kind of permanent intergovernmental conference. Its task was to establish and implement a joint recovery program that would enable the member states "to attain . . . without outside help of exceptional nature, an adequate level of activity."

While the Convention was being drafted, England acted to limit the powers of the organization. She wanted the secretary-general to have only a consultative role, whereas the United States and France preferred to see him endowed with more extensive powers.[2]

Once the Convention was signed, England intended to apply it in a limited fashion. From the very outset, she tried to restrict the role of the O.E.E.C. in the distribution of American aid, insisting that discussions with the United States should take place within the framework of bilateral accords rather than within that of the Convention.

Similarly, England believed that the organization was not qualified to draw up a plan for Western European recovery that would be in harmony with the various national plans. In February 1949, Belgium suggested that the power to make decisions relating to economic planning be expressly conferred upon the organization.[3] Since this solution was discarded in April 1949, the French government commissioned Jean Monnet to work out, with his opposite number in London, Sir Edwin Plowden, the basis for an economic union between France and England that might serve as the nucleus for a European economic union. The attempt failed.[4]

The Liberation of Trade and Payments

The O.E.E.C. was most effective in the domain of intra-European trade and payments. In 1950 it inaugurated the European Payments Union (E.P.U.), a clearing and credit institution for the settlement of current transactions on a multilateral basis. The O.E.E.C. removed quantitative obstacles from the path of trade. A certain economic solidarity between the European countries developed which promoted the growth of trade. All the member states benefited.

But the weakness of the French monetary and fiscal policy proved the main obstacle to the smooth functioning of the intra-European system of trade and payments.

Between 1945 and 1949, the franc lost six-sevenths of its nominal value. Although France received more assistance from the United States than any other European country, she had the greatest difficulty in meeting her commitments concerning the liberation of her trade and payments. In 1952, the inflationary effects of the war in Indochina, plus the rising costs of raw materials resulting from the Korean War, led Antoine Pinay, then premier

[2] Max Beloff, *New Dimensions in Foreign Policy* (London: George Allen & Unwin, 1961), 38, 39.

[3] Achille Albonetti, *Préhistoire des Etats-Unis d'Europe* (Paris: Editions Sirey, 1963), 49.

[4] Etienne Hirsch, "L'Angleterre fera-t-elle antichambre?" *Cahiers de la République*, no. 51, Jan. 1963, 9.

and minister of finance, to establish quotas. In 1954, just as the policy of free trade was being resumed, the Algerian War replaced the struggle in Indochina. Once again inflationary trends developed. France's deficit within the European Payments Union increased. In 1957, Paul Ramadier called for a complete resumption of quotas. Indirect devaluation was effected through subsidies for exports and levies on imports, but this did not substantially improve the country's finances.

The Fourth Republic was unable to insure a balance in its external payments. From 1945 to 1958 the total deficit rose to eleven billion dollars. Forty-four per cent of this deficit was financed by American aid. The rest was taken care of by borrowing abroad and by drawing on gold and currency reserves.[5]

The mishaps of the French economic and monetary policy weakened its resolve and hampered its action in favor of the construction of Europe.

The Council of Europe

On May 10, 1948, a congress was held at the Hague. Churchill's personality dominated the proceedings. The congress unanimously voted in favor of convoking a European Assembly to be elected by the parliaments of the member states.

The resolution was presented to the Consultative Council of the Brussels Treaty, where French and British views clashed. On July 19, Bidault suggested to his colleagues that a European interparliamentary assembly be created to make recommendations to the governments for the establishment of an economic and customs union. The suggestion was rejected by the British government. On October 26 it made a counterproposal for the creation of a European Committee of Ministers. On January 28, 1949, the Council reached a compromise solution. Without legislative or constituent powers, the Assembly would be parliamentary in nature, and purely consultative. Authority would be vested in the Committee of Ministers.

The treaty creating the Council of Europe was signed on May 5, 1949. The members of the Council were the five original signatories of the Brussels Treaty. They invited five more nations to join them—Denmark, Norway, Sweden, Ireland, and Italy.

The National Assembly ratified the treaty by a large majority—423 to 182. Only the Communists voted against it.

The Assembly of the Council of Europe was so composed that it represented the views of the national parliaments rather than those of the countries themselves. It was quickly to become a political forum where

[5] André de Lattre, *Les finances extérieures de la France* (Paris: P.U.F., 1959), 358, 359.

certain French proposals were debated—the Schuman Plan in the economic domain, the Pleven Plan in matters of defense.

Schuman's Declaration of May 9, 1950

"Europe cannot be forged all at once, nor by an over-all reconstruction; Europe will be created by concrete achievements which first will establish real solidarity. To unify all the European nations would require the elimination of the secular conflict between France and Germany; any action undertaken must first of all affect France and Germany."

"To this end . . . the French government proposes to place all Franco-German coal and steel production under a common High Authority, in an organization open to the participation of the other countries of Europe."

"By pooling basic commodities and by establishing a new High Authority whose decisions will create a tie between France, Germany, and the other member states, this proposal lays the first concrete foundations for a European federation, the indispensable prerequisite of peace."

The statement, which Robert Schuman read to the press, took everyone by surprise. For one thing, the procedure was unprecedented; no one had been told about it beforehand, neither the ministers involved, the professionals of the coal and steel industries, nor Parliament.[6] For another, what he said was unusual: the problem of Franco-German relations was approached in a new spirit, a spirit that transcended national rivalries and paved the way for a joint undertaking. That very morning the foreign minister had informed Chancellor Adenauer, knowing that the Federal Republic would agree.

This move was the work of two men—Jean Monnet, who inspired it, and Robert Schuman, who assumed political responsibility for it.

Like many revolutionary ideas, the notion of a coal and steel pool corresponded to a current of thought that shaped the objectives of its authors.

In 1949 the idea of coordinating the basic European industries was mentioned at meetings of the Council of Europe in Strasbourg and the United Nations Economic Commission in Geneva. Furthermore, the United States was urging France to eliminate restrictions on German industry, especially metallurgy, and to clarify her stand on the integration of Germany into Western Europe. At about the same time Washington discussed the question of rearming Germany, whose military potential and industrial power were based on coal and steel.[7]

[6] Pierre Gerbet, *La genèse du plan Schuman* (Lausanne: Université de Lausanne, 1962), 30.
[7] *Ibid.*, 15.

Control of German industry could only grow weaker with the passage of time. Had not the moment come to find some form of joint administration? This question was already being raised in certain French political circles.

The Purpose of the Coal and Steel Pool

The creation of a Franco-German coal and steel pool would serve convergent economic and political goals. Furthermore, the formulation of economic goals would facilitate the acceptance of controversial political goals.

The French steel industry was afraid it would be outstripped by a rival with greater productive capacity, more highly concentrated units, and more competitive prices. The coal-steel ratio in France and Germany was such that the two economies were complementary rather than competitive. The French steel industry imported German coke and Germany's steel industry imported French iron ore. It therefore seemed expedient to create a vast mining and industrial complex embracing not only the Ruhr and Lorraine but also the Walloon part of Belgium, Luxembourg, and the north of France—a region artificially divided by political frontiers. A common market in coal and steel would profit by the economic advantage of larger territory in a highly industrialized and densely populated area.

Such an economic policy would forge powerful common interests between the national economies. West Germany would be bound to France and to Western Europe by organic ties. France would get full credit for generosity by offering her hereditary enemy the prospect of reconciliation. From the point of view of security, this solution was substituted for the reverse alliance since the military threat had now moved to the East. It also provided insurance against a possible rapprochement between West Germany and the Soviet Union. The Germans were badly shaken by defeat. Their new democratic institutions had no roots. It might therefore be possible to consolidate these institutions into a community larger than a truncated nation.

In short, by substituting organic bonds for the traditional rivalry, Robert Schuman's proposal tended to satisfy France's need for security in the face of the German potential. An association between France and Germany would promote the long-term goal of a federated Europe.

Institutional Measures

The magnitude of the objective called for new methods and means.

Robert Schuman told the National Assembly on July 25: "We persist in believing that the mere coordination of governmental efforts is not enough."

The recent past justified his assertion: the failure of economic planning within the O.E.E.C., the Council of Europe's lack of political power.

The foreign minister's concept of the necessary institutions was summed up by the three options indicated by André Marchal on how to build European unity: the mechanism of the market or organized integration; a union of sectors or a union of nations; whether to give priority to political or economic considerations.[8]

The discussion of these options pointed up the significance of the new terms that had appeared in the political vocabulary—integration, supranationalism—compared to the old and vague terms of confederation and federation.

The first option was one of economic policy. Should the obstacles to trade between the countries in question be eliminated? Or should a certain number of measures be taken to adapt the economic structures in order to cushion the shock of a return to free trade? The present solidarity of the members states would disappear if the free movement of people, merchandise, and capital—the desired economic objective—had damaging and consequently unacceptable social consequences. Integration would produce solidarity. In its literal sense, integration meant the consolidation of all the parts into a single whole. In its initial economic sense, solidarity meant vertical industrial concentration. In the new sense of the word, integration signified "the process . . . of abolishing discrimination between economic units belonging to different national states."[9]

The second option involved the domain where integration was to be applied. Should one approach it piecemeal, should it be limited to the coal and steel sectors, or should the approach be worldwide and apply to all national economic activities? The authors of the Schuman Plan opted for a union of sectors. This might seem surprising. Only the creation of a general common market could confer on each of the nations involved the advantages of an economy of sizable dimensions, especially by lowering costs and prices. The economic policy of one integrated sector embracing several nations might very well conflict with national economic policies for all the sectors of a particular nation. This objection, which was economic in nature, was overlooked, however, because the political difficulties in launching an economic and customs union seemed so overwhelming. The economic union concluded in 1944 with the Benelux countries progressed slowly. The Franco-Italian Treaty of March 26, 1949, establishing a customs union had to be abandoned because of the objections voiced in industrial and professional circles.

[8] Marchal, *L'Europe solidaire*, 150.
[9] Bela Belassa, *Theory of Economic Integration* (Homewood, Ill.: Richard Irwin, 1961), 1, quoted by André Marchal, *L'Europe solidaire*, 185.

The third option on how to build Europe pertained to integration, its nature and purpose and its role in determining the order of priorities. Was the creation of political institutions for purposes of economic union the highest priority? Or, on the contrary, should efforts first be made to achieve economic integration in the hope eventually of achieving political union? Friedrich List, writing in the nineteenth century, had this to say: "Commercial union and political union are twin sisters: one cannot be born without the other." This was also Schuman's opinion. The new institution and the pooling of basic commodities seemed to him "the fundamental bases for a European federation." Political integration may be defined as the process whereby the political organs of nations transfer their loyalty to a new decision-making entity whose institutions have an authority transcending that of national institutions. Political integration is therefore a deliberate step in the direction of a federal type of state.

Reactions to the French Proposal

Because of its tone as well as its substance, Schuman's declaration caused a shock.

The American government immediately expressed approval for a move that was in harmony with the basic objectives of its foreign policy ever since the Marshall Plan: the reconstruction of a strong, unified Europe.

When Chancellor Adenauer was informed of the declaration, he hailed it as "a magnanimous gesture on the part of France toward Germany." The German government was quick to perceive the advantages of the French plan: Germany would be joining the new institution on a footing of equality with her partners. Supported by a parliamentary majority, Adenauer gave his formal approval on May 16. Only the Socialist Party dissented. It refused to identify Europe with the capitalist system. German businessmen looked forward eagerly to the end of restrictions on the production of basic commodities.

Would England accept the principle of a supranational authority that had the approval of her continental neighbors? Jean Monnet went to London on May 15. A British communiqué of June 2 stated that the government "is unable to accept in advance the principles underlying the French proposal." On June 13, the Executive Committee of the Labour Party published a brochure entitled *European Unity* which explained the British position. The authors claimed that "in terms of origins, language, institutions, customs, political views and economic interests, they felt closer to Australia and New Zealand than to Europe." They believed that close economic cooperation between England and the Continent would not be beneficial since the industries involved did not complement one another. Actually, they were afraid that in a federated Europe the Socialist parties might be in the minority and that therefore the social reforms recently enacted in England might be jeopardized.

French public opinion generally applauded Schuman's declaration. *Le Monde* observed: "The French plan is based on the assumption that Franco-German entente must be the focal point of any European union. This view seems sounder than the opinion that future Franco-German relations will depend on a unified Europe."

Both the Left and the Right, however, openly dissented. The Communists talked about German economic preponderance. At the Socialist Party Congress, Guy Mollet voiced alarm over the collaboration of French and German capitalists. He was afraid of an offensive against Protestant and labor-oriented Great Britain. Pierre-Etienne Flandin reflected the opinion of the traditional Right when he said: "We are offering Germany, after having beaten her, what she would have imposed on us, had she won." General de Gaulle had greeted with enthusiasm on March 16, 1950, Chancellor Adenauer's proposal for a political and economic union of France and Germany. "In short, this amounts to a revival of Charlemagne's venture on modern, economic, social, strategic, and cultural foundations." Speaking at Metz on May 19, he alluded sarcastically to the foreign minister's proposal: "De Gaulle says we must create a new economy, and then we are handed this mumbo-jumbo about coal and steel in the name of some vague combine, without knowing where we are going."

As for the industrial circles, they were divided. The steel industry's trade association expressed surprise at not having been consulted and said it preferred cartels to an international organization. Communist-influenced trade unions sided with the French Communist Party. Socialist and Christian trade unions approved the government's move and demanded that representatives of the working class be included in the membership of the High Authority.

Negotiation and Ratification of the Treaty

To prevent delaying tactics from Britain, Robert Schuman invited the governments that agreed to the principle of the French proposal to publish a joint communiqué. This communiqué, issued on June 3, stated that the six governments "have as their immediate goal the pooling of coal and steel production and the setting up of a new authority whose decisions will be binding" on the states concerned.

The prospect of German rearmament hung over the negotiations that began in Paris on June 20. The Federal Republic hoped to obtain freedom of action in steel production in exchange for its adherence to the Schuman Plan. The French government subordinated its acceptance of the principle of German rearmament in any form whatsoever to the signing of the coal-steel pool treaty. The Americans therefore had to exert pressure on the Germans to get them to accept measures to de-cartelize which would satisfy the French. It was the intervention of John McCloy, the American high commissioner in Bonn, that forced the Federal Republic to consent on March 14, 1951, to de-cartelization proposals which resembled the ones put forward by the Allies in December 1950.[10]

At Germany's request, it was agreed that the signing of the treaty would not prejudice the future status of the Saar. The Benelux countries and Italy, fearful of being dominated by a Franco-German coalition, secured an enlargement of the High Authority's membership from five to nine. Finally, the Benelux countries, in the absence of any real political federation, were apprehensive of giving the High Authority exclusive power to determine a common policy. They therefore insisted upon the establishment of a Council of Ministers to bring before the High Authority the points of view of the member states.[11]

The treaty was signed in Paris on April 18, 1951. Immediately thereafter the French government informed the Germans that it would suggest the abolition of the International Authority for the Ruhr as soon as the High Authority was qualified to take over.

In November the Economic Council and the commissions of the National Assembly were requested to examine the treaty. The Economic Council voted in favor by 111 to 15, with 29 abstaining. The representatives of the C.G.T. (Confédération Général du Travail) opposed the treaty. Unwilling to align themselves with the Communists, the employers' representatives abstained. In principle, they opposed any control by an agency not recruited from their own ranks. In any case, they were highly suspicious of international planning. They objected particularly to Article 65 of the treaty which prohibited ententes. The Assembly's commissions on foreign affairs, labor, industrial production, and finance favored ratification. The economic affairs and defense commissions were opposed.

The Assembly debate began in December. The majority elected on June 17, 1951, excluded the Communists and the R.P.F. The Socialists participated in the government. Guy Mollet, vice-president in the Pleven cabinet, was responsible for matters pertaining to the Council of Europe. Robert Schuman

---

[10] William Diebold, Jr., *The Schuman Plan* (New York: Frederick A. Praeger, 1959), 70–73.
[11] *Ibid.*, 63.

remained foreign minister. Unlike the German Socialists, whose critical attitude had not altered since May 1950, the French Socialists rallied to the idea of supranationalism and were resigned to England's absence. The position of the traditional Right was as yet unknown. Paul Reynaud came out warmly in favor of ratification, but General Aumeran opposed the re-integration of Germany into the European community of nations. Pierre André, a spokesman for the steel industry, warned against the danger created by England's nonparticipation and the threat of Germany's industrial power. He make a motion to adjourn, which the R.P.F. seconded. The Gaullist arguments were presented by Jacques Soustelle and Léon Noël. Soustelle objected to the treaty on the ground that it "turned over a major industrial sector to a stateless, uncontrolled technocracy." Noël criticized the Schuman Plan as being too restrictive both geographically and economically because it limited the industrial sectors. "Instead of placing France and Germany in the lead, Europe should first organize itself politically." The government, he said, merely offered "fragments of a general policy."

On December 13, the Assembly took the decisive action of rejecting the motion to adjourn by a vote of 376 to 240. The opposition comprised 103 Communists and Progressists, 116 R.P.F., and only 20 deputies of the traditional Right. The foreign minister, expressing a deep conviction, declared: "Although the Community involves the usual, inevitable risks, they are counterbalanced by such an important political advantage that we should and can take them." He hazarded two predictions. The first was soon realized: "The establishment of the Community will in no way alter our own plans for modernization and re-equipment; rather, it will stimulate them." The second prediction gives pause even today: "If Europe is capable of greater cohesiveness and discipline, it will become all the more valuable within the Atlantic Organization."

Status and Functioning of the E.C.S.C.

The treaty set up institutions that channeled the confrontation between national and communitarian points of view. The first were expressed by the Council of Ministers. The second were developed by the High Authority, an independent organ.

Although the institutions of the E.C.S.C. had a certain impact on industrial structures and on the commodity markets covered by the treaty, the governments, none the less, assumed sole responsibility for the general economic policies of their respective countries. Consultations between the High Authority, the Council of Ministers, and the governments made for a highly complex system of decision-making.

In the light of experience, one might say that a timid concept of economic integration on the basis of cooperation between industrial sectors contrasted sharply with the bolder political concept of Franco-German reconciliation.

To further the process of European reconstruction, should the economic basis for integration be enlarged, or should supranationalism be broadened to include political domains?

The second question was raised before the E.C.S.C. Treaty was signed. The first question was raised before the end of the transitional period.

8

Setback and a
New Start for Europe

From the E.C.S.C. to the E.D.C.

A CLOSE CHRONOLOGICAL and institutional correlation existed between the European Coal and Steel Community and the European Defense Community. In August 1950, three months after Schuman's declaration, Winston Churchill obtained from the Consultative Assembly of the Council of Europe a resolution calling for the creation of a European army. In October 1950, pointedly referring to the intervention of Churchill—who was expected to be the next prime minister—René Pleven laid before the National Assembly the plan that was to bear his name. It was the counterpart in the domain of defense of the Schuman Plan. The institutional pattern was the same: an elected executive, called the High Authority in the E.C.S.C., became the E.D.C.'s Commissariat; the Assembly was composed in a manner similar to that of the E.C.S.C.; there was a single court of justice.

The debate in the French National Assembly over the E.D.C. began in earnest in February 1952, two months after the ratification of the E.C.S.C. Treaty and a few days before the Lisbon meeting of the North Atlantic Council. The Assembly voted in favor of the E.D.C. but made its approval contingent on two main conditions: close association with England and "subordination of the European army to a supranational political power with limited but real jurisdiction."

This somewhat ambiguous vote in no way altered the political conception, which was based on integration rather than cooperation. But it did call into question two of the options in the Schuman Plan. One was the geographical enlargement of the communities; the other was the subordination of the political to the economic.

The E.C.S.C. was based on the establishment of an industrial continental market whose nucleus would be France and Germany. Consequently, England's nonparticipation did not cause much regret. But the E.D.C. was planning to rearm Germany, and England's participation would be desirable as a counterbalance.

In the E.C.S.C. the short-term goal of economic integration would pave the way for the ultimate goal of political integration. In the E.D.C., the Commissariat, the executive organ of the proposed European Ministry of Defense, would be responsible solely to the Assembly. The need was felt to subordinate the army to politics, to cap the E.D.C. and also the E.C.S.C. with a political community that would be more plainly of the federal type than either of the two sectoral organizations.

It was feared that the desired geographical enlargement might not be achieved in the absence of a political authority. Without reviewing the debate on the European army, already discussed in conjunction with European unification, let us examine two aspects that clarify the controversy over European construction—the attitude of England toward the E.D.C., and the fate of the plan for a political community.

England and the European Army

On May 27, 1952, the day the E.D.C. Treaty was signed, the British government put its signature to two diplomatic documents. The first was a treaty between England and the member states of the E.D.C. It stipulated that if a member of the E.D.C. were the object of armed aggression in Europe, England would automatically give it military assistance. The second was a protocol annexed to the NATO Treaty stipulating that an armed attack against one of the member states of the E.D.C. would be considered an attack against all the parties to the treaty.

The two documents were a far cry from the provisions the National Assembly had hoped to obtain in February 1952.

Successive French governments had attempted to get from London the assurance that British troops assigned to the Continent would be kept there and that England would collaborate closely with the E.D.C. On March 11, 1953, the British government offered to send an English delegation to the Commissariat and to appoint a representative to the E.D.C. Council of Ministers. It refused, however, to become involved in any joint Community decision-making. The offer did not satisfy the French. Bidault began to lose confidence in the success of the undertaking.

Throughout the long ministerial crisis that lasted from the fall of the

Mayer cabinet to Laniel's assumption of office, every premier was committed to refrain from requesting the National Assembly to ratify the treaty as long as no satisfactory assurances had been obtained from England regarding her association with the E.D.C. Yet Winston Churchill's speech to the House of Commons on May 22, 1953, should have removed all uncertainty: "We are not members of the E.D.C. and we have no intention of becoming integrated into a European federal system. . . . We are with them but not part of them."[1]

On the basis of a British proposal of September 1953, new negotiations were begun. They terminated on April 13, 1954, on the eve of the fall of DienBienPhu. In a convention concerning England's cooperation with the E.D.C., a consultative procedure was suggested that referred specifically to the number of British forces stationed on the European continent. The British government promised to appoint representatives to the Council of Ministers and to the Commissariat of the E.D.C., but the gesture was made when the game was already over.

On August 30, 1954, the National Assembly rejected the E.D.C. This decision, said the *Times* on August 31, "gives England a second chance to take the lead in Europe."[2] Anthony Eden suggested that Germany be admitted to NATO thanks to the broadening of the Brussels Treaty. To obtain the consent of Mendès-France, he announced on September 29 that England would continue to maintain on the European continent the number of troops presently posted there, and that she would not withdraw them against the wishes of the majority of the members of the Brussels Treaty. Despite the special safeguards—a grave overseas crisis, or external financial difficulties—this commitment was presented as "a very important step forward."

To be sure, the British government never wanted to belong to the E.D.C., in spite of Field Marshal Montgomery's urging. Although England bargained for the price of her cooperation, she was careful, throughout the lengthy controversy in France, not to oppose the treaty openly. The British were anxious not to thwart the Americans, who were determined champions of the E.D.C. But England revealed her true leanings by granting France, within the framework of the Western European Union—an intergovernmental organ—the assurances she had refused since 1952 to give the E.D.C. By creating a common army, the E.D.C. planted the seeds for a political federation. And by constantly postponing the concession to France of the guarantees she wanted, which could at any moment have caused a shift in the majority of the National Assembly, England eliminated the danger of establishing a continental bloc, which the plan for a European political community might have foreshadowed.

[1] H. J. Heiser, *British Policy with Regard to the Unification Efforts on the European Continent* (Leyden: A. W. Sythoff, 1959), 63.

[2] *Ibid.*, 67.

The Plan for a European Political Community

On December 10, 1951, the Consultative Assembly of the Council of Europe recommended "the creation of a political authority, subject to the democratic control of a parliamentary Assembly, whose jurisdiction will be limited to defense and foreign affairs, sectors in which the exercise of joint sovereignty has been rendered necessary by the constitution of a European army and its employment within the Atlantic framework." The motion before the National Assembly, adopted in February 1952 and cited earlier, referred to the same concern. Thus, Article 38 was inserted in the E.D.C. Treaty to pave the way for the study of a definitive political organization founded on the principle of the separation of powers and comprising, in particular, a bicameral representative system.

In September 1952, Robert Schuman and Alcide de Gasperi suggested to the E.C.S.C. Council of Ministers that it should invite the Assembly of this organization—which would be set up in the same way as the future E.D.C. Assembly—to draft a blueprint for a European political community. The Assembly, afterwards called the *Ad Hoc* Assembly, entrusted the task to a constitutional commission presided over by Heinrich von Brentano.

The commission's plan was adopted by the Assembly on March 9, 1953. It provided for a Chamber of the peoples elected by universal suffrage, a Senate elected by the national parliaments, a European Executive Council whose president was elected by the Senate, and a Council of Ministers. This new Community was gradually to absorb the E.C.S.C. It would exercise control over defense and foreign relations, and coordinate economic and financial policies. It would take the necessary steps to create a general Common Market.

Speaking for the E.C.S.C. Council of Ministers, Bidault let it be known that the governments were not inclined to follow the deputies of the *Ad Hoc* Assembly along the path they had outlined. The plan was ambitious because of the federal nature of its institutions and the scope of its political and economic functions. It was superimposed on the very complex and bitterly disputed E.D.C. institutions. In the climate of opinion that prevailed in France at that time, it had very little chance of being seriously considered. The E.C.S.C. ministers asked their assistants to study the plan at their October meeting in Rome. Because of internal dissension in the Laniel cabinet, on instructions were sent to the French delegate. In November, the ministers asked a commission to draft a new plan but it was never to see the light of day.

The Crisis of 1954

The vote in the National Assembly on August 30, 1954, marked a low point in the struggle for European unity in France. Nationalist feeling was strong. The E.C.S.C., far from constituting the first pillar of a vast federal edifice, appeared as the isolated outpost of an army that was perhaps not routed, but was at any rate in retreat.

Had France by 1954 given up the fundamental options of Schuman's 1950 declaration—reconciliation with Germany, reconstruction of Europe through integration? Her E.C.S.C. partners had every reason to wonder. It is surprising to the historian that anti-German feeling in France, far from being revived by the rejection of the E.D.C., had on the contrary been weakened. The controversy had been a fixation, an abscess. The reconciliation was profound and lasting. The settlement of the Saar question on terms favorable to Germany did not provoke an outburst in France. England did not replace Germany as France's privileged ally.

On the future of European integration, however, the reaction was more subtle. The road to a military Europe had been closed for a long time—and the road to a political Europe as well—because opposition to a European army was also opposition to a prefederal concept of foreign policy. But the road to an economic Europe remained open. France had already begun to take that road with the E.C.S.C. She was to continue on it. European economic integration—"la relance Européenne"—began in the spring of 1955, as soon as the Paris Accords on Western European Union were implemented.

The Messina Conference

The Benelux countries took the initiative in promoting a new start for Europe, or "la relance Européenne," as it was called. Their governments wanted to test France's intentions in regard to integration. In this they were encouraged by a cautious statement Edgar Faure made on April 5, 1955, in favor of a European policy: "I want it to be pursued without any dogmatism." In a speech of April 21, J. W. Beyen, foreign minister of the Netherlands, advocated a study of general economic integration. It was to be supranational in character, another version of the plan he had drawn up in 1953. His project, which had been approved by Belgium and Luxembourg, was transmitted on May 18 to the other members of the Council of Ministers of the E.C.S.C. at a meeting in Messina on June 1.

Meanwhile, the E.C.S.C. Assembly met in Strasbourg from May 6 to 14th. Jean Monnet declared that the two methods envisaged for European reconstruction—the integration of new sectors, and a general economic integration—could be implemented without contradiction. In November 1954, the president of the High Authority had let it be known that he would not ask for a renewal of his mandate, which was due to expire on February 10, 1955. In May 1955 the Gaullist ministers in the Faure cabinet opposed the reappointment of Monnet, who was then planning to retain the presidency of the High Authority. Under the circumstances, Edgar Faure decided to submit the candidature of René Mayer as Monnet's successor. This choice met with an easy approval in Messina.

The ministers then proceeded to study the Benelux memorandum. According to the document, "the progress made by the E.C.S.C. revealed the need to widen the Common Market to include areas similar to those already covered by the organization. The Benelux countries believe, however, that a widening of the Common Market would not be successful unless a more general integration were attempted." To this end, they suggested the creation of an economic community to work toward a Common Market by the gradual elimination of quotas and tariffs and the harmonization of financial, economic, and social policies of the member countries. In referring to the integration of industrial sectors, the Benelux memorandum expressed the opinion that transport and sources of energy should be studied and a joint authority responsible for the peaceful use of atomic energy should be created. The German and Italian governments favored a general Common Market rather than integration by industrial sectors. Antoine Pinay, who represented France at Messina, agreed to study the goals and methods outlined in the memorandum. The proposals for a gradual reduction in tariffs and the coordination of economic policies appeased the French, who had voiced certain objections.

The resolution adopted on June 3 at Messina declared that "the governments recognize that the time has come to enter a new phase in the construction of Europe. They are of the opinion that European construction must first be achieved in the economic domain." It went on: "We must work toward the establishment of a united Europe, through the development of common institutions, the gradual merger of national economies, the creation of a Common Market, and increasing harmonization of social policies." A committee of intergovernmental delegates was asked to prepare the way for a Common Market and a joint organization for the peaceful development of atomic energy. This six-power committee was presided over by the Belgian foreign minister, Paul-Henri Spaak. Its headquarters were in Brussels. Finally, England was invited to send a representative, with the firm understanding that this would in no way commit her to the Messina resolution.

The Spaak Report

The political climate was very favorable when the committee began its work. Delegates to the joint E.C.S.C. Assembly were divided into three political groups that cut across nationalities: Liberals, Christian Democrats, and Socialists. At the May 1955 meeting, Guy Mollet, president of the Socialists, stated that his group was ready to join in any effort to widen the jurisdiction of the E.C.S.C. The German Socialists, who until then had expressed certain misgivings, willingly joined the institution because of its antitrust policy and its efforts to help industrial conversion. This change in the attitude of the German working-class was confirmed in October when Jean Monnet founded the Action Committee for a United States of Europe. The committee consisted of representatives of the three political parties of the joint Assembly, employer's associations, and employee unions (with the exception of Communist unions). Its purpose was to promote the construction of Europe and, for the immediate present, to help implement the Messina resolution.

Spaak's committee met for the first time on July 9 in Brussels. From the very outset there was deep dissension between the British representative and his colleagues in regard to structure and objectives. England liked the cooperative procedure proposed for the O.E.E.C. but objected to the establishment of a common external tariff that would entail drastic changes in her commercial policy toward the rest of the world, especially the Commonwealth. When the heads of delegation met on November 7 it was quite clear that England had no intention of joining the Common Market. Spaak made it plain that participation in the work of the committee implied a desire to implement the Messina resolution. The British delegate withdrew without a word of encouragement to the others.[3]

Differences of opinion cropped up between the French and their partners during the three meetings of the Spaak committee. The French were asking for safeguards, for a longer transitional period, and for some correlation between the tariff reductions and the harmonization of social and economic legislation.

Guy Mollet was elected premier on January 2, 1956. In his investiture speech of February 1 he said that plans for a general Common Market would be completed as quickly as possible under conditions that would insure the necessary transitions and adjustments. He also favored the proposed establishment of Euratom (the name given to the future European Atomic Energy Community). He concluded with the following appeal: "I solemnly urge the Assembly to make the idea of European unity a great bond rather than as heretofore a bone of contention."

Paul-Henri Spaak asked Pierre Uri and Hans von der Groeben to draft a report on the work of his committee. This remarkable document, known as the "Spaak Report," and studied by the heads of delegations in April 1956, was both a resumé of the suggestions of experts and an analysis of the philosophy of the Common Market. It provided a solid basis for future negotiations. In May, Spaak discussed it before the E.C.S.C. Assembly at

[3] Miriam Camps, *Britain and the European Community (1955–1963)* (Princeton: Princeton University Press, 1964), 45.

Strasbourg. A lively debate resulted from Michel Debré's criticism of the conception of a Europe of the Six, a conception Debré had objected to earlier apropos of the E.D.C. With Debré alone dissenting, the Assembly voted unanimously in favor of the Common Market. At the end of May the delegates met in Venice. Christian Pineau, the French foreign minister, approved the initiation of preliminary negotiations on the two treaties, one creating the E.E.C., the other Euratom.

The Negotiations and Debate on Euratom

After the Spaak Report was adopted by the heads of delegations, negotiations for the creation of the Common Market and Euratom began in earnest. The Benelux countries, supported by Germany and Italy, were determined to link the two lest the French government should agree to Euratom but not to the Common Market.[4]

Early in July the government asked the National Assembly for a debate on European integration ("la relance Européenne") in the light of the Spaak Report. The discussion centered mainly on Euratom.

There were two controversial issues: France's right to manufacture atomic arms, and the more or less supranational nature of the new institution. This last naturally involved the connection between the E.C.S.C. and Euratom, and also England's possible participation.

Originally, Jean Monnet had entertained the hope that the member states of the future organization would, with American backing, commit themselves exclusively to research on the peaceful uses of atomic energy. But some Gaullist, Radical, and Moderate deputies held that France could and should manufacture nuclear weapons. Mindful of this current of opinion, Christian Pineau had stipulated, when the Spaak Report was adopted, that the member states should regain their freedom in military matters five years after the treaty went into effect, without requiring any prior consent from their partners. This clause entitled France to do as she pleased about nuclear weapons. Yet the Gaullists wanted more; they insisted that France should be free forthwith to manufacture atomic weapons. Jacques Chaban-Delmas, the minister of public works, threatened to resign unless the Mollet government promised to insert this provision.

The Gaullists also opposed any organic connection between the E.C.S.C. and Euratom. The link between the two organizations was justifiable on economic grounds. Besides, Europe needed to lay down a common energy policy. The opposition was motivated by political considerations. The Gaullists rejected the supranationalism of the E.C.S.C. They insisted that it would have to be abolished or attenuated. Those who believed in atomic

4 *Ibid.*, 54.

nationalism pointed out that France, who was ahead of her partners in nuclear research and had her own uranium deposits, might be giving up more than she was receiving in any communitarian enterprise.

If this argument was valid for France, it was much more so for England who was considerably ahead of France and had a much closer relationship with the United States in the field of nuclear science. Such was the answer that Christian Pineau gave Mendès-France when the latter objected to the idea of limiting Euratom to six members only. Mendès-France wanted English participation in a seven-power Community similar to the W.E.U. The parliamentarians who desired association with England were also afraid that Germany would eventually dominate Euratom. Although in 1956 Germany was behind France, she had a greater industrial potential in chemistry and metallurgy. Debré, who elaborated on this thesis before the E.C.S.C. Assembly on May 11, was answered by Louis Armand. Armand argued that the European nations could either unite to form a large atomic group or else become satellites of the United States. In the latter event, Germany would quickly become America's most powerful partner.[5] Thus, in the domain of nonmilitary atomic science as well as in other areas of European unity, fear of Germany and the desire for association with England were apparent.

The debate began in the National Assembly on July 5. The government was concerned about the military controversy, fearing that memories of the E.D.C. would be rekindled. It invited two experts, Francis Perrin, commissioner for atomic energy, and Louis Armand, one of the initiators of Euratom, to explain to the deputies the technical aspects of the peaceful utilization of nuclear energy. American technological expertise was overwhelming. A comparison between America and France showed that the ratio of investment was 60 to 1, whereas it was 60 to 9 for the United States and England. American isotope separation plants consumed more electricity than did all of France. A comparison of the number of experts in each country showed approximately the same ratio of 60 to 1.

Maurice Faure, secretary of state for foreign affairs, who had been charged with negotiating the two treaties, answered the Social Republicans on behalf of the government. He agreed that it was necessary to separate Euratom from the E.C.S.C. But on the peaceful uses of nuclear energy, he said: "France is free to make a bomb or not to make one. The decision is up to her government and her Parliament." At the end of the debate, the premier announced that France would promise not to explode an A-bomb before January 1, 1961, and that national enterprises should be given priority in the allocation of fissionable materials.

[5] *Le Monde*, May 27–28, 1956, quoted by Daniel F. Dollfus and Jean Rivoire, *A propos de Euratom* (Paris: Les Productions de Paris, 1959), 160.

Speaking of France's general European policy, Guy Mollet said that the unification of Western Europe was politically imperative for France. Only a united Europe could speak with authority to the two giants, the United States and the Soviet Union. He added: "My deep conviction, which has not changed for many years, is that only the integration of Germany into a European entity . . . with authority over her, and all other member states will provide a lasting solution to the German question."

The Socialists moved that the government continue the negotiations on Euratom. The motion was adopted by 332 to 181, with 72 abstaining. It constituted a commitment, as the premier noted. The dissenters comprised 150 Communists and Progressists, and 27 Mendès-France Radicals. Among those abstaining were 20 Independents, and most of the Poujadists. Of the 21 Social Republicans, 15 voted with the government.

The further negotiations on Euratom, based on the government's statement and the Assembly's motion, raised no major difficulty.

The Negotiations and Debate on the Common Market

Publication of the Spaak Report facilitated negotiations between France and her partners. It also lent harmony to the debate in the National Assembly. The plan for a Common Market was presented as a cohesive and balanced whole, embracing every factor of production and all sectors of the economy. The preamble stated: "The purpose of the Common Market is to create a vast area for a common economic policy, a powerful productive entity that will permit continuous expansion, increasing stability, rapid improvement in the standard of living, and the development of harmonious relations among the participating nations."[6] Like the men who later drafted the treaty, the authors of the report dealt first with functions and then with institutions. They drafted the procedural rules that would enable the institutions to make decisions within their competence; they did so without paying undue attention to doctrinaire theories.

The negotiators were eager to act quickly so that the treaty would be signed while the Mollet government was still in power and before the German elections, slated for the fall of 1957. To these internal considerations must be added the external concerns of the Six. One was the Suez affair, which attested the impotence of Europe and gave added impetus to efforts at integration. The other was the announcement made by England before the O.E.E.C. Council in July 1956 that she intended to explore the possibility of setting up a free-trade area comprising the future customs union of the Six and the rest of the O.E.E.C. member states. As Miriam Camps observed, Great

---

[6] Comité intergouvernemental créé par la Conférence de Messine, *Rapport des chefs de délégation aux ministres des affaires etrangères* (Brussels, 1956), 13.

Britain's interest in a free-trade area was reassuring to those states that were reluctant to embark on any undertaking without England's participation; it also stimulated a greater effort by those who were afraid that difficulties would arise over the Common Market once negotiations for a free-trade area had been initiated.[7]

On the advice of businessmen, and because of economic conditions at home, France made certain demands during the final phase of the negotiations.

The French government asked the advice of the Economic Council. Its answer, on July 12, was approval of the plan for a Common Market. Jean Deleau of the agricultural sector read the report. Ninety-nine voted in favor, thirty-five against, and eighteen abstained. This was significant. The farmers and the non-Communist trade unions—(C.F.T.C.) Confédération Française des Travailleurs Chrétiens, and (F.O.) Confédération Force Ouvrière—were in favor; the managerial staff union and the C.G.T. were against. Eight of the fourteen representatives from private industry dissented; the others abstained.

The Economic Council expressed some concern about the disparity between foreign and domestic prices. It also voiced reservations about the duration of the plan and the passing from one stage to another in the transitional period; the coordination between the harmonization of social legislation and the freeing of trade; the desire of France to continue to tax imports and to subsidize exports; the organization of the European markets for agricultural commodities. After much deliberation, the Council asked for the inclusion of the overseas territories in the Common Market.

To overcome the resistance of industrialists and insure the cooperation of agricultural circles, the government invited qualified representatives of employers' associations workers' and farmers' unions to participate in the negotiations. It obtained an important concession—the extension of the transitional period from twelve to fifteen years. Passage from the first to the second stage of the transitional period represented a compromise: it would not occur automatically, as Frances partners had hoped. The goals for the first stage, as detailed by the treaty, would have to be realized before the second stage began. Decisions to this effect were to be unanimous. France's partners conceded that the harmonization of social legislation should include the length of paid vacations and equalization of pay for men and women. They refused, however, to agree to France's practice of paying overtime. In view of the fact that France's currency was overvalued, her partners accepted the maintenance of taxes and subsidies, but on condition that a joint examination of the economic situation should be made annually. Thus, France's partners demonstrated their desire to facilitate her transition from protec-

[7] Camps, *Britain*, 69.

tionism to free trade. The discussions Mollet held with Adenauer in November 1956 were in large part responsible for the successful conclusion of the accords.

Discussions on agriculture underscored the need to institute a common agricultural policy that would transcend national boundaries. The draft treaty outlined the major features of such a policy.

In January 1957 the Mollet government proceeded to debate the major principles of the Common Market in the National Assembly. For the first time parliamentary circles indicated their wish to see French economic policy take a new direction.

Advocates and opponents of the treaty concurred in denouncing the shortcomings of protectionism and the weakness of the French economy. They differed, however, on the methods for remedying the situation.

Mendès-France insisted that economic recovery at home should precede the construction of European unity. He reproached the government for not having implemented the necessary reforms promptly and for having exposed a fragile economy to outside pressures. Prefacing his remarks with the pessimistic statement that the Community would not achieve its goals, he expressed concern that French capital would benefit Germany, whose industry was more profitable. He added that there was a danger that unemployed Italians would come to France, where full employment was assured. In addition, he feared two things: the competition of France's partners who "wanted to preserve the commercial advantages that their social backwardness had won them"; and the pressure France's partners would exert to persuade her to devalue her currency. Should there be a great disparity in prices, the standard of living would decline. Reiterating his criticism of supranationalism, he contended that "a democracy abdicates if it delegates its powers to an external authority."

René Pleven and other speakers observed that, in any case, to rectify the balance of payments it would be necessary to increase French exports and that once the Common Market was set up this would become a necessity.

Government spokesmen expressed the belief that outside pressure would facilitate internal reforms. According to Maurice Faure, "France cannot isolate herself from the rest of Europe without giving up economic reform and an increase in her standard of living. For France, Europe is not the easy way out but rather the road to salvation."

Guy Mollet told the Assembly that its vote in favour of the Common Market would constitute a commitment to ratify the treaty.

The motion accepted by the government was adopted by 322 to 207, with 42 abstaining. It called for a common agricultural policy and integration of the overseas territories. The motion expressed the hope that the Common Market would be included in a free-trade area to which Great Britain would adhere and for which—a pious wish—"there would be guarantees equivalent to those contained in the Common Market treaty." Finally—and this was constructive—it asked the government "to pursue in view of the prospective Common Market, a policy of selective investments that would modernize the French economy."

Opposed to the motion were 149 Communists and Progressists, 14 Mendès-France Radicals, 4 Social Republicans, and all the Poujadists. Of those abstaining, 5 were Radicals, 11 Independents, and 12 Social Republicans (Gaullists).

Negotiations among the Six were resumed in February. They focused primarily on tariff problems, the voting procedures of the Council of Ministers, and methods of associating the overseas territories. The general level of the future external tariff was to equal the mathematical mean of French, German, Italian, and Benelux tariffs. It was agreed that the tariff rate for certain products on which no agreement had been reached prior to the signing of the treaty would be settled by the Six during the first stage of the transitional period. (This was the "G List".) The Benelux countries obtained certain guarantees from the "qualified majority" vote of the Council of Ministers to the effect that they would not be outnumbered in the balloting by the three larger nations. The greatest difficulties arose over association with the overseas territories. France asked that the products originating in the overseas territories be given preferential treatment within the Community *vis-à-vis* similar goods imported from third countries. Germany opposed this because of the higher prices that prevailed in the French franc zone. Finally, the Six agreed to apply to their trade with the overseas territories the advantages they granted each other: but the convention of association was concluded for a trial period of five years in view of the evolution of the political status of the territories concerned.

The German industrialists severely criticized the considerable concessions granted to French protectionism. Ludwig Erhard, economics minister, voiced his objections openly and agreed to join the Common Market only because of political considerations and pressure by Adenauer.

Both treaties were signed in Rome on March 25, 1957.

Ratification of the Rome Treaties

The Mollet government fell in May 1957, allegedly over financial questions but actually because of the Algerian war. The National Assembly chose Maurice Bourgès-Maunoury as Mollet's successor. He had been minister of national defense in the Mollet cabinet. Like his predecessor, Premier Bourgès-Maunoury was a firm advocate of European unity. Pressed by the imminence of the German elections, Bourgès submitted the two treaties for ratification in July.

The debate on Euratom was preceded on July 3 by an almost unanimous vote in the National Assembly, only the Communists dissenting, that approved a five-year plan to develop atomic energy. The plan covered the 1957–1961 period and earmarked funds for the construction of a plant to separate isotopes. The discussion was calm.

The debate on the European Economic Community restated the arguments that had been presented to the National Assembly in January. With great clarity, Alain Savary, the general reporter, outlined the major needs of the French economy: "It is essential for the government to establish a policy of selective investments and to draft such a plan in conjunction with the Common Market. . . . The champions of autonomy should tell us how to make our economy competitive, how to remedy the balance of payments without the gradual stages, the facilities, and the guarantees of the Treaty of Rome." He reminded the Assembly opportunely that "the trend toward the freeing of trade is strong and lasting because it is encouraged by the great powers and by the specialized international agencies."

Mendès-France, on the other hand, believed that France was in no position to meet the competition of the Common Market and that she would be unable to do so by January 1, 1959, the date stipulated by the treaty. To prove his point he adduced the reestablishment on June 18, 1957, of import quotas which had become necessary because France could not comply with the O.E.E.C.'s trade regulations. In conclusion, he said: "Political morality, the dignity of France, and her self-interest demand that we refrain from making commitments we are unable to honor."

In response, Pierre-Henri Teitgen said that only the Common Market could force France to reform her economy and finances. Maurice Faure stressed the communitarian spirit of the treaty.

The effect of German reunification on the fate of the Common Market was also mentioned. According to Christian Pineau, "there is no way to tie a reunified Germany to the Common Market for the simple reason that such a Germany does not exist." The foreign minister added: "Should German reunification inject a new factor into the picture, it would be well to remember that France has the same rights as Germany."

Approval of both treaties was voted by 342 to 239. Dissenting were 149 Communists and Progressists, 19 Radicals, 16 of 21 Social Republicans, 35 Poujadists, and a few isolated members of the Center and the Right.

Two years after the Messina Conference, France approved the creation of the E.E.C. by a large majority. This action contained the seeds of a revolution in the economic life of France and continental Europe.

9

Euratom

Origins

THE CREATION OF EURATOM must be viewed from two standpoints: America's policy of eliminating secrecy from the civilian use of nuclear energy; and Europe's fear of a shortage of energy.

In a speech before the United Nations on December 8, 1953, President Eisenhower offered American help in research on the peaceful application of atomic science to all the countries who wanted it. This decision, reached shortly after the Russians exploded their first H-bomb, was an attempt to forestall a similar offer from the Soviet Union. On August 30, 1954, the MacMahon Act was amended to make possible the sharing of nuclear materials and information with foreign countries. At the Geneva Conference of 1955 the Soviet Union made a similar change in its policy.

The two nuclear superpowers also sponsored the creation of an International Agency for Atomic Energy with headquarters in Vienna. The agency functioned within the framework of the United Nations. Its purpose was to establish relations between East and West in the domain of civilian atomic energy and to control the peaceful utilization of the nuclear materials that would be provided. Between 1955 and 1958 the United States concluded numerous bilateral accords pertaining to research and a few concerning the delivery of atomic reactors.[1]

The industrialized nations of Western Europe were extremely interested in the application of nuclear techniques. Numerous reports by experts emphasized the danger—greatly exaggerated at the time—of a shortage of

[1] Bertrand Goldschmidt, *L'aventure atomique* (Paris: Fayard, 1962), 103–22.

energy. Ever since the war, England had concentrated on both the peaceful and military uses of nuclear energy. France had studied its peaceful application since the establishment of the Commissariat of Atomic Energy. She had every intention of reserving the right to explore the possibilities of its military use. The Paris Accords of October 23, 1954, gave Germany the right to engage in civilian atomic research. It was altogether natural that the Six, who were bound to one another by a treaty that established a Common Market in coal, and who had very inadequate oil resources of their own, should consider pooling their technical and financial resources in order to create an atomic Common Market.

But this idea immediately caused a British reaction within the framework of the Organization for European Economic Cooperation (O.E.E.C.). Following a report made by this organization in 1956 and approved by its Atomic Energy Commission, the Council of the O.E.E.C. established in December 1957 the European Agency for Nuclear Energy. Its main purpose was to organize technical cooperation by creating joint enterprises.

Objectives and Functions

According to its sponsors, Euratom had more ambitious objectives. According to Pierre-Olivier Lapie, it should "promote the creation of a new industry by providing it with scientific, technical, material, commercial, and institutional foundations."[2] The common objectives of the Six, however, were limited by the situation and intentions of the nations involved. France alone had a military program which precluded any clause that called for abandoning plans to acquire atomic weapons. Electrical production in Germany and Belgium was in the hands of private industry, and this in turn meant that plans to pool the production of atomic power had to be abandoned.

Three men were charged by their respective governments with drafting plans for Euratom—Louis Armand, Franz Etzel, and Francesco Giordani. They suggested building power stations for the production of enriched rather than natural uranium. In a report of May 1957 they demonstrated that enriched uranium produced by Europe would cost considerably more than buying American-produced uranium; at any event this was true in calculating the construction of the first plant. As a consequence, France's partners decided to buy uranium 235 directly from the United States.[3] France had no intention of submitting to any outside control in the use of her own resources; she was quite advanced technologically and possessed uranium

[2] Pierre-Olivier Lapie, *Les trois communautés* (Paris: Librairie Arthème Fayard, 1960), 143.
[3] Daniel F. Dollfus and Jean Rivoire, *A propos de Euratom* (Paris: Les Productions de Paris, 1959), 137.

mines in her overseas territories as well as at home. The French situation called for restrictive clauses in a joint policy to stock fissionable materials.

There were also differences in price policies. France gave priority to her autonomy and security in a planned system under the aegis of a public organization, the Commissariat of Atomic Energy, whereas Germany, under the guidance of private industry, thought in terms of costs. It was therefore not possible to establish a system of communitarian planning for the development of atomic energy.[4] Euratom was committed to a series of five-year research projects, the first to be determined by the treaty. These projects, in addition to those of the member states, were designed to set up an integrated program. In industrial matters, Euratom advised on proposed public and private investments and made every effort to coordinate them. In short, its responsibility was to launch the common enterprises of its members.

The structure and institutions of Euratom were patterned on those of the E.C.S.C. but took into account the experience of the coal and steel pool and the attitude of the Gaullist opposition in France. Therefore the political authority was assigned to the Council of Ministers, which was to determine research programs by unanimous vote and resolve budgetary problems by majority rule. The Council was to base its decisions on proposals made by the Commission which, since it enjoyed powers similar to those of the E.E.C., could formulate policy. The Parliamentary Assembly and the Court of Justice had jurisdiction over all three Communities.

In conclusion, since atomic energy had both civilian and military uses, the duality of Euratom's goals tended to restrict the field of activity as well as the means of an organization geared to peaceful ends but whose activity often had political implications.

[4] Georges Vedel, "L'Euratom," *Revue économique*, Mar. 1958, 215.

10

The European Economic Community

Goals and Methods of the Common Market

ARTICLE 2 OF THE Treaty of Rome reads: "Through the establishment of a Common Market and the gradual coordination of the members' economic policies, the Community will seek to promote the harmonious development of economic relations . . . and continuous and balanced expansion; to hasten an improvement in living standards and encourage closer relations among nations."

The Spaak Report defined the objectives of the Common Market in almost identical terms. To achieve these goals, the document said, it was absolutely necessary to merge the separate markets. Such a merger would, "through an increasing division of labor, eliminate the waste in the utilization of resources and, by giving greater assurance of access to supplies, help to give up unprofitable productions." It further added: "In many branches of industry, national markets offer no opportunity to achieve the optimum production which monopolistic enterprises permit. The advantage of a large market is that it reconciles mass production with the absence of monopoly."[1]

How would it be possible to achieve a merger of markets, a smooth transition from national markets to a single Common Market?

The Common Market had to be defined in relation to the outside world, and it had to achieve an adequately homogeneous internal structure.

The customs union which created a common external tariff met the first

[1] Comité intergouvernemental créé par la Conférence de Messine, Rapport des chefs de délégation aux ministres des affaires étrangères (Brussels, 1956), 13.

105]

prerequisite, economic union the second. Economic union covered a large area which can be subdivided into several categories: the free movement of the factors of production, the setting up of fair conditions for competition, the adoption of an economic policy that would apply both generally and to specific industrial sectors.

The method of attaining these goals was to guarantee a gradual adjustment of the national economies within certain time limits. The successive stages would be reached more slowly than in the coal and steel Common Market because the entire domestic economy would be affected. Deadlines were set in order to hasten the necessary national reforms.

A set of reforms designed to achieve a Common Market "would be inconceivable unless there were common regulations and actions and an institutional system to coordinate them."[2]

The method defined by the Spaak Report led one to wonder if the treaty was a regulatory one or merely a blueprint. Actually, it was a combination of the two. Precise regulations and deadlines were laid down to eliminate tariffs between the member states and to establish a common external tariff. The various forms of economic union were defined in much broader terms, as directing principles, so that the treaty could be implemented exclusively through regulations that delineated its true nature.

The Institutions

Most of the responsibilities of the European Economic Community devolved upon two key institutions, the Council of Ministers and the Commission.

The Council of Ministers, comprising representatives of the member states, was to assure the coordination of the members' economic policies and implement the decisions arrived at jointly by the governments. Usually decisions were to be reached by unanimous vote during the first stage of the transitional period. A majority vote (twelve out of seventeen votes, according to the following distributions: France, Germany, Italy, four votes; Belgium, the Netherlands, two votes; Luxembourg, one vote) was to suffice for most important questions during the third stage.

The Commission was to consist of nine members appointed by the governments. It was to administer the treaty, supervise the smooth functioning and development of the Common Market, make recommendations, and offer advice. Its relations with the Council were determined by Article 149. The Commission would suggest, the Council decide. As long as the Council had not decreed, the Commission could alter the initial proposal. Inversely, the Council could not amend the Commission's proposal save by unanimous

[2] *Ibid.*, 14.

decree. This ingenious system—"a proposal-decision without amendment," according to Robert Lemaignen—stimulated the governments to act, and the mere preparation of a proposal made it possible to identify the opposition and consequently to make the necessary adjustments.[3] The Commission's right to take the initiative made possible a fruitful dialogue between representatives of communitarian institutions and those responsible for national interests.

The Assembly and the Court of Justice were to serve the E.C.S.C., Euratom, and the E.E.C. The Assembly was empowered to debate and to control the administration of the Commission, but was denied legislative powers. Article 138, Section 3, empowered the Assembly to draft plans for election by direct universal suffrage, the procedure to be uniform for all the member states. This prudent stipulation was designed to pave the way for a European Assembly elected by universal suffrage. The Court of Justice was to play an important role through its supervision of those treaty regulations that governed competition.

The Political Significance of the Treaty of Rome

Did the operation of the Common Market's institutions make the Community a supranational organ? Did the process of economic integration bring the Europe of the Six closer to a federation? If we are to assess the political significance of the Treaty of Rome, these questions must be answered.

The European Economic Community was without doubt less supranational than the E.C.S.C. The word supranational was eliminated from the political vocabulary in order to temper the virulence of the rightist opposition in France. The Council of Ministers, an intergovernmental executive body, was endowed with powers superior to those of the Commission, a communitarian organ. If, according to Hans J. Morgenthau, the test of sovereignty is possession of "the supreme law-creating and law-enforcing authority,"[4] then the Commission did not have legislative powers. According to two American lawyers, the Common Market exercised an exclusive and final power over everything related to certain important governmental functions but remained essentially "a functional rather than a territorial authority."[5] Raymond Aron set forth three criteria for the assessment of supranationalism in the European Communities: the relinquishment of the principle of unanimous vote; the direct relationship between the Common Market's

[3] Robert Lemaignen, *L'Europe au berceau* (Paris: Plon, 1964), 103.

[4] Hans J. Morgenthau, *Politics among Nations*, 3d ed. (New York: Alfred Knopf, 1960), 313.

[5] Morton A. Kaplan and Nicholas de B. Katzenbach, *The Political Foundations of International Law* (New York: Wiley, 1961), 139.

legislative powers and the citizens or enterprises of the member states; the conclusion of agreements with other countries.[6] During the transitional period the area to which these criteria applied was slated to expand. Thus, after the third stage, the important decisions of the Council of Ministers would be made by a qualified majority. Similarly, the adoption of communitarian regulations, particularly those governing agriculture and competition, would lead to communitarian legislation and to new jurisdictional powers for the Commission. Finally, the tariff and commercial policies would become communitarian after the common external tariff had been put into effect.

Thus the Treaty of Rome included supranational provisions that were already operative and capable of development. Was the dynamism of the institutions powerful enough to force the member states to cross the Rubicon? Opinions were divided. Raymond Aron's answer was negative: "The development of the Common Market into a true federation results neither from a juridical nor an historical necessity," for this would be to assume that economics control and encompass politics.[7] André Marchal, on the other hand, stated that economic unification calling for drastic structural changes was far less reversible than political integration.[8] With greater subtlety of thought, Marjolin observed: "In building an economic Europe, one is also building a political Europe."[9] To be sure, the important economic decisions —and the Treaty of Rome embodies many—exert a real political influence. But no matter how many balance-of-power or timetable provisions the treaty may contain, no decisions will be made unless the member states can muster enough political will to overcome the temptation of immediate gains in order to work toward a future common good. When applied to European unity, this political will rests on an ideology that places the common good of the federation above the desire for national power.

Such an ideology did exist after the Treaty of Rome was signed. It was perceptible in the common concern of governments to complete the economic edifice by the parliamentary control of a European Assembly elected on the basis of universal suffrage. It was evident in one specific case—the desire to safeguard the identity of the Common Market from the British plan for a free-trade area.

The Common Market and the Free-Trade Area

After the withdrawal of her representative from the Spaak Committee in November 1955, Great Britain suggested on December 6 that the O.E.E.C.'s

[6] Raymond Aron, *Paix et guerre entre les nations* (Paris: Calman-Lévy, 1962), 730.
[7] *Ibid.*, 732.
[8] Andre Marchal, *L'Europe solidaire* (Paris: Editions Cujas, 1964), 236.
[9] Robert Marjolin, *Communautés Européennes*, July 1963.

powers be increased. It asked the O.E.E.C.'s Council of Ministers to thrash out the question of the relations of the Six with the other nations of Western Europe. In July 1956 the Council set up a special study group to examine ways and means of instituting a multilateral association between the future customs unions and the other European nations. The O.E.E.C. committee's report, published in January 1957, contained a plan for a European free-trade area. With agriculture excluded, the sole purpose of the association would be the elimination of commercial trade restrictions. But Britain's request in March 1957 to withdraw some of her troops posted in Germany increased the Continent's distrust. At that time the political advantages of economic association with England seemed very tenuous.[10]

On October 18, 1957, the O.E.E.C. Council of Ministers began negotiations in earnest. Reginald Maudling, a member of the British cabinet, presided. Led by Maurice Faure, the French delegation presented a negative memorandum in February 1958. The French Economic Council unanimously voted to reject the plan for a free-trade area. The Maudling Committee ceased to function in April 1958 as a result of the French political crisis.

The Political Rivalry between England and the Continent

The juridical, commercial, and economic arguments for or against the British proposal concealed a political rivalry connected with the balance of power in Western Europe.

Actually, England feared the establishment of an integrated economic unit on the Continent and the possibility of a large political unit. The population of the Community equalled that of the United States. It accounted for one-fourth of the world's trade, approximately one-third of the world's food and raw materials imports, and one-third of the world's export of manufactured goods. The economic importance of "Little Europe" was greater than that of the Commonwealth. Before the end of the transitional period, because of its customs and economic union, it would be more cohesive than the group of nations and territories connected with England by monetary and commercial ties. This new entity might very well become the principal spokesman in Europe *vis-à-vis* the United States.

Great Britain's tactics thus consisted in surrounding the Common Market with a wide free-trade area in order to increase the number of participants and reduce the commitments that would be acceptable to all.

France feared the coexistence of the two organizations. The broader and looser of the two might stifle the smaller and more restrictive. How could France expect her partners to accept the numerous safeguard clauses and

[10] Miriam Camps, *Britain and the European Community (1955–1963)* (Princeton: Princeton University Press, 1964), 111, 114, 115, 121.

harmonization measures that had been formulated in response to her express wishes? Her partners' trade relations were largely with the rest of Europe and their exports were competitive. Germany and Italy, for example, did not need such clauses to benefit from tariff reductions in a free-trade area.

France's tactics therefore consisted in making all kinds of technical objections. She demanded separate accords on each product instead of general agreements. She also asked for a three-year interval between tariff reductions within the Community and for a similar arrangement in the free-trade area.

French ratification of the Treaty of Rome in July 1957 and the establishment of the Brussels Commission in January 1958 linked the Six more closely. While the British concentrated on working out a common policy, they continued to underestimate the strength of the movement toward European unification.

In short, the diplomatic battle between the champions of a Common Market and those of a free-trade area was "more like an internal conflict of policy than a quarrel among sovereign states."[11]

[11] Aron, *Paix et guerre,* 456.

11

European Construction and
France in 1958

Economic Recovery and Solidarity

THIRTEEN YEARS after the German surrender in 1919, Europe experienced a worldwide economic crisis, intra-European trade decreased, and the national economies tended to remain isolated from one another. In 1958, thirteen years after the German capitulation of 1945, Western Europe was a prosperous, competitive economic area that was rapidly expanding. In 1952, because of the parallel recovery of investments and exports, the deficit in the current balance of payments was eliminated. Thereafter there were surpluses. This favorable balance was more sound than the one that had existed before the war because it no longer depended on income from investments abroad. It was based on the sale of commodities and services, on competitive prices and third-party markets, although trade with the United States showed a large deficit. Intra-European trade developed very quickly through the elimination of quotas and the establishment of a multilateral system of payments. The gross national product increased far more rapidly in Europe than in the United States. Most of the countries had improved and stabilized their currency between 1947 and 1949, and several had adopted a *de facto* external convertibility of their currency.

To be sure, considerable differences existed between the principal European nations. The defeated countries, Germany and Italy, triumphed in the postwar economic competition because of ample reserves of labor, a high rate of investment, and wise management of their public finances. All this enabled them to realize their goal, "expansion amid stability." England forfeited her chances of expansion in order to maintain the pound sterling as a reserve currency and as a tie between the members of the Commonwealth. France consumed and invested more than her resources warranted. She showed signs of a new economic vitality, but the chaos in her public finances and the cost of the Indochinese and Algerian wars impeded currency reforms and price stabilization.

In short, the importance of England compared to the Continent, particularly to the Europe of the Six, decreased. Among the Six, Germany, although truncated, was none the less the strongest of the partners because of her dynamism and her industrial potential. Finally, the old colonies, even those that progressed peacefully toward independence, proved a burden to the homelands because of investments in the growing infrastructure and the decline in preferential trade.

European economic recovery was due to several factors: American military protection, which enabled Europeans to work effectively in an atmosphere of almost continuous security; the temporary but substantial aid provided by the Marshall Plan; reciprocal European aid in trade and payments; the general improvement in the productive capacity of every country and every sector of the economy.

Thus, to a certain extent, Europe was making up for the losses and waste of the war. It was recovering its traditional commercial functions. Yet it did not enjoy the same advantages as the United States, whose technical superiority prevailed in a multitude of old and new branches of activity.

At that time a sense of economic solidarity was growing in Europe. In a variety of ways, Europe was trying to overcome the obstacles to domestic trade.

The first manifestation of this new sentiment was induced by the American gesture of solidarity. The Marshall Plan, which expressed American idealism as well as concern, comprised certain mechanisms that linked external with mutual aid. The European states within the European Payments Union conducted inquiries, debated the merits of their respective policies, and made collective recommendations to each of the nations. They learned in this way to stand solidly together instead of quarreling. Twice obliged to suspend freedom of trade with her partners, France continued to benefit none the less from the general advantages of the system. In 1957, at the height of a crisis in her balance of payments, she received help from both the United States and the other nations of Europe.

The word cooperation describes the first step toward economic solidarity which the Organization for European Economic Cooperation (O.E.E.C.) was instrumental in creating.

The word integration describes a further step toward economic solidarity. The problem was no longer merely to facilitate the regulation of international commercial and financial operations, but rather to create a Common Market, i.e. a customs union plus an economic union. The Common Market was to function among a few nations that were closely linked geographically and had attained a similar level of development.

The E.C.S.C. was the first instrument of integration but it covered only the coal and steel sectors. Integration by sectors was the method also used to set up Euratom. But the real instrument of integration, which by 1958 had not been tested, was the European Economic Community. It was designed to establish a general Common Market.

Two kinds of international economic organizations marked the two steps toward economic solidarity. Seventeen Western European nations collaborated within the intergovernmental organizations of the O.E.E.C. and the E.P.U. Of these, six embarked on the road to integration via three institutions that tended towards supranationalism: the E.C.S.C., Euratom, and the E.E.C.

How did the coexistence of two kinds of economic institutions affect the political situation? And how did the coexistence of military and political institutions, to which all or some of the Western nations belonged, affect the political situation?

Political Solidarity and Uncertainty

To assess the political situation of Europe in 1958, one must compare it with the situation that prevailed in 1932.

Political divisions in Europe were deep-seated in 1932. Briand's efforts to effect a Franco-German rapprochement in 1929 failed. Rivalry and distrust were increasing at a time when National Socialism was preparing to overthrow parliamentary rule. The Anglo-French alliance remained precarious.

In 1958 the political solidarity of Western Europe was evident outside the Atlantic Pact; within it, the Franco-German reconciliation was further proof of solidarity.

Signed in 1949, the Atlantic Pact protected Western Europe, neutrals as well as signatories, against a possible aggressor. European solidarity resulted from American protection against the Soviet menace. It increased when tensions between the two blocs increased, and decreased when the danger seemed less imminent and tensions diminished. Fear of a common threat was not strong enough to warrant the creation of a European army.

Schuman's declaration of May 9, 1950, was the generous gesture that led to Franco-German reconciliation. In 1952 this gesture was embodied in a supranational institution, the E.C.S.C. Its openly proclaimed purpose was to build "the first concrete foundations for a European federation." Franco-German reconciliation was sturdy enough to withstand the French Parliament's rejection of the European Defense Community in 1954. In 1957, motivated by the same political considerations, European ideology had sufficient vitality to create the European Economic Community.

The institutions of the Europe of the Six were therefore hybrid in nature: their immediate goal was to promote economic integration, their long-term objective was to promote political integration.

More modest was the goal of the Council of Europe, designed "to achieve a closer union between its members." The Consultative Assembly created in 1949, to which almost all the Western European nations belonged by 1958, was a political forum, not a legislative body.

Linked together for defense, reconciled, governed almost everywhere by democratic regimes, Western Europe none the less suffered from two uncertainties.

One, strategic in nature, resulted from the rivalry between the United States and the Soviet Union. The other, institutional, stemmed from the political will of Europeans.

The first uncertainty had to do with the division of Germany and Europe. The Atlantic Alliance guaranteed the status quo of Yalta and Potsdam. It made no atempt to push back the Soviet Union. Europe remained divided into two spheres of influence. The Western sphere was protected by the Americans, the Eastern sphere was dominated by the Russians. European and German unification depended not on the will of the two Europes but on the wishes of the two superpowers.

The second uncertainty was due to the absence of purely European political and military institutions. United in defense but dependent on the United States, Western Europe between 1949 and 1958 did not set up the institutions which, functioning within the Atlantic Alliance and in opposition to the Soviet Union, would have given it the necessary political weight commensurate with its restored economy. And this was so because in Western Europe, where internal tensions existed, nationalist and traditionalist forces checkmated federalist and innovating forces. The attempts to build a unified Europe revealed conflicts in ideologies and interests. The conflict between the champions of political and economic integration and the advocates of mere cooperation pitted the nations against each other, divided political parties and economic interest groups.

To measure the relative strengths, in 1958, of each camp on the question of European construction, we must outline the strategy used to promote integration and the counterstrategy employed to foster cooperation between 1948 and 1958.

The Ideology and Strategy of Integration

The French sponsors of European integration professed a political and economic ideology which they shared with certain political parties and socioprofessional groups in France and in the other countries of the Six. They also had outside support. With varying success they attacked successively on a series of fronts. This attack constituted the strategy of integration.

The doctrine of the European Movement, outlined in 1948 at the Hague Congress, was explained many times by Robert Schuman and Jean Monnet.

The ideas that led Schuman to believe in the necessity of European construction were assembled in a slim volume that appeared after illness had forced its author to give up all political activity. The Schuman doctrine was based on a new concept of international relations. "Instead of persisting in the old nationalism, in a grudging, distrustful independence, we are linking the interests, decisions, and destinies of this new community of states, which heretofore have been rivals. This new policy rests on solidarity and increasing trust." The European Community, he added, will not be patterned on a Holy Alliance; "it will be founded on democratic equality transferred to the domain of relations between nations. The right of veto is incompatible with such a structure, which assumes the principle of majority rule and excludes the dictatorial exploitation of material superiority. This is the meaning of supranationality; people are even now too inclined to view it only as a relinquishment of freedom and fail to see all that has been acquired in terms of authority and guarantees." Alluding to Bergson's ideas, he wrote: "Democracy is evangelical in essence because its prime mover is love." Speaking of Maritain, Schuman reminded his readers that the rationalists of the eighteenth century proclaimed and popularized the rights of man and the citizen. In essence Christian, these principles were inscribed in the first democratic constitution, that of the United States. Here the bond between Christianity and democracy was deeply felt and evident in everyday political life. Schuman concluded by predicting that "a generalized democracy, in the Christian sense of the word, will reach its full flowering in the construction of Europe."[1]

No lasting democracy is possible without its appropriate institutions. New institutions conforming to joint regulations and capable of serving the Community will render effective the desired solidarity between nations. On this point, Jean Monnet cited the Swiss philosopher, Amiel: "Only institutions . . . can accumulate collective experience; on the basis of this experience and this wisdom, individuals submissive to the rules will see that although their nature will not change, their conduct will be gradually transformed." He observes that "the weakening of the Continental nations is due not only to their divisions but also to the ease with which they challenge the workings of their institutions."[2]

[1] Robert Schuman, *Pour l'Europe* (Paris: Les Editions Nagel, 1963), 45, 47, 63, 77.
[2] Jean Monnet, *Les Etats-Unis d'Europe ont commencé* (Paris: Robert Laffont, 1955), 43, 44, 45.

Whereas this political ideology is based on federal democracy, the economic ideology is based on organized liberalism. Observing that the Europe of today is no longer living according to the rhythm of the modern world, Jean Monnet held that the establishment of a large internal market should enable Europeans to take advantage of the technological revolution that reduces costs, and prices for the benefit of the mass of consumers. "The gradual replacement of the least efficient production for the best will be one of the essential effects of this Common Market, one of the major pre-requisites of the kind of progress that determines a rise in living standards." A broad market "reconciles the struggle against monopolies and the maintenance of competitive enterprises with the development of enterprises large enough to employ the most modern techniques." However, "the advantages that each can gain from a Common Market can be fully realized only if it appears to be a permanent justification." There is no point in eliminating quotas if they are to be replaced by customs, nor customs if the tariffs on transport are discriminatory. Nor is there any point in eliminating discriminatory tariffs if the market is to be divided among the producers' cartels. "Such measures," said Jean Monnet, "are inseparable from one another. And it is precisely these measures that distinguish the establishment of a Common Market from fragmentary free-trade measures that are always revokable and almost always can be offset by protectionist devices." Thus institutional methods establish or restore domestic and foreign competition.[3]

The political and economic ideology of integration represented the convergence of three major European cultural currents: Christianity, Liberalism, and Socialism. It is not surprising that in France, Robert Schuman's foreign policy leaned heavily on the "third force"—M.R.P., Radicals, members of the traditional Right, and Socialists—in other words, on a coalition of Center parties favoring parliamentary democracy against the extremist parties, Communists and Gaullists, who opposed it.

On the question of European integration, the Center parties were not always in agreement. The M.R.P. voted unanimously for ratification of the three treaties: the E.C.S.C. in 1951, the E.D.C. in 1954, and the E.E.C. in 1957. Unanimously in favor of the E.C.S.C. and the E.E.C., the Socialists were evenly divided over the E.D.C. The Radicals voted unanimously in favor of the E.C.S.C. but were evenly divided over the E.D.C., while one-third voted against the E.E.C. One-fifth of the traditional Right rejected the Schuman Plan, over one-third rejected the European army, and a few isolated members voted against the Common Market. The French employers, generally opposed to the E.C.S.C. in 1951, had reservations about the Common Market in 1956 but rallied to it in 1957. The non-Communist trade unions (C.F.T.C. and F.O.) favored both economic institutions. The farmers supported the E.E.C. as early as 1956.

[3] *Ibid.*, 97, 115, 111, 81.

At the time of the May 9, 1950, declaration, the Christian Democratic parties had an absolute majority in Germany and Italy. Despite Socialist opposition, Adenauer had little trouble in securing parliamentary ratification of the E.C.S.C. President de Gasperi also had an easy time in spite of the opposition of a strong Communist Party and some Socialists.

In the Benelux countries, Christian Democrats, Socialists, and Liberals were at one in regard to foreign affairs. In 1955 the German Socialist Party approved the idea of European integration. German economic circles were more favorable to a wide free-trade area than to a rigidly regulated Common Market, but they went along with the government. In October 1955 Jean Monnet founded a powerful pressure group to further the cause of integration, the Action Committee for a United States of Europe. It included representatives of Christian, Socialist, and Liberal parties, employers' associations, and non-Communist trade unions from the six nations. The existence of this Committee speeded the ratification of the Treaty of Rome.

External as well as internal factors exerted an influence on the construction of Europe.

The global strategy that pitted the Western democracies against the Soviet Union and its satellites naturally led the United States to hope for a strong and united Europe. Mindful of its military and technological superiority, it feared above all that West Germany's heavy industry might be neutralized or fall under Russian control. The best guarantee against such a threat was Franco-German reconciliation and the organization of a political federation around these two continental states. For this reason the United States, to whom the federal concept was familiar, sponsored Robert Schuman's 1950 plan and its various ramifications. American intervention, which was very much in the forefront during the debates on E.D.C., was far more discreet during the planning of the Common Market.

On the other hand, European integration aroused systematic hostility in the Soviet Union. Yet it was precisely the fear of a Soviet invasion that solidified Europe. Soviet pressure, as a consequence, had an effect that was the very opposite of the one intended. At the height of the cold war, Stalin was a powerful federating force. When tensions relaxed, the Soviet threat diminished and there was less urgency to establish close political ties.

Global strategy influenced the strategy of integration. From 1950 to 1958, Jean Monnet was responsible for the offensives to promote European construction. In 1950 he concentrated on the economic front, especially the two vital sectors of coal and steel. In the opinion of Robert Ducci, these were marvelously well chosen sectors from a tactical point of view; at any rate they satisfied the immediate concern of Germany and France, but they were too limited to permit strategic maneuvers on a large scale. American pressure for German rearmament forced France to make a difficult choice between a German national army and a European army. Monnet opted for a European army. There was no longer any question of integration by sectors. The sovereign prerogatives of the states in the domain of foreign affairs would have to be pooled. Thus, those who had championed the E.D.C. were led to elaborate a federal constitution of sorts in the form of a plan for a European Political Community. It did not survive the counterattack of the nationalist forces in France. European economic recovery was achieved by abandoning all political plans. Monnet advocated a new approach by industrial sectors as well as research in atomic energy for peaceful ends. The Benelux countries took the initiative in suggesting a general economic approach to the Common Market which the French government supported. Thus, boldness on the political front was followed by caution on the economic front.[4]

Throughout the long battle for Europe, the champions of integration on the Continent had to take the measure of the advocates of mere association.

Ideologies and the Counterstrategy of Association

For very different reasons, the Communists, the Gaullists, and the British government opposed European integration.

The Soviet Union opposed any form of European unity, whether by association or integration. The Marxist-Leninist ideology and the rivalry of the two blocs led the Russians to combat any move that might give greater cohesiveness to the states of Western Europe. They opposed it through the national Communist parties and by diplomatic mean. The French Communist Party, a tool of the Soviets, and isolated from the majority since 1947, urged its deputies to vote against ratification of the treaties of association—the O.E.E.C. in 1948, the Council of Europe in 1949. It joined forces with the Gaullists to oppose ratification of the treaties integrating the Europe of the Six in 1952 and again in 1957.

The Gaullist ideology was essentially nationalist. "The nation is the fundamental political reality," Michel Debré proclaimed.[5] Yet, according to de Gaulle, states are "the least impartial and the most self-seeking entities in the world."[6] His own policy is that of national ambition. The theory of integration, Debré declared, "stemmed from a political conception—the Europe nation—that is contrary to the nature of things. . . . Europe is not a nation but a collection of nations. . . . Supranationality has become an escape from national responsibilities. One cannot simultaneously forge a European state and refashion the French state. The second of these, France, is being abandoned for the sake of the first."[7]

[4] Achille Albonetti, *Préhistoire des Etats-Unis d'Europe* (Paris: Editions Sirey, 1963), preface by Roberto Ducci, 18, 19.

[5] Michel Debré, *Ces princes qui nous gouvernent* (Paris: Plon, 1957), 144.

[6] Charles de Gaulle, *Mémoires de guerre* (Paris: Plon, 1959), III, 200, 90.

[7] Debré, *Ces princes*, 119, 126, 130.

Several times, especially in Lille on June 29, 1947, de Gaulle declared that Europe must be organized into a single whole in order to thwart any attempt at hegemony and achieve a balance between the two blocs. However, "Europe will not be forged unless France assumes leadership, and I mean a France on her feet and without apron strings" (Paris, February 11, 1950). On several occasions, de Gaulle also advocated a confederated Europe. He made his position clear at a press conference on February 25, 1953: "Instead of thinking about an intolerable and impractical merger, let us practice association. We have lost years indulging in daydreams. Let us begin by making an alliance with the free states of Europe." Thus Gaullist Europe would consist of an association of nations "that must collaborate and also keep a close watch over each other" under French guidance.[8]

Since the basis of politics is the satisfaction of ambitions, the relations between nations depend on alliances of the traditional kind, which are therefore revokable. Such an ideology, one that refuses to rise above the national concept, that rejects institutions capable of developing solidarity and trust, is a pure and simple expression of the will for power.

General de Gaulle's haughty nationalism did not impel him to refuse American aid under the Marshall Plan, but it did make him hesitate over the bilateral Franco-American accord that implemented it: in the vote for ratification on July 7, 1948, most of the Gaullists abstained. In 1949 these same deputies supported the creation of the Council of Europe. But Charles de Gaulle did not temper his criticisms of this institution, which "has no value for action" and whose "lack of responsibility" he denounced in his press conference of November 14, 1949.

His criticism was acrimonious, his opposition to supranational European institutions total. The Gaullist tactic was to join the Communists and to wrest from the Third Force a certain number of votes, especially from the right Center. His arguments stressed fear of German hegemony, England's nonparticipation, and the danger of granting power to stateless technocrats. In the December 1951 balloting on the E.C.S.C., the Gaullists joined the Communists in opposing it but had very little support from the traditional Right. After 1952 the Socialists left the government and only a fraction of the Gaullists supported the majority. The E.D.C. was attacked on three levels: from within the government, in the Parliament at Debré's instigation, and by public opinion through the general's comments and press conferences. A stateless army apparently was more dangerous than a communitarian steel industry. To defend the French Union, the French Army must remain an indivisible entity. A German national army was preferable to a European army because "there never has been an army that did not derive from the

---

[8] *Ibid.*, 136.

state."[9] These arguments won the approval of a large number of Socialists, and some Radicals and traditional Rightists. Their votes enabled the Gaullist and Communists to carry the day against the E.D.C. on August 30, 1954.

When the Western European Union and Germany's entry into NATO were voted on, December 29, 1954, the Gaullists and Communists parted company. But they joined forces again in July 1957 in opposing the ratification of the two Treaties of Rome that created the Common Market and Euratom.

The successive cabinets that launched and perfected plans for "the new start for Europe" ("la relance Européenne") included Gaullists. They naturally acted as a brake. Throughout the Brussels negotiations the Gaullist minority in the French Parliament aroused anxiety. As a consequence, the advocates of integration limited the scope of atomic cooperation to peaceful ends, discarded the idea of a federal tax that would benefit the E.E.C., and abandoned plans to set a deadline for the election by universal suffrage of the Parliamentary Assembly of the Six. Although de Gaulle could not prevent the establishment of a Common Market, he managed to deprive it of some of its political substance.

British ideology cannot be defined in a single word. It was neither nationalist nor federalist. Because of their experience with the decentralized administration of a multiracial empire, the English knew better than to indulge in nationalist excesses. Having developed a flexible system for their Commonwealth, they mistrusted the rigidities of a federal constitution. They felt no need for close political ties with Europe since their alliances and institutions had heretofore protected them from foreign invasion. To be sure, their own internal constitutional practices rested on the three cultural currents that combined to strengthen the federal idea on the Continent. England was the highly regarded exemplar of political liberalism; her puritan morality was Christian in inspiration; for a long time she had instituted a Socialist distribution of income. The Labour Party and the Conservatives, however, based England's foreign policy on three axioms that derived from her membership in the Commonwealth, the Anglo-American Community, and Europe.

The first axiom was the maintenance of the Commonwealth as a constellation of states under British guidance. It was because of the Commonwealth that England was a world power. But in 1958 this organization had no common foreign policy. Some of its members were neutral, others were associated with the West. The United States insured the defense of Canada by the Atlantic Pact, the defense of Australia and New Zealand by the ANZUS, and collaborated with England through SEATO for the defense of Southeast Asia. The Commonwealth was no longer as united economically as it had

[9] Charles de Gaulle, speech at Nancy, Nov. 25, 1951.

been in the past. Imperial preference was declining. England opposed any European economic organization that might weaken the trade connections between the members of the Commonwealth.

The second axiom was maintenance of the privileged relationship with the United States. This ancient bond, which had grown closer during the war, united partners of very unequal strength. England depended on the United States for the defense of her territory and the protection of her currency. For the United States she was an adviser who was always heard but whose counsel was not always heeded. In principle, England was opposed to any multilateral relationships in the Western world that might jeopardize her bilateral relationships with the United States.

The third axiom was the maintenance of a balance of power in Europe. This balance would be disturbed if France and West Germany, united with the other Common Market countries, established an economic bloc more powerful than the Commonwealth, and perhaps a political bloc that might become Europe's principal spokesman in dealing with the United States.

Adherence to these three axioms tended to protect England's threatened position as a world power. The deep-seated insularity of the British made it difficult for them to realize that their position would be best protected if England assumed leadership in Europe. In this respect, British policy was consistent. The Labour Party until 1951, then the Conservatives, restrained solely by America's persistent interest in European construction, made every effort to limit Europe's capacity to organize for cooperation and integration.

It was due to England that from its beginning in 1948 the O.E.E.C. had only limited powers. Thereafter the British government reduced further its field of activity: the O.E.E.C. was not to become involved in economic planning, the reduction of tariff barriers, or the coordination of credit policies. In 1952, at the expiration of the Marshall Plan, its usefulness was challenged. It was because of England that the Assembly of the Council of Europe remained purely consultative instead of becoming a European federal Parliament, as France had suggested. It was the impotence of the O.E.E.C. and the Council of Europe that spurred France to follow the path of pre-federalism. But in June 1950 the Labour government rejected the principles of integration and supranationality that were the cornerstone of Schuman's declaration of May 9, 1950.

France was not particularly disturbed by England's absence from the coal and steel pool, but she was very eager for British participation in a European army, as a counterbalance to Germany. It was Churchill who first suggested a European army at the Council of Europe in August 1950. In May 1952 the Conservative government signed a convention with the member states of the E.D.C. which was no great improvement over the methods of cooperation prescribed by the Atlantic Pact. At the same time, Anthony Eden tried, for the benefit of Britain, to make the Council of Europe the framework for all European activities, including the supranational institutions of the Six. In May 1953, Churchill told the House of Commons: "We have no intention of becoming integrated into a European federal system." In April 1954 a new convention was signed between England and the Six E.D.C. countries but it was scarcely better than the convention of May 1952. In September 1954, immediately after the rejection of the E.D.C. by the French National Assembly, England agreed to give France, within the framework of the W.E.U.—an intergovernmental organ—the assurance that she would continue to maintain on the Continent the same number of troops that were currently stationed there, an assurance she had refused to give within the framework of the E.D.C.—a supranational organ. In February 1957, England, who had never attempted to breathe life into the W.E.U., asked her partner's permission to withdraw a sizable number of troops posted in Germany.

From 1955 to 1958, England's open opposition to any plan for the economic integration of the Six came on the heels of her surreptitious opposition to the military and political undertakings of the 1951 to 1954 period. Her strategy consisted in proposing alternatives to plans for integrating the Six that would interest all or most of the O.E.E.C.'s members. Immediately after the Messina Conference of June 1955, England suggested strengthening the powers of the O.E.E.C. In July 1955 she responded to the Euratom project by asking O.E.E.C. to consider the creation of an agency for technical nuclear cooperation. The result was the establishment in December 1957 of the European Agency for Nuclear Energy. In July 1956, after the Six adopted the Spaak Report as a basis for discussion of the Common Market, England requested the O.E.E.C. to make a study of a wide free-trade area that would include the Six and the other states of Western Europe. In October 1957 she proposed negotiations, to be supervised by the Maudling Committee, for the simultaneous establishment of the Common Market and a free-trade area. She was trying in this way to detach the free-trade states in the Europe of the Six—Germany and the Netherlands—from the protectionist ones. To Germany and the Netherlands she pointed out that they would enjoy the commercial benefits of a reduction in tariffs without being penalized by the limitations of France's safeguard clauses.

One is struck by the parallelism between Britain's external opposition and the Gaullists' internal opposition to the construction of an integrated Europe.

Balance of Forces in 1958

The controversy over Europe was geopolitical in nature between the principal nations, and ideological in the sphere of public opinion. The geopolitical quarrel pitted England against the Continent; the ideological quarrel pitted nationalism against federalism.

In 1958 the power relationship of the geopolitical forces was less complicated because of the Atlantic Pact. The states of Western Europe were protected against the Soviet threat by American weapons, both nuclear and conventional. No territorial demands pitted one nation against another. Their rivalry was essentially economic and affected primarily trade relations. Only countries like England and France that retained overseas territories had direct military responsibilities there, independently of the Atlantic Pact. Germany was in the best position in regard to economic competition: increasing growth rate of the gross national product, productive investments, industrial potential, flourishing exports, stable currency. France occupied a middle position: a dynamic economy, military responsibilities overseas, a weak currency. England's situation was the most critical; production and exports were practically at a standstill, her preferential ties with the Commonwealth were growing looser. The gradual implementation of the Common Market, with all the advantages of a broader economy, would threaten England's future and benefit the Continent.

One cannot, however, measure the political power of a nation exclusively in economic or military terms. The spread of cultural values, the efficacy and stability of institutions, loyalty to alliances, political imagination—all these are components of a moral authority that makes itself felt in diplomacy as well as in global strategy.

In this respect, memories of the war were a moral liability for West Germany, although she was divesting herself of them little by little. But the special restrictions on the Federal Republic's sovereignty, the division of Germany between East and West, the precarious position of Berlin, were among the factors that tended to decrease the importance of the German nation. In 1958, in spite of her prosperity, Germany could not aspire to leadership in Europe.

Unlike Germany, England on the morrow of the war enjoyed considerable prestige. In 1958 this asset had not entirely disappeared but neither had it been enhanced. Twice England had a chance to assume the lead in Europe— in 1948 and in 1954. She failed to avail herself of it. She had no part in the ideological ferment of the Continent.

The moral authority of France was declining at the end of the war owing to a long period of decadence that was political, military, and economic rather than cultural. Her reconciliation with Germany, her efforts after 1950 to build European unity, won her an influence such as she had not enjoyed since the French Revolution. The appeal for solidarity, for a forgetting of insults, and a restraint of national selfishness—all these were generous ideas that impressed public opinion inside and outside Europe. They took shape in institutions adapted to the times and to the needs of the nations. Ideas and institutions were Europe's rare, new contributions to a political organization torn by two wars within the space of thirty years.

Until 1958 the special position of England placed a strain on the equilibrium of the Continent's two ideological forces, federal and national. Despite the warnings of the independent liberal press, successive British governments, preoccupied by their relations with the Commonwealth and the United States, did not realize that the establishment of a prefederal regime would be democracy's best safeguard on the Continent. After the signing of the E.D.C. Treaty in 1952, England's European policy reinforced the Gaullist opposition to the Fourth Republic. It was partly responsible for the formation in 1954 of a German national army which might eventually become the tool of an ambitious foreign policy.

To be sure, unconditional surrender dealt a lasting blow to German nationalism. But one cannot help wondering whether, in order to overcome Germany's ancient demons, it might not have been wiser to have set up a political federation. This could have been accomplished by constituting a common army quickly instead of making gradual preparations for a federation through the Common Market.

In 1958, however, the Christians and Socialists who advocated a federal union of Europe were the only real political forces in West Germany.

In France, the champions of integration were clearly beating a retreat by 1958. United on foreign policy since 1955, the Christians, Liberals, and Socialists were divided on economic policy and on the war in Algeria. Some of them failed to understand that the battle of Europe was being waged in Algiers and that the monetary welfare of France was a prerequisite to the establishment of the Common Market. The split in the Center parties paved the way for the nationalist Right.

Great currents of ideas force their way through obstacles. Would the idea of European unity, already weakened by the fear of German rearmament, be destroyed by the fear of decolonization? Would it be saved by the very strength of the institutions it fostered?

Frenchmen held the answer to this question in their own hands. Divided on all major problems, they had in their ranks the most eminent champions and detractors of a united Europe.

III

Decolonization

12

The Worldwide Movement and the
French Attitude

Definition and Trends

A MOVEMENT OF SECESSION for some, of liberation for others, decolonization was a return to international public law in the relations
between colonizers and colonized. The principle of equality replaced
domination, contractual relations replaced power relations.

The national idea reached the dependent territories through the school,
the press, and the customs of the ruling oligarchy. The right of self-determination for peoples stemmed from the 1789 Declaration of the Rights of Man.
Deeply entrenched in the colonies, Christian missions preached the brother-
hood of man, which implied equality. These ideas were implemented in the
twentieth century by the native clergy.

In the nineteenth century, English liberalism, Christian and democratic in
inspiration, established self-government for the white residents of the
Dominions. In the twentieth century the doctrine spread to coloured people.

The American brand of anti-colonialism invoked the same principles as
the British, imbued as it was with memories of the war for independence. On
the morrow of World War II, American public opinion openly criticized the
colonialist policies of the European nations.

The Soviet Union's anti-colonialist struggle, subversive in its implementation, was of Marxist inspiration. To pave the way for revolutionary
Socialism, local Communist parties backed the nationalist movements in all
of Europe's overseas possessions.

Nurtured externally by Christianity, Western democracy, and Marxism,
nationalism found a powerful internal stimulant in native religions and

ideologies. In 1945 the resurgence of Islam in North Africa and the Middle East, of Gandhi's ideas in India, and the impact of the Japanese occupation in Southeast Asia converged to weaken the authority of the European colonial powers.

These powers, to be sure, preserved their material and intellectual superiority over the dependent peoples, but the latter could claim an indisputable ideological superiority. "The nationalists . . . believe in the sanctity of their cause more strongly than their adversaries believe in the legitimacy of their domination,"[1] wrote Raymond Aron.

From Brazzaville to San Francisco

The French conception of decolonization became plain at the Brazzaville Conference in February 1944. It was inserted between two diplomatic documents dealing with the same subject, the Atlantic Charter and the Charter of the United Nations.

The Atlantic Charter, signed in 1941 by Roosevelt and Churchill, defined the goals of the two great Western democracies. According to Article 3, the United States and England "respect the right of all peoples to choose the form of government under which they will live; and they wish to see sovereign rights and self-government restored to those who have been forcibly deprived of them." Because of its generality, this declaration could be adduced by dependent overseas populations as well as by peoples under German or Japanese occupation.

The great powers were already preparing to internationalize somewhat the tutelage of colonialized people. Reacting to this movement, the Brazzaville Conference made recommendations designed to "affirm and guarantee the intangible political unity of the French world." The basic principle was clearly enunciated: "The aims of the civilizing mission accomplished by France in her colonies preclude the idea of autonomy or any possibility of evolution outside the French empire; the idea of a possible, even ultimate establishment of self-government in the colonies must be discarded." Free France rejected internal autonomy, and therefore, even more, independence. De Gaulle stated that the purpose of the conference was to clarify the conditions that would permit the overseas populations "to become integrated into the French Community." P.-F. Gonidec has observed: "The conference is steeped in tradition. The notion of empire is strongly affirmed."[2]

According to the authors of these recommendations, what was the substance of integration? On the political level, it was a satisfactory repre-

[1] Raymond Aron, *Paix et guerre entre les nations* (Paris: Calmann-Lévy, 1962), 230.

[2] P.-F. Gonidec, *Droit d'outremer* (Paris: Montchrétien, 1959), I, 335.

sentation of the colonies in the future French Constituent Assembly. On the level of the administration of territorial interests, it was the creation of assemblies of elected representatives with consultative and also some decision-making power. On the economic level, the purpose of integration was to raise the living standard through the development of agricultural and industrial production.

This concept was far behind the already timeworn practices of the British Commonwealth, mentioned earlier. It was also far behind the Charter of the United Nations, signed on June 26, 1945, in San Francisco by most of the sovereign states, including France.

One of the primary objectives of the Charter was "to develop friendly relations between nations, based on respect for the principle of the equality of rights of peoples and their right to self-determination." (Article 1, Sec. 2.)

Furthermore, the Charter addressed a special declaration to the non-autonomous territories. According to Article 73, the mother countries "regard it as their sacred mission . . . to grant the political aspirations of native peoples and to aid them in the gradual development of their free political institutions."

Section VIII of the Constitution of 1946

After a referendum in the spring of 1946 had resulted in the rejection of the initial draft constitution, a second Constituent Assembly was elected on June 2, 1946.

The Mouvement Républicain Populaire (M.R.P.), which had just triumphed in the elections, chose one of their members, Paul Coste-Floret, to serve as general *rapporteur* for the second draft of the constitution. Coste-Floret presented a detailed text dealing with the French Union—Section VIII—that was inspired by the authoritarian and centralized conception that de Gaulle, then a member of the opposition, had outlined in his Bayeux speech of June 16. On August 28, Edouard Herriot attacked the draft as "the expression of a mindless and anarchical federalism" which would make France "a colony of her former colonies."[3] On the same day, de Gaulle declared that this draft would pave the way for "foreign domination through the destruction of the Union." The M.R.P.'s attitude stiffened because a good many of its members were Gaullists at the time. Herriot's criticism was echoed by many Centrists and Rightists.

The text voted by the second Constituent Assembly was adopted by referendum on October 21, 1946, although in the overseas territories the nays outnumbered the ayes by 335,000 to 258,000.

[3] Quoted by P.-F. Gonidec, *ibid.*, 351.

Members of the Constituent Assembly could emulate the British example, as embodied in the Charter of the United Nations, and provide for an evolution of the territories toward internal autonomy and eventually toward independence. They could follow the recommendations of the Brazzaville Conference and provide for an improvement in the status of individuals, thus attenuating or even eliminating inequalities between subjects and citizens.

The first conception, called association, assumes a confederal structure (patterned on the Commonwealth) for all the mother countries and their dependencies; the second, called assimilation or integration, is conceivable within the framework of a unitary state.

On the whole, and despite certain concessions made to the doctrine of association, Section VIII of the constitution provided for a certain degree of integration while preserving the definite preeminence of the mother country over the territories. This conception is entirely in harmony with the Napoleonic centralization of the French governmental system. It appears in the membership of the French Union, in its institutions, and in the status of individuals.

The old French empire consisted of two kinds of possessions: the incorporated colonies, an integral part of the French Republic; and states outside the French Republic, i.e. protectorates and countries under the mandate of the League of Nations.

The constitution of 1946 made the same distinction, although its terminology was somewhat different. According to Article 60, "The French Union is formed on one side by the French Republic which comprises metropolitan France, the departments and overseas territories, and on the other by associated territories and states."

In the thinking of the members of the Constituent Assembly, overseas departments meant Algeria and the four old colonies; overseas territories meant the French colonies of Africa and Madagascar; associated states and protectorates meant Vietnam, Cambodia, Laos, Tunisia, Morocco; associated territories under mandate of the United Nations were Togo and the Cameroon.

Contrary to the declared intentions of the constitution's preamble, Section VIII did not insure the equality of collectivities because (according to Gonidec) the French government was "the real directing organ of the Union."[4] Nor did it insure equality of individuals: French nationals retained a privileged position in the French Union, especially from an electoral point of view.

The natives, however, rebelled against the real inequality among collectivities and among individuals. They demanded internal autonomy, even independence, alluding to the evolutionary nature of the status and the declared

4 *Ibid.*, 372.

[130

intentions of the preamble. At the same time public opinion in metropolitan France gradually perceived the political and economic consequences of assimilation.

This twofold opposition triumphed over the ultra-conservatism of the local civil servants and destroyed the artificial and ambiguous edifice of the French Union.

The struggle for decolonization began in different ways and with varying success throughout most of the old empire. War in Indochina, political crises in Tunisia and Morocco, war in Algeria, liberal reform in Black Africa—these punctuated the stages of a futile battle that had not ended when the Fourth Republic fell. At every stage, external events played an important role in the hostilities as well as in the negotiations. At every stage, public opinion, poorly informed about the local circumstances and the international situation, resigned itself to the inevitable and pointed an accusing finger against its institutions and the political forces in power.

13

The Indochinese War

Indochina in 1945

INDOCHINA IS PEOPLED by three ethnic groups, unequal in size. The natives of Cambodia and Laos (three million and one million inhabitants respectively in 1945) are "Hinduized." The ancient empire of Annam, or Vietnam, embraces the territories or Ky, of Tonkin, Annam, and Nam-Bô (Cochin China) and has twenty-two million inhabitants.

Beginning in A.D. 939, after ten centuries of Chinese domination, Vietnam enjoyed more than nine centuries of independence before the French conquest. "The Vietnamese people are aware of a long, independent past, of their dynamism. They know they belong to a civilization which is not surpassed by that of the West except in the matter of technology," Philippe Devillers has written.[1] Influenced morally and intellectually by the Chinese, Vietnam had none the less retained its own national identity.

The French conquest shattered the political unity of Vietnam. In 1874 Cochin China became a French colony. Annam and Tonkin were converted into protectorates under the nominal suzerainty of the Emperor of Annam. The same thing happened to Cambodia and Laos, which retained their respective suzerains. The Indochinese Union, established in 1886, was a juridical and political instrument in the hands of the governor-general, who was responsible to the colonial minister rather than to the minister of foreign affairs. Throughout the territory controlled by the Union, a system of direct administration was established.

[1] Philippe Devillers, *Histoire du Vietnam de 1940 à 1952* (Paris: Editions du Seuil, 1952), 30.

In June 1940 (immediately after the Franco-German armistice was signed), a Japanese threat loomed over the land, which was without a political structure based on popular choice. In August the Vichy government granted Japan certain military facilities in exchange for the promise to respect French sovereignty in Indochina. In July 1941 the Darlan-Kato Accord broadened these privileges to include the use of the airports and naval bases.

Admiral Decoux, the governor-general, resisted the Japanese demands and tried to stimulate national sentiment in Vietnam.

In 1941 Nguyen Ai Quoc, the future Ho Chi-minh, formed a new political party, the Vietminh. Its members were drawn from Communist and Nationalist groups that had emigrated from South China. In an arresting brochure, the Vietminh set forth their political program. It consisted of ridding the country of French and Japanese Fascists. It claimed independence for Vietnam and urged cooperation with the democracies that opposed Fascism and aggression. It envisaged the establishment of the Democratic Republic of Vietnam. According to Philippe Devillers, the Vietminh have never deviated from their initial program.[2]

They set up an underground organization and won the confidence of the Chinese national government by supplying information about the Japanese and the French.

On March 9, 1945, the Japanese government addressed an ultimatum to Admiral Decoux. The French troops were annihilated. The Emperor of Annam, Bao-Dai, congratulated the Japanese and offered his collaboration. He set up a government whose sole purpose was to prevent the Japanese from administering the country directly.

On the morrow of the bombing of Hiroshima, Ho Chi-minh unleashed his guerrillas, whom he had organized clandestinely. Thereafter they were called the Vietnamese armies of liberation. On August 25 Bao-Dai abdicated in favor of the Vietminh, who already controlled all of Vietnam. On the 29th, Ho chi-minh set up a provisional government and assumed its presidency. Bao-Dai was to be the "Supreme Adviser." The Communists had a majority in this coalition government and controlled the principal ministries. On September 2 Vietnamese independence was proclaimed. The program of 1941 was now to be implemented.

Reconquest

Would an attempt be made to reconquer Indochina after the Japanese occupation and despite the reluctance of the United States whilst the claim to independence was put forward by the Nationalists and Communists? Or

[2] *Ibid.*, 98.

would an attempt be made to establish between France and her former possessions another kind of relationship based on independence and technical and economic aid?

In a declaration of March 24, 1945, the Provisional Government of the French Republic announced its intention of preserving political control in Indochina. It set up an Indochinese Federation that included Cochin China, Annam, Tonkin, Cambodia, and Laos, with a federal government presided over by the governor-general. French and native ministers were to be responsible to the governor-general.

At the Potsdam Conference of July 1945 the Americans and Russians assigned the task of disarming the Japanese to the British in southern Indochina up to the sixteenth parallel, and to the Chinese in the North. When Japan surrendered in August, de Gaulle decided to send the expeditionary force he had trained to help fight the Japanese. He appointed General Leclerc commander-in-chief and Admiral d'Argenlieu high commissioner.

On August 20, 1945, Bao-Dai sent de Gaulle a message: "I beg you to realize that the only way to safeguard the spiritual influence of France and her interests in Indochina is to acknowledge openly the independence of Vietnam. You must give up the idea of reestablishing French sovereignty or French administration in any guise."

Leclerc entered Saigon on October 5. Preceded by the commissioner of southern Indochina, Jean Cédile, he was supported by the commander of the British troops, General D. D. Gracey. Within a month Leclerc was in possession of the cities and major routes of Cochin China. In February 1946 he extended his control to southern Annam, Cambodia, and Laos.

On August 22, Jean Sainteny, the commissioner for Tonkin, landed alone at Hanoi. The first Chinese troops entered the city on September 9. Ho Chi-minh repressed the revolutionary excesses in order to win the confidence of Chiang Kai-Shek. Cleverly enough, he managed to dissolve the Indochinese Communist Party. The Vietminh won a big victory in the elections of January 6, 1946.

Convinced that "Indochina is first of all a Chinese problem"[3] and that the expeditionary force could not win against the combined Vietminh and Chinese forces, Leclerc decided to negotiate. While making preparations for the peaceful landing of his troops in Tonkin, he initiated talks with the Chinese and Vietnamese governments.

The Gouin ministry, which took office after de.Gaulle's resignation on January 20, 1946, approved Leclerc's plan.

The Sino-French Treaty was signed at Chungking on February 28. The Chiang Kai-Shek government recognized French sovereingty in Indochina

[3] Quoted by Devillers, *ibid.*, 205.

and agreed to withdraw its troops from Tonkin and northern Laos before March 15. In exchange, France promised to abolish the "Capitulations" and to establish a free port in Haiphong for trade with China.

Negotiations with the Vietnamese resulted in an accord signed on March 6, 1946, by Ho Chi-minh and Sainteny. The French government recognized the Republic of Vietnam "as a free state and as a member of both the Indochinese Federation and the French Union, with its own government, parliament, army and finances." This declaration fulfilled one of the major aims of the Vietminh—independence. As for the additional claim—"the union of the three Ky's," that is, of the three sections of Vietnam: Tonkin, Annam, and Cochin China—"the French government promises to ratify any decisions reached by popular referendum." Finally, an agreement between Leclerc and Giap outlined the method by which the French forces would be returned to the territory under Vietminh control. Thus, the army had paved the way for a liberal policy.

Philippe Devillers noted that in March 1946 France "was the first nation, before Holland, England, and even America, to come to a firm agreement with Asiatic nationalism."[4] But this unprecedented opportunity was never to be thoroughly exploited. Leclerc and Sainteny were far ahead of Saigon and Paris.

D'Argenlieu openly criticized the accord of March 6. Backed by most of the colonial administrators, he based his policy on the declaration of March 24, 1945. His object was to divide Vietnam. To this end, on May 30, 1946, he recognized the Cochin Chinese Republic, which was autonomous and hostile to the Vietminh.

Ho Chi-minh and the Vietnamese delegation flew to France on May 31 to negotiate a firm agreement with the French government. Simultaneously, the elections of June 2 altered the picture in France: the Socialists lost ground whereas the M.R.P. increased its representation; a resurgence of the Radical and Moderate forces gave the Constituent Assembly a more Rightist orientation.

Georges Bidault headed the new government. Marius Moutet was minister of state for the French Union. The Fontainebleau Conference began on July 6 with not a single French politician having been asked to confer with Ho Chi-minh. The head of the Vietnamese government told the press: "The relations between France and Vietnam must be determined by treaty. And the treaty must be based on the fundamental principle of the right of our people to self-determination." Max André, president of the French delegation, replied: "Our conception of the French Union is not that of an alliance but of an association of states closely united by common organs."[5] The

[4] *Ibid.*, 241.
[5] Quoted by Devillers, *ibid.*, 296, 297.

Vietminh refused to accept the Indochinese Federation as the possessors of sovereign rights over the state of Vietnam. On August 1 at Dalat, Admiral d'Argenlieu convoked a conference on the Indochinese Federation but did not invite a Vietminh representative. The Fontainebleau Conference broke up. Unable to procure ratification in Paris of the March 6 accord because it failed to win support in Saigon, Ho Chi-minh signed a secret pact with Marius Moutet on September 14. It referred exclusively to economic and cultural relations between France and the Vietminh. On the eve of his departure, Ho Chi-minh made a final appeal: "Do not let me leave like this! Support me against those who are trying to go further than I. You will never regret it."[6]

The situation in Indochina had deteriorated during the long absence of Ho Chi-minh. American recognition of the independence of the Philippines went almost unnoticed in Paris. But in Southeast Asia it made a deep impression. Part of Cochin China fell under Vietminh control. As a consequence, on November 10 the president of the autonomous republic created by d'Argenlieu, Dr. Thinh, committed suicide. According to Bernard Fall, in Tonkin Ho Chi-minh had to choose between capitulation to colonialism or the espousal of orthodox Communism.[7] Having lost face at Fontainebleau, he convoked a Constituent Assembly that adopted a draft constitution containing no reference whatsoever to the French Union.

Tensions increased between the Vietnamese and French authorities. The creation of a French customs office at Haiphong produced difficulties. Refusing to call a meeting of the joint commission, for which the pact of September 14 had made provision, General Valluy, acting high commissioner, demanded the bombardment of Haiphong on November 23. On the 28th, shortly before the government resigned, Admiral d'Argenlieu obtained approval for this operation from Georges Bidault and the Interministerial Committee for Indochina. Urgently recalled to Saigon, Sainteny tried to negotiate with Ho Chi-minh. On December 15 Ho Chi-minh sent Léon Blum a judicious message suggesting the cessation of hostilities. The message, which was "delayed en route," did not reach Paris until the 26th. Meanwhile, on December 19, Giap's troops had fiercely attacked the French forces at Hanoi. The war had begun.

War without War Aims

Heading an all-Socialist cabinet, Léon Blum took office on December 18. In an article in the *Populaire* on December 10, he had urged a "sincere agreement based on independence." In his investiture address he stated that order

---

[6] Quoted by Jean Sainteny, *Histoire d'une paix manquée* (Paris: Amiot Dumont, 1953), 209.

[7] Bernard Fall, *Le Vietminh* (Paris: Armand Colin, 1960), 36.

must be restored before a free state could be established. He sent Marius Moutet and General Leclerc to Indochina. In an autograph letter to Moutet, which was accompanied by a memorandum dated December 31, Ho Chi-minh again proposed a cessation of hostilities. He also suggested immediate talks. The letter, however, never reached its destination; the two men did not meet. Early in January, Leclerc stated: "Anti-Communism is a means to an end that will have no backing as long as the national problem remains unresolved." Following the advice of de Gaulle he refused the post of high commissioner which Léon Blum offered him upon his return. Moreover, he never received the governmental assurances he had requested.[8]

On January 22, 1947, Paul Ramadier succeeded Blum. He spoke in the same vein as his predecessor: "We will put an end to it (the war) as soon as order and security have been assured." Since the attack at Hanoi, the French press, poorly informed, had been giving vent to violent feelings. As Philippe Devillers has pointed out, "Not a single French newspaper sent a correspondent to Tonkin during the critical period."[9] The foreign press had changed its tone since the accord of March 6, 1946. On January 22, 1947, the *New York Times* commented: "France is the only European country that is trying to hold on to her colonies in Asia by the use of force."[10]

During the ensuing months the major events that occurred outside of France had no effect whatsoever on her policy in the Far East.

On February 20, 1947, the British government fulfilled its promise of 1940. In a statement that has since become famous, it announced its decision to transfer its powers and to get out of India at a specified date. On the advice of the last viceroy of India, Lord Mountbatten, the time for departure was advanced almost a year. India and Pakistan were granted full independence within the Commonwealth on August 15, 1947.

Like Indochina, Malaya had been invaded by the Japanese. The Communist Party there had trained guerrillas. In 1948 England gave the colony a federal Legislative Council with seats shared out amongst local ethnic groups and economic interests. The British also endowed Malaya with a federal Executive Council whose native members were appointed after consultation with the various political parties. Both councils were to some degree representative.

Holland, on the other hand, was engaged in a struggle against Indonesia, which had controlled Java and Sumatra ever since the Japanese surrender. A police action began in July 1947. The United Nations attempted to arbitrate the affair but its efforts proved futile. Holland engaged in a second police action in December 1948, but under pressure from the United States

---

[8] Devillers, *Histoire du Vietnam*, 367, 369.
[9] *Ibid.*, 358.
[10] *Ibid.*, 373.

and the United Nations, she renewed her efforts to arrive at a negotiated solution. The result in 1949 was the total transfer of sovereign rights to Indonesia. The status quo was maintained, however, in western New Guinea.

In China the Communists were gaining ground at the expense of the nationalists. In November 1945, President Truman had sent General Marshall on a mission of conciliation. Marshall returned to Washington in January 1947 to report utter failure. During a tour of inspection, General Wedemeyer observed in July 1947 that Chiang Kai-Shek was incapable of carrying out the necessary political and economic reforms. Civil war broke out in 1948. In 1949 Mao Tse-tung captured Peking.

Events in Asia influenced the Indochinese, who were convinced that the French position was anachronistic. Both the Nationalists and the Communists were fortified by this belief. But the developments in China carried more weight with the extremists among the Vietminh.

Successive French governments were more anxious to justify their refusal to negotiate than to define war aims. "These aims were exclusively negative," Jean Lacouture and Philippe Devillers noted. They put it this way: "We cannot allow . . . the natives to rule themselves, dismember the empire, and let the people fall into the hands of the Communists. Nor can we expose the Catholic minorities to possible danger or deprive the West of raw materials."[11] The French governments could not decide whether the Communists or the Nationalists were the real enemy, or how much to concede to them. How would independence affect the French Union? The opposition was equally hesitant. In a press conference on November 17, 1948, de Gaulle expressed the opinion that time was on France's side.[12]

These uncertainties were apparent in the negotiations between Ho Chi-minh and Bao-Dai.

French political parties were divided on the question of which group to treat with. The Communists and a large minority of the Socialists wanted a resumption of the talks with Ho Chi-minh. The M.R.P., influenced by Admiral d'Argenlieu, preferred to negotiate exclusively with the Nationalists.

On March 27, 1947, Emile Bollaert, replacing the admiral as high commissioner, moved successively in both directions.

Toward the end of April 1947, the Vietminh's foreign minister, Hoang Minh-Giam, offered to negotiate on the basis of the resolution adopted at the Congress of the French Socialist Party. The Communist ministers were expelled from the Ramadier government on May 4. This led Bollaert to draft very severe conditions for an armistice. Bollaert's emissary, Paul Mus,

---

[11] Jean Lacouture and Philippe Devillers, *La fin d'une guerre* (Paris: Editions du Seuil, 1960), 11.

[12] Quoted by Lacouture and Devillers, *ibid.*, 20.

believed that the French authorities were making a grave mistake in respond-
ing to a proposal for the suspension of hostilities "by insisting, before the
commencement of negotiations, on the total surrender of forces that had not
been defeated."[13] Ho Chi-minh's answer was blistering: "There is no room
for cowards in the French Union. And I would be a coward were I to accept
these conditions."[14]

On August 23, the coalition cabinet, which consisted of Socialists,
Radicals, and M.R.P.—the third force—decided to eliminate the Vietminh
from the negotiations. It accepted Bao-Dai's solution, which was supported
by the colonial officials and certain *colons*. On September 10, in his Ha-Dong
speech, Bollaert offered Vietnam, Cambodia, and Laos "freedom" within
the French Union rather than independence. There was no longer any
will to interpose an Indochinese Federation between these states and France,
as had been done in 1946. On the other hand, diplomacy and the army
remained under the jurisdiction of metropolitan France.

On November 21 the Schuman cabinet took office. The M.R.P. demanded the portfolio for overseas territories, and it was given to Paul
Coste-Floret.

On November 25 and 27, 1947, Laos and Cambodia declared their adherence to the French Union and relinquished control of their foreign policy.
In the Along Bay declaration of December 6, Bollaert obtained a similar
commitment from Bao-Dai in the name of Vietnam. The accord was facilitated
by the high commissioner's prior stand on the unification of the three Ky's,
henceforth considered an internal Vietnamese problem. Having become
emperor once again, Bao-Dai formed a provisional government and counter-
signed, again in the Along Bay, the protocol of June 5, 1948, which formally
recognized the independence of Vietnam and its right to unity. But before
the status of Cochin China could be changed the National Assembly would
have to ratify the accord. The chronic weakness of the Fourth Republic
delayed the ratification, which Bao-Dai awaited in France.

On April 8, 1949, Vincent Auriol, as president of the French Union,
informed Bao-Dai that France would not object to the inclusion of Cochin
China in Vietnam if it were approved by a referendum. Despite the opposition
of Communist and R.P.F. deputies, in May 1949 the National Assembly
ratified a law to integrate Cochin China with Vietnam, to recognize a unified
Vietnam, and to confer upon Cambodia and Laos the status of associated
states within the French Union. In September 1949 the methods of transferring powers to the associated states were debated at the Pau Conference
where France was represented by Jean Letourneau, minister for the overseas
territories in the Bidault cabinet. The accords fixing membership conditions

---

[13] Paul Mus, *Vietnam, sociologie d'une guerre* (Paris: Editions du Seuil, 1952), 315.
[14] Quoted by Mus, *ibid.*, 316.

for the three states in the French Union—an associative relationship provided for in Article 61 of the constitution—were approved by a law of February 2, 1950. The system of protectorates was thus officially done away with. The Indochinese were critical of the statute because it gave the associated states only a quasi-autonomy for internal affairs and limited international rights.

To be sure, France ended up by granting Bao-Dai in 1950 what she had refused Ho Chi-minh in 1947. But having misjudged the extent of the peoples' loyalty to the Vietminh, she did not know how to transform non-Communist Vietnamese nationalism into an active force. On the contrary, by her hesitations and restrictions, France undermined the authority of Bao-Dai, which was already in jeopardy at the time of his return to office.

Meanwhile, the military situation was deteriorating. To be sure, the war minister, Paul Coste-Floret, told *Figaro* on May 14, 1948: "I believe that from now on there will cease to be a military problem in Indochina."[15] His opinion, however, differed markedly from that of General Leclerc. In January 1947, Leclerc estimated that 500,000 men would be needed—the entire annual contingent—to liquidate the insurrection quickly.[16] But only the Vietnamese units were recruited. These auxiliary troops found themselves in a difficult position in dealing with the Vietminh, who were already entrenched in many of the mountain areas.

"Actually, the war had no leadership," wrote Jean Lacouture and Philippe Devillers. They added: "The government was waging war but it did not seem to take the trouble to provide itself with the requisite means."[17] The refusal to send the required number of conscripts precluded a military solution. "The decision to keep our conscripts out of the Indochinese war was a fatal error from many points of view, and one that France alone committed: neither the Netherlands, England, nor the United States hesitated to send their troops to New Guinea, to Palestine, to Malaya, and to Korea, respectively. The presence of French troops would have forced the political leaders to rethink the Indochinese problem more frequently and thoroughly."[18]

The International War

The choice between war and peace was made unwittingly. The transition from an aimless to an international war came as a shock.

On January 14, 1950, Ho Chi-minh recognized the Chinese People's Republic. His government was immediately recognized by Mao Tse-tung. On

[15] Alfred Grosser, *La IVe République et sa politique extérieure* (Paris: Armand Colin, 1961), p. 260.
[16] Lacouture and Devillers, *La fin*, 25.
[17] *Ibid.*, 24.
[18] Bernard Fall, *Indochine 1946–1962* (Paris: Robert Laffont, 1962), 366.

January 30, the Soviet Union recognized the Democratic Republic of Vietnam. On February 7 the United States recognized Vietnam (that is, the Bao-Dai government), Laos, and Cambodia, which were elevated to the rank of independent states within the framework of the French Union by the law of February 2, 1950. In February, General Giap announced on the radio that the period of guerrilla warfare was over and that the real war was about to begin.

"The eventual success of a revolutionary movement depends upon the determination of the 'external base' to play a part until the very end," according to the geopolitical theory of Bernard Fall.[19] Communist China was playing this role in regard to Ho Chi-minh. "Armed and equipped by China, Vietnam was now ready to take the initiative militarily."[20] In October 1950, five Vietnam divisions, the first large units, occupied the Tonkin delta. The first serious defeats occurred near the Chinese frontier: Dongke, Lang-Son and Cao-Bang fell to the hands of the Vietminh on September 18, October 3, and October 18.

Meanwhile another conflict began in Asia on June 25, 1950. North Korean troops, backed by Communist China, crossed the thirty-eighth parallel. The United States immediately lent its support to South Korea. At the same time an American military mission was sent to Indochina. American aid was beginning to function. On December 23, 1950, a treaty was signed between the United States, France, and the associated states. In the space of a year, the colonial war had become part of the rivalry between the two blocs. The United States and the Soviet Union confronted each other through the intermediary of Indochina and Korea.

The fall of Lang-Son and Cao-Bang aroused French public opinion. Debate in the National Assembly began on October 19. For the first time a voice was raised in Parliament to complain of the inconsistency of French policy and to demand decisive action. Pierre Mendès-France flatly declared: "There are only two possible solutions. The first is to achieve our objectives in Indochina by means of political power. If we follow this course . . . and, if we are to obtain a quick military success we will need three times the number of troops presently stationed there, and appropriations must be tripled. The alternative is to seek a political accord with the enemy. . . . An accord means concessions, sizable ones, far more extensive, of course, than those that might have sufficed earlier." Speaking again on November 22, Mendès-France said he preferred direct negotiations to a growing internationalization of the conflict. He stressed the serious damage done to France's position in Europe by her involvement in Asia. In a motion adopted by a vote of 337 to 187, the Assembly decided "to furnish the government with sufficient means to

[19] *Ibid.*, 362.
[20] Lacouture and Devillers, *La fin*, 28.

enable the associated states to put their national armies on a war footing as quickly as possible." It asked the government "to stress to the free nations the international nature of the conflict precipitated by the Vietminh, who are challenging the entire future of Southeast Asia. It must also emphasize the necessity of collaboration in order to meet the present threat and find the way to . . . a lasting peace."

The only positive result of the debate was the government's decision, reached on December 6, 1950, to name General de Lattre high commissioner as well as commander-in-chief of the army. The new civilian and military leader would have to do battle on three fronts. From France he demanded reinforcements, and he claimed that the loss of Tonkin would mean the loss of all of Indochina, although the army chiefs of staff did not agree with him. He also asked that a large force be sent to Asia forthwith and that the period of compulsory military service be increased to two years. The objection was raised that France's contribution to the defense of Europe would thereby be decreased. After a few month's delay, the Queuille government agreed in March 1951 to send reinforcements from Africa—French officers and non-commissioned officers as well as native troops. The fundamental decision was thus again postponed while "contact was established between Africa and an anti-colonialist revolution."[21] In September 1951 de Lattre asked the United States for increased aid. The prestige of his name guaranteed success. The delivery of arms was speeded up. The general halted the Vietminh advance in Tonkin and defended the "useful delta." At the same time he publicly advocated independence for Indochina. In a speech on April 19, 1951, he made his views plain: "I have come here to win your independence for you, not to restrict it." He cautioned the French government against the dangers of a war fought so far from home and the threat of Chinese inter-vention. Illness interrupted the mission of this fine soldier. De Lattre's political views were the same as those held by General Leclerc five years earlier. He died on January 11, 1952.

This was a bright interlude, but it proved shortlived. Thereafter the diplomatic and military situation steadily deteriorated.

General Raoul Salan succeeded de Lattre as commander-in-chief. To Jean Letourneau's duties as minister of the associated states were added that of high commissioner.

In March 1953 Vietminh troops penetrated the Plaine des Jarres and sealed off Tonkin. The war spread to all Indochina. General Henri Navarre, who succeeded Salan as commander-in-chief on May 8, 1953, followed the plans prepared by his predecessor. They consisted of setting up a more powerful battle corps than that of the enemy.

After the death of Stalin, relations between the United States and the

[21] *Ibid.*, 31.

Soviet Union became considerably less tense. Was the time ripe for an international settlement of the Southeast Asian conflict? This was to be discussed at the Bermuda Conference where the president of the United States was to meet with the British and French heads of government. But the conference had to be postponed because of the protracted ministerial crisis in France. Two of the three premier-designates rejected by the National Assembly, Paul Reynaud and Pierre Mendès-France, favored negotiations. The third, Georges Bidault, was opposed. On June 26 Joseph Laniel was accepted as head of the government and Bidault became his foreign minister. Laniel announced that he would explore the possibility of ending the war. This change in the direction of French policy was confirmed on July 3 when powers were transferred to the associated states.

On July 27 an armistice was proclaimed in Korea but the Indochinese problem was left up in the air despite the efforts of the French government to persuade the Americans to settle both questions simultaneously. Bao-Dai was becoming more demanding. In September he convoked a political congress that demanded total independence for Vietnam and withdrawal from the French Union. Thus France, even if victorious, would no longer enjoy even a nominal sovereignty in Indochina.

Faced with this situation, parliamentary opinion quickly veered.

Another debate took place in the National Assembly on October 27. Joseph Laniel analyzed the positions of the various parties on the question of an international negotiation—China, the United States, the Vietminh— and concluded that "if one day Ho Chi-minh and his team . . . should seem inclined to make proposals, the French government and the other interested governments . . . would have to assess their merits and come to a joint decision on how they should be handled." By a vote of 315 to 252 the Assembly called upon the government "to do whatever might be necessary to bring about negotiations and the general pacification of Asia." As Alfred Grosser has observed, "the majority seemed to prefer an internationalization of the peace."[22] The opposition included Communists, Socialists, and a third of the Radicals. Antoine Pinay abstained and Mendès-France was not present. The recent disturbances in North Africa—the sultan of Morocco was overthrown in August, and guerrilla warfare was spreading to Tunisia— influenced the French government's attitude.

The day after the Assembly debate, a Swedish journalist, the Paris correspondent of the *Expressen,* sounded out Ho Chi-minh. Ho's answer was published in the *Expressen* on November 29: "If the French government learned its lesson during the war years and wishes to conclude an armistice and resolve the Vietnam problem by negotiation, the Democratic Republic of Vietnam and its people are quite ready to study the French proposals."

[22] Grosser, *IVᵉ Republique,* 290.

But unlike the French Parliament, Ho Chi-minh preferred to negotiate directly with the enemy.

Defeat and Partition

Peaceful intentions on both sides, differences of opinion on whether the eventual accords should be bilateral or multilateral—these marked the attitudes of the adversaries at the close of 1953.

The Laniel government was quite divided on how to proceed. René Pleven advocated direct negotiations. In December, he suggested to the premier that Alain Savary should sound out the intentions of the Vietminh. Laniel agreed but came up against the opposition of Bidault, who said to Savary early in March: "Ho Chi-minh is about to surrender. We are going to defeat him. Let's not strengthen his hand by this kind of contact."[23]

Moreover, preparations for international negotiations were under way. At the Bermuda Conference in December, Laniel and Bidault obtained the support of Eisenhower and Churchill for a Big Four conference with the Soviet Union, to be held in Berlin. This conference, which began on January 25, decided in the middle of February that a settlement of the Indochinese question would be a subject of discussion in Geneva on April 15 between France, the associated states, the United States, and England on the one hand, and the Soviet Union, China, and the Vietminh on the other. Military events, however, moved more quickly than the diplomatic preliminaries.

General Navarre's operational plan of July 1953 depended for its execution on reinforcements from metropolitan France and from the Vietnamese army. The reinforcements from France were insufficient, those from Vietnam were problematical. On December 3 Navarre, noting indications of an impending attack against Laos, decided "to engage in the battle of the northwest by centering his defense on the base of DienBienPhu, which must be saved at all cost."[24] DienBienPhu was located in a hollow three hundred kilometers from Hanoi and it was inaccessible by land, save by portage. Joseph Laniel, in retrospect, has noted: "By accepting, and not choosing, the site of the combat, we lost at one fell swoop all the advantages we enjoyed by virtue of our tremendous superiority in artillery, armored tanks and aviation."[25] Navarre justified his decision by adducing the necessity of defending Laos, whose security against any outside threat France had agreed to guarantee in a treaty of cooperation signed on October 23. The secret report of the Committee of Inquiry on DienBienPhu was later to state: "The

[23] Quoted by Lacouture and Devillers, *La fin*, 47.
[24] Joseph Laniel, *Le drame indochinois* (Paris: Plon, 1957), 38.
[25] *Ibid.*, 53.

government played no part in the decision to occupy DienBienPhu or in the battle that resulted from this decision."[26]

The Vietminh unleashed their attack on March 13 in the hope of achieving maximum results before the Geneva Conference got under way. By March 28 the airstrip could no longer be used and supplies had to be dropped by parachute. The airstrip was occupied on April 23; after that the use of parachutes became impossible.

On March 20, General Ely had been sent to Washington to obtain massive American aid. His talks with Admiral Radford suggested the possibility of direct intervention by American bombers. This might yet save the camp, which was cut off. An official request for such intervention was made on April 5. The American government replied that its help would depend on British cooperation. On April 26 England announced her refusal to become involved because of the impending Geneva Conference.

France came to this conference on April 29 aware that her military position was critical; the fall of DienBienPhu was imminent. In addition, her diplomatic position was precarious because the Western camp was divided.

The French government hoped for an armistice that would not jeopardize the final settlement. Such a settlement between the belligerents could be concluded when the time was up. But no armistice was possible without the approval of China, who was backing the Vietminh effectively, or without the Soviet Union. Yet France had nothing to offer China in exchange: international recognition of China and her entry into the United Nations depended on the United States, not on France. Presumably, France could influence the Soviet Union by immediately refusing to ratify the treaty for the European Defense Community, which had been hanging fire for several months because of deep divisions in public opinion and in Parliament. On the one hand, abandonment of the negotiations would cause a serious crisis between the United States and France, and on the other, the Soviet Union anticipated a clash of the two extremes in the National Assembly which would lead to rejection of the treaty when the question was debated.

Hostile to the idea of armed intervention, the American government accepted the idea of a cease-fire in the hope that the Vietnamese would subsequently resume the fight themselves. England envisaged the possibility of partition, a solution that the Vietnamese naturally rejected.

The camp at DienBienPhu fell on May 7. The climate of opinion in France was defeatist, and the dissemination of the news by the world press inflated still more the importance of this inevitable reverse.

On May 25, Pham Van-Dong, foreign minister of the Vietminh, began to make overtures with an eye to partition. Georges Bidault was opposed to

[26] J.-R. Tournoux, *Secrets d'Etat* (Paris: Plon, 1960), 460.

such a solution, but the matter was again discussed by the military experts on June 10, just before the fall of the Laniel cabinet. Meanwhile, a final and futile attempt was made to obtain American intervention. It was refused on June 8 by Eisenhower for fear that such a move might unleash a general atomic holocaust.

Simultaneously—and how can one fail to see how ridiculous such a gesture was at such a time?—France initialed treaties of independence and association with Vietnam. The independence of Vietnam was acknowledged for the fifth time, but without any reservations as to the sovereignty of the state.

On June 12 the Laniel cabinet was overthrown by a vote of 296 to 306.

On June 18, Pierre Mendès-France assumed office by a vote of 419 to 46, with 143 abstaining (76 of these were M.R.P. deputies loyal to Bidault). Mendès-France said he would not count the 100 Communist votes in computing his majority. Because of his former accurate criticisms of France's Indochinese policy, Mendès-France had been entrusted with this thankless task.

Negotiations took a new turn with Mendès-France in the saddle. His tactics were determined by the military situation. Hanoi could not be defended, the road to Haiphong was threatened, and the military leaders were calling for a quick solution. It was not until July 27, after the accords had been concluded, that the premier revealed the true situation to the National Assembly. It was this situation that led him to set a time limit for the negotiations—one month—and to create "a psychological atmosphere that would be equivalent to a military truce."[27]

Mendès-France exerted direct military pressure on the enemy by declaring that France would protect her expeditionary force by sending the regular conscripts if no honorable peace were concluded. He accepted straight off the idea of partition, and proceeded to hold direct talks with the Vietminh. In order to have Anglo-American support he asked the United States, finally won over to the idea of partition, and England to spell out the terms for their approval of the future accords. These conditions were made known on June 29. They proved acceptable to the French government, which could now speak for the Western world.

The accords were concluded on July 21. Partition was effectuated at approximately the seventeenth parallel. Militarily this solution benefited Vietnam and hurt the Vietminh. Cambodia, Laos, and South Vietnam attained independence. The French and Vietnamese troops were given three hundred days to evacuate the northern zone. Elections in both zones were set for July 1956. A system of international control was established.

The National Assembly ratified the accords on July 23, 1954, by 462 to

[27] Lacouture and Devillers, *La fin*, 225.

13; 140 deputies, including the M.R.P., abstained. The Independents either voted against or abstained.

The Balance Sheet

Thus the international war was concluded by a peace based on partition. The accords were signed by the belligerents with the consent of the indirect adversaries.

One year after Stalin's death and the Korean peace, the Soviet Union and China were eager to put an end to the second local struggle in Asia. The United States, for its part, refused to be dragged into a general war. The indirect adversaries were therefore at one in wishing to see the conflict terminated.

France saved her expeditionary corps, salvaged her economic interests to some extent, lost almost all her political influence in Indochina, and compromised her position within the French Union. South Vietnam became a protégé of the United States and North Vietnam a satellite of China. The historic frontier separating China from Southeast Asia now included Tonkin and a part of Annam.

France's persistent refusal to grant Vietnam unity and independence—a refusal she justified by calling the war a struggle against Communism—benefited both China and Communism substantially.

In assessing the results, one must assign the responsibilities. They seem to have been shared, but unequally.

General de Gaulle was responsible for the decision to attempt the reconquest of Indochina, for the authoritarian doctrine that defined the future status of the Indochinese Federation, and for choosing the man who initiated the policy. Admiral d'Argenlieu systematically applied this doctrine and became its propagandist for the M.R.P. and the Right until he was recalled in February 1947. He incessantly opposed the diplomatic accord concluded in March 1946 by General Leclerc with Ho Chi-minh. Once war had begun, the Gaullist deputies voted against a liberal status for the associated states.

The Socialists were hesitant and divided. After de Gaulle's resignation in January 1946, the Gouin government kept an even keel between d'Argenlieu and Leclerc until the elections to the Constituent Assembly. Toward the end of 1946 and the beginning of 1947, Léon Blum and Ramadier subordinated the resumption of negotiations with Ho Chi-minh to the reestablishment of order. It was not until August 1947, under the Ramadier government, that the cabinet decided to negotiate, not with Ho Chi-minh but with Bao-Dai.

The M.R.P. were opposed to an accord with the Vietnam. After the 1946

147]

elections and the appointment of Bidault as head of the Provisional Government, their influence increased. It was a member of the M.R.P., Paul Coste-Floret, who became the minister for overseas territories in the Schuman cabinet of November 1947. And it was another member of the M.R.P., Jean Letourneau, who was put in charge of Indochinese affairs, first as minister for overseas territories in the Bidault cabinet of 1949, then as minister for the associated states from 1949 to May 1953—in other words, during most of the period of the international war. During this period successive French governments had refused to send the contingent General de Lattre requested in 1951. Georges Bidault bore the larger share of responsibility for this. As premier of the Provisional Government in 1946, he had failed to create an atmosphere propitious for the successful conclusion of the Fontainebleau Conference with Ho Chi-minh. As premier in June 1953, he opposed the idea of negotiating with the Vietminh. As foreign minister in Laniel's cabinet early in 1954, he persisted in opposing negotiations, against the better judgment of Laniel and Pleven. As head of the French delegation at the Geneva Conference, he rejected the idea of partition.

Actually, no political party was unanimous or consistent in supporting real independence for Vietnam. Only a handful of individuals recommended a realistic and liberal solution to the problem—Leclerc and de Lattre during their missions in 1946 and 1951, and the premier-designate, Paul Reynaud, in 1953. Only one man—Pierre Mendès-France—alerted public opinion in 1950 to the real issues and explained that the alternative to independence was total war. Thereafter, he incessantly urged that negotiations be opened with the Vietminh. But he was not called upon to deal with the situation until it was too late, after the fall of DienBienPhu.

In this account of a lost cause, three successive events stand out, three situations that were followed by unwise political decisions arrived at without regard for military realities.

The first of these was reached in July 1946 at Fontainebleau. The chance to consolidate the Leclerc–Ho-Chi-minh accord of March of that year by playing the trump card of Vietnamese independence from China was lost.

The second decision came in August 1947 when the cabinet resolved to negotiate with Bao-Dai instead of Ho Chi-minh. To select this spokesman for Vietnam was to court disaster because Bao-Dai did not have the backing of the Vietnamese people.

The third option was exercised in November 1950 when, after Mendès-France's prophetic speech, the National Assembly voted against sending additional troops. It also urged American aid—in other words, continuation of the international war.

14

Shake-up in ℓAfrica

Over-all View

THE UPHEAVALS THAT BESET the French Union on the morrow of the war also affected the protectorates of Tunisia and Morocco, the three overseas departments that constituted Algeria, and the overseas territories of Madagascar and French-speaking Tropical Africa (former French West and Equatorial Africa).

The liberation of the Islamic countries was a major trend in the global evolution following the war. The Maghreb (northwest Africa) could not remain outside this trend. Since 1945 it had at its disposal a tool for propaganda and concerted action, the Arab League. Since 1952 it had a leader, Nasser. The nationalist chieftains of Tunisia, Morocco, and Algeria sought political support from the Arab League. The insurrection in Madagascar was not unrelated to the political developments in India, Indochina, and Indonesia. In French Tropical Africa, nationalism developed at a slower pace because of the lower rate of literacy.

Tunisia

The nationalist Neo Destour Party was founded in 1934 by Habib Bourguiba, who emerged as a strong leader and demanded independence after 1945.

In 1950 Robert Schuman, the foreign Minister, seemed to be guiding the French government toward a policy of liberalism and internal autonomy. The French *colons*, on the other hand, were invoking the principle of "co-sovereignty" in order to participate in the administration of the Tunisian institutions. In December 1951, Schuman was forced to execute an about-face and to affirm "the definitive nature of the bond that unites France and Tunisia."[1] The contest had begun. Jean de Hautecloque, who had been appointed resident-general of Tunisia in January 1952, resorted "to the kind of methods employed by big business during the last century in dealing with strikes."[2] He had Bourguiba arrested and later meted out the same treatment to the premier, M'Hammed Chenik. In 1954 the Tunisians openly revolted: there was terrorism in the cities and armed groups of fellaghas were formed in the countryside. On July 31, 1954, a few days after the agreement to partition Indochina was signed in Geneva, Pierre Mendès-France went to Tunis and said to the bey: "The internal autonomy of Tunisia will be recognized and proclaimed by the French government without any reservations."

On August 27, the National Assembly voted approval of the government's policy in North Africa by 419 to 112, with 88 abstaining. The greater part of the independents were in the opposition, and two-thirds of the M.R.P.'s abstained. The conventions establishing the new status were signed on June 3, 1955. But recognition of Moroccan independence in November 1955 led to the granting of similar status to Tunisia. The Protectorate Treaty of 1881 was abrogated on March 20, 1956. Bourguiba deposed the bey in 1957 and became premier and chief of state. Throughout the post-independence period, Franco-Tunisian relations were dominated by the Algerian war.

Morocco

The Istiglal, or Independence Party, was founded in 1943, a few months after a meeting between President Roosevelt and the sultan of Morocco, Mohammed Ben Youssef. In a speech in Tangiers on April 10, 1947, Sidi Mohammed assumed the leadership of the Moroccan nationalist movement. The new resident-general, General Alphonse Juin, cited in his memoirs the instructions he received in May 1947 from the foreign minister. Bidault anticipated "a palace take-over either through voluntary abdication or dethronement caused by the French authority itself."[3] The Franco-Moroccan crisis had begun. The sultan's claims for independence were countered by threats from the residents-general, who leaned heavily on Glaoui, the leader of the Berber tribes. General Augustin Guillaume, Juin's successor, arrested and banished the sultan on August 20, 1953. Terrorism and counter-terrorism increased. Frenchmen were massacred at Oued Zem on August 20, 1955, the anniversary of Sidi Mohammed's departure and exile.

[1] Quoted by Alfred Grosser, *La IVe République et sa Politique Extérieure* (Paris: Armand Colin, 1961), 267.

[2] Jean Lacouture, *Cinq hommes et la France* (Paris: Editions du Seuil, 1961), 146.

[3] Alphonse Juin, *Mémoires* (Paris: Plon, 1960), II, 141.

Premier Edgar Faure organized a meeting at Aix-les-Bains to pave the way for independence. It was held under the aegis of Antoine Pinay and was attended by representatives of the different political parties in Morocco. Faure obtained a guarantee from the exiled sultan. The Gaullist opposition within the government and in the National Assembly refused to accept the projected reforms. The vacillation of the French government virtually assured the restoration of the sultan. After a meeting at la Celle-Saint-Cloud on November 6, 1955, between Sidi Mohammed and Antoine Pinay, it was announced that negotiations for independence were about to begin. Returning to Morocco, Sidi Mohammed was proclaimed King Mohammed V. The accord on independence was signed on March 2, 1956.

In Morocco, as in Tunisia, the persistent refusal to grant internal autonomy merely led to a sudden award of independence.

Algeria before the Rebellion

Before the war, Algeria was controlled politically by the Europeans. Under the leadership of Ferhat Abbas, the locally elected Muslims attempted to broaden their political rights without infringing on French sovereignty. In November 1942 Abbas conferred with Robert Murphy, the special envoy of the United States to the French authorities in Algiers. This meeting, like the one between the sultan of Morocco and President Roosevelt, led the nationalist leader to focus his attention on internal autonomy. The Manifesto of the Algerian People, published on February 10, 1943, revealed this shift.

The considerable disparity in the living standards between the European and Muslim communities (respectively one million and eight million strong) grew more pronounced as a consequence of the maldistribution of income and the Muslim population explosion. Owing to a very poor harvest, the Muslims suffered from undernourishment in the spring of 1945. It was in an atmosphere of intense racial tension that an insurrectionary movement broke out in Sétif on May 8, 1945. It spread to Constantine. "The number of French dead attests the blind violence of this uprising; the number of Muslim dead reveals the pitiless violence of the repression."[4]

Ferhat Abbas decided to pursue the movement by confronting the French Parliament. In August 1946 he laid before the Constituent Assembly a draft constitution for the Algerian Republic, as a member of the French Union. Using the concept of federalism, he asked for internal autonomy and completely excluded the idea of assimilation. In the course of the debate, he said: "In 1936 I did not find Algerian nationality among the Muslim masses. However, I find it there today."[5]

[4] Roger Le Tourneau, *Evolution politique de l'Afrique du nord musulmane* (Paris: Armand Colin, 1962), 350.

[5] Quoted by Jean Lacouture, *Cinq hommes*, 301.

A new status for Algeria was put to a vote in the National Assembly on September 20, 1947. Algeria was to remain a part of the French Republic, a policy of assimilation was to be pursued, and the trend toward internal autonomy was to be discouraged. The Algerian Assembly was given the right, however, to implement a certain number of reforms for which the nationalists were clamoring. The Muslim deputies in the National Assembly refused to participate in the debate. But the motion was passed by a vote of 325 to 86. The Gaullists and Moderates opposed it; the Communists abstained.

In the municipal elections of October 1947, the R.P.F. candidates easily triumphed in the first college (where the voters were French citizens) after de Gaulle's speech in Algiers on October 12: "Any policy which, on the fallacious pretext of an evolution in reverse, has the effect of reducing the rights and duties of France here, or of discouraging the inhabitants of French origin, who were and remain the pervading influence of Algeria; or finally, any policy that leads French Muslims to believe they can separate their destiny from that of France, actually only opens the doors to decadence."

In the 1948 elections to the Algerian Assembly, the extreme Right won in the first college (mostly composed of French citizens), and the candidates of the administration captured 43 of the 60 seats in the second college (Muslim voters). As a consequence, this assembly did not consider the reforms called for by the statute.

Neither the Franco-Moroccan crisis of 1947 nor the Franco-Tunisian crisis of 1950 exerted an influence on the attitude of the French government in Algeria. The political parties did not carry the Algerian problem to the French public, although they were to do so during the Algerian rebellion, which will be examined in the next chapter.

Madagascar

A Nationalist movement had been active in Madagascar ever since 1929. In the elections to the first Constituent Assembly in November 1945, both nationalist candidates, Raseta and Ravoahangy, won mandates. In March 1946, a few days after the signing of the Sainteny–Ho Chi-minh accord, the two Malagasy deputies submitted to the Assembly a draft law that would confer on Madagascar the status of an associated state. Reelected by a 78 per cent vote to the second Constituent Assembly, they asked the government to hold a referendum on the status of the island. Their party, the Mouvement Démocrate de la Révolution Malgache (M.D.R.M.), triumphed in the legislative elections of 1946 and in the elections to the provincial assemblies in January 1947. The first instructions received by the new governor-general, Marcel de Coppet, ordered a fight against the M.D.R.M. In the wake of an uprising that took place during the night of March 29, 1947, the governor-general arrested the Malagasy deputies and proceeded to repress the insurgents with great brutality. His successor, the M.R.P. deputy Pierre de Chevigné, pursued the same policy. The official count was 90,000 dead.[6]

The French *colons* demanded that the Malagasy deputies and senators be tried despite their right to parliamentary immunity. The accused were condemned to death on October 4, 1948, by the Criminal Court of Tananarive. The conduct of the trial was such that the president of the National Assembly, Edouard Herriot, protested to the president of the Republic. The death sentences were commuted to detention in a fortress. The state of siege, proclaimed in 1947, was not raised until 1956.

French-Speaking Tropical Africa

The French colonial regime in French Tropical Africa was based on direct administration. Unlike the British colonies, none of the territories had local elected assemblies. Section VIII of the 1946 constitution introduced a fortunate innovation: the creation in each overseas territory of so-called representative assemblies, usually elected on the basis of a limited suffrage and in accordance with the dual college system. Moreover, the territories elected deputies to the French National Assembly. Thanks to the territorial assemblies of which they were rightful members, the African deputies of the various parties (especially the most powerful of them, the Rassemblement Démocratique Africain (R.D.A.) founded by Félix Houphouët-Boigny), "disposed in each territory of a rostrum, a secretariat, and a legal propaganda workshop. Should the need arise, they could also call for demonstrations."[7]

The growing influence of the R.D.A., the Algerian rebellion, the rapidity of political progress in English-speaking Africa, and the pressure of the United Nations in favor of a more liberal regime for the associated territories (Togo and Cameroon)—all these combined to spur the governments to shake off the torpor that had prevailed in French-speaking Tropical Africa from 1948 to 1954.

1955 was a year of municipal reform. 1956 witnessed the enactment of the "Loi Cadre" for the overseas territories. It was drafted by Gaston Defferre, minister for the overseas territories in Guy Mollet's cabinet, in collaboration with Houphouët-Boigny, the first African deputy to hold a minister's portfolio. This measure. which introduced the single college as well as universal suffrage, and gave the government broader powers to achieve administrative reforms, was adopted by the National Assembly on June 20, 1956, by a large

[6] Olivier Hatzfeld, *Madagascar* (Paris: P.U.F., 1960), 94.

[7] Robert Delavignette, *L'Afrique Noire française et son destin* (Paris: Gallimard, 1962), 128.

majority: 446 to 98. The opposition consisted mainly of the Moderates. The 1957 decrees implementing the law gave each territory a government council, presided over by a representative of the French Republic, but composed of elected members who shared in the executive power. P.-F. Gonidec, commenting on the reforms of 1956 and 1957, wrote: "The idea of territorial autonomy was accepted. The policy of centralization and assimilation was abandoned."[8]

In the elections of March 31, 1957, to the territorial assemblies, the R.D.A. obtained a majority of the seats. The Congress of the R.D.A., meeting in Bamako in September, voted a resolution demanding the immediate creation of a federal "Franco-African Community." This demand was supported by Léopold Sedar Senghor of the Parti du Regroupement Africain (P.R.A.) at a conference in Dakar in March 1958. The need was felt to alter the "Loi Cadre" and to modify Section VIII of the constitution.

Having learned something from the experience in Indochina, Madagascar, and North Africa, the Fourth Republic knew how to pave the way for the future of French Tropical Africa. It was aided in this by the sense of responsibility of the African politicians, many of whom had been trained in France. The testimony of Adlai Stevenson, head of the American delegation at the United Nations, is striking: "I am accustomed," he said in 1957, "to native spokesmen wanting to see me and to speak with me frankly, but I have never heard a black African speak of France with ill will."[9]

[8] P.-F. Gonidec, *Droit d'outremer* (Paris: Montchrétien, 1959), I, 323.
[9] Quoted by André Blanchet, *Itinéraire des partis africains depuis Bamako* (Paris: Plon, 1958), 110.

15

The Fourth Republic and the Algerian War

Initial Goals of the Algerian Rebellion

THE REBELLION BROKE out in the Aurès, one of the most destitute regions in Algeria. Its beginnings were marked by subversive acts and the massacre of Europeans. On November 1, 1950, the leaders of the rebellion issued an appeal to the Algerian people to combat colonialism. At the same time they announced their intention of achieving national independence. The goal was "the reestablishment of a sovereign, democratic, and social Algerian state within the framework of Islamic principles." Direct action was to be undertaken inside Algeria; abroad support was to be sought from the Muslim world and from the United Nations. The Algerian rebels organized the National Army of Liberation (A.L.N.). Their political arm was the National Liberation Front (F.L.N.) which was directed by Ben Bella from headquarters in Cairo.

Taken by surprise, the former Nationalist parties at first were hopeful but reserved judgment. But the influence of the rebels on the Moslem population grew, thanks to coercion and propaganda. This influence was given added impetus from the outside by the Bandung (Indonesia) Conference which met in April 1955. Attended by representatives of African and Asiatic states, it also included some F.L.N. observers.

As early as the spring of that year, the insurrection spread to Kabylia. On August 20, the second anniversary of the deposed Moroccan sultan's exile, the F.L.N. launched a widespread operation in North Constantine, the site of the 1945 uprising. F.L.N. troops, supported by the Muslim masses, attacked several European centers. Atrocities were committed in the course of the attacks as well as during their repression. Ferhat Abbas had gone to Paris early in August 1955 to warn French political circles against the violence that was about to be unleashed. Neither the premier, Edgar Faure, nor General de Gaulle received him.[1]

Meanwhile, the F.L.N. won a twofold moral victory within and outside Algeria. On October 26, one of Abbas's aids in the Union Démocratique du Manifeste Algéréen (U.D.M.A.),* Doctor Benjelloul, called a meeting in Algiers of all Muslim members of various French elective bodies as well as of the Algerian Assembly. Having obtained a pledge from the sixty-one representatives present "to support any decision reached by the majority," Benjelloul secured the passage of a motion stating that the policy of integration had seen its day and affirming that "the vast majority of the population now adhere to the Algerian national doctrine." Thus, the Muslims who had been elected with the moral support of the French administration were now deserting.

The Algerian affair was brought before the United Nations by a group of Afro-Asiatic nations. On September 30, the United Nations General Assembly decided, by a vote of 28 to 27, with 5 abstaining, to include the matter in its agenda. Although it was subsequently removed because of serious objections from the French delegation, the international character of the Algerian problem was thus made amply clear.

Pacification

The first debate on the rebellion in the National Assembly occurred on November 12, 1954. The premier leaned heavily on the letter of the constitution: "One does not compromise when it is a matter of defending the internal peace of the nation, the unity, the integrity of the Republic. The departments of Algeria constitute a part of the French Republic. They have been irrevocably French for a long time." Later, he added: "Several deputies have compared French policies in Tunisia and Algeria. I must affirm that no contrast, no comparison can be more erroneous, more false. Algeria is France." How could Mendès-France, the author of the Carthage declaration, advance a legal argument to support a position on Algeria which was the very opposite of the one he had taken on Tunisia? How could he so misjudge the affinity between nationalist movements throughout Muslim North Africa?

Probably because his government was so upset by the rejection of the E.D.C., Mendès-France felt the need to seek help from the most nationalist

---

[1] Jean Lacouture, *Cinq hommes et la France* (Paris: Editions du Seuil, 1961), 313.

* Translator's note: The U.D.M.A. was an Algerian party organized in 1945 by Ferhat Abbas; it supported an autonomous Algeria joined to France by a federal tie.

elements in the Assembly. He selected the new governor-general from the ranks of the Gaullists. Jacques Soustelle was appointed to the post on January 26, 1955, a few days before the cabinet fell; his new duties were confirmed by Edgar Faure.

Shortly after his arrival in Algeria, Soustelle declared: "France would no more leave Algeria than she would leave Provence or Brittany." He described the fight against the rebels as pacification. While the Algerian Nationalists aimed for independence, he demanded a return to order.

Pacification requires powers and means. The "state of emergency" law enacted on April 3, 1955, suspended the public liberties. The number of troops was increased from 50,000 to 120,000 by the transfer of conscripts from Indochina and from German garrisons. Furthermore, both before and after the 1955 disturbances, the reserves were called up.

Soustelle intended not only to pacify Algeria but also to integrate it closely with France. He suggested the creation of a single electoral college by granting Muslims political rights equal to those enjoyed by the Europeans of Algeria. The Europeans rejected both the principle of integration and the single electoral college. After the Constantine massacres, the *colons* began to set up organizations for self-defense.

The October 1955 debate on Algeria in the National Assembly "gives the impression of great complexity and of a refusal to adopt a clear-cut policy."[2] The government received a vote of confidence. The tally was 308 to 254, with 20 abstaining. The opposition consisted of Communists, Socialists, and about half of the membership of the Radical party. A few weeks later, in a proclamation issued at La Celle-Saint-Cloud, the government accepted the return of the sultan and recognized the independence of Morocco.

Edgar Faure decided to dissolve the National Assembly and to postpone the elections in Algeria.

The electoral campaign waged by the Left used Guy Mollet's slogan, "An idiotic war, with no way out." Mollet became premier on February 1, 1956.

Guy Mollet in Algiers on February 6, 1956

Even before his investiture, Guy Mollet let it be known that he intended to appoint General Catroux—the man who negotiated the return of the exiled sultan—to the post of resident-minister. Speaking before the Assembly, the premier promised to "strengthen the indissoluble union between Algeria and metropolitan France, to respect the 'Algerian personality,' to achieve total political equality for all the inhabitants of Algeria," and to organize free elections as quickly as possible.

[2] Roger Le Tourneau, *Evolution politique de l'Afrique du nord musulmane* (Paris: Armand Colin, 1962), 402.

The choice of Catroux, plus the announcement of Mollet's program, provoked a fierce outcry among the French of Algeria. They manifested their belated enthusiasm for Jacques Soustelle at the moment of his departure, having suddenly discovered in him the champion of French Algeria. They lost no time in showing their anger toward Guy Mollet when he landed in Algiers on February 6.

Taken aback by his hostile reception, Mollet replaced Catroux by Robert Lacoste. "When he left for Algiers he thought only of calming the Muslims, but events were to make him think only of calming the Europeans," Jacques Fauvet has written.[3] Mollet yielded to the overwhelming power of Algiers and to the support given it in France. A lawyer, Jean Baptiste Biaggi, spoke for Algiers at a press conference at the Hotel Aletti: "We have aroused Algeria, now we will arouse metropolitan France."[4]

February 6 signaled the end of all efforts to implement a liberal policy. Mollet made a threefold proposal: "A cease-fire, elections, and negotiations." His purpose was obvious. Would not a cease-fire mean the end of rebellion, which would be unacceptable to the rebels? Was it possible to reestablish order so that free elections would be held? Would not the newly elected Muslims demand independence, just as the sixty-one Muslim deputies had done? Would not immediate recognition of the "Algerian personality" be the prelude to recognition of an Algerian state?

Internal and External Rebellion

The end of a liberal policy meant the disappearance of the moderate elements in the opposition. On April 22 Ferhat Abbas arrived in Cairo to announce his adherence to the F.L.N. His decision had tremendous repercussions.

The rebellion was reorganized internally as well as externally at the Soummam Valley Congress held in August 1956 in Algeria. From then on supreme political authority was vested in the Conseil National de la Révolution Algérienne (C.N.R.A.). The collective character of the insurrectionary executive, the Committee of Coordination and Execution (C.C.E.) was proclaimed. A rebel administration was set up with its own political commissioners and tax collectors. Conditions for a cease-fire were laid down: recognition by France of the indivisibility of Algeria (including the Sahara), recognition of Algeria's national and unlimited sovereignty, and recognition of the F.L.N. as Algeria's sole representative.

Having acquired independence, the Tunisian and Moroccan governments could not refuse to support the F.L.N., but they hoped to find some

[3] Jacques Fauvet, *La IVe République* (Paris: Arthème Fayard, 1959), 317.
[4] Quoted by Jacques Barsalou, *La mal aimée* (Paris: Plon, 1964), 263.

basis for an understanding with France. It was in this spirit that a North African conference, suggested by Mohammed V, was to be held in Tunis on October 22. But the plane from Rabat, carrying Ben Bella and his F.L.N. companions, was rerouted to Algiers, with the knowledge of the resident-minister. Whatever the motive might have been—to quash the rebellion or torpedo the Tunis Conference—the consequence was a protracted interruption in the secret negotiations started with the F.L.N.

The Suez expedition began on November 1. On August 14 Lacoste had telegraphed Mollet that France "has everything to gain in Algeria by embarking on this military expedition with Great Britain." The withdrawal of the French and British troops from the canal, forced by the combined pressure of the United States, the Soviet Union, and the United Nations, was regarded by the entire Arab world as a diplomatic defeat for France.

The early months of 1957 witnessed a recrudescence of terror in Algeria. Thanks to their foreign bases, however, the rebels were able to increase their supply of arms and improve their military organization. During the month of March 1957, Tunis became the headquarters of the C.N.R.A. Ferhat Abbas was called to serve on the Committee of Coordination and Execution.

Military Operation and Psychological Warfare

Having opted for a policy of coercion, the government asked the National Assembly to give it full powers. These were voted on March 16, 1956, by a large majority. The Algerian statute was suspended and the Algerian Assembly dissolved. All the powers heretofore exercised by the governor-general and the legislative bodies were now in the hands of the resident-minister. The arrival of fresh troops in August 1956 swelled the number to 400,000.

Little by little, the army assumed administrative and police responsibilities in much of the territory. Its most dynamic elements, seasoned by guerrilla warfare in Indochina, gradually fashioned the tools and techniques of psychological warfare and also defined and defended a certain Algerian policy.[5]

The "cinquièmes bureaux," created to assist the army staff in 1957, conducted the psychological warfare. Actuated by paternalism toward the Muslim population, they favored integration. In Algiers, the psychological branch of the army was a network of information with a political bureau, the Dispositif de Protection Urbaine (D.P.U.). It was an instrument to fight terrorism and to spread propaganda, according to Colonel Roger Trinquier.[6]

[5] Raoul Girardet, *La crise militaire française 1945–1962* (Paris: Armand Colin, 1964), 188–91.

[6] Roger Trinquier, *Le coup d'état du 13 mai* (Paris: L'Esprit Nouveau, 1962), 36–37.

Thanks to the D.P.U., General Massu won in a few days the "battle of Algiers" that liberated the city from terrorism in 1957.

By the end of 1957, the rebellion was no longer capable of paralyzing the life of the great cities by continuous attacks. The French forces could not, however, wipe out all the pockets of resistance in the mountainous regions or destroy the A.L.N. reserves massed in Tunisia. The bombardment of Sakiet Sidi Youssef on February 8, 1958, by the French air force raised the question of whether it was entitled to exercise the right of pursuit on Tunisian territory. This move on the part of the French air force was endorsed by the government. Tunisia filed a complaint with the Security Council of the United Nations.

The Muslims, subjected to the Nationalist propaganda of the rebels and to the integrationist propaganda of the army, awaited the outcome of a war of which they were the principal victims. The European population helped to maintain order in territorial units composed of reservists who freely dispensed their arms and even kept them in their homes. According to Philippe Hernandez, "Lacoste's responsibility for placing the French of Algeria in a permanent state of insurrection is overwhelming."[7]

Economic Problems

In addition to broadening the duties of the army, the resident-minister embarked on a program of agrarian reform and public works designed to reduce unemployment. Rural life had been thoroughly disrupted by the military operations. The camps sheltered as many as a million and a half displaced persons.

Despite the discovery in 1952 of natural gas and oil deposits in the Sahara, the economic situation in Algeria showed no significant improvement for the time being. The sizable investments in the Sahara were mentioned by some Frenchmen as a further reason for continuing the war. The export of hydrocarbons, however, depended primarily on internal stability and on the maintenance of trustful relations between France and North Africa.

"The existence of the Algerian rebellion modifies the economic conditions under which French sovereignty can be maintained," read one anonymous report drafted by high officials of metropolitan France. It concluded: "An appreciable improvement in the living standards of the Muslim people, which in any case would not be sufficient to insure the decline of nationalism in Algeria, would certainly entail a considerable decrease in the living standards of metropolitan France."[8] To provide full employment for a

[7] "Histoire de la Guerre d'Algérie," *La Nef*, Oct. 1962, Jan. 1963, 39.

[8] "Quelques données du problème algérien," *Report of the High Officials* (Paris, June 1957), 4.

population that was increasing at the rate of 2.9 per cent annually, and to raise income at the rate of 6 per cent per Muslim inhabitant, would force France to assume a financial burden of eight billion (new) francs by 1980.

The Political Alternatives in 1957

The prolongation of the war led to a debate in metropolitan France on the status of Algeria. The alternatives were integration, independence, or partition—each entailing radical changes.

Jacques Soustelle was the principal champion of integration. He advocated a complete merger of the French and Algerian economies and a total equality of rights and duties for both peoples. We have just indicated the approximate cost that complete equalization of Franco-Algerian economic life would entail for metropolitan France. Political equalization presupposed "the presence within the two (French) parliamentary assemblies of elected Algerian deputies designated in such a way and in such numbers as to insure an equality of sovereignty for France and Algeria."[9] This could only lead to the partial "Arabization" of the French Parliament.

Raymond Aron's theory of independence rested on the sociological, economic, and political impossibility of integration. The Muslim community of Algeria was not part of a liberal civilization. With Tunisia and Morocco independent, Algeria could not remain an integral part of France. "To recognize the Algerian personality is actually to accept the fact that tomorrow an Algerian state will become a reality." Hence, France's war aims should include not only Algerian independence but also a way of bringing it about that would avert unbearable humiliation for France. Her war aims must also include a betterment of the chances of establishing good relations between the new Islamic states and the West.[10]

A few publicists mentioned the possibility of partitioning Algeria. They cited the many historical examples of partition accompanied by population transfers effected on the basis of race or religion: India and Pakistan in 1947, Jordan and Israel in 1948. In November 1956 Maurice Allais noted that it was impossible to deprive the Muslims of the right to self-government. But it was equally impossible, he pointed out, to abandon the Europeans of Algeria or those Muslims who sided with France. He suggested that the French be given political power in one zone and that the Muslims be granted a similar monopoly in another, the zones to be determined by international arbitration.[11]

[9] Jacques Soustelle, *Aimée et souffrante Algérie* (Paris: Plon, 1956), 245, 252.
[10] Raymond Aron, *La tragédie algérienne* (Paris: Plon, 1957), 27.
[11] Maurice Allais, *Les Accords d'Evian* (Paris: L'Esprit Nouveau, 1962), 331–33.

None of the three radical doctrines was received favorably by Parliament or by public opinion, and none was seriously considered by successive governments. Instead, while continuing the war, France sought no solution other than further assimilation.

The *"Loi Cadre"*

After the fall of the Mollet cabinet in May 1957, Maurice Bourgès-Maunoury drafted, with the help of Lacoste, the text of the "Loi Cadre." It was submitted to the National Assembly on September 30.

The draft reaffirmed that Algeria was "an integral part of the French Republic" but added that the "Algerian personality" must be respected. Algerians, Frenchmen, and Muslims were to designate their elected members in a single electoral college. The various communities were to have representatives in all the assemblies. Algeria was to be divided into five autonomous territories and provision was made for a federal organ to tie these districts together by majority vote. Some matters would remain under the jurisdiction of metropolitan France. These included foreign affairs, defense, currency, justice, public services, mines, and fuel, among others.

In short, the "Loi Cadre" maintained the principle of French sovereignty in Algeria but attempted to establish a balance of sorts among the communities.

The authors of the "Loi Cadre" referred to this regime as federalism. Although the measure provided for eventual federalism within Algeria, it did not prescribe such a system for the relations between Algeria and France. In the opinion of Roger Le Tourneau, the text of the "Loi Cadre" merely "pointed up the awkward situation in which the French leaders found themselves and the need they felt to put an end to France's 'do-nothing' attitude."[12]

Jacques Soustelle called upon the Right to oppose the Bourgès-Maunoury draft law. It was rejected by 279 to 253. The Gaullists, Poujadists, many Independents and peasants, including Antoine Pinay and Roger Duchet, a third of the Radicals, and the entire Communist Party voted against the measure.

The new premier, Félix Gaillard, drafted a second version that gave the Europeans greater guarantees within the territorial councils. It was accepted by Jacques Soustelle. On November 19, 1957, the National Assembly adopted this version by a vote of 269 to 200. Pierre Mendès-France made several very valid criticisms of the statute: it represented a retreat from the position taken in 1947; it was granted, not negotiated; order would never be reestablished "unless there was real and sincere contact with the people."

[12] Le Tourneau, *Evolution politique*, 245.

The law was not to go into effect until February 5, 1958, after the Senate had voted, which meant that it was never to be implemented.

May 13, 1958

The bombardment of Sakiet showed that the government lacked authority over the army. France and Tunisia, however, accepted the good offices of the United States and England in settling the affair. Negotiations were begun to effect the withdrawal of French troops from all of Tunisia, except for the base at Bizerta. But the National Assembly refused to approve this solution and the Gaillard government resigned on April 15. A long ministerial crisis ensued. The president of the Republic appealed to a champion of integration to form a cabinet, but the leaders of all the major political parties objected to the choice of Jacques Soustelle. Georges Bidault and René Pleven refused to assume the premiership. Finally, President Coty appointed Pierre Pflimlin, who was supposedly in favor of negotiations with the F.L.N.

The political situation was tense in Paris and in Algiers. Spokesmen for the French population, headed by Alain de Sérigny, were devoted to a conservative conception of colonialism. For tactical reasons, however, they made overtures to Soustelle and to certain military leaders who favored integration. Part of the Algerian army was hostile to "the system" which it regarded as conducive to abandonment, to a new and intolerable humiliation. The army's department of psychological warfare championed integration. Gaullist propaganda had two main spokesmen. Jacques Chaban-Delmas, minister of national defense in the Bourgès-Maunoury and Gaillard cabinets, was represented in Algiers by a member of his personal staff, Léon Delbecque. Jacques Soustelle, acting through the Union for the Renovation and Safety of French Algeria (Union pour le Renouveau et le Salut de l'Algérie française), successfully wooed the Algerian veterans.

The appointment of Pflimlin consolidated the opposition. On May 9, General Salan, Commander in Chief, sent to General Ely, chief of staff, a warning about Algeria that also went to the president of the Republic: "The French army in its entirety would feel the abandonment of this national patrimony to be an outrage; its reaction to despair could not be foretold."

On May 11, in *Dimanche-Matin*, the weekly edition of *L'Echo d'Alger*, Sérigny addressed an appeal to General de Gaulle. On May 12, organizations of the "ultras" of Algiers asked the public to demonstrate on the following day, when Pflimlin was to be invested.

During the evening of May 13, a group of students, led by Pierre Lagaillarde, occupied the Government General building, the office of the Algerian ministry. General Massu announced to the crowd the formation of a Committee of Public Safety (Salut Public). Delbecque, who had just arrived in Algiers, read a proclamation by Salan announcing that he was "temporarily taking in hand the fate of French Algeria." He then called upon the crowd to acclaim the army and General de Gaulle. In Paris, Félix Gaillard, the interim premier, conferred civil powers on Salan, a move confirmed by Pierre Pflimlin immediately after he was invested by a vote of 274 to 129. The opposition included a majority of the traditional Rightists plus the Poujadists. A hundred and thirty-seven Communists abstained.

On the morning of May 15, General Salan addressed the Algerian crowds that were still gathered on the steps of the Forum. Pressured by Delbecque, he ended his speech by shouting: "Vive de Gaulle!"[13] This exclamation was to determine the fate of the party. That same evening de Gaulle, through the agency of his political secretariat, issued a statement to the country: "I hold myself ready to assume the powers of the Republic." On May 16 thousands of Muslims from the Casbah flooded the Forum in response to Colonel Trinquier's bidding: "We are Frenchmen and we want to remain Frenchmen."[14]

After the turbulent days in Algiers, the government fluctuated between repressing the uprising by blockading Algeria and preparing for General de Gaulle's assumption of power. The army and the police eluded the government in metropolitan France. Preparations were being made for parachutists to descend on Paris. Parliament was caught between its fear of the parachutists and its fear of Charles de Gaulle. Meanwhile, the general temporized. He knew that not a single citizen would defend the regime. The primary purpose of his May 19 press conference was to calm public opinion. Watching the growing disintegration of the parliamentary regime, the general waited until the representatives of the political parties appealed to him directly. Satisfied that the forces on the move were about to descend on Paris, he delayed making use of them because he did not want it said that he took power illegally. On May 27 he published the now famous communiqué: "Yesterday I undertook the regular process necessary for the establishment of a republican government capable of insuring the unity and independence of the country." Pflimlin resigned on May 28. De Gaulle was invested as premier on June 1 by a vote of 329 to 222; the opposition included 83 non-Communists. On June 2 he was given full legislative and constituent powers. The Fourth Republic was dead.

The Balance Sheet

What were the effects of the war when the change of regime took place?

[13] Jean Ferniot, *Les ides de mai* (Paris: Plon, 1958), 45.
[14] Trinquier, *Le coup*, 141.

In Algeria, the military situation can be described as insoluble for two reasons: the rebels could not act together in large numbers; and the French army could not break up the rebel political-administrative organization. The political situation was dominated by increasing conflict between the communities. Whatever the significance of May 16 might be—the will to fraternize in the face of possible integration, or relief at the prospect of peace—the Muslim masses were apparently divided, a sizable minority having been won over to the idea of independence. Despite the tactical alliances concluded on the eve of the uprising, the majority of Algerian Europeans none the less rejected the liberal reforms and, even more, actual integration.

In France, the continuation of the Algerian war forced the government to withdraw several divisions from the NATO forces. The high cost of the war was one of the major causes of inflation and of the fall of the franc from 1955 to 1958. As for the parliamentary system, the Algerian war caused the rise and fall of a multitude of ministries. Guy Mollet capitulated in the face of the opposition in Algeria which, on February 6, 1956, forced him to change the direction of his policy. Bourgès-Maunoury, Gaillard, and Pflimlin resigned or fell over the Algerian question.

Why did the Algerian policy of the Fourth Republic fail?

The coexistence of two communities, divided by religion, personal and economic status, and demographic pattern, created intrinsic difficulties that were aggravated by the Muslim population explosion and the resurgence of the Arab world. These difficulties, especially peculiar to colonies containing a minority group of settlers, were ignored as long as French domination went unchallenged. Subsequently, they were underestimated.

The Fourth Republic's initial mistake was its persistent refusal to grant Algeria internal autonomy. The status of an associated state, which the Moslem members of parliament had suggested in 1947, was denied. The Statute of 1947 that called for some measure of assimilation between Algeria and metropolitan France, and for the recognition of "the Algerian personality" was not applied. The fiction of Algeria as "an integral part of the French Republic," based on the letter of the constitution, was maintained until the advent of the "Loi Cadre" of 1958. Internal autonomy would not, of course, have eliminated all the conflicts between the two communities, but it would probably have made possible their gradual and peaceful resolution.

The Fourth Republic tacitly rejected integration. This solution appealed neither to the nationalists, who wanted a homogeneous Muslim state, nor to the Algerian Europeans, who were hostile to further assimilation. Nor did it appeal to metropolitan France, which was beginning to assess the cost. But the idea of integration, which Soustelle advanced so forcefully in Parliament and which was advocated by the most dynamic elements in the Algerian army, was not refuted by the various French governments. This ambivalence betrayed weakness and was therefore a mistake.

Finally, the major error made by the regime was its refusal to realize the consequences of its relationship with three North African countries that belonged to the Islamic world. There was a fundamental contradiction between willingness to grant Tunisia and Morocco independence in 1955 and the determination to maintain an authoritarian and centralized regime in Algeria in 1958. Raymond Aron's warning of 1957 was never heeded: "I maintain that it is madness to send an army of 400,000 men to Algeria after having granted independence to Morocco."[15]

The attitude of the authorities in Algeria was that of a series of refusals amounting to a total denial of reality. The truth was unbearable because it was tragic. A choice had to be made between prolonging the war and granting independence (the latter involving the departure of a large section of the European population). Faced with an option that it could not bring itself even to state clearly, the government called up additional troops in an effort to continue the war. But it was unable to define its war aims. Consequently, it could not allay the weariness of the public or the anxieties of the army.

All the political parties must share the blame for this lack of civic courage. A large section of the traditional Right, led by Roger Duchet, was influenced by the "ultras" of Algeria, for whom Alain de Sérigny was the spokesman. The same was true of some leading Socialists like Robert Lacoste, or Radicals like André Morice, or M.R.P.'s like Georges Bidault. Since 1955, the vague liberal tendencies *vis-à-vis* Algeria of the various governments lead by a Socialist or a Radical were fiercely opposed by the Gaullist deputies. Jacques Soustelle, who had returned from Algiers in January 1956, led the group. In 1947 General de Gaulle unreservedly supported the position of the Algerian French. He had not addressed the public since June 30, 1955. It almost seemed as if he were encouraging his friends to denounce any liberal reform as a betrayal of the French cause in order to hasten the fall of the regime. Since Soustelle was a champion of integration, his attacks against those provisions of the "Loi Cadre" that favored the Muslim claims can only be explained as part of a policy of destruction.

The new regime was brought to power by circumstances that produced both "(civilian) champions of a conservative and reactionary policy in Algeria and (military) champions of a policy of integration."[16] It was also brought to power by the tacit support of public opinion in metropolitan France, weary of parliamentarianism and war. But the reality of the Algerian problem remained: the temporary solution of internal autonomy was no

[15] Aron, *La tragédie algérienne*, 54.
[16] Ferniot, *Les ides de mai*, 37.

longer viable. The choice was between prolonging the war and independence. Would the new regime realize, as Raymond Aron had pointed out, that "the loss of Algeria is not the end of France?" Would it adopt the war aims urged by Aron: to seek out in Algeria, now that Tunisia and Morocco were independent, spokesmen whose nationalism was not xenophobic; to fight to avoid dishonor but not to prevent the Algerians from becoming independent; and finally, to substitute cooperation for domination?[17]

Such was the painful challenge that the Fifth Republic would have to take up from the faltering hands of the Fourth.

[17] Aron, *La tragédie algérienne*, 30, 32.

16

Decolonization and France in 1958

Centralization and Decolonization

THE COLONIAL EMPIRE of the Third Republic was an authoritarian and centralized organization. According to section VIII of the 1946 constitution the Fourth Republic and the French Union presented the same characteristics.

But in a highly centralized system it was very difficult to reconcile the need of the overseas peoples for autonomy with the need for unity under the aegis of metropolitan France. French political thought, which tended to be unitary, rejected any delegation of power. It was not receptive to gradual reforms, or reforms that varied according to the territory.

In the absence of a decentralized structure, the protectorates and dependent territories were extremely tempted to demand full national sovereignty, since attainment of the status of an associated state was viewed merely as a step in this direction. Inversely, metropolitan France vacillated when faced with the immediate consequences of independence, or the economic consequences of integration—in other words. of assimilation pushed to an extreme.

The Application of Section VIII of the Constitution

Although Section VIII of the constitution was not in itself a good instrument for decolonization, nonetheless the French authorities did not make the most of whatever it had to offer.

The authorities engaged in a delaying action in regard to demands for internal autonomy—which was similar to the status of an associated state—as well as to subsequent demands for independence.

The accords concluded with Vietnam, Cambodia, and Laos in 1950 gave these associated states only partial internal autonomy, which was followed by independence in 1953. Madagascar was refused the status of an associated state in 1947. So severe were the repressive measures that no further active demands were made until 1956. This severity served to discourage the North African representatives to the National Assembly from making similar demands. But neither the bey of Tunisia nor the sultan of Morocco had any intention of joining the French Union. In their opinion, internal autonomy was certainly a first step toward independence. But more than this, it conformed to the spirit of the protectorate treaties, a spirit that was betrayed by the practice of direct administration. The Algerian Muslims elected to the National Assembly demanded that Algeria be made an associated state. The Statute of 1947, however, rejected any move toward autonomy, and the "Loi Cadre" of 1958 maintained the principles of French sovereignty.

This delaying action, judged in itself and independently of the world outside of the French Union, resulted in two failures, one partial success, and one total success.

Under de Gaulle, the Indochinese war was a war of reconquest; under the Fourth Republic it was a war of decolonization. The mistakes made were serious—the choice of the spokesmen, the absence of any specific war aims, the lack of adequate measures or skillful leadership in the conduct of operations. The war in Algeria, which in 1954 followed on the heels of the Indochinese war, was different in kind: it was a war of liberation for the Muslims, and a conflict between two ethno-religious communities. Because France had marshaled more powerful forces, the conduct of military operations improved, but the war aims were never stated. By 1958 the government was incapable of continuing the war to final victory, and unable to stop it through negotiation.

Wars had occurred throughout the entire life of the Fourth Republic. The first (Indochina) was a political and military failure; the second (Algeria) a political failure. But the decolonization of Tunisia and Morocco may be considered a partial success in the sense that, after resisting reform for a long time, the government granted internal autonomy to Tunisia and independence to Morocco before local rebellions broke out. Too much temporizing, especially in regard to Morocco, led to too much haste.

The Indochinese experience did not foreshadow the Algerian war, but the events in North Africa furnished instructive lessons to those who were responsible for French policy in French Tropical Africa. After years of a "do-nothing" attitude, sensible reforms were implemented.

Decolonization in the International Context

Viewing the policy of decolonization in its international context, two observations are in order. On the one hand, the policy was affected only slightly by external events. On the other, it altered substantially the international position of France.

The deliberate refusal to take outside events into account was especially striking in the case of Indochina. "The original cause of the war and of the final catastrophe," Raymond Aron has observed "was the patriotic but blind determination to maintain a French presence despite everything that was happening in Southeast Asia"[1]—the liberation movement, which began in 1945; and China's subjection to Communism in 1950. The war, which became international from the moment France requested American aid, was ended in 1954 by the partition of Vietnam. This solution was arrived at with the tacit consent of the indirect adversaries in the conflict, the United States and the Soviet Union.

In December 1951, on the morrow of Egypt's denunciation of the Anglo-Egyptian Treaty of 1936, the French government suggested the idea of co-sovereignty to the Bey of Tunisia. The day before, Libya had announced its independence.

The Algerian war was the principal cause of the Suez expedition. The expedition represented a show of force. But by the end of the colonial period, no average-sized power could succeed in such an enterprise without incurring the risk of a serious diplomatic setback.

The policy of decolonization, however, had direct and grave consequences for the international position of France, particularly for her alliances. The war in Indochina forced France to withdraw troops from NATO, considerably reducing her contribution. With part of France's army posted in Germany and an expeditionary force in Indochina, some politicians began to take a very critical view of the constitution of a European army. It might, they felt, deprive France of freedom of action within the French Union. The prolongation of the war, the fact that it had become international, made France dependent on American aid. Finally, after the defeat at DienBienPhu, the Soviet Union had to be dealt with tactfully. This situation probably increased the number of deputies in the National Assembly who were hostile to the ratification of the European Defense Community Treaty.

The Algerian war had international repercussions. The Suez expedition produced tension between France and the United States; this in turn engendered suspicion of NATO in France. Every year the Algerian affair was discussed in the NATO General Assembly. The French were openly criticized in the presence of spokesmen for the underdeveloped countries. It was

---

[1] Raymond Aron, *L'Algérie et la République* (Paris: Plon, 1958), 76.

hardly surprising that the Algerian war was soon to become the main pre-occupation of most Frenchmen. The problem of European unity seemed secondary, despite its importance for the future of France. The financial drain of the war hampered France in her efforts to adapt her economy to the requirements of the Common Market.

Political Forces and Decolonization

Under the Fourth Republic forces favorable to European unity clashed with those opposed, whereas the question of decolonization did not give rise to similar tensions. With the exception of the Communists, no political party in France included in its program the concession of internal autonomy to the overseas possessions without at the same time stipulating all sorts of conditions and restrictions. Very few politicians believed that voluntary association could or should replace French domination. This rigid attitude was due primarily to the relationship that existed more or less consciously in people's minds between the decreasing influence of France in Europe and the prospect of world power that preservation of her colonial empire would ensure.

Bismarck had encouraged the colonial conquests of the Third Republic, which sought prestige for its officers and administrators. During the early days of the Fourth Republic, the phenomenon of compensating for weakness by a show of strength played a similar role. After the defeat in 1940 and the German occupation, the survival of the French Union seemed a tangible proof that France was still a world power.

But education and the construction of roads did not slake the thirst of colonized peoples for independence. Some observers noted this and totted up the costs. To the huge investments already made overseas must be added the growing expense of preventing or combating rebellions. People were gradually becoming convinced that in the twentieth century colonialism no longer paid off. To be sure, those businessmen who profited from the power-fully protected market in the French Union, or who received orders for the manufacture of munitions, did not object to colonial wars. But although the thesis on decolonization which Raymond Cartier propounded in 1955 failed to gain strong support, it did force many Frenchmen to reconsider the economic consequences of integrating Algeria with metropolitan France.

General de Gaulle's idea of an overseas policy was to reject both internal autonomy for the colonies and "any possibility of progress outside the French Empire." He formulated his doctrine in the categorical language of the Brazzaville Conference of 1944. In August 1945 it was de Gaulle who decided to reconquer Indochina. It was he who instructed Admiral d'Argen-lieu, in accordance with the declaration of March 24, 1945, to maintain the policy of domination, especially by creating an Indochinese Federation. After his resignation, de Gaulle supported every move Admiral d'Argenlieu made until the admiral was recalled. Thereupon he advised the more liberal General Leclerc to refuse to serve as high commissioner. In 1946 de Gaulle opposed Section VIII of the constitution of the French Union. In his opinion, it would "disrupt the Union and lead to foreign domination." In 1947 he opposed the Statute for Algeria which the National Assembly had approved. In Algiers he confirmed his hostility to a regime which he considered too liberal.

All the governments of the Third Force (the Third Force had been established in 1947, after the eviction of the Communists) were violently attacked by de Gaulle and his political friends whenever there was an opportunity to reach a liberal decision on the French Union. Gaullist deputies voted against the 1950 law granting the status of associated states to Vietnam, Laos, and Cambodia, even though their prior arguments had led to a considerable reduction in the scope of the statute. After 1952 Gaullist deputies joined the government. They consistently exerted themselves to stall liberal solutions to pending problems. They approved the deposition of the sultan in 1953. Until the very last moment they opposed peace negotiations with the Vietminh. Although in 1954 they supported the Geneva accords on the partition of Indochina and the grant of internal autonomy to Tunisia, in 1955 they opposed the arrangement concluded by General Catroux and the sultan. Their opposition brought about the return of Mohammed V and the sudden concession of total independence to Tunisia and Morocco.

During the Algerian rebellion, General de Gaulle refrained from taking sides. But one of his henchmen, Jacques Soustelle, played a decisive role. As governor-general of Algeria in 1955, Soustelle was the self-appointed defender of integration, whose economic and political cost Parliament was gradually coming to realize. In 1957, Soustelle mobilized the rightist deputies in the National Assembly against Bourgès-Maunoury's draft of the "Loi Cadre." He accepted Gaillard's version of the law which, according to Mendès-France, represented a retreat from the Statute of 1947.

The authoritarian conception of the French Union was consistently supported by the M.R.P. In this respect, Georges Bidault's views closely resembled those of Charles de Gaulle. As president of the Provisional Government of the French Republic in 1946, Bidault won acceptance of Section VIII of the constitution in its second version. At the Fontainebleau Conference he failed to create an atmosphere conducive to a successful completion of the negotiations with Ho Chi-minh. As early as 1947 he contemplated deposing the sultan of Morocco. In 1953, as foreign minister, he had his way about the sultan. In 1953 and again in 1954 he opposed negotiations with the Vietminh and rejected the idea of partition until the Laniel cabinet fell. In the National Assembly Bidault sided with the Gaullists on all the important matters affecting Algeria. Jean Letourneau, minister for the associated states from 1949 to 1953, was largely responsible for the attitude of the M.R.P. on Indochina.

Full credit for a realistic appraisal of the problem of decolonization must go to Mendès-France. Because of his courageous attitude in the National Assembly in 1950, he was asked in 1954 to negotiate the Geneva accords on the partition of Vietnam. His offer shortly afterward to grant internal autonomy to Tunisia saved France from the necessity of fighting a rebellion there. When the Algerian rebellion erupted, Mendès-France took a firm stand, which he was subsequently to modify. In 1956 he resigned from the Mollet government because he disagreed with the premier on the conduct of the war in Algeria. The Radical Party was deeply divided on the question of North African policy. In a cabinet which itself was divided, Edgar Faure won approval of independence for Morocco.

Like the Radical Party, the Socialists harbored both liberal and authoritarian tendencies. Having campaigned to end the war, Guy Mollet, backed by Robert Lacoste, yielded on February 6, 1956, to "the imperious power of Algeria." He suggested "a cease-fire, elections, and negotiations," but this only led to a prolongation of the war. On the other hand, he made every effort to prevent a broadening of the conflict in French-speaking Tropical Africa. Supported by Gaston Defferre, he won acceptance in 1956 for the "Loi Cadre," which granted internal autonomy to the overseas territories.

The traditional Right was also divided, but the majority of its members leaned toward an authoritarian policy. Antoine Pinay exhibited a liberal attitude toward Morocco in 1954, but in 1957 he joined Roger Duchet in opposing the first draft of the "Loi Cadre" for Algeria. In 1953 Joseph Laniel advocated negotiation in Indochina but he was unable to impose his views on his foreign minister.

In short, most French politicians were opposed to decolonization. Successive governments, accused by de Gaulle and his friends of abandoning French colonial interests, were unable to formulate a consistent policy or explain to the public the often painful alternatives that inescapably confronted the nation. Thoroughly shaken by the Indochinese war, the Fourth Republic succumbed to the war in Algeria.

17

Conclusion: The Foreign Policy
of the Fourth Republic

French Regimes and Foreign Policy

FROM THE DEATH of Louis XVI until the Liberation, France had many
regimes. Three of these fell because of disastrous foreign policies: the
First Empire, the Second Empire, and the Third Republic.

Foreign policy is devised and executed in relation to the external world.
It is like a moving body, endowed with a force of its own and traveling over
a field of energy. The moving body will achieve its objective if the pilot
constantly assesses the exact relationship between internal and external forces
as well as every possible combination of them. Working with material and
psychological data, foreign policy—a symbiosis of strategy and diplomacy—
calls for a hardheaded, global, and coherent view of realities and of the means
and goals capable of modifying them.

The repeated failures of French foreign policy during the last century and
a half may lead one to suspect that our compatriots have an inaccurate, fragmentary, and therefore incoherent vision of the outside world.

Born in a new world, its position weak, would the Fourth Republic be
more clearsighted than the Third? Had its ruling class learned enough from
the recent troubles to chart its future course? This was the crucial question
at the end of World War II.

The Fourth Republic was enclosed between the two reigns of Charles de
Gaulle. It did not spring into being on the day Paris was liberated, nor on the
day the president of the Provisional Government of the French Republic resigned. Its legacy was a well-defined foreign policy; but an international system
was now taking form that differed radically from that of the Treaty of Versailles.

Gaullist Policy and the Bipolar International System

During his fifteen months of office, from October 1944 to January 1946, de Gaulle mapped out his foreign policy; rejection of an alliance with England; a reverse alliance with the Soviet Union because of the German threat and the Anglo-Saxon attempt at hegemony; inclusion of France among those powers that would decide the fate of Europe and decide on global policy matters; denial of internal autonomy for the overseas territories; reconquest of Indochina.

De Gaulle had three basic goals: recognition of France as one of the great powers; a France independent of the two victors of World War II; integrity of the French Union.

In implementing his ideas, however, de Gaulle erred in his choice of allies. France's position as a major power was acknowledged because of England's support and despite the opposition of the Soviet Union. He also erred in his assessment of the balance of power. The world was quickly moving toward a bipolar international system which would force France to take sides rather than to play the role of arbiter. And finally, de Gaulle erred in his conception of the French Union. This mistake was to cause the fall of the Fourth Republic.

The rivalry between the United States and the Soviet Union was evident at the Potsdam Conference of July 1945. The discord between the victors reached its peak at the Moscow Conference of March 1947. The Fourth Republic actually came into being in May 1947 when the Communists were evicted from the government. The geographical position of France, her institutions, her way of life, placed her squarely within the Western bloc. The Western bloc was beginning to be organized and France was already playing a part in it. The foreign policy of the Fourth Republic differed from that of General de Gaulle.

The establishment of the Western bloc confirmed the division of Germany and Europe. It required the organization of a collective West European defense, under the aegis of the United States, which in turn demanded a change in the status of West Germany.

It also presupposed closer economic and political ties between the European allies of the United States—in other words, a move toward European unity. But it did not presuppose the defense of colonial empires. The principles of the United Nations Charter, American ideology, Europe's weakness after defeat, the geographical boundaries of the Atlantic Pact—all these combined with Communist subversion to hasten decolonization. And decolonization itself had moved from the purely internal to the international domain.

Foreign Policy and Gaullist Opposition

The foreign policy of the Fourth Republic featured three major themes: collective defense, European construction, and decolonization.

On each of these, General de Gaulle took a stand against the regime. He concentrated his attacks on foreign rather than on domestic policy, probably expecting that it would be his foreign policy that would return him to office. The Fourth Republic managed to live with the general, who opposed it through public opinion, through Parliament, and, after 1952, through ministers who were loyal to him in the government. The foreign policy of the Fourth Republic must therefore be looked upon as resulting from two forces: the combined strength of the Center and moderate Right, represented by coalition governments constantly threatened in a regime of government by assembly, and the monolithic force of the hermit of Colombey himself. De Gaulle's strength derived from his strong will and his hold over public opinion; it was buttressed in the National Assembly by the support of the Communists and the turncoats from other political parties.

In 1947, Gaullist opposition to the foreign policy of the Fourth Republic was active only in matters pertaining to decolonization. Its spokesmen criticized Section VIII of the constitution, especially the Statute of Algeria, and the political options regarding Indochina.

The first attack on a traditional domain of foreign policy came in June 1948 and was directed at the future status of Germany. Although de Gaulle did not criticize the tenor of the Atlantic Pact when it was signed, he reiterated in May 1949 his serious misgivings about independence for West Germany. He was very sarcastic about Robert Schuman's declaration of May 9, 1950. His friends joined the Communists in voting against ratification of the European Coal and Steel Community in December 1951. An extremely virulent campaign was waged against the European Defense Community in 1952, mainly because of its supranational character. In December 1954, however, the Gaullists and Communists parted company on the question of the Western European Union and Germany's entry into NATO. They joined forces again in July 1957 during the balloting on ratification of the Common Market and Euratom treaties. Several clauses of these Treaties, relating to a prefederal construction of European unity, had been eliminated because of Gaullist opposition.

While attacking the European policy of the Fourth Republic, General de Gaulle and his cohorts systematically opposed any steps toward decolonization. Here, they generally parted company with the Communists. In 1950 the Gaullist deputies voted against giving Vietnam, Cambodia, and Laos the status of associated states. In 1953 they likewise opposed a motion calling for negotiations with Indochina. They approved the banishment of the sultan in

1953. Mendès-France's government alone won their approval: in 1954 they supported the Geneva accords on the partition of Indochina and the concession of internal autonomy to Tunisia. But their negative attitude was again apparent when they assailed the arrangements concluded by the sultan of Morocco and General Catroux. It was this opposition that was responsible for the haste in granting total independence to Morocco and Tunisia. After 1955 de Gaulle refrained from taking any position, but until the very last days of the Fourth Republic, Michel Debré and Jacques Soustelle advocated the maintenance of French authority in Algeria.

Taking advantage of the tension which the Algerian policy created between the United States and France, the Gaullists deputies openly criticized the Atlantic Pact. Instead, they demanded an exclusively national form of defense which, the possession of nuclear weapons by France would help realize.

Foreign Policy and the Atlantic Alliance

The foreign policy of the Fourth Republic was determined primarily by the decision in 1947 to join the American-dominated Western bloc.

France took a stand *vis-à-vis* her principal partner on the three main issues: collective defense, European construction, and decolonization. With regard to collective defense, France had to take Germany into account; she had to consider England in matters relating to European construction.

The foundation of the Western bloc was the Atlantic Pact. France initiated the treaty together with England, and was a loyal partner. The principal difficulty that arose between her and the United States stemmed from the American demand that West Germany should be rearmed. Public opinion was divided in France. It was this split that led the government—after suggesting the formation of a European army in order to avoid the reconstitution of a German one—to consent, after four years of debate, to the creation of a German army and to Germany's entry into NATO. But France's effective participation in a common defense was limited by the assignment of most of her forces to other theaters of action—to Indochina and then to Algeria.

Collective defense and the economic and political consolidation of Western Europe were the dual objectives of American policy: the Marshall Plan and the Atlantic Pact reinforced one another. The United States congratulated itself on the Schuman declaration of May 9, 1950, which sealed the Franco-German reconciliation. It supported the French move to accelerate the economic unification of Europe through supranational organizations endowed with broader powers than the first European organizations, which were intergovernmental in nature.

177]

Fearing the establishment of an economic and perhaps political unity on the Continent, England refused in 1950 to participate in the negotiations that led to the formation of the E.C.S.C. In 1955 she placed all kinds of obstacles in the way of the Common Market negotiations—obstacles that culminated in the division of Western Europe into two groups of states, the Six led by France and Germany, and the "non-Six," headed by England.

It was in regard to decolonization that France and the United States diverged politically. The United States wished to further independence for the nonautonomous territories, in accordance with the United Nations Charter. France placed herself in the paradoxical position of denying her colonies both internal autonomy and the right of secession, yet acknowledging their right to self-development. Her wars were waged to protect colonialism. Whereas metropolitan France was part of the Western bloc, overseas France remained outside it. The Atlantic Pact did not apply to overseas possessions. After 1951, owing to the war in Korea, France obtained financial if not military help from the United States. During the Algerian war and because of it, she embarked on the Suez expedition without consulting the United States. Under pressure from America, she had to abandon it.

In outlining the Fourth Republic's major foreign policy problems and in showing how they were affected by internal opposition and external alliances, one is struck by an inconsistency between the colonial policy on the one hand and the Atlantic and European policies on the other. This inconsistency emerges more clearly when we analyze the means and above all the ends of French foreign policy.

The Means of Foreign Policy

Any coherent foreign policy must establish ends that are related to means and must create the means to achieve these ends.

Raymond Aron has called attention to three fundamental elements in a state's power—in other words, its capacity to impose its will or to prevent others from imposing theirs: the milieu, the resources, the collective influence. "The power of a collectivity depends upon the area of its activity and its capacity to utilize the resources, both human and material, with which it is endowed."[1] How should one assess these three elements in relation to France in 1947, at a time when the Fourth Republic came into being, when the system of the two blocs was crystalizing? And how had they evolved by 1958? An answer to these questions will shed some light on the means available to French foreign policy.

By milieu or area of activity we mean the size of the territory and its geographical position. Metropolitan France was but a fraction of the area

[1] Raymond Aron, *Paix et guerre entre les nations* (Paris: Calmann-Lévy, 1962), 65.

contested by the two rival blocs in their planetary strategy and diplomacy. Yet it was of great strategic importance from the standpoint of communications between the United States, the principal ally, and Western Europe, which the Atlantic Pact was designed to defend. As for overseas France, it was immense and spread over four zones—Indochina, Madagascar, French Tropical Africa, and North Africa—of which only the latter was rather close to the mother country. Strategically, it was an element of weakness for military operations outside the Atlantic Alliance.

In assessing manpower resources from the standpoint of foreign policy, only the metropolitan population should be considered because the overseas territories were asking for internal autonomy or independence and the official policy of the French Union was opposed to both. The national population was one-fourth that of the United States and approximately equal to the population of Great Britain, West Germany, or Italy. France's birth rate had increased and the loss of manpower due to the war was less than in 1919. In terms of population, France was a nation of average size.

The term average, imprecise though it is, can also be applied to natural resources. The agricultural potential of metropolitan France was considerably greater than that of the three European countries that were equal to it in size; its mining and fuel industries were inferior to Germany's but superior to Italy's. What matters, however, is the extent to which these industries were exploited. After a half century of protectionism and underinvestment, the agricultural yield was low, considering the quality of the land, and the industrial equipment was clearly inferior to that of England or Germany. The resources of the overseas territories were modest, and little had been done to develop them. Military considerations apart, the French Union was an economic liability for metropolitan France.

The capacity for collective action—that is, the discipline of France's citizens, their solidarity in the face of trouble, their talent for administrative, economic, and military organization—had been altogether inadequate during the span from the Treaty of Versailles to World War II. After the trauma of defeat and occupation, fresh conflicts disturbed the body politic. The constitution of 1946 established a regime of government by assembly. The prerequisites for effective collective action had not been realized, nor would they be throughout the life of the Fourth Republic because of the absence of stable institutions and civic spirit: opposition to the regime was not alone to blame.

A solid economic and financial foundation would have contributed to the efficacy and continuity of foreign policy, but it too was lacking. Between 1944 and 1947 the monetary policy got off to a bad start, although investments began well. This trend was to continue. The franc was still not stabilized as late as May 1958 whereas most European currencies had been stabilized by 1949. Import quotas were reestablished in France in 1957 although they had been eliminated by most European countries four years before. There was a chronic deficit in the balance of payments although France received proportionately more economic aid until 1952 than any of the other Marshall Plan nations. To be sure, economic growth in France was more rapid than in England but it was achieved in an atmosphere of chronic inflation. In 1958 West Germany surpassed France because of her dynamic economy as well as her financial stability. Her rate of investment was higher and she was ahead in science and technology.

In 1947 France's military potential in conventional weapons was very low. From 1950 to 1954 she participated in the rearmament efforts undertaken by all the European members of NATO. Because of the war in Indochina, however, France contributed very little to the collective defense of Europe and therefore to that of her own territory. Her relative share in the Alliance's defense plans was reduced by the war in Algeria. In 1958 France had an army that was well-trained in guerrilla warfare but she had fewer armored divisions than West Germany, who furnished the largest number of troops for NATO'S central front. While England was exploding her first H-bomb in 1957, France was setting aside large sums for military nuclear research.

In short, when the Fourth Republic was making its début, France had a geographical area that was widely spread out, and an average amount of resources that were inadequately exploited. Because of institutional and psychological factors, her capacity for collective action was rather limited. Unlike the other European countries, especially West Germany, she failed, under the Fourth Republic, to make the most of the limited resources of a second-rate power within the Western bloc.

With such limited capacities, could France entertain grandiose ambitions?

The Objectives of Foreign Policy

Any political entity that is endowed with a will aspires to survive, to continue to exist. Its first objective is security. But power or force, the means to obtain security, can become an end in itself. Glory based on pride can, in turn, become a well-defined objective. To this statement of abstract objectives must be added a formulation of concrete goals: the material conquest of space and men, the conquest of the spirit in the form of an ideological victory. Depending upon the time and place, space and men can be elements either of security and power, or of insecurity and weakness. Glory is elusive because it is subjective: "Accomplished facts will never appease the doubts of whoever aspires to glory." An idea, on the other hand, has substance for the believer. Such is, in essence, Raymond Aron's analysis of the eternal objectives of foreign policy.[2]

[2] *Ibid.*, 82–86.

In the bipolar system characterized by the rivalry of two continent-states, the United States and the Soviet Union, the Western bloc that formed around the United States was seeking security. The territory and the peoples of Western Europe were the prize for which the two superpowers competed. To win these spelled power. The bloc's organization for collective defense, and consequently the military and political organizations of Western Europe, were the measures taken to insure this victory; they constituted security and power. The conflict was also ideological; it pitted liberal and democratic capitalism against Marxist collectivism.

Meanwhile, another idological struggle was being waged outside the two superpowers' direct spheres of influence. On the political level, this struggle pitted the budding nationalism of the dependent territories—which were demanding individual and collective equality—against the older nationalism of certain Western European nations, which were trying to preserve their hegemony. On the ethno-religious level, the struggle pitted the yellow, black, or Arab races against the white—Buddhism or Islam against Christianity. The conservative attitude of the colonizer was not inspired by a need for security (a colonial war waged far from the homeland tends to weaken the nation), or by a desire for power (the responsibilities of an empire are greater than the benefits), but by an idea—a yearning for glory. It was important to prevent the amputation of the overseas possessions because they lent world-wide prestige to the nation.

As part of Europe, as the home of the French Union, France pursued three goals simultaneously in charting her foreign policy.

The first was to make sure that in the immediate present French territory would be safe from an attack by the Soviet Union, using either conventional or strategic weapons. To prevent such an attack, France became an active participant in the Atlantic Pact. The efficacy of the Pact was based on the integration of conventional weapons by all members and on the nuclear power of the United States. The democratic and anti-Marxist ideology coincided with the objective of security.

The second goal was to insure the short-term prosperity and the long-term security of France as part of Europe. To accomplish this, a federation of Western Europe was mapped out which hopefully would acquire, because of its size, an economic and military power equal to that of the superpowers. The federation was to preserve its ties with the United States but hoped to free itself from American domination. In pursuing this goal, the new ideology of a federation vied with the old nationalist idealogy. Survival and power were the goals that inspired the union of average-size nations that heretofore had been rivals.

The third objective was to preserve the overseas possessions within the authoritarian and centralized French Union. But this involved a fundamental contradiction: the denial of internal autonomy was not consistent with the acknowledged right of self-determination. The overriding tendency to deny self-determination proved far stronger than the willingness to grant it. This attitude generated serious crises in all the overseas possessions and shooting wars in two of them, Indochina and Algeria.

The simultaneous pursuit of these three objectives was dangerous because it led to a dispersal of resources and to conflicts of ideology.

Colonial strife forced France to assign a substantial portion of her economic and military resources to her overseas territories. This increased her financial dependence on the United States, whose additional aid she had constantly to request. It also brought about an increasing military dependence on the United States because the conventional forces for the defense of metropolitan France were reduced by the wars to a minimum. France's position within NATO, especially *vis-à-vis* Germany, was weakened. The wars also weakened France's ability to compete with her O.E.E.C. partners and with the Europe of the Six. The dispersal of French resources did not lessen the security of France because of the Alliance, but it did diminish her power within the Alliance and in Europe. Her colonial policy provoked ideological controversy at home. NATO'S collective defense represented a struggle for a democratic ideal, but resistance to decolonization was a struggle against the right of self-determination, which is an integral part of the democratic ideal. There was therefore a certain ideological conflict (apart from bilateral relations with the United States) between the collective defense of the Western bloc and the French resistance to decolonization. Even more marked was the incompatibility between the construction of European unity and French colonial policy. Collective defense was founded on the federalist ideology, and in the midst of the twentieth century it attempted to transcend the nationalist ideology that had prevailed in Europe ever since 1900. French colonial policy was founded on a nationalist ideology so narrow that it reproved and opposed overseas nationalism, and rejected internal autonomy. Yet internal autonomy was a halfway house between dependence and independence; it was acceptable and viable if it could be introduced in a federal and egalitarian system rather than in an authoritarian and centralized one.

In short, under the Fourth Republic France pursued objectives that were too ambitious for her limited resources. What is more, she pursued objectives that could not be reconciled because of the conflicting ideologies that underlay them. The inadequacy of ends in relation to means and the incompatibility of conflicting goals led to two major crises, in 1954 and in 1958. The crisis of 1954, which occurred at the tail end of the war in Indochina, culminated in a setback of political Europe, and bore within it the seeds of a German nationalist resurgence. The crisis of 1958, caused by the prolongation of the war in Algeria, culminated in the overthrow of a regime that did not know how to make the most of its means, limit its ambitions, or observe the rules for a unified foreign policy based on a combination of strategy and diplomacy.

The Balance Sheet of the Fourth Republic

The regime was ephemeral: only twelve years separated the resignation of General de Gaulle in January 1946 from his return to power in May 1958— only eleven years actually, if we take as a starting point the elections of November 1946, after the constitution was adopted, or the eviction of the Communists from the government in May 1947. These eleven years witnessed both successes and failures in foreign policy.

On the credit side of the ledger was the regime's frank preference for the Western bloc and its more hesitant decision to further the construction of a united Europe. The Fourth Republic must be credited, along with England, for the negotiations that culminated in the Atlantic Pact. It was also the first government of Europe to offer Germany reconciliation and to suggest methods more radical and more effective than mere cooperation for the economic and political unification of Europe. Moreover, France contributed the psychological and institutional foundations necessary for European unification. Franco-German reconciliation had obviously been attained, but the institutional program was only partially achieved. Opinion was divided on how to rearm Germany. This division resulted in rejection of the European Defense Community, which in turn delayed the political unification of Europe. Incompetent handling of public finances and currency problems obstructed and delayed the economic unification of Europe. Despite France's weaknesses, her moral position was considered by the allies to be strong, thanks to her diplomatic initiatives. England's refusal to become involved on the Continent and the fact that Germany remained divided served to strengthen still further the position of France.

On the debit side of the ledger was the failure of France to pursue a liberal and consistent policy of decolonization. Unlike England, who had become inured over the years to the decentralized administration of the Commonwealth, and had gradually granted her colonies internal autonomy (which eventually led to independence attained peacefully), France allowed herself to be dragged into two successive colonial wars. They weakened her economy and undermined her political influence in Europe and in the Atlantic Alliance. She was ill prepared to meet the inevitable crisis that followed the European defeat of 1945, an event that marked her transition from a world power to a continental power, from a first-rate to a second-rate nation.

To judge the Fourth Republic equitably, one must take into account factors of time and space. Temporally, the Fourth Republic compares favorably with the Third. Despite political instability, errors in administration, dispersed efforts, and inconsistent goals, France gave evidence of renewed vitality, a desire for expansion, and a creative imagination that were in marked contrast to the profound military, political, economic, and demographic decadence of the Third Republic. Spatially, only a brief comparison of France with other countries of the same size can be outlined here. England sacrificed her economy to her currency whereas France sacrificed her currency to economic expansion. England discovered peaceful ways to decolonize whereas France did not. England failed to understand that her future, in the long run, was in Europe whereas France understood this but was unable to get her élite to agree unanimously. Their successes and failures were of a different nature, but France came out favorably in the balance. Her relative importance increased in Western Europe. The relative importance of West Germany increased simultaneously, in accordance with the historic axiom that the vanquished recover more quickly than the victors. West Germany, contested by the two superpowers, entertained no ambitions for independence outside the European union or the Atlantic Alliance. She was free from the hazards and the bondage that were inseparable from the possession of overseas territories. A high degree of political stability and of competence in the management of her economy insured a strong currency and rapid expansion.

In short, the balance sheet of the Fourth Republic's foreign policy shows that its chief defects were an inadequacy of means and an inconsistency of ends. On the whole, its record was positive: the regime disappeared, but France had asserted herself.

The Europe-Overseas Dilemma

The dilemma France faced can be stated in the following terms: should she give priority to a global policy based on her colonial possessions, or to a continental policy determined by the balance of power in Europe and in the world?

This dilemma was not new. Often in the past France had vacillated between her continental vocation and her maritime ambitions. In the eighteenth century, weakened by the wars of Louis XIV and threatened on the Continent by Austria or Prussia, she lost her first colonial empire to England. After the war of 1870 France established a new empire, but throughout the history of the Third Republic, France always gave priority to continental interests and was careful never to involve the country in a colonial conflict.

The profound changes wrought by the war of 1939–1945 should have led the Fourth Republic to pursue a similar policy and to act prudently.

In the multipolar system of the Versailles peace, France remained a great continental power; Germany continued to be the potential enemy, England, the ally. British naval superiority was still the colonial empire's bulwark of defense in case of war. The empire provided more colonial troops for metropolitan France than the homeland could post overseas to protect its possessions. Yet the revolt of Abdel-Krim in Morocco in 1925 was a warning that the situation could be reversed.

In the bipolar system of the cold war, a tremendous disparity in resources separated the United States, leader of the Western bloc, from its principal lieutenants, England, France, and eventually West Germany. The potential enemy was the Soviet Union. The defense of metropolitan France was identified with the defense of Western Europe. The defense of the French Union rested on France alone.

The Fourth Republic wanted to keep the French Union intact, and to accomplish this it was prepared to use arms if necessary. Hence France entrusted to her allies, especially the United States, the task of defending the homeland.

In so doing, was France protecting her fundamental long-term interests? An objective answer to this question depended on the future of colonial empires and on the future of average-sized nation-states such as they were in 1950.

Colonial empires were everywhere under attack. For ideological reasons, the United States did not approve of perpetuating them. For strategic reasons, the Soviet Union wanted to see them disappear. Local national movements demanded economic progress as well as political independence. But the real obstacles were the colonizers themselves. The peoples of Asia and Africa had deep-rooted reasons for desiring liberation. "In imposing their ideas and their civilization, the Europeans justified the revolt of the colonies and thereby also deprived themselves of the complacency of conquerors."[3]

Because of internecine wars, the nation-states of Europe ceased to play a decisive role in global diplomacy or strategy.

Considered individually, they did not have at their disposal a complete panoply of strategic and conventional weapons, nor a sufficiently large market to make the most of their people's resources. The idea of a federal state stemmed precisely from the design of endowing Western Europe with the power that individual nation-states no longer possessed and that would redound to the advantage of their people. China's power became manifest after her unification in 1949. European power might become manifest if the Continent were unified peacefully under the aegis of the Atlantic Alliance.

Since the start of the cold war considerable changes had occurred, especially in the number, hierarchy, and alignment of states and territories. In states that had recently achieved independence and in territories that were

[3] Raymond Aron, *L'Algérie et la République* (Paris: Plon, 1958), 83.

still dependent, young nationalist movements formed groups on the basis of ethnic and religious affinities, according to the type of civilization to which they belonged. The Arab League was the first of such groups. In English- and French-speaking Black Africa, the common band of being Negro brought the people closer together. The concept of the nation, which European colonizers had introduced overseas, led to that of civilization, and it was around this concept that ideas were crystallizing. The various civilizations that lived side by side and came into contact with one another because of the technical, industrial, and military superiority of the West, could survive and forge ahead only if they too adopted the technology and administrative structures that had enabled the West to progress. Regional alignments and the tendency to pool technological know-how were additional motives for the nation-states of Europe to collaborate. These nation-states belonged to the same civilization, which was of Christian inspiration, liberal, and socialist. By uniting with all the states and territories that were forming new groups, they could devise a common strategy and a new approach to relationships—based on cooperation rather than on domination—and thus draw closer the concept of nation to that of civilization.

In this international context, the United Nations became a rostrum for the young nations and for non-Western civilizations. The authoritarian French Union seemed an anachronism and a source of weakness. The establishment of a federated and unified Europe promised prosperity and power.

The Past and the Future

The following question arises: why did the French élite oppose the movement for decolonization? Why was it divided on the question of unifying Europe? In other words, why, in the face of the Europe-overseas dilemma, did Frenchmen under the Fourth Republic fail to make a decision that was commensurate with their means and consistent with their long-term interest, as well as with those of the peoples of the French Union?

To blame General de Gaulle for the choice, or rather the persistent refusal to choose, is too easy. To be sure, de Gaulle did bring all his weight to bear on events; he did influence them. But his skill and willpower would not have sufficed had they not been reinforced by real situations, historic traditions, deep-seated feelings, and ideological beliefs.

Three observations should help to clarify this point, although they are by no means complete.

The first observation has to do with the specific facts pertaining to French colonialism in North Africa.

The three North African countries were colonies containing a minority group of settlers. Five to ten per cent of the population were of French or European origin, therefore Christian. They were living alongside of an overwhelming Muslim majority whose status differed distinctly from their own. A large proportion of the posts held by Europeans in the various sectors of the economy could have been filled by unemployed Muslims who were living at a bare subsistence level. Independence would deprive many Europeans of their jobs. Eventually and inevitably, they would have to be transferred to France. The situation was quite different in the Dominions of the white Commonwealth, whose population was entirely European, or in the English- and French-speaking territories of Black Africa, where the white population consisted primarily of a handful of administrators or businessmen. In South Africa, where independence had been achieved long ago, the ruling classes of the Dominion were able to arrange the coexistence of blacks and whites to suit their own convenience. To be sure, the problem was a delicate one, but it was less explosive than the difficulties that beset Christians and Arabs living side by side at the time of the Islamic renaissance. Inseparable from independence for North Africa was the tragic alternative which the governments of the Fourth Republic did not have the courage to disclose to the French public on either side of the Mediterranean.

The second observation centers on mental attitude, the direct result of French education. French youths are brought up on history. From elementary school through the university, they are immersed in dreams of the grandeur that was France. They learn about the campaigns of Louis XIV and the brilliance of court life at Versailles, but they are not taught the price that an entire generation of Frenchmen had to pay for the Sun King's glory. The remember the victories of Napoleon, who led his troops all the way to Moscow, but they forget that twenty years of warfare during the revolution and the Empire sapped the nation's vitality. In terms of wealth and population, the relative position of France in Europe has been declining ever since 1660. But does a single textbook point out that this decline was due to two glorious undertakings in which there was a great disparity between means and ends? The student's persistent dream of grandeur leads eventually to the citizen's refusal to face the truth and assume responsibility to accept present-day political realities. Whenever the few responsible politicians who have coldly analyzed the relationship between means and ends spell out the implications, they are neither heard nor heeded. On the other hand, political lies or omissions always find a large audience. The slogan in 1920 was "Germany will pay"; in 1955 it was "Algeria is France." Abdicating responsibility is an old game. If the facts do not coincide with optimistic prognostications, someone else is to blame. The Americans were responsible for German rearmament, for the loss of Indochina. In this kind of psychological climate, the French Union became an alibi, a way of continuing to live "only for France," the France from Dunkirk to Tamanrasset. In 1950, Pierre Mendès-France told the truth about the Indochinese war. He was placed in office solely to negotiate the peace of 1954. Not a single politician told Parliament the plain hard facts about the confrontation between France and Islam in North Africa. Raymond Aron was the only political writer who exhibited any lucidity.

The third observation refers to the conception of power in France. Authoritarian and centralist, this conception can be traced to the jurists of the Capetian kings. It found expression in the Napoleonic administration and reached florescence in our contemporary planned economy. In no other industrialized country are the local authorities and the nationalized enterprises as closely controlled by the state as they are in France. The refusal to delegate powers is omnipresent. It can be ascribed to a basic lack of trust in the citizen and this, in turn, deprives him of a sense of responsibility. It pits "the citizen against the constituted authorities," as the title of a book by Alain puts it. Moreover, politicians and bureaucrats become hostile and confused when they have to go over the heads of a unitary state's administration to delegate powers either to a subordinate official or to a higher authority.

Faced with the disintegration of the French Union, the authorities refused to grant internal autonomy—in other words, to delegate power to the overseas territories. This refusal, which we have denounced so frequently in this book, hastened the collapse of the French Union. There were some, as we have shown, who sincerely believed that integration would prevent dismemberment. They tried to apply their ideas to Algeria. To be sure, a colonial conquest can achieve integration if the conquerors forcibly impose their religion, laws, and customs. But who are to be integrated by a decision reached in metropolitan France? Europeans and Arabs, Christians and Muslims, believers in two ancient, powerful, and rival religions, populations that are economically and ethnically disparate. France could not, in the space of a few years, assimilate ten million Algerian Muslims who, in some respects, feel closer to Egypt and the Middle East than to the homeland. Integration imposed by metropolitan France on peoples of such different backgrounds, where a minority is dominant and the majority yearns for independence, was not a realistic solution.

Inversely, given the chaos and divisions in Europe, the post-1950 governments of the Fourth Republic advocated the integration of Europe by persuasion rather than by force. Unlike the proposed integration between the overseas territories and metropolitan France, European integration involved peoples alike in their civilization, religion, ethnic type, economic structure, and approximate standards of living. The integration of Europe was to be fashioned not by a unilateral decision, but by discussion, arbitration, and constant negotiation. The long-term objective was federation. The method consisted in gradually formulating joint decisions on the basis of majority vote. This is supranationalism. It presupposes a delegation of power. But delegation upward in European affairs elicits the same objections as delegation downward in overseas affairs.

During the period of the Fourth Republic, political and administrative centralization obstructed both decolonization and European unification. Unwillingness to face reality, combined with unwillingness to delegate power, leads to day-dreams, to political stagnation. The past was overwhelming, the present disappointing, the future uncertain. Could the old dreams of glory find fulfillment in the present structures so that future reforms could be dispensed with, even though they might contain the seeds of future power?

The Europe-overseas conflict was a dilemma involving divergent foreign policy goals; it was also a conflict between the past and the future. Colonialism as a form of domination was a thing of the past. The federated continent-state was a thing of the future.

Frenchmen, divided on the goals of foreign policy and the ideologies related to them, failed to avail themselves of the patience and persistent effort that lead to great achievements. The crisis of the regime, which sprang from these divisions, brought to power a man of the past. De Gaulle had opted for the perpetuation of the French Union. He denounced the Atlantic Alliance as an American protectorate. He opposed a supranational Europe. He was largely responsible for the inconsistencies of French foreign policy goals. The fear of being charged with treason by the one man who symbolized resistance to the invader paralyzed successive governments of the Fourth Republic, which were tempted to rid themselves of the burden that was colonialism.

Weary of the war in Algeria, disgusted with the regime of government by assembly, France gave herself to de Gaulle. Once the great man was in power, would he look to the future?

BOOK TWO

THE
FIFTH
REPUBLIC

I

Decolonization and Cooperation

1

The End of the Algerian War

From the Election to the " Peace of the Brave"

ON JUNE 1, 1958, General de Gaulle was elected premier by the National Assembly. The vote was 329 to 224, with 32 abstaining. On June 3 he was authorized to propose a new constitution. He was given full powers. In metropolitan France they would lapse at the end of six months. In Algeria they would last as long as he held office. On June 4 he arrived in Algiers. He named Salan delegate-general but told him: "I am the minister of Algeria."

The self-imposed silence that de Gaulle had maintained since June 30, 1955, made it impossible to guess his intentions. In his speech of June 4 he did not commit himself to a specific political formula. He announced, however, that "in not less than three months, . . . all Frenchmen, including the ten million Frenchmen of Algeria, will be called upon to decide their own fate."

He added that these ten million Frenchmen, "united in a single electoral college, will be asked to choose their representatives." Finally, he "opened the doors of reconciliation" to those who, as he himself acknowledged, had fought courageously. An initial objective would be the right of self-determination for all Algerians (meaning both French and Moslems). There were three ways to achieve this: a single referendum for both France and Algeria; elections in Algeria in a single electoral college; negotiation with the rebels. On his way to Oran, de Gaulle said he hoped that all Algeria would participate in the referendum "in order to show that it is organically and forever French." At Mostaganem, impressed by the demonstrations of the Muslim population, he cried out at the end of his speech: "Vive French Algeria!" He was never to utter these words again.

The initial aims of General de Gaulle were clear. The referendum would strengthen the personal position of the premier in metropolitan France and in Algeria; the elections would demonstrate the progress of pacification to world opinion and to the F.L.N. Afterward, the government would assert its authority over the army, rebuild the Algerian economy, and open a dialogue with the rebels.

The new constitution, drafted in August, was completed on September 4. It was not applicable to Algeria which nevertheless participated in the referendum of September 28. Unlike the voters of metropolitan France, the Algerians were not called upon to approve the constitution. Unlike the voters of the overseas territories, they were not asked to join the Community that had replaced the French Union. Instead, they were to manifest confidence in France and in General de Gaulle who would determine the future status of Algeria. Prior to the referendum, a single electoral college was established and the right of suffrage was granted to Muslim women. In his speech at Algiers on August 29 General de Gaulle indicated the importance of the referendum: "If you vote 'yes' you will show that you wish to conduct yourselves entirely as Frenchmen and that you believe that the necessary evolution must take place within a French framework."

On September 19 the F.L.N. replied to the referendum by establishing an Algerian government-in-exile. It was headed by Ferhat Abbas and included civilians, some of French, others of Arabian culture, as well as military men. Ben Bella, a prisoner in France, was proclaimed vice-president. The government was immediately recognized by the Arab countries, including Morocco and Tunisia, and by China. It urged the Algerian population to abstain on September 28 and declared: "The Algerian people have not waited to be 'granted' independence. They assume it. They proclaim it." The order to abstain was not, however, obeyed. Out of 4,412,000 registered voters, 3,357,000 (76 per cent) voted 'yes' and 118,000 voted 'no.' In view of the referendum's success, the F.L.N. made more conciliatory declarations and announced that it was ready to begin informal discussions with the French government under the military and political conditions of a cease-fire, without demanding "preliminary independence" but with an eye to negotiating for it.[1]

In his press conference of October 23, General de Gaulle responded to these overtures by offering a "Peace of the Brave." It would be achieved either by on-the-spot negotiations for a cease-fire or by negotiations with the rebellion's organization abroad whose representatives had been invited to

[1] *Année politique 1958*, 127.

come to France. As for the political conditions, they must be decided by the Algerians themselves, following free elections in which every tendency could find expression. These words had great repercussion throughout France and abroad. The Provisional Government of the Algerian Republic (G.P.R.A.) responded with a refusal, motivated by the political as well as the military character of possible negotiations on the entire status of Algeria.

De Gaulle's intentions in regard to this status were uncertain. In this same press conference of October 23 he said: "Future solutions will be based on the courageous identity of Algeria and its close association with the French fatherland." It was up to the Algerian citizens to manifest their will in the forthcoming legislative elections. The elections, with a single electoral college, took place at the end of November. The voters balloted for mixed lists composed of Muslims (two-thirds) and Europeans (one-third). The possibility of bargaining between the government and the G.P.R.A., plus the uncertainty about the status of Algeria, led the Europeans to reassert their desire for integration whereas the bulk of the Muslims, disappointed in their aspirations for peace, did not understand the need for a new electoral consultation. The electoral campaign was conducted without enthusiasm. The lists that favored integration won.

On December 12, de Gaulle named Paul Delouvrier delegate-general and General Maurice Challe commander-in-chief. At the close of this first stage the head of the government had benefited from a quasi-plebiscite on his name and had strengthened his authority, but had not asked for the approval of a policy. This policy was not mentioned in the speech of October 3 at Constantine, which merely affirmed, in terms similar to those of the press conference of October 23, that: "in any case, the future of Algeria . . . will be built on a double foundation: the retention of its identity and its close solidarity with the French fatherland." Claude Paillat reported that de Gaulle, in receiving General André Zeller who had resigned a few months earlier, said to him at the end of June: "See here, Zeller, integration is meaningless, independence is a disaster. There is only one middle solution, association."[2] In December 1958, the nature of the association was undetermined. But de Gaulle had put his men in their places with orders to Challe to concentrate the army on its operational tasks and orders to Delouvrier to launch a program of economic development.

Military Operations and Economic Development

Challe directed the military campaign that bears his name with three main objectives in mind: to maintain the impermeability of the barriers, to destroy

[2] Claude Paillat, *Dossier secret de l'Algérie* (Paris: Le Livre Contemporain, 1961), 75.

the rebel bands inside the country, and to continue the work of pacification. The first objective was achieved. Attempts to get through the barriers failed in February–March as well as in November–December 1959. The second objective necessitated the regrouping of the reserves in order to make them "the spearhead of an offensive strategy"[3] and to carry out a series of offensives from west to east in the very zones where the rebels had taken refuge. These operations were successful in the Oran Province in February and March, in Algerois in April and June, in Kabylia in July, in North Constantine in September and October 1959, in Ouarsenis in March, and in Atlas in April 1960.[4] Pacification progressed, aided by the enrollment of Muslims in the regular and supplementary units, the regrouping of the Muslim civilian population, and the extension of the role of the army in educational, medical, economic, and administrative domains.

Challe "quickly perceived that Paris expected of him not a total military success by use of arms but an improvement in the situation that would make it possible to negotiate from a position of strength."[5] The instructions he gave to the army in March 1960, on the eve of his recall to France, confirmed that the purpose of the struggle was to keep Algeria French. These instructions were in no way modified by his successor, General Crépin. As Raoul Girardet observed: "The orders issued to the army on the subject of pacification and intensification of the struggle against the rebellion remained unaltered for more than two years."[6] The result of this was an uneasiness that Claude Paillat analyzed in the following terms: "The official declarations that came from above were full of ambiguities. They made the army feel in a vague way that the directives of the high command did not correspond precisely with those of the chief of state."[7]

Improvement in the economic conditions of the Muslims, like improvement in the military situation, represented a trump card in any eventual negotiation. At Constantine on October 3, 1958, de Gaulle outlined in broad terms a five-year program. In December 1958 Paul Delouvrier announced that the government would set aside one billion new francs per year to equip Algeria. The plan was vigorously implemented in 1959 and 1960. As a consequence of the changing political situation, however, private industrial investments came to a halt. On the other hand, the extraction and transportation of Sahara oil and natural gas continued to develop in spite of the fighting.

[3] J. Fauvet and J. Planchais, *La fronde des généraux* (Paris: Arthaud, 1961), 50.
[4] Jean-Paul Benoit, "Chronologie de la guerre en Algérie," "Histoire de la guerre d'Algérie," *La Nef*, Oct. 1962, Jan. 1963, 13.
[5] Fauvet and Planchais, *La fronde*, 51.
[6] Raoul Girardet, *La crise militaire française 1945–1962* (Paris: Armand Colin, 1964), 207.
[7] Paillat, *Dossier secret*, 363.

Oil and gas pipelines were laid. The production of petroleum, which in 1958 had been less than one million tons, was approaching fifteen million tons by 1961.

By sponsoring both public and private investments the government apparently promoted, if not a French Algeria, at least a largely autonomous Algeria associated with France.

What Is Self-Determination?

Early in 1959 de Gaulle, elected president of the Republic, designated Michel Debré as premier but reserved for himself supreme responsibility for Algerian affairs. On January 30, repeating his proposal of the "Peace of the Brave," he declared that the destiny of Algeria "is essentially up to the Algerians themselves." In his press conference of March 25, he said that France "is working for a transformation in which Algeria will find its new identity" and that the destiny of Algeria "will be linked with that of France." Meanwhile the statements made by de Gaulle to Pierre Laffont, the deputy from Oran, and which the latter reported in his newspaper, *L'Écho d'Oran*, on April 29, aroused disquiet among the "pieds-noirs."* "Those that cry the loudest for integration today ... merely want to have 'Papa's Algeria' returned to them; but 'Papa's Algeria' is dead and those who do not understand this will die along with it." The municipal elections of April took place in an atmosphere of indifference with relatively few people going to the polls—only 40 per cent of the voters in Algiers. On May 9 at Blois, de Gaulle declared: "We are about to engage in negotiations that may be decisive." The possibility of contacts with the F.L.N. accentuated the uneasiness of Europeans who were celebrating the anniversary of May 13 without enthusiasm. On August 16, Ferhat Abbas declared that "the only possible solution is an independent Algeria" and that "France has no intention of negotiating seriously."[8]

In a major statement by de Gaulle on September 16, 1959, the key word, self-determination, was uttered. "We shall resolve the Algerian problems," he said, "by the free choice that the Algerians themselves will make as to their future. ... I believe that recourse to self-determination must be proclaimed from this day forward." Having stated the principle, he mentioned three possible solutions: "Secession, which some think will lead to independence ...; complete Francization as it is implied in the equality of rights ...; government of Algerians by Algerians, backed by the help of France and by a close union with her. ... In the latter event, Algeria will require a federal

---

* Translator's note: nickname of the French colonists.
[8] *Année politique 1959*, 282.

regime which alone can enable the diverse communities—French, Arab, Kabyl, Mozabite, etc.—that reside in the country to obtain guarantees for their own ways of life within a framework of cooperation. . . ." Once the speech was delivered the exegesis began. Which solution did the general prefer? Independence would be "disastrous." De Gaulle concocted an elaborate definition for Francization—a new term for French Algeria or integration—but he made no qualitative judgment. The overriding impression was that he preferred the middle-of-the-road solution of association.

In Algiers the "activist" movements tried to get the Algerian parliamentarians to protest against this statement and vote against the government. But the debate in the National Assembly revealed that the great majority of the deputies approved de Gaulle's Algerian policy. Only nine deputies, among them Léon Delbecque and J. B. Biaggi, resigned from the U.N.R. (Union pour la Nouvelle République). The balloting on October 15 gave the government a huge majority: 441 for, 23 against, 88 abstaining. Three-fourths of the Independents gave de Gaulle a vote of confidence.

The French authorities of Algiers were in an awkward position. On October 28, de Gaulle sent a message to the Algerian army, explaining the necessity for self-determination "after a delay that will probably be of several years' duration." On October 30, Paul Delouvrier declared: "I must emphasize again that we are fighting for a French Algeria."[9]

The F.L.N. had Ferhat Abbas answer de Gaulle. He formally acknowledged Algeria's right to self-determination but added that voters could not choose freely "under the pressure of an army of occupation." He said he "was ready to discuss with the French government the political and military preconditions for a cease-fire as well as the necessary preconditions for the implementation of the rights to self-determination." This was his way of demanding recognition as the sole spokesman for the Algerian people.

"To ask the Muslims of Algeria whether they want to be French or not is to acknowledge that, at least temporarily, they no longer are French, or that they are French only on sufferance. Yet . . . such a doctrine inevitably forges Algerian nationality and makes the establishment of an Algerian state—one that will ultimately be independent—unavoidable. If the French put the question to the Muslims, it is because they have decided to leave, or are resigned to the idea. Thenceforward the issue is decided and pacification becomes impossible." This was Raymond Aron's analysis and it led him to conclude that de Gaulle, in granting self-determination, agreed to eventual independence for Algeria.[10] This interpretation is confirmed by Claude Paillat's account of an interview which de Gaulle accorded on January 19,

[9] *Ibid.*, 284.
[10] Raymond Aron, preface to *Année politique 1960*, 6.

1960, to Marc Lauriol, a deputy from Algeria. "See here, Lauriol," the general reportedly said in reference to the Muslims of Algeria, "those people aren't French! ... What they expect me to do is to give them Ferhat Abbas."[11]

Thus de Gaulle secretly opted for independence even as he offered a theoretical choice between three eventual alternatives. The government spoke two different languages: one was for consumption in metropolitan France, which would have been relieved to accept a negotiated peace even at the price of independence for Algeria; the other was for the French in Algeria and for the army who had been told by the military leaders that the troops were fighting for French Algeria. This ambiguity served the designs of the F.L.N., which had every reason to continue the war, knowing that the psychological campaign was doomed to failure and that the prolongation of hostilities would force de Gaulle to be less rigid about negotiating.

From the Barricades of Algiers to the Referendum on Self-Determination

The year 1960 was highlighted by the week of the barricades in Algiers, the abortive negotiations of Melun, *de facto* recognition of Algerian independence, and the announcement of a referendum on self-determination.

The insurrection of the barricades broke out on January 24 upon the recall of General Massu, corps commander of the Algiers army, who had made hostile remarks about the policy of self-determination to a German newspaperman. The troops were ordered to clear the streets of Algiers. The insurgents tried to enlist the army's cooperation in forcing the government to relinquish its policy. A fraternization of sorts was established between the troops, to whom Challe repeated on the 27th that the army was fighting so that Algeria would remain definitively French, and the insurgents, who were moved by Delouvrier's emotional speech of the 28th. In a televised address on January 29, de Gaulle reaffirmed his conviction that the promotion of self-determination was the only policy worthy of France. He reminded his audience that the rebel organization "claims that it will not agree to a cease-fire unless I first negotiate with it about the political future of Algeria, which would be tantamount to establishing it as the sole legitimate agency and setting it up in advance as the government of the country." He added flatly "This I will not do." Then, addressing the French of Algeria, he asked: "How can you listen to the liars and conspirators who tell you that in granting a free choice to the Algerians, France and de Gaulle want to abandon you, withdraw from Algeria, and surrender it to the rebellion? You can be

---

[11] Paillat, *Dossier secret*, 336–37.

sure that . . . nothing will please de Gaulle more than to see the Algerians opt . . . for the most French of available solutions." These words reassured the army which, on the whole, had remained loyal. The surrender of the entrenched camp took place on February 1.

Soustelle quit the government on the 5th, and a certain number of general officers who were suspected of sympathizing with the insurgents' cause were recalled to France. The government agency in charge of psychological warfare was suppressed. Territorial units were dissolved. The army was thus relieved of its political responsibilities. From the 3rd to the 5th of March, de Gaulle was in Algeria for personal conversations with commanders of units in the hinterland. On this trip, which was called "the mess inspection," he emphasized the necessity of a total victory for French arms. He added that he counted on the army to achieve pacification and control the period of transition. General Challe was recalled to France in April. He left his directives to the army, a political testament that concluded that the objective of war was to aid the various communities that people Algeria "to build alone and in concert a French, modern, humane Algeria."

The success of the Challe plan impelled Si Salah, one of the rebel military chiefs, to put forward the basis for a general cease-fire, thus confirming the army's premise about a possibility of a split between the internal and external fronts of the rebellion. Si Salah was received in secret session by de Gaulle on June 10 but the meeting had no sequel and Si Salah returned to the *maquis* where he was strangled by his own men.

On the other hand, de Gaulle did renew his offers to the external (political) front of the rebellion on June 14. On June 20, the G.P.R.A. announced that it was sending a delegation presided over by Ferhat Abbas, it being understood that Abbas would discuss political issues and confer with de Gaulle. His emissaries were received rather coldly at the prefecture of Melun on June 26. The negotiators could not come to an understanding. The French excluded all political negotiations before a cease-fire. The F.L.N. rejected a cease-fire that was not accompanied by guarantees for self-determination. Neither side had altered its position since the offer of the "Peace of the Brave" in October 1958. Under the circumstances, de Gaulle refused to meet Ferhat Abbas. The discussions came to an end on June 29. So far as the chief of state was concerned, they doubtless served to accustom the army and public opinion in both France and Algeria to the possibility of real negotiations.

On September 5 de Gaulle opened his press conference by saying: "There exists an Algeria, an Algerian entity, an Algerian identity." Then he asked: "This being so, what solution will the Algerians agree to?" His answer was plain. "I tell you that as I see it, they will want Algeria to be Algerian." But there was an alternative to an Algerian Algeria. "The only question that will arise, in my opinion, is whether Algeria will be Algerian despite the French, by seceding, breaking away from France, or whether it will be Algerian in association, in friendly union with France."

As always, the change in de Gaulle's vocabulary signified an alteration of his policy. In September 1959, he had envisaged three possible solutions: secession (or independence), Francization (or integration), or autonomy (the government of Algerians by Algerians in association with France). In September 1960, de Gaulle indicated that independence was imminent by using the slogan "Algerian Algeria"; then he made a distinction between independence by secession, such as Guinea had acquired in September 1958, and independence by association, as introduced in the May 1960 amendment to the 1958 constitution and immediately granted to the African and Malagasy Republics.

The speech of November 4, 1960, confirmed this interpretation. Algerian Algeria "means . . . an Algeria that . . . will have its own government, its own institutions and laws." The words "Algerian Republic" were uttered. Self-determination, which presupposed a referendum, was the way to achieve one or the other form of an Algerian Algeria, but in fact de Gaulle had resigned himself to Algerian independence.

The next step was to appoint a team whose mission it would be to pave the way for independence by association. On November 22 Louis Joxe was named minister of state for Algerian affairs. He was to carry out the direct orders of the chief of state. Jean Morin was named delegate-general of the government in Algeria, replacing Paul Delouvrier. On November 16 an official communiqué announced a referendum on Algeria. De Gaulle and Joxe arrived in Algeria on December 9 to be greeted by an atmosphere of revolt. For the first time, Muslims paraded up and down the streets of Algiers and Oran, holding aloft the green flag of rebellion. The Europeans shot at the demonstrators. Their resentment against metropolitan France increased as the time for the referendum of January 8, 1961, approached. The following question was put: "Do you approve of the draft of the law submitted to the French people by the president of the Republic on self-determination for the peoples of Algeria and on the organization of government prior to self-determination?" In his speech of December 20 de Gaulle analyzed the significance of the referendum. "The French people are being called upon to decide whether they will allow . . . the Algerians to decide their own fate once peace has been restored." He stressed the point that "everything compels the Algeria of the future to associate with France." He added that "our people's affirmative answer to the referendum will also represent a call for an end to the fighting and a peaceful confrontation." The Communists and of course the champions of a French Algeria, grouped around Jacques Soustelle and Georges Bidault, urged their followers to vote "no." The Socialists and Popular Republicans united with the U.N.R. to urge their adherents to vote "yes." The Radicals and the Independents were divided. They made no recommendations to their voters. On January 6, 1961, de Gaulle issued a final appeal: "I turn to you, rather than to intermediaries. . . . This is a matter between each of you and myself." In metropolitan France 75 per cent of the voters responded with a "yes." The number of abstentions was greater than it had been in the referendum of 1958, amounting to almost one-fourth of all the registered voters. In Algeria, the abstentions were much more numerous—40 per cent of the registered voters—and the proportion voting "yes" was smaller—69 per cent. The F.L.N. tried to boycott the referendum but only in the large urban centers did its followers obey orders. The Europeans returned a massive vote of "no." When the referendum was over, the European population of Algeria realized that it was isolated both from metropolitan France and from the Muslims of Algeria.

The Preliminary Negotiations and the Putsch of the Generals

By returning a "frank and massive" "yes" the voters of metropolitan France and the Muslims of Algeria had, according to de Gaulle, declared in favor of Algerian independence. The way was therefore clear for serious negotiations. On February 22, 1961, secret contact was made between Georges Pompidou and Ahmed Boumendjel. Three weeks earlier de Gaulle had invited Bourguiba to meet him. He received him on the 27th at Rambouillet and enlisted the good offices of the Tunisian president. The commencement of official discussions with the G.P.R.A. was announced on March 30. In his press conference of April 11, the president of the Republic made overtures to the G.P.R.A.: "This state will be what the Algerians want it to be. I am personally convinced that it will be sovereign in both domestic and foreign affairs. And let me say once again that France will place no obstacle in its way." In the hope of forestalling a rupture, he uttered a vague threat: "We will draw the proper inferences regarding the desire of certain peoples—and we already know to which areas they belong—to be part of France. They have as much right to self-determination as the others. . . . We will therefore first have to regroup them to insure their protection." The *putsch* of the generals adjourned the discussions.

During the night of April 21–22, four retired generals, two of whom were former commmanders-in-chief in Algeria—Maurice Challe and Raoul Salan—seized power in Algiers. "I am in Algiers to keep our promise," Challe said in his proclamation, "the promise the army made to safeguard Algeria so that our dead will not have died in vain." Salan had emigrated to

Spain, but his opinions were well known. Challe's conduct, however, was surprising. After his departure from Algiers in April 1960, he had become commander-in-chief of NATO's Central European forces. In November 1960, the day after de Gaulle's speech alluding to the "Algerian Republic," Challe had offered to resign, but this was kept secret for two months. He made his decision after de Gaulle's speech of March 11, 1961, and fixed the date for the execution of the plan which the colonels, who were removed after the week of the barricades, had prepared for the seizure of power both in Algiers and in Paris.

The public buildings in Algiers were occupied during the night of April 21–22. The insurgents encountered no organized resistance but were obliged to use part of their forces to block the barracks that housed units loyal to the government. They took Oran. The situation in Constantine was confused.

In Paris, the police seized the members of the army's general staff who were responsible for the metropolitan plot. De Gaulle remained calm in the face of the storm, which "brought out his capabilities and skill."[12] A state of emergency was proclaimed. On Sunday, April 23, de Gaulle addressed a brief message to the nation. He condemned the authors of the insurrection and released the soldiers from their duty to obey them. He invoked Article 16 of the constitution which gave full powers to the president of the Republic whenever the republic's institutions or the integrity of its national territory were threatened. The labor unions unanimously decided to stage an hour-long protest strike on Monday the 24th.

By the end of the day on the 23rd, Challe had under his control about fifteen regiments, but not all the subaltern or noncommissioned officers had rallied to these units. The indecision of the troops became more pronounced in Oran and Constantine on the 24th, while the navy dissociated itself entirely from the insurgents. On the 25th Challe, followed by the commanders of the mutinous units, gave himself up. Salan went into hiding. Three generals and more than two hundred officers were relieved of their commands.

While the insurrection lasted the conscripted soldiers exerted pressure on their officers. The army, except for the shock troops, who were convinced that the victory which had seemed so close in April 1960 had been stolen from them, was not ready for sedition.[13] The majority of the officers preferred a wait-and-see policy. The government's firm stand, the success of the strike in metropolitan France, the attitude of the army contingent—all these swept away hesitation and stifled the plot.

[12] Fauvet and Planchais, *La fronde*, 157.
[13] *Ibid.*, 248.

Negotiations and the Subversion of the O.A.S.

Eleven months separated the collapse of the generals' *putsch* on April 25, 1961, and the signing of the Evian Accords on March 18, 1962. This interlude was highlighted by negotiations between France and the G.P.R.A., by the unilateral declarations of the president of the Republic, and by the subversive acts of the Organization of the Secret Army (O.A.S.) in Algeria and in France.

Among foreigners and the Muslims of Algeria, de Gaulle's prestige was at its zenith in late April. On the other hand, the morale of the French of Algeria was at its lowest point, despite the immediate resumption of attacks by the O.A.S. Would this fleeting moment be seized to begin serious negotiations at long last? De Gaulle hoped so. His address of May 8 resumed the themes of his speech of April 11: recognition of the internal and external sovereignty of Algeria, a threat of realignment in case of secession and rupture.

Negotiations began on May 20 at Evian. That very day the French government ordered a unilateral thirty-day truce in Algerian territory. Offensive operations would not be resumed. The first week of discussion was devoted to a face-to-face presentation of the basic issues. Disagreement centered on the meaning of self-determination, the future status of minorities; the participation of the various currents of opinion in the elaboration of new institutions, and finally on the political regime for the Sahara. The F.L.N. claimed that the referendum must allow the Algerian people to express their desire for independence; France looked upon it as a means of ratifying preliminary agreements to guarantee cooperation. The French government wanted the political rights and guarantees to be given to the European community of Algeria as a whole. Insisting on the integrity of the Algerian people, the F.L.N. held, on the contrary, that Algerian nationality must result from an option: Frenchmen in Algeria who did not wish to become Algerian nationals could remain in Algeria, but they must have the status of foreigners. Furthermore, the F.L.N. wanted to be recognized not merely as the spokesman of the fighting forces but also as the sole representative of the Muslim community. The French delegation wanted the Sahara to remain a separate political entity within Algeria. The F.L.N., on the contrary, stressed the integrity of Algerian territory, at the same time distinguishing between the principle of sovereignty and the right to exploit the resources in hydrocarbons. In view of the obstacles, the French delegation decided on June 13 to adjourn the discussion.

Thereupon both the government, in a statement of June 28, 1961, and de Gaulle, in the course of a visit to Lorraine on June 29 and July 2, reminded the people of the two kinds of alternatives: either a sovereign Algerian state, associated with France and aided by her, within which "the two communities would cooperate in the service of Algeria" (Verdun); or a realignment, to protect "those Algerians who do not want to be part of a country in the throes of chaos and who would like to remain linked to France." (Épinal). Since his press conference of September 16 on self-determination, de Gaulle had been holding in reserve the solution of partition. It was his opinion that the threat of partition would produce organic cooperation between the communities.

The F.L.N. had always been opposed to partition. In accordance with the logic of nationalism, it underscored the integrity of the territory and the integrity of the Algerian people. It was ready to invoke self-determination, but without acknowledging the existence of an organic French community. De Gaulle's insistence on calling for a regrouping led the G.P.R.A. to mobilize Muslim public opinion. On June 30 it published the following statement: "The threat of partition is designed to encourage the creation of zones of French sovereignty within our country." July 5 was proclaimed a "national Day against Partition." More than three hundred people were killed or wounded in Algeria that day. In the National Assembly the Muslim deputies displayed their solidarity by refraining from participating in the debates.

The idea of partition was almost unanimously condemned in Parliament, especially by Guy Mollet. In the National Assembly on June 29 Georges Bidault did likewise. In the Senate, Gaston Defferre came out against it on July 5. Speaking for the government, Louis Joxe did not defend this solution with much conviction. Alain Peyrefitte, Gaullist member of the National Assembly, discussed the debates in a book published in December 1961. It seemed to him "that evacuation would be difficult to avoid if there was no regrouping."[14] He argued with good reason that self-determination should not mean the annihilation of a minority by the majority and that "identification of the majority with unanimity and the absence of any right of veto for the minority is conceivable only in an ethnically and politically homogeneous population."[15]

Parliament's negative reaction did not facilitate the French delegation's task when discussions resumed at Lugrin on July 17, at a time when the French-Tunisian conflict over the base of Bizerta was growing bitter. The areas of disagreement were like those that had figured at Evian. The discussions were interrupted on the 28th at the request of the F.L.N., which refused to consider any basic question as long as its demands concerning the Sahara were not met.

[14] Alain Peyrefitte, *Faut-il partager l'Algérie?* (Paris: Plon, 1961), 7.
[15] *Ibid.*, 154.

Following the failure of the negotiations at Evian and Lugrin, the Conseil National de la Révolution Algérienne (C.N.R.A.), the highest organ of the F.L.N., met in Tripoli and proceeded to reshuffle the Provisional Government of the Algerian Republic (G.P.R.A.). Ben Khedda, a representative of the Marxist trend in the liberation movement, replaced Ferhat Abbas, who spoke for the bourgeois elements and was subsequently removed from office. This reshuffling attested a desire to endow the new Algeria with political institutions and an economic structure similar to those of the peoples' democracies, to pursue a policy of noninvolvement in the diplomatic domain, and to answer the French government's demands with a formal refusal.

Meanwhile, the French authorities in Algeria were being deprived of more and more of their real power. The Muslims obeyed the orders of the F.L.N., the French of Algeria obeyed the commands of the Organization of the Secret Army (O.A.S.), which was supported by officers and enlisted men who had deserted, as well as by members of every class of the European population. The power of the O.A.S. was so great by November and December 1961 that people wondered whether a Franco-Algerian agreement, even if signed, could be applied on the spot.

Alluding to the situation in January 1962, Edgar Faure wrote: "Things have come to such a pass that negotiations can no longer be conducted on the basis of a compromise. To bargain at this point would no longer be to negotiate but to break off relations."[16] This statement was already true after the discussions at Evian and Lugrin, which represented the last chance to settle the conflict honorably. Robert Buron observed that at the Council of Ministers on August 31, 1961, de Gaulle had said: "Our policy—and I'm surprised that people refuse to realize this—is one of disengagement."[17] The word was mentioned again on September 5. In the course of this press conference, the general made his first major concession to the nationalist thesis. It concerned the Sahara: "Our line of conduct is one that safeguards our interests and takes realities into account. These are our interests: the free exploitation of the oil and gas which we have discovered and will continue to discover. . . . The realities are that there is not a single Algerian, I am sure, that does not believe that the Sahara should belong to Algeria." This unilateral concession was presented as a kind of bonus for association between France and the new Algeria. A further step was taken after the bloody riots of November 1 in Algeria and Ben Bella's hunger strike. In the course of a trip to Corsica and Provence, de Gaulle admitted that the F.L.N. had on its side "most of the Algerian population" (Bastia, November 7). A second

[16] Edgar Faure, preface to *Année politique 1962*, 11.
[17] Robert Buron, *Carnets politiques de la guerre d'Algérie* (Paris: Plon, 1965), 120.

major concession, the public acknowledgement of the F.L.N. as the sole representative, was thus accorded unilaterally. Thereupon, secret contacts were resumed between the French government and the F.L.N., such a procedure having been thought preferable to official negotiations.

De Gaulle's speech of December 29 confirmed his policy of disengagement. He announced the repatriation in January 1962 of two divisions and some of the air forces. The beginning of the year was marked by a new outburst of terrorism.

On February 5, de Gaulle let it be known that the negotiations were nearing an end. He refrained from mentioning the organic cooperation of the communities. This tacit renunciation of the creation of minority institutions in Algeria was the third major concession to the F.L.N. and constituted an acknowledgement of the unity of the Algerian people.

Secret contacts were resumed at les Rousses on February 12 and 13. The French delegation, headed by Louis Joxe, included two other ministers who had been former members of Parliament under the Fourth Republic, Robert Buron (M.R.P.) and Jean de Broglie (Independent). The plans for the accords were studied in Paris and in Tripoli. The final Evian negotiations took place from March 7 to 18.

The Evian Accords

On March 18 de Gaulle and Ben Khedda simultaneously announced a cease-fire and the conclusion of the accords. The general was intent on justifying the principle of association: "The imperative needs and desires of Algerians for everything that will contribute to their development, their current need for economic, technical, cultural progress, the presence in their midst of a large number of people of French origin who play an important role today and are expected by France to play an even more important role in local activities, the strength of the Muslims who come from the opposite shores of the Mediterranean to work or study in our cities all these make it mandatory for Algeria to associate itself with our country." Ben Khedda stressed that "the terms of the accords conform to the revolutionary principles we have affirmed time and again: 1. The territorial integrity of Algeria on the basis of its present borders, which excludes any open or secret attempt to partition the north of Algeria, and also any attempt to sever our country from the Sahara; 2. the independence of Algeria . . .; 3. the unity of the Algerian people—this has been recognized; France will give up the idea of an Algeria composed of diverse communities . . .; 4. recognition of the G.P.R.A. as the sole spokesman and authorized representative of the Algerian people." Ben Khedda added: "We have resolved the problem of the Europeans of Algeria within the framework of sovereignty for the

Algerian state. We have discarded the notion of 'community' and the principle of double citizenship, which would impair the future unity of the Algerian state and jeopardize its evolution."

The accords comprised measures pertaining to the transitional period—the implementation of a cease-fire, the exercise of full powers before the balloting, the regulations of voting procedures for the plebiscite on self-determination—and also regarding the asssociation of an independent Algerian state with France. The cease-fire accords prohibited recourse to violence. They provided for the freezing of the F.L.N. forces in their present positions and ruled that the French forces would take steps to station troops in such a way as to avoid any contact. From the start of the cease-fire until the balloting on self-determination, the Provisional Executive (its members, predominantly Muslims, were to be appointed by the French government but with the official approval of the G.P.R.A.) would have *de facto* sovereignty; whereas France would retain only nominal sovereignty. As for the balloting on self-determination, the choice was no longer to be between the maintenance of the status of a French province, independence by breaking all ties with France, or independence by cooperation with France. Only one question would be asked of the Algerian voters: "Do you wish Algeria, now an independent state, to cooperate with France under the conditions set forth by the declaration of March 19, 1962?" This was not a choice but the predetermination of a solution recommended by both parties to the agreement.

What did the solution calling for independence and cooperation involve? The sovereign Algerian state would guarantee the safety of persons and property. Reprisals for war damage were prohibited. Having acquired a common legal status, French Algerians and Muslims would be given a three-year period in which to choose between becoming Algerian nationals and remaining in Algeria as privileged foreigners. France and Algeria would accord each other preferential commercial treatment and Algeria would continue to belong to the Franc Zone and to insure freedom of transfer. All Frenchmen would be entirely free to take with them their goods or capital, if they decided to leave Algeria. Should their legal rights be curtailed as a consequence, for example, of agrarian reform, they would receive "a prior equitable indemnity." French concerns in Algeria would be allowed to continue doing business without discrimination. The Sahara oil code would be enforced for all mining claims already accorded and preferential rights would be given to French companies in the distribution of new permits. In exchange for these guarantees, France promised for a three-year period to give as much financial aid as it had in the past, and to provide cultural and technical assistance. On the military level, France would retain its air force and naval bases at Mers-el-Kébir for fifteen years and its atomic testing site in the Sahara for five. Robert Buron noted that this clause conflicted with the policy of noninvolvement laid down by the G.P.R.A. Yet, during the talks at Rousses "our spokesmen knew that this was a first and essential condition in any effort to come to an understanding and they were resigned to accepting it."[18]

Parliamentary debates began on March 20, tinged sometimes with violence and always with sadness. Three major questions were raised: The first was asked by Maurice Faure: "Are our accords binding on the future government of Algeria, and to what extent?" Louis Joxe gave an embarrassed answer: this was not a matter of an "accord concluded by one state with another. . . . The accords submitted to the people of Algeria will involve Algeria itself and . . . they will be imposed upon the Algerian state." The second question was whether France could invoke constraining sanctions in case the terms of accord were not carried out. According to Pascal Arrighi, "everything depended upon whether the future Algerian government would show some moderation in return for French aid." The third question had to do with the protection of Algerians of the Muslim faith who were not French citizens. Several speakers voiced concern for the fate of those Muslims who had sided with France. Once again Joxe gave an embarrassed answer: "Legally speaking, all Algerians are French as soon as they set foot in France. . . . The fact that they are free to move about entitles Muslims to the assistance, if they should need it, that France gives to all its people."

Neither the Assembly nor the Senate voted on this issue.

In an article in *Le Monde*, the opinion of the opposition was summarized by Alfred Fabre-Luce: the Evian accords "established an F.L.N.-dominated government without any prior consultation; they narrowly limited the amount of time during which the French army would remain in Algeria, and offered minorities guarantees that could be swiftly revoked. It was capitulation without defeat."[19] Ben Bella's statement to the April Congress of the F.L.N. seemed to confirm this view: "The compromise peace concluded at Evian will result in a blocking of the revolution if the provisions of this accord are not revised in such a way as to serve our national interests."

The Period of Transition

The referendum was to take place on April 8. The following question was put to the French voters: "Do you approve of the law submitted to the French people by the president of the Republic concerning the accords to be concluded and the measure to be taken on the question of Algeria, in

[18] *Ibid.*, 221, 242.
[19] Alfred Fabre-Luce, in *Le Monde*, Mar. 29, 1962.

accordance with the government's declarations of March 19, 1962?" All the parties advised their members to vote "yes," with the exception of the Independents, who left the decision to the voters. The people answered with an overwhelming "yes" in favor of peace. The affirmative ballots represented 65 per cent of the registered voters and 91 per cent of all the votes cast. The results were more favorable than the outcome of the referendum of January 8, 1961, on the question of self-determination.

After the arrest of Salan at the end of April, the French community gave up the struggle. The O.A.S. resorted to a scorched-earth policy that culminated in the burning of the University of Algiers. The Provisional Executive, installed on April 7, began negotiations on May 18 with the head of the O.A.S. of Algiers, Jean-Jacques Susini. An agreement was concluded on June 17. Violence soon subsided but the exodus of the population quickened. The majority of the emigrants left Algeria on July 1. By the end of 1962, only 200,000 French nationals remained.[20] As soon as the Evian accords were signed the F.L.N. advanced its troops. Robert Abdesselam said this about the cease-fire on April 26: "What has happened is the very reverse of the situation envisaged by the accords. It is the Army of National Liberation that in effect occupies all of Algeria and it is the French troops who are frozen in their present positions." Under these circumstances there could be no guaranteed protection for the Muslims that were loyal to France, whether they were local representatives, bureaucrats, members of reserve units, or conscripts. There were in all 200,000 to 250,000 men, approximately a million people if we include their families. Stripped of arms, the reserves were at the mercy of their compatriots. The instructions of the high commissioner and of the commander-in-chief, which Abdesselam quoted in the National Assembly on April 26, warranted his statement that "the number of 'faithful' to be repatriated was, at all costs, to be kept extremely low." And in fact only 12,000 men—40,000 including the members of their families—were sent to France.[21] The phrase, "disgraceful abandonment," which Abdesselam used, was not too strong.

At the start of the campaign for the referendum on self-determination due to take place on July 1, de Gaulle made an astounding speech. On May 8 he said: "When we grappled with this problem in 1958, we found that . . . an attempt at usurpation was taking shape in Algiers. . . . At the same time, the Muslim rebellion . . . offered the French community only one choice: a traveling bag or a coffin." Jean Lecanuet's comment is pertinent: "To denounce the May 13, 1958 usurpation to which he owed power and which he carefully failed to condemn at the time; to speak of a traveling bag or a

[20] *Année politique 1962*, 341.
[21] Marcel-Edmond Naegelen, *Une route plus large que longue* (Paris: Robert Laffont, 1964), 126.

coffin when the Algerian refugees were pouring into France to escape terrorism; to depict an Algerian policy that took four years to solve (only to culminate in the negotiated solutions that May 13 tried to prevent) as continuity and sternness . . . —all these features of his speech not only reveal absurd paradoxes and a desire to remake history for his own glorification, but an evasion of the facts."

Efforts to organize an Algerian "Party of Europeans" failed. Susini urged the Europeans to vote "yes." The Party of the Algerian People, a new version of the M.N.A. of Messali Hadj, was excluded from the electoral campaign. In the referendum of July 1, 99.72 per cent of all the ballots cast (representing 91 per cent of the registered voters) were affirmative.

The proclamation of the independence of Algeria took place on July 3. The jurisdictions that had been preserved by the French government since the Evian accords were transferred to the Provisional Executive. "After French disorders had marked the end of French sovereignty, Algerian disorders marked the introduction of Algerian sovereignty."[22] A conflict that arose between Ben Khedda and Ben Bella grew bitter. Ben Bella controlled the Province of Oran, won over Kabylia, and triumphed over Ben Khedda in Algiers with the help of Colonel Boumedienne's troops. Civil war was brought to an end on September 5 amid cries of "baraket" ("that's enough"). On September 20 elections to the National Constituent Assembly were held. They merely ratified the list of candidates designated by Ben Bella's political bureau. The democratic people's Republic of Algeria was proclaimed on September 25; the first Algerian ministry presided over by Ben Bella was constituted on the 29th; and Algeria was admitted to the United Nations on October 8.

The Balance Sheet

The Algerian war had lasted four years under the Fifth Republic. A massive exodus of French nationals, abandonment of the Muslims who had remained loyal to France, many Frenchmen left to the mercies of a government of Marxist inclination, whose chief made no secret of his intention to "revise" the Evian accords—such was the situation at the end of the period of transition.

How can one explain this "capitulation without defeat?" It was a difficult game to play, of course. De Gaulle had been brought to power by both the champions of integration (the French nationals of Algeria and the élite of the professional army) and by the advocates of peace—the bulk of public opinion in metropolitan France. He could not satisfy all of them nor could he do everything at once.

[22] Edgar Faure, preface to *Année politique 1962*, 11.

On three different occasions France's position *vis-à-vis* the F.L.N. was relatively favorable. In September 1958, after the first referendum, all the French and a majority of the Muslims expressed their confidence in the general. During the summer of 1959, successful military operations directed by Challe dangerously weakened the internal rebellion. In April 1961, the failure of the revolt of the generals gave the chief of state additional prestige. De Gaulle failed to take advantage of any one of these three situations to reach a speedy agreement. In October 1958 he began by offering the "Peace of the Brave." He believed that the proposal of an armistice coming from him prior to any political negotiation would be accepted immediately by the rebels. He was disappointed by their categorical refusal. Was it this disappointment that prompted him to postpone any option on the future status of Algeria? The policy of pacification according to the Challe plan, and industrialization according to the Constantine plan, would have been consonant with internal autonomy—if that were still possible—as well as with independence for Algeria in association with France.

In his speech of September 1959 on self-determination, de Gaulle adopted a method, offered a triple option, made a secret choice, and uttered a threat. Thereupon he made and also provoked ambiguous and contradictory statements. The option he offered the voters was integration, secession, or association. His secret choice was independence by association rather than independence by secession. The veiled threat was to regroup with the purpose of preventing secession. In case of association, de Gaulle expected to obtain the organic cooperation of the communities, in other words a minority status, of the Lebanese type, for the European community. His words were ambiguous because de Gaulle fostered, for the benefit of the army and the French nationals in Algeria, the myth of a solution in which he himself did not believe, the myth of a French Algeria. From September 1959 until the recall of Challe in April 1960 ambiguity reigned. But after his allusion to an "Algerian Republic" in November 1960 de Gaulle no longer could speak in ambiguous terms. From then on the cards were on the table, and many Europeans sought refuge in subversion or in the shock troops that were preparing the putsch of April 1961.

The decision to negotiate on the basis of independence by association was made toward the end of 1960. Actual negotiations were begun at Evian in May 1961, immediately following the putsch. The situation was far less favorable than in September 1959 after Challe's military victories. The veiled threat to regroup was more clearly formulated in June 1961 but it grew less and less meaningful as French authority in Algeria weakened as a result of the O.A.S. attacks. Ten months elapsed between the first and the second Evian meetings. Two major concessions had been made in de Gaulle's unilateral declarations of September and November 1961 to the

F.L.N. and were therefore not subject to bargaining: the political union of the Sahara with Algeria, and the right of the F.L.N. to be the sole representative of the Muslims in November. The concession that was to have the most serious consequences, because it fixed the conditions for a cease-fire, was agreed to in February 1962; it meant surrendering the organic status of the European community. This was to result, after the Evian accords were signed, in an exodus of French nationals and in the total "Algerianization" of the territory.

The Fifth Republic's policy is open to criticism on four counts: the delays in negotiation, the concept of a referendum on self-determination, the use of the threat to regroup, and the refusal to accept international arbitration.

In a war of decolonization, time works against the mother country. If the general had made his private choice by September 1959 why did he wait until the end of 1960 to negotiate? The deliberate ambiguity of his statements did him no service in the long run. A conflict with the French of Algeria was inevitable. The longer it was postponed the weaker French authority became in its dealings with the Algerian rebels. And why did he let ten months elapse between the first and second Evian accords, since recognition of the F.L.N. as the sole representative of the Muslims and union with the Sahara were inevitable?

Although the principle of self-determination, or the right of the Algerians to decide their own fate, is an excellent thing, its application was dangerous for the French community because of the single electoral college. And it is true that the solution of independence by association, which was first de Gaulle's secret, then his avowed preference, was necessary in order to preserve the rights of the minority in a basically federal regime. But a single electoral college "made it possible for the Muslim majority to decide the fate of the French minority."[23] The majority vote of a single electoral college denudes the federal solution of its substance.

From that point on, the "organic cooperation of the communities," or, to put it differently, the minority status of the Europeans of Algeria, could be negotiated only with the aid of a threat to regroup. It was a belated threat because in 1961 a change occurred in the relative strength of the armed forces which was deleterious to France; it was also a threat that was not understood by the French of Algeria or by metropolitan France since both were impervious to federalist conceptions. The parliamentary debates of July 1961 show that the French politicians did not perceive that regrouping would give the European minority and the pro-French Muslims a chance to secede in case the F.L.N. refused to grant them a bona fide federal status.

[23] Maurice Allais, *Les Accords d'Evian* (Paris: L'Esprit Nouveau, 1962), 135.

Experience shows that international guarantees facilitate the establishment and maintenance of minority status for an ethnic-religious group. The Algerian problem is an international one insofar as it concerns the entire Muslim world and the security of the Atlantic Alliance (since Algeria lies within the geographical zone covered by the pact). But de Gaulle always maintained that the Algerian problem must be solved by France alone, without the interference of foreign countries. In his opinion, international arbitration was not to be countenanced because it would have reflected on the full sovereignty of the French nation. "From the moment that the French state decided not to exercise this sovereignty, Algeria was handed over to the Algerian state—in fact, to the G.P.R.A.—automatically and without any restrictions."[24]

The weariness of the public in metropolitan France served de Gaulle's purpose. Once the French had left, he planned to carry out a broad policy of cooperation with the new states in North and Black Africa upon whom France had bestowed independence. Independence and generalized cooperation afforded France a new kind of freedom and a new field of action. This is the meaning of Edgar Faure's remark in his preface to *l'Année politique 1962*: "Thus, if one looks carefully at the objectives of French foreign policy—its European and worldwide ambitions—one may say that success of a kind resulted from the very magnitude of the failure."[25]

[24] René Courtin, in *Réforme*, Apr. 7, 1962.
[25] Edgar Faure, preface to *Année politique 1962*, 11.

2

From the Franco-African Community to Independence

THE LAW OF JUNE 3, 1958, called upon the goverment to draft a constitutional law to the following effect: "The Constitution must permit the organization of the Republic's relations with the peoples associated with it." Actually, the difficulties resulting from decolonization under the Fourth Republic, from the Algerian war and the application of the "Loi Cadre"* of 1956 on overseas territories, required a complete recasting of section VIII of the constitution of 1946. In his speech of June 13 de Gaulle added to the number of "enormous problems" he had to face that of "organizing, in accordance with the federal principle, our country's ties to the peoples of Africa and Madagascar with whom we are associated."

The Constitutional Consultative Committee, established by the law of June 3, included deputies from the two large parties of Black Africa, the Rassemblement Démocratique Africain (R.D.A.) and the Parti du Regroupement Africain (P.R.A.). Félix Houphouët-Boigny, minister of state, helped to prepare the governmental draft. The two parties differed about the immediate future of French-speaking Tropical Africa. Complying with the resolution adopted at the Congress of Bamako in 1952, the R.D.A. urged that between France and the overseas territories an egalitarian federal state should be constituted. It should be composed of autonomous states with a federal government and parliament. The P.R.A., which recently had

* Translator's note: The "Loi Cadre" of 1956 provided for universal adult suffrage and greater local participation in government. It paved the way for the achievement of independence by the overseas territories.

acquired a parliamentary nucleus in the National Assembly, held its constitutive assembly on July 25 at Cotonou. The final resolution, supported by Senghor, demanded immediate independence for the peoples of French-speaking Tropical Africa and the admission of the African states and France into a confederation. A few days before, on July 18, the R.D.A. and the P.R.A. deputies had agreed to request the head of the government to recognize the right of their countries to self-determination—in other words, their right to independence. On July 29 a lively debate took place in the Constitutional Consultative Assembly between the champions of federation and the advocates of confederation. De Gaulle, speaking before the committee on August 8, firmly rejected the P.R.A.'s suggestion of a confederation and stated in unequivocal terms that the overseas territories would have a choice between secession and association with the Community. (He indicated a marked preference for the word "community" rather than "federation.") Had he then adopted the R.D.A.'s notion of an egalitarian federation? This was the basic question.

According to the constitution of 1958, the republic comprised metropolitan France and the overseas provinces and territories. The preamble stated that "the Republic offers those overseas territories that manifest a desire to belong to it, new institutions . . . conceived with a view to their democratic evolution." Article I states: "The Republic and the peoples of the overseas territories, who voluntarily adopt the present Constitution, establish a Community" whose institutions are defined in section XII of the constitution.

Theoretically, the overseas territories were free to choose one of four solutions: the status quo within the republic; the status of an overseas province; the new status of a member state of the Community; and lastly, secession which, under the name of independence, consisted in breaking all ties that bound them to France. French-speaking Tropical Africa and Madagascar rejected the first two solutions. In this referendum on the constitution, an affirmative vote was an act of free choice signifying acceptance of the principle of association with the Community, whereas a negative vote meant refusal, and consequently secession.

The member states were granted internal autonomy and the Community was empowered to handle foreign policy, defense, monetary matters, and joint economic and financial questions. The president of the Republic was to preside over and represent the Community. Moreover, he was to preside over the executive council of the Community, which included heads of the governments of member states and ministers in charge of the Community's joint affairs. The executive council had no decision-making power and was not to be responsible for the government of the states. The Senate, composed of delegates from the legislative assemblies of the member states, was to function in a consultative, not in a legislative capacity. All of the Community's legislation was to be drafted in accordance with the rulings of the president, which would require no countersignature.

What was the nature of the Community? Was it an egalitarian federation? Michel Debré, in his report on the new constitution to the Council of State, was the first to speak to the question: "It is a regime based on the authority of those politicians who are responsible for each state, the supreme arbiter being the president of the Community." The minister of justice added: "This Community needs a central power that will be responsible to the president of the Republic."[1] To be sure, the Community had certain features of a federal regime: the division of responsibilities between the states and the Community, the states' participation in the founding and functioning of common institutions. But it lacked the characteristics of a federal state, which consists in "the existence of common organs endowed with real decision-making power on governmental and legislative levels."[2] In reality, the Community did not have a federal legislature, and the federal executive comprised only the president, not the executive council, a collegial body.

Contrary to Article I of the constitution, the Community was not based on the equality of peoples. The predominance of the French Republic was evident in the fact that the president of the Republic and the president of the Community were one and the same, and in the concentration of executive and legislative powers in the hands of the president. "Actually," wrote P.-F. Gonidec, "the Community was nothing more than another version of the French state"[3]—an authoritarian and centralized French state. Section XII, like all the other sections of the constitution, was designed to coincide with the views of Charles de Gaulle.

The presidential regime of a Community can be an explosive one. Marcel Merle wrote: "The experience of other federal states shows that solidarity between the member states is based first on homogeneity, then on contiguity, and finally on the equality of the other contracting parties." Merle added that the Community failed to meet a single one of the three conditions. Would it be necessary to resort to the security measures provided in Section XII—that is, the possible transfer of responsibility for the Community to one of its members? Or would the right of secession have to be invoked?[4] The answer to this question was given even before the referendum of September 28, 1958, was held.

---

[1] Michel Debré, Report to the General Assembly of the Council of State on August 27, 1958, to present the new constitution.

[2] P.-F. Gonidec, *Droit d'outremer* (Paris: Montchrétien, 1959), II, 217, 221.

[3] *Ibid.*, 222.

[4] Marcel Merle, "La constitution et les problèmes d'outre-mer," *Revue Française de Science Politique*, 1959, 159, 161.

The Referendum—Guinea Votes "No"

Before definitively deciding on the text of the constitution, de Gaulle made a tour of Africa from August 20 to August 27 to advise and sound out the politicians and voters of the overseas territories. On the 22nd at Tananarive, he declared: "The provisions that are being suggested to the peoples . . . exclude no single solution, not even that of secession," and further on: Procedures for revision will also be made available for those who prefer to go their own separate way." In Brazzaville, on the 24th, he outlined the purpose of the new institution: "I believe that this Franco-African Community is indispensable to our common political power." At Conakry, the talks de Gaulle had with Sékou Touré, the real head of the government in a one-party state, were very strained. A representative of the R.D.A., imbued with syndicalist ideas, Sékou Touré occupied a position to the left of his party. For several months he had been demanding independence for his country. He had created a species of people's democracy in Guinea. On August 23, the governor, Mauberna, handed de Gaulle the text of a controversial speech— which he did not deign to read—that Sékou Touré was about to deliver and to which the audience reacted strongly.[5] "We prefer poverty with liberty to wealth with slavery," Sékou Touré shouted. And again: "We expect to exercise our right to independence to the fullest degree but we expect to retain our ties with France. . . . The new relationship must be devoid of any paternalism." To which de Gaulle replied: "Independence has been mentioned. I will say this louder here than anywhere else—independence is available to Guinea. It can have it by voting 'no' to the proposition that has just been made; in such an event, I guarantee that metropolitan France will have no objection." Relations were broken off and all attempts at reconciliation failed. De Gaulle refused to see Sékou Touré again. He departed for Dakar where demonstrators in the crowd likewise shouted for independence. The general spoke to them: "I want to say a few words to those carrying placards. Here is what I wish to say: If they want independence let them say so on September 28."

In a solemn introduction of the constitution on September 4, the general confirmed the categorical position he had taken: "Every territory will have the means either of accepting France's proposition by its vote in the referendum, or of refusing it and in this way of breaking all ties with France." The principle was explicit: independence and membership in the Community were incompatible.

The leaders of both African parties urged their followers to vote "yes" in the referendum. In spite of the pressure exerted by his friends of the

[5] Jean Lacouture, *Cinq hommes et la France* (Paris: Editions du Seuil, 1961), 334, 342, 350.

R.D.A., Sékou Touré voted "no." But to show that he was not saying "no" to France, he suggested that the governor of Guinea should immediately proclaim that Guinea desired association with the Community on the basis of Article 88 of the constitution that stated: "The Republic or the Community can conclude accords with the states that wish to become associated with it in order to develop their civilization." The purpose of this text was obviously political. It involved the prolongation, through economic and cultural ties, of a solidarity that had existed between France and those of her former possessions that had attained independence. But the governor's message to Paris received no reply.[6]

The referendum was a huge success. Of the 14,000,000 registered voters in all the overseas territories, 9,200,000 voted "yes" and only 600,000 voted "no." The proportion of affirmative to negative votes was more than 92 per cent in ten territories, 78 per cent in two others. In Guinea, 95 per cent voted "no." Africans vote for a man or for a symbol. The people of Guinea voted for Sékou Touré.

"Then," Jean Lacouture wrote, "began the history of the second 'no,' France's 'no' to Sékou Touré." On August 23 at Conakry, de Gaulle said to his ministers and to the governor: "All right, the matter is plain: we will leave on the morning of September 29." He kept his word. A representative of the French government, Jean Risterucci, arrived at Conakry on September 28 on a special mission. He announced the repatriation of French officials, the suspension of all investments, and the total suppression of budgetary assistance to Guinea.[7] On October 2 Guinea announced its independence. On October 9, Sékou Touré repeated his offer of association with the Community. De Gaulle answered that he would first have to consult the Community. In his press conference of October 23, the general expressed contempt for Guinea. "Guinea, in our view, is a mutation but we don't know what kind." France refused to recognize Guinea and abstained from voting on its admission to the United Nations on December 12. After a first mission failed, three protocol agreements on cultural, financial, and technical questions were finally signed on January 7, 1959, and ambassadors were exchanged. The agreements have not been implemented and resentment persists. France's conduct all too often has not been devoid of a "churlish pettiness."[8]

Although the referendum solved the problem of attaching the twelve overseas territories to the Community, it did not settle the question of territorial groupings which set the P.R.A., the champion of "primary federations," against the R.D.A., which was hostile to them. Actually,

[6] *Ibid.*, 357.
[7] *Ibid.*, 352, 358.
[8] André Blanchet, "La Guinée sans la France," *Le Monde*, June 3, 1959.

between October and December 1958, each individual territory opted for the status of member state within the Community. These states adopted their constitutions between January and April 1959. The constitutions provided for a single legislative assembly and a head of state endowed with broad powers.

On December 21, 1958, de Gaulle was elected president of the Republic and president of the Community. Early in 1959, he proceeded to set up the organs of the Community, the Executive Council and the Senate, and to make presidential decisions in a centralizing spirit, in order to lay down the foreign and defense policies of the Community: "The foreign policy of the French Republic and of the Community is unique." "The army responsible for the defense of the Community is one and indivisible." (February 9, 1959.)

Furthermore, he set himself the task of guiding the two states administered by the United Nations, Togo and Cameroon, toward independence. These two states did not participate in the referendum nor were they members of the Community. Decrees promulgated on December 30, 1958, gave them a transitional status with the understanding that they would attain total independence by 1960. In English-speaking Black Africa, provisions were made for Nigeria to achieve full independence during the course of the year.

Independence in the African and Malagasy Republics

At the end of 1959, the legislative and constituent assemblies of the new African states decided in favor of individual membership in the Community, but these decisions did not settle the debate over territorial groupings that were designed to avert the "Balkanization" of Africa. There were three groupings, each different in nature, by the beginning of 1959. The first comprised the four states that emerged from former French Equatorial Africa. On June 23 these states founded the Union Douanière Equatoriale (U.D.E.) The second grouping originated in Senegal, whose leaders hoped to achieve a republic, called the Federation of Mali, combining Senegal, the Sudan, Dahomey, and Upper Volta. Only Senegal and the Sudan became members of the federation, whose constitution was adopted on June 10. The third grouping was founded at the initiative of the Ivory Coast and called itself the Conseil de l'Entente. It hoped to achieve economic and administrative cooperation by means of a customs union and the joint administration of transports. The Entente was created on April 4 between the Ivory Coast and Upper Volta; Niger and Dahomey joined it shortly thereafter. Thus, six of the seven states of former French West Africa were organized into two entities that corresponded roughly to the zones of influence of the two major African political parties; one was oriented toward Dakar under the influence of Senghor, and the other toward Abidjan under the influence of Houphouët-Boigny. The Islamic Republic of Mauritania, whose population was white, alone remained isolated from these movements.

Senghor's P.R.A. changed its name from Parti du Regroupement Africain to Parti de la Fédération Africaine (P.F.A.) in March 1959. On July 3 it passed a resolution at its constitutive congress at Dakar demanding the transformation of the Community into a "Multi-National Confederation," thus reaffirming the thesis maintained by Senghor the year before in the Consultative Constitutional Committee. At the Congress of the R.D.A. of September 5, Houphouët-Boigny reiterated his preference for a rigidly organized Franco-African entity. At the session of the executive council of the Community on September 10 and 11, two theses were debated. The premiers of Senegal and the Sudan leaned on their right to independence to demand that responsibility be transferred by negotiation from the Community to the Federation of Mali, in accordance with Article 78 of the constitution. In his press conference of November 10, de Gaulle came round to the idea which he had rejected in 1958—independence by association: "France's policy in regard to these countries is to respect and recognize their right to self-determination and at the same time to offer them the opportunity of forming an entity with France in which they would have France's assistance and France would have their participation in her worldwide activities. . . . The Community, for everyone, is effective independence and guaranteed cooperation." Negotiations with Mali began on December 13. On December 15 the Malagasy Republic asked for independence. The accords transferring responsibility were signed on April 2, 1960, for Madagascar, on April 4 for Mali. They stipulated that participation of the member states in the Community would rest henceforward on a contractual and not a constitutional basis. France would contribute her aid and the member states would cooperate in matters of foreign policy and defense.

The Community, which had been a presidential regime, was changed to a confederation. This "renewal" required a revision of the constitution, and the government proceeded to undertake it. Article 86 was completed by adding the following stipulations: "A member state of the Community can, by means of accords, become independent without thereby ceasing to belong to the Community. An independent state that is not a member of the Community can, by means of accords, become a member of the Community without sacrificing its independence." This text was adopted without enthusiasm on May 12, 1960, by the National Assembly. The Socialists, Radicals, and a large group of Independents voted against it; the M.R.P. joined forces with the U.N.R. It was adopted May 18 by a slight majority in the metropolitan Senate, after Edouard Bonnefous had put the following pertinent question: "Is it possible to follow in Algeria a policy different from the one that has been established for the rest of Africa?" On June 2 it won the almost unanimous approval of the Senate of the Community.

The bestowal of independence on Mali and Madagascar gave rise to bitterness among the leaders of the states in the Conseil de l'Entente. They believed that de Gaulle's acceptance of independence within the Community constituted a negation of the concept of a federal Franco-African Community that Houphouët-Boigny had always upheld. They further believed that broad internal autonomy and the symbolic recognition of independence within a strong and lasting federal organization would insure the stability and hasten the political maturation of the young and as yet fragile states. But a position of such wisdom was no longer acceptable to the voters. One had to go a step further than Mali. On June 3 Houphouët-Boigny in the name of the Ivory Coast and of his colleagues of Niger, Upper Volta, and Dahomey, handed de Gaulle a letter asking that all the responsibilities reserved for the Community be transferred to each of the states of the Conseil de l'Entente prior to any accord for association. They demanded that the attainment of independence be dissociated from the establishment of special ties with France. De Gaulle agreed in principle and made the following comment in his address of June 14: "We have recognized the right of self-determination for all those who are dependent on us. To refuse this right would be to deny our ideals and to provoke interminable struggles . . . for advantages that would inevitably crumble in our hands." The accords for the transfer of responsibilities were signed July 11, 1960. The independence of the four states was proclaimed early in August. The states of French Equatorial Africa adopted a procedure similar to that of Mali. Their independence was likewise proclaimed in August.

These rapid institutional changes had repercussions on the various groupings of states. The Conseil de l'Entente emerged all the stronger whereas the Federation of Mali fell apart on June 18. France recognized Senegal's independence. In September as a consequence of this, the Sudan, which still called itself the Republic of Mali, denounced its agreements of cooperation with France.

On September 21 the General Assembly of the United Nations unanimously voted the admission of the eleven African and Malagasy states sponsored by France—the question of Mauretania having been tabled as a consequence of Morocco's objections. The heads of the delegations from Africa paid their respects to France and to General de Gaulle, whose absence was remarked and regretted.

"One can no longer properly speak of the Community, if we understand by this term a political entity superior to states and having a constitution and institutions of its own," said Raymond Aron. All that is left, he added, was a number of French-speaking African republics with special ties to France.[9]

The authoritarian and centralizing structure of section XII of the constitution of 1958 was more fragile and ephemeral than that of section VIII of the constitution of 1946. The Community disappeared in three stages. Even before it had been ratified it was weakened by the "no" of Guinea, which set itself up as the protagonist for the liberation of Africa; it was shattered a year later by the Federation of Mali's request for independence; it was dissolved at the end of twenty months by the demands of the states of the Conseil de l'Entente. Two of the former overseas territories, Guinea and the ex-Sudan Mali, inclined toward the Soviet bloc.

The French Coast of Somali

According to section XI of the 1958 constitution, the overseas territories were to be collectivities within the French Republic. In the referendum of 1958, the people of French Somaliland had opted for the status of overseas territory. On August 25 and 26, 1966, when de Gaulle visited Djibouti on his way to Cambodia, violence erupted there. The demonstrators demanded independence. However, if France lost possession, the territory would at once be claimed by the Republic of Somali and Ethiopia since both used the port of Djibouti. De Gaulle immediately decided to organize a referendum for 1967. The people would be asked to choose between internal autonomy with continued aid and total secession. Displeased by the manifestations that occurred during his visit in 1966, the chief of state took the same categorical position in regard to the territory that he had assumed in 1958 in regard to Guinea; he excluded the possibility of independence by association and left only the choice of independence by secession. The referendum took place on March 19, 1967. The supporters of internal autonomy polled 22,000 votes as against 14,000 votes for the secessionists.

The disturbances in Djibouti pointed up the fragility of the ties that linked France with the few "dependent territories" she still retained. The political climate of New Caledonia, which de Gaulle visited a few days after his stop in Djibouti, also left much to be desired. The authoritarian structure of section XI of the constitution of 1958 was in turn threatened.

[9] Raymond Aron, preface to *Année politique 1960*, 9.

3

Cooperation

Purpose and Methods

COOPERATION WAS A NEW approach to the problem of relations between the former fatherland and the new states that had achieved political independence; more generally speaking, it was also a new approach to the relations between industrialized and developing countries. Little by little, as decolonization became an accomplished fact, a feeling of solidarity grew in men's minds. The Fifth Republic, which was obliged to finish the work of decolonization that the Fourth Republic had begun, drafted in less than two years plans for a policy of cooperation. The report of the Commission headed by Jean-Marcel Jeanneney was published in 1963; it defined the purpose, reasons, and methods for the new policy.

The economic objective of cooperation was to reverse the trend toward an increasing disparity between the living standards in poor and rich countries.

The need for human solidarity and universal well-being, the prospect of participating in a general evolution rather than in geographically compartmentalized sections of economic activity, should induce the rich states to give appropriate intellectual and material aid to the developing countries and "to help the assisted countries to become true nations." Seen from this perspective, "cooperation unites economics, strategy, and policy."[1]

The Fourth Republic had begun a policy of cooperation with Tunisia and Morocco in 1956, the year they achieved independence. The idea of

[1] "La politique de coopération avec les pays en voie de développement," *Report of the Study Commission*, established by the decree of March 12, 1963 (Paris, 1963), 8, 35, 47.

independence through cooperation was adopted by the Fifth Republic in its policy toward French-speaking Tropical Africa as early as 1960, after the disintegration of the Community. But the nub of de Gaulle's policy of cooperation lay in the bonds that linked Algeria and France, which the Evian accords defined. The difficulties caused by the Algerian war and subsequent Franco-Algerian cooperation affected the relations of France with Tunisia and Morocco. Finally, de Gaulle broadened the focus to include cooperation with the territories outside of the former French Union. This was an important element in his global strategy.

Two methods of cooperation were implemented concurrently. The first was bilateral and was the method preferred by the governments of the Fifth Republic. It satisfied the aims of a purely nationalist strategy. The second method was multilateral. It called for association of the African republics and Madagascar with the European Economic Community, in accordance with the principle established in response to the demands of the Fourth Republic and incorporated in the Treaty of Rome.

French-Speaking Tropical Africa and Madagascar

Regardless of whether they were signed before or after the bestowal of independence, the treaties of cooperation concluded by France with each of the African republics and with Madagascar created, on a contractual basis, privileged relations between these states and France. The purpose of the treaties was both political and economic.

On the political level, they obligated the signatories to consult each other about the matters of foreign policy. The treaties were usually accompanied by accords for military assistance that obligated France to supply army personnel, and by defense agreements stipulating that if the African states requested it to do so, the French army would intervene to reestablish order. Thus, in February 1964, French military intervention reestablished the government of Gabon which had been overthrown by a *coup d'état*. France's willingness to supply army personnel was due in part to the eagerness of several chiefs of state to put an end to the uprisings that threatened Congo-Brazzaville, Dahomey, and Togo in 1963. The defense agreements provided for the stationing of French troops in certain areas for a fixed period of time. In July 1964, it was decided to reduce their numbers. The African premiers' visits to Paris, by their frequency and solemnity, tended to emphasize political solidarity within a framework of cooperation.

Economic and cultural solidarity resulted from accords on education, technical assistance, and financial aid that were concluded over a five-year period. The states were requested to prepare annual investment plans or programs to be submitted to the Fund for Assistance and Cooperation

(F.A.C.), an organization responsible for apportioning the necessary sums. The financial policy consisted in increasing the amount of aid connected with the purchase of equipment and gradually to substitute loans at low interest for outright gifts. It also consisted in reducing subsidies for balancing the states' budgets; these were considerable in 1960 but tended to be negligible by 1965. At France's suggestion, six states—the Ivory Coast, Upper Volta Mauritania, Senegal, Dahomey, and Niger—established in May 1962 the West African Monetary Union. It was endowed with a unique central bank and, later, with a unique currency (Communauté Financière d'Afrique, C.F.A.) to which France gave unlimited guarantees. Monetary cooperation enabled the states to attenuate some of the consequences of the "Balkanization" of French-speaking Africa.

In the commercial domain, the African republics and Madagascar received preferential treatment from France. Similar arrangements were included in the multilateral preferential system established by the Treaty of Rome. This consisted of an association of overseas countries and territories with the European Economic Community. The initial convention on association was limited to five years because of the expectation that an evolution in the political status of the territories would ensue. As early as 1961, interparliamentary meetings prepared political circles in Europe and Africa for the elaboration of a new convention based on parity for the various states. The convention concluded at Yaoundé in July 1963 between the six states of the Common Market and eighteen developing states, fourteen of which belonged to the Franco-African Community, sanctioned the maintenance of the free trade zone established by the first convention. Financial and technical cooperation was broadened. The system of multinational and regional cooperation that resulted from the new association tended to tighten the ties between the African states themselves. Mali was among the associated states whereas Guinea, whose commercial and cultural relations with France had improved after Algeria achieved independence, refused to sign the Yaoundé convention. For a long time the English-speaking African states were hostile to the association. In 1965, however, the largest of them, Nigeria, entered into discussions with the E.E.C. whose power of attraction asserted itself in the field of Euro-African cooperation.

European political structures could not be transposed to Black Africa. The Africans were adopting a territorial principle which was alien to the tribal concept of power, and they went too far in developing the administrative practices introduced by the French authorities. They substituted the single-party system and authoritarian control of the state for the parliamentary regime.

Meanwhile, the tribal disputes that had been stifled under colonial rule were resumed after independence. The French-speaking Black African republics enjoyed only a few years of peace. There was a rash of *coups d'état*: in Togo in 1963, in Dahomey and in the Central African Republic in 1965, in Upper Volta in 1966, and once again in Togo early in 1967. But the chiefs of state, except those from Guinea, Mali, and Congo-Brazzaville, were more moderate than extreme. Thus—save for the above-mentioned states, and a few scattered incidents—the direction of foreign policy in general conformed to the views of the former rulers. In the spring of 1961, most of the young republics expressed the hope that the discussions at Evian between France and the F.L.N. would lead to a peace treaty with Algeria.

In February 1965, after two ephemeral cabinet changes, thirteen French-speaking republics founded the Organisation Commune Africaine et Malgache (O.C.A.M.) with its headquarters at Yaoundé. Two republics failed to join it—Guinea and Mali—even though Soviet economic aid which had been given to Guinea in 1959 and to Mali in 1960 was unsuccessful. China also attempted to exert a political influence in Black Africa through diplomatic missions and offers of technical assistance. France's recognition of China in 1964 did not have any notable impact because, within the space of a few years, the Chinese "cooperators" became unpopular in most of French-speaking Black Africa, with the exception of Congo-Brazzaville.

Tunisia and Morocco

Soon after he assumed power, de Gaulle undertook to establish good relations with Tunisia and Morocco. On June 2, 1958, he sent cordial messages to President Bourguiba and to King Hassan II. He lost no time in launching a series of negotiations to settle outstanding problems. The most delicate of these was Tunisia's demand for the evacuation of French troops. Following an incident at the Algerian-Tunisian border, Tunisia asked the Security Council of the United Nations to protect its frontiers. On June 17 a Franco-Tunisian accord was concluded. It stipulated that all the French military forces stationed in Tunisia, except those in Bizerta, would be withdrawn within a four-month period. It also announced the opening of negotiations on the future status of Bizerta. The terms of the accord were approximately identical with those that the Gaillard government (which had been overthrown on this issue by Gaullist opposition) had envisaged a few months earlier, in conjunction with an Anglo-American good-will mission. Following the conclusion of the accord, Tunisia withdrew its request. On June 14 a more limited accord was concluded with Morocco for the withdrawal of French troops from western and southern Morocco.

Tunisia and Morocco, who had invited the representatives of the F.L.N. to a North African conference at Tunis on June 17, recognized the Provisional Government of the Algerian Republic as soon as it was created on

September 20, 1958. On October 1, both states joined the Arab League. By this act they apparently discarded the opportunity of joining the Franco-African Community, a move made possible by Section XIII (Article 88) of the 1958 constitution. Tunisia and Morocco thereby manifested their solidarity with the Maghreb and the Arabic-Muslim world.

Political relations between France and Tunisia alternated between trust and provocation. In October 1959, perhaps in connection with the Franco-Tunisian commercial accord, Bourguiba expressed satisfaction with de Gaulle's announcement of a policy of self-determination for Algeria. In 1960 he protested against the explosion of an atomic bomb by France in the Sahara and immediately made demands in regard to Bizerta which were given partial satisfaction. In February 1961 de Gaulle invited Bourguiba to Rambouillet, hoping for his support in connection with the resumption of negotiations with the F.L.N. On July 5, after the failure of the first Evian accords, Bourguiba delivered a vigorous speech on the subject of Bizerta. On the 18th, the day after the resumption of Franco-Algerian discussions at Lugrin, he encouraged several thousand people to stage a demonstration in favor of blocking the base. De Gaulle answered on the 19th by sending parachutists. The counterattack was bloody. Tunisia broke off diplomatic relations, and on July 20 it appealed to the Security Council. The Council ruled in favor of an "armed forces' retreat to prior positions," which caused a conflict between France and the United Nations. On instructions from Paris, the admiral in command of the Bizerta base refused to receive the United Nations' secretary-general, who was conducting an on-the-spot investigation. Moreover, after he had made certian suggestions to the French government, Dag Hammarskjöld received a blistering letter from the minister of foreign affairs. It seemed that Bourguiba, anticipating that the Lugrin talks would collapse, wanted to break off relations with France and join the Arab chiefs of state. As for de Gaulle, he responded to the affront with a violence that shocked French and international public opinion. He chose none the less to confront Bourguiba rather than to allow the United Nations to arbitrate. On July 22 an accord was concluded between the two parties for a cease-fire; negotiations for evacuation of Bizerta culminated in an additional accord on September 29. Meanwhile, the General Assembly of the United Nations voted an Afro-Asian resolution morally condemning France. There were sixty-six votes supporting it, including four NATO members (Denmark, Iceland, Norway and Turkey) and nine French-speaking African republics, including Madagascar. Bizerta was evacuated once and for all on October 15, 1963.

Economic relations between France and Tunisia were administered by a customs union. But after independence this union was no longer viable owing to the difference in the structures of the two economies and the entry of France into the Common Market. In September 1959, following a request from Tunisia, a preferential commercial and tariff convention replaced the former customs union. The convention survived the Bizerta affair.

In August 1963, France granted Tunisia financial aid. In April 1964 Bourguiba asked the French government to begin negotiations for the repossession by Tunisia of the lands that had belonged to colonial France. This request was in harmony with the expropriation measures that Ben Bella had taken in Algeria. France suspended all financial assistance and denounced the commercial convention of 1959. As a result of the latter action, Tunisian exports to France immediately decreased by two-thirds.

The rigor of the economic reprisals against Tunisia contrasted sharply with France's long-suffering attitude toward Algeria. And this was all the more striking because Tunisia's political attitude toward the Western democracies was favorable, whereas Bourguiba's relations with Nasser and the Arab League were frequently strained.

France's relations with Morocco were less stormy even though in 1959 Morocco had maintained a wait-and-see attitude toward the policy of self-determination in Algeria. In 1960 Morocco requested and obtained the withdrawal of the remaining French troops; by the beginning of 1961 the Casablanca and Agadir bases were evacuated. In 1960 Morocco, backed by the Arab League, claimed Mauretania, but France did not take this seriously. During the month of June 1963, King Hassan II paid an official visit to de Gaulle. It was a prelude to the conclusion of a Franco-Moroccan agreement to cooperate. This showed that the French colony in Morocco (155,000 people) was now more important than its counterpart in Algeria.

Because of the "open-door" policy laid down by the Act of Algeciras, Morocco was less integrated than Tunisia into the French economy. Unable therefore to give it preferential treatment, France had instituted tariff quotas, especially for wine and wheat. This system was continued after independence. Some of these quotas were reduced in 1960 but were restored and even augmented in 1962. This resulted in an increase in exports to France. The cooperation agreement concluded in July 1963, provided for an increase in technical and cultural assistance and for financial aid whose sum was approximately equal to that allocated to Tunisia a little later. In October 1963 Morocco, like Tunisia, embarked upon a program of agrarian reform similar to Algeria's. The Moroccan state expropriated more than one-third of the land owned by Frenchmen. The agrarian reform resulted in a flight of capital, the disappearance of foreign exchange, and the restriction of imports from France. In July 1964 an agreement for the partial indemnification of the French colonials was concluded, after which France resumed the financial aid she had suspended. Political relations between France and Morocco became tense in November 1965 over the kidnapping, on French territory, of Mehdi Ben Barka, the head of the opposition in Morocco.

Morocco, whose pro-Western sympathies were as pronounced as those of Tunisia, definitely received better treatment than the latter in the domain of commerce. Although the technical and cultural assistance accorded to the two former protectorates was rather generous, the financial aid earmarked for these two basically agricultural states seems very modest in comparison to that given to Algeria, whose resources in hydrocarbons yield a large revenue.

Algeria

Algeria was in a critical economic state when it became independent. After the departure of the French, economic activity was slowed down in all sectors of the exchange economy, while the migration of a large number of people because of the war disturbed the subsistence economy. The government tried to elude the financial as well as the political and social obligations imposed on it by the Evian accords.

Two thousand French nationals disappeared during the summer of 1962 and numerous acts of aggression were committed against the *harkis*.* In March 1963 the government adopted a nationality law which created two categories of citizens: Algerians who, before independence, had had the civil status of Muslims or nationals, and Europeans of Algeria who had chosen Algerian nationality. This distinction, which contravened the Evian accords, tended to create an exclusively Arab-Muslim nation. Few French acquired the Algerian nationality. The number of French nationals residing in Algeria fell to 150,000 by the beginning of 1964.

After the voluntary or forced departure of Frenchmen, their agricultural properties were declared "vacant" by decree. The exploitation of these lands was entrusted to administrative committees appointed by the Algerian government. On March 19, 1963, Ben Bella announced that 1,200,000 hectares of vacant property were being transferred, by unilateral decision, to the administrative committees. Acting again without the consent of the French government and in violation of the Evian accords, the Algerian government expropriated on March 30 the lands of the colonist magnates who had continued to farm their fields. A French protest lodged on April 5 was purely pro forma. The last French agriculturalists, numbering about five or six thousand, were dispossessed of their land in October 1963. They were to be partially indemnified by an appropriation deducted from France's subsidy to Algeria for equipment.

* Translator's note: *harkis* are Algerian Muslim auxiliary fighters, many of whom are mounted on horses.

An Algerian decree of May 9, 1963, placed under the protection of the state private property of all categories—agricultural, commercial and industrial—"whose acquisition, exploitation, or utilization may disturb the order and peace of society." This decree was used in September 1963 to nationalize without indemnification Algeria's last three French daily newspapers. This discriminatory measure threatened the freedom of speech of the French in Algeria. In October and November several large enterprises were nationalized, and the definitive nationalization of vacant property was announced.

Soon the military clauses were under attack. Ben Bella spoke haughtily on April 16, 1963, one month after the explosion of an atomic bomb in the Sahara: "Confronted with the fire of reality," he declared, "there are certain clauses (of the Evian accords), military clauses, for example, that we cannot accept." On May 2 France promised that she would not explode any more bombs in the Sahara. By June 1964, one year prior to the stipulated date, France had evacuated all her troops from Algerian territory. This was the moment Ben Bella chose to assert that "the temporary presence of French troops in the Mers-el-Kébir and Sahara bases will soon be dealt with."

The regulations pertaining to hydrocarbons were an unfailing source of dispute although Algeria reaped the lion's share: a tax of $12\frac{1}{2}$ per cent on all the oil it exported; one-half of the profits made by the large oil companies and $40\frac{1}{2}$ per cent of the capital stock of Repal, one of the largest petroleum concerns. The first infringement of the French mining regulations involved the owner's right to transport, which was governed by rules relating to the exploitation of oil deposits. In July 1963, Trapal, a company founded by seventeen oil producing concerns in Algeria, requested authorization to lay and administer a third pipeline to connect Hassi-Messaoud to Arzew, near Oran. The Algerian government demanded a share of the capital. Then, in April 1964, immediately after Ben Bella's visit to de Gaulle in March, it decided to employ a British firm to lay the pipeline and to construct a gas liquefying factory that was to be under the management of the Algerian state. The contract for the construction of an oil refinery was awarded to an Italian firm.

In July 1964, the Algerian government ruled that 50 per cent of the receipts of all the oil companies must remain in Algeria. This not only contravened the provisions of the Evian accords but also went counter to the general practice of all the oil-producing countries in the Middle East that favored the free flow of capital.

By May 1964 negotiations were underway for a revision of the oil regulations in the Sahara. The Franco-Algerian hydrocarbon agreement of July 29, 1965, granted Algeria new and substantial fiscal advantages as well as better regulations for the prospecting and exploitation of oil deposits.

Although existing concessions were retained and new ones accorded, the taxes on oil companies were almost doubled and Algeria's share of the Repal company's capital stock rose from 40½ to 50 per cent. A cooperative association composed of French and Algerian state enterprises was founded. It received vast fields with the understanding that the work of prospecting was to be shared. Approximately 80 per cent of the research cost was to be paid by the French company, but the exploitation of any oil the cooperative might discover was to be shared equally by the two partners. This amounted to a semi-nationalization of deposits even though French capital and French technicians would make their discovery possible.[2] France invested roughly six to seven billion francs in Sahara oil companies. In 1964 she consumed 65 per cent of Algeria's crude oil at prices that exceeded those prevailing in the world markets. Consequently, in the French protected market, the price of oil, not including the tax, was 65 per cent higher than in Germany.[3] According to the terms of the new agreement, France was to buy oil over a fifteen-year period at a fixed price. This would protect the state of Algeria against a probable decline in world prices. As for natural gas, the producers would be reduced to selling at a price that left them a very small part of the profit. Algeria, on the other hand, would make a substantial profit on the methane it exported to France. As one international oil publication put it, all these provisions represented an "almost irresistible bait" for Algeria.[4]

From 1963 to 1965, the financial assistance provided by France averaged one billion francs a year; to this must be added large advances from her treasury. After 1966, in accordance with the terms of the new oil accords, financial assistance was fixed at 200 million francs per year over a five-year period, and the taxes on oil were greatly increased. In December 1966 a financial agreement cancelled two-thirds of Algeria's debt to France.

Franco-Algerian commercial relations were based on a bilateral preferential system. France negotiated with Algeria a series of agreements on agricultural products, especially wine, to be bought at French domestic prices until September 1963 when an Algerian tariff was scheduled to go into effect. This Algerian tariff granted France's partners in the Common Market preferential treatment that was equivalent to one-half of the reduction allotted to French products. Thus, from a tariff point of view, Algeria was treated as a member of the E.E.C. even though legally it did not belong to it.[5]

In summary, the degree of Algerian economic dependence on France was considerable. The remittances of some 700,000 Algerian workers in France

---

[2] *L'opinion economique et financière*, July 25, 1965, 839.

[3] Paul Fabra, "Les accords franco-algériens," in *Le Monde*, July 30, 1965.

[4] *Petroleum Press Service*, Sept. 1965.

[5] André Van Ruymbeke, "Les relations economiques de l'Afrique du nord," in *Communantes et Continents*, Jan.–Mar. 1965.

accounted for approximately one-fifth of the national income. Algerian public investment funds came entirely from French sources and from taxes on oil; three-fourths of Algerian exports went to France and were generally paid for at prices higher than those that prevailed in the world markets. Nonetheless, the socialization of the economy through the confiscation of assets belonging to the French of Algeria did not enrich the Muslims. On the contrary, their national income decreased.

On the domestic level, the first years of independence were marked by a violent struggle for power and the establishment of a totalitarian regime. In August 1963 the parliament adopted a constitution based upon the single-party system, whereupon Ferhat Abbas resigned from the presidency of the Algerian Assembly. In September Ben Bella was elected president of the Republic. In October he obtained the special powers sanctioned by the constitution. In 1964 Ben Bella ousted from the government the last members of the G.P.R.A. and exiled a large number of his opponents.

Ben Bella's foreign policy aimed at eliminating the aftermath of colonialism, first in Algeria and then in the Third World. He was prepared to support the demands of pan-Arabism and to practice an anti-Western neutralism with the aid of Russia and especially of China. Algeria became a center of revolutionary activity for all of Africa.

His speech of October 1, 1963, made his attitude toward France crystal clear: "We are not against cooperation. . . . It should be understood, however, that such cooperation must be freed from everything that symbolizes our subjection." On February 25, 1964, shortly after France recognized China, Ben Bella commended de Gaulle: "France is about to take political options which we applaud. . . . " On March 13, 1964, Ben Bella was the guest of de Gaulle at the Chateau de Champs. The purpose and results of the meeting were kept secret. It was doubtless at Champs that the decision was made to revise the Sahara oil regulations. This meeting enabled Ben Bella to boast of the guarantee de Gaulle gave him prior to the F.L.N. Congress which, on April 16, was to approve the socialist options of his government. For de Gaulle the meeting served to underscore his concern for the uncommitted Third World just as he was leaving for Mexico—a trip that was followed in the autumn by a tour of South America.

The secretary of state for Algerian affairs, Jean de Broglie, in his speech of November 4, 1964, revealed with candor the essentially political purpose of Franco-Algerian cooperation: "Algeria is also and above all the 'narrow door' through which we must pass to reach the Third World. A quarrel between France and some other state of North Africa is nothing more than bilateral tension. A quarrel with Algeria would transcend the limits of Franco-Algerian relations and might wreck our diplomatic goals throughout the entire world."

On June 19, 1965, Ben Bella was relieved of power by Colonel Honari Boumedienne, first vice-president of the Council and minister of war. After a few months, Boumedienne was confronted with the same problem that had preoccupied his predecessor: to rid Algeria of all foreign enterprises and all cooperation with France.

In May 1966, the major mining concerns were nationalized. In October 1967, the Algerian national banks were to enjoy a monopoly in all financial transactions. This naturally forced all the foreign banks to fold. The American and British oil companies were placed under the jurisdiction of the state in 1967. The same fate awaited the French oil-distributing companies in May 1968. The implementation of the 1964 agreements on hydrocarbons ran into difficulties. Concerns that had been nationalized were not indemnified. Commerce between France and Algeria dwindled and was increasingly based on a system of barter and exchange.

Little by little, the French government withdrew. It imported less Algerian wine. In June 1968, because of the employment situation in France, the government decided to implement rigorously the 1964 agreement on the emigration of Algerian labor.

The anticipated evacuation of the Mers-el-Kébir naval base—which was in no way protected from atomic attack—was announced in October 1967 and carried out early in 1968.

Other Countries in the Third World

In 1963 and 1964 de Gaulle began a series of diplomatic maneuvers designed to prove to the uncommitted Third World France's competence as a leader compared to the two hegemonic powers, the United States and the Soviet Union.

Offers of economic cooperation for political ends were made to Central Africa, Southeast Asia, and South America. In December 1963 a cultural and technical agreement was concluded with the Congo (Leopoldville). De Gaulle wanted to be present in this French-speaking state, which, as a consequence of disturbances following decolonization, was vulnerable to the rivalry of the United States, the Soviet Union, and China. In a statement made on August 29, 1963, on the Vietnam situation, de Gaulle said he wished to see "the whole of Vietnam . . . use all its energy to become independent of external forces" and declared that France was ready "to take the necessary steps for close cooperation with this country." None the less, relations with South Vietnam became strained in 1964 because France favored neutralization (she was of course incapable of promoting it). The theory of neutralization attracted Cambodia, whose chief of state, Prince Norodom Sihanouk, decided in November 1963 to put an end to the program of American aid.

Pierre Messmer, the minister of war, went to Pnom-Penh in January 1964 and offered Cambodia military assistance, increased cultural aid, and lent his support to the convocation of an international conference to guarantee the country's neutralization.

1964 was the year for Latin America. De Gaulle went to Mexico in March and to ten South American states in September and October. To the governments of all of these countries he talked about the benefits to be derived from economic aid given without political strings of any kind. He also discussed the need for economic diversification in developing countries and the possibility of stabilizing the markets for raw materials. One basic political theme was stressed everywhere: rejection of any form of hegemony. However, Georges Pompidou, commenting on the results of the presidential visit to the South American countries, acknowledged that "France is not in a position to intervene massively in their development."

Thus, cooperation fell heir to the difficulties wrought by decolonization; but, like colonization, it became a tool of power politics.

4

Cooperation and France in 1968

Financial Burdens

D E GAULLE'S POLICY of cooperation entailed sacrifices. In financial order to assess this policy accurately, a comparison must be made between the cost and the economic advantages obtained or anticipated, as well as the purely political gains which France could expect.

Because of this policy, France assumed both direct and indirect obligations; she also sacrificed valuable assets. The direct obligations are measurable and have fluctuated very little in absolute value since 1958. From 1959 to 1965 the amount of financial aid, both public and private, contributed by France to the Third World averaged 1,300 million dollars per year. The amount was the same for 1958.[1] The direct cost of cooperation replaced the money spent in earlier years for the economic and social requirements of colonization. In 1962 Algeria received 42 per cent of the bilateral aid, Black Africa and Madagascar 30 per cent, Tunisia and Morocco 4 per cent, the rest of the Franc Zone 8 per cent, and countries outside of the Franc Zone 14 per cent.[2] This aid represents more than 10 per cent of the total amount invested annually in France.[3] Aid was 2.31 per cent of the national income

[1] A) "Les moyens financiers mis à la disposition des pays les moins développés," 1956–1963, 154; B) "Efforts et politiques d'aide au développement," Examen 1965, pp. 143, 147, Examen 1966, p. 175, *Organization for Economic Cooperation and Development (O.E.C.D.).*

[2] "La politique de coopération avec les pays en voie de developpement," *Report of the Study Commission*, established by the decree of March 12, 1963 (Paris, 1963), 73.

[3] *Ibid.*, 50.

in 1962, 1.94 per cent in 1963 and 1964, 1.88 per cent in 1965. During this same period the contributions made by the United States, England, and Germany to the Third World averaged 1 per cent of their respective national incomes.[4] The direct cost of cooperation for France, in relation to her resources, is therefore twice as much as that of the three great industrial nations of the Western world.

The indirect cost of cooperation consists in the purchase of foodstuffs and raw materials at higher prices than those that prevailed in the world markets: wheat and wine in the three North African countries, tropical products in Black Africa and Madagascar, oil in Algeria. These burdens tie the French economy closer to Africa; they perpetuate and develop a system of over-pricing which inevitably makes French exports less competitive in the inter-national market. Given the fact that the overpricing of tropical foods was scheduled to cease after 1967, in accordance with the regulations laid down by the Convention of Association between the E.E.C. and the eighteen African states and Madagascar, the indirect cost to the French economy stems essentially from the wine and oil agreements with Algeria.

Finally, losses have resulted from the Algerian government's con-fiscation of French property and from its failure to pay any indemnity. Farms as well as industrial and commercial property figure among the losses. The semi-nationalization of oil has had similar consequences. A by-product of France's tolerant attitude toward Algeria is the confiscation of the colonists' property in Tunisia and Morocco.

In short, the policy of cooperation has been more disadvantageous to the French economy than to its principal industrial competitors, whose direct costs are lower and who have neither indirect costs to contend with nor loss of assets.

The Economic Consequences Today

Has this costly policy been beneficial to the states France has assisted? One must be prudent in answering this question. Cooperation is a long drawn-out affair. It consists in training men for administration and entrepre-neurship. A distinction must be made between the recent evolution of the assisted states and the prospects opened up by long-term planning.

Because of the generosity of France and her concentration on countries within the Franc Zone, the French-speaking peoples of North and Tropical Africa receive a far more direct assistance than other underdeveloped countries do: $18.50 per inhabitant in 1961 compared to $6.00 per inhabitant in the rest of the Third World.[5] But this direct aid is earmarked primarily for

[4] B) Examen 1965, *O.E.C.D.*, p. 61.
[5] "La politique de cooperation," *Report of Study Commission*, 57.

Algeria, whose share is ten times greater than that of Tunisia and Morocco combined. The gap is even greater between the North African countries if indirect costs are taken into account.

From the standpoint of efficiency Algeria, which has received the lion's share, has made the poorest use of it. The financial and economic difficulties of Tunisia and Morocco are due in part to the contagion of Algerian collectivism. Compared to North Africa, French-speaking Tropical Africa has received little basic equipment and also little assistance in the exploitation of its natural resources. Nevertheless, and despite the additional handicap of political partition, French Tropical Africa's evolution, though uneven, has been quite rapid in certain states such as the Ivory Coast and Gabon which know how to attract and retain foreign capital for the exploitation of their natural resources.

Long-Term Economic Prospects

Two fundamental obstacles hinder the long-term development of the Third World. The first is declining agricultural production. According to a report of the Food and Agricultural Organization (F.A.O.), during the 1965–1966 season the production of food in the Far East, Latin America, and Africa was substantially lower than before the war.

The second obstacle is the decrease in the price of raw materials which has of course hurt food-producing countries. The overproduction of raw materials in relation to demand caused a fall in prices. On the other hand, owing to growing inflation in the industrialized countries, the price of manufactured goods rose. The result was a commercial imbalance in countries that produced basic foodstuffs. This was dangerous both in terms of revenue, since international trade accounts for a considerable proportion of the Third World's national income, especially in Africa, and in terms of payments, because of the rapid increase of the underdeveloped countries public debt.

The task of increasing farm production in the underdeveloped countries, of reorganizing the market for raw materials in order to bring it in line with the market for manufactured goods, was too difficult for France to accomplish on her own. She needed the cooperation of the larger industrialized countries—her partners in E.E.C., the United States, England and her E.F.T.A. (European Free Trade Association) partners. In short, multilateral rather than bilateral cooperation was required.

Methods

The French government realized the advantages of multilateral cooperation but hoped to exploit, for political purposes, the potentialities of bilateral cooperation. Yet it did invoke multilateralism on several occasions.

In 1961, continuing the work of the Fourth Republic, the Fifth Republic obtained the adoption of the Convention of Association between the E.E.C. and the eighteen African states and Madagascar. Agreements were concluded at Yaoundé in 1963.

In 1961, two French ministers, Wilfrid Baumgartner and Edgard Pisani, stressed the need for a global approach to the problem of regulating prices and improving the world market for basic products. During the Kennedy Round, the tariff negotiations which mainly involved the United States, the E.E.C., and the E.F.T.A., offered international experts a chance to study the question. On France's initiative, the six countries of the Common Market delivered a mandate to the Brussels Commission to this effect

However, in 1965 multilateral aid to the public sector of underdeveloped countries was only 3½ per cent of the total French expenditure for that purpose.[6] France showed a marked preference for bilateral aid as a means of exerting political influence; but this is usually too costly because the donor, in seeking political results, neglects the dictates of economic realities. There is a certain analogy to be drawn here between the United States' bilateral aid to Latin America and that of France to North and Black Africa. Some critics accuse both countries of neo-colonialism. What, then, is the real mainspring of France's policy of cooperation?

The Third World—A Power Tool?

De Gaulle's ambition is to pursue a global policy in the name of France. In his view, cooperation represents an instrument of power rather than the prerequisite of solidarity. He believes that since France has a freer hand than the hegemonic powers of both East and West, and since she has had no colonial ties since 1962, she can exert an influence in the uncommitted Third World. (By "uncommitted" he means not subservient to any of the world powers or, at any rate, ready to reject their tutelage).

How can France capture this huge, turbulent clientele, upon whom dollars are showered and who are constantly beset by Soviet and Chinese propagandists? There is only one way: to cooperate at all costs with the country against which for almost eight years France waged her last colonial war. If France succeeds in catching Algeria in her net she can also capture the Third World. To prevent all foreign interference, cooperation must be bilateral. France has offered "irresistible bait" in the form of the Evian accords of 1962 and the oil agreements of 1965. She will have to accept all the affronts, the rebuffs, the open and deliberate violations of clear-cut recent agreements. She has to be submissive and humble. She must turn the other

---

[6] B) Examen 1966, *O.E.C.D.*, p. 175.

cheek. France has not shown a shred of pride in her relations with Algeria. Through what "narrow door" will her grandeur find its way?

Ben Bella realized this. He cashed the subsidies, confiscated France's assets, demanded co-ownership and co-management of the oil, and practically prohibited the use of the Sahara launching sites. He was in a position to use blackmail, he knew it and took full and impudent advantage of it. His Elysée host could but bow to events and hope that this recruiting sergeant would bring him more clients. Boumedienne followed his example but less successfully.

Yet all de Gaulle's efforts proved futile because the financial sacrifices France made did not profit the Algerian people; because the amount of help that a country like France, whose own resources are modest, can give to countries outside of Africa, to Latin America or Southeast Asia, for example, is negligible.

France has become an ally of Cambodia and has acquired an intermittent client in the Congo (Leopoldville). But after the general's trip to Latin America, the chiefs of state he had seen there hastened to grant interviews to the local American ambassadors. French policy toward the Third World has not hampered the United States in its exclusive sphere of influence, the Western hemisphere. It did not convert France, a middle power, into a great one.

II

Defense and Alliances

5

New Elements in Global Strategy

The Ballistic Revolution

GENERAL DE GAULLE resumed power at a time when the strategy of the great powers was undergoing a complete transformation because of the technological revolution. Not only were piloted airplanes used but also long-range ballistic missiles that could deliver thermonuclear bombs. The gradual appearance of China on the international scene was also part of this revolution.

The replacement of the atom by the hydrogen bomb considerably increased the destructive powers of nuclear weapons. The addition of the missile to the airplane considerably increased the rapidity with which a bomb could be transported. Thus all at once there was an increase in firepower and a contraction of the time of war.

A distinction must be made between intermediate-range ballistic missiles (I.R.B.M.) and intercontinental ballistic missiles (I.C.B.M.). The missiles can be launched from underground silos or from atomic submarines. These new weapons were perfected between October 1957, when the first sputnik was launched by the Russians, and December 1960, when the first American atomic submarines armed with Polaris missiles were put into service.

By the end of 1967, the United States had 750 intercontinental Minuteman missiles and 250 Minuteman II's in underground silos, 54 Titan II missiles, and 41 atomic submarines, each equipped with 16 medium-range Polaris missiles. The Soviet Union apparently had 450 to 475 intercontinental missiles, 700 to 750 medium-range missiles, and 50 atomic submarines each armed with 3 or 4 missiles.[1]

[1] *The Military Balance 1967–1968* (London: The Institute for Strategic Studies, 1967), 5, 7, 27.

It takes thirty minutes for a Minuteman to travel the distance that separates the United States from Russia and seven minutes for missiles fired from Soviet launching platforms to reach their targets in Western Europe.[2]

The ballistic revolution points up the enormous advantage of possessing offensive as distinguished from defensive weapons—a fact that was already clear during the first stage of the nuclear age, that of the piloted plane. These new weapons have important implications for the deployment of force, the strategy of deterrence, and strategic doctrine.

Deployment of Strategic Forces

Before the ballistic era the superiority of the American strategic air force, both in numbers and equipment—supersonic bombers with a 6,000-mile range—gave the United States an almost foolproof insurance against enemy planes. The ring of so-called peripheral air bases around the Soviet Union also protected Western Europe.

Soviet medium-range missiles, however, were a direct threat to Europe. The United States suggested that certain of their allies should build launching platforms for medium-range missiles and keep their least vulnerable air bases for supersonic planes. Launching platforms were installed in England (Thor missiles), in Italy and Turkey (Jupiter missiles), and became operational in 1958 and 1960 respectively. By 1963 they were obsolete as a result of the increased number of American intercontinental missiles. Intercontinental ballistic missiles, in effect, constitute a direct and mutual threat for the United States and the Soviet Union; they can be flown over the North Pole from launching platforms on territories belonging to each of the two great powers.

Finally, nuclear-missile submarines in their adjacent waters threaten both of the two great powers. The United States has naval bases in Great Britain and in Spain for atomic submarines that patrol the Mediterranean, the North Sea, and the Arctic Ocean.

Thus the defense of the United States and its allies of the Atlantic Treaty rests on the quadruple system of strategic weapons deployed over two theaters of operation separated by several thousand miles. A direct Russo-America encounter would be fought principally with intercontinental ballistic missiles, supersonic bombers having become relatively obsolete. A Russo-European war would be fought principally with intermediate-range ballistic missiles backed up by atomic submarines.

The Russians have given priority to building intermediate-range missiles to be used against Europe. But the psychological effect of their apparent

[2] Marc de Lacoste-Lareymondie, *Mirages et réalités* (Paris: Editions de la Serpe, 1964), 128.

progress in the field of missiles, and especially in space exploration, has caused grave concern in the United States. In 1958 a controversy arose over the missile gap. Immediately after the election of President Kennedy the construction of intercontinental missiles increased. Exposed for the first time to a direct threat, the Americans thought it expedient to have at their disposal a surplus of such weapons.

Another reason for the surplus is the disparity between the strategic position of Warsaw Pact states and that of the members of NATO. The first group is a compact continental bloc that lends itself to a certain concentration of forces. The states in the second group are located in two zones that are very distant from one another. Consequently, although they have a unified command, they must rely on their own resources.

The European zone is the most threatened owing to its proximity to the Soviet launching platforms. Furthermore, there is a disparity within the Atlantic Alliance between the strategic position of the United States and Canada on the one hand, and that of Western Europe on the other.

Still another disparity stems from the fact that military secrets are kept better in the Soviet Union than in the West. This has led the United States to increase the number, dispersal, and mobility of its weapons of retaliation.[3]

Since ballistic missiles can reach their target quickly, an enemy subjected to a first strike must be able to retaliate by an almost instantaneous second strike. A network of Distant Early Warning lines is therefore mandatory in the deployment of offensive weapons.

Two such networks have been constructed. One is for the protection of North America and has a series of radar stations, the most distant of which extend from Alaska to Greenland. The other is for the protection of Western Europe; its radar stations stretch from Norway to Turkey. Both of these have been installed and are operated by American forces. At present they are designed to detect enemy bombers which can be intercepted by ground-to-air missiles armed with homing devices and carrying nuclear bombs.

Ballistic missiles are more difficult to detect and—at least for the time being—are impossible to intercept. As a result of the research currently underway both in the United States and in the Soviet Union, anti-missile missile networks are planned but not yet operational. Since a missile is therefore more than likely to reach target, the superiority of offensive weapons remains presently a basic characteristic of nuclear warfare.

In the future, both American and Russian aerial alert networks will use heavy satellites; consequently, both countries are dependent upon technological advances. Competition between the two in the conquest of space is therefore an important aspect of geopolitical supremacy.

---

[3] Raymond Aron, *Paix et guerre entre les nations* (Paris: Calmann-Lévy, 1962), 642.

The strategy of the two great powers tends more and more to become global because of the possibility that their new equipment, both planes and missiles, will be able to reach every corner of the world. Strategic theory in the missile age must necessarily be adapted to new offensive and defensive conditions.

Deterrence

In view of the considerable advantage that possession of ballistic missiles gives to the attacker, only the threat of retaliation will give pause. According to General Beaufre, "The purpose of deterrence is to prevent an enemy power from deciding to use its weapons by making preparations that constitute an effective threat."[4] This psychological result is obtained by comparing the stakes with the risk. The destructive danger to both men and resources is enormous in any kind of atomic competition. Therefore it is imperative to determine "which stakes are worth a risk of this kind." It is at this point that the concept of an atomic threshold emerges. "Wisdom requires . . . that we fix the atomic threshold rather high; it also requires that we preserve a certain flexibility." It would not be logical to risk a war for a small stake, or to fail to preserve a margin of maneuverability to avoid putting the enemy in a position of having to choose between losing face or pushing the panic button.[5]

Therefore an essential distinction must be made between an offensive strategy and a strategy of deterrence. In the most recent phases of the cold war between America and Russia, only the strategy of deterrence has been used.

Raymond Aron has written: "A deterrent force exists solely at the moment it is capable of inflicting retaliation and therefore of surviving an enemy attack that one wants to deter."[6] But a real capacity for retaliation presupposes a certain set of conditions that has been defined by an American theoretical strategist, Albert J. Wohlstetter. He says that deterrent systems must have "the ability to survive enemy attacks, to make and communicate the decision to retaliate, to reach enemy territory with fuel enough to complete their mission, to penetrate enemy active defenses, that is, fighters and surface-to-air missiles, and to destroy the target in spite of any 'passive' civil defense in the form of dispersal or protective construction or evacuation of the target itself."[7]

[4] General Beaufre, *Dissuasion et stratégie* (Paris: Armand Colin, 1964), 21.
[5] De Lacoste-Lareymondie, *Mirages et réalités*, 141–43.
[6] Raymond Aron, *Le grand débat* (Paris: Calmann-Lévy, 1963), 48–50.
[7] Albert J. Wohlstetter, "The Delicate Balance of Terror," *Foreign Affairs*, Jan. 1959, 216.

After 1959 only the Americans and Russians were in a position, because of their weapons, to deter one another. Each country's capacity for retaliation was considerable. This fact stabilized the situation. Such is the paradox of the nonemployment of atomic weapons: it forces both sides to approach the question of strategy in a new spirit. Nuclear weaponry has a political rather than a military history. Strategy and politics have become more closely complementary than in the past.

McNamara's Doctrine

The two nuclear powers were obliged to adapt their strategy to recent technological findings and to the fluctuations in their relative strength.

Until 1953 the United States maintained a complete advantage in regard to deterrence of the Soviet Union. Until 1957 the power of deterrence of the two countries was approximately equal and this left the United States with a considerable advantage because American territory was relatively less vulnerable. From 1953 on, John Foster Dulles preached the doctrine called "massive retaliation," according to which "in case of aggression at some point of the border between the two blocs, retaliation would be neither local nor conventional but the United States would have the choice of the place and the weapons."[8]

After ballistic missiles were added to nuclear weapons and a situation of approximate nuclear parity was established, American strategic theory was based on two factors: one was the ability to launch second strikes; the other was the objective of this second-strike force. Real deterrence exists only when the belligerent, attacked by a first strike, still has at its disposal sufficient means for a second strike. The attacker would generally have as its target the enemy's means of retaliation and would therefore practice a counter-force strategy. As for the country attacked, depending upon its means of retaliation, it could either try to destroy the enemy's forces or aim for his population and his industrial resources—in other words, it could practice a counter-city strategy.

It is precisely because both the United States and the Soviet Union are for the most part invulnerable, owing to their shelters and to their nuclear-missile submarines, that the situation has become extremely stable. None the less, an atomic war could break out accidentally or through a misunderstanding. In order to prevent this, it is important to maintain communication with the enemy, especially in times of political crisis. It is for this purpose that a "hot line" was hooked up between Washington and Moscow in 1963. Atomic war could also break out as a consequence of an

[8] Aron, *Le grand débat*, 33.

escalation from conventional weapons to tactical atomic, then to strategic weapons. And finally it could break out irrationally, because some one made a thoughtless decision.

American theorists, speculating about the relative strength of the two great powers, led the American secretary of defense to formulate in 1962 the doctrine of graduated response. It rests on the principle that the first phase of a nuclear war would be the destruction of enemy forces rather than of civilian populations, even if the enemy strikes first. But flexible response requires a centralized system of command and control. "The requirement of central control is interpreted by the Pentagon to mean the integration of strategic nuclear forces in a way that forecloses the technical possibility of independent use," Henry A. Kissinger wrote.[9] McNamara was therefore against the use of national nuclear forces and the total autonomy it would entail for those countries that possess the weapons. He had serious reservations about the placing of tactical nuclear weapons in the hands of first-line units because of the difficulty of centralizing their control. In January 1963 McNamara stated that American strategic doctrine showed a preference for the conventional forms of defense for use in Western Europe. Land forces in effect limit the threshold of nuclear stockpiling. The corollary of this is that a non-nuclear Soviet military attack would be countered by purely conventional weapons.[10]

In short, the doctrine is one of moderation and discretion—a refusal to accept the inevitability of nuclear war. It advocates a selective war, one that requires considerable mastery of the system of communication and command. It is a doctrine that has often been misunderstood in Europe, where it has provoked strong reactions.

European Reactions

Prior to the time when massive retaliation became possible, Europeans felt secure, believing that they would be protected by the United States in case of need. At the same time, of course, they feared the possibility of an apocalypse. But now that they are faded with the possibility of graduated response, Europeans are beginning to wonder whether they can count on America's determination to defend them with all the means at her disposal. They are afraid that graduated response will enable a Soviet attack to devastate Europe in a war waged with conventional weapons. And they are even more afraid that the United States might refuse to involve their strategic

[9] Henry A. Kissinger, *The Troubled Partnership* (New York: McGraw-Hill, 1965), 101.

[10] Kissinger, *Troubled Partnership*, 128.

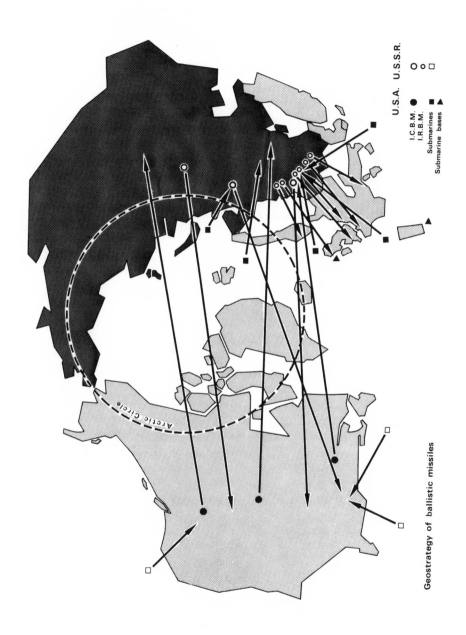

U.S.A.   U.S.S.R.

I.C.B.M.   ○   ○   □
I.R.B.M.   ●   •   ■
Submarines   ■
Submarine bases ▲

Geostrategy of ballistic missiles

Arctic circle

forces lest the Soviets retaliate by attacking them in their own country, which has become vulnerable. They are less sure of an automatic American intervention since the decision would be made in Washington, not at NATO; American nuclear weapons are national, not integrated arms. Europeans anxiously complain that under current conditions their position is more threatened than that of America. Their densely populated countries are endangered by Soviet intermediate-range missiles. Apart from the concentrations of population, Europeans lack atomic shelters and their warning time is shorter.

In view of the recent vulnerability of the United States, what military measures can the European NATO nations take since their vulnerability is even greater? There are several possible solutions. The first is to reinforce the arsenal of conventional weapons so that the integrated defense of NATO would be better able to deter an enemy attack and provide protection in a non-nuclear war. This calls for financial sacrifices. The second solution, at least for some of the European nations, is to develop, with American help, an effective system of retaliation for Western Europe. This would call for not only financial but political sacrifices since the strategy of deterrence and attack requires more stringent weapon control. The third solution is recourse to national rather than collective military measures.

It remains for the larger states to create deterrent forces of their own, these national forces being considered either as auxiliaries to the American strategic system or as entirely autonomous in their action. England chose the first formula. France, as early as 1960, made known her intention to choose the second.

The Americans have been trying to persuade Europe to adopt the first solution. They cannot act for Europe in matters requiring political reform and sacrifice of sovereignty, which the second solution would entail. Failing such reforms, they are studying ways and means of associating their European partners not with the decision on when to use such arms, which they believe is indivisible, but with the shaping of the strategy of deterrence. In this respect their attitude is influenced by the fear—which they share with the Russians—of a spread of nuclear weapons.

The Risks of Proliferation

The dangers of proliferation are self evident. The relative confidence in the rational behavior of the enemy, on which the relations between the major powers are based, would disappear in the face of a multiplication of national atomic weapons whose use would depend on a decision of each head of state.

Those nations that have recently acquired nuclear weapons do not have a real deterrent power that would enable them to survive a first strike. Their means are limited. Their strategy would have to be counter-city rather than graduated response.

The dangers of proliferation are not imaginary. Very soon the reduced cost of manufacturing nuclear reactors and the simplification and diffusion of fission techniques will make thermonuclear arms available to nations of average means whose technical and financial capacities will stimulate their political drives.

Moreover, the two major nuclear powers tend to become interdependent because of the danger inherent for both in a thermonuclear war, and this makes such a war less probable. Therefore, they naturally refuse to be dragged into total war against their wishes. It was in this spirit that the United States and the Soviet Union signed in 1963 the Treaty of Moscow limiting nuclear experiments and in 1968 the Nonproliferation Treaty. China and France, unequal in size as well as in potentialities, refused to sign both treaties and are attempting to counter American-Russian complicity and to break up the current bipolarity. China's rise to the rank of a world power, the certainty that it will soon be a major atomic power, France's desire for military and political independence—these factors are having a profound effect on global strategy, which until now has been determined by the rivalry of only two great blocs that were not without fissures but on the whole rather cohesive.

Rivalry and Subordination in the Thermonuclear Age

The revolution in nuclear weapons has modified the relations of the two major powers with each other as well as with their respective clients.

The relations of the nuclear powers with each other are characterized by considerable political stability and technological competition. An armed invasion of Europe by the Soviet Union seems unlikely because the defense systems of each side are substantial. The Soviets prefer an indirect offensive strategy in the form of subversive warfare rather than direct strategy.[11] But the nuclear balance could change at any moment should a technological breakthrough occur. "Anti-aircraft, anti-missile, and anti-submarine techniques could make spectacular progress by means of satellites when they have achieved—and the time is not too distant—adequate development." A military confrontation between the United States and the Soviet Union is continuing in the domain of space exploration, the first achievement of which is a systematic observation of enemy territory.[12]

[11] Beaufre, *Dissuasion*, 47–147.
[12] General Beaufre, "La guerre de l'espace est commencée," *Réalités*, Nov. 1965.

"Communist solidarity, like Western solidarity, does not include atomic weapons" because of the magnitude of the risks and the need for a centralized control of military operations.[13] The great powers hope to preserve for themselves the control of nuclear weapons whereas certain of their allies are pursuing a policy whose purpose is to procure atomic arms of their own. The general stability protects the allies as well as the neutrals so that, according to Kissinger's observation, "a country gains little from being allied and risks little by being neutral."[14] It was this observation that led de Gaulle to build a national nuclear force under the protection of the American deterrent. None the less the research done in middle-sized countries like France or England is ten or twenty years behind the times; besides, both scientific personnel and funds for scientific research are limited. As a consequence, these countries are building first-generation vehicles, whereas the great powers already have second-generation vehicles in operation and are completing the research for third-generation ones. Thus, despite the efforts of the middle-sized powers, the gap between them and the great powers continues to increase on all levels—technological, military, and strategic. In this global game a special place must be reserved for China, which is certainly no longer a middle-sized power compared to the principal European nations, but cannot as yet be compared to the two great powers.

The Latent Hostility between China and the Soviet Union

In 1950, at the time of the accords signed by Stalin and Mao Tse-tung, the Soviet Union conceded China's right to Manchuria, Port Arthur, and Dairen, thus renouncing the zone of influence it had established in 1945 at the expense of Japan. Thereafter, the Soviet Union gave China limited financial aid and such extensive technical assistance that Russian technicians played a considerable role in the Chinese government. The Korean and Indochinese wars reinforced China's prestige in Asia. At the same time, Stalin's death inclined the Chinese toward greater independence.

At the time of Stalin's "second death," friction between the two big Communist states became apparent. Mao Tse-tung did not concur in Khrushchev's severe judgment of Stalin, pronounced at the Twentieth Congress of the Soviet Communist Party in 1957. On the contrary, the Chinese Communists supported the theory of permanent revolution. This position was taken at a time when, after the failure of a liberal movement, the extremists came to power in China with the establishment of people's communes. The "Great Leap Forward" was designed to enable the Chinese,

[13] Aron, *Paix et guerre*, 606.
[14] Kissinger, *Troubled Partnership*, 16.

like all other peoples whose economy is underdeveloped, to find the straight path to Communism without taking the roundabout course of Soviet Socialism. In this way, China claimed to be the leader of the proletarian nations. The Chinese thought the Soviet Union should use the power it had acquired in 1957 through the possession of intercontinental ballistic missiles to speed up the revolutionary movement in underdeveloped countries and even in Western ones.[15] The Soviet leaders, on the other hand, felt that atomic warfare could be avoided; their policy toward the West was therefore conducted with caution and, whenever the circumstances allowed, there was a relaxation of tensions.

In September 1958 the Chinese bombarded the island of Quemoy in the Formosa Straits in order to gain possession of it. The Russians persuaded them not to land and at the same time Khrushchev, in a letter to Eisenhower, threatened the Americans with atomic retaliation should they take up arms against the Chinese. Sino-Soviet solidarity was thus proclaimed but with a view to a peaceful solution of the conflict. In September 1959 the. Soviet Union expressed disapproval of China over the Sino-Indian conflict. Finally, after his trip to the United States and his personal meetings with Eisenhower at Camp David, Khrushchev went to Peking for the tenth anniversary of the Chinese Republic. He appealed for moderation: "We have no need of war. . . . At present, the heads of certain capitalist governments are beginning to evidence a more realistic view of the international situation."

Open Opposition

The political and ideological conflict between the Chinese and Soviet philosophies first became apparent in February 1960, at a conference of the Warsaw Pact states, and then in June at the Rumanian Communist Party Congress, and finally in November, at the meeting of all the Communist parties in Moscow. The Russians withdrew all their experts from China. In October, 1961, at the Twenty-Second Soviet Communist Party Congress, the conflict grew bitter over the general orientation of the Communist world and the strategy of war and peace in the atomic age.

Whereas after Khrushchev's trip to Peking in 1959 China spoke of the Soviet Union as the "leader of the Communist camp,"[16] from 1960 on it officially challenged Russia's monopoly in the interpretation of Marxist-Leninist doctrine. It wanted the national parties to unite in a definition of Communist strategy and tactics, which meant giving the Chinese Communist Party the right to judge Soviet policy.[17]

[15] Jean Laloy, "La politique etrangère de l'U.R.S.S.," Lectures Delivered at the Institut d'Etudes Politiques, Paris, 1962–1963, p. 401.
[16] "Message à Vorochilov," *Année Politique 1959*, Oct. 9, 1959, 519.
[17] Laloy, "Politique étrangère," 408.

In 1960 at Moscow the Chinese refused to believe that the imperialists did not desire a nuclear war and declared that the power of deterrence could be used in local wars. The Russians reiterated their opinion that the use of force was no longer necessary to promote revolution and that atomic war was not inevitable. They expressed the belief that it was in the interest of the Socialist camp to coexist peacefully with the West in order to overcome the risk of war and to free resources for more effective economic competition with capitalism.[18] Since the Soviet Union was one of the two major nuclear powers it tended to revise its world strategy in order to prevent an all-out war. "The universal danger created by thermonuclear weapons profoundly affects the Marxist ideology."[19]

The quarrel over both doctrine and strategy continued after the public debates on the Cuban affair in October 1962. After Khrushchev retired, China openly criticized the Soviet Union. It accused it of succumbing to two errors—"adventurism" and "capitulationism"—both inspired by a blind admiration for nuclear arms.[20] Shortly afterward the Soviet Union expressed disapproval of the Chinese offensive against the province of Assam in India

In 1962, border disputes arose between China and Russia in the province of Sin-Kiang, and the Chinese claimed the region of Khabarovsk in Siberia.[21]

Meanwhile China rallied the Communist parties of the Far East: North-Korea, North Vietnam, Indonesia, Laos, Burma, Thailand, Malaysia, Singapore, Japan.[22] In this way it proclaimed its role as a world power.

In November 1965, an agency of the new China disseminated a document accusing the leaders in Moscow of collaborating with the United States "for world domination." In January 1966, the Soviet Union, with the tacit consent of the United States, was the arbiter of a conflict in Kashmir where for many years Pakistanis had opposed Indians. China supported Pakistan. Kosygin's intervention at the Conference of Tashkent led to the collapse of Chinese activities in Central Asia. In March 1966, China rejected the invitation to attend the Twenty-Third Soviet Communist Party Congress and in this was backed up by several Communist parties in Asia.

China's Atomic Bomb

China was demonstrating its strategic potential if not yet its power. On October 16, 1964, it exploded a uranium bomb in Sin-Kiang. This explosion

[18] David Floyd, *Mao against Krushchev* (New York: Frederick Praeger, 1963), 113–14.
[19] Laloy, "Politique étrangère," 406.
[20] Floyd, *Mao against Krushchev*, 161.
[21] Robert Guillain, *Dans trente ans la Chine* (Paris: Editions du Seuil, 1965), 187, 188.
[22] *Ibid.*, 187.

did not surprise the Americans, who had announced its imminence shortly before, nor the Russians, who for a long time had known the nature of China's intentions. In 1957 a Russo-Chinese atomic agreement had been concluded. Khrushchev had promised to give his ally bombs and the secret of how to make them. In 1959 the Soviet Union broke off the agreement.[23] China continued its experiments at the price of heavy financial sacrifices which doubtless gravely affected the economic crisis it was experiencing. It naturally refused to sign the treaty concluded in 1963 by the United States and the Soviet Union on the curtailment of nuclear testing.

On October 27, 1966, China launched a missile with a warhead capable of hitting a target over four hundred miles away. On June 17, 1967, she exploded her first thermonuclear bomb. Thus China, four years after its entry into the atomic club, evidenced a marked technological advance over France. As soon as its missiles are operational it will be able to threaten its immediate neighbors with strategic weapons. But not until 1975 will it be in a position to threaten the United States or Europe, unless some unforeseeable technological breakthrough occurs.

China and World Strategy

Unified for the first time since the beginning of the industrial era, having overcome major economic difficulties occasioned by the withdrawal of Russian technicians, and having demonstrated by the bomb its scientific abilities and political ambitions, China has joined the ranks of the great world powers.

In many respects China's full potential has not yet been realized. The country could be adversely affected by a population growth that might outstrip its resources.

The Sino-Russian conflict "is a dispute between two great and proud people over their position and power in the world."[24] It can be explained by a combination of national and ideological factors. The Russian state has no further territorial claims to make. The Chinese state is not satisfied: Formosa, Hong Kong, border disputes with the Soviet Union and with India, exclusion from the United Nations. The Communist system is monolithic in principle but China and Russia represent two stages of revolution. " 'Maoism' could be defined as exaggerated Stalinism. A people poorer than the Russians must, at the cost of even greater efforts, become industrialized more rapidly."[25]

---

[23] *Ibid.*
[24] Floyd, *Mao against Kruschev*, 191.
[25] Klaus Mehnert, *Pékin et Moscou* (Paris: Stock, 1963), 44.

For the first time the Communist world is divided. This could prove an advantage to the West. Global strategy no longer is practised as it was in 1950, in the framework of a rigidly bipolar system. China is a third pole and Europe, if it in turn becomes unified, might become a fourth. And the Vietnam war is not quite like the Korean war. It pits the United States against China as distinct from Russia. Will the West know how to take advantage of the conflicts and contradictions of the Communist world? This is one of the reasons, but not the only one, why de Gaulle decided to recognize the Chinese People's Republic on January 27, 1964.

6

East–West Tension and Détente

The Berlin Crisis and Germany's Status

THE WEST GERMANS were the first to wonder whether, in view of the new atomic balance of power, the Russians would alter their German policy. In July 1958 the Bundestag voted in favor of a meeting of the four powers in Berlin to reexamine the German problem. The following September the Western powers sent a diplomatic note to the Soviet Union.[1] The response was quick and blunt. On November 10, in a speech at Moscow, Khrushchev brought up Berlin's four-party status. On November 28 he mentioned it again in a diplomatic note, demanding that the status of West Berlin be changed to that of a free city. If this were not done within six months, he wrote, the Soviet Union would have more to say on the subject to the German Democratic Republic.

Voices were also raised in America. On January 28, 1959, speaking before the Foreign Affairs Committee of the House of Representatives, John Foster Dulles stated: "The Allies are agreed that they will risk war rather than allow themselves to be evicted from West Berlin." After Harold Macmillan's trip to Moscow, the four foreign ministers decided to meet in Geneva in May to discuss Germany's status. Members of delegations from both East and West Germany would be present as advisers.

Ever since the signing of the Atlantic Treaty, Western policy toward Germany had been based on three principles: (a) the integration of Western Germany into the military, political, and economic institutions of the West;

[1] Jean Laloy, "La politique étrangère de l'U.R.S.S." Lectures Delivered at the Institut d'Etudes Politiques, Paris, 1962–1963, p. 353.

(b) the imposition of certain limitations on German rearmament with a view to eventual negotiations with the East; (c) the possibility of German reunification in the event of a general agreement between East and West.

On May 14, Christian Herter, who succeeded John Foster Dulles on April 18, presented the Western plan for Germany. It defined for the first time the method and successive stages of eventual reunification. Berlin was to be unified first, and then the rest of Germany. A reduction of foreign forces would guarantee a free election. The elected Constitutional Assembly would pave the way for a German government empowered to sign a peace treaty.

The Soviet plan, on the other hand, was to ask the two German states to conclude a peace treaty with the Eastern and Western powers; the two German states alone were qualified to speak in the name of Germany since it was their representatives who had signed the act of surrender in 1945. Such a treaty could lead to reunification because it would bring together the two Germanies. In the interim, Berlin would be declared a free and demilitarized city. Thus unified, Germany would be neutralized: foreign troops would no longer be allowed to remain on her soil.

Each side rejected the other's proposals. However, on August 3, just before the end of the Geneva Conference, it was learned that Eisenhower had invited Khrushchev to visit the United States. After the tensions and differences between the four nations, a dialogue between Americans and Russians was to take place. The Europeans feared that an understanding might be reached without them. They knew that for a long time one objective of Soviet policy had been to deal directly with the United States. Early in September Eisenhower left for Europe to reassure his allies; on September 13, prior to his departure, Khrushchev saw to it that a rocket was fired to the moon.

Khrushchev was impressed by American living standards. He admitted to Adlai Stevenson: "Now I see how the slaves of capitalism live. They live very well." In a speech on September 24, he said: "We would like to maintain friendly relations with the American people and with the American government, and I make no distinction between the two," thus denying the Marxist theory that the leaders of capitalism do not represent the people. The Soviet Union was acknowledged as possessing as much power and prestige as the United States.

To these psychological returns that were the product of public contact must be added the improved political prospects that resulted from the meetings of the two leaders at Camp David (September 25–27). Eisenhower and Khrushchev suggested to their British and French colleagues that a summit meeting be held at the end of the year in Paris to discuss outstanding problems: Germany, Europe, peaceful coexistence, disarmament. The Soviet

Union gave up the idea of fixing a deadline for discussion of the Berlin Problem.

Khrushchev immediately went to Peking to make sure that China was not opposed to a policy of détente that would lead to a summit conference. On October 31, shortly after his return to Moscow, he addressed a session of the supreme Soviet in a manner that conformed to "the spirit of Camp David." He also expressed approval of the French policy: at the Geneva Conference de Gaulle had stipulated that he would consent to German reunification only on condition that the German people "do not call into question their present frontiers"—the Oder-Neisse line.

De Gaulle had invited Khrushchev to visit France before the summit conference. Now, wanting to make sure that France's first atomic bomb had been exploded before the visit, he suggested that the Russian premier wait until the spring of 1960.

The summit conference was scheduled to begin on May 15. But an American U-2 plane on a reconnaissance flight over Russian territory was shot down by anti-aircraft. When Khrushchev arrived in Paris he demanded that Eisenhower apologize publicly for the incident, claiming it was not enough merely to suspend all reconnaissance flights. The summit meeting never took place. The U-2 incident was only a pretext. Two factors explain the Russian about-face: Khrushchev's conviction that the Western powers would not agree to the new status he favored for Berlin; the need to appease the opponents of his policy of détente in Moscow and in Peking.[2]

The status quo lasted until the American presidential elections. In January 1961 John Kennedy took over; in February he suggested to Khrushchev that they confer. The meetings took place on June 3 and 4 at Vienna, two months after Kennedy's Bay of Pigs fiasco. The moment was not propitious and the atmosphere was not favorable. The two national leaders disagreed about nuclear tests, disarmament, and Germany. Khrushchev demanded a solution for Berlin before the end of 1961. In his speech to the American nation on June 6, Kennedy said: "Neither we nor our Allies can forget our obligations to the inhabitants of West Berlin."

Once again tension increased. On July 8 Khrushchev announced an increase in the Soviet Union's defense budget. Kennedy replied on the 28th by asking for increased military expenditures. Departures from East Germany increased; during the month of July, 30,000 refugees crossed its border.

On August 13, the German Democratic Republic closed the border between East and West Berlin. On August 17, a note from the Western powers protested "the unilateral change in the four-party status of Berlin."

---

[2] Raymond Aron, preface to *Année Politique 1960*, p. x.

Kennedy and Macmillan decided to begin negotiations with the Soviet Union on the German question. De Gaulle and Adenauer felt that the Russians must first agree not to violate the status of Berlin. In September the East German authorities started to build the wall that separates the two sections of the city.

At the Twenty-Second Congress of the Soviet Communist Party held in Moscow from the 17th to the 31st of October, Khruschev mentioned the possibility of new negotiations on the German problem and the future of Berlin, but did not allude to the deadline set (December 31). Adenauer, who had paid Kennedy a visit on November 20, tried on December 9 to persuade de Gaulle to agree to new negotiations. The effort failed. In his speech of February 5, 1962, the general reaffirmed his refusal "to negotiate about Berlin or Germany as long as the Soviet Union persists in its threats and demands and creates a situation that precludes a real relaxation of international tensions." He had said the same thing in his press conference on September 5, 1961.

Nevertheless talks were resumed between January and April 1962. However, they were confined to the Americans and the Russians. An American memorandum offered two new suggestions: the establishment of an international body comprising the representatives of the occupying powers and the two Germanies to supervise access to West Berlin; the conclusion of a nonaggression agreement between NATO and the signatories of the Warsaw Pact. This was divulged by the German press, whereupon the negotiations were interrupted. Was the West German government responsible for the leak to the newspapers? In any case it feared that the American government would be willing to recognize East Germany.

After the Cuban crisis, the Soviet Union provoked no further incidents in regard to the German problem. However, on June 12, 1964, it did conclude a treaty of friendship with the German Democratic Republic. In a joint communiqué issued on June 26 the Western powers declared that the treaty could not affect the four power agreements on Germany and Berlin.

The Near East and Africa

Russo-American rivalry for the support of the uncommitted Third World, especially the countries of the Near East and Africa, was likewise in evidence but it was less acute than the competition over Germany.

In July 1958 a *coup d'état*, encouraged by the Soviet Union, resulted in the assassination of the king of Iraq and his prime minister, Nuri Said. The Soviet Union moved the Iraqi pawn with an eye to establishing a protectorate of sorts over Egypt. The West reacted swiftly. The Americans landed troops in Lebanon and the British sent airborne units to Iraq. Through John Foster

Dulles, Eisenhower informed de Gaulle of his intentions. The affair had no serious consequences. Because of the movement for Arab unity, the countries of the Near East were determined not to become involved in the rivalry of the great powers.[3] In August 1964 the area was again the scene of disturbances owing to the British Commonwealth's movement toward disengagement "East of Suez." The Yemeni lodged a complaint against England with the Security Council of the United Nations. The Council decided against England by a vote of nine to two (the United States and England), with France abstaining. France's attitude was probably due to her desire to show the non-committed nations that she was independent of the United States. But England resented the gesture. In similar circumstances at the time of the Franco-Tunisian differences at Sakiet (1958) and Bizerta (1961), it had refused to condemn France.

British, French, and Belgium decolonization in Africa created a void which the Americans and the Russians were eager to fill, if only to hamstring each other. Although active in Mali and Guinea, it was primarily in the Congo (Leopoldville) that the Soviets attempted to obtain a foothold. Here the poverty of the local élite, after the hurried departure of the Belgians, made the situation ripe for anarchy. The Russians supported Lumumba, the prime minister of the Congo; the United States backed Kasavubu, president of the Republic; Belgium favored Tshombe, who was the leader of the secessionist state of Katanga, where most of the Belgian capital was invested. After Lumumba's death, the Adoula government demanded protection from the United Nations. Dag Hammarskjöld, secretary-general of the United Nations, advocated the armed intervention of the world organization. On several occasions during the years 1960 and 1961, ballots were cast; each time France voted on the side of the Communist countries, denying the United Nations' right to use force, and later refusing to share the cost of the military operations. Obsessed by the desire to prevent the Sovietization of the Congo, and unwilling to alienate even the neutralist African governments, America is counting on the United Nations. De Gaulle regrets that the Western powers cannot agree on a common policy which might have prevented Soviet infiltration and rendered unnecessary any intervention by the United Nations.[4] He showed his contempt for the role of the United Nations in his press conferences of September 5, 1960, and April 11, 1961.

The Cuban Crisis

The revolution that brought Fidel Castro to power in Cuba in January 1959 was initially nationalist and hostile to the United States, but not

[3] Laloy, "Politique étrangère," 373–75.
[4] Raymond Aron, preface to *Année politique 1960*, p. x.

Communist. Castro confiscated American property in Cuba and, in July 1960, filed a complaint with the Security Council against the United States. The Russian delegate backed him up. By its subversive acts so close to the United States and to the latter's sphere of influence, the Soviet Union was pursuing an indirect strategy.

In January 1961 the United States broke off diplomatic relations with Cuba. On April 17 anti-Castro expeditionary forces based in Florida landed in Cuba. The invasion had apparently been prepared by the American government. Castro immediately appealed to the General Assembly of the United Nations. On April 18 Khrushchev informed Kennedy that the Soviet Union would give Cuba every assistance in repelling aggression. On April 22 the anti-Castro expeditionary force capitulated. This fiasco reflected badly on the United States. On May 1 Castro proclaimed Cuba the first Socialist republic of the New World. On December 1 he formally announced his adherence to Marxist doctrine.

In July 1962 the Soviet Union installed in Cuba launching platforms for ground-to-air intermediate-range ballistic missiles. Early in September Kennedy revealed this to the American people and called up 150,000 reserves. On September 13 he declared: "If Cuba . . . becomes an appreciably powerful base for Soviet aggression, the United States will take whatever military action is necessary to insure its own safety and that of its allies." On October 15 American aerial photography obtained proof of the existence of the launching platforms. Moreover, twenty-five Soviet cargo ships, protected by submarines, were sighted in the Atlantic.

The Soviet challenge tended to alter the relative strength of the two great powers. American territory could be threatened from Cuba just as Western Europe was already menaced by I.R.B.M.'s based in the Soviet Union.

The American response to the Soviet challenge was vigorous but also cautious. On October 22 Kennedy instituted a blockade of arms destined for Cuba and warned that should missiles fired from Cuban territory reach the United States, the Americans would retaliate by firing on Russian territory. On the 25th Kennedy sent a secret message to Khrushchev demanding the dismantling of the bases and threatening a landing in Cuba. On the 28th Khrushchev acquiesced: "The Soviet government . . . has issued a new order directing that the so-called offensive armaments should be dismantled and returned to the Soviet Union."

Why this retreat? Khrushchev had not taken seriously Kennedy's warning of September 13. The United States was quite capable of achieving its objective—the destruction of the launching platforms—by unleashing a purely local war and using only conventional weapons. Raymond Aron has observed: "Because the Soviets could not defend themselves on the spot, they had to choose between withdrawal, retaliation elsewhere, and escalation."[5] But they were not prepared to employ non-nuclear weapons at another spot—Berlin, for example. The danger of a generalized nuclear war was averted. Khrushchev sought a compromise: the dismantling of the Soviet bases in exchange for an American promise not to invade the island.[6]

The Cuban affair demonstrated that in the face of mutual threats of nuclear war, local superiority in conventional arms played a deterrent role and raised the nuclear threshold. It also showed that in the presence of such threats, the goal was compromise, not defeat of the adversary.

From an interview with Ambassador Hervé Alphand on December 4, it is plain that at the time of the Cuban crisis de Gaulle informed Kennedy that he approved his firm policy. The incident confirmed the general's belief that France should be able to act independently in the domain of nuclear strategy.

Quite different was the French attitude when the American government landed marines in Santo Domingo in 1965 to oppose the return of the ex-president, Juan Bosch. At the meeting of the Security Council in May, the French representative condemned the American intervention.

Negotiations on Disarmament

The race in thermonuclear armaments did not slow down efforts under-way since 1954 to seek peace through disarmament.

Two groups were active: one, consisting of nuclear powers—the United States, England, and the Soviet Union—studied methods of detection as well as ways and means of halting nuclear testing; the other, the so-called Committee of Ten (subsequently Eighteen), concerned itself with a plan for general disarmament.

Both groups met at Geneva. Negotiations persisted despite the Berlin and Cuban crises, which had created such serious tension between the two world powers. The problem of nuclear testing and the more general one of disarmament were debated before the Political Committee of the United Nations.

In October 1958 the Political Committee gave its attention to the suspension of nuclear testing. The Soviets had suspended their tests since March 31 and were hoping to resume them. The Americans suggested a one-year suspension. The French requested that the nuclear powers cease stockpiling, adding that if this were not done, they would develop their own nuclear power. With France abstaining, the American resolution was adopted. Nevertheless, the Soviet Union resumed its nuclear tests on October 2.

---

[5] Raymond Aron, *Le grand débat* (Paris: Calmann-Lévy, 1963), 170.
[6] General Beaufre, *Dissuasion et stratégie* (Paris: Armand Colin, 1964), 77.

In September 1959, while Khrushchev was visiting the United States, the United Nations set up the Committee of Ten. It was composed of the representatives of five Eastern and five Western countries. On October 29 it unanimously adopted a resolution calling for total and general disarmament under international supervision. In March 1960, a Western, three-stage plan for general disarmament was approved by the Nato Council and submitted to the Committee of Ten. A new Western plan was worked out in June. The Soviet government refused to examine it on the date previously agreed upon—June 27. This was shortly after the Khrushchev-Kennedy meeting. As a consequence, work on the plan was halted. However, the two powers resumed their collaboration soon after the Berlin crisis, on December 20, 1961, when they suggested that the General Assembly of the United Nations should enlarge the disarmament committee from ten to eighteen by adding the representatives of eight neutral countries. The resolution was unanimously adopted, and a meeting of the committee was scheduled for the spring of 1962. Khrushchev wanted a summit meeting of the eighteen states, but on February 17 de Gaulle wrote him to suggest negotiations between "those powers that possess nuclear weapons or will soon have them." Khrushchev declined a four-power conference. On March 5 the French foreign minister announced that France would not participate in the disarmament conference. On March 7 *Le Monde* made the following comment on this decision: "Whereas in the past France's policy has always been to voice the aspirations of small countries, General de Gaulle seeks agreement only among the great powers."

At the Disarmament Conference that took place in August 1962, the American and British delegation presented two alternatives: a general treaty prohibiting all nuclear testing; and a limited treaty prohibiting tests in the air, in cosmic space, and in the waters. This twofold plan made a favorable impression on the neutrals.

Meanwhile, the Americans and Russians negotiated intermittently on the cessation of nuclear testing and on testing itself. It should be noted that the Russians conducted a series of nuclear tests in September 1961 during the Berlin crisis; the detonation of a fifty-megaton bomb on October 3 concluded these experiments; the Americans resumed their tests in April 1962 at the time of the Cuban crises; the Russians again exploded more bombs in July 1962. On November 4, when the Cuban crisis was over, the United States announced the cessation of tests in the atmosphere.

The Treaty of Moscow on the Partial Nuclear Test Ban

After the Cuban crisis, the Soviet Union decided to accept the second Anglo-American proposal of 1962; on August 5, 1963, it signed a treaty with the United States and England for the cessation of nuclear testing. According to the treaty, only underground tests would be permissible. In the present stage of scientific knowledge, such tests cannot be detected. They can, however, be verified by on-the-spot inspection but this the Russians refused to accept.

The treaty contains one broad clause: it is open to every nation. It also contains a restrictive clause: a signatory must give three months' advance notice if it should wish to renounce it.

What is the political significance of the treaty for American-Soviet relations and for the relations of each of the two powers with its allies?

The treaty publicly manifests a kind of solidarity between the two powers capable of starting a thermonuclear war and also anxious to prevent one. Kennedy was convinced of the need for such solidarity. To be sure, the two potential adversaries have antithetical political philosophies. But over the years both have shown wisdom and caution in their relations with each other. Since the signing of the treaty there has been a little more mutual confidence, a little less suspicion. The moratorium on nuclear testing is an example of restraint brought about by an implicit understanding. Before the Cuban crisis, an agreement reached in June 1962 foreshadowed cooperation in the domain of meteorological and television satellites. In May 1963, an accord was concluded for the peaceful exploration of space. In April 1964 the two nations proclaimed simultaneously their intention of reducing the manufacture of fissionable materials for military use—a reduction fully justified by the existence of considerable stockpiles exceeding the "requirements" of total warfare. In May 1964 the two nations concluded a consular agreement. The fear of spying has decreased now that each of the two rivals can photograph the military bases from cosmic space. The installation of the "hot line" between Washington and Moscow attests a common anxiety to prevent a misunderstanding or accident from triggering a nuclear conflict. Finally, the treaty is looked upon as a political instrument likely to slow down the proliferation of thermonuclear arms.

A majority of the Western, Eastern, and neutral nations signed the treaty, although West Germany expressed some hesitation. Three nations refused to sign: China, Albania, and France.

There was nothing surprising about China's attitude. To sign the treaty would mean to opt for peaceful coexistence to which China was opposed. Albania followed China's example.

The government of West Germany was divided. Some of its members were afraid that the treaty would strengthen the international status of the German Democratic Republic, and that a policy of détente would perpetuate the partition of Germany. Loyalty to the Atlantic Treaty, however, was the decisive factor, and on August 19 Bonn signed the treaty.

De Gaulle's firm intention of acquiring nuclear power for France explains his refusal to sign.

The Vietnam War and Southeast Asia

The Berlin and Cuban crises pitted the United States against the Soviet Union. The Vietnam war pitted the United States against China. The first confrontation of the two powers occurred in 1958 over Quemoy, in the Formosa Straits. Influenced by Russia's policy of moderation, China gave up the idea of effecting a landing there.

Initially, the Vietnam conflict was a civil war between the People's Republic of the North and the South Vietnam Republic. The Geneva Accords of 1954, which ruled that the country be divided at the seventeenth parallel, stipulated that elections would be held within a two-year period. The purpose of this provision was to insure self-determination, the possible reunification of the North and South, and the establishment of a single neutral state. But Ngo Dinh Diem, president of South Vietnam, refused to organize elections. In the North Ho Chi-minh did not give up the idea of reunification; to obtain it, he resorted to subversive acts by backing the southern opposition, the Viet Cong. Guerrilla warfare broke out around 1956.

The Americans, replacing the French, increased their military staff as subversion spread; they further expanded their activity in 1961, shortly before Diem declared a state of emergency. In November 1962 a disagreement between Diem and the Americans resulted in Diem's fall from power and his death. Thereafter South Vietnam had a series of unstable governments that lacked popular support. In 1964, General Maxwell Taylor was appointed United States ambassador to South Vietnam. The American command, which had set up headquarters in Saigon as early as 1962, ordered aerial attacks against the communication lines of the North. Escalation began. In February 1965 American pilots took an active part in the operations; in March, United States marines landed and installed powerful bases, while entire units of the North Vietnamese army fought in the South. China and the Soviet Union were furnishing arms to the North Vietnamese. Early in 1968 the United States had an army of 450,000 men in South Vietnam but was unable to prevent the Viet Cong from taking over a large part of the country.

In several of the states of Southeast Asia subversive movements, stoked by a nationalist ferment and influenced by the Chinese, made their appearance. For several years three factions—Western, neutralist, and Communist—confronted each other in Laos in a situation tantamount to civil war. After protracted negotiations with each other and with the great powers, the contending factions managed in 1962 to form a coalition government that was committed to no military alliance. Cambodia proclaimed its neutrality, then in 1963 demanded the convocation of an international conference to safeguard it. The conference could not be arranged. In May 1965 Cambodia broke off diplomatic relations with the United States. In 1964, to protect its interests and to be ready for trouble in Cambodia and Laos, the United States sent armed forces to Thailand. Supported by China, Indonesia opened hostilities against Malaysia, which was backed by the United States and England. In January 1965, Indonesia left the United Nations because Malaysia joined the Security Council. The eviction of the Indonesian Communist Party in 1966 put an end to the conflict but the situation in Malaysia remained troubled, especially after Singapore withdrew from the Federation of Malaysia, a development in which China doubtless had a hand.

Thus, the reunification of Vietnam was not the only thing at stake in the conflict. Rather, the pivotal issue was the determination of both China and the United States to establish spheres of influence in Southeast Asia. China had managed to shape the enormous mass of its population into a powerful political organization. Through local nationalist movements and the dissemination of the communist ideology, it attempted to win over to its side other large agglomerations of people, less well organized and as yet politically uncommitted. China wanted to extend its influence toward the south where it hoped that Indonesia, which until recently had been sympathetic to Communism, would join it; and toward the west, throughout pro-American Thailand and pro-Chinese Burma, in order to threaten India with the eventual support of Pakistan.

The United States opposed the Chinese thrust to the south and the west. It had just won an indirect victory when Indonesia changed sides. And it intended to protect Malaysia and India and safeguard Australia and New Zealand with which it had concluded a treaty of alliance in 1951 and 1952. Assisted by England, Australia, and New Zealand—the latter two countries provided contingents for the Vietnam war—it organized the defense of the Indian and Pacific Oceans with the aid of a chain of naval and air bases.

Toward the conflict between the United States and China, the Soviet Union adopted an attitude of prudence. It was not displeased to note the measures taken by the United States to limit Chinese expansion. Wishing to avoid any direct conflict with the United States, it gave the North Vietnamese only limited military assistance—in the form of anti-aircraft missiles. At the same time it issued verbal protests against American escalation.

In the conflict between the United States and China over Vietnam, the success of peace negotiations will be determined by the two great powers rather than by the immediate adversaries. China demanded the departure of all American troops prior to any negotiation, according to an interview which Edgar Snow had with Mao Tse-tung in January 1965. But the North Vietnamese made no such demand. In his Baltimore speech of April 1965, President Johnson said that the United States will not prescribe any prior conditions, in form or in substance, for initiation of negotiations, but he refused to accept the Viet Cong as spokesman. In his declaration of February 1965, Kosygin demanded, in the name of the Soviet Union, a rigid application of the Geneva Accords of 1954.

The European allies of the United States entertained serious reservations about the war in Vietnam. A segment of British public opinion was opposed to a continuation of hostilities but successive English governments realized that the United States, in balking Chinese ambitions, was defending the interests of the Commonwealth in the Indian and Pacific Oceans.

General de Gaulle had different objectives. He hoped not only that France would regain a foothold in the Far East, but that she would reestablish herself there as a great power, or at least as a power not identified with the United States. With this in mind France recognized China on January 27, 1964.

Summary

Since 1958 three developments have troubled the relations of the great powers: the Berlin and Cuban crises and the war in Vietnam.

The Berlin crisis made several things clear. One was the fragility of Soviet domination over the German Democratic Republic: to prevent a mass exodus it was necessary to build a wall. Another was the stability in the thermonuclear age of an absurd strategic situation that would not have been possible in the pre-nuclear age.[7] A third was Western vacillation in regard to Germany. The erection of the Berlin wall and the failure of the West to react firmly shocked public opinion in Germany. NATO was making no progress on the problem of unification, and some West Germans were beginning to wonder whether some other approach should be tried.[8]

The Cuban crisis shed light on the thermonuclear age. It showed the role that non-nuclear weapons can play in raising the atomic threshold. The Americans were strong enough to win a local non-nuclear war; the Russians had been forced to withdraw. After this emergency, Europeans became convinced that "the two main nuclear powers will avoid a direct military confrontation for an indefinite period." This should serve to convert NATO from a purely defensive alliance into a political organization with well-defined objectives.[9] Total escalation seems less likely. Fear of massive destruction should impel the Soviet Union to strive increasingly for a détente. After Cuba the Russians ceased to issue threats about Berlin. They signed the Treaty of Moscow for the cessation of nuclear tests.

---

[7] *Ibid.*, 159.

[8] Henry A. Kissinger, *The Troubled Partnership* (New York: McGraw-Hill, 1965), 89, 90.

[9] *Ibid.*, 9.

The Vietnam war is non-nuclear. Immediately at stake is the political control of Southeast Asia. Domination of India and the Australian subcontinent is the long-term objective of the contestants. The war is therefore limited but of prime importance; it pits the United States against an ambitious and dissatisfied China. The East-West conflict of the 1950s has moved from Europe, where the rivalry of the two great thermonuclear powers has produced considerable stability, to Asia. China's growing influence made itself felt, long before the country had operational strategic weapons, through indirect and subversive activities. So far, the war in Vietnam has not affected the Russo-American détente. The Soviet Union's restraint is due to internal factors—the instability of its leadership, the evolution toward a consumers' society—and to the ideological and political impact of the Sino-Soviet split.

Such is the context within which de Gaulle, in the name of France, was conducting a strategic operation in the grand manner. He began cautiously, but he daily grew more bold. He intended to win for France a place among the great nuclear powers. To accomplish this, France must be armed, her eminence must be acknowledged, she must make a show of independence within and outside the framework of alliances. As long as she was waging a war in Algeria, caution was necessary. The first indication of her independence came in connection with the status of Germany: in 1959, alone among the Allies, de Gaulle accepted the Oder-Neisse line. However, during the Berlin and Cuban crises he exhorted the United States to stand firm against the Russian threat. When the question of disarmament arose he did everything he could to gain recognition for France as a potential nuclear power: in February 1962 he suggested a four-power conference, which the Soviet Union rejected; he decided not to participate in the deliberations of the Committee of Eighteen on disarmament. His audacity prevailed after 1963. Alone among the members of NATO, de Gaulle refused to sign the Treaty of Moscow. As long as the nuclear powers refused to desist from stockpiling and exploding missiles, France would retain complete freedom of action. In 1964 he challenged Washington and Moscow by granting diplomatic recognition to China. Later, he openly criticized American escalation of the war in Vietnam. French dissidence in the Western camp deliberately paralleled Chinese dissidence in the Eastern camp. De Gaulle, wrote Henry A. Kissinger, sees "little risk and considerable potential gain in political independence," because "measures contradictory to those of the United States are thus in a sense supported by the American nuclear umbrella. . . . Neutrals enjoy most of the protection of allies and allies aspire to have the same freedom of action as do neutrals."[10]

This glimpse of de Gaulle's reactions to the conflicts in which the United States, the Soviet Union, and China are involved gives but a fragmented

[10] *Ibid.*, 17–18.

view of his aims in the area of defense. His policy was evident within the Atlantic Alliance. The transition from ally to neutral—perhaps even to opponent—occurred piecemeal: the proposal of a three-power directorate in 1958, the creation of a national deterrent force, the several challenges of 1963, the rapprochement with Eastern countries, the withdrawal from NATO in 1966, several moves in planetary diplomacy in 1967.

7

The Proposal of a Western Three-Power Directorate

De Gaulle, Defense, and the Alliances from 1949 to 1958

D E GAULLE RESUMED OFFICE at a time when the strategy of the great powers was undergoing a basic change. The smaller nations, like France, did not share in this change, but the fundamentals of their defense policy were affected.

Had the general's ideas about defense and alliances changed since the signing of the Atlantic Treaty? In his press conference of November 17, 1949, he declared: "It would be unthinkable to allow the defense of France to be guaranteed or the direction of her military efforts to be determined by any country other than France herself." We know the role de Gaulle played in the rejection of the European Defense Community. In his press conference of November 12, 1953, he denounced the E.D.C., which would "create a stateless army of Frenchmen and Germans," and declared that the alliance with the United States had become a species of protectorate. He added: "France must find out whether an understanding can be reached with the Soviet Union." On August 26, 1954, speaking about the E.D.C. he exclaimed: "To make the Atlantic Treaty seem like a good alliance and not a bad protectorate—such is the great mission that destiny offers France."

On June 1, 1958, in his investiture address to the National Assembly, de Gaulle denounced "the increasing degradation of the state" and cited, among other examples, "our international position disparaged within the very core of our alliances." He intended to see to it that his government would be able "to answer for . . . the independence of the country." In his radio talk on June 13 he enumerated his objectives: "To take our proper place in the

Western world to which we belong but to which we are not limited; to act in a manner appropriate to France and conducive to her interests and security."

Were independence and political action appropriate to France compatible with the Atlantic Treaty and with the world strategy of the major nuclear powers? This was the big question.

Feelers

France's position within the Atlantic Treaty was, according to de Gaulle, a subordinate one. To rectify this the treaty would have to be revised on the strategic as well as on the military level. This was the substance of de Gaulle's conversation on June 16, 1958, with Paul-Henri Spaak, secretary-general of NATO. He elaborated on this thesis in the course of interviews with Secretary of State John Foster Dulles on July 4 and 5. To Dulles's objections that Germany and Italy would demand similar treatment in NATO, de Gaulle replied that they were continental states whereas France had the makings of a global power. Finally, he maintained that cooperation—in contrast to integration—was the only practical basis on which relations between allies could be founded.[1] The general played host to Chancellor Adenauer at Colombey on September 14 and sought to win West Germany over to his views. A communiqué issued subsequently declared that "Franco-German cooperation was the basis of European construction" and that it would "reinforce the Atlantic alliance and promote the well-being of all nations." Adenauer apparently accepted de Gaulle's conception of cooperation and his idea that France should play the role of a world power.[2]

The Memorandum of September 24, 1958

After these preliminary feelers de Gaulle decided that the time had come to pinpoint his ideas. On September 24 he sent a confidential memorandum to Eisenhower. On October 24 the major points of the memorandum were revealed by *Der Mittag* of Düsseldorf and subsequently developed by *Le Monde* on November 11 and 13. Without in any way contradicting the substance of the *Le Monde* article, the French government admitted that de Gaulle had sent personal messages to Eisenhower and Macmillan on the subject of the Atlantic Alliance. The text of these messages had been given to the other European allies.[3] But the general never published the actual text of the memorandum sent to Eisenhower. In his book, *The Three Lives of*

---

[1] David Schoenbrunn, *The Three Lives of Charles de Gaulle* (New York: 1966), 294.

[2] *Ibid.*, 298.

[3] *Année politique 1958*, 452, 453.

Charles de Gaulle (published in 1965), David Schoenbrunn, having doubtless received his information fromWashington, analyzed de Gaulle's correspondence with Eisenhower and subsequently Kennedy. The facts he adduced in a chapter entitled "The Hour of Reckoning with the Anglo-Saxons" were not denied by Paris. De Gaulle's subsequent statements and actions tally with Schoenbrunn's account which is largely quoted hereafter.

In his memorandum of September 24, 1958, de Gaulle criticized the manner in which the alliance functioned, suggested changes, and threatened to take action if his suggestions were not heeded. He criticized the handling of past crises, such as the Lebanon incident, and stressed the danger France incurred by being an ally of the United States; he complained that France, "a power with worldwide interests and responsibilities," was not sufficiently informed or consulted about many of the decisions made by the United States. His suggestion was to "create a tripartite organization to take joint decisions on global problems"—the three parties being the United States, England, and France. This organization would be empowered to draw up strategic plans and also to implement them especially in regard to "the use of atomic weapons anywhere in the world." He threatened that France "would subordinate" her participation in NATO to considerations for her "world interests" and her right to "equal participation" in global strategy.

Eisenhower, replying on October 20, acknowledged that the Soviet Union and its allies threatened the entire free world, but he added that the regional pacts took this fact into account. He reminded the general that these treaties would further the habit of consultation among allies. He urged de Gaulle "to avoid anything that might impair or destroy the growing confidence in such consultation between members of NATO" or give our allies the impression that "basic decisions affecting their own vital interests are being made without their participation." He did, however, open the door to negotiation. On December 15, Dulles paid a visit to de Gaulle in Paris. De Gaulle confirmed Dulles's impression that the words "joint decisions" contained in his memorandum meant the right of veto. Dulles suggested that three-power joint action might be tested in Africa, to which de Gaulle replied: "Of course a common policy in North Africa would necessarily be a French policy."[4] France never sent a representative to the three-party committee de Gaulle himself had suggested.

This passage of arms between de Gaulle and Eisenhower is indicative of the extent of their differences. De Gaulle made two claims. One had a bearing on the political direction of the alliance, which was determined by Anglo-Saxon interests. Since France was a world power this problem should be settled by a three-power committee. The creation of such a committee

---

[4] Schoenbrunn, *Three Lives*, 303.

would mean official acknowledgement of France's eminence. His second claim went even further. In demanding the right of veto over the use of American deterrent forces, de Gaulle was claiming France's right to have a permanent say in American global strategy. This was excessive if we remember that France had not yet exploded her first trial bomb, that her contribution to the alliance's conventional weapons was less than that of Germany, and that de Gaulle was speaking, not in the name of Europe, or of the six European nations, but solely in the name of France. Doubtless his demands were made with the idea of provoking a refusal which would then justify France in her gradual resumption of freedom of action.

First Gestures of Disengagement

On March 7, 1959, de Gaulle launched his first offensive against NATO by serving notice that the French government intended in time of war to withdraw some of its naval forces from the Mediterranean. It is difficult to justify technically a transfer to French command in time of war since this is the very moment when a unified command would prove most desirable. Nor did the immediate needs of the Algerian war require such a transfer because the units involved played no part in the general conflict. De Gaulle's press conference of March 25 only added to the confusion: "NATO's eventual sphere of action does not extend south of the Mediterranean. The Middle East, North and Black Africa, Madagascar, the Red Sea, etc., are not part of it. Who can deny that France might eventually find herself obliged to intervene in these countries? She would have to do so independently of NATO. But would this be possible if she did not have at her disposal the use of her fleet?" This statement contains two errors. First, by virtue of Article 6, inserted at the express request of France, Algeria was part of NATO's sphere of action. Furthermore, there was nothing to prevent France from using her naval forces in the Mediterranean in order to intervene in the Middle East or in Africa since, in time of peace, these naval forces were under national command. The confusion thus created was deliberate. The gesture of March 7 had a political rather than a military significance. This became clear at de Gaulle's press conference: "I believe that the Alliance would be all the more vigorous and powerful since the large nations would be united in the kind of cooperation in which each state assumes its own responsibilities, rather than in a system of integration in which nations and governments would be more or less deprived of their functions and responsibilities in matters concerning their own defense."

In the interval between de Gaulle's provocative gesture of March 7 and his press conference of March 25 a second exchange of secret letters took place between the general and Eisenhower. De Gaulle advised Eisenhower to be firm with Khrushchev about Berlin; but the primary purpose of his letter was to reiterate the theme of his September 24, 1958, memorandum, especially "the vital need to cooperate in joint political, diplomatic, and strategic plans everywhere in the world." To which Eisenhower immediately replied: "I attach the greatest importance to the maintenance of our military situation through a maximum degree of close and concrete cooperation . . . within NATO." Since the president of the United States had referred expressly to NATO as the strategic organ of cooperation, the president of the French Republic carried the debate to the French public in the terms we have just cited.

A second controversy pitted France against a unified Atlantic command: the installation of American launching platforms and the stockpiling of intermediate-range missiles for American units stationed in France. De Gaulle hoped to establish a close connection between the award of such facilities to the Americans and France's right to share in atomic strategy decisions. In June 1959, after de Gaulle's refusal to allow the stockpiling of missiles, General Norstad decided to withdraw American fighter bombers since they had to be stationed close to the missile depots. Thereupon the French government made public its intention not to "take on any new commitments toward NATO," which meant it refused to allow the installation of launching platforms on its soil. In December, the fighter bombers were transferred from France to Germany.

The third controversy stemmed from France's refusal of the American offer to pool information on the technology and use of tactical missiles with thermonuclear warheads. France refused because these were to remain under American control. England, Germany, Holland, and Turkey accepted the offer. In July 1959 they signed accords to this effect with the United States. Greece and Italy subsequently signed similar accords. It was not until September 1961, at the time of the Berlin crisis, and in connection with the stationing of troops in Germany and the reinforcement of an interallied means of defense, that France decided to follow suit. In 1959, a fourth military controversy arose over NATO's unification of air defenses. The revolutionary changes in detection techniques and the increased speed of planes and missiles led interallied officials to request the pooling of the facilities needed to install a network for a Distant Early Warning System. This network, to be completed by 1960, was to extend "from Norway to Turkey." Responsibility for launching an air defense was to be entrusted to a single command. The first proposal evoked no objections from the French government. The same was not true of the second, which the French government regarded as a measure leading to integration. But the air space over the countries of Europe is too restricted for isolated defense; and the time lapse too short to allow for an intergovernmental consultation. It was suggested that French defenses should remain under national command but that they should be coordinated at the highest level with the interallied defense system. After lengthy negotiations, this solution was adopted with the approval of the NATO Council in September 1960.

Early in September 1959, when Eisenhower was making a tour of the principal European capitals prior to Khrushchev's visit to the United States, he and de Gaulle discussed problems pertaining to the organization of NATO. The communiqué on the Eisenhower-de Gaulle talks, issued on September 3, was couched in vague language. The two chiefs of state had examined "ways of improving cooperation between the two countries in regard to the world as a whole, especially methods of consultation on essential problems, political as well as military." No special organ of consultation was established. Thus, in the space of one year, despite two exchanges of letters with Eisenhower, despite the implementation of his threat to loosen his ties with NATO (which took four different forms), despite his confidential talks with the president of the United States, General de Gaulle had not been able to impose his views on Eisenhower. He thought the time had come to attack directly the congenital flaw in NATO—integration.

The System of Integration Has Had Its Day

In October 1959 de Gaulle published Volume III of his *Memoirs*. Political commentators pored over the "vast plan" he had formulated for his country at the time of the Liberation: "To collaborate with the West and with the East; if need be to form alliances with one side or the other, but never to accept any sort of dependence." To implement this plan, de Gaulle wished "to bring together for political, economic, and strategic purposes, the states bordering on the Rhine, the Alps, and the Pyrenees," in order "to forge from such an organization a third planetary power and, if need be, to make it serve as the arbiter of the two rival Soviet and Anglo-Saxon camps."[5] David Schoenbrunn wondered whether the publication in 1959 of ideas which the general attributed to the time of his first reign was designed to serve as a warning to the Anglo-Saxon nations.[6]

Be that as it may, on November 3, 1959, de Gaulle's speech to the École Militaire sounded the death knell of the generally accepted NATO principle. It expressed his determination: "The defense of France must be French. . . . If a country like France should be called upon to wage war, it must wage its own war. . . . Naturally, the defense of France will be combined with that of other countries, if necessary . . . but it is indispensable that France be responsible for her own defense, that she defend herself for her own ends,

---

[5] Charles de Gaulle, *Mémoires de guerre* (Paris: Plon, 1959), III, 179.
[6] Schoenbrunn, *Three Lives*, 320.

and in her own way." And he gave the following justification for his determination: "If one allowed France's defense to cease to exist within a national framework over a protracted period of time, if defense of France were to be joined or fused with some other system, then it would not be possible to preserve a state of our own." He went on to speak of the military and strategic consequences: "That is why we cannot accept the idea of a war, or even of a battle, in which France would no longer be France and would not be acting in her own interests, for her own share, and according to her wishes. The so-called system of 'integration' . . . has had its day. . . . Our strategy must be coordinated with that of other nations. But each country must share in the decision-making." For the first time de Gaulle clearly spelled out his strategic doctrine; he linked it to his concept of France's independence. He stressed the subordinate nature of alliances. His speech pointed up his two objectives: to condemn integration and to justify the possession of a national striking force. "The consequence of all this is that we must . . . provide ourselves . . . with a force capable of serving our own ends. It goes without saying that such a force must include atomic weapons." His two objectives dovetailed: an integrated alliance was unthinkable if the use of a deterrent force were to be decided solely by the countries that had it.

At the NATO Council sessions of December 15 to 17, 1959, the controversy over integration continued; the question of NATO's political leadership was not settled. Nor was it settled when Eisenhower and de Gaulle met on December 19. This encounter took place outside of the framework of the Western summit conference; its purpose was precisely to make preparations for the 1960 summit meeting which Khrushchev was to attend that spring. On December 28 and 29, French foreign policy issues were debated in the National Assembly. The Alliance's global mission was discussed as well as the decisions or intentions of the government regarding its fleet in the Mediterranean, its air defense, and the stockpiling of nuclear bombs. Maurice Faure expressed approval of a readjustment in the Atlantic Pact but regretted that these revisions were requested "under conditions that have resulted in weakening the alliance whereas we should have worked toward a stronger alliance."

During the month of June a fresh series of secret letters were exchanged between de Gaulle and Eisenhower. The general's third letter stressed "strategic global cooperation" and France's hope of having "an equal voice in joint decisions on the use of nuclear arms."

Eisenhower proposed a meeting of the three Western powers to study the French demands for a "global strategy." This was a step in the right direction, in de Gaulle's opinion. In a fourth letter to Eisenhower toward the end of June, he made a counter-suggestion: the setting up of a three-power committee "to make plans for a global strategy . . . and to reorganize the

Atlantic Treaty." To this Eisenhower responded by saying that no useful discussion of the reorganization of NATO would be possible until de Gaulle wrote a report detailing his suggestions. He noted that twice in the course of conversations about the Atlantic Treaty de Gaulle had promised to send him such a report, but that so far he had not done so.[7]

Public Attacks against NATO

This was the end of the controversial secret correspondence between Eisenhower and de Gaulle. The general decided to publicize the debate. In his press conference of September 5, 1960, he enlarged on the doctrine he had outlined in his speech of November 3, 1959. He launched a direct attack against NATO and served a warning on Eisenhower's successor (American presidential elections were slated for November, 1960). According to de Gaulle, at the time NATO was created, "the nations of Western Europe . . . postponed until some later date the rebirth of their national identities within the framework of the international order, or perhaps gave up entirely any hope of such a rebirth. And so the alliance was founded on the precept of integration, that is, a system in which the defense of each of the European nations, with the exception of England, was devoid of national characteristics, . . . in which the principle weapons, nuclear arms, were available solely to the Americans." For the last ten years the possibility of war had been growing, and the nations of continental Europe had become increasingly conscious of their identities. "Under the circumstances, France believes that what has been accomplished in ten years in this narrow sphere and on the basis of integration must be brought up to date." Two changes must be made: first, "NATO must be limited to the European sphere alone." There must be some sort of plan "among the world powers of the West . . . as to their political and eventually strategic policies outside of Europe, particularly in the Middle East and in Africa." The second change concerns "integration for the defense of Europe. . . . Without in the least abrogating the principle of the alliance we have concluded . . . it seems to us that the defense of a country must be national in nature." The two demands were incompatible: how could one ask for a broadening of political and even strategic cooperation and at the same time demand independent control of the means of defense?

The same inconsistency was evident in de Gaulle's remarks in his press conference of April 11, 1961. The organization of NATO must be altered in two essential ways: (1) "The right and duty of each of the continental European powers to have a national defense of its own must be recognized. It is intolerable that a great nation should leave its fate to the decisions and

[7] *Ibid.*, 310.

actions of another nation"; (2) "The question of the use of nuclear arms by the two Western powers who have them must be thoroughly explored. . . . The continental European nations, who are far more exposed to danger, must know precisely with what weapons and under what circumstances their overseas allies will wage war alongside them."

The diplomatic debate on NATO was resumed in May 1961 at the time of President Kennedy's official visit to Paris. Kennedy suggested to de Gaulle that a three-power military directorate be set up to elaborate a common program for Berlin and Laos, the areas then being threatened. De Gaulle never appointed a French delegate to discuss these questions with the English and American representatives. Probably it was public recognition of France's eminence that interested him primarily. According to Schoenbrunn, Kennedy "suspected de Gaulle of having developed the theory in order to make his deeply rooted desire for self-aggrandizement appear rational." Shortly after the erection of the Berlin wall, de Gaulle sent a secret letter to Kennedy in which, after first expressing his ideas on what the allied attitude toward Russia should be, he alluded to NATO in the same terms as in his letters to Eisenhower. Kennedy did not reply to the remarks about NATO but a little later wrote to de Gaulle on the subject of nuclear policy. He said he would be willing to examine any suggestions that would satisfy France's need for nuclear arms but that he was anxious to avoid establishing a precedent that might lead to a proliferation of atomic weapons. The American solution was to give France the necessary means in exchange for a promise that she would not engage in nuclear testing. De Gaulle turned the offer down. But in January 1962 he again wrote to Kennedy to suggest the creation of a three-power political planning group and a military staff to make provisions for "joint decisions and actions" particularly in regard to the "nonaligned nations." But the detailed memorandum he promised was never sent.[8]

In his speech of February 5, 1962, de Gaulle observed that France must be the effective ally of America, "for the present." Alluding to the direction of his foreign policy, he said: "Doubtless . . . this new course will enable us to oppose the network of prior agreements that assigned to us the role of a so-called integrated nation, in other words, a second-rate nation."

There was no further mention of a three-power directorate. The speech of February 5 contained the same phrases de Gaulle had used in his *Memoirs*. "France . . . must help to build Western Europe into an organized union of states so that, little by little, on both sides of the Rhine, of the Alps, perhaps even of the Channel, a political, economic, cultural, and military entity can be established that will be the most powerful, prosperous, and influential in the world."

[8] *Ibid.*, 317.

Was the Gaullist demand for a three-power directorate a means or an end in itself? Certainly the general's constant preoccupation was to mold France into a great power and to force the United States to acknowledge her as such. But the very excessiveness of his demand opens it to other interpretations. What de Gaulle asked was that American world strategy be subject to the approval of the French chief of state; furthermore, the general refused to formulate proposals for reform; he refused to participate in the work of a three-power committee; his desire to direct the policy of the Alliance and his systematic criticism of any form of integration were contradictory. The American refusal to make France officially an equal partner of the United States gave de Gaulle two choices. One was to denounce NATO as sub-servient to American nuclear power and to reject military integration, which might limit the free use of France's future nuclear weapons; the other was to make France the most powerful of all the middle-sized nations in the organized union of European nations, and the leader of a Western Europe that would not be subordinate to the United States.

As early as 1960 the absolute independence of the future French nuclear force was proclaimed. Early in 1961 de Gaulle began discussions for the constitution of a political Europe in harmony with his views. By the beginning of 1962 the rejection of integration was not so much a threatening gesture as an end in itself.

8

The National Deterrent Force

Political and Strategic Justifications

ON OCTOBER 23, 1958, a few weeks after his memorandum to Eisenhower on the political direction of NATO, de Gaulle held his first press
conference. He explained his plans for French atomic power, announced
forthcoming nuclear tests, and concluded: "Besides, when we will have
become an atomic power, which will not be long from now, we shall have far
better means of making our influence felt in those areas that all mankind
holds dear: world security and disarmament." On November 3, 1959, in an
address before the École de Guerre in which he emphasized his condemnation
of integration and his views on the defense of France, he declared: "Consequently, during the next few years, it is obvious that we must have a force
strong enough to act for us, what is called 'a strike force' capable of being
deployed at any time, anywhere. It goes without saying that such a force must
include atomic arms—whether we manufacture them ourselves or buy
them—but they must belong to us; and since it is possible to destroy France
from any point in the world, our atomic force must be able to make itself felt
any place on earth."

The press conference of November 10, 1959, dealt primarily with the
cessation of nuclear testing to which the Soviets and the Anglo-Saxons had
agreed. France, in de Gaulle's opinion, could but approve this step, "but if
anyone has the notion of asking her to give up the idea of having her own
atomic weapons while others possess them and develop them in large quantities, there is no chance that we would agree." Alluding to the possibility that
the two rival powers might reach an understanding to divide up the world,

de Gaulle declared: "The truth is that by equipping herself with nuclear arms, France is serving the cause of world peace." In his Washington press conference on May 31, 1960, de Gaulle once again stressed France's role and her national identity: "This implies that France, too, will be endowed with nuclear weapons since other nations have them, that France's capabilities, her territory will be dependent on herself alone; although the destiny of France is linked with that of her allies, it remains in her own hands." This theme of national autonomy in regard to armaments was repeated at Strasbourg, in a speech delivered on November 23, 1961, to army personnel: "France must preserve her will, her image, and her future for her own ends. This requires atomic weapons . . . for our military might. . . . A great nation that does not have such weapons when others do has no say in its own destiny. . . . There are no longer conflicts or hazards anywhere in the world that do not concern a world power, and consequently France."

At a press conference on April 11, 1961, a new note was sounded for the first time. Alluding to a reorganization of the Alliance, the general said: "The question of the use of nuclear arms by the two powers that have them must be thoroughly explored. . . . For the nations of continental Europe (which are by far the most threatened) must know exactly with what weapons and under what circumstances their overseas allies will wage war for them." And at his press conference of May 15, 1962, de Gaulle once again deplored the state of uncertainty about the fate of Europe that the Alliance had allowed to prevail. Since both America and Russia had the capacity to strike each other directly, "no one knows today when, how, or why one or the other of these great atomic powers will use its nuclear weapons. This statement should suffice to make it plain that everything—the defense of France, the battle for Europe, even a world war, as it was conceived when NATO was constituted —is now open to question." In view of the situation, a French national deterrent force "completely changes and will continue to change the conditions of our defense and of our intervention in distant lands, as well as the contributions we can make to the security of our allies."

In summary, two arguments were advanced in favor of atomic weapons for France. The first was political: no nation can be ranked a great power unless it possesses the supreme weapon and, what is more, unless it alone controls its use. Only then is it able to determine its own fate and proclaim its total sovereignty. The second argument was strategic: the United States has become vulnerable to attack. Western Europe is in greater danger than its protector. Might not the United States be tempted to disengage itself from the European theater of operations? NATO has shown a total indecisiveness in dealing with the following important question: under what conditions will an American deterrent force intervene? Therefore France must take every precaution; she has grave doubts about the way an alliance integrated in matters pertaining to conventional weapons would function, especially since such an alliance is dependent, in all matters affecting thermonuclear weapons, on America's decision.

What Kinds of Nuclear Weapons?

On February 13, 1960, the first French A-bomb was exploded at Reggana in the Sahara. A second bomb was exploded on April 1. On July 18 the government drew up a legislative proposal for the procurement of certain kinds of military equipment. The discussion in the National Assembly was scheduled for October. We will come back to the debates later. The text defined the national military policy and earmarked appropriations for the years 1960–1964. Military policy was to be based on three instrumentalities of defense: a national deterrent force; a conventional offensive force (mechanized divisions, airborne divisions, warships, airplanes); and an operational defense of its territory (regional and provincial units).

Strategic deterrence would consist of a first-generation and a second-generation force. The first-generation force covering the years 1963–1969 included fifty Mirage IV A planes equipped with fifty- to sixty-kiloton atom bombs.

In mid-1959 the French government had considered ordering the Mirage IV B, which is much heavier than the IV A and has a greater flying range. The Mirage IV B was to have been equipped with Pratt and Whitney turbo-reactors, licensed by Snecma with the permission of the American government. A few months later the order was cancelled either because American authorization was withdrawn or because of financial considerations. France was thus the first nation that had begun to build atomic weapons without a precise strategic plan for the delivery of the bomb against a prime enemy.[1] Indeed, the Mirage IV A has a limited range of 2,500 kilometers. If it is refueled in flight by aerial tankers the range is increased to 4,800 kilometers. The legislative proposal earmarked appropriations for the purchase of twelve American C 135 F aerial tankers. They were ordered in June 1962, with the authorization of President Kennedy. On May 1, 1962, a fifty-kiloton bomb was exploded underground at Hoggar. This test was a prototype of the Mirage IV's A-bomb. The first Mirage IV planes were operational by October 1963. By the end of 1965 the strategic air command had two squadrons in service, each containing twelve Mirage IV A's and four C 135 F's.[2]

[1] Leonard Beaton and John Maddox, *The Spread of Nuclear Weapons* (London: Chatto & Windus, 1962), 89.

[2] *The Military Balance* (London: The Institute for Strategic Studies), *1963–64*, p. 12; *1965–1966*, p. 17.

The second-generation strategic deterrent force included intercontinental ballistic missiles with a range of 3,000 kilometers. They were equipped with thermonuclear warheads. The launching platforms consisted of three nuclear submarines which, according to the legislative proposal, were to be operational by 1969, 1971, and 1973, respectively. The H-bombs were to be made of uranium-235 manufactured in part in the isotope separation factory of Pierrelatte. But it could not produce at full capacity until 1970. Thermonuclear tests were to be carried out in the archipelago of Gambiez, 1,200 kilometers from Tahiti. The first submarine would not be ready for action until 1971–1972. The plan to make H-bombs was postponed and A-bombs, reinforced with titanium, were manufactured instead.

The interval between the first- and second-generation force was spent in manufacturing surface-to-surface intermediate-range missiles. The first solid-fueled French missile, called Agate, was tested in the summer of 1961. It will be operational in 1970. It is generally believed that in September 1959 the United States government prohibited all American companies from co-operating with France in her plan to acquire ballistic missiles.[3]

The Parliamentary Debates

The legislative proposal for the creation of a French atomic power provided a time schedule that was to extend well beyond 1964. The projected calendar of the two-stage building plan called for completion long after 1970. The statement of objectives, however, did not define the strategy to be used for the employment of these new weapons. The parliamentarians had no information save that contained in extracts from speeches made by de Gaulle prior to the debates. On October 13, 1960, Michel Debré discussed the legislative proposal before the National Assembly. He emphasized the imperfections of the Atlantic Pact: its geographical limitations, its exceedingly inegalitarian political and strategic organization, the drawbacks of integration. He justified the proposal on several counts: the impetus it would give to scientific research, France's responsibilities in Africa, the limitations of interallied cooperation in matters pertaining to atomic weapons. "The French government is said to be hostile to an integrated deterrent force. But nobody accepts such an integration, nobody even envisages it. For a long time there will be only national atomic forces, and these cannot be integrated." Couve de Murville stressed the objectives of international foreign policy: "What we must aim for is a share in atomic strategy, a share in the supreme command."

In the opinion of the opposition, the government's plan was dangerous from the point of view of foreign policy and ineffective from the point of view

[3] Beaton and Maddox, *Spread*, 94.

of defense. In defending a motion censuring the plan, Guy Mollet accused the government of failing to answer the following question: Had it tried by negotiation to achieve an integration of atomic armaments before resorting to this national program of defense? He noted that England had consented to launching platforms, the double key system, and American bomber bases. "What is that if not integration?" he asked. In the Senate, Edouard Bonnefous opted for an integrated continental striking force. Jean Lecanuet exclaimed: "Yours is a nationalist policy whereas ours is communitarian." At the third reading of the measure in the Assembly, Paul Reynaud predicted that a French nuclear force would open the way for a German one. René Schmitt and Jules Moch criticized the choice of Mirage IV. Bombardment by a piloted plane was a thing of the past, they said. Strategic targets would not be reached. Thoughtful planning should be based on the use of unmanned missiles. Several speakers observed that France was neglecting her conventional armaments and was not fulfilling her obligation as a member of NATO. The debate was lively. Three motions to censure the plan were made; they received, successively, 207, 214, and 215 votes. The first motion attacked "the new concept of European and Atlantic policy proposed by the government." The opposition consisted of Communists, Socialists, a majority of Radicals, half of the Independents, and only a third of the M.R.P. The plan was adopted, however, through the procedure of the blocked vote. François Valentin observed that although the procedure was legal, it "annihilated the true nature of the law which is designed to express the general will of the voters."

In July 1962 another debate took place over the special budget which contained large appropriations for the construction of the Pierrelatte factory. Prime Minister Georges Pompidou, imitating his predecessor, sought recourse in the blocked vote. He said: "The day may soon come when political union will be established and this will of course raise questions of defense. French possession of atomic armaments will be an essential trump card for the cause of defense. Afterward the question of a nuclear force within a European framework can be considered." This was a surprising statement, coming as it did three months after France's partners had rejected a plan for political union of the six nations that had de Gaulle's approval. Once again a motion of censure was passed by 206 votes, the distribution according to party being approximately the same as in 1960.

The Efficacy of Deterrence

The value of a given deterrent force can be assessed in conjunction with the objective criteria laid down by Wohlstetter (Book II, Chapter 5), which we must apply to the French force.

According to this theory, no deterrence is possible unless a strategic force is capable of a second strike, that is, of retaliation. If such a force is not able to retaliate, deterrence is impossible; the only choice left, then, is an offensive strategy. To be sure, the French force could cause massive destruction by a first strike, provided its objective was counter-city. But would such a force be able to retaliate if the potential enemy were the Soviet Union?

The first-generation force consisted of the Mirage IV whose range was not sufficient to reach Russian territory without the aid of aerial tankers purchased in America. To reach the target the Mirage would have to be refueled in flight, which would mean flying over friendly territory. It could be detected by air alert networks unless it flew at a low altitude. It would be exposed to surface-to-air missiles equipped with homing devices, and the principal cities of the U.S.S.R. are surrounded by such missiles. Out of a total fleet of fifty Mirages, only twenty or thirty would be available. A small number of them could accomplish their missions with fifty-kiloton A-bombs.

The second-generation strategic force would include three or at the most four atomic submarines. It was estimated that one out of three would be at sea at any given time.

Meanwhile, to justify a small independent deterrent force, the theory of "proportionate deterrence" was invoked. According to those who preached this theory—and General Gallois was among them—"the mere relationship between the stakes a country represents and its capacity for retaliation should suffice to deter a possible enemy from risking a conflict. In other words, if France should have the necessary means of inflicting a global amount of destruction on Russia, consistent with its economic potential, the Soviet conquest of France would result in a stalemate."[4]

The damage caused on Russia by a few fifty-kiloton A-bombs would not compare with France's economic potential. Moreover, the military efficacy of a few atomic submarines is altogether questionable.

France, therefore, does not meet the first criterion of deterrence. Nor does she meet the second criterion—the invulnerability of the forces of retaliation. The Mirage IV's are entirely vulnerable to ballistic missiles. As for atomic submarines, their invulnerability is dependent on the technical gamble that from now until 1972 no anti-missile missile capable of intercepting Polaris-type missiles will be perfected.[5] Yet both the Americans and the Russians are working on the problem.

The third criterion has to do with decision-making, even after the attack. NATO's network of telecommunications, built by American technicians, consists of eighty-two stations strung out from Norway to Turkey. Yet the

[4] Marc de Lacoste-Lareymondie, *Mirages et réalités* (Paris: Editions de la Serpe, 1964), 181.

[5] Raymond Aron, *Le grand débat* (Paris: Calmann-Levy, 1963), 128.

time lapse for warning of an attack is very brief. A radar belt around French frontiers could not perform this service, even if France had the technical and financial means to install it.[6]

The fourth criterion concerns the capacity to survive, which is related to the size of the territory and the density of the population. With 170 bombs of varying power, many of which might be less than a megaton, it would be possible to destroy all French population centers with more than 200,000 inhabitants. In comparison to the Soviet Union, France actually has no capacity whatsoever for survival.[7]

Thus the French deterrent force does not meet the fourth criterion for deterrence. It can intervene only in a first strike capacity. In other words it must adopt an offensive strategy. What concepts would govern such a strategy?

Strategic Concepts

The technical limitations on France's capacity to retaliate force her to launch a first strike counter-city attack. How can the existence of such a force, whose use is determined solely by France, affect the relations of France with her potential enemy, the Soviet Union, and with her principal ally, the United States?

The French doctrine in regard to the enemy is that of massive retaliation. It is based on the notion that deterrence is achieved by two factors: the weapon and the will. The potential aggressor must be absolutely certain that any serious attack or threat on its part would provoke a nuclear war. This is a systematization of John Foster Dulles's plan to reserve for America, whose thermonuclear weapons are superior to those of its opponent, Russia, the right to choose the weapons. But can this plan be applied by France, whose status is that of a minor nuclear power? In other words, is a French second strike credible? It seems highly doubtful. To launch thirty Mirage IV's against the Soviet Union, one must be prepared for the total destruction of France. "With such means at the disposal of the Soviets, if France were to attempt to deter them—something even the American force could not do—her action would simply convice the enemy that she had gone completely mad." So wrote Raymond Aron. And he added that when it came to a test of wills, the head of the country that was entirely destroyed would no longer be on an equal footing with the head of the country that merely suffered some loss.[8]

---

[6] De Lacoste-Lareymondie, *Mirages*, 184.
[7] *Ibid.*, 185–86.
[8] Aron, *Le grand débat*, 121, 152.

Can the striking force of a minor country play a useful role in an alliance?
Two theses have been presented in this connection.

According to the so-called triggering theory, the role of such a force
would be not to take the place of the American one, as in the preceding case,
but to impose nuclear escalation under circumstances that would be of
secondary importance for Americans yet vital for Europeans. The partisans
of this theory assume that the United States would use only conventional
weapons for the defense of Europe, reserving its strategic forces for the
defense of its own territory. These theorists are determined to accept
American guarantees yet cynical enough to try to impose their decisions on
the United States. But one might assume that the kind of solidarity that
exists among enemies will also affect the relations of the major atomic
powers.[9]

General Beaufre believes that the doctrines of massive retaliation and
triggering are oversimplifications. What interests him is the theory of a
multilateral deterrent force. In particular, he is looking into the influence
that a third partner with a small retaliatory force might have on the situation
of the two main adversaries. The latter presumably represent a balance of
power, that is, each has the capacity, when retaliating, to inflict terrible
destruction on the other. The addition of a third power, the supposed ally of
either of the two major powers, can have strategic consequences that far
transcend its actual nuclear strength. A third power will limit to a certain
extent the freedom of action of both major powers and will therefore
augment strategic stability. General Beaufre does not deny that the existence
of an independent nuclear force entails a risk; the third partner might react
in a confused way, or it might be very inept at playing the game of multilateral deterrence. One must therefore reduce conceptual conflicts between
allies to a minimum and plan a common strategic doctrine. "An independent
force ceases to be dangerous only when it has allies."[10]

The Nature of Alliances

Strategic doctrines must be evaluated in terms of the nature of alliances.
Is an alliance influenced by atomic armaments and by the rules governing
deterrence?

The traditional purpose of alliances is to alter the balance of power and to
obtain promises of mutual assistance. Does the existence of nuclear weapons
justify a loss of faith in the security offered by alliances? General Gallois

[9] De Lacoste-Lareymondie, *Mirages*, 193.
[10] General Beaufre, *Dissuasion et stratégie* (Paris: Armand Colin, 1964), 93, 94, 98,
102.

answered this question categorically. The power of the atom condemns alliances. The danger of destruction of both men and resources is so great that one can count only on oneself. "To gamble on trust when the stakes are human lives and national independence is a crime." The author of this theory of alliances asserts that national solidarity is infinitely greater than international solidarity. In view of the American belief that hostilities will eventually break out in Europe he sees the need for a national force of deterrence.

One must be leery of tendentious interpretations of Americans' interests in Europe, of their theory of action, and of the reliability of their strategic power. It is an error of judgment to think that the European theater of operations is merely of secondary interest to the United States. Soviet supremacy in Western Europe would alter dangerously the balance of deterrent forces, to the detriment of the United States. To insinuate that the Americans would use massive retaliation to defend their fatherland and a strategy of graduated response to defend Europe is to interpret McNamara's doctrine incorrectly. Graduated response would be used in both instances. To be sure, one must differentiate between the United States and Europe, but this difference is irreducible because it is a result of geography.[11] To suggest that no reliance can be placed in the American threat unless American territory is directly attacked is to attach too little importance to the restraint of the Soviet Union, which does not dare to attack a position as exposed as that of Berlin. Finally, if it is true that no country willingly commits suicide for the sake of another, why should France be better qualified than the United States to protect the other European states?

The truth is that the pressures of modern technology destroy traditional notions of national sovereignty. "NATO's nuclear dilemma has developed because there is an increasing inconsistency between the technical requirements of strategy and political implications of the nation-state."[12] This observation by Kissinger tallies with Raymond Aron's conclusion: "It is not alliances generally that are condemned by the existence of thermonuclear arms but alliances of the traditional type. Great nations are capable of protecting smaller ones, but they obviously will not be willing to do so if the latter claim the right to unleash a holocaust. Alliances will either evolve toward communities or they will dissolve; they will not return to their prenuclear practices."[13]

In this philosophical controversy about international relations in the nuclear age, the discussion has revolved around the question of trust. The

[11] Aron, *Le grand débat*, 142.
[12] Henry A. Kissinger, *The Troubled Partnership* (New York: McGraw-Hill, 1965), 117.
[13] Aron, *Le grand débat*, 272.

immediate justification for a French nuclear force was perhaps that it might convince the United States of the necessity for a dialogue with Europe on the matter of strategy; the long-term justification was that such a force, combined with England's, might constitute the nucleus of an apparatus for retaliation which would be able to survive a Soviet attack. But the conflict over American strategic hegemony that began in 1958 continued after 1963 in quite a different spirit. As a consequence, a good deal of harm was done to security in general because of the French attitude. The French theory of national nuclear autonomy weakened the effectiveness of American deterrence because it tended to loosen the ties between Western Europe and the United States. It aroused grave concern among those Europeans who were sincerely attached to the principles of the Atlantic Alliance. And it confirmed in others a neutralist attitude that led to the abdication of all responsibilities in the face of American hegemony. It also stimulated nuclear proliferation, and this might some day prove a temptation to Germany. In short, by the end of 1962, France was not only isolated within the Alliance, she was a dissident voice there because of the total incompatibility between the American theory of a single command and de Gaulle's insistence on the nonintegration of the French national force. Meanwhile this force was developing under the cover of American guarantees.[14]

[14] *Ibid.*, 201, 202.

9

The Year of Defiance

Kennedy's Grand Design

GENERAL DE GAULLE and President Kennedy had two very divergent conceptions of the Atlantic Alliance and the international order, particularly in regard to Europe. A federated Europe would have put an end to internal rivalries, bound Germany indissolubly to the West, acted as a counterweight to the Soviet Union, and given the United States an adequate partner. On December 30, 1961, Dean Rusk outlined the guiding principles of American policy toward Europe: "In 1947 the American government decided that it would link the recovery of Europe to efforts at European unification. We chose quite consciously not to play a balance-of-power game with the nations of Europe but to build toward a strong partnership in the affairs of the west."[1]

On July 4, 1962, Kennedy made a statement about the interdependence of the United States and a unified Europe: "In such a Europe we would have a partner with whom we could deal on a completely equal footing regarding the immense tasks that the establishment and the defense of a community of free nations entail." In his speech of June 25, 1963, at Frankfurt, Kennedy was more explicit: "Only a closely united Europe can prevent a fragmentation of the Alliance." The United States would assign to an integrated Europe the responsibilities it denied to a nation-stage coalition. Kennedy intimated that

[1] Dean Rusk, "Some Issues of Contemporary History," *U.S. Department of State Bulletin* (Washington, D.C.: U.S. Government Printing Office, 1962), Vol. XLVI, No. 1177, Jan. 15, 1962.

he was ready to concede to a united Europe the nuclear autonomy he had refused to grant to a national nuclear force.

Kennedy's plan for an Atlantic partnership was announced at a time when de Gaulle's personal power was growing. The Algerian war was over. The Legislative Assembly elected in November 1962 had a majority that supported his foreign policy. In his address before the Assembly on December 11, the general said: "Within the framework of the Atlantic Alliance—which is now indispensable for the defense of the free world—it is inconceivable that France should not have a modern military force of her own." The Alliance was no longer a permanent element of French policy.

Without revealing his over-all geopolitical views, the general embarked upon a series of actions, some positive, others negative. These actions were related to the place of England and Germany in Europe; to the Gaullist conception of Europe and France's place *vis-à-vis* the great powers: the United States, the Soviet Union, and China. All these initiatives, which had considerable impact on the European scene, were undertaken within a short period of time, from January 1963 to January 1964. Underlying all he did was an attitude of defiance toward Kennedy's Grand Design and, more generally, defiance toward American policy throughout the world.

The Rejection of the Nassau Accords

Toward the end of 1962 England was involved in two important discussions: one was economic and long-range, her admission in the European Economic Community, the other, military, concerning the equipment of her bombers with ballistic missiles.

In 1957 England's first disappointment was having to give up making a missile called Blue Streak because it proved too expensive. Instead she ordered Skybolts, air-to-surface missiles that were manufactured in the United States. In 1962 McNamara decided that the American forces no longer needed Skybolts because they had long-range Minuteman missiles protected by underground silos. How would it be possible to reconcile the fiction of an independent British force of deterrence with the American desire to integrate NATO's strategic forces, especially at a time when maintenance of this fiction was essential to the survival of the Conservative government? Macmillan and Kennedy met from December 18 to 21, 1962, in Nassau, the capital of the Bahama Islands. They agreed on the following solution: the United States would provide England with Polaris missiles and England would manufacture, with the help of American technology, nuclear submarines and nuclear warheads. The British Polaris submarines would be assigned to NATO's multilateral force, which the United States and Great Britain would set up with the help of the other allies. England was committed to use her nuclear force "for the international defense of the Western Alliance," but would resume her freedom of action should her government "decide that the highest national interests are at stake." The Labour Party viewed these accords as proof that British independence was dead.

Before leaving for the Bahamas, Macmillan met de Gaulle in Rambouillet on December 15–16. When Macmillan was asked whether England, once she had been admitted to the European Community, would contribute to the defense of Europe, he replied that perhaps she would.[2] From Nassau Kennedy sent de Gaulle a personal letter on December 21, 1963, offering France Polaris missiles under conditions similar to those offered to England. De Gaulle, replying on January 2, 1963, said he would consider the proposal. But he did not hesitate for long. He was shocked by both the form and content of the Nassau Accords. The proposal had been negotiated between "Anglo-Saxons" and the news had been immediately released to the press. There was a striking contrast between England's tenacity in laying down economic conditions for her entry into the Common Market and the speed with which she accepted a nuclear future with the United States. "Britain's application was bound to raise the question whether it was consistent with the aspirations of a united Europe for one of its members to have an exclusive relationship with the United States on so vital a subject as nuclear strategy," Kissinger has observed.[3]

The press conference of January 14, 1963, killed three birds with one stone. First, de Gaulle vetoed England's entry into the Common Market on grounds that were primarily political. He predicted that if England and subsequently other states were admitted, "a colossal Atlantic Community, dependent upon and controlled by the United States, will be established definitively and it will lose no time in swallowing up the entire European Community." Secondly, he stressed his doubts about the eventual intervention of the United States in Europe. "The Americans . . . are faced with the possibility of direct destruction. Therefore, the immediate and, one might add, the privileged defense of Europe . . . will be . . . of secondary importance. . . . In view of this, no one in the world, especially no one in America can say where, when, how, and to what extent American nuclear arms will be used to defend Europe." This being so, why should France give up the idea of herself possessing the most effective weapons? Thirdly, de Gaulle rejected the notion of a multilateral force because of the problem of central command—the American deterrent forces were under the orders of the president of the United States. There followed a further, technical argument: Polaris missiles were useless to France if she had neither

---

[2] *Année politique 1962*, p. 608.

[3] Henry A. Kissinger, *The Troubled Partnership* (New York: McGraw-Hill, 1965), 86.

submarines to launch them nor thermonuclear warheads with which to equip them.

After the press conference Kennedy's proposal for an Atlantic partnership between the United States and a united Europe, including England, ceased to be a newsworthy topic.

The Franco-German Treaty of Cooperation

While de Gaulle isolated England from Europe, he also tightened the bonds, both military and political, that united France with West Germany.

During the first meeting of Adenauer and de Gaulle in 1958, the German chancellor had tacitly consented to a French leadership of sorts in Europe. He had no desire to see Germany pursue an autonomous foreign policy. Immediately after the Berlin crisis of 1961, the Americans and the English were in favor of negotiating with the Russians. But de Gaulle supported Adenauer in his refusal to do so. Germany was in constant fear of an understanding between the two major powers which would perpetuate her division. France thus appeared to be the defender of West Germany's interests. The atmosphere thus created was conducive to the success of de Gaulle's visit to Germany from the 4th to the 9th of September 1962. In a speech before the war college at Hamburg, de Gaulle declared: "We are confronted with a colossal world threat. The Atlantic Alliance, which was organized for the purpose of coping with it, is of no value unless Frenchmen and Germans on both sides of the Rhine are in agreement. . . . Because of our situation as well as the common danger, it is therefore essential to the union of our two countries that our armies cooperate organically for a single and identical defense." The foundations of the Franco-German Treaty of Cooperation were laid during the course of this visit. The treaty was signed in Paris on January 22, 1963, a few days after the press conference in which de Gaulle rejected Kennedy's Grand Design.

The treaty covered such areas as foreign affairs, defense, and education. In matters of defense, the objectives were to pool strategic doctrines, to exchange military personnel, and to develop an armaments program.

In German political circles, however, de Gaulle's repeated attacks against American military supremacy engendered some doubt whether the treaty was consonant with the spirit of the Atlantic Pact. For this reason, when the treaty was ratified on May 16, 1963, the Bundestag unanimously voted to insert a preamble enumerating the principal aims of German foreign policy; included was the phrase: "a common defense within the framework of the North Atlantic Alliance and the integration of the forces of those countries that are members of the Alliance." The opposition in the French National Assembly tried in vain to introduce a similar statement.

Franco-German cooperation for defense was off to a bad start. The preamble nullified the bilateral nature of the treaty, which was so important to de Gaulle. The disagreement was public before the treaty came into force.

Which Europe?

With Germany raised to the rank of a privileged ally and England repudiated by France and left in the Anglo-Saxon camp, what sort of Europe did de Gaulle hope to build?

There are three keys to his oft-articulated ideas: a Europe of nation-states; a European Europe; Europe from the Atlantic to the Urals. The first refers to the nature of European institutions, the second to Europe's relations with the United States, the third to the geographical boundaries of Europe.

The Europe of nation-states was the clearest of his formulas: a Europe practicing cooperation rather than integration. A plan for a union of states had been developed in accordance with Gaullist ideas shortly after the first conference of chiefs of state that met in Paris in February 1961. This plan was rejected on April 17, 1962. One reason for the failure was that the five partners of France wished to insert a reference to the Atlantic Alliance regarding a common policy of defense—which was one of the purposes of the union—and de Gaulle objected. But the relinquishment of the plan did not in any way alter the general's position; this he made amply clear in his press conference of May 15, 1962: "There can be no other Europe save that of the states, except naturally for myths, fiction and parades." The Franco-German treaty of cooperation was drawn up in accordance with the concept of a Europe of the states.

His second formula was mentioned in his press conference of July 29, 1963, the day before the United States and the Soviet Union signed the Treaty of Moscow. De Gaulle feared that the two major powers might come to an understanding without his becoming a party to it. He affirmed that France "wants to be France in a Europe that must be European." Evoking "the beginning of a conflict between a European empire, possessor of vast Asiatic territories"—Russia—and an overpopulated and ambitious China, he continued: "The United States, which after all has no claims to make on the Soviets after Yalta and Potsdam, suddenly sees tempting opportunities opening up to it; for example, all the separate negotiations between the Anglo-Saxons and the Soviets. The agreements limiting nuclear testing seem to be extending to other, essentially European problems (in the absence so far of the Europeans themselves), and obviously do not represent the views of France."

On July 23, 1964, de Gaulle expressed his views most explicitly. "The reasons for which the Alliance has placed Europe in a subordinate position are becoming less and less convincing with each passing day. Europe must assume its share of responsibility." And, in the same press conference, his definition followed: "A European Europe exists by and for itself; it must have its own policy in the world arena." From Strasbourg on November 22, 1964, de Gaulle launched an appeal to the other side of the Rhine, in order to justify both the Franco-German treaty and a European Europe: "simply the achievement with Germany's help of a great ambition, which is at once very old and very new—the constitution of a European Europe that will play an independent, powerful, and influential role in the free world."

He then proceeded to define the geographical borders of a Europe composed of states and no longer subject to American domination. "Europe from the Atlantic to the Urals" is perhaps the oldest expression in the Gaullist vocabulary and for a long time it was the most mystifying. It seems like something lifted from a turn-of-the-century textbook in geography (freshman year). References to this concept abound. The first dates from May 29, 1949: once Europe has been constituted in accordance with agreements between France and the German states, "it will be possible to fashion all of Europe, once and for all, including Russia—should she change her form of government." More precise is his statement of March 16, 1950: "I am convinced that if France—once she is on her feet and properly directed—appealed to Europe to constitute itself, especially with Germany's assistance, the atmosphere of Europe, from the Atlantic to the Urals, would change entirely; even those in office on the other side of the Iron Curtain would respond to the resulting situation. The key to the liberation of Europe lies in Europe itself." There is a similarity between these statements and a passage in Volume III of de Gaulle's *Memoirs*: "The unity of Europe can be built in the form of an organized association of its peoples from Iceland to Istanbul, from Gibraltar to the Urals." On November 22, 1959, a month after the publication of Volume III, de Gaulle declared at Strasbourg: "If the peoples of Europe on either side of the Iron Curtain could come to an agreement among themselves, we would be certain of peace on earth." On April 7, 1960, de Gaulle went to London. Addressing Parliament, he expressed the hope that "the future will make it possible for Europe to lead its own life with the help of a balance between the two parts of it that have different forms of government." He spoke in the same vein on April 25 before Congress in Washington. Thereafter these declarations multiplied. In his radio talk to the nation on June 8, 1962, he said: "Let us hasten the day when totalitarian regimes, having lost their virulence, will enable us to lower the barriers, and all the peoples of our Continent will find themselves in harmony with one another, in an atmosphere of friendship." Finally, there was the press

conference of July 29, 1963, which has already been cited: "France...believes
... that the day will come when a real and even a sincere détente will entirely
change East-West relations in Europe; and when this day arrives, France will
make constructive suggestions for peace, stability, and the future of Europe."

How does one put together the pieces of the Gaullist puzzle? Western
Europe must not have powerful institutions. Should they solidify, France
would have less freedom of action; Europe would find it more difficult to
extend her borders. Western Europe must be independent, less subordinate
to the United States; any kind of military integration would tighten the
bonds of dependence. Europe, including Russia if possible, must be unified.
The Europeans themselves would forge Europe. The Americans should have
no part in this. European unity achieved by means of a direct American-
Russian détente was out of the question. De Gaulle himself would make the
necessary suggestions for the reconstitution of Europe. He was counting on
the support of the Germans, who desired reunification. Such seemed to be,
in the year 1963, de Gaulle's plan.

The Rejection of the Moscow Agreement

In the Europe of de Gaulle nothing must hinder France from becoming a
nuclear power. On August 5, 1963, he refused to sign the Treaty of Moscow
on the cessation of nuclear testing. He explained his reasons at his press conference of July 29, 1963. The mutual agreement to refrain from nuclear testing
made experimentation less probable, he conceded, but there was nothing
to prevent the United States and the Soviet Union from continuing to manufacture missiles and delivery vehicles. The treaty "in no way affected the
terrible threat that hangs over the world as a result of the nuclear arms
possessed by two rivals." It was "only of minor practical importance." De
Gaulle therefore would not sign it nor would he change his mind about
procuring strategic weapons for France "without which her security and
independence would no longer be hers." Only if the nuclear powers—
whom France would soon invite to study the problem of effective disarmament—gave up making and exploding missiles and producing delivery
vehicles, would he change his mind. Thus de Gaulle returned to his idea of a
four-power conference; he had referred to it once before, in February 1962,
just prior to his decision not to participate in the disarmament conference of
the eighteen states. The spirit of the Franco-German bilateral treaty was
adversely affected when Germany submitting—unlike France—to pressure
from Washington, adhered to the Treaty of Moscow on August 19.

The press conference of July 29, 1963, like that of January 14, served to
express once again the general's doubts about an American intervention in
Europe and his criticism of the structures of the alliance: "It is altogether

natural that America should consider its survival the principal aim of a conflict. It is natural, too, that she consider the time, extent, and method of nuclear intervention solely in terms of this paramount concern. But this is precisely why France must have her own nuclear weapons. Consequently, France is obliged to modify drastically the conditions and modes of her participation in the Alliance; the Atlantic organization was founded on the principle of integration and this principle is no longer valid for France."

Recognition of China

In the Gaullist world it is required that France deal directly with all first-rate powers. The war in Vietnam offered France an opportunity to return to the Far East and to play a role there quite different from that of the United States. On August 29, 1963, just prior to the fall of the Diem government, de Gaulle made a statement expressing his hope for peace and unity "throughout all of Vietnam." On January 27, 1964, to dramatize his opposition to American foreign policy, he recognized China. At that time China was engaged, through the intermediary of smaller states, in a local war against the United States. In principle, recognition was a wise decision. In his press conference of January 31 the general invoked "the weight of evidence and common sense." He added: "No political reality exists within Asia that does not interest or affect China." The decision to recognize China, which otherwise made sense, became perverted by the spirit that animated it. "It's a shame," François Mitterrand pointed out, "that the diplomatic recognition of China has all the earmarks of a challenge to Washington and to Moscow. These countries are merely guilty of having attempted to establish the foundations of peaceful coexistence." Such was the interpretation given to the general's decision, which was made without prior consultation with the United States and West Germany.

The year 1963–1964 was marked by defiance: refusal to admit England to the Common Market; rejection of America's offer of missiles; conclusion of the bilateral treaty with Germany; efforts to create a Europe independent of the United States; plans for a European association that would include Russia; recognition of China. All these were so many facets of a major quarrel initiated by de Gaulle against the Americans—more than a quarrel really, a cold war.

10

The Road from West to East

The NATO Multilateral Force

THE 1963–1964 ACTS OF DEFIANCE were indicative of the new direction of French foreign policy. Thereafter de Gaulle made clear France's disengagement from the West and the beginning of her commitment to the East.

Ever since the press conference of January 14, 1963, a quarrel had been brewing in NATO, especially between France and the United States. It was occasioned by the plan for a multilateral deterrent force announced in an Anglo-American communiqué issued after the Nassau Conference. Since 1960 the American government had been studying the feasibility of creating a NATO Multilateral Force equipped with seaborn Polaris missiles. On January 14 de Gaulle analyzed the composition of the force in these terms: "The question is one of constituting a so-called multilateral atomic force to which Great Britain will contribute all the weapons she has or will have and to which the Americans will contribute a few missiles." He proceeded to outline the rules governing membership and control. "This multilateral force will be assigned to the defense of Europe and will be subject to American control." Most of the American nuclear weapons would not belong to the Multilateral Force; they would be under the direct orders of the president of the United States. The general could not accept such "a situation. It is not consistent with the principle . . . of disposing of one's own deterrent force. To pay the cost of a multilateral force under foreign control would be to contravene the principle of our own foreign policy and defense."

This attack on a policy that was still in the planning stage roused the Americans to action. The Multilateral Force was conceived with two things in mind: it was America's answer to a French autonomous force, and it was designed to bind the most committed of all the European allies, West Germany, to NATO's deterrent strategy.

On April 8, 1963, the Soviets protested, declaring that the purpose of a multilateral force "is to distribute nuclear arms to NATO and to satisfy the demands of the Federal Republic for equality in nuclear armaments."

It was decided to set up a committee to explore the problem more thoroughly. The committee consisted of a small number of European states, including the Federal Republic, which had expressed a sustained interest in the plan, and England, which reserved final judgment. In April 1964 the committee suggested the constitution of a fleet of twenty-five surface ships each carrying eight A-3 Polaris missiles. By the end of October it was decided that 40 per cent of the operation costs would be paid by the United States and 40 per cent by West Germany. Washington had counted on London's concurrence; the smaller countries were expected to follow suit. Thus France would find herself isolated. But the British elections of October 1964 brought about a change of attitude that disappointed the Americans. The incoming Labour Party opposed both a national and a multilateral force. On November 23 Harold Wilson declared that the American proposals "would add nothing to the power of the Western camp," and that in any case the United States' right of veto in the matter of using such a force would be decisive.

Meanwhile, the French government counterattacked. On November 3 Couve de Murville declared in the National Assembly: "One might well wonder whether this force, instead of strengthening the Alliance might not introduce . . . the germs of conflict for which no one could say that France is responsible." On November 5, Georges Pompidou issued a warning to Germany: "If the Multilateral Force should culminate in the creation of a German-American alliance of sorts," this would not be consistent with the Franco-German Treaty of Cooperation. On December 16 Harold Wilson, addressing the House of Commons, confirmed that, with the exception of a few bomber planes held in reserve for strategic missions in Asia and east of Suez, British nuclear forces, both planes and submarines, would be assigned to NATO. Under the circumstances, Johnson ceased to pressure the allies for the constitution of a force which, in the opinion of Manlio Brosio, secretary-general of NATO, could be created by only a fraction of the NATO members but could not be integrated into NATO without the unanimous consent of all of its members.[1]

One might well wonder why the Americans used the Multilateral Force as the principal theme of their policy toward NATO. Their motives were complex: fear of proliferation; the desire to give formal acknowledgment to

---

[1] *Année politique 1964,* 302.

the nuclear ambitions of West Germany; the hope of creating, with the help of England, the core of a European nuclear force that would be distinct from the American force; finally and above all, the wish to resolve the fundamental and controversial problem of nuclear control within the Alliance.[2] The Multilateral Force, however, was not the right answer to the problem. To be sure, West Germany demanded political equality within NATO but she could not have acquired nuclear weapons by a unilateral decision without compromising her chances of reunification. According to Henry A. Kissinger: "The United States put forward a proposal based on a theoretical conception of *German* desires that the Germans felt obliged to accept because they did not want to thwart *American* wishes."[3] The idea that Germany might share in a nuclear fleet revived fears in Western Europe. The Multilateral Force could not constitute the nucleus of a European force as long as the United States was part of it and as long as it represented a divisive factor between France and Germany. Finally, the Multilateral Force did not basically change the problem of nuclear control since the United States retained its right of veto and the French national force remained autonomous. The United States tried, by a technical expedient, to solve the political problems of defining common objectives in the domain of nuclear strategy and of East-West relations.[4]

The French Deterrent Force

Since the question of the Multilateral Force was not of immediate interest to de Gaulle, he concentrated on establishing a French force. Taking full responsibility for his promise, he defined and asked for further definitions of the way the weapons should be used; he justified to the country the existence of a national nuclear force, and he secured appropriations for his program.

A decree of January 19, 1964, fixed the functions of the commander of the strategic air forces. This officer was made "responsible for the execution of the operations of these forces under instructions given by the President of the Republic" (Article 5). The provisions of the decree increased the powers of the chief of state at the expense of the prime minister.

In his press conference of January 14, 1963, de Gaulle appropriated as his own the theory of proportional deterrence. "Atomic power has the unique attribute of absolute efficacy. . . . Even if it does not achieve its full potential. . . . French atomic power, from its inception, will have the dismal and terrible capacity to destroy in a few seconds millions and millions of men.

[2] Henry A. Kissinger, *The Troubled Partnership* (New York: McGraw-Hill, 1965), 141–42.

[3] *Ibid.*, 144.

[4] *Ibid.*, 154–57.

This fact cannot fail to influence to some degree at least the intentions of a potential aggressor." In his press conference of July 23, 1964, the general reiterated this thesis: "As far as the immediate defense of each of us is concerned, given a certain nuclear capacity, a comparison of the respective weapons is only of relative value."

In July 1964, the *Revue de Défense Nationale* published the text of a lecture delivered by General Ailleret, army chief of staff. In the event of a Soviet act of aggression, he said, France must retaliate with all the means at her disposal. He spoke in favor of the theory of massive retaliation, rejecting the American doctrine of flexible response.

In his television speech of April 16, 1964, de Gaulle again justified the acquisition of national atomic weapons. For France "to deprive herself of her own means of deterring the enemy from attacking, when she is quite capable of acquiring them, would be to deliberately attract lightning without having a lightning rod. And it would also be to rely on a foreign protectorate for her entire defense, her very survival, to say nothing of her political policies. Besides, there is no assurance that help would be forthcoming." The theme of the "strategic and therefore political dependence" of countries that do not possess nuclear arms "in contrast to the heavily armed giants that are not a threat to us" was repeated in his press conference of July 23, 1964. "From now on," he said, "the path of deterrence is open to us."

In the autumn the government laid before the National Assembly a second legislative proposal for military equipment. In explaining its action, the government indicated that, in the event of war, "the operations of our combined forces will, in principle, be combined with those of our allies. French forces must be in a position to intervene within and outside of Europe . . . within and outside of the framework of the Alliance." The accent was on independence. Operations would be combined, but not the actual forces, because that would mean integration. The rapporteur for the legislative proposal pointed out that the constituted authorities had decided to manufacture a surface-to-surface strategic ballistic missile and create tactical nuclear weapons. He stated that the priority given to deterrence will be maintained. Consequently, appropriations for conventional weapons were being drastically cut. In the course of the debate, François Mitterrand said he refused to choose between two bad solutions, a national or a multilateral force: "Absolute deterrence is not possible if the enemy knows that despite our capacity to cause partial damage, he can destroy us completely. . . . Nor is it achieved if he knows that France has neglected to take the proper precautions to insure the survival of her own population." To which Georges Pompidou replied: "It is not indispensable that we should be the equal of an enemy; it is enough if the damage we can inflict on him is sufficient to deter him from striking." The measure was passed in the Assembly on December

3, by a vote of 278 to 178, with 22 abstaining. The opposition included Communists, Socialists, the Rassemblement Democratique, and a majority of the Centre Républicain. A hostile vote by the Senate was wiped out by a second balloting of the National Assembly on December 15.

The first stage of the Pierrelatte plant was inaugurated in January 1965. The work of setting up the necessary installations for nuclear tests was done in Mururoa in the South Pacific instead of in the Sahara. On April 16 the United States was asked to close its consulate at Papeete, on the nearby island of Tahiti.

Disengagement from NATO

While he continued to see to the construction of a national force of deterrence and to thwart plans for the constitution of a multilateral force, de Gaulle was making decisions that tended to reduce France's commitments to NATO. He refused to discuss certain strategic problems at NATO and emphasized his doubts about the amount of protection NATO could give its members.

On June 21, 1963, the French naval forces assigned to NATO were withdrawn. Apparently this move was decided upon without prior consultation with the Federal Republic. On April 27, 1964, French officers were recalled from the interallied general staff. It was not appropriate, the general said, for these officers to shoulder responsibilities for organizations upon which French units were no longer dependent. In September 1964 NATO naval maneuvers in the Atlantic were carried out without the participation of French surface ships. In May 1965 France informed her partners that she would no longer take part in NATO's "Fallex" strategic maneuvers.

At its April 1963 session in Ottawa, the NATO Council decided to engage in a long-term study of the Alliance's major strategic problems. The French government refused to approve the appointment of a French delegate whom the secretary-general of NATO had chosen as a member of the committee. In November 1965, at Robert McNamara's suggestion, ten of NATO's ministers of defense set up a special nuclear committee. Its purpose was to get as many member states as possible—including non-nuclear nations like West Germany—to work out the Alliance's strategy. France refused to join the group.

Meanwhile the general continued to criticize NATO. On July 23, 1964, he attacked European docility as well as American domination: "The reasons for which the Alliance has placed Europe in a subordinate position are becoming less and less convincing with each passing day"; and later: "The possession of nuclear weapons gives America and Soviet Russia such a sense of security, and what is more, so much justification for exercising their

hegemony within their respective camps, that they will not part with them."
On November 22 at Strasbourg, he asked whether a European people should,
"by playing the role of auxiliary, put its very existence into the hands of a
power, however friendly, that is located in an alien world." The tone of his
television talk of December 31, 1964, was categorical: "Our country, which
seeks to dominate no one, intends to be its own master. . . . While rejecting
any system which, under the guise of 'supranationalism,' or 'integration' or
'Atlanticism,' would actually subject us to a well-known hegemony, we are
ready none the less to cooperate amicably with each of our allies." In a television speech of April 27, 1965, he sounded an isolationist note: "The re-
emergence of a nation whose hands are free, which we have become, plainly
modifies the world interplay which, since Yalta, seems to have been limited
to two partners." In his press conference of September 9, 1965, de Gaulle
defined one of his general objectives: "We can and therefore should have a
policy that is our own. What kind of policy? Above all we must remain above
any enfeoffment." Having stated the objective, he went on to spell it out:
"Thus, as long as we deem the solidarity of Western peoples to be necessary
for the defense of Europe, our country will remain the ally of its allies. But
our commitments of long ago will expire by 1969 at the latest. The NATO
provisions prescribing 'integration,' which subordinate our country and place
our destiny in the hands of a foreign authority, will lapse." Thus, French
withdrawal from NATO was foreshadowed and an outside date set.

At this point one might wonder about De Gaulle's political conception of
the significance of an alliance. An alliance must be so constituted that "no
outside pressure will determine the policy" of a nation "with free hands"—
an expression that was repeated, in this context, in the course of an interview
granted to Michel Droit on December 14, 1965. Once again the general
gave his pragmatic views: "We are forced to take the world as it is and to live
with such a world. What does that mean? It means that France need not
exclude any possibility for herself." To be the ally of her allies meant, all
things considered, not to exclude the possibility of ceasing to be an ally.

Tension in Franco-German Relations

As France disengaged herself from NATO and affirmed her complete
freedom of action, West Germany drew ever closer to the United States.
German foreign policy, which for fifteen years was inspired and implemented
by Chancellor Adenauer, was based on friendship with France and the
United States. The cold war between Germany's two friends, which became
more obvious just as the Franco-German Treaty of Cooperation was signed,
forced the Federal Republic to choose. The scales were tipped in favor of the

United States. The presence of American troops and strategic weapons in Europe constituted, in the eyes of the Germans, the sole effective protection for their territory, the only guarantee that the status quo would be maintained in Berlin. The protection afforded by the French deterrent force seemed very slight in comparison.

Moreover, the Americans made every effort to assure the Germans of their firm determination to intervene in Europe in the event of a nuclear conflict with the Soviet Union.

In June 1963 John Kennedy went to Germany. In a speech at Frankfort he declared: "Some say that the United States will not honor its commitments. Our commitments in Europe are indispensable for the defense of our common interests and yours." In Berlin he aroused enthusiasm when he said: "Ich bin ein Berliner." The French minister of information, Alain Peyrefitte, answered for de Gaulle: "Who can say what Kennedy's successor will think about this fifteen years from now?" And he reminded the public that during the two world wars America waited before intervening in 1917 and again in 1941. The United States might withdraw its forces from Europe at any time, Peyrefitte said. In commenting on the Moscow Pact de Gaulle (as seen above) expressed doubts about American intervention in Europe.

France had two complaints against the Federal Republic: its membership in the Multilateral Force, and its blindness to the need for a European foreign policy independent of the United States. To his ministers de Gaulle left the task of criticizing the Multilateral Force while he spoke for an independent Europe and repeated his unwillingness to accept integration within the framework of the Atlantic Alliance. On July 23, 1964, he expressed publicly his disappointment in the Franco-German Treaty of Cooperation: "We are forced to note that . . . so far no common line of activity has resulted from it. . . . For the moment Bonn does not believe that our policy should be European and independent. . . . Meanwhile, until the Germans see the light, France will continue to pursue such a policy on her own." In a speech at Strasbourg on November 22, 1964, he justified the reconciliation of the two countries, citing "the achievement, with Germany's help, of a great ambition, which is at once very old and very new—the constitution of a European Europe that will play an independent, powerful, and influential role in the free world." Anticipating these remarks, Chancellor Erhard had refused, in a speech at Fürth on November 21, to promote the disintegration of NATO.

At the end of 1964 the plan for a Multilateral Force was tabled, but the ties between Germany and the United States grew stronger. De Gaulle realized that he could not rely on the Federal Republic to second him in constituting "a Europe of states," detached from America, and with himself as its leader. He was therefore led to accentuate his line of policy.

On the one hand, he emphasized increasingly his disappointment in Germany and for the first time expressed his concern about it. In a press conference held on September 9, 1965, he observed that the Treaty of 1963 "covers many matters which so far have remained in a state of cordial suspension. Nevertheless, in such domains as cultural and youth exchanges, it has brought desirable results." On December 14, in an interview with Michel Droit during the presidential campaign, de Gaulle said: "And then there is Germany, which is changing. We have absolutely no idea where her ambitions will take her. Naturally, we hope she will follow the right course, and we have good reason to believe she will, but we cannot be certain."

On the other hand, the general indicated more plainly his intention of reconstituting the Europe of his dreams, the Europe of his past.

Toward a Gaullist Europe

In his Strasbourg speech of November 22, 1964, the chief of state stressed that the people's democracies were becoming more liberal: "Finally, as for the future, . . . the internal and external evolution of the Eastern totalitarian bloc (under the elemental pressure of men who hope to recover their dignity and of peoples who wish to regain their national freedom) gives us reason to hope that one day all of Europe will be drawn together, will be stabilized, solving its problems and marshaling its vast resources for progress and peace." In his press conference of February 4, 1965, he stressed the ties between the status of Germany and that of Europe: "The German problem is essentially the European problem." He went on to explain the French point of view: "For France, everything today can be summarized in three closely related lines of action: to help Germany to become a force for progress and peace; and if she does, to help her achieve reunification; to follow whatever course will allow her to realize this." He emphasized that "the present indeterminate status" of Germany "cannot last forever." He indicated the way to put an end to it: "What should be done cannot be accomplished in one day unless there is understanding and cooperation among the nations that have always been, are, and always will be deeply concerned about the fate of their German neighbor—in short, the peoples of Europe." Thus, Germany's status and that of Europe must be determined by the European nations concerned, including Russia, and without the help of the United States. The following sentence confirmed this interpretation: "The peoples of Europe must plan first to consult, then to determine jointly—lastly to guarantee jointly the solution of this problem, which is essentially that of their Continent. Only thus can Europe be reborn, only thus can a balance be maintained in Europe; it is the only road to peace and cooperation in every part of the territory that nature has attributed to it."

The mystifying phrase "from the Atlantic to the Urals" was thus made crystal clear. The general was speaking of course of a geographical Europe, or rather of a Europe as it appeared in every historical Atlas that did not go beyond the year 1913. In his press conference of September 9, 1965, he alluded once again to a general European settlement and a settlement of the German question: "We do not hesitate to predict that the day will come when all of Europe will be ready to solve its own problems and, above all, the problem of Germany; when it will reach a constructive understanding, from the Atlantic to the Urals. A general agreement is the only way to do this." Such an agreement would be sought by de Gaulle and the Soviet Union, but without interference from the United States. In order to forge a unified Europe with the assistance of Russia a Western Europe must not be constituted with the help of the United States. From 1961 to 1963 England had been the Trojan horse of this Americanized fraction of Europe; for this reason she was being excluded from the Common Market. In 1964 Germany had rejected the idea of a European and independent Europe. It was therefore necessary to weaken the European Economic Community, the instrument used by the United States to influence the Continent.

In effect, the creation of a Gaullist Europe required the political stagnation of Schuman's Europe, even at the cost, temporarily at least, of economic progress. On June 30, 1965, when the question arose of financing a joint agricultural policy, de Gaulle deliberately provoked a crisis within the Common Market. It was inadmissible, in de Gaulle's opinion, that certain decisions of the E.E.C. Council should, according to the Treaty of Rome, be determined by majority vote during the third stage of the transitional period, i.e. from 1966 on. He also thought excessive the powers and role of the Commission. He therefore provoked on June 30, 1965, a crisis in the Common Market about the financing of the common agricultural policy. Refusing to comply with the stipulations of the treaty, France seceded from the Council.

In his press conference of September 9, 1965, de Gaulle demanded a revision of the conditions for "cooperation" that had been established by the six Common Market countries. He wanted, he said, to put an end to the "misleading myths" of supranationalism. The presidential election of December 1965 showed how strongly the French voters favored the construction of a unified Europe. Thus the general, although still of the same mind, was obliged to agree that France would resume her place in the Council of the E.E.C. (January 1966, at Luxembourg).

What was happening to Franco-British relations? They were subjected to a hot and cold shower. In September 1965 de Gaulle refused to allow the Bank of France to cooperate with banks of the other industrialized countries in their effort to support the pound sterling. But in the spring of 1966 he let it be known through the under-secretary of state for foreign affairs that

France would not oppose a new request by England to join the Common Market.

Neutralism in Southeast Asia

Between 1964 and 1966 de Gaulle's European policy was fraught with ambiguities. He went all out for a unified Europe while at the same time plumping to some extent for a Europe of the Six, especially in the domain of agriculture. His Asian policy was much clearer; it was neutralist.

At the meeting of the Southeast Asia Treaty Organization (SEATO) in April 1964, France supported the neutralization of South Vietnam—in defiance of the United States—and approved Cambodia's refusal of SEATO's protection. In his press conference of July 23, 1964, de Gaulle declared that military action was unthinkable in Vietnam. He invoked instead the Geneva Accords of 1954. In February 1965 the general accepted a Russian proposal that France and the Soviet Union should cooperate to restore peace in Southeast Asia. In May 1965 France recalled her representatives on the general staff of SEATO. In June 1965 Saigon broke off diplomatic relations with Paris. At the meeting of the General Assembly of the United Nations in September 1965, Maurice Couve de Murville, speaking in the name of France, proposed China's admission to the United Nations. In a letter to Ho Chi-minh dated February 8, 1966, and made public a few days later, de Gaulle stipulated that Vietnamese independence would be "guaranteed by a ban against foreign intervention . . . in exchange for a policy of strict neutrality on the part of the Vietnamese authorities." He added: "We exclude the possibility of a military solution and we do not approve the prolongation of the war, *a fortiori* its spread, on the pretext that this will produce a solution." Thus the general, having broken off French ties with SEATO, completely disassociated France from American policy in Southeast Asia.

Rapprochement with the East

France's rapprochement with the East was the natural consequence of her attitude toward American policy in Southeast Asia; it was also consistent with her neutralist position and with her gradual withdrawal from the Atlantic Pact. Consistent, too, was her desire to constitute a European Europe in contrast to a Western Europe completely dependent upon the United States. De Gaulle wanted to see all of Europe, including Russia, unified and capable of settling the status of Germany with an eye to her eventual reunification.

However, to pursue these objectives with an alliance that was only partially "integrated" was not a simple matter. First France would have to prove to the Soviet Union that she wanted really to break off her commitments to NATO and to rid herself of all dependence. Apparently, conclusive proof was to be furnished by the declaration de Gaulle made at his press conference on September 9, 1965. France, he announced, planned to withdraw from NATO before 1969. Thereafter, France had to convince the Soviet Union that it was in Russia's interest to relax her hold on Eastern Europe and to put an end to the uncertain position of Germany by joining France in guaranteeing a new status for that country. De Gaulle expressed his views on this new status in his press conference of February 4, 1965. On April 8 Valerian Zorin took up his post as Russian Ambassador. One might have thought that the arrival of such an outstanding public figure would lead to exploratory conversations on the subject. Such conversations did take place during Andrei Gromyko's official visit to Paris at the end of April and during Couve de Murville's visit to the Soviet Union from October 28 to November 2, 1965. Finally, public opinion had to be prepared for such a change in France's foreign policy. With this in mind de Gaulle dwelt on such themes as the attenuation of the Russian threat to Western Europe, the wisdom of resuming friendly relations with the Soviet Union, and the desirability of establishing amiable relations with all the states of Eastern Europe.

Accordingly, in his televised speech of April 16, 1964, the general said that although the Soviet threat to France was very real, it was not necessarily permanent. "As long as the Soviet Union's ambitions and form of government confront the free world on both sides of the Atlantic with the threat of a terrible war, France will be in danger of destruction and invasion. We have no assurance that our American allies, who are themselves directly threatened with annihilation, will be able to protect us." At a press conference on July 23, 1964, he spoke in the same vein about Western Europe: "It is doubtless wise for France to maintain her alliance with the United States since both countries will continue to be concerned about the North Atlantic as long as the Soviet threat persists." At his press conference of September 9, 1965, however, de Gaulle made a careful distinction between the Atlantic Alliance, to which under certain conditions he was willing to adhere, and NATO, an instrument for domination, which he rejected. He said: "As long as we believe that the solidarity of Western peoples is necessary for a possible defense of Europe, our country will remain the ally of her allies." Already the tone had shifted and the threat had become a mere possibility. In the interview of December 14, 1965, the likelihood of an attack on Western Europe had dwindled: "Until recently . . . Western Europe appeared to be threatened by the East; this menace has not yet completely disappeared."

The theme of renewed friendship with the Soviet Union was discreetly alluded to in de Gaulle's press conference of September 9, 1965: "We attach great importance to our new relations with Russia." And in his speech of December 11, 1965, after Couve de Murville's trip to Russia, the general spoke with greater warmth: "France . . . is attached to Russia—regardless of transient regimes—by many natural affinities and common interests."

The idea of developing closer relations with Eastern Europe was mentioned for the first time in his speech of December 31, 1964: "As their internal evolution leads the Eastern states more and more toward peace, our contacts with them will increase." In his press conference of September 9, 1965, the general expressed his satisfaction with the visit to Paris of Ion G. Maurer, Rumanian premier. He also expressed pleasure over the imminent visit of Jozef Cyrankiewicz (from September 9–16), the Polish premier. During his presidential campaign de Gaulle alluded to these contacts on several occasions. On December 14 he said: "We are also on ever closer terms with Eastern Europe, because it exists and because there is absolutely no reason why we should not have peaceful relations with it." In his end-of-the-year speech, he stated: "Having recovered independence, which in no way affects our friendships or our alliances, we can now . . . develop even more extensively our economic, scientific, technical, and political relations with the countries of Eastern Europe."

Without affecting existing alliances? In view of the deterioration of France's relations with the United States the question is a valid one.

The Cold War with the United States

Actually, the cold war with the United States had assumed a world-wide character. All the stages of the route from West to East which we have just described contributed to this: opposition to the creation of a Multilateral Force; insistence on the possession of a national deterrent force; emphasis on dissociation from NATO: attempts to convince the German Federal Republic to associate with France in a policy of independence toward the United States; plans for the settlement of the German question without interference from the United States; the adoption of a neutralist attitude in regard to Southeast Asia; direct contact with the Soviet Union and the Eastern states of Europe; the constitution of a new order in all of Europe, including Russia; the establishment of a balance "throughout our Continent, based on understanding and cooperation among all the peoples who live as we do" (press conference of April 27, 1965). All these were so many attempts, both negative and positive, to destroy what had been accomplished by the Atlantic Pact or envisaged in the plan for an Atlantic partnership. This wide range of actions and efforts, however, did not account for the great difference between John

Kennedy's Grand Design and the gradually emerging Grand Design of Charles de Gaulle. Nor can we overlook, more particularly, a whole series of actions and pronouncements bearing on the relations between France and the United States. These comprise the deliberate refusal to hold bilateral summit meetings; the adoption of a hostile attitude toward the United States in its traditional spheres of influence; the mounting of an attack against the monetary supremacy of the United States; and finally, the issuance of a warning to the French public against the danger of being dragged into war by the United States.

The more the general had summit meetings with the chiefs of the small and middle-sized states, the more he avoided contact with the president of the United States. He had somehow managed to avoid inviting Kennedy to Paris at the time of his last trip to Europe in June 1963, a few months before his assassination. When he attended Kennedy's funeral, Johnson invited him to come to Washington in January 1964. De Gaulle answered ambiguously, raising questions of protocol. The two presidents have never met since then.[5] Thus, political differences have never been thrashed out between the two chief executives, whereas British prime ministers and the German chancellor have had frequent conversations with the president of the United States.

De Gaulle's attitude is all the more striking in view of the fact that he took the time to go to Mexico in March 1964 and to visit ten Latin American republics from September 20 to October 16 in the same year. In Latin America he denounced, albeit cautiously, the pressure exerted by the two superpowers. On May 4, 1965, the French representative on the Security Council of the United Nations condemned American intervention in Santo Domingo. This was plainly an act of hostility toward the United States since the island is at least as important as Cuba for American security.

In February 1965 de Gaulle took the cold war to an entirely different battlefield—that of the international monetary system and the supremacy of the dollar. Putting his faith in the gold standard, de Gaulle severely criticized the gold exchange standard which in his view favored and accounted for the large American investments abroad. He declared: "We therefore deem it mandatory to establish international exchanges, like those that existed before so many misfortunes befell the world. These exchanges must rest on an indisputable monetary basis that does not bear the imprint of any one nation." On February 11, France unilaterally abandoned the Gold Exchange Standard. The Bank of France was instructed to convert most of its dollars into gold. The solidarity of the central banks of the large industrial countries, which is invaluable in times of monetary stress, was affected by this action.

[5] David Schoenbrunn, *The Three Lives of Charles de Gaulle* (New York: Atheneum, 1966), 323–26.

During the closing months of 1965 de Gaulle, proceeding by innuendo, launched a major offensive against the United States on the issue of the Atlantic Alliance. During the past three years he had objected to the pact mainly because of the uncertainty of American intervention in the event of a Soviet attack. As Soviet aggression grew less and less likely, he hit upon another pretext for criticism: an alliance with the United States might drag France into a general war. On November 30, at the beginning of the presidential campaign, de Gaulle mentioned this danger for the first time: "The new French Republic, although still an ally of her allies and a friend of her friends, is no longer willing to be subordinate to any one of them. Such a status would not be worthy of France and might, under certain circumstances, automatically involve her in a war not of her choosing." He expressed the same views, almost in the same words, in speeches on December 11 and December 31, 1965.

Thus, for de Gaulle, an integrated alliance spelled subordination. It offered nothing but insecurity in the unlikely event of Soviet aggression in Europe. But in the far more likely event of a Sino-American war, such an alliance risked involvement. These, in effect, were the general's hypotheses when he predicted that the war in Vietnam would spread. Such were the arguments he used as he moved from dissociation to withdrawal.

11

Withdrawal from NATO and the Trip to Moscow

The Basic Decision

ON SEPTEMBER 9, 1965, de Gaulle hinted that France would withdraw from NATO no later than 1969. After his presidential campaign and a year prior to the legislative elections, he decided to hasten the moment. His press conference of February 21, 1966, contained a fresh challenge, similar in style to his defiant speeches of 1963. Once again he alluded to the difference between the Treaty of the Atlantic Alliance, which was still in effect for France, and the policies adopted subsequently. The latter were no longer "satisfactory under the present circumstances." By present circumstances he meant his estimate that the Russian threat to Europe had dimmed, and that the Russian threat to the United States made America's intervention in Europe extremely uncertain. Thereupon the general evoked—not by innuendo as he had done in November 1965, but in precise terms—the danger of being dragged into a war. His purpose was to put an end to the integration of French forces and installations with a military system subject to American command: "The wars that America is waging in other parts of the world—yesterday in Korea and Cuba, today in Vietnam—may be escalated to such an extent that a general holocaust will ensue. If this happens, Europe, whose strategy in NATO is that of the United States, would automatically be involved in a struggle not of its choosing." France wanted to be the mistress of her own destiny; she was in a position to assume broad political and strategic responsibilities because of her atomic power. She intended "to continue to modify the current arrangements" with an eye to "re-establishing a more normal situation, that of her sovereignty. Then everything that is

French—whether on the ground, in the air or on the seas, . . . and all foreigners who happen to be in France will be under the exclusive control of the French government."

Measures for Implementation

Once the basic decision was made public, measures were taken to implement it.

On March 7 de Gaulle sent a personal message to Johnson announcing France's intention of "modifying the form but not the basis of our Alliance." In effect, France was to remain a member of the Alliance concluded in 1949: "Save for circumstances which, in the course of the next three years, may change the fundamental basis of East-West relations, France in 1969 and thereafter will be resolved as always to fight alongside of her allies should any one of them be the victim of unprovoked aggression." On the other hand, "France expects to recover her full sovereignty over her own territory which, at the moment, is encumbered by the permanent presence of allied military forces, and by the use that is being made of her skies. France will also cease to participate in an integrated command and will no longer make her forces available to NATO."

In this way de Gaulle retained the pledge of mutual assistance but underlined the requisite condition (unprovoked aggression) and added a new reservation (a change in the fundamental basis of East-West relations). At the same time he withdrew from the permanent organization which consisted in three factual situations: (a) the presence of American troops in France (26,000 men and twenty-nine bases and depots); (b) the assignment of French officers to an integrated command (especially to the General Staff Committee, to the supreme command of allied forces in Europe, and to the Central European command); (c) the loan to NATO in time of war of two French divisions stationed in Germany.

Only three of his ministers had been informed of his intentions; none the less, on March 9, de Gaulle's decision was formally approved by the entire Council of Ministers.

A communiqué on the same day by the minister of information paraphrased the French memorandum of March 7 that was sent first to the United States and then to the other member nations. The memorandum asserted that it would be futile to negotiate since France's partners all seemed to be partisans of the status quo. France was therefore obliged "to take whatever measures seemed necessary and which are in no way incompatible with her participation in the Alliance." She was willing, however, to study with her allies the links it would be necessary to establish between the French and the NATO command; she would continue to station French troops in Germany

in accordance with the agreements of October 23, 1954; and she was prepared to discuss the practical questions connected with the application of
these measures.

A second memorandum of March 29 set a date, July 1, for the withdrawal
of French forces in Germany under Atlantic control and for the recall of all
French personnel from the integrated command. The removal from France
of Atlantic, American, and Canadian headquarters and bases was to take
place on April 1, 1967.

The Juridical Point of View

France's unilateral decisions affected her multilateral relations with her
partners of the Atlantic Pact (Washington Treaty, 1949), and the Western
European Union (Paris Accords, 1954); her bilateral relations with the
United States (secret agreements concluded between 1951 and 1958 on
troops, bases, and communications systems), and with Germany (Treaty of
Cooperation, 1963).

Article 12 of the Atlantic Pact stipulates: "After the treaty has been in
effect for ten years or more, the contracting parties will consult each other at
the request of any one of them, with a view to revising the treaty; consideration will be given to current factors affecting peace and security in the region
of the North Atlantic." The American answer to the French memorandum
of March 29 pointed out that the allies had recently invited the French
government to submit reform proposals for revision of the treaty. It also
noted that the NATO organs of the treaty from which France was withdrawing were created by a unanimous decision of the Atlantic Council,
including the formal approval of France. As for the five secret agreements on
bases and facilities granted to the Americans in France, it was stipulated in
each of the first four that they would be honored "as long as the North
Atlantic Treaty is in effect, unless both governments should decide by mutual
agreement to give it up." The fifth agreement, of December 6, 1958, which
was concluded after de Gaulle's return to power, referred to the communications system and stipulated that in the event of dissension, the agreement
would be cancelled after a two-year period. The American note proposed
that the United States use the two-year period to remove its facilities and
evacuate its bases.

The German answer to the French memorandum, dated May 3, stated
that withdrawal of French NATO troops from Germany affected the entire
system of treaties and decisions established by the Atlantic Council between
October 3 and 23, 1954. These had linked the right of foreign troops to be
stationed in Germany to their membership in NATO. Germany therefore
demanded that new accords be concluded with France on the basis of equality
and reciprocity. It must be noted that France's decision had been reached

without prior consultation with Germany, although such consultation was prescribed by the Franco-German Treaty of Cooperation.

According to international law, France had contravened simultaneously the North Atlantic Treaty of 1949, the treaty of the Western European Union of 1954, and the Franco-German Treaty of 1963.

The Impact of the Debate

The juridical considerations, however, were less important than the political issues.

The French decision challenged the fundamental principle of the Alliance. The structure of the Alliance was rejected by a member state of prime importance in Western Europe; France's role was important because of her political and economic as well as her strategic global position.

The uneasiness in the Alliance developed into a major crisis. This in turn precipitated a public debate between France and her partners and among Frenchmen. It pitted against each other the supporters and adversaries of General de Gaulle's unilateral decision.

The debate centered around the reasons for his decision and its consequences. Three reasons were advanced; one had to do with the structure and functions of the Alliance, i.e. the very nature of a system of alliances in the atomic age; the contrast between integration and cooperation between a protectorate and independence. The second reason had to do with the nuclear strategy of the Alliance; the third with the dangers to which the European states were exposed: Soviet aggression and the possibility of being dragged into a war by the United States.

The decision must be examined from two different angles. How would it affect the military strength of the Alliance, especially its deterrent force? Would the decision lead to French neutralism in Europe and possibly even to a reversal of alliances?

These are the questions that must be explored in a realistic appraisal of the French government's decision. The ground work for this decision was laid long ago, but the final objective was known only by Charles de Gaulle. The announcement (made on January 12, 1966, by Ambassador Valerian Zorin) of the general's forthcoming official visit to Moscow—scheduled for June 20—points up the importance of the change in French foreign policy.

Independence or Integration?

Independence must be the supreme aim of the foreign policy of a power such as France. Integration makes members of an alliance the satellites of the strongest power. Such are, in simplified form, the major refrains of de Gaulle's foreign policy. What direction did his policy take on the morrow of

France's withdrawal from NATO? The dilemma of independence versus integration, depending upon whether it is viewed from a national or a collective point of view, was twofold: within the present NATO system of integration, has France preserved her freedom of action in foreign affairs? Is an integrated alliance in the atomic age more effective than an unorganized one?

On March 18, France's fourteen NATO allies issued a statement affirming their adherence to the principle of integration and their intention of strengthening the existing Atlantic organization. On April 14, in an address before the National Assembly, Georges Pompidou replied: "For several years we have repeatedly affirmed our loyalty to the Atlantic Alliance—that is, to the treaty of 1949—and our wish to reexamine the integrated organization that has been superimposed upon it." It was plain that there was total disagreement.

Actually, the Atlantic Alliance and the integrated organization in no way limited France's freedom of action. The exclusion of England from the Common Market, the refusal to sign the Moscow Pact, the recognition of China—all these decisions were contrary to the wishes of the United States but they did not adversely affect the organization. On April 14 Couve de Murville confessed to the National Assembly: "It has been said over and over again that NATO never prevented our nation from pursuing its own political policies. On the whole, this is true." He quickly added, however: "The question is not so much whether we were able to do what we wanted but rather whether we would be dragged into doing what we did not want to do," meaning of course, becoming involved in a war because of the United States.

On April 13 Georges Pompidou stated: "Inasmuch as integration in peacetime is an instrument for collective war, it is the offspring of the cold war and helps to perpetuate it." This idea is tendentious. Far from perpetuating the cold war, integration is a defensive mechanism that paves the way for détente.

For the concept of integration Pompidou substituted the notion of an "alliance freely consented to" and Couve de Murville stated: "It is absurd and harmful to say that an unorganized alliance becomes automatically worthless." And further on: "I am sure that if the Atlantic Alliance had been in existence before the last war, Paul Reynaud would not have had to launch an appeal into the void as we know he did when he asked President Roosevelt for help." Recent history, however, belies this. In 1939 Czechoslovakia and Poland learned the value of treaties with France that were not part of an organized joint defense. In the event of aggression, ordinary agreements are of little value. In a letter written on March 23 in response to de Gaulle's letter of March 7, President Johnson believed that "the members of the alliance must prepare the structures of command, draft the strategic and tactical plans, and identify the forces to be assigned to NATO as a precaution against a crisis. . . . NATO's arrangements should reflect the technological and strategic imperatives of our day."

On April 20 Georges Pompidou replied that the NATO Council meetings generally made only minor decisions. "The system gets jammed when major and especially strategic decisions are made."

Nuclear Strategy and the Defense of Europe

Georges Pompidou remarked that in 1954 the approved strategy of the Atlantic Council was massive retaliation and that officially there had been no change, whereas the supreme command favored flexible response. "It was enough for McNamara to repudiate Dulles's ideas, for a strategy never approved of by the NATO Council to become the strategy of the supreme command" (speech of April 20). This strategy "actually consisted in allowing the United States to limit its initial field of operations and to shield its own territory from the depredations of a potential aggressor." Such a strategy "might expose us to nuclear attack first and then to invasion" (speech of April 13). Paul-Henri Spaak admitted that "one of the weaknesses of the Alliance was the uncertainty about its strategic doctrine." France never made a sustained effort to remedy this. On the contrary, in various ways "France opposed the reexamination, discussion, and redefinition of the Alliance that had been planned at the Ottawa meeting in 1963."[1]

In a speech before the National Assembly on April 14, René Pleven said: "If we want our atomic force to have some significance . . . we must reach an agreement with our allies . . . on the best way to use a deterrent force." He believed that there was no real contradiction in the two theses because a distinction had to be made between a major aggression and a border incident. It was also necessary, he insisted, to make preparations for common action in a crisis and examine the various strategic possibilities.

"Nobody can predict the form a world war will take. All we do know is that atomic weapons are the essential element and that they are not and can never be integrated. They are and will remain a national weapon." These two statements by Couve de Murville deserve a few comments.

As to the first statement, it is altogether conceivable that the Russians or the Americans might develop an anti-missile missile. This would make once more conventional weapons indispensable in Europe, in crises other than border incidents.

As for the second statement, a distinction must be made between the United States and the European states. It is true that the United States will

[1] *Figaro,* May 9, 1966.

never grant to any one else the right to veto decisions it might be forced to make in some other part of the world. The long debate between Eisenhower and de Gaulle on the possibility of a three-power directorate attests to this. As for the European states, they can give up the idea of national nuclear forces only if they agree to build "a European defense organization" in order to pursue a common foreign policy.

Once again the differences between France and the other European states are evident. "Our European partners are not necessarily hostile to the idea of a purely European defense organization. They only insist that such an organization should not appear to be directed against the United States," Raymond Aron wrote.[2] The objection to a European undertaking, Couve de Murville told the National Assembly, is that the European nations "would have to try to construct together a common economy, a common foreign policy and a common defense." The minister was obliged to admit that "our partners do not share our views." According to them, the appropriate forum for the discussion of international defense and international policies is NATO. "Nothing would be more antinomic than the concepts of European and Atlantic integration. . . . Let no one say that if Europe is integrated it will become the second pillar of the Atlantic world, on a par with the United States. These are ready-made ideas that cannot survive three minutes of close scrutiny." The French government refused to examine the effect of European integration on the relations between Western Europe and the United States, just as it refused to study a common strategic doctrine. Actually, France's offensive against the United States was followed by a similar offensive against the European states. The French government hoped in this way to convince some of these states to follow its example and withdraw from NATO. Its assessment of the risks incurred by members of the Alliance contributed to this end.

Soviet Aggression or American Involvement?

The premier analyzed the latent conflicts in the following terms: "The threat to Western Europe has been attenuated; Asia has replaced Europe as the arena where the major powers will confront each other."

The diagnosis is correct. There is a Russo-American détente in Europe and a Sino-American conflict in Southeast Asia. But Europe must decide whether this détente means that the Russian threat has disappeared and whether the tension in Southeast Asia entails the danger of involvement in an American war.

The détente in Europe is recent. The last Berlin crisis occurred in 1961, the Cuban crisis in 1962. The present attitude of the Soviet Union is not

[2] *Figaro*, May 13, 1966.

immutable: a dictator might reappear or Peking might make its influence felt in Moscow. Global competition persists between the West and the Communist world. And the numerical disparity between Soviet forces and those of Western Europe is still overwhelming. In the Europe of today, this is offset solely by American troops and nuclear weapons.

Will the Atlantic Pact, which is a regional alliance, and the permanent organization that stems from it, drag France into a conflict outside the sphere of the treaty? Juridically, the Pact is categorical: France is not committed.

Looking at the problem factually, we can say that recent local conflicts attest the freedom of action of America's European partners: Korea, the Congo, Cuba, and now Vietnam.

Let us analyze the possibility of a conflict between the two major powers. Whether neutral or an ally, France might very well become involved in a Sino-American war because such a war would quickly spread. If she were an ally of the United States, she would be less exposed to the danger of invasion and destruction because all the allies would profit by a collective system aimed at deterring the enemy from using the worst of his weapons.

In the event of a war in Europe, France, which is still a member of the Alliance, would take "whatever action she thought necessary," according to Article 5 of the North Atlantic Treaty. But French intervention is quasi-automatic according to Article 4 of the Treaty of Brussels (which became Article 5 by virtue of the ruling of October 23, 1954). It stipulates: "If one of the contracting parties should be the object of armed aggression in Europe, the others will contribute all possible aid, including military assistance, in accordance with the stipulations of Article 51 of the Charter of the United Nations." France was thus legally bound by the revised Treaty of Brussels. She could not in fact avoid involvement in a war in Europe as long as French troops were stationed in Germany.

In short, the motives for French withdrawal from NATO, which de Gaulle gave in his press conference and which his ministers repeated before the National Assembly, are not convincing. Either France is a faithful ally and her departure from NATO is of purely symbolical importance; or she is a nominal ally inclined to join the neutralists, and her affiliation with the Alliance cannot be justified.

An account of the debates in the National Assembly, and an examination of the effect French secession had on the deterrent force of the Alliance, should shed some light on this problem.

The Discussion in the National Assembly

The reasons for French withdrawal from NATO were discussed on April 13, 14, and 20 in the National Assembly; also debated was the kind of diplomacy that the decision might make possible. Raymond Mondon, speaking for the Independents, voiced the anxieties that the prospect of such a diplomacy aroused in the ranks of the majority.

Mondon spoke with understanding about the feelings of many Frenchmen. He expressed the hope that de Gaulle's impending trip to Moscow would be followed by a meeting between him and Johnson. With no less naiveté he asked why the government decided to quit NATO before the date fixed by the accords. François Mitterrand reminded his audience of the many times de Gaulle had reversed his policy toward Russia. In 1962 he had denounced Russia as that "colossal world threat" and inveighed against the oppression that hung over Central and Eastern Europe as a consequence. Mitterrand accused de Gaulle of having only one line of action: "A firm determination to pursue a policy of isolation based upon the notion that nationalism is the truth of our day." The most trenchant remarks were made by René Pleven. He reproached the government for presenting the deputies with a *fait accompli*; what could Parliament do but accept it? "As for our allies, they simply have to pack up and leave." He expressed surprise that no attempt had been made to negotiate either with our allies or with their enemies: "Your haste proves your determination to create the irreversible, that is, in our view the irreparable." He emphasized the impact of this decision which he condemned: "You are handing the U.S.S.R. a royal gift: the dismissal of American and Canadian troops. What are you getting in exchange? NATO will be weakened but not the Warsaw Pact. . . . France played her trump card before going to Moscow in June."

The opposition introduced a motion censuring the French withdrawal. Only 137 voted in favor—the Socialists, the Rassemblement démocratique, and thirty-four of the fifty-four Centre démocratique. In spite of their concern, the Independents supported the majority as did the Communists. "The crisis is not behind but ahead of us," said René Pleven, in commenting on the vote.

How did de Gaulle's decision affect the Alliance and the relations between East and West?

The Effects of the Decision on the Alliance

The withdrawal of France from NATO altered the distribution of its military forces and affected the defense measures taken by the allied command.

It was inevitable that France's secession from NATO should result in the lessening of NATO's influence in Western Europe. Faced with dismemberment on the Continent, England should strengthen her military and political ties with the United States and Germany. The Federal Republic should become the continental pivot of the Alliance. An industrial power, with a goodly supply of conventional weapons, it was in a position to increase its military demands for possession of nuclear weapons or its political demand for reunification. This should lead the United States to establish a highly integrated Anglo-German-American coalition. The NATO organs for planning and control should be simplified. The smallest member states of the Atlantic Pact would either be tempted by neutralism or would align themselves with the coalition. The southern flank of the Alliance—Portugal, Greece, and Turkey—might be tempted to follow France's example.

The defense arrangements of the interallied command were necessarily affected by the French decision and its practical consequences—the assignment and deployment of conventional troops and the functioning of the infrastructure's network.

France's withdrawal decreased the number of troops available to the NATO command in time of war. This occurred at a time when both the United States and Great Britain were reducing their forces, America because of Vietnam, and England because of difficulties with its balance of payments. At the same time, the Federal Republic was under pressure from France in regard to the stationing of French troops on the German side of the Rhine. In response to a German memorandum of May 3, the French government announced on May 18 that the question was political, not juridical. It wanted to know whether the German government still wanted France to station troops on its territory in view of the fact that these were no longer subject to the NATO system of joint command.

French withdrawal impeded the deployment of the interallied forces in a Central European sector that was cut off from French territory. Yet this area was strategically of paramount importance. Because of the absence of French troops, the distribution of conventional NATO forces was reduced in depth. Troops stationed in Germany depended exclusively on the North Sea ports. The same was true of the American troops available to NATO in an emergency. If the right to fly over French territory was withdrawn, direct air liaison between the northern and southern sectors of Western Europe would become more difficult. Planes would be obliged to make a long detour over Spain, since both Switzerland and Austria were neutral. The right to fly over French territory, which in the past had been granted for a one-year period, was put on a month-to-month basis by a May 3 decision of the French government.

As long as France was a member of the Alliance, she as well as her partners found it most advantageous to share in the Early Warning system. This alert system naturally had to be integrated. As René Pleven observed, without the Early Warning system "our strategic force would be deaf and blind and could be destroyed on the ground."

The task of the Alliance was therefore made more difficult by French withdrawal from NATO. The defense of the Western world would have to depend increasingly on America's deterrent force, particularly on its long- and intermediate-range ballistic missiles.

Yet the United States, in protecting West Germany, would also be protecting France—provided, of course, that the other European members of NATO did not follow the example of France and ask the United States to withdraw its troops and abandon its bases.

Consequences for the Deterrent Force

The problem of deterrence is affected by military factors—the nature and strength of the force involved, the plans for their deployment; and by political factors—the cohesiveness of an alliance and the mutual trust of its members.

Seen from this perspective, the French secession weakened Western deterrence. The Atlantic Alliance was militarily less effective, at least as an instrument of conventional warfare. It was politically divided.

Speaking of the absolute primacy of deterrence in a nuclear age, General Beaufre observed that "the danger has changed in form: instead of romantic and brutal invasions, the risks we incur today are those of subtle political shifts that bring about changes in the balance."[3] French withdrawal from NATO resulted in just such an imbalance. Moscow was quick to realize this. On March 31, Waldeck Rochet, the secretary-general of the French Communist Party, speaking before the Twenty-Third Congress of the Communist Party, acclaimed General de Gaulle. René Dabernat wrote: "The Atlantic crisis gave the Soviet Union the greatest victory it had ever achieved without waging war."[4]

The full extent to which Western deterrence will be weakened depends upon how France envisages her special status as an ally detached from the organization of the Alliance.

What was the significance of the removal of NATO's headquarters and bases from France? Gilles Martinet interpreted it as an indication of "France's belief that she might, under certain conditions, avoid a conflict involving her allies"—a Berlin crisis, for example.[5] This interpretation was corroborated by the premier's statement of March 28 in a televised speech. Georges Pompidou, discussing the kinds of incidents that could involve France in a war, said: "If a conflict should arise between the United States on one side, and China and Russia on the other, a world war, a nuclear war, might ensue.

[3] General Beaufre, *Dissuasion et stratégie* (Paris: Armand Colin, 1964), 153.
[4] *Combat*, Apr. 5, 1966.
[5] *Le Nouvel Observateur*, Mar. 16, 1966.

A war situation could arise in Asia as well as in Europe. . . . I believe that if we are not integrated into the American system we will have a better chance of avoiding war." Thus, French neutrality in the event of a European war was no longer an academic question. Maurice Couve de Murville's emphasis on an "unprovoked war" implied that France reserved the right to decide whether or not a war in Europe was "unprovoked." To be sure, the treaty of 1949 did not guarantee automatic assistance, but the same is not true of the revised Treaty of Brussels (1954). France, as we know, "need not foreclose any possibilities that might be to her advantage." Therefore she could decide, with no more than one month's warning, to prohibit her allies from flying over her territory; she could recall her troops from West Germany. The French government asked Bonn for an agreement about the new status of French troops stationed in Germany. When the German government requested a redefinition of the responsibilities of these troops and their relationship to the interallied command, France refused to supply it. Under the circumstances, France might also withdraw her troops from West Berlin. Thus the status of Berlin, which was regulated by the Potsdam Accords, could be modified unilaterally by France. The Soviet Union would be in a position at any time to renew its pressure on Berlin, knowing that France would almost certainly remain neutral.

Indeed, the eventual withdrawal of French troops stationed in Berlin was mentioned unofficially during the Franco-German discussions about the status of French forces in West Germany.

Since her withdrawal from NATO, France has been really "a nation with free hands." Although protected by the treaty, she is bound by practically no commitments whatsoever to her allies. This fact undermines somewhat the credibility of Western deterrence.

The Kremlin Speech

The logical sequel to withdrawal from NATO was a rapprochement with the East. De Gaulle, who had not conferred with a president of the United States since Kennedy visited Paris in 1961, went to Moscow on June 21, 1966.

The trips Couve de Murville had made to Warsaw on May 18 and to Prague on June 25 were designed to prepare the way for some common position in regard to the status of Europe and Germany which France, the Soviet Union, and the Iron Curtain countries could agree on.

Two Soviet statements suggest a certain similarity of views about Europe. On April 27 in Rome, Andrei Gromyko, minister of foreign affairs, proposed a pan-European conference for the purpose of resolving the problem of security on the Continent. On May 20, Jouri Joukov, the Paris correspondent of *Pravda*, reminded his readers that "as early as 1960 General de Gaulle had said that an attempt should be made to unify the two sections of the European Continent in order to achieve collaboration from the Atlantic to the Urals." He deplored the existence in France of "forces that wished to give a different meaning to the word 'Europe' by excluding the Soviet Union."[6]

De Gaulle's speech at the Kremlin on June 21 confirmed his intention of establishing a new European order based on Paris and Moscow. It was not enough that East-West relations had evolved from a state of permanent tension to peaceful coexistence. "New relationships must be established that will lead to détente, to understanding and to collaboration." Referring to the status of Europe, the general said: "France is not satisfied with this rigid confrontation of two organizations"—that is, two massive blocs, the Atlantic and Warsaw Pacts. "Europe reconstituted as a fruitful whole, no longer paralyzed by sterile division . . . is the first prerequisite of a rectified international situation. . . . The establishment of an understanding between the states that until now have been antagonistic is primarily . . . a European problem." In this way de Gaulle reiterated his now familiar ideas about the dismantling of the blocs—Europe from the Atlantic to the Urals, a European Europe. Referring to the status of Germany, de Gaulle said: "The arrangements that must some day be made for German reunification and for the security of our Continent are a European problem."

Finally, in alluding to the "ways and means" of achieving these political objectives, the general expressed the belief that "France and the Soviet Union must begin collaborating today in the expectation that all Europe will work in concert." Thus a Franco-Soviet entente was to be the prelude to a pan-European conference.

The East's Response

To measure the gap between General de Gaulle's objectives and the results of the Moscow meetings one must analyze the Franco-Soviet communiqué of June 29 and the statement published in Bucharest on July 8 at the close of the conference of members of the Warsaw Pact.

The first document mentioned the status of Germany discreetly. It merely suggested that opinions should be exchanged on the subject. The question was treated more explicitly in the second statement: peaceful settlement of the German question and the security of the Continent will be possible only if "at the very outset the existence of the two German states is acknowledged."

[6] Quoted in *Combat*, May 21, 1966.

The Soviet Union and the majority of the satellites were dominated by fear of West Germany. Russian weapons, the East German bastion, and the American NATO troops stationed in the Federal Republic, provided security against the German threat. Moreover, a "confrontation of the two organizations" would enable the Soviet Union to retain its hold not only on East Germany but also on Poland and Czechoslovakia. During Couve de Murville's trip to Warsaw in May 1966, André Fontaine wrote: "If détente occurs at Warsaw, it is expected to come from an understanding between the blocs to regard the German problem as a *fait accompli*, rather than from a disintegration of the blocs."[7] Since French withdrawal from NATO had increased Germany's influence in that organization, it was important that the bonds uniting members of the Warsaw Pact be tightened. On the other hand, Rumania, whose borders adjoined neither of the two Germanies, hoped for the breaking up of the two blocs. In opting for the coexistence of the two Germanies, the Bucharest conference declared itself in favor of maintaining the two blocs.

Meanwhile, explicit if not sincere approval was given to a European Europe. The text of the Franco-Soviet statement reads: "The two governments agree that European problems must be considered primarily within a European framework." In the same spirit, the Bucharest conference suggested the "convocation of a general European conference to study the related questions of European security and the achievement of general European cooperation." The matter of who was to participate in such a conference was treated with calculated vagueness. According to the *Le Monde* correspondent in Bucharest, this seemed to suggest that the United States would play a role.[8]

Opposition to German reunification, maintenance of the two blocs, the presence of the United States in the determination of European settlements, the acknowledgment that a Europe from the Atlantic to the Urals was mere fiction—such was the response of the East to de Gaulle's Moscow trip.

Why should this surprise us? De Gaulle spoke solely about territorial problems that concerned the entire Western world. He raised these questions with the Russians, who assessed the extent of American supremacy more realistically than he did. And in speaking of these matters, de Gaulle was not armed with concessions from Germany because these would have required American consent. He merely said in Moscow that the scope of a Franco-Russian entente would be determined by Soviet interests. The leaders of the Kremlin, whose relations with China were precarious, had no desire to risk a major crisis with the United States over Europe and Germany, especially since they were altogether satisfied with the status quo. A limited agreement

[7] *Le Monde*, May 21, 1966.
[8] *Le Monde*, July 10, 1966.

with de Gaulle weakened the Atlantic Alliance without in any way obliging the Russians to break off relations with the United States.

Toward a French Neutralism

This limited agreement was spelled out in a Franco-Soviet communiqué: "The two governments have decided to continue to hold consultations at regular intervals. Such consultations will have a bearing on European and other international problems of common interest." The joint communiqué was bolstered by the announcement that a direct line of communications would be established between the Kremlin and the Elysée. This was reminiscent of the 1963 Franco-German Treaty of Cooperation which also provided for periodic consultations on foreign policy and defense. To be sure, no formal Franco-Soviet treaty was drafted, but the solemnity of the statement signed by the two chiefs of state suggested the tone of a nonaggression pact.

France thus found herself in the ambiguous position of a member of the Atlantic Pact, protected by the United States yet able to invoke this communiqué in order to remain neutral should a crisis arise between America and Russia.

The ambiguity of France's position, which Lord Gladwyn described as "national neutralism,"[9] weakened Western deterrence. The Atlantic Alliance became less powerful militarily. The deployment of conventional NATO forces was reduced in depth. The Soviet attitude toward the German problem proved that French secession was indeed "a royal gift" to Russia. France received nothing in exchange. But she retained, none the less, the protection of the Alliance. And because of this, her example might prove contagious. Those members of the Atlantic Pact that were already tempted to remain neutral would incline more and more in that direction. The ambiguous position of France increased German uncertainties. Wooed by the United States, Germany was beset by conflicting pressures.

Meanwhile members of the Alliance, shocked by the general's conduct, reacted to French neutralism. The Alliance could survive only by defining and pursuing its long-term objectives regarding the status of Germany. It could no longer be satisfied with a defensive military success which insured containment of Russia without war. It was obliged to approach the problem of relations with the East—that is, the German problem—through diplomatic channels: this the Atlantic Council acknowledged in Brussels on June 8, 1966.

[9] Lord Gladwyn, in a speech to the Congress of the Association of the North Atlantic Treaty, Munich, Sept. 1966.

12

Planetary Diplomacy

Siding against Israel

THE LEGISLATIVE ELECTIONS of March 1967 reduced the government's majority. Would de Gaulle's ideas on foreign policy become more moderate or more extreme? Actually, advancing age plus absolute power led the general to proceed more vigorously than ever. The opening of the legislative session coincided with a series of diplomatic escalations that assumed planetary proportions. The first move had to do with England and is discussed elsewhere in the book. The second, involving the Middle East, concerned both Israel and Arabian oil.

To the latent conflict between Israelis and Arabs, which began with the creation of the state of Israel, must be added the continuous rivalry between Americans and Russians. After the British withdrawal from Suez, the United States was the sole guarantor of Western Europe's principal source of oil. The Russians, for their part, wanted access to the Mediterranean. In 1956, at the time of the Anglo-French Suez expedition, France was Israel's ally. In concluding the Evian Accords of 1962, de Gaulle based his policy toward the Third World on a close alliance with independent Algeria. Israel, however, was the largest purchaser of French tanks and combat planes.

On May 22 Nasser ordered a blockade of the Gulf of Aquaba, where Elath is situated. It is the only port on the Red Sea through which Israel can procure oil. The blockade was an act of aggression against Israel, who had announced that such a move would constitute a *casus belli*. Nasser was defying the United States, England, and France: in 1957, they had guaranteed freedom of navigation in the Gulf of Aquaba.

On May 24 France asked the three permanent members of the Security Council—the United States, England, and the Soviet Union—to cooperate with her in seeking a solution to the crisis. The United States and England immediately agreed, but the Soviet Union ignored the request.

On June 2, de Gaulle made his position plain in a statement unequivocally repudiating the 1957 agreement on the Gulf of Aquaba. In the name of France, he declared: "Any state that is the first to resort to arms anywhere will not have the approval or even the support of France." He let it be known that if the Israelis began hostilities, they would receive no arms from France. The tenor of de Gaulle's remarks seemed to absolve Egypt, who had initiated the blockade, and to condemn Israel in advance should it retaliate.

Israel was the great victor of the six-day war. The cease-fire of June 8 was the result of an agreement in the Security Council between the United States and the Soviet Union. It was not a four-power agreement. France immediately prohibited the shipment of arms to Israel.

Eager to compensate for Egypt's military defeat by a diplomatic victory, the Soviet Union requested and obtained a special meeting of the United Nations General Assembly to consider the crisis in the Middle East. On June 17, on his way to New York, Kosygin stopped in Paris. Would de Gaulle take advantage of his special relations with the Soviet Union to facilitate an understanding between the two superpowers?

There was no indication of this in the communiqué issued by the French cabinet on June 21. Analyzing the local responsibilities in the conflict, de Gaulle "blamed" the Arabs for their threats and "condemned Israel for starting the war." Proceeding to the question of worldwide responsibility, he charged that "the war unleashed in Vietnam by American aggression" accounted for "China's haste to arm" and also "affected the psychological and political process which resulted in the Middle East conflict." This condemnation of both Israel and the United States determined his solution. On the local level, France "will not accept any changes produced by military action," thus undermining Israel's position in the United Nation debate. On the global level, "there is no chance of arriving at a peaceful settlement as long as the war in Vietnam continues." Having expressed his views, de Gaulle attempted to prevent a dialogue between the two superpowers.

Nevertheless, such a dialogue did take place on June 23 and 25. Kosygin and Johnson met in Glassboro, New Jersey, half way between New York and Washington. Perhaps the detonation of China's first thermonuclear bomb had something to do with the meeting. In any event, the two men were in agreement about the need to maintain peace and to recognize Israel's right to exist.

The two superpowers, however, intended to take each other's measure in the General Assembly of the United Nations. The Soviet Union supported the Yugoslav resolution demanding immediate and unconditional evacuation of the territories occupied by Israel. The Latin American resolution, which the United States supported, linked evacuation to the cessation of hostilities between Arabs and Jews. On July 5, France voted in favor of the Yugoslav resolution, thus breaking away from all the NATO states except Greece and Turkey. She tried to get the twelve French-speaking African states to join her but only four allowed themselves to be persuaded.

General de Gaulle thus moved, in quick successive stages, from apparent neutrality toward the belligerents to a position of total solidarity with the Arab countries. His analysis rested on the conviction that the peaceful coexistence of the two superpowers was about to end, whereas in reality direct contact between the Americans and Russians was soon to materialize and prove beneficial.

French public opinion, which in 1956 had unreservedly approved the Suez expedition, was disturbed by this abandonment of Israel, and especially by the embargo on the shipment of fifty Mirages that had been bought but not delivered prior to the end of the lightning war. There was dissension even within the government.

At a press conference on November 27, 1967, de Gaulle explained French policy in the Middle East. He described the Jews as "an élite people, sure of themselves and domineering," and the state of Israel as "warlike and determined to achieve self-aggrandizement." He reminded his listeners that after the Algerian war, France had resumed her ties of friendship and cooperation with the Arab peoples of the East. This, he added, represented "a basic tenet of our foreign policy." Finally, observing that France's voice had not been heard, he declared that "any settlement must be based on the evacuation of all territories taken by force."

The tone of his remarks, rather than what they implied about the direction of French foreign policy, aroused a good deal of feeling. Although the public realized that France's desire to ensure friendly ties with the Arab world was motivated by concern for her relations with the Third World as well as by her need for oil, de Gaulle's views about the Jewish people and the state of Israel evoked criticism. This obliged the general to disclose his correspondence with the former Israeli prime minister, Ben Gurion, dated December 6 and 30. In a short book published early in 1968 on de Gaulle, Israel, and the Jews, Raymond Aron charged that the general, by his statements, "knowingly, deliberately opened up a new period in Jewish history and perhaps in anti-Semitism."[1]

The Quest for Arabian Oil

Through the Compagnie Française des Pétroles (C.F.P.), the French state possessed, by virtue of its 35 per cent voting right, a minority share in each

---

[1] Raymond Aron, *De Gaulle, Israel, et les Juifs* (Paris: Plon, 1968), 18.

of the two international oil consortiums operating in Iraq and Iran respectively.

The French government was anxious to procure new sources of oil independently of the large Anglo-American companies. It was therefore trying to come to an agreement with the governments of the Middle East, or with the national oil companies recently established by these governments.

Following the pattern of the 1965 agreement with Algeria on hydro-carbons, the French government immediately used the E.R.A.P. (Entreprise de Recherches et d'Activités Pétrolières, an oil company financed by the state that had been dealing with Iran since 1965) not as a concessionary company but as an entrepreneurial prospector for oil.

In November 1967, in the same spirit, negotiations were begun between the E.R.A.P. and the National Iraq Oil Company. An agreement signed on February 4, 1968, gave the E.R.A.P. the right to prospect for oil in a zone which until 1961 had been part of the concession granted to the Iraq Petroleum Company, the international consortium of which the C.F.P. was a member.

During the negotiations the French government decided to lift the ban on the delivery of arms to Iraq. Although in June 1967 Iraq was not officially at war with Israel, Iraqui troops fought on the Jordanian front. The French decision was resented bitterly by the Israelis. The connection between the contract for oil prospecting and the shipment of arms was obvious.

On February 7, 1968, General Aref, head of the Iraqui state, paid a visit to General de Gaulle. France was hoping to obtain further advantages in the form of a concession to the C.F.P. in the oilfields in North Roumailah, famous for its huge reserves. This hope was doomed to disappointment but de Gaulle none the less reminded his guest of "the ancient and natural affinity which our people and the Arab peoples have never ceased to feel for one another." The Franco-Iraqui communiqué of February 10 represented a further escalation of the offensive against Israel. It announced the joint opinion of the two heads of state regarding a settlement in the Middle East: "There can be no settlement without a *prior* evacuation of all the territories occupied since the beginning of hostilities." In other words, de Gaulle was encouraging the Arabs' intransigent attitude instead of urging moderation on both parties. He encouraged the race in armaments by the manner in which he discriminated between the Israelis and the Iraquis. The quest for Arabian oil was inspired by de Gaulle's desire to be free of the tutelage of the large oil trusts and to weaken American influence in an area where the Soviet Union seemed to favor an Israeli-Arab conflict.

Long Live Free Quebec!

Like all heads of state, de Gaulle was invited to visit the 1967 Exposition in Montreal. After three months of negotiation, and contrary to the rules of etiquette in such matters, de Gaulle demanded and obtained permission to travel throughout the province of Quebec before visiting the capital at Ottawa. In permitting de Gaulle to portray himself as the emissary of French culture, the Canadian government assumed he would be circumspect in regard to the demands for autonomy that certain circles in Quebec were making.

On July 24, aboard the cruiser *Colbert*, the general arrived in Quebec in uniform. Addressing the French Canadians, he spoke of "the advent of a people who, in every domain, desire self-determination, who wish to take their destiny into their own hands." The following day, in front of the City Hall of Montreal, he alluded to his travels throughout the province, then said: "I found myself in an atmosphere of liberation." Using the slogan of the champions of independence for Quebec, he proceeded to shout, "Long live free Quebec!" ("Vive le Québec libre!").

On July 26, after due deliberation, the Canadian government published a communiqué which read in part: "Certain of the president's statements tend to encourage a small minority of our population who seek to destroy Canada, and as such they are unacceptable to the people and government of Canada." The same day, speaking at the University of Montreal, the cradle of the separatist movement, de Gaulle told his audience that their country was "the neighbor of a colossal state whose very size is a challenge to your own identity." Offended by the Canadian government's reply, the general informed Prime Minister Lester Pearson that he would not go to Ottawa.

In a speech on July 29, Daniel Johnson, the prime minister of Quebec, referred to the general's visit and requested the convocation of a Constituent Assembly to draft a new constitution that would give full autonomy to Quebec.

An official communiqué was published on August 1, after a meeting of the French cabinet. De Gaulle criticized the oppressive regime and the ensuing discriminatory one that had victimized the "French Canadians" since 1763 and 1867 respectively. Then, "without any equivocation," he informed "the French Canadians and their government that France intends to help them achieve the liberating goals which they have set themselves."

This diplomatic escalation astonished the French people. Why did de Gaulle, in defiance of the rules of hospitality, meddle in the domestic affairs of a foreign country, and one that was an ally besides, to the point of assuming the mission of freeing Quebec? The analogy between Charles de Gaulle's affinity with French-speaking peoples and the *Deutschtum* of the Third Reich was noted by leading newspapers.

On September 20, the French government decided to establish, in conjunction with the government of Quebec and "on the basis of parity, an intergovernmental organization for joint action" that would set up ministerial conferences and regular meetings at the highest level. The procedure would be analogous to that followed in implementing the Franco-German Treaty of Cooperation of 1963 and the joint Franco-Soviet declaration of June 29, 1966. A step toward recognition of Quebec's independence had been taken.

At his November 27, 1967, press conference de Gaulle reverted to the themes of his visit to Quebec—British political control and the American economic threat. He justified his conduct by saying: "The passion for liberation was so strongly expressed that it was clearly the duty of France, represented in my person, to respond with solemnity and without equivocation." He predicted the "advent of Quebec to the rank of a sovereign state" and expressed the hope that "the solidarity of the French community on both sides of the Atlantic will be consummated."

Replying to these remarks on November 28, Lester Pearson protested anew against unwarranted meddling. He reminded his people of what de Gaulle had said during an official visit to Canada on November 19, 1960. On that occasion, the general referred to the solidarity and stability of "a state that has discovered the means of uniting two societies very different in origin, language, and religion."

In a speech of December 31, 1967, de Gaulle tendered his good wishes to all the children of France, including "those of the French nation in Canada." In a televised interview accorded to Michel Droit on June 7, 1968, on the morrow of the general strike, he posed as a revolutionary and boasted, among other things, of having "inaugurated the liberation of Canada."

Feelers in Eastern Europe

General de Gaulle's remarks about Canada caused great astonishment because very few Frenchmen are interested in the linguistic and cultural conflicts that divide Canada. But his speeches in Poland and in Rumania surprised no one because they expressed his conception of Europe extending from the Atlantic to the Urals. The game, however, was a delicate one. How could Franco-German collaboration and the special relations that existed between France and the Soviet Union be reconciled with the encouragement given to the states of Eastern Europe to recover a certain measure of their autonomy? The purpose, of course, was to hasten the disintegration of the Eastern bloc in the same way in which France had dislocated the Western bloc.

Arriving in Warsaw on September 7, 1967, de Gaulle repeated once again that the Polish borders must remain unchanged. In making this point, he was supporting the conservative diplomacy of the eastern countries, which favored the maintenance of the territorial status quo. He was warmly acclaimed. Very cautiously he began to preach "a relaxation of tensions, then an understanding, and finally cooperation in western, central and eastern Europe, which may result in a contractual settlement of the important problem of Germany." And he advised Poland to follow the example of France and to safeguard and develop the essence, influence, and power of the nation, "no matter how mighty the colossuses of the Universe may be." In his welcoming speech, the Polish prime minister, Edward Ochab, had stated that the first prerequisite of an international détente was "recognition of the realities, Germany being one of these realities." At Gdansk, formerly Danzig, de Gaulle spoke with greater clarity: "France has no advice to give to Poland but . . . she hopes, she expects, that you will take a longer and broader view than you have done so far." Alluding to the status of Europe and Germany in a speech before the Polish Parliament on September 11, he expressed the hope that "a European order . . . will gradually be established in which all the nations of the Continent will participate and whose solidarity they will guarantee." Wladyslaw Gomulka's answer was plain: from her historic experiences Poland drew the conclusion "that is best expressed by her adoption of the road which leads to friendship and alliance with her great neighbor to the east, the Soviet Union." This alliance, together with the treaties of mutual assistance concluded with the states of Eastern Europe, especially with the German Democratic Republic, "is the cornerstone of the policy of the Polish Popular Republic and the principal guarantee of its security." Further more, the Franco-Polish pact of 1939 "had failed to protect either France or Poland." Gomulka chose to base his foreign policy entirely on that of the Soviet Union and to subordinate a possible settlement of the German problem to the simultaneous existence of the two German states. A Franco-Polish declaration published on September 12 mentioned the possibility of convoking a European conference on security but alluded in the vaguest of terms to the German problem.

Of all the members of the Warsaw Pact, Rumania has demonstrated the greatest independence of the Soviet Union during the past few years. Would General de Gaulle's remarks about dismantling the military blocs be received more favorably there than in Poland?

On May 15, 1968, speaking in Bucharest at a luncheon given by Nicolas Ceaucescu, secretary-general of the Rumanian Communist Party and chief of state, de Gaulle praised Russia, "whose worth and power make her an essential pillar of a reunited Continent." He cited Moscow as one of the capitals of the European continent from whence would emanate 'the great movement that will unite Europe for peace and progress." On that same day, speaking before the Great National Assembly, de Gaulle reminded his audience that France was withdrawing "not from her western friendships, of course, but from Atlantic subordination of any kind—political, military, or monetary." At Craiova, on May 17, he stated: "We must refashion Europe from one end to the other, without any iron curtain." Ceaucescu responded by paying homage to the Soviet Union, "which plays a remarkable role in the global arena," and went on to suggest that "the existence of two German states should be recognized."

In Bucharest as in Warsaw, de Gaulle clarified his conception of "all of Europe." It included not only the nations of eastern Europe but also, and above all, Russia. In both capitals de Gaulle observed that the theory of a divided Germany had lost none of its force and that his appeal for an emancipation of the satellite countries was heard but not heeded. There was, of course, ample evidence of a popular desire to reconcile Marxist Socialism with freedom of expression. But such liberal tendencies bowed to the reality of Soviet military power and to the need for the kind of security that the Warsaw Pact and the bilateral agreements between the Soviet Union and the various republics furnished.

Vietnam Peace Talks in Paris

"The disgrace of war and foreign intervention in Asia must cease!" Thus did de Gaulle express his feelings at a press conference on May 16, 1967. During the second half of 1967, American public opinion changed. Robert McNamara, the American secretary of defense, who was to resign a few months later, told the United States Senate on August 25 that he did not believe that an escalation of the air war would induce the North Vietnamese to negotiate.

On December 30, 1967, Nguyen Duy-Trinh, North Vietnam's foreign minister, declared: "As soon as there is a cessation of the bombing and of other acts of war against the Democratic Republic of Vietnam, Hanoi will open negotiations with the United States on all the problems that concern both parties." On January 16, 1968, the North Vietnamese delegate to France, Mai Van-Bo, confirmed this statement. He said: "We will begin talks with the United States after an unconditional cessation of the bombing." On January 29 the Vietcong unleashed a major attack, called the Tet offensive, against all the cities of the south. Doubtless they wanted to be in a position of strength should negotiations begin. The American military machine was badly shaken. A few months before the election of a new president, the American public began once again to question the objectives of the war and the chances of victory.

On March 31, President Johnson announced both his intention not to run for reelection and his decision to stop the bombing of North Vietnam with the exception of Khe Sanh, where the American outpost required protection. He appealed to Ho Chi-minh. On April 4 the North Vietnamese government announced it was ready to appoint a representative to negotiate with the Americans.

As early as April 3 General de Gaulle took a stand which he expressed in the following terms: "The public announcement of a cessation of the bombing of North Vietnam, although this halt is neither unconditional nor general, appears to be, on the part of the president of the United States, a first step toward peace and consequently an act of political courage and reason."

On May 5, after several weeks of discussion about where the negotiations should take place, the two adversaries agreed to meet in Paris. This choice was justified by the fact that all the parties concerned with the result of the negotiations—especially China and the two Vietnams—had diplomatic representatives in Paris. Unquestionably, this was a victory for the French government. Was this a reward for discreet services rendered the two adversaries through their respective chancelleries? At present we do not have sufficient information to answer this question. But one is struck by the change in France's attitude after President Johnson's historic announcement.

What Was the Motivation?

The short interval between the legislative elections of March 1967 and the general strike of May 1968 was marked by worldwide diplomatic activity on the part of France. She denied England entry into the Common Market. She waged the gold war against the Anglo-Saxons. She opposed Israel in the Middle East and attempted to encourage the liberation of Quebec. She urged Poland and Rumania to emancipate themselves. Finally, she renewed her criticisms of the war in Vietnam.

What was the motivation behind these spectacular moves?

Charles de Gaulle could not accept the fact that the global balance of power depended on whether conflict or harmony reigned between the two giants, America and Russia. He believed that the power of the United States was greater than Russia's. Therefore he did not maintain an equal balance between the two rivals.

In entering the preserves of Eastern Europe—he referred to it as central Europe in order to emphasize that Russia, the pillar of European unity, was part of Europe—he showed great consideration of the Soviet Union. His appeals for emancipation were discreet; the response was disappointing, even if we take the long view.

But he showed no such consideration for the United States. Instead, he attacked it on all fronts. England was as dependent on the United States in 1967 as she had been in 1963. She needed American assistance for defense and even more for the support of her currency. Noting all this, de Gaulle kept

Britain out of the E.E.C. He wanted Europe to include the Soviet Union and to be altogether independent of the United States. England would oppose such a twofold scheme. Her entry into the Common Market would strengthen the Atlantic bloc, a military, economic, and political entity dominated by the Americans. Observing that the international monetary system was deteriorating, he hoped to accelerate its decline. He encouraged the gold rush in order to weaken the pound and subsequently the dollar. Speculating on Russo-American rivalry in the Middle East, he sided with the Arabs against the Israelis—that is, with the Soviet Union against the United States. He tried to prevent a dialogue between the two superpowers. Intervening in favor of the separatists in Quebec, he tried to weaken Federal Canada, the natural ally of the United States, and to pit the French-speaking province against its powerful American neighbor.

Did General de Gaulle's realpolitik achieve its geostrategic objectives? So far as England is concerned, the answer is no. Isolated from the Europe of the Six, she would become more dependent than ever on the United States. The answer was also negative in regard to the international monetary system. The aftermath of the May 1968 general strike stopped the offensive of the franc against the dollar. The results were also negative in Canada: if Quebec seceded, it would fall even more completely under the economic and cultural domination of the United States. There were likewise no gains in the Middle East; the Glassboro meeting signaled the greatest improvement in East-West relations since the Cuban affair. To be sure, the position of the Soviet Union in the Middle East was strengthened by the conflict there, but this was due far more to America's involvement in Vietnam than to General de Gaulle's backing.

In short, the only victory of France's planetary diplomacy during the brief life of the 1967–1968 National Assembly was the choice of Paris as the meeting place for peace talks on Vietnam.

13

Defense without eAlliance?

Local Conflicts and Spheres of Influence

THE CHANGE IN America's Vietnam policy, plus the crisis that has persisted in the Middle East ever since the six-day war, could not fail sooner or later to affect the spheres of influence of the two great powers.

The American decision to open peace negotiations with Vietnam foreshadowed the eventual withdrawal of the United States from Southeast Asia. Whatever methods were being contemplated to contain the expansion of China, it seemed clear that America would gradually reduce its military forces in Vietnam. This did not mean that Soviet influence would automatically increase in Southeast Asia.

The involvement of the United States in Vietnam has, however, definitely facilitated Soviet penetration in the Middle East. Ever since the six-day war, the Soviet navy, consisting early in 1968 of about forty ships, has been constantly cruising in the Mediterranean, not far from the American Sixth Fleet. The Russian vessels have easy access to supplies at Port Said and Alexandria in Egypt and at Latakia in Syria. Russian economic and military aid to Algeria has made Mers-el-Kébir a potential Soviet base ever since it was evacuated by the French navy. On December 24, 1967, the Soviet Union signed an important oil agreement with Iraq. Finally, the military potential of Israel's enemies, the Arab states, has been restored. France's persistent refusal to deliver the Mirage IV to Israel influenced the American decision of July 1968 to provide Israel with a certain number of planes.

Increasing rivalry between the United States and the Soviet Union in the Middle East has not prevented them from cooperating in regard to anti-missile missile networks, nor from collaborating actively in the preparation of a nuclear nonproliferation treaty. It is in the light of this cooperation—which has curiously grown ever since the French withdrawal from NATO—that we must examine the recent evolution of the Atlantic Alliance and of French defense policy.

Antiballistic Missiles

From the start of the nuclear age, the question of deterrence for both the United States and the Soviet Union has rested on the possession of increasingly powerful offensive weapons. During the last few years, however, the two superpowers have perfected a weapon capable of giving protection against the enemy's retaliatory raids. The enormous cost of a complete antimissile missile (A.B.M.) network has caused both powers to delay the execution of their programs. Early in 1967 the Soviet Union decided to build a thin A.B.M. network around Moscow. On September 18, 1967, the American secretary of defense, Robert McNamara, announced that the United States had reached a similar decision. The two networks have some common features: they do not provide effective defense against either of the two major nuclear powers (this would require a dense network) but do offer a shield against possible Chinese attack.

Having exploded her first H-bomb in June 1967, and her second in December 1968, China seems to encounter difficulties in implementing her ballistic missiles program. She is still not safe from nuclear blackmail which has hitherto prevented her from intervening in the conventional armed conflict in Vietnam. She refuses to yield to the rules of deterrence and continues to reproach the Soviet Union for its policy of peaceful coexistence with the United States. This decision of the Americans and the Russians, on which the two rivals must have agreed in advance, was equivalent to an unwritten treaty of cooperation directed against China. The immediate result was to lessen the value of the atomic forces possessed by second-rate powers like England and France, whose system of reprisals no longer had a deterrent capability comparable to that of the potential enemy of the Atlantic Alliance, the Soviet Union. As a consequence, Western Europe has become more and more dependent on the United States for its security. According to André Fontaine, France will find it "increasingly difficult to convince any European nation that it will be better protected by her striking force than by the American umbrella."[1]

The Nonproliferation Treaty

A common and constant concern of the United States and the Soviet Union has been to prevent the spread of nuclear weapons. The likelihood of

[1] André Fontaine, "A.B.M.," *Le Monde*, Sept. 29, 1967.

proliferation increases as more and more generators of nuclear energy are put to use, and as the production of plutonium becomes widespread in the industrialized countries.

Immediately after the signing of the Moscow accords on the nuclear test ban treaty on August 5, 1963, negotiations to draft a nonproliferation treaty were begun. Considerable progress was made early in 1965 when the United States gave up the idea of a multilateral deterrent force that was to include Federal Germany in the nuclear strategy of the Atlantic Alliance.

Negotiations were pursued on three levels: between the two superpowers and England; within the Geneva Committee of Eighteen on disarmament, an offshoot of the United Nations; in the Atlantic Council, where the United States consulted its allies. On August 24, 1967, the United States and the Soviet Union filed the initial version of the treaty in Geneva. On January 19, 1968, the second version was published. It took into account a number of objections raised by the non-nuclear nations. On June 13, 1968, this draft was approved by the General Assembly of the United Nations. Ninety-five affirmative votes were cast as against four negative votes and twenty-one abstentions including France. Fifty-nine nations signed, in Washington, Moscow, and London.

The two nuclear powers that had refused to sign the nuclear test ban treaty in 1963—China and France—refused again in 1968. Both countries rejected American and Russian hegemony.

France pronounced the treaty on disarmament an illusion, arguing that it merely served "to prevent those who had no weapons from acquiring them." The French attitude was negative: to reject a possibly inadequate treaty but one that is none the less a step toward peaceful coexistence is to pursue a policy of pessimism. The French attitude was also dangerous: it tended to encourage certain German ambitions.

Actually, the nonproliferation treaty affected Federal Germany more than any other European nation. For the Soviet Union, the main purpose of the treaty was unilateral discrimination in the domain of nuclear armaments which Germany accepted without demanding eventual reunification in exchange.

Today Federal Germany—who is not on the first list of the signatories of the treaty—is the most powerful nation of continental Europe as measured by the use of nuclear energy for peaceful purposes. Her primary concern is to make sure that she will not be prevented from making further technological gains. She likewise is anxious to circumvent industrial spying by the International Agency for Atomic Energy as it fulfills its commitments to the non-nuclear nations in regard to the control of atomic energy activities.

Another concern of Federal Germany, shared, as the first is, by Italy, is to leave the way open for the possible creation of a European Community for

Atomic Defense. Germany received some assurance from the United States to this effect, but the treaty does not provide for a formal "European clause." However, the signatories are entitled to revise their commitments after five years.

While the non-nuclear nations are not to acquire or manufacture nuclear weapons, the nuclear powers are to refrain from furnishing nuclear weapons to other countries. New clauses were added. One of these refers to the total exchange of scientific and technical information about the peaceful uses of nuclear energy. Another, inserted at the request of France's Euratom partners, tends to give Euratom, acting in behalf of the International Agency for Atomic Energy, the right to control the atomic activities of its member states.

A final provision links the signing of the treaty to "the pursuit of negotiations in good faith to bring about a cessation of the armaments race." And indeed, on the very day the treaty was signed, Johnson and Kosygin announced forthcoming negotiations for a limitation of offensive and defensive nuclear weapons.

The Evolution of the Atlantic Alliance to August 1968

Monetary problems, the war in Vietnam, progress toward nonproliferation, and the withdrawal of France from NATO—all these influenced not only the strategic and political doctrine of the Atlantic Alliance but also the distribution of its conventional forces.

In May 1967 England proceeded to reduce somewhat the number of troops assigned to Germany because of balance of payment difficulties. In the spring of 1968, as a consequence of her gradual withdrawal from the Far East, she reversed the trend and increased her land forces in Germany and her navy and air forces in the Mediterranean.

In May 1967 the United States, for its part, transferred three brigades and four squadrons of fighter bombers from Germany to Vietnam. Finally, in July 1967, the economic recession in Germany forced the country to postpone arrangements to ready a small part of its land forces.

As for France, on August 30, 1967, she informed the member states of NATO that authorization for allied military planes to fly over her territory would be renewed on an annual rather than a monthly basis after January 1968. This concession was made in exchange for allowing France to participate in a new interallied radar network, NADGE (NATO Air Defense Ground Environment), for long-range detection. Without it the French deterrent force would have been paralyzed. Shortly thereafter, the commander-in-chief of NATO received a letter from the head of the French military staff. France wished to inform NATO, it read, that the French troops posted to Germany would cooperate with the allied armies only if Paris decided that a clearly marked act of aggression had occurred.[2]

As for the strategy of the Alliance, the Atlantic Council made two important decisions which would not have been possible had not France withdrawn from NATO. At a meeting on December 16, 1966, it set up a Nuclear Defense Committee open to all the member states of NATO. It also established a more restricted Nuclear Planning Group. The purpose of these organs was to bring the non-nuclear nations of the Atlantic Alliance into close collaboration in the elaboration of a nuclear strategy the execution of which would be the responsibility of the United States. In addition, at a meeting on December 14, 1967, the Atlantic Council officially adopted the strategy of graduated response which had been American strategy ever since 1961. The opposition of France, which favored the strategy of massive retaliation, had forced the abandonment of the doctrine evolved by McNamara, which NATO would have implemented in case of war because of America's nuclear preponderance within the Alliance.

On the other hand, decisions of a political nature were reached with the full agreement of France. The most important decision was the adoption of the "Harmel Report" on December 14, 1967. Named after the Belgian foreign minister who proposed it, this report dealt with the future tasks of the Alliance, especially with the policy of détente between East and West. According to the report, the Alliance has a twofold function during a period of peaceful coexistence: to maintain sufficient military force and political solidarity to deter aggression; and to seek more stable relations in order to resolve pending political problems. Military security and détente were in no way inconsistent; rather they complemented one another. How could such a détente best be emphasized?—By pursuing a multilateral action through the Alliance, or by means of bilateral contacts? France expressed the opinion that "as sovereign states, the allies are not bound to subordinate their policies to a collective decision." She was afraid that a European policy of centralized détente would not give her full freedom of action. She conceded, however—and in this she was in agreement with her partners—that "the search for a relaxation of tensions must not be allowed to culminate in a rupture of the Alliance."

A communiqué issued by the Atlantic Council on June 25, 1968, represented a further step along the road to rapprochement with the East. The communiqué suggested "a balanced and mutual reduction of forces between East and West." But in this same communiqué the Council expressed concern over the measures taken in May by the German Democratic Republic regarding the avenues of access to West Berlin. It reaffirmed the special

---

[2] *The International Herald Tribune*, Sept. 19, 1967.

responsibilities devolving on the four powers in regard to the German question. This declaration gave some comfort to those who were disturbed by the privileged relations that existed between France and the Soviet Union.

The French Armament Policy

After her withdrawal from NATO, France concentrated on the development of her deterrent force. In the course of a debate in the National Assembly on October 24, 1967, Pierre Messmer, Minister of the army, provided the following information: The deterrent force comprised three generations, but their state of preparedness was not uniform. Only the squadron of sixty Mirage IV's was operational. The second generation consisted of a ground-to-ground missile system whose launching platforms were to be buried in silos in the Haute-Provence. The nuclear warhead had been tested in 1966, the rocket in 1967. It would carry a load of 150 kilotons and would have a range of 2,500 kilometers. The first unit would be operational by 1970. The third generation would consist of four nuclear submarines equipped with sea-to-ground missiles capable of carrying 500 kilotons over a distance of 2,000 kilometers. The first submarine, launched on March 29, 1967, would be operational by 1970. The second, at present in dry dock, would be ready by 1972.

Tactical atomic missiles were being perfected for the land army. The missile Poseidon, with a charge of from ten to twenty-five kilotons and a range of one hundred kilometers, would be operational by 1972. Finally, in July 1968 France launched a new series of nuclear tests in the Pacific Ocean. The first French two-megaton thermonuclear bomb was exploded on August 25, sixteen years after its American counterpart. It was still far from being operational, however.

In analyzing the prospects of the French nuclear arsenal, Jacques Isnard has written: "If we accept the most optimistic hypothesis, France will have a nuclear capacity of about thirty megatons around 1975. In other words . . . what one American bomber carries today in its storage tank."[3]

The prospects for conventional arms were likewise unfavorable because the government had earmarked increasing amounts for strategic weapons. Pierre Messmer admitted that the modernization of the land army toward the close of 1967 was three years behind the schedule established in 1964. Retrenchment in the purchase of naval matériel for the conventional fleet has been so extensive that the auxiliaries of the strategic navy may very well prove inadequate when this force becomes operational. Finally, in 1967, the

[3] Jacques Isnard, *Le Monde*, July 11, 1968.

government had to give up the plan of building a swing-wing combat plane* in collaboration with England.

On the morrow of the social crisis of May 1968—whose repercussions on the national economy will be extremely severe—the problem of the cost of equipping a strategic force inevitably arises. Should the French army apportion the necessary funds over a longer period of time? This would prolong from 1971 to 1975 the use of the Mirage IV squadron, while the manufacture of an intercontinental ballistic missile in the megaton power range would be delayed until 1990.[4]

After the November 1968 monetary crisis, the government decided to spread the cost over a period of time. On November 26 it announced that the tests in the Pacific scheduled for 1969 would not take place.

Defense on All Fronts

France has often proclaimed her doctrine of a national strategic force. Would not the development of such a force, limited as it has been by budgetary and technological considerations, lead to a further loosening of the ties that link France to the Atlantic Alliance? On September 15, 1967, Louis Vallon, a member of Parliament who reportedly has de Gaulle's full confidence, published an article advocating the withdrawal of France from the Atlantic Pact by August 1968. He concluded: "We must either resist the American hegemony by opening Europe to the East or become enclosed in a small, integrated Europe, subordinate to the United States."[5] Manlio Brosio, secretary-general of NATO, immediately expressed concern about the intentions of the French government. According to André Fontaine, the foreign minister would confine himself to the terms of the letter General de Gaulle addressed to President Johnson on March 7, 1966.[6] Brosio, however, reminded France that not until the month of August 1969—not 1968—did a member state have the right to withdraw from the Alliance, and even then, a year's notice was necessary.[7]

On December 4, 1967, the Centre d'Etudes de Politique Etrangère issued a document that detailed the various possible forms for a reorganization of Europe over a long period of time, provided stability and security prevailed.

* Translator's note: Technically a "variable geometry aircraft," it is commonly called a "swing-wing" to suggest where the geometry varies on the plane. In flight and cruising at supersonic speeds the wings are swept back in the form of a delta to reduce the drag. In landing and take-off the wings are spread wider to increase the lift.

[4] Jacques Isnard, *Le Monde*, June 16, 1968.
[5] Louis Vallon, "Notre République, 1968," *Notre République*, Sept. 15, 1967.
[6] André Fontaine, *Le Monde*, Sept. 23, 1967.
[7] *Le Monde*, Sept. 17, 1967.

Three models—détente, entente, and cooperation—were presented, all of them readily associated with de Gaulle's statements about East-West relations. The first called for the maintenance of the two alliances, the Atlantic and Warsaw Pacts. The efforts of the member states in both blocs would be oriented toward détente, in conformity with the conclusions of the Harme Report. But détente was open to criticism because the Americans would assume leadership in Western Europe and this would culminate in a Russo-American condominium over all Europe. The second model, which called for an entente, resembled the Rapacki plan which the United States had rejected in 1958. It would be preceded by a series of steps to reduce stockpiles of nuclear weapons and by a diminution of conventional forces in all the countries of the two Europes where foreign troops were posted. The third model, that of cooperation, provided for the replacement of the two military alliances by a pan-European security system guaranteed by the United States and the Soviet Union. Germany would be reunified in the form of a confederation. It is easy to recognize in this third solution the objective de Gaulle had set forth in his February 4, 1965, press conference on the status of Germany and Europe. Does the author's preference for cooperation as a solution tend to confirm the fears aroused by Louis Vallon's article?

An article in the *Revue de Défense Nationale* of December 1967, penned by General Ailleret, army chief of staff, produced the strongest reaction and brought into question whether France still belonged to the Atlantic Alliance. Ailleret discussed the important subject of strategy, defined by de Gaulle in his speech of November 3, 1959—in other words, independent nuclear defense. In the present state of this disordered world, he said, it was impossible to tell who might tomorrow be the enemy of France and who her ally. Therefore, he contended, "an *a priori* alliance would not give France a general guarantee of security." In his view, the French goal should be "to achieve as much strength as possible in an autonomous and individual way." And he indicated how to accomplish this: France must have at her disposal "significant quantities . . . of megatomic ballistic missiles with a world-wide range." Such a force would no longer be aimed in a single direction but would be capable of intervening everywhere. Thus, defense on all fronts would be substituted for a defense "governed" by the great ally of France.[8]

General de Gaulle, inspecting the military schools on January 27, 1968, confirmed the statement of his chief of staff by saying, "Our strategy must concern all fronts."

Is this feasible, since France will be unable for many years to produce intercontinental thermonuclear missiles? At the beginning of 1968, France had

---

[8] General Ailleret, "Défense 'dirigée' ou défense 'tous azimuts,'" *Revue de Défense Nationale*, Dec. 1967.

not formally withdrawn from the Atlantic Alliance, but she appeared to have chosen the path of defense without alliance.

The Invasion of Czechoslovakia

On August 21, 1968, the armed forces of the Soviet Union, supported by East Germany, Poland, Hungary, and Bulgaria, invaded Czechoslovakia. For several months the Czechoslovakian government and the Czech Communist Party had been doing their utmost to achieve a compromise between Marxist socialism and freedom. On October 16 a bilateral accord imposed by the Soviet Union legalized for an indeterminate period the presence of Russian troops on Czechoslovakian soil.

The main reason for the Soviet decision to invade Czechoslovakia was the Communist oligarchy's fear of being confronted in Eastern Europe as well as in Russia itself with a current of opinion that favored greater political freedom. The Soviets hoped that military occupation would serve to conceal any symptoms of political weakness. The strengthening of the Warsaw Pact clearly served Russian imperialism rather than international Communism. The Eastern bloc would once again be made watertight.

America reacted with caution. The military operation had taken place within the Russian zone of influence. The United States government was anxious not to jeopardize Soviet-American cooperation in the nonproliferation of nuclear weapons. The two superpowers must keep communications open.

At the request of the Federal Republic, the Atlantic Alliance Council of ministers met one month earlier than scheduled, in order to examine the political and military consequences of the new coup in Prague.

Militarily, the occupation of the Bohemian plateau constituted a forward strategy consisting of the deployment of Soviet divisions further west, facing the German Federal Republic.

Politically, Russia was formulating a new doctrine, that of the limited sovereignty of those countries that were part of a "Socialist Community" whose interests should be identified with the interests of its Soviet mentor. The Soviets exerted pressure on the Balkans; this led Albania to withdraw officially from the Warsaw Pact, and Yugoslavia to make military preparations.

The North Atlantic Council issued a communiqué, on November 16, reaffirming its determination to seek a peaceful solution to the German question and to safeguard Berlin. It threw out a warning: "Any Soviet intervention that has a direct or indirect influence on the situation in Europe or in the Mediterranean will cause an international crisis whose consequences will be grave." The warning was aimed primarily at preventing any action against Yugoslavia or Austria. The communiqué further stipulated that the member states of NATO had decided to reassess their means of defense. It affirmed that the East-West détente, which the Harmel report had advocated a year earlier, remained a long-term objective. Finally, it reminded the member states that, according to the 1949 treaty, the Alliance would continue indefinitely.

The occupation of Czechoslovakia served to unite the Alliance more closely than ever. The member states that had been the most neutralist, such as Norway and Denmark, subscribed unreservedly to the terms of the communiqué. What has been France's attitude since August 21?

We Will Remain in the Alliance

The Prague coup caused a painful but cautious revision of French defense policy.

A government communiqué of August 24 condemned the Soviet intervention as being "contrary to the sovereignty of states and to the rights of human beings." It observed that in advocating the solidarity of socialist states Russia was actually pursuing a policy based on the existence of blocs. "France has freed herself from any such conception of the world," but she remained faithful to a policy of détente.

In a press conference on September 9, de Gaulle repeated the same theme. "Since 1958 we Frenchmen have worked incessantly to put an end to a system based on the existence of two blocs. . . . Thus . . . we have gradually broken away from the military organization of NATO, which subordinates the Europeans to the Americans. . . . The recent events in which Czechoslovakia has been . . . the stage and the victim appear blameworthy to us because they are absurd in terms of the prospects of European détente." The general's conclusion was disconcertingly optimistic: "What has occurred in Czechoslovakia demonstrates that our policy, although apparently frustrated for the moment, is consistent with underlying European realities, and therefore is a good one."

On September 28, de Gaulle went to Bonn for a half-yearly meeting under the Franco-German Treaty of Cooperation, but his defense minister did not accompany him; thus he could avoid all serious military talks with Chancellor Kiesinger.

De Gaulle visited Turkey from October 25 to 30. To President Sunay, who claimed that the Atlantic Alliance was necessary to the security and freedom of both Turkey and France, de Gaulle answered that the two countries were determined "to maintain their integrity and independence." The general added that their alliances "could take many different forms." These two countries, signatories of the communiqué published on October

30, were both members of the same alliance; meeting two months after the Prague coup, they managed to bring off the curious feat of never mentioning the treaty that insured their defense.

It was also surprising that on November 16 France should sign the communiqué published by the North Atlantic Council at the close of the meeting. This document, which is summarized above, reflected the allies' firm and determined attitude toward the Soviet Union. However, France did express one reservation regarding the indefinite continuation of the Alliance: "Unless events should modify in some basic manner the relations between East and West, the French government believes that the Alliance must continue as long as it is necessary." This sentence is almost an exact repetition of the message de Gaulle sent to Johnson on March 7, 1966, when France withdrew from NATO. But the reservation expressed in 1968 did not have the same effect as that of 1966. Earlier, de Gaulle was hoping that a Franco-Soviet rapprochement might lead to a reversal of alliances. After Prague, that possibility did not seem at all likely, and the reservation was repeated solely pro forma.

On December 5, Pierre Messmer, the minister of defense, speaking for the government on military policy told the National Assembly: "We are in the Atlantic Alliance and we will remain in it." He immediately added, as if to apologize, "Although we willingly accept alliances as long as they are defensive, we reject what is termed integration."

The omni-directional defense, so named in December 1967, was discreetly done away with in December 1968. France would not denounce the North Atlantic Treaty in 1969.

14

The Atlantic Alliance and France in 1968

The Relations of the Two Superpowers and the Balance of Military Power

IN 1968, AS IN 1958, the territorial status of Europe remained unaltered. But the relations between the United States and the Soviet Union had undergone drastic changes because of the fluctuating crises and periods of détente in and outside Europe, to say nothing of the rapid advances in nuclear armaments achieved by China.

Under Khrushchev, the Soviet Union again raised the question of the status of Berlin and Germany. The crisis, which began in November 1958, culminated in August and September 1961 in the erection of the Berlin wall. Pursuing his offensive, in July 1962 Khrushchev directly threatened the United States by installing launching platforms for intermediate-range rockets in Cuba. The Americans, who would have won a localized war in Cuba merely by using conventional weapons, reacted so strongly that the Russians had to back down. From then on, the threats to Berlin ceased.

After this nuclear test of strength, Khrushchev sought an understanding with the United States. In July 1963 the two major powers signed the Treaty of Moscow. It provided for a cessation of nuclear tests with the exception of those carried out underground. Despite the transformation of the civil war in Vietnam into a conventional conflict that pitted the United States against China through the intermediary of the Southeast Asian states, the two superpowers nonetheless signed a nonproliferation treaty in July 1968.

The recurring crises between the United States and the Soviet Union were resolved for three fundamental reasons. First, despite their divergent political philosophies, both the Russians and the Americans were not eager to risk mutual annihilation in a nuclear war. Second, the Soviet Union had become the enemy of China in the domain of ideology as well as in the competition for spheres of influence. Third, the military power of the United States and of the Soviet Union had reached approximate parity.

The Soviet Union preserved considerable superiority in conventional forces. Toward the close of 1967 it had twenty-six divisions posted to Eastern Europe (twenty in East Germany, two in Poland, four in Hungary), backed up by sixty divisions in European Russia.[1]

By the beginning of 1968 the American strategic forces comprised 1,054 intercontinental rockets buried in silos and 37 atomic submarines, each equipped with 16 intermediate-range Polaris missiles. The Soviet forces comprised 520 inter continental rockets in hardened silos, 700 to 750 intermediate-range missiles, and 45 atomic submarines, each equipped with 3 rockets.[2]

The military balance of power was due to the progress of the United States in the domain of nuclear armaments. After 1960, as a consequence of the controversy over the missile gap, the American government accelerated the construction of ballistic missiles and atomic submarines. Today it possesses weapons that are equal in effectiveness and superior in number to those of the Soviet Union.

The Americans are concentrating their efforts on long-range rockets in order to threaten the Soviet Union from their home base. They are defending Europe by submarines that operate from bases in England and Spain and patrol the North Sea and the Mediterranean.

The Russian effort is concentrated on intermediate-range rockets that threaten Western Europe directly. Since 1966 the Soviet Union has considerably increased its stockpile of long-range rockets for use against the United States.

The intercontinental missiles of both superpowers could, if necessary, be used against China. As for the thin network of anti-missile missiles which both the Americans and Russians decided to create in 1967, it will unquestionably serve to protect each of the superpowers against possible Chinese aggression. Global geostrategy is tending toward a tripolar system.

Both the United States and the Soviet Union have an over-kill power. Their relations are marked by mutual vigilance in an atmosphere of peaceful coexistence and by a common distrust of China. Because of its geographical position, Western Europe is more vulnerable than the United States to a direct attack, whether by use of conventional or strategic weapons.

However, the current détente—the reasons for which we have enumerated —means that Europe, protected by the United States within the Atlantic

[1] *The Military Balance, 1967–1968* (London: The Institute for Strategic Studies, 1967), 6.
[2] *Ibid.*, 45.

Alliance, is less vulnerable to a direct military attack than it was in the 1950s. To be sure, the Soviet Union is not likely to reduce its military or police forces.

The conflict between traditional Marxist ideology and those Eastern Europeans who cherish a socialism consistent with freedom led the Soviets to invade Czechoslovakia in August 1968 and to occupy it militarily for an indefinite period. In view of the present situation of nuclear parity, Russia will resort more and more to indirect strategy, to subversion directed against the West. She will seek bloodless victories by political means. Soviet penetration of the Mediterranean ever since 1967 is one example of this strategy.

In the face of this kind of indirect threat, has Western Europe achieved a measure of autonomy in matters of defense? Or, to put it differently, what is the balance of military power within the Alliance?

The Balance of Military Power within the Alliance

In 1968, as in 1958, the United States played a leading part within the Alliance in financial responsibility as well as defense arrangements.

In 1966 the United States spent 9.2 per cent of its gross national product for defense; England, France and Germany spent 6.4 per cent, 4.4 per cent, and 3.6 per cent respectively. Most of the other European members of the Alliance spent between 3 and 4 per cent.[3]

The conventional Alliance forces assigned to NATO for the Central European front consist of twenty-five divisions, twelve of which are German, six American, three British, two Belgian, and two Dutch. France has five divisions, all under national command, two of which are stationed in Germany. Thus, Germany has the largest number of conventional forces on the central front. These forces are closely coordinated with the American forces from a logistic point of view.

The American divisions stationed in Germany have tactical atomic weapons. The European divisions stationed in Germany, in the Benelux countries, in Italy, Greece, and Turkey, also have atomic arms, but they are subject to both American and national control under the double key formula. According to a statement made by McNamara in Rome on September 23, 1966, the number of tactical atomic weapons in Europe had tripled since 1961 and now comes to seven thousand.[4] The presence of these weapons has increased the firing power of the conventional forces. It has also increased the responsibility of the United States for the over-all effectiveness of these forces.

[3] *Ibid.*
[4] *Ibid.*, 47.

The Alliance's strategic forces actually boil down to the American force. Only the Americans are strong enough to deter effectively a Soviet aggression. England has H-bombs but no ballistic missiles in underground silos. She will have a fleet of four atomic submarines equipped with American Polaris rockets. Two submarines became operational in 1968. Even more than in 1958 the British strategic force can be regarded as an adjunct of the American force. France has A-bombs and Mirage IV supersonic planes. She is constructing a nuclear submarine but it is not yet operational. The French force, for which the government claims total autonomy, does not conform to the objective criteria of deterrence. The American and Russian decisions to establish thin anti-missile missile networks will have the effect of downgrading the British and French forces even more in comparison with those of the two major powers.

In short, in 1968 the territorial integrity of Western Europe rests on the American guarantee, borne out by the presence of troops and atomic weapons on European soil and in European waters. This is reflected in the Alliance's strategy and command.

Strategy and Command

Until 1957 the strategy of the Alliance was based first on the American monopoly and then on America's nuclear preponderance. Under the circumstances, the Alliance accepted America's doctrine of using massive retaliation to meet any Soviet aggression.

Between 1957 and 1960 this strategy was complicated by the stockpiling of ballistic missiles and atomic submarines, and by a rough nuclear parity between the United States and the Soviet Union.

The American doctrine of graduated response, elaborated in 1961, was based on the contention that there could be no real deterrence unless a belligerent, attacked by a first strike, had at its disposal the capacity to strike second. To avoid such extreme measures, substantial conventional forces were necessary. This would raise the atomic threshold. It would thus be possible to adapt response to attack, to choose among several operational plans, and to apply the doctrine of graduated response in combination with cautious escalation. This moderate doctrine, which denied the inevitability of atomic war, was not adopted by the Alliance until December 1967, that is to say, shortly after France's withdrawal from NATO. France did not deviate from the doctrine of massive reprisals. Graduated response was more difficult to implement at a time when the allies were reducing the number of conventional forces assigned to the Alliance, thus lowering the atomic threshold.

Graduated response calls for great mastery of the command system. From this premise the Americans drew the conclusion that control and strategic decision-making were indivisible. Technically, their reasoning was correct: in times of crisis, quick action is necessary. Politically, the consequences were grave. The Europeans, more exposed to danger than the Americans, had less confidence that an intervention decided in Washington would automatically ensue. "In times of crisis, whoever reserves an exclusive right to command would, by virtue of that very fact, be inclined to reserve a political monopoly as well," Jean Laloy noted.[5]

Between 1960 and 1964 the Americans tried to set up a multilateral deterrent force. The plan failed in the face of French opposition. Such a force would not have altered the strategic decision-making process since the United States reserved the right of veto for its use. Toward the close of 1966, the creation within the Alliance of a Committee on Nuclear Defense enabled the non-nuclear nations to join the Americans in strategic planning and consequently in international crisis management. The strategic decision regarding the use of nuclear weapons remained in the hands of the United States.

Apart from this recent amendment of limited scope, the Europeans had no satisfactory solution for the political challenge that resulted from the technical necessities of atomic strategy. The best solution would have been to draw the proper inferences from the fact that technological problems and the cost of effective nuclear weaponry exceeded the capacities of a single European nation but possibly not of a Western Europe moving toward political integration. France, electing to counter this challenge by an individual rather than a communitarian response, developed a national and independent atomic force.

The Attitude of France

In 1954 General de Gaulle assigned to France the mission of "making sure that the Atlantic Pact establishes a good alliance and not a bad protectorate." As soon as he returned to power he gradually effected the changes he desired and for which he had made preparations well in advance. During the electoral campaign of February 1967, Maurice Couve de Murville, in response to questions asked by Alfred Fabre-Luce, revealed that as early as 1958 he had been informed of the general's intention to withdraw from NATO.[6]

The kick-off took place in September 1958, on the morrow of the Fifth Republic's first referendum. De Gaulle suggested to Eisenhower the

[5] Jean Laloy, *Entre guerres et paix, 1945–1965* (Paris: Plon, 1966), 257.
[6] Alfred Fabre-Luce, *L'homme journal* (Paris: Gallimard, 1967), 229.

establishment of a three-power directorate, including England, that would formulate global strategic plans. France would thus be recognized as a world power. This suggestion, which would have meant granting France the right to veto decisions concerning the use of the American deterrent force, was rejected. In November 1959 de Gaulle announced his own strategic doctrine: the independence of France was incompatible with the idea of an integrated alliance and required a separate deterrent force. Little by little, de Gaulle dissociated France from her bonds with the permanent organs of the Alliance. In January 1963, after the legislative elections that gave him an acquiescent majority, he refused the American offer of Polaris missiles. In August 1963 he refused to sign the Moscow Pact which would have limited France's freedom to conduct nuclear tests. In 1964 French atomic weapons became operational but were limited to a strike-first capacity. He adopted the theory of massive retaliation, which the Americans had discarded. In February 1966, on the morrow of his reelection as president of the Republic, de Gaulle announced the withdrawal of France from NATO, but not from the Alliance. This entailed the removal from France of NATO headquarters and American troops. The role of the French troops stationed in Germany had come into question. In June 1966 the general signed a Franco-Soviet declaration in Moscow. Because of its tone and solemnity, it was somewhat akin to a nonaggression pact. In January 1968 de Gaulle confirmed the assertions of his chief of staff that France must adopt an "all-azimuths" strategy, in other words, one that would be independent of any system of alliance. In July 1968 he refused to include France in the treaty on nonproliferation of nuclear weapons.

In December 1968, four months after the occupation of Czechoslovakia by the Soviet Union, de Gaulle authorized his defense minister to declare: "We are in the Atlantic Alliance and we will remain it it."

Thus, for three years, France has been in the ambiguous position of being a member of the Atlantic Pact, protected by the American deterrent force, yet capable of remaining neutral in the event of a major crisis between the United States and the Soviet Union. She has thought of herself as a "nation with free hands," as de Gaulle has repeatedly described her since 1965. In the domain of strategy, her doctrine of freedom can be summed up as follows: neither integration nor subordination to the United States, but an opening to the East. Until the Russian troops entered Prague, Gaullist France seemed the instigator of the disintegration of the Alliance.

The Attitude of the Other European Members of the Alliance

The enjoyment of foreign military protection during an entire generation, as well as the persistence of internal political divisions, served to weaken the Western Europeans' sense of civic responsibility. It was surprising that one of the centers of human civilization, endowed with a very high standard of living, should not have attempted to protect itself, and should have been unable to provide itself with the appropriate means of defense through collective efforts.

The declaration of March 1966 made by the fourteen members of the Atlantic Pact affirmed their loyalty to the principle of military integration after France's withdrawal from NATO, but it concealed many different points of view.

Several smaller states were mindful that the traditional neutrals—some of whom, like Sweden and Switzerland, were well armed, while others, such as Austria and Ireland, were not—were just as much protected by the United States as were its allies. The invasion of Czechoslovakia in 1968 put an end to neutralist tendencies.

Italy was divided for a long time between her desire to share in planning Atlantic strategy and the pressure the powerful Communist Party exerted until 1968 to reduce armaments.

England was undergoing a profound internal crisis as a result of the break-up of the Commonwealth, the failure to adjust some branches of her economy to meet modern industrial competition, and her exclusion, on two different occasions, from the Common Market. She relied on the United States to supply her with strategic weapons. She depended primarily on the United States and also on Western Europe to bolster her currency. Having reduced her military commitments in Europe in an effort to maintain her bases in the Far East, she reversed her military policy in 1968, accelerated withdrawal east of Suez, but had every intention of remaining in the Mediterranean. Since Harold Wilson's conversion to a European policy, the Labour government, which was not able to gain entry into the E.E.C., could neither follow a foreign policy distinct from that of the United States nor become the spokesman of Western Europe in the domains of political construction or defense.

West Germany, which occupied a front row in the Alliance because of its conventional weapons, became third in political importance after France's secession from NATO. In spite of this recent promotion, and in spite, too, of its military progress, the German Federal Republic found itself in an awkward position as a member of an alliance whose purpose was to contain Russia and to maintain the status quo in Europe.

Since 1966, West Germany has been concerned about the uncertain role of French troops stationed on her soil. Between 1966 and 1968 she was worried about the reductions of American troops which had already been effected or were about to be. After the Soviet divisions penetrated Czechoslovakia, she realized that the military threat on her eastern flank had become more serious and that the strengthening of the Warsaw Pact made the possibility of reunification even more remote.

Germany was still torn between her need for security which only the United States could guarantee, and her hopes for reunification which only the Soviet Union could fulfil. French opposition to the ideal of an integrated Europe served to deepen the Germans' desire for a unified nation. Thus, the problem of German reunification became one of the major current problems of the Atlantic Alliance.

The Reunification of Germany

The question of German reunification had been debated many times between the East and the West. The possibility of negotiations had never been thoroughly explored because the stakes were high and the conflicting positions seemed irreconcilable. The present position of France and the evolution of thinking in Germany forced the Alliance to reexamine the question.

The stakes were both military and political. East Germany constituted a protective shield for the Soviet Union. Without it, Russian troops would be forced to occupy Poland or to retreat into Soviet territory. For the Atlantic Alliance, West Germany constituted a strategic area indispensable for the deployment of conventional forces, as well as a source of fresh troops. Both the Americans and the Russians hesitated to withdraw their forces because of the uncertainty about the political direction a unified Germany would follow, particularly since she would be by far the most important nation of the European continent, both in population and in industrial power. The East Germans have repeatedly demonstrated their desire for the freedom and prosperity which their compatriots in the West enjoy. The political risk is therefore greater for Russia than it is for the West. This would not be the case if a major economic crisis were to occur in the Western world; or if the West Germans were to be swept up in a kind of nationalist fervor that would make them willing to sacrifice the cause of freedom for that of unity.

The political and military risks of reunification are so great that neither the Russians nor the Americans so far have been willing to incur them because of the profound change such an operation would cause the East–West balance. Until now they have preferred the status quo. The defensive nature of the Alliance inclines the West to this position. Russia would hold the trump card in any negotiation since she alone can grant or refuse reunification. She is demanding a high price on the grounds of the great political danger involved. So far the West has not wanted to pay the price— total neutralization—because of the unthinkable military danger.

The attitude of the Soviet Union is still dominated by fear of Germany. The presence of American troops in West Germany, the integration of German troops into NATO, prevent the formulation of an independent West German strategy. The presence of Soviet troops in East Germany guarantees the security of Poland against the Federal Republic. Therefore all of Russia's efforts since 1955 have been aimed at obtaining the implicit or explicit recognition of East Germany—in other words, the consolidation of the status quo. Khrushchev's memorandum to Kennedy of June 4, 1961, contained a spurious suggestion for reunification and a sincere proposal for the signing of a peace treaty with the two German states, which later could be invited to confederate. In actuality, the Soviet Union would consent to German reunification only if it were in a state of extreme weakness or extraordinary strength—neither of which is the case at present; or in exchange for some important military concession, neutralization, for example. Jean Laloy believes that "the neutralization of Germany through her division" is the real meaning of all the plans for a confederation of the two German states.[7]

The declaration made by the signatories of the Warsaw Pact on July 4, 1966, on the morrow of de Gaulle's visit to Moscow, confirms this interpretation. The communiqué published on April 26, 1967, after a conference held by the same states at Karlovy-Vary (Carlsbad, Czechoslovakia) was even more explicit. It contained a program for the creation of a collective security system in Europe. The program was based on recognition of the existence of two sovereign and equal German states. It provided for the withdrawal of foreign troops and the creation of a denuclearized zone in Central Europe.

The classical Western position—from which the general has dissociated himself—consists in tying the Federal Republic to the West by a network of political, military, and economic institutions but limiting its nuclear armaments in order to keep the door open to reunification. Reunification must be achieved by the free expression of the will of the entire German people. The last suggestion made by the West in 1959 was to postpone free elections until some future date, to be preceded by an agreement on Berlin and by certain limited steps towards world disarmament. In the course of the Rusk-Gromyko bilateral discussions of 1962, which did not commit all of the Western world, the Americans envisaged mutual nonaggression accords between the states of the Atlantic and Warsaw Pacts. Actually, the West's interest in possible reunification is based on the hope of seeing a liberal regime established in East Germany. The problem is how to reconcile a certain measure of military disengagement with the security of Western Europe.

[7] Laloy, *Entre guerres*, 359.

The present attitude of France was expressed by de Gaulle in a press conference on February 4, 1965. It was confirmed in his speech to the Kremlin on June 21, 1966. De Gaulle was no longer trying, as in 1962, "to settle the fate of all of Europe" starting from Franco-German solidarity, but he did want to solve the German problem "through the concerted action of the peoples of Europe" and to settle the question of armaments "by accord with all of Germany's neighbors," in other words, by neutralization. He envisages, at a later stage, a kind of European system, uniting Western and Eastern states, including the Soviet Union and excluding the United States. The American participation in the European settlement would be limited, to say the least. The American troops, having withdrawn from France, would withdraw also from West Germany. According to this scheme in its present form, de Gaulle refuses the recognition of Eastern Germany and, in this respect, his position differs from that of the Soviet Union. De Gaulle also wishes to set up at the same time "the whole of Europe and the whole of Germany" and, in this, his position differs from that of the Western Powers. Such a united Europe and united Germany would be under Soviet rule.

The official position of the Federal Republic is to reject both neutralization and recognition of East Germany. Reunification must not be pursued at the cost of security and can be achieved only with the diplomatic support of the Western powers. For a long time the Socialist Party was tempted to exchange reunification for neutralization; but since 1960 it has supported the government's policy. Public opinion is certainly far more sensitive to the problem of reunification now that the prospects for a political union of Western Europe grow dimmer, especially since 1963. One current of opinion maintains, along with Karl Jaspers, that the aim of West Germany's foreign policy must be to obtain a regime of freedom for the East Germans, in exchange for recognition of the present frontiers of Germany.[8] This suggestion would be acceptable to East Germany, once the Communist regime was suppressed there, because a movement toward fusion would be irresistible. The speech made by Rainer Barzel, leader of the Christian Democratic group in the German Parliament, in New York on June 16, 1966, heralded the advent of a new approach to the problem. The essence of Barzel's suggestion was that a distinction must be made between the question of reunification and that of Russian troop withdrawals from the East and American troop withdrawals from the West. A reunified Germany would find herself in a position similar to Austria's between 1945 and 1955: foreign troops would be stationed on German soil "within the framework of a European security system."[9] For the first time a German politician must

[8] Karl Jaspers, *Liberté et reunification* (Paris: Gallimard, 1962), 57.
[9] *Le Monde*, June 17, 1966.

be credited with saying that German reunification is not compatible with complete equality of rights.

Since the beginning of 1967 the coalition government of Chancellor Kiesinger has pursued a policy of détente toward the Eastern countries, encouraged in this by General de Gaulle. However, improved relations between Federal Germany and certain states of Eastern Europe aroused suspicion in the Soviet Union. East Germany's participation in the invasion of Czechoslovakia can only serve to further delay any hope of reunification.

"Yesterday the reunification of Germany was out of the question. Today it is on the agenda, but it may well remain on the agenda for years."[10] This remark by Raymond Aron derives from the multiplicity of incompatible theses. How can a future reunification be reconciled with the political construction of Europe? Can the numerous and dynamic German people remain forever divided? Will they be content, once reunified, to remain forever neutral? These questions underline the difficulties of the problem. The status quo is therefore tempting, though not justifiable. In order to subsist, the Atlantic Alliance must face a challenge that is political and diplomatic rather than military. Without any views on the future of Germany, it will not be able to meet the threat of subversion by the Soviet Union.

The Atlantic Alliance, although it will continue for the present, will have to contend not only with a political and diplomatic threat, but with a military one as well.

Crisis and Prospects of the Alliance

The crisis of the Atlantic Alliance was caused as much by its victories as by its failures.

The Alliance met the Soviet military threat and maintained the territorial status quo in Europe. But, although it protected Federal Germany, it did nothing to facilitate reunification; although it protected all of Western Europe it did nothing to right the imbalance between the protected states and the American protector, nor did it oppose the centralization of strategic decision-making, which was entirely in American hands.

France must be assigned a heavy responsibility for the Alliance crisis, but she is not solely to blame. The obstacles to German reunification are the result of the rivalry between the two superpowers. Perhaps some day this will be attenuated by continuous efforts to ease tensions between them. But the method of reunification which France proposed would lead to a neutralized Germany in a Europe dominated by the Soviet Union. The

[10] Raymond Aron, *Figaro*, June 23, 1966.

imbalance within the Alliance could only have been modified by the political integration of Western Europe. But France opposed supranational concepts and kept England out of the Common Market. Criticism of the McNamara doctrine is justified—not of the idea of graduated response, which is sound —but of the centralization of strategy, which is not so sound. But the creation of an independent strategic force is no answer to centralization.

The Alliance crisis culminated in France's withdrawal from NATO in 1966. After the Harmel report in 1967, the tasks of the Alliance expanded, because the détente became an additional objective along with deterrence. After the invasion of Czechoslovakia, which drew the member states closer to one another, deterrence became a primary objective. The close of 1969 will raise the question of membership. At this time each state will have to decide whether or not it wants to withdraw from the Alliance. At the close of 1968, one begins to wonder about the military and political prospects.

From a military point of view, the Alliance is faced with the problems of troops, strategy, and weapons.

Early in 1968 it seemed probable that there would be a reduction in the number of American troops stationed in Europe, so that the number of divisions stationed on the Central European front could be decreased from a theoretical twenty-five to twenty or perhaps fewer. Such reductions may be merely unilateral short of any similar decision in the East. The occupation of Czechoslovakia has led members of NATO to give up any idea of decreasing the number of their troops; rather there will be a redeployment of forces, in view of the new strategic situation which has lowered the atomic threshold. The problem of weapons is twofold: the rationalization of manufacture, and the possible constitution of a marginal deterrent force in Western Europe. With this in mind, some people cherish the notion of a technological community that would centralize the military commands of the member states, or even a European Community of Atomic Defense. Both of these would require mutual political confidence and a delegation of powers to a single supranational authority. Such ideas are inconsistent with the nationalist conceptions of the Fifth Republic, yet without the participation of France they could not be effectuated.

Moreover, the lack of a political will in Western Europe tends to accentuate the imbalance between the European partners of the Alliance and the United States. At this very moment the signing of a nonproliferation treaty only serves to underscore the gap between the nuclear and the non-nuclear powers. Similarly, the creation of thin anti-missile missile networks downgrades the deterrent forces of England and France in comparison with those of the two superpowers.

From a political point of view, the Alliance is faced with two insoluble problems: East-West relations and German reunification. Centrifugal tendencies in Eastern Europe have led the Soviet Union to tighten the military constraints of the Warsaw Pact. Détente, therefore, can no longer constitute a short-term objective. More than ever, East Germany is the key to the Soviet system of defense, so that any discussion of reunification must again be postponed. Because of the fear of a nuclear holocaust, however, and in spite of the Soviet Union's return to the idea of the Eastern bloc as a hegemonic system, East-West relations in the long run should evolve within the general framework of reconciliation and the elaboration of a more satisfactory status for Germany and for Europe.

III

Europe

15

The Launching of the
Common Market

Opposition to the Establishment of a Wider Free-Trade Area

IN BOOK ONE OF THIS VOLUME we described the initial phases of the diplomatic battle that pitted France against England after 1955. The bone of contention was the construction of an economically united Europe. France, after some hesitation, championed the Common Market, while England advocated a free-trade area. After the ratification of the Treaty of Rome, England urged the establishment in Europe of a large free-trade area embracing the European Economic Community and the other members of the O.E.E.C. The matter was debated by the Ministerial Committee of the O.E.E.C., presided over by Sir Reginald Maudling, a member of the British cabinet. In April 1958 the committee suspended its meetings because of the French political crisis.

After May 13, France's partners in the O.E.E.C. were concerned with the question of whether de Gaulle, who had hotly criticized the Treaty of Rome, was really interested in getting the Common Market under way. They also wondered about France's ability, given the critical state of her balance of payments, to put into effect by January 1, 1959, the tariff regulations prescribed in the Treaty of Rome. Or would she have to invoke the safeguard clauses?

Both fears were dissipated, one by the Franco-German rapprochement, the other by the French monetary reform.

The following communiqué was issued on September 14 after the first de Gaulle-Adenauer meeting at Colombey-les-Deux Églises: "We are convinced that close cooperation between the German Federal Republic and the French Republic will be the keystone of any constructive effort in Europe." The first sign of such cooperation between the Six was the adoption on October 8 of a memorandum on the organization of a common market with an eventual free-trade area. According to this document, it was necessary to harmonize the tariff and trade agreements made within the two organizations, and to emphasize their institutional differences. This approach, however, was not acceptable to England. As a consequence, the debates at the Maudling Committee encountered difficulties. On November 14, Jacques Soustelle, the minister of information, unexpectedly torpedoed the talks when he told the press: "France, unlike England, believes it is impossible to create a free-trade area by introducing free trade between the six Common Market nations and the eleven other members of the O.E.E.C.; it is impossible because there is no uniform tariff for the seventeen nations, and no harmonization in the economic and social domains." This unilateral declaration led to a suspension of the negotiations and eventually to their failure. The British proposal offered the member states trade advantages comparable to those enjoyed by members of the Community. However, the eleven would not be obliged, as were the Six, to establish a single external tariff and pursue a single economic policy. It was therefore feared that a larger and less restrictive organization would water down the more limited and exacting Community organization. The French especially were afraid that the Germans, attracted by the advantages of a market that embraced all of Western Europe, might neglect the obligations inherent in the principles of an economic union. The English overestimated their ability to negotiate. It had become apparent to everyone, even to the Germans, that the British hoped to take full advantage of their privileged position as members of both the Commonwealth and the European free-trade area. Moreover, they underestimated the strength of the movement toward European unity; and they did not assess correctly the impetus given this movement by Adenauer's decision (in spite of the opposition of his minister of economics, Ludwig Erhard) to sacrifice certain German commercial interests to the higher cause of a political entente with France.

On November 26, General de Gaulle took it upon himself to pay a call on Chancellor Adenauer at Bad Kreutznach. Fresh signs of a political entente between the two countries were apparent after this visit. In going to see Adenauer, de Gaulle wished to assure the German government that France would not invoke the safeguard clauses of January 1, 1959, in order to avoid the time schedule established by the Treaty of Rome for the reduction of tariffs. In exchange he hoped to obtain assurances that the Federal Republic would not insist on reopening negotiations with England on the question of a free-trade area. The two governments agreed to present joint proposals to their Common Market partners. These proposals were adopted on December 3 at the Council of Ministers of the Six at Brussels. They underscored the decision, which had been made public, that France would immediately free as much as 40 per cent of her trade with members of the O.E.E.C. The proposals were liberal in their conception. First, the Six decided to extend to all the member states of the General Agreement on Tariff and Trade (G.A.T.T.), the 10 per cent reduction in tariff rates they accorded each other. Secondly, they decided to grant to all the member states of the O.E.E.C., on a reciprocal basis, the 20 per cent increase in quota restrictions on manufactured goods which they accorded each other. But they reserved for themselves alone the stipulations that quota restrictions on manufactured goods should represent a minimum of 3 per cent of the national production of any given item. At a meeting of the Maudling Committee on December 15, England reproached France for increasing her quotas for the benefit of the Six before having met her obligations as a member of the O.E.E.C. This included the freeing of at least 75, not 40 per cent of her trade. England asked for acceptance of the principle of preferential treatment among all the states of the O.E.E.C., whereas France wanted to continue it solely among the Six. She did not want to extend these advantages to third-party nations. The meeting broke up in disagreement. England decided to hasten a return to the convertibility of the pound sterling. But the radical monetary reform initiated by the French government on December 28, 1958, enabled it on January 1, 1959, to increase to 90 per cent the proportion of its foreign trade to be freed. This decision left England no further cause for complaint.

The Devaluation of the Franc and the New Economic Policy

When the principles of the Common Market were first implemented, the monetary and economic situation of France was critical as compared to that of her partners. Even since 1949, her partners had stabilized their currencies, whereas never since World War II had France reorganized her monetary system. She was therefore in no position to redress the balance of foreign trade. In June 1958, Antoine Pinay, whom de Gaulle had appointed minister of finance, floated a loan like the one that had won the confidence of French investors in 1952. This brought a stringent reduction in the circulation of money and provided the necessary respite for the preparation of even more important measures. Pinay accepted most of the proposals put forward by a committee of experts headed by Jacques Rueff. The monetary reform consisted in combining devaluation with internal deflation and sweeping measures to free trade and payments. Economic subsidies and price pegging were abolished; wages were frozen. The 17.5 per cent devaluation of the franc, coming on the heels of the 20 per cent 1957 devaluation, was calculated to stimulate exports. The freeing of 90 per cent of French trade enabled the country to respect its commitments within the O.E.E.C. and to use the pressure of foreign competition to influence domestic prices. The establishment, in concert with the principal European nations, of the convertibility of currencies placed France in the same situation as her partners in regard to foreign investments. In short, France discarded her traditional protectionist policy and embarked on the path of liberalism.

Seen as a whole, the measures were coherent, judicious, and courageous. They had an immediate effect on the launching of the Common Market and on England's conduct in regard to it.

The Communitarian Doctrine and the British Reaction

On January 13, 1959, in a speech before the European Parliamentary Assembly, the president of the Commission, Walter Hallstein, replied with a smile to the accusation of discrimination leveled by critics of the Common Market, particularly critics of England: "If two people marry, this is discrimination toward others. The only way to avoid it is to do away with the institution of marriage."[1] In February, he handed the ministers of the Six a memorandum on the relations of the Community with third-party nations. According to this document, which was used by the ministers as a basis for discussion, there were only two satisfactory systems of multilateral free trade: "A customs union (or, to be more precise, an economic union) that insures to all the participants a uniform status in regard to the provision of supplies, or worldwide free trade that guarantees the same kind of equality." In a second memorandum of September 1959, the Commission pointed out that it would be in the interest of the Community, once it was consolidated, to pursue a liberal trade policy toward the third countries.

For a few months the British continued to envisage a unique multilateral system for Europe, within the framework of O.E.E.C. Such was the refrain of Maudling's speech of April 27, 1959, before the Consultative Assembly of the Council of Europe. But at the same time England was exploring another solution which consisted in grouping around her a certain number of European nations in a small free-trade area. A preliminary conference was held at Stockholm on June 13. It was attended by seven nations: England, Sweden, Norway, Denmark, Switzerland, Austria, and Portugal. An agreement was concluded in the same city on November 20. To obtain it, England had to agree to grant to several of her partners, especially Denmark, sizable tariff concessions for certain agricultural products. The purpose of the European Free Trade Association (E.F.T.A.) was consistent

[1] *Année politique 1959*, 307.

with Britain's initial concept: to abolish tariffs between member states while at the same time preserving individual national tariffs and national control of trade policies.

Both the Six and the United States regarded the Stockholm agreements as a defensive measure taken by England in opposition to the Common Market and as a purely commercial arrangement devoid of any long-term political significance.

After the creation of the E.F.T.A., the British attempted to establish working relations between it and the E.E.C. within the framework of the O.E.E.C. French political circles, however, thought that the O.E.E.C. was not an appropriate forum for a discussion of European trade policies. This opinion was shared by the Commission.[2] It was agreed to transform the O.E.E.C. The change consisted in broadening the geographical framework of the organization. Instead of remaining purely European, it became Western by virtue of the full participation of the United States and Canada. It restricted its sphere of action in regard to both monetary and commercial matters because of the coexistence of the E.E.C. and the E.F.T.A. The principal task of the new Organization for Economic Cooperation and Development (O.E.C.D.), created by the convention of November 14, 1960, was to coordinate the aid given by Western industrialized nations to developing states. In July 1961 England decided to ask for membership in the E.E.C. Her decision to do so was influenced by the limited nature of the American commitments to the O.E.C.D., and by the moral support the United States lent to the E.E.C., because of the implicit political objectives contained in the provisions of the Treaty of Rome.

The Acceleration of the Industrial Common Market

The failure of the wider free-trade area, followed by the creation of a small one, was noted with satisfaction in French industrial circles. French businessmen were leery of direct commercial competition without the assurance that economic and social policies would be harmonized, in accordance with the provisions of the Treaty of Rome.

General de Gaulle saw the Common Market as a possible means of helping France to become a dominant power on the Continent. Early in 1960 his outlook coincided with that of the Commission, which wanted to consolidate an institution that was still fragile. On February 13, well ahead of the time schedule, and before the next session of the G.A.T.T., the Council of Ministers approved a common external tariff. On March 2, the Council reached an agreement regarding the tariffs applicable to the famous

[2] Miriam Camps, *Britain and the European Community* (Princeton: Princeton University Press, 1964), 241–42.

"List G" of products appended to the Treaty of Rome. The duties on this list had been established by negotiation among the Six and the rates were fixed by them at a level lower than the arithmetic mean of the national duties.

The moment seemed opportune for the Commission to suggest that the member states speed up the establishment of an industrial Common Market. All six nations were enjoying a rare period of monetary stability and economic expansion. Their economic policies were becoming more coordinated. An economic policy committee was set up to study and compare the economic indicators. The recommendations of the Commission were approved almost unanimously by the European Parliamentary Assembly on March 28 and discussed by the member nations. At the Council of Ministers, Germany and the Netherlands seemed disinclined to accelerate the removal of tariff barriers for fear of hampering their trade with England and with other members of the E.F.T.A. France supported the Commission's proposals; they were adopted by the Council of Ministers on May 12. On December 31, 1961, by the end of the first stage of the transitional phase of the Common Market, tariffs on industrial products, between member states would be reduced by 50 per cent instead of the 30 per cent stipulated in the treaty. On the same date quotas for industrial products would be removed; this was also several years ahead of the treaty's schedule. Finally, it was decided that on December 31, 1960—a year in advance of the time schedule—the first steps would be taken toward the ultimate replacement of national tariffs by a common external tariff. Considering that French tariffs were higher than those of Germany and the Benelux countries, these arrangements attested the more liberal direction of French economic policy.

The decisions reached in May 1960 were implemented at the stipulated time. However, at the close of 1961, in accepting relatively rigid antitrust regulations, France had to take into account the German point of view.

The Beginnings of a Common Agricultural Policy

The simple methods of tariff reductions for industrial goods became far more intricate when applied to agricultural products because of the variety and complexity of the aid that the various nations accorded their own farmers. The Treaty of Rome required the member states to define and then apply a common agricultural policy that was based essentially on the organization of markets.

This policy was of major importance to France. The continuous increase in production obliged the nation to export its surplus produce. But these opportunities for export were bound up with the organization of a communitarian preferential market, the E.E.C. as a whole and Germany in particular suffering from a sizable food shortage.

In June 1960, proposals for a common agricultural policy were presented to the Council of Ministers by Sicco Mansholt, in the name of the Commission. The scheme envisaged the free movement of agricultural products within the Community and the establishment for them of a common trade policy and a common price level. On November 15, 1960, these proposals were approved by the member states. A common protectionist policy now had to be worked out. The Commission suggested an innovation, a "levy" that would be equal in amount to the difference between the current price paid by the importer and the generally lower price offered by the exporter. After an initial opposition by Germany, the levy was accepted on December 20, 1960. In 1961, plans for fixing market prices for each category of products ran into difficulties. Michel Debré, addressing the National Assembly, warned: "We have the right and the duty to demand that the treaty be applied in the agricultural domain before it results in a common economic policy." At the Council of Ministers in Brussels on July 3, France held that the second transitional stage of the Common Market must await the achievement of definite progress in the agricultural domain. The first stage ended on December 31, 1961. Two weeks later the Council of Ministers adopted a series of regulations concerning the organization of markets, the communitarian financing of subsidies for exports, and for the reform of agricultural structures. Germany was called upon to make the greatest sacrifices because her farmers were protected and her consumers benefited from imports from countries with low production costs. The French exerted considerable pressure because it was necessary to define a common agricultural policy before deciding whether or not to admit England to the E.E.C. She had requested admittance in July 1961.

In his press conference of February 5, 1962, de Gaulle congratulated himself on the progress toward a common agricultural policy: "We were not willing . . . to create a Common Market that did not include agriculture. . . . Otherwise, France, an agricultural as well as an industrial nation, would have experienced a terrible upheaval in her economic, social, and financial stability. On the contrary, we saw to it that this serious omission in the Treaty of Rome was remedied in all essential respects." Actually, far from having neglected agriculture, the Treaty of Rome devoted much attention to it (articles 38 through 47) and defined the methods and objectives. The implementation of the program required the enactment of important communitarian legislation. The texts approved on January 14, 1962, merely constituted the first step.

Be that as it may, the Common Market as an institution passed the test, in advance of the time schedule, of the first transitional stage; it was ready for the second.

The Magnetism of the European Economic Community

The speeding up of the industrial Common Market and the inauguration of a common agricultural policy attested the continuing desire of governments to implement the treaty; it also showed the approval of the Common Market by industrialists, farmers, and trade unionists.

The success of the new institution cannot be measured by the high rate of economic growth in the member states: the prosperity of the industrialized nations on the Continent predated the signing of the 1957 treaty; but it certainly can be measured by the spectacular growth of trade among the member states. This progress may be ascribed not only to favorable circumstances, the direct effect of reduced tariffs, and the abolition of quotas, but also to the conduct of businessmen. Spurred by the prospect of increased competition, they sought new outlets in a broader market. Lastly, the success of the Common Market may be measured by the attraction exerted by the Community on the outside world. Walter Hallstein wrote in July 1962: "Look at the great effort of various nations to gain entry into the Common Market, to become partners in it, or to determine in agreement with it the main lines of the commercial and economic policies of the free world!"[3]

On June 8, 1959, Greece asked for association with the Common Market under Article 238 of the Treaty of Rome. Turkey followed her example on July 31. An agreement of association was signed with Greece on July 9, 1961. These two developing nations were thus able to benefit from a Marshall Plan of sorts offered by the industrialized nations of the European continent.

The transitional system of association instituted by the treaty to favor the overseas territories of France and Belgium was transformed when sixteen nations acquired independence. After a meeting of European, African and Malagasy parliamentarians in Strasbourg in June 1961, the Commission sent to the Council of Ministers a communication dealing with the future of the association system.

The first joint meeting of the Council of Ministers of the E.E.C. and the African and Malagasy leaders was held in Paris on December 6, 1961.

The most striking evidence of the attraction exerted by the Common Market came to light on July 30, 1961, when England requested membership in the Community under Article 237 of the treaty. Ireland and Denmark, whose ties with England were very close, immediately followed suit. The three neutral states of the E.F.T.A.—Sweden, Austria, and Switzerland—could not, for political reasons, request membership, but on December 12 and 15, 1961, they did ask to be admitted as associates to the E.E.C. Thus,

[3] "La première étape du Marché Commun," Report on the Implementation of the Treaty (Jan. 1958–1962), E.E.C., July 1962.

two years after the signing of the convention of Stockholm and shortly before the end of the first stage of the Common Market's transitional period, three states of the E.F.T.A., including the leader of that organization, applied for membership in the Community; and three others requested the status of associates. The E.F.T.A. seemed to be breaking up even before it got under way.

The Community soon became the principal trade partner of the United States within the G.A.T.T. The establishment of a common tariff enabled the Community to offer, on a reciprocal basis, a linear tariff reduction of 20 per cent on industrial products. This had been suggested in 1958 by Douglas Dillon, then American undersecretary of state. On May 29, 1961, a multilateral conference got under way to study an exchange of tariff concessions. On January 16, 1962, an important agreement was reached in Brussels between the United States and the Community. It foreshadowed a sizable tariff reduction on both sides of the Atlantic.

In addition to the economic and psychological factors we have mentioned, a conjunction of circumstances accounted for the success and influence of the Common Market. For the first time since the Liberation, there was a strong government in France. It was able to impose a program of financial austerity and remove the shackles of trade; this in turn enabled France to meet the time schedule laid down by the Treaty of Rome. De Gaulle leaned heavily not only on his own followers but also on those former political parties of the Fourth Republic that favored Western European unity. Two other political factors have already been mentioned: Chancellor Adenauer's support of General de Gaulle's policy; and agreement between de Gaulle and the Brussels Commission. The speeding up of the industrial Common Market and the implementation of a common agricultural policy were due to the combination of these three factors.

The success of the Common Market has not, however, converted de Gaulle to a communitarian conception of Europe. On the contrary, the deliberate weakening of both the European Coal and Steel Community and Euratom, on the one hand, and on the other, the efforts to create among the Six a political union of states, were indications of the general's deep attachment to a European policy based essentially on national sovereignty.

16

Trouble in the Specialized Institutions

The Coal and Steel Community and the Coal Crisis

THE COAL AND STEEL COMMUNITY AND EURATOM, because of their limited fields of competence, were minor institutions compared to the E.E.C. whose function was to direct the general economic policy of the Six. The difficulties encountered by the specialized institutions contrasted sharply with the success of the Common Market.

In 1958 the Coal and Steel Community experienced a serious coal crisis. At a time when worldwide consumption of fuel was steadily increasing, coal was piling up on the floors of the coal mines. The cost of coal production was rising. Consequently, coal could not compete with oil. After the Suez affair, several member states ordered large quantities of coal from the United States on medium-term contracts. The High Authority of the Coal and Steel Community, which was not competent in the area of commercial policy, did not oppose the move. In Belgium, the crisis was most acute because of the country's low rate of productivity. In the spring of 1959, the High Authority wanted its Council of Ministers to declare a state of "obvious crisis." This would facilitate, under Article 58 of the Treaty of Paris, the establishment of production and import quotas. On March 17 a large majority of the Consultative Committee, including German industrialists hostile to any kind of quota, voted against the plan. The European Assembly backed it, but faintheartedly. When the plan was presented to the Council of Ministers on April 23, it was voted down by the German government.

On May 14, a second, less drastic plan was rejected by France, Germany, and Italy, their votes outnumbering those of the Benelux countries.

Discussion centered on whether the High Authority should order a reduction of coal production or call for intergovernmental accords. Jean-Marcel Jeanneney, representing France in the Council of Ministers, declared that it was not the task of a supranational authority to limit the production of large business concerns; the matter was one for individual governments to decide. On May 15, Michel Debré spoke in a similar vein before the National Assembly: "I believe that the responsibility of governments to their elected representatives is such that it will be very difficult, even for the sake of international cooperation, for governments to allocate to independent authorities the right to regulate matters for which, after all, they must answer to their own nations."

By refusing to acknowledge the existence of a crisis, the Council of Ministers made it impossible to apply Article 58 of the Treaty of Paris. The Council did take certain steps on July 31: the Coal and Steel Community offered aid to unemployed Belgian coal miners; a government subsidy was granted to collieries; and a certain number of Belgian mines were closed. On December 15, the situation having seriously deteriorated, Belgium requested and was granted authorization to establish quotas for the purchase of coal from her Coal and Steel Community partners. Thus the Belgian coal market was isolated and remained so until 1962—a situation not at all consonant with the treaty's principle of the free circulation of goods. The solution hit upon was actually protectionist and nationalist rather than communitarian or supportive of free trade.

In his press conference of September 5, 1960, de Gaulle used the crisis to criticize supranational institutions. "These organs are technically useful but they do not and cannot have authority; therefore they are not politically effective. . . . As soon as . . . a big problem crops up, one realizes that some 'high authority' actually does not have authority over a variety of areas. Only nations have such authority. We saw this not so very long ago during the coal crisis." This was an ill-chosen accusation because it was the nations, especially France, that hindered the workings of the communitarian institution.

Euratom and the Nuclear Reactors

"Euratom is an institution of applied science inscribed in the political structure of the Europe of the Six."[1] The mission of this institution was to promote the construction of atomic centers for the civilian use of atomic energy in order to stimulate research and education. The purpose of these centers was to produce nuclear power.

[1] Jules Guéron, "Politique européenne de recherches et de diffusion des connaissances," *Education européenne*, No. 41, May–June 1966, p. 5.

Euratom met with difficulties in the accomplishment of this mission. These were due to the preexistence of national programs for research and production and also to changes in supply and demand in the market for energy.

When Euratom was launched, national centers for research and industrial installations already existed. In France they were quite large, thanks to the impetus given by the French Commissariat of Atomic Energy. Other member states also had sizable centers. Some of these were in Germany, which had been authorized in 1955 to study the utilization of atomic energy for peaceful ends.

However, construction of atomic centers (the "Wise Men's" report of 1957 contained a plan for fifteen million kilowatts' capacity to be installed by 1967) was slowed down because power resources, once so scarce, were rapidly becoming abundant. Continental Europe could now afford to import a growing amount of oil at relatively low prices. Industrialists, who had been asked to build powerful reactors that would produce nuclear electricity at competitive prices, had no idea how such reactors would perform technically or how long they would last. They were therefore unable to estimate the true cost of atomic energy.[2]

Moreover, the contractors hesitated to participate in a program to construct nuclear centers launched in 1959, according to the provisions of the Euratom-United States agreement of November 8, 1959. Even guarantees of performance and donations of material, plus the prospect of loans from the United States, failed to persuade them. The Commission was finally obliged to suggest that Euratom should share the financial costs of construction. Pierre Guillaumat, minister of state in charge of scientific research, was opposed to this for two reasons: from the point of view of scientific research, the participation of Euratom would contribute nothing; furthermore, the measures under consideration favored the construction of American rather than French reactors. Étienne Hirsch, who in February 1959 succeeded Louis Armand as the president of the Euratom Commission, replied that it was Euratom's task to weigh the industrial uses of nuclear energy. It was both possible and desirable to build French reactors within the framework of the existing agreement. The Atomic Energy Commissariat (A.E.C.) rejected this solution. In an effort to end the impasse, Hirsch obtained participation in the first Euratom program without the enactment of supplementary appropriations. The revised program was adopted by the Council of Ministers on July 3, 1961, by a majority vote, in spite of the opposition of France. On December 20, 1961, the Hirsch-Guillaumat controversy culminated in the replacement of Hirsch by Pierre Chatenet as the president of Euratom.

[2] J. G. Polach, *Euratom: Its Background, Issues and Economic Implications* (New York: Oceana Publications, Inc., 1964), 120, 123.

Euratom embarked on a study of new types of reactors, especially the production of breeder reactors. In 1959, at a time when this type of reactor, which was destined to have a great future, was still unknown in Europe, Euratom proposed a partnership with the French Atomic Energy Commissariat. At that time no other atomic center was in a position to compete with the A.E.C. By using Euratom, France could have become a European center of development in this domain. The A.E.C. refused. The chance to launch a unique European enterprise was lost. When in 1961 the A.E.C. finally changed its mind, Germany had already begun to build a sizable installation and Italy had submitted plans for a comparable program. As a consequence, Euratom concluded in 1962 three partnership contracts in direct violation of the communitarian principle.

Euratom and Research

To fulfill its responsibilities in determining the best type of reactor for every use, and to broaden the category of reactors that would be useful in Europe, Euratom earmarked research appropriations for a series of five-year programs. The first covered the years 1958–1962. Some of the appropriations were for research contracts designed to support certain features of national programs, but the lion's share was earmarked for joint research projects. Most of the contracts were linked to the Euratom-United States agreement envisaging a research program whose costs would be shared by both parties.

Some suitable means had to be found for purely communitarian research. Taking into account the dispersion and slowness of research in individual European nations, which contrasted sharply with the concentration of means and the technical progress that characterized the United States, the Euratom Commission agreed to transform one of the existing national centers into a joint research center. Preferably, such a center would be located in a country that had several centers and where no heavy construction program was already under way.

For this reason Euratom chose Grenoble. In 1959 the French government declined the invitation. The Commission was therefore obliged to divide the joint research between four separate centers. The largest was established at Ispra, in Italy. This solution was a poor one because of distance and dispersal of effort.

In short, France, which had demanded the presidency of the Commission and had made considerable technical progress by 1959, could have become the leader of Euratom. Her stand on a common research center and the manufacture of power reactors redounded to the advantage of her partners, especially Germany, which became, in the domain of nuclear energy, the beachhead of the United States in Europe. But some of the solutions adopted for research and construction did not fulfill the maximum technical and economic objectives of the Community.

The Obstacles to a Common Policy for Energy

The coal crisis and the difficulties in launching Euratom pointed up the lack of a common policy in regard to energy. It also revealed the harmful consequences of the chaos resulting from the divergent aims of member states and from the scattering of talent throughout three different communities.

The divergence of aims was obvious. The Six were not able to come to an agreement over the duties on oil in the common external tariff. To protect her coal industry, Germany wanted to charge a high rate for the right of entry, whereas France, for budgetary reasons, preferred the imposition of heavy internal oil duties. In Germany power was part of the private sector; in France, most of it was government controlled. L'Union Générale des Pétroles was established in April 1960. A government refining and distributing company, its object was to sell the products of state concerns that exploited the oil resources of the Sahara. The French government organized this Union not to nationalize oil but rather to compete more successfully with the powerful Anglo-Dutch and American companies. It also wished to obtain preferential treatment for oil produced in the Franc Zone.

In the national markets, various kinds of power sources competed in different ways. In the Common Market as a whole, the Coal and Steel Community was competent for coal, Euratom for nuclear energy, and the E.E.C. for non-nuclear electricity, oil, and natural gas. The Treaty of Rome made no provision for a common policy in regard to uses of power; therefore there was no legal basis upon which such a policy could be implemented.

At the suggestion of Piero Malvestiti, president of the High Authority, an interexecutive committee on power was set up on November 29, 1959. On June 22, 1962, it issued a memorandum regarding ways and means of instituting a common policy on power resources. It proposed the establishment of an open Common Market for power resources within the Community. This seemed too innovative for the Council of Ministers of the Coal and Steel Community; they rejected it on October 10, 1962.

Meanwhile leading European circles became more and more mindful of the relationship, exemplified by the United States, between the dynamism of an economy and the abundance and low cost of power. They also noted the institutional obstacles that stood in the way of a common policy on coal and oil. In the course of 1960, the presidents of the three communities,

Hallstein, Hirsch, and Malvestiti, decided in favor of fusion of the three organizations. The idea was taken up by the Netherlands in a discussion among the Six on the subject of European political unity.

The European University

The aim of Euratom was not merely to promote research but also to disseminate knowledge. Article 9 of the treaty provided for the training of specialists and for the creation of an "institute at university level." A temporary committee was set up by the Council of Ministers on October 14, 1959, to consider the establishment of a European university; it presented its report in May 1960. It advocated the creation of a third-cycle institution (doctoral program only), comprising a small number of departments, focused primarily on the social sciences. Speaking on May 12, 1959, before the European Parliamentary Assembly, the former Italian foreign minister, Gaetano Martino, explained that the purpose was to "further the formation and diffusion of a true European conscience." In the opinion of Étienne Hirsch, president of the temporary committee, a European university would make possible "the cohabitation, on an equal footing, of professors and students from different nations." At a meeting of the Council of Ministers on June 20, 1960, five governments were ready to accept the recommendations of the temporary committee. But Couve de Murville, speaking on behalf of France, questioned the communitarian nature of the proposed institution and sought assurance that the member states would assume financial responsibility for it. The plan was tabled because the Council of Ministers could not reach an agreement.

It was revived in a different form under different circumstances. At the suggestion of de Gaulle, a meeting of chiefs of state took place in Bonn on July 19, 1961. The purpose of the meeting was to expedite political cooperation between the Six. Also on the agenda was the question of cooperation in the domain of higher education and research. A communiqué announced "the establishment by Italy of a European university at Florence, to whose intellectual life and costs the six governments would contribute." Euratom was dispossessed. On December 21, 1962, the Parliamentary Assembly voted a resolution expressing regret that the Council of Ministers did not accept suggestions that would have placed the university within the framework of the Treaty of Rome and given it an autonomous structure. Although the Italian government appointed an organizational committee the affair made no progress, mainly because of the failure to formulate a plan for political cooperation by the Six.

17

Political Europe without
Supranationality

Political Construction and Economic Integration

THE RAPIDITY WITH WHICH THE TREATY'S TARIFF REGULATIONS
were applied to the Common Market led some political observers to
wonder about the possibility of constructing a European political union.
The unification of Europe had hitherto been confined to the economic
domain. Ever since the rejection in 1954 of the treaty instituting the European Defense Community, this road had been closed.

Two methods were considered: development of the communities, or a
new government action.

The first method, advocated by the Action Committee for a United
States of Europe, involved the adoption of three projects: a merger of the
executives of the three existing communities; the creation of a European
university within the framework of these communities; and the election of a
European Parliament on the basis of universal suffrage. The first two projects have been discussed in the preceding chapter. The third had a greater
political significance and was backed up by an identical provision in the
Treaties of Rome and Paris. It read: "The Assembly will develop plans
for an election on the basis of direct universal suffrage in accordance with
a uniform procedure for all the member states."

On October 23, 1958, the Commission for Political Affairs of the
European Parliamentary Assembly charged a committee with the responsibility of working out the requisite plans. The text adopted by the Commission in March 1960, and by the Assembly in May, was presented to the
Council of Ministers of the Six on June 20. During the transitional phase

[382

of the Common Market, only two-thirds of the parliamentarians were to be elected on the basis of universal suffrage. The authors of the project were anxious to avoid the danger of government by assembly before a strong European executive power was established. Similar prudence led the authors to state that, since the scope of existing communities was essentially economic, the Assembly, however elected, could not assume purely political responsibilities and would not be constituent.

It was clear from the work of the Strasbourg Assembly that any real progress in the construction of a European political union would require either extension of the scope of the existing communities or the creation of a new authority for foreign affairs and defense. In either case, governmental intervention would be necessary.

It came from General de Gaulle. And it was not based on the Community concept.

The Organized Cooperation of the States

The ministerial statement of Michel Debré, read before the National Assembly on January 15, 1959, outlined the Gaullist theory of an organized cooperation of states: "France, although not claiming a power equal to that of the great empires of the world, considers that she must assume the stern responsibilities of a country determined to play a leading role. . . . For the future of our nations we must arrange regular and continuous consultations between chiefs of state. This is the way to true solidarity. This is the way that leads to a united and great policy." The first application of this method of intergovernmental consultation was a decision made on November 23, 1959. The Council of Ministers of the Six, alluding to a joint proposal made by France and Italy, declared: "The six foreign ministers have agreed to hold regular consultations on international policies."

On May 31, 1960, on the morrow of the failure of the four-power summit meeting, de Gaulle commented on this event; he also defined his position. He alluded to the organization of the free peoples of the old Continent that enjoyed the protection of the Atlantic Alliance. "To help make Western Europe into a political, economic, cultural and human entity, organized for action, progress, defense—this is what France is trying to do. . . . The nations that become associated must not thereby cease to retain their identity; the path we shall travel must surely be that of an organized cooperation of states, the prelude, perhaps, to the establishment of an imposing confederation."

These remarks were mentioned by the premier in the course of the foreign policy debates that took place on June 14 and 15 in the National Assembly. In Michel Debré's opinion, the essential requirement was "a political partnership of states, nations, fatherlands, for the purpose of governmental cooperation." In passing, Debré criticized the recent resolution of the European Parliamentary Assembly: "It is very hard to see what the election of a political assembly by means of universal suffrage will add in view of the existing technical organs or commissions of top civil servants." On July 25, Debré announced to the National Assembly a forthcoming move toward the organized cooperation of European governments.

De Gaulle proceeded to sound out France's partners. The first statesman to whom he disclosed his doctrine of a practical politically unified Europe was Chancellor Adenauer, who was his guest at Rambouillet on July 29. According to André Fontaine, the general suggested periodic meetings of chiefs of state and heads of government; the establishment of permanent intergovernmental commissions for foreign affairs, defense, economics, and cultural matters; revision of the Euratom and Coal and Steel Community Treaties; and a referendum in the six countries on the new treaty.[1] Apparently Adenauer, although not altogether convinced by de Gaulle's arguments, was nonetheless interested. The attitude of the German cabinet, however, was extremely reserved. An economic commission that prepared the ground for the decisions of the chiefs of state and government heads would only weaken the executives of the three communities. A commission for defense seemed designed to weaken NATO. De Gaulle's criticisms of this organization and his intention of establishing a national deterrent force lent plausibility to such an interpretation. At the end of August and during the early part of September, de Gaulle contacted the Italian and Dutch chiefs of state. They expressed similar reservations. The Atlantic Organization seemed to them the appropriate agency for European military collaboration. The Netherlands demanded British participation.

Ignoring these reservations—Belgium and Luxemburg were to be consulted later—de Gaulle made public in a press conference of September 5, 1960, his concept of a European political union. He contrasted Europe as it was with the Europe of everyone's dreams. The states were the only reality; they "alone have the right to command and the authority to act." The dreams were represented by "certain more or less extra-national organs. These organs have a certain technical validity but do not and cannot have authority; therefore they lack political efficacy." The states could use these specialized organs to lay the groundwork for their decisions, and possibly the states would follow, but "these decisions ... belong to them alone; they can be made only through cooperation." France believes such cooperation to be "desirable, possible and feasible in the political, economic, cultural and military domains." A solemn European referendum would lend

[1] André Fontaine, *Revue du Marché Commun*, Feb. 1961, p. 63.

the indispensable attribute "of cooperation and democratic innovation to this rebirth of Europe."

Because of de Gaulle's personality and the position of France in Europe, de Gaulle's move was of prime political importance. It called for a total change of objectives and methods in constructing European unity. The long-term goal of a confederation would replace the prudent move toward a federation. A formal agreement between governments would replace the dialogue between a communitarian executive and a nation-based Council of Ministers. The general made every effort to reassure his partners. One of his intimates, Alain Peyrefitte, published a series of articles on the future of Europe in *Le Monde*. Invoking history, he reminded his readers that "confederations have a tendency to become federations." Sketching the future, he pointed out that one of the characteristics of the new system would be gradualism; a period of unanimous decisions would be followed, after the referendum, by the majority decisions of the chiefs of state and the government heads.[2] On October 2, in Metz, Debré declared: "The government's European policy, as defined by General de Gaulle, is a continuation of the experiment begun a few years ago and known as 'integration,' especially in the economic domain."

Debré and Couve de Murville went to Bonn on October 7. Before engaging in discussions along the lines indicated by de Gaulle, Adenauer requested some assurance about France's intentions in regard to NATO. A communiqué issued on October 8 stated that "the discussions once again showed that the Atlantic Alliance is the foundation of European security, and that the collective effort of all the members of the Alliance, motivated by a common will, is necessary to guarantee this security." The advocates of integration were attracted by the possibility of reviewing the question of European political unification. On November 22, Jean Monnet wrote to the members of his Action Committee urging support for the principle of summit meetings as a first step toward European unity; but, he specified, the existing communities must be preserved and the way to a federal type of evolution must remain open. Monnet's opinion apparently influenced Adenauer's decision to back the general.[3] It remained for the chiefs of state and the government heads to discuss the matter face to face.

European Summit Meetings

The first European summit meeting took place in Paris on February 10 and 11, 1961. The Dutch expressed very strong reservations about the

[2] Alain Peyrefitte, "L'avenir de l'Europe," *Le Monde*, Sept. 14–17, 1960.

[3] Irving M. Destler, "Political Union in Europe 1960–1962," Woodrow Wilson School of Public and International Affairs, Washington, D.C., Sept. 28, 1964.

creation of a permanent organ that gave no assurances in regard to its relations with the three communities. Once again they demanded British
participation in all political consultations. Joseph Luns, the Dutch foreign
minister, observed that the E.E.C. had only six members because only six
nations accepted the idea of economic integration. If these countries formed
a political confederation, England must be invited to join it. The final
communiqué was cautious in referring to general principles. The Six were
seeking "the proper means of organizing closer political cooperation" and
hoped to "lay the foundations of a union that would develop gradually . . .
and that could be broadened subsequently." The door was left ajar for
England. An eventual federation might become a possibility. Questions of
defense were not mentioned. The communiqué announced the establishment of a commission composed of the representatives of the six governments, subsequently called the Fouchet Commission in honour of its French
chairman. At the next summit meeting, the commission was to submit
proposals concerning both political organization and the development of
the existing communities.

The chiefs of state and government heads held their second conference
at Bonn on July 18. They examined the report of the Fouchet Commission.
According to the communiqué, they decided "to meet at regular intervals
to exchange views, harmonize policies, and arrive at a common position, in
the hope of furthering the political union of Europe and strengthening the
Atlantic Alliance." They believed that "their cooperation would facilitate the adoption of such reforms as might be needed to increase the effectiveness of the communities." They added that "cooperation of the Six
must transcend the political framework" and broaden its scope to embrace
education, culture, and research. De Gaulle did not have his way about the
references to the Atlantic Alliance, the referendum, revision of the treaties
governing the communities, or the creation of intergovernmental commissions
for economic and military questions; but he did obtain the consent of his
partners for an intergovernmental form of political union, organically
separated from the communities and not strictly limited in scope.[4]

Negotiations for a Union of States

The Fouchet Commission met on November 10 to discuss a preliminary
draft treaty for a union of states. Accepted as a basis for discussion, this
draft was received rather favorably by Germany, Italy, and Luxembourg.
A delicate point was contained in Article 16 providing for a general revision
of the treaty at the end of three years. "This revision shall have as its

---

[4] *Ibid.*, 46.

principal object the establishment of a unified foreign policy and the gradual constitution of an organization within the Union that will centralize the European communities." The terms were ambiguous and could be interpreted as a move toward supranational reform or subordination of the communities. Meanwhile, major difficulties were raised by the Dutch, who refused to include a common defense policy as one of the objectives. The Dutch also laid down as a prior condition the participation of Britain in the negotiations. They reaffirmed their slogan: "No British-type Europe without the British." So vehement were they that on July 31 England requested entry into the Common Market. On October 10, when the negotiations began, Edward Heath stated in Brussels that England fully agreed with the objectives and policies of the authors of the Bonn declaration. Speaking for Belgium, Paul-Henri Spaak, who had recently returned to the ministry of foreign affairs, supported the Dutch position.

The Quai d'Orsay, however, hoped to conclude a treaty of union before the end of negotiations with England in order to make clear that this union was of French inspiration. Certain concessions therefore had to be made. This task fell to Christian Fouchet. He circulated a second and unofficial draft. Although it was not published, it was looked upon as an expression of the French position. The clause pertaining to revision was phrased in such a way as to guarantee the establishment of communitarian institutions. The document was well received.[5] On December 15, at a meeting of the Council of Foreign Ministers, it was agreed that membership in the E.E.C. would *ipso facto* entail membership in the Union of States.

So far the atmosphere had been auspicious. A communication of January 18, 1962, from Christian Fouchet to his colleagues contained the second official draft (but the third text). It filled France's partners with consternation. The new document was a retreat not only from the unofficial draft of December but from the first official draft of November. The Atlantic Alliance was not mentioned. Both defense and economic policy were again listed as being within the purview of the Union of States. The guarantees to the communities had disappeared. And finally, it was specified, contrary to the compromise arrived at by the Council of Ministers on December 15, 1961, that admission to the Union of States would not automatically result from membership in the communities. Thus a new barrier was raised against England. Every controversial point that had been debated ever since de Gaulle's initial contacts with the heads of government in the summer of 1960 was settled in a way that coincided with the wishes of the French head of state. The author of this accomplished fact was indubitably de Gaulle himself. What motives could have inspired him to nullify eighteen months

[5] *Ibid.*, 53–59.

of laborious discussions? Did he hope to obtain additional concessions from those who had already yielded so much? Did he feel he could not accept a draft that did not faithfully reflect his principles? His televised speech of February 5, 1962, tends to support the second interpretation: "We are actively attempting to extricate Europe from the realm of ideology and technocracy and to induce it to face political realities.... We are suggesting to our partners an over-all organization to further the co-operation of states, without which there cannot be a united Europe, save in dreams, parades, or fiction."

Meanwhile the five delegations of France's partners had put together a draft treaty that resembled the unofficial text given out by Christian Fouchet in December. The most striking passage in this document was a revised clause stipulating that "majority rule would be gradually introduced in determining the will of the Council."

Despite very divergent opinions, the Fouchet Commission resumed its work on February 20. Negotiations moved ahead because the three major states were anxious to conclude them. Italy felt that a European Union of States would enable her to exert a greater influence on the major decisions of the West. The Federal Republic believed that close ties with France would strengthen its position with the United States on the question of Berlin. On March 15 the Fouchet Commission adopted a third official draft treaty containing alternative proposals on all the controversial points. De Gaulle, who on February 15 had conferred with Adenauer in Paris, went to Turin on April 4 to meet President Segni and Foreign Minister Fanfani. Of major importance was the request made by Edward Heath (in a speech delivered in London on April 10 before the Council of the Western European Union). He asked that England be permitted to participate without delay in negotiations on the political structure of Europe. Heath accepted the idea that the Union of States "should take a joint position on problems of defense." But he contended that "any European defense policy must be closely tied to the Atlantic Alliance." In saying this he was expressing a conviction and concern shared by the five partners of France, although they had not made this clear since the summer of 1960. Heath's speech merely strengthened de Gaulle's conviction that England would only participate in a European organization closely associated with the United States. There was profound disagreement about the direction to be given to a political union.

At the Council of Foreign Ministers in Paris on April 17, it was precisely over the question of England's participation in the Union of States that the split between France and her partners occurred. Spaak and Luns accepted Italy's compromise proposals regarding the Atlantic Alliance and the economic scope of the Union but they refused to approve the treaty draft if England were not to be part of the European Economic Community.

Couve de Murville, who presided, suspended the debate. In May and June the Italian government together with Ambassador Attilio Cattani (who succeeded Fouchet as president of the study commission) made several fruitless attempts at conciliation.

Throughout the negotiations, the Dutch opposed the Gaullist plan for a fundamental reason: the balance of power. Belgium joined them after November 1961. The two governments argued that a federal regime must respect the identity of the smaller states. The intergovernmental system proposed by de Gaulle would lead to a partnership of the two most powerful nations of the European continent. The inclusion of England in a political union would be a safeguard against the danger of a Franco-German entente; it would also protect Western Europe against the danger of dissociation from the United States. Such was the gist of Spaak's remarks on April 19: unable to achieve a supranational Europe consonant with his convictions, he preferred to make concessions to the French point of view if the price of such concessions was the inclusion of Great Britain.[6]

Political Europe according to de Gaulle

The collapse of negotiations did not cause de Gaulle to deviate from his line. Quite the contrary. The press conference of May 15, 1962, gave him a chance to reaffirm his conception of an organized cooperation of states and to attack the doctrine of integration. This done, he stressed the fears of his foreign interlocutors as well as the concern of the parliamentary opposition within France.

In de Gaulle's opinion, the positive results of the Common Market justified his conception of a politically unified Europe. "It is the states and the states alone that created this economic Community ... that made it an effective reality." The Community resulted from the economic and financial recovery of France and from the inclusion of agriculture. But economic construction was not enough. "Western Europe must be organized politically. If this were not done, the economic Community itself would be unable to function and survive indefinitely." Thereupon de Gaulle repeated his idea of creating political, defense, and cultural commissions with their own rules and regulations. As for the concept of integration, it was unrealistic and dangerous. "In the absence of a federating country with sufficient power, influence and skill in Europe today ... we fall back on a kind of hybrid in which the six states are willing to submit everything for decision by some kind of majority. ... There is no way, at present, for a foreign majority to constrain recalcitrant nations." In the name of realism,

[6] "Le dossier de l'Europe politique," presented by the European Parliament, Bureau d'information des communautés européennes, January 1964, p. 42.

389]

de Gaulle categorically rejected majority rule. Besides, "in this so-called 'integrated' Europe there might be no policy whatsoever." And the real danger was that Europe might "be subjected to the power of some outside force" that did have a policy. "Such a federating country might exist, but it would not be European." Political integration would result in subjection to the United States.

In short, de Gaulle discarded the notion of a supranational Europe because it limited France's political freedom. He excluded England from a union of European peoples because she wanted all European defense policies to be directly linked to the Atlantic Alliance. He rejected all political and military ties between Europe and the United States that were related to the functions of the Alliance. The remarks he made to the press that same day were revealing. In exchange for nuclear protection, "Europe would entrust to the United States the command of its forces and consequently the determination of its policies and defense strategy. This is what is called integration." A French deterrent force would enable French defense "to be once again truly national" and strategically free. Thus de Gaulle's rejection of European integration was combined with his rejection of Atlantic military integration.

The press conference of May 15 created a stir within the government. Pierre Pflimlin immediately resigned and took four M.R.P. ministers with him. On the other hand the Independent ministers, led by Valéry Giscard d'Estaing, refused to quit the government despite a summons to do so from their parliamentary group. It had balloted on the issue on May 22—the vote was fifty-seven against thirty-one, with thirty abstaining. Thus, while one section of the traditional Right supported the general's foreign policy, the M.R.P. opposed it. In a speech at Annemasse in the Haute Savoie on May 20, Pflimlin pointed out that the opposition was not systematic. He added: "A Europe of states . . . takes us back to the nineteenth century, to the Congress of Vienna. . . . Actually, a political union would have no future were it subject to the rule of unanimity."

On June 12 Edouard Bonnefous spoke in the Senate about the Gaullist conception of a united Europe. "It would be a Continental Europe based on a Franco-German protectorate, protected by a French striking force. It would stretch from the Atlantic to the Urals; in other words, it would be closed to the West and open to the East. Even if it did not claim to be neutral, it would inevitably tend to become a third force because it would act independently of the Atlantic group." Jean Lecanuet remarked that it was impossible to conceive of progress by stages if the kind of Europe one wished to build was not determined in advance. Couve de Murville declared: "What we envisage is an evolutive process." "Evolving toward what?" Lecanuet asked. "We will see," the minister retorted.

The National Assembly fared no better. On June 13 the Foreign Affairs Commission called for a vote after the debate. The minister refused. At that point, Maurice-René Simonnet read a message on behalf of the opposition. Entitled "Manifesto of the Europeans," its text was as follows: "We, the undersigned French deputies, having been unable to express our views by a vote, declare our desire to see France follow the path of European unity, which we conceive of as a democratic community of peoples, and not as a series of outworn diplomatic conferences between government leaders. We reaffirm that only a United Europe, a partner of the United States and on equal footing with it within the Atlantic Alliance, can safeguard . . . our freedom and peace." The text won 296 signatures. The motion censuring the creation of a French striking force had obtained 207 votes. But the manifesto did not involve the parliamentarians' political responsibility to the same extent as did the vote of censure. The opposition appeared stronger than it actually was.

General de Gaulle's diplomatic efforts had one beneficial effect: they placed before the public the problem of the political structure of Europe. The length of the negotiations and their subsequent failure attested the difficulty, if not the impossibility, of finding some compromise between an organized cooperation of states and integration. To raise the issue of the political institutions of Europe was to cause those who believed in one or the other to question the nature of alliances and defense as well as the geographical dimensions of Europe.

The interrelationship of these problems is equally apparent and important in another protracted series of negotiations that overlaps with the one we have just described: negotiations for the entry of England into the European Economic Community.

18

The European Economic Community
without England

England Revises Her Position

EARLY IN 1959, even before the establishment of the European Free
Trade Association at Stockholm, the weekly *Economist* raised the
question of England's entry into the Common Market. This was the moment
to reexamine Winston Churchill's axiom that England belonged to three
sets of states: the British Commonwealth of Nations, the Community of
Anglo-Saxon peoples, and Western Europe—in that order. Early in 1960
a committee of high officials, presided over by the permanent secretary of
the treasury, concluded that England should become a member of the
E.E.C., primarily for political reasons. England was destined to lose her
relative power and influence in comparison with both the United States
and the Commonwealth. Should the E.E.C. prove successful, the most
direct means of tying Europe closely to the United States in an Atlantic
partnership would be England's membership in the Community.[1] On July
23, in a debate in the House of Commons, the foreign secretary, Selwyn
Lloyd, hinted at the possibility of British membership in the E.E.C. He
enumerated what were to be Britain's three preoccupations when the
negotiations began: the Commonwealth, the E.F.T.A., and domestic
agriculture.

Thereupon Harold Macmillan put out a series of diplomatic soundings.
On August 10 he saw Chancellor Adenauer, late in January 1961 he visited

[1] Miriam Camps, *Britain and the European Community* (Princeton: Princeton
University Press, 1964), 281.

General de Gaulle at Rambouillet; finally, early in April he approached President Kennedy, who encouraged him in his endeavors.

In his speech of July 31, 1961, before the House of Commons, Macmillan finally expressed qualified acceptance of the principles inscribed in the Treaty of Rome. But before this speech he had already made certain moves: in June he had conferred with the Council of the E.F.T.A. and early in July with the Commonwealth countries. Macmillan said: "The problem is both economic and political. Although the Treaty of Rome contains economic clauses, it has nevertheless an important political goal, that of promoting the unity and stability of Europe. . . . Should the establishment of closer ties between the United Kingdom and the E.E.C. nations alter the time-worn and historic ties that bind the United Kingdom to the other Commonwealth nations, the harm would be greater than any anticipated gain." The final decision regarding England's entry would depend upon the outcome of the negotiations. For domestic reasons, such as England's imperial policies, Macmillan reiterated that England's position was not to be construed as a choice between Europe and the Commonwealth. This ambiguous statement did not convince the Labour Party. It refrained from voting on the issue of entry into the Common Market on August 3. The same ambiguity was to prevail during the three stages of the negotiations: an exploratory phase; an active and fruitful one, especially so far as Commonwealth problems were concerned; and a disappointing interlude primarily devoted to British agricultural problems.

The Exploratory Phase

Western Europe reacted favourably to the English request for membership. In his press conference of September 5, de Gaulle was somewhat cautious but also encouraging: "We are aware of the complexities of the problem, but everything leads us to suppose that this is the moment to begin to think about it. As for myself, I am only too pleased not only for the sake of my country but also for that of Europe."

At the request of the French government, the seven governments decided to open discussions. They would be advised by the Brussels Commission. The procedure was cumbersome because the Six had to take a common stand on every British demand or proposal.

The seven-power round-table conference began on the morrow of Edward Heath's Paris declaration of October 10. Heath stated that the problem of adapting the British system to membership in the Common Market could be resolved by the addition of protocols to the treaty. To this the Six immediately replied that "these protocols must not alter the tenor or the spirit of the treaty and should have bearing solely on the transitional regulations."[2] Heath quickly assured them England was not seeking preferential treatment for her trade with the Commonwealth or her domestic agriculture. Speaking to the first point, Heath said that England could not join the Common Market if the stipulations were likely to entail serious losses in trade for certain Commonwealth countries. Accordingly he suggested that such losses should be offset by supplying "comparable outlets"—that is, markets of comparable size within the enlarged community. The Six replied that after the expiration of the transitional period they would not allow special preferential trading links between the Community and the Commonwealth. On the question of agriculture, Heath was willing to agree that England should follow the continental system of price support for produce. But he hinted that he would like to see England participate in the formulation of the system. This was a vain hope. France deliberately held up the seven-power negotiations until she had extracted an agreement from the Six on the Community's joint agricultural policy. She was afraid that England and Germany, the two largest importers of food products, would prevent her from achieving her goals.

Negotiations were resumed at the end of February. The British, insecure about opinion at home and worried about the reaction of the Commonwealth countries, foolishly hesitated before suggesting compromise measures. Negotiations did not become lively until the early days of May 1962.

The Period of Activity (Problems of the Commonwealth)

On May 29 a preliminary accord was reached for the gradual elimination of United Kingdom preferences for manufactured goods from the old white Dominions—Australia, New Zealand, and Canada.

A second agreement was concluded on August 3 on exports from India, Pakistan, and Ceylon. At the suggestion of the French delegation, the Six accepted a plan to enlarge existing outlets for manufactured products from these developing countries. This was to be done within the framework of a comprehensive trade agreement with the Community. The Six next conceded to Commonwealth countries in Africa and the Caribbean the same terms they had granted to their own former dependencies.

Although the problem of agricultural products from tropical zones was more or less satisfactorily settled, difficulties arose over the treatment of products from the temperate zones—Canada, Australia, New Zealand. These countries competed directly with the products of the Community, especially cereals, meat, and dairy foods. England had abandoned her demands for guaranteed "comparable outlets," but she now asked for

[2] Report to the European Parliament on "L'etat des négociations avec le Royaume-Uni," E.E.C., Brussels, Feb. 1963, p. 14.

"reasonable outlets"—a very ambiguous term. France was reluctant to give England guarantees of outlets for "White Commonwealth" producers. Moreover, backed by the Commission, but opposed by some of her partners, she claimed that England should not be exempt from the levy on products from temperate zones in the Commonwealth. Her purpose was to uphold the principle of preferential treatment for the Community, established in January 1962. Finally, the French subordinated any agreement with England on agricultural exports from the old white Dominions to a definitive entente among the Six on the financing of agriculture. The British delegation rejected the compromise solution suggested by the Commission. The question was left in the air when negotiations were suspended on August 5, one month before the beginning of the Commonwealth Conference in London.

Macmillan visited de Gaulle at Champs on June 1 and 2. The general was surprised by the Prime Minister's intention of giving priority from now on to England's European role and his readiness to take his chances on the reaction of the Commonwealth. At a press conference of May 15, de Gaulle reaffirmed his concept of a formal cooperation of states. The following day, Macmillan emphasized his allegiance to a confederated Europe that would possess its own means of military defense. But apparently the subject of a Franco-British agreement on nuclear armaments was not discussed.[3]

What were the effects of President Kennedy's declaration of July 4 on the interdependence of the United States and a united Europe? To Kennedy's way of thinking, the two entities should pursue a common foreign policy. In de Gaulle's opinion, Europe should have its own foreign policy. One cannot help wondering whether the July 4 declaration did not serve to confirm de Gaulle's fear that England's membership in the Community might obstruct his plans for the future of Europe. Kennedy's enthusiasm for British membership seemed highly suspect to the general.

The Commonwealth Conference opened on September 10. The atmosphere was heavy with undertones of the election struggle between the Conservatives and Labour. Macmillan rejected the suggestion of certain of his colleagues that the whole vital issue of England's entry into the Common Market should be dealt with on a bipartisan basis.[4] Gaitskell passionately opposed entry into the Common Market. The conference, nonetheless, managed to avoid forfeiting the results achieved so far by negotiation. A communiqué of September 3 acknowledged that the final decision was up to the British government. The Commonwealth countries were in no position to suggest an alternative solution. In October the annual congress of

---

[3] Camps, *Britain*, 428, 429.
[4] Nora Beloff, *The General Says No* (Baltimore: Penguin Books, 1963), 134.

the Labour Party assumed a hostile attitude, whereas the Conservative Party, by a large majority, gave Macmillan a full vote of confidence.

The Disappointing Phase (British Agriculture)

The debates were centered on British agriculture. The Community system insured profitable domestic prices to farmers by means of a levy against foreign imports. In the British system, on the other hand, consumer prices were identical with those of the world market. These so-called world prices were artificially lowered because of subsidies from the overseas producer countries. British farmers were paid the difference between the guaranteed and the market price in the form of government subsidies known as "deficiency payments." The British delegation naturally wanted the gap between the price level of production and that of consumption to be reduced very gradually. It therefore made two demands: maintenance of all food guarantees and subsidies during the transitional stage; extension of the transitional stage for certain specified products. The Six, however, contended that from the time of England's entry into the Common Market, she would have to apply the rules laid down by the common agricultural policy, and that she must do so in time to meet the deadline of the transitional stage, which was January 1, 1970. Nor would the French delegation depart from this position. On the other hand, the British could not agree to accept the various compromise solutions suggested by the Commission. Negotiations were deadlocked. At this point, on December 11, a committee headed by Sicco Mansholt was formed to examine the effects of the various plans for adjusting British agriculture to the Community system.

Meanwhile there were changes of international policy that affected the third phase of the negotiations, just as they had the second. Ever since April 17, 1962, when talks of a political union among the Six collapsed, and also since Kennedy made his statement about the interdependence of the United States and a united Europe (July 4), de Gaulle had been edging closer to Germany and farther away from the Anglo-Saxons. It was during his triumphal visit to Germany that he first suggested to Adenauer the possibility of a Franco-German Treaty of Cooperation. The treaty was to be drafted in a spirit similar to that of the six-power union agreement.

Far less pliable was France's attitude toward England. Although de Gaulle alluded to a Western European union (in his televised speech of December 31) "prepared to welcome, at some future date, an England that should and would join it definitively and without reservations," he was actually filled with misgivings. The tenor of his talks with Macmillan at Rambouillet on December 15 and 18 and Macmillan's visit with Kennedy at Nassau on December 18–21 accounted for his feelings.

The Rambouillet and Nassau Conversations

At Rambouillet, de Gaulle and Macmillan discussed European defense and England's entry into the Common Market. De Gaulle apparently expressed some doubt about England's ability to effectuate the necessary adjustments to the prevailing Common Market system. Macmillan purportedly informed de Gaulle about the probable replacement of Skybolts by Polaris missiles; the Americans had found the Skybolts inadequate. It is doubtful that either of the two men suggested that French and British research and nuclear weapons should be combined.[5]

During the Nassau meetings, England's entry into the Common Market and British nuclear armament were discussed. According to Nora Beloff, the Americans had no intention of concluding an agreement with the British until after the completion of the Brussels negotiations. Kennedy had apparently been mistaken about Macmillan's chances of bringing these negotiations to a successful conclusion. He had reluctantly agreed to deliver the Polaris missiles to England. Against his better judgment, Kennedy also yielded to Macmillan's request (which the prime minister had made for internal political reasons) that he announce publicly that England would be permitted to use these missiles should 'it be in her national interest to do so. Macmillan had hoped in this way to preserve the image of British sovereignty.[6]

"The Nassau meeting, ... whose purpose was to settle a serious Anglo-American crisis," was convincingly presented by the general to his continental partners as an attempt to impose "Anglo-Saxon hegemony" and to settle European affairs "in the absence of the Europeans themselves."[7]

The General Says No

In a press conference of January 14, 1963, de Gaulle made public two closely related decisions: his refusal to accept Kennedy's offer of Polaris missiles and his refusal to admit England into the Common Market.

As we have seen in the discussion of the Fifth Republic's defense policy, de Gaulle waited until the early days of January before making his first decision. This was probably also true of his second decision. French press commentaries designed to soften public opinion impelled Heath to go at once to Paris. On January 11 he asked Couve de Murville whether the French government would oppose England's admission to the Common

---

[5] Camps, *Britain*, 468, 469.
[6] Beloff, *General*, 159.
[7] *Ibid.*, 164.

Market if the unresolved technical problems were settled satisfactorily. The answer was, "Certainly not." [8]

The press conference of January 14 was held on the same day that negotiations were resumed in Brussels. It was significant that de Gaulle dealt successively with three major topics: the English request for entry, NATO and the Nassau Accords, and Franco-German collaboration. On the "truly important" subject of England, de Gaulle began by explaining the "real facts of the problem." The first fact: "The Treaty of Rome had been concluded between Six Continental states which were all economically similar" and politically interdependent. The second fact: the treaty had "begun to be implemented practically" when "agriculture was introduced into the Common Market" at the request of France. The third fact: England, having first refused to create such an institution, and then having hampered its operation, now requested entry "on its own conditions." The fourth fact: "The nature, structure, and conditions that prevailed in England were basically different from those of the other Continental countries." The fifth fact: the British system of subsidies was incompatible with the Community's system of preferential treatment for the agriculture of the Six.

Given all this, one can but question the British intentions. Moreover, what would be the consequences of her admission? And what if other states should be tempted to follow her example? "The problem is this: Can Great Britain actually find a place within the framework of a common tariff policy, can she give up preferential treatment for the Commonwealth countries, cease to claim that her agriculture must have special privileges, and still nullify the agreements with other countries that belong to the free-trade area?" This problem had not been solved. England alone could resolve it. The questions raised had to do with the way a Common Market would function were it to be broadened to include most of the states of Western Europe. "If so, then what we have to envision is quite a different Common Market." The cohesion of its members would not long withstand the challenge of its economic relations with the United States. "The Common Market would definitely become a colossal Atlantic Community dependent upon and controlled by America, which would soon absorb the entire European Community. This is not at all what France had worked for and has accomplished; France wants a truly European institution." At this point, de Gaulle repeated his doubts about England and suggested, as a possible alternative solution, her association rather than membership in the Common Market.

Faced with this disheartening analysis of England's acts and intentions, the British government could either withdraw its request because of French opposition, call for a summit conference to force a major politico-military

[8] Camps, *Britain*, 471.

confrontation, or continue to negotiate in order to put France in the position of ending the negotiations.[9] Macmillan chose the latter way out and Heath, with his usual phlegm, followed suit.

On January 15, Heath met with the ministers of the Six, as planned. He accepted, a little tardily, December 31, 1969, as the outside date for the close of the transitional period for British agricultural goods. On the sixteenth, he made a series of proposals regarding those tariff questions that had been left dangling. On the seventeenth, in the presence of the ministers, Couve de Murville requested a suspension of negotiations. The five other E.E.C. delegations opposed the move. Hallstein, speaking on behalf of the Commission, which was the treaty's watchdog, refused to agree to the suspension. On the eighteenth, the Council of Ministers adjourned until January 28. Chancellor Adenauer, who had come to Paris on January 21 to sign the Franco-German Treaty of Cooperation, made no great effort to insure the continuation of negotiations.

The final rupture occurred at Brussels on January 29. Two phrases summed up the debate. One was uttered by Couve de Murville: "We are seeking to maintain neither a small nor a large Europe. Rather, our aim is to determine whether the Europe we are creating is a truly European Europe." The other phrase was pronounced by Heath: the negotiations, he said, were being terminated "by the decision of only one party."

The Responsibility for the Rupture and Its Effect

The adversaries were speaking for posterity. But one could not claim, as de Gaulle did, that any further discussion would be a waste of time, nor that an agreement was about to be reached, as Macmillan maintained. The controversial issues left dangling were important—the treatment of agricultural products from the Commonwealth temperate zones, the transitional arrangements for British agriculture, tariff regulations for raw materials, the steps to be taken with an eye to the E.F.T.A. countries. The Commission's report to the European Parliament on February 23, 1963, contained the following comment on the negotiations with the United Kingdom: "At times solutions to problems depended primarily on moves the British government should have made, at others on proposals that should have been worked out by the Six themselves." Moreover, the United Kingdom's request for admission entailed an obligation on its part not only to accept the treaty but also to admit the considerable progress the treaty had accomplished since its signing.[10]

9 Camps, *Britain*, 480.

10 Report to the European Parliament, "L'etat des négociations avec le Royaume-Uni", 100, 101.

Had the British government used all the means available to accomplish its purpose? In view of her attitude after 1955 toward the three communitarian institutions, "Great Britain should have known that suspicion would be aroused by her belated request."[11] Throughout this entire period she had employed delaying tactics; the factor that doubtless contributed the most to molding and strengthening the Community of the Six was the long series of negotiations with England.[12] In Nora Beloff's opinion: "History will surely decide that Macmillan also had his part in the final rupture. The long delay in starting negotiations; the even longer delay in building up British confidence in the European venture; the absence of any firm political commitment until the Government seemed to face imminent electoral defeat; the stalling for so many weeks on how to subsidize bacon and eggs; the innate reluctance to take risks and trust foreigners—all these prepared the setting for the final disaster."[13] The former American secretary of state, Dean Acheson, judged British policy severely. At West Point on December 5, 1962, he said: "Great Britain has lost an empire and has not yet found her role. She has tried to play a role distinct from that of Europe, based on her special relations with the United States and on her position as head of the Commonwealth, which has no political structure."

England's double system of relations determined her attitude toward the Continent. She never opted frankly between the Commonwealth and the Community. She attempted to preserve her relations with the Commonwealth to the end, even as she toyed with entry into the Community. The primary consideration in favor of admitting England should have been her influence in Europe and in the United States. It would have lent an Atlantic character to the enlarged Community.

And it was precisely awareness of the Anglo-American interdependence that was the dominant factor in de Gaulle's decision to end the negotiations. His first reaction to the British request had been one of skepticism. The general stressed the letter of the treaty and the required measures to implement it in order to make sure that England would not weaken the customs union, the economic union, or the Community's system of preferential treatment. But de Gaulle distrusted Kennedy's enthusiasm for a seven-power or ten-power Community. The Trade Expansion Act, announced in January 1962, was approved by Congress in September. The general regarded it as an American instrument for the economic domination of Europe. It provided for a large free-trade area which would threaten the autonomy of the Community, especially in regard to agricultural policy. Kennedy's July 4 statement on the interdependence of the United States and a united Europe

[11] Pierre Drouin, *L'Europe du Marché Commun* (Paris: Julliard, 1963), 248.
[12] Camps, *Britain*, 508.
[13] Beloff, *General*, 147.

—the two entities to be equal partners—was not at all to the general's liking. What was to prevent the present inequality from increasing? On December 21 of the same year, England has proved willing to place her nuclear weapons under the absolute control of the United States. She would therefore become the United States' Trojan Horse in Europe—an obstacle to an independent Europe.

The decision to exclude England from the Common Market involved an international risk that only the Franco-German Treaty reduced: France's isolation within a Common Market whose progress would be slowed. But the decision involved no internal risks. On the economic side, the industrialists hoped that tariffs would be maintained to protect them from British competition, and the farmers assessed the danger of a seven-power common agricultural policy. In the political domain, de Gaulle was benefiting from the peace in Algeria and the results of the legislative elections of November 1962 that gave him a docile majority in the National Assembly. The "European" opposition had been crushed.

The moment was therefore propitious for the next step in the Gaullist conception of Europe: that of a European Europe. The key passage in his press conference of January 14, 1963, was the following: "What France had wanted to achieve, and had achieved . . . is a truly European entity." This was also Couve de Murville's refrain at Brussels on January 29: "We . . . are seeking to ascertain whether the Europe we are constructing is a European Europe."

It is quite clear that this expression signified a Europe independent of the United States, or tending toward such independence. In such a Europe, with England subordinate to America, and France associated with a Germany that had not yet recovered her full military sovereignty, would not France, who sponsored an organized cooperation of continental states, be in a position to play a preeminent role?

The rupture, nonetheless, satisfied no one. It created confusion and engendered stagnation. America had to give up the idea of an Atlantic association. England could not reconstitute her former Commonwealth. The Benelux countries rejected a formal cooperation of states out of loyalty to Great Britain and the United States. The geographical expansion of the Common Market was blocked by England's exclusion. Germany, led by her aging chancellor, tried to reconcile the irreconcilable—Franco-German cooperation with Atlantic integration.

19

Franco-German Cooperation

The German Problem in 1958

THE TRADITIONAL PROBLEM Germany posed for France before World War II was that of containing her territorial expansion and of preventing her from oscillating abruptly between the East and the West in a multi-polar system.

The presence of the Soviet Union in Central Europe and the division of both Europe and Germany altered the traditional pattern. Ever since the establishment of the two antagonistic blocs, and especially after the signing of the North Atlantic Treaty, the policy of the Western powers toward West Germany was founded, as we have said earlier, on three principles: integration of the Federal Republic into a Western complex of military, political, and economic institutions; the imposition of certain limitations on German rearmament; preparation for the eventual reunification of Germany in the wake of a general agreement between the East and the West. After 1958 three factors influenced the West German situation. The launching of the Common Market tightened the bonds that linked Germany with her partners in the E.E.C.; Soviet pressure over the problem of Berlin tended to call into question the quadripartite status of the city; and, finally, General de Gaulle attempted to impose his personal conceptions about the functioning of the Atlantic Pact and the political and economic construction of Europe.

The general's attitude toward Germany fluctuated between distrust and confidence. His friendly feelings toward Chancellor Adenauer, which were reciprocated, plus the international situation, impelled him to center his strategic policy on Franco-German cooperation. He began to implement this policy from the time of his interview with Adenauer at Colombey, on September 14, 1958.

In view of Germany's dependence on the West, the chancellor had no intention of conducting an autonomous foreign policy. On the contrary, he sought the moral support of a more independent continental partner.

The general purpose of the Franco-German rapprochement was, from the French point of view, to insure West German support for the launching of the Common Market. This was important to the French economy. De Gaulle also wanted an ally when the time came to implement his ideas on the construction of Europe. In return, France would back the Federal Republic in its resistance to Soviet pressure; she would also support any attempts contemplated from time to time by England and the United States, to accept a compromise solution over Berlin and the status of Germany.

We have looked at the Berlin crisis from the viewpoint of relations between the East and the West. We will now examine it more closely from the angle of Franco-German relations.

France and the Berlin Crisis

The crisis that began after Khrushchev's speech on November 10, 1958, was acute in 1958–1959 and again in 1961–1962. Both times the Soviets issued an ultimatum. In between, a period of relative détente intervened.

The Soviet memorandum of November 27, 1958, suggested to the Western powers that West Berlin should become a demilitarized free city. If no agreement could be reached within six months, the Soviet Union would deal directly with the German Democratic Republic on the matter. The Western powers were ready to discuss the status of Berlin but only within the context of a general settlement of the German question. In the course of the winter the Soviet Union seemed to have given up its rigid time schedule but declared that if no peace treaty were to be signed by the two Germanies, it would conclude such a treaty with East Germany alone.

While John Foster Dulles was declaring the intention of the Allies "to risk war rather than to allow themselves to be evicted from West Berlin," Harold Macmillan was traveling to Moscow. This was in February 1959 and the trip was made to sound out the Soviet government. Macmillan had had no prior consultation with the Germans. The communiqué published on March 3, after his visit, concluded that it would be useful to study the "limitation of armed forces and armaments, conventional as well as nuclear, in some region of Europe chosen jointly." Adenauer reacted adversely to this suggestion. Backed by General Norstad, supreme allied commander in Europe, he denounced any form of disengagement in the West.[1]

[1] James L. Richardson, *Germany and the Atlantic Alliance* (Cambridge, Mass.: Harvard University Press, 1966), 268–69.

General de Gaulle chose this moment to expound his views on the Berlin crisis and on the entire German problem. In a press conference of March 25, he reminded his listeners that three closely connected questions has been raised by Moscow: West Berlin's communications system; the formal division of Germany into two states; the neutralization in Europe of a zone that would consist primarily of Germany. Before entering into more detailed discussion, he defined the climate of Franco-German relations: "Germany, as she exists at present, in no way threatens us. ... We even believe that she constitutes as essential element in the life and progress of Europe and of the entire world. Furthermore, ... France and Germany have decided to cooperate. On this point, Chancellor Adenauer's policy coincides with our own." He went on to speak of West Berlin; he could not allow, he said, the city to be subjected to "the Pankow system." He refused to recognize East Germany as a sovereign and independent state, since it existed solely by virtue of Soviet occupation. There followed an important declaration: "The reunification of two segments into a single Germany that would be entirely free seems to us the normal destiny of the German people, provided they do not challenge the present frontiers— and that eventually they favor integration into a contractual organization of all of Europe dedicated to cooperation, freedom and peace." Finally, he formally declared himself against the neutralization of Germany.

Thus in 1959 de Gaulle was the only one of the three Western Allies— and he is still the only one today—to recognize the Oder-Neisse line as the eastern border of Germany. But he was skillful enough to assume this position while stressing the need for reunification. Moreover, he backed Germany in her rejection of the English suggestion of "disengagement."

The second acute phase of the Berlin crisis began two years later, at the time of the Vienna meeting between Khrushchev and Kennedy. On June 4, 1961, the head of the Soviet government handed the president of the United States a memorandum inviting the Western powers to sign at an early date a peace treaty either with a unified German state or, if no understanding on reunification could be reached between the two Germanies, with one of the two separate states. In speeches on June 15 and 21 Khrushchev announced that the Soviet Union would sign a treaty with East Germany before the end of the year if no agreement had been reached on reunification. On August 13, the East German government closed its frontiers between the East and West sectors of Berlin. In September, disregarding Western protests against "a unilateral change in the quadripartite status" of the city, it built a wall separating the two sectors.

The United States was inclined to negotiate with the Soviet Union, as it had in 1958-1959, but not on the basis of Khrushchev's memorandum. The German government was worried about American intentions, which it could not oppose openly. The passive acceptance of the Berlin wall shocked the German public. It undermined, at least temporarily, German confidence in the promises of the Allies. Some apparently believed that there might be a real inconsistency between Germany's national aspirations and her Western orientation.[2]

On September 5 de Gaulle took quite a different view from that of the Americans. In his press conference the general said: "Let the Soviets stop threatening, let them help to reestablish a détente instead of hindering it. . . . Then the three Western powers can examine with them all the problems of the world, especially that of Germany." There was an embarrassing switch of ministers in the West German government. Gerhard Schroeder was appointed the new foreign minister. Adenauer went to see Kennedy in November and obtained from him assurances that the anticipated negotiations would be limited to the question of Berlin. Excluded from all discussion was the problem of Germany's status.[3] By December Adenauer had still been unable to persuade de Gaulle to participate in the negotiations. In a televised speech of February 5, 1962, the general confirmed his decision "not to negotiate on Berlin or Germany so long as the Soviet Union does not put a stop to its threats and injunctions and bring about an actual easing of the international situation."

From January to April bilateral negotiations were under way between the Americans and the Russians. They went beyond the question of West Berlin because the Americans suggested to the Russians that the states that had signed the Atlantic and Warsaw Pacts should exchange pledges of nonaggression. The German press carried the news; it caused quite a stir. Adenauer openly criticized the American plan for international control of Berlin. Kennedy, on the other hand, argued that since the United States assumed the lion's share of the cost of protecting the city, it had the right to explore any possibility of a negotiated settlement. Just as tension came to a climax, de Gaulle again reiterated his views on the German problem and Franco-German relations.

Franco-German Solidarity

His press conference of May 15, 1962, contained nothing new on the German problem: "Given the altogether precarious equilibrium between East and West, our attitude about Germany is that at present the time is not ripe to change the accomplished facts there."

[2] Henry A. Kissinger, *The Troubled Partnership* (New York: McGraw-Hill, 1965), 69.
[3] Richardson, *Germany*, 292.

A new note was sounded on the nature and aims of Franco-German relations. "There is a solidarity between France and Germany. The immediate security of the two peoples depends on this solidarity. One has but to look at the map to be convinced of this. Any hope of uniting Europe in the political, economic, and military domains rests on this solidarity. Therefore the destiny of all of Europe, from the Atlantic to the Urals, depends upon this solidarity. For if it is possible to establish in Western Europe an organization that is solid, prosperous and dynamic, then we can once again look forward to equilibrium in Europe with the Eastern states; and once again we can look forward to a truly European cooperation, especially if, at the same time, totalitarianism ceases to poison the sources."

Thus Franco-German solidarity was made to appear as the key to the construction of Western Europe and, ultimately, of all Europe.

During the ensuing months, the tightening of Franco-German political bonds was the primary objective of both Chancellor Adenauer and General de Gaulle. From July 2 to 9 the chancellor paid an official visit to France. The general returned the courtesy, visiting Germany from September 4 to 9. Both visits were marked by warm official welcomes and enthusiastic public demonstrations.

In answer to President Luebke's welcoming speech upon de Gaulle's arrival in Bonn, the general responded by extolling the union of France and Germany, first "in face of the Soviet desire for domination"; next as a "bulwark of power and prosperity" for an alliance of the free world; finally, "it should ease tensions by heralding an international understanding that will enable all of Europe (whenever the East renounces its policy of world domination—an outmoded idea today) to create equilibrium, peace and progress from the Atlantic to the Urals. The necessary condition for such a union is a vigorous, strong Western European Community, essentially a single and identical Franco-German policy."

On September 7, speaking in Hamburg to the officers of the German Staff College, de Gaulle explained the purpose of Franco-German military cooperation. "And now a colossal world threat has arisen. The Atlantic Alliance that was organized to contain it will be useless unless Frenchmen and Germans on both sides of the Rhine are in agreement." He quoted the German writer, Zueckmayer: "Yesterday it was our duty to be enemies, today it is our privilege to be brothers."

The official communiqué published in Bonn on September 7 stated that France and Germany "are convinced that their future is bound up with the gradual development of a united Europe." It announced that "practical steps will be taken by the two governments to tighten the bonds that already exist in a great many domains." The ensuing negotiations were based on a French memorandum of September 19 which suggested that an institutional character should be given to Franco-German cooperation by carrying out some of the provisions of the Fouchet plan. The German answer of November 19 stressed that military cooperation between the two nations should be worked out within the framework of NATO. This, however, would make the union less significant politically. The two foreign ministers met in Paris on December 16–17 to put the finishing touches to a treaty of cooperation. Thus de Gaulle, having failed to convince the Six of the E.E.C., hoped to achieve a Union of States on a bilateral basis.

A few days before signing the treaty de Gaulle held his famous press conference of January 14, 1963. He used the occasion to reject publicly the American offer of Polaris missiles and to exclude England from the Common Market. In enthusiastic terms he described the exemplary if not exclusive nature of the Franco-German rapprochement: "Two great peoples who fought each other terribly and for a long time are now drawn together in an identical impulse of affection and understanding. . . . What is actually happening is a kind of mutual discovery between two neighbors in which each perceives the value, merit and dynamism of the other." He alluded to the solidarity that unified them in matters of security, economic trade, and culture. Referring to Adenauer's trip to France and his to Germany, he said that he was "more than ever convinced that the new pattern of Franco-German relations rests on an incomparable popular foundation."

But did it not also rest on a certain ambiguity at the top? To be sure, the chancellor, who preferred a formal treaty to a simple accord, accepted more easily than his foreign minister, Schroeder, the exclusion of England from the E.E.C. But on January 10 he informed the American government of his willingness to see Germany participate in the multilateral atomic force urged upon the European members of the Atlantic Alliance after the Kennedy-Macmillan talks at Nassau. French and German views therefore conflicted on the question of the Atlantic defense.

The Franco-German Treaty of Cooperation of 1963

Actually, 1962 marked the high point of the coordination of Franco-German policies. The treaty was signed in January 1963. In the same year differences over its implementation emerged.

The document was obviously inspired by the conception of a "co-operation of states," which de Gaulle had detailed in his press conference of September 5, 1960, and again, after the failure of the six-member Union of States, in a press conference of May 15, 1962. The treaty provided for meetings twice a year between chiefs of state and heads of government; quarterly meetings between foreign ministers; regular meetings between the authorities of the two countries responsible for defense, education, and youth. The meetings would cover a large field. "The two governments will consult each other . . . on all important questions of foreign policy and primarily on matters of common interest, with the object of arriving at a joint decision, insofar as this is possible." Problems relating to the European Community, East-West relations, and questions arising within NATO were listed under the heading of matters of common interest. In the domain of defense, the competent authorities were to make every attempt to adjust their strategic doctrines, increase exchanges of army personnel, and work together on armaments.

The Bundestag debate on ratification revealed the serious reservations of the majority political parties. The Christian Democrats and the Liberals were not inclined to accept the treaty unless it was preceded by a preamble. The text adopted on May 16 noted that the Franco-German Treaty "does not affect the rights and obligations of the multilateral treaties" concluded by Germany. It also expressed the Bundestag's determination "to accomplish the great tasks of the Federal Republic's foreign policy by implementing this treaty," especially "a particularly close collaboration between Europe and the United States, . . . a common defense within the framework of the North Atlantic Alliance, and the integration of the armed forces of those nations that are members of the alliance; European reunification along the path opened by the creation of the European Communities, including Great Britain as well as any other nations wishing to join; finally, the consolidation of these Communities."[4] Thus the vast differences between the foreign policies of the two countries were pointed up.

The ratification debate in the French National Assembly on June 12 and 13 gave the opposition a chance to emphasize this divergence. A motion to adjourn was proposed in the Assembly and couched in the following terms: "The Assembly . . . realizes that it is necessary to reaffirm France's desire to persist in building a democratic community of European peoples based upon the gradual and limited transfer of sovereignty to communitarian institutions." The motion was voted down by 277 against 183 (41 Communists, 67 Socialists, 37 Rassemblement Démocratique, 32 Centre Démocratique out of 55). Ratification of the treaty was voted by 325 to 107, with 42 abstaining; the members of the Rassemblement Démocratique abstained while the Centre Démocratique voted in favor of the motion.

Did de Gaulle entertain doubts about the alignment of the two foreign policies? On July 2, the day before a trip he was to make to Bonn for one of the regular consultations, he addressed the two houses of Parliament. What he said attested to a certain skepticism: "The treaties, you know, are

---

4 "Le dossier de l'Europe politique," presented by the European Parliament, Bureau d'Information des Communautés Européennes, January 1964, p. 50.

like young girls and roses: they only last a brief time. Should the Franco-German Treaty fail to be applied, well, it would not be the first time in history that this has happened."[5]

In the area of defense, the treaty was applied only in regard to exchanges of personnel. The German government avoided any bilateral discussion of tactics and strategy, believing that such matters should be thrashed out by NATO. The United States and England exerted strong pressure on Germany to buy American and English matériel. They did so both for the sake of balance of payments—the German purchases would pay for the cost of stationing allied troops in Germany—and for general political reasons— France's gradual disengagement from NATO. German-American military cooperation was developing at all levels—tactics, strategy, logistics, and armaments. An agreement concluded on November 14, 1964, made the German armed forces dependent on the United States for their military equipment.[6]

However, the most serious bone of contention between France and Germany in 1963 and 1964 was the possible creation of a multilateral force. Earlier, in dealing with the Fifth Republic's defense policies, we examined the reasons for the American suggestion of a multilateral force, as well as France's reasons for opposing it. Germany supported the idea because of three major aims: to have a hand in the Alliance's strategy of deterrence with only nominal political risk; to take a first step toward European military integration, which English and French nuclear arms could subsequently supplement; to bind the United States more closely to the defense of Europe.[7] This was clearly unacceptable to the French government. When at the close of 1964 negotiations for a multilateral force seemed about to cause a rupture between France and Germany, the German government drew back and the plan was discarded.

Another important difference between the foreign policies of France and Germany lay in their respective attitudes toward the Moscow Pact of August 5, 1963, on the cessation of nuclear testing. The Federal Republic's initial reluctance to sign this treaty was due to its fear that the provisions might reinforce the current international status of East Germany. These fears were dissipated after the United States and England explicitly declared that East Germany's inclusion in the treaty in no way implied that she would be recognized as a state.

Nor did West Germany wish to be identified with de Gaulle's gesture of defiance when, on January 27, 1964, he recognized China.

5 André Passeron, *De Gaulle Parle* (Paris: Fayard, 1966), 340.
6 Kissinger, *Partnership*, 207.
7 Richardson, *Germany*, 70.

Thus, throughout 1963 and 1964, Germany was aligned with the United States on the principal foreign policy questions. She believed that European independence must not be procured at the price of loosening her ties with America. Moreover, Germany attached greater importance to American protection than to French.

In a press conference of July 23, 1964, de Gaulle expressed his disappointment with the results of the Franco-German Treaty. He said: "So far no common policy has emerged as a result of the treaty." He also gave his explanation: "Bonn is not convinced, at least for the time being, that this policy must be European and independent."

In a speech at Strasbourg on November 22, 1964, the general issued a final appeal to Germany. His justification for the reconciliation of the two countries was "the achievement in common of a great ambition which is at once very old and very new: the construction of a European Europe, one that will be independent, powerful and influential in the modern world."

A European Settlement of the German Problem

His appeal having gone unheeded, the general again gave his over-all view of Germany at a press conference of February 4, 1965. Reminding his listeners that "the German problem is essentially a European problem," he declared: "For France, everything today can be summarized in three closely related lines of action: to help Germany to become a force for progress and peace; and if she does, to help her achieve reunification; to follow whatever course will allow her to realize this." On the second question, he said that "an unresolved German problem" twenty years after Germany's capitulation "cannot last forever." He added that "a real peace, *a fortiori* the fruitful relations between East and West, cannot be established as long as German anomalies persist." On the third question, which had to do with ways and means, he said: "What should be done cannot be accomplished in one day unless there is understanding and cooperation among the nations that have always been, are, and always will be deeply concerned about the fate of their German neighbor—in short, the peoples of Europe. These people should first investigate together, then settle in common, lastly offer a joint guarantee for the solution of a question concerning primarily their continent. Only thus can Europe be reborn, only thus can a balance be maintained in Europe: it is the only road to peace and cooperation in every part of the territory that nature has attributed to it." Two major conditions were mandatory to a settlement: first, "Russia must evolve in such a way as to envisage her future not in terms of a totalitarian constraint imposed upon herself and others, but of progress achieved in common by individuals and free peoples"; second, "Germany must acknowledge, to begin with, that the solution of the German problem necessarily implies a frontier and arms settlement reached by agreement with her neighbors in both East and West." In conclusion, de Gaulle said that the German problem "can be solved only by Europe because it is Europe's concern. This, in the last analysis, is the essential objective of French policy on this continent."

We can measure the distance de Gaulle traveled between 1962 and 1965. To be sure, he still spoke of German reunification within the framework of an independent Europe stretching from the Atlantic to the Urals. But his method had changed. There was no longer any question of "settling the destiny of all Europe" by close ties between France and Germany, whose union would constitute a "bulwark of power." On the contrary, the German problem was to be settled by "the combined action of the European peoples." And by other factors as well. It was not enough for Germany to acknowledge her existing frontiers. The question of her armaments would have to be settled "by an agreement with all her neighbors"; in other words, Germany would have to be neutralized—a solution that was discarded in 1959—and a general settlement would have to be guaranteed by the European peoples.

Thus, the first question raised in the press conference of February 4, 1965, was clarified. "To act in such a way that Germany will become a reliable force for progress and peace." No longer was the general seeking to protect France against Soviet ambitions by a Franco-German union; now he was protecting France against German ambitions by a Russo-French guarantee—a guarantee between the two nuclear powers of the Continent. This new angle was confirmed by two passages in a televised interview de Gaulle gave the journalist Michel Droit, on December 14, 1965: "Germany, which is changing and about whose ambitions we know nothing, absolutely nothing," and again: "the Germans who cannot and should not supply themselves with nuclear weapons."

Why did General de Gaulle stress the reunification of Germany? One explanation of his attitude has been given by Alfred Grosser. "If France is to retain her privileged position on the Continent, Germany must not have atomic weapons. Yet her powerful position might lead her to acquire them, especially if France should refuse Germany the right to political and military integration; this will be the moment for Germany to present her national demands." It was neither easy nor desirable to subject the Federal Republic to discriminatory treatment. West Germany would not willingly give up her claims unless she could look forward to reunification. Moscow would not consent to reunification if West Germany demanded atomic equality. "A reunified Germany should have a status that will guarantee the security of her eastern neighbors." A limitation of German sovereignty in the military domain "will compensate for her demographic and industrial advantages over France."[8]

The Dialogue with the East on the German Problem

Believing that Russia had evolved to the point where a direct exploration of the German problem could be undertaken, de Gaulle initiated Russo-French talks on the foreign ministers' level. They took place in Paris from April 26 to 30, 1965, and were resumed in Moscow from October 28 to November 2. In his press conference of September 9, and again during the presidential election campaign, de Gaulle made several allusions to the lessening of the Soviet threat to Western Europe. He spoke of the growing friendship between France and Russia and of the progress of France's relations with other nations of the East.

These declarations were a prelude to his plan to visit Moscow. He announced his intentions on January 12, 1966; he was in Russia from June 20 to 29.

In a speech before the Kremlin on June 21, the general expressed the hope that new relations between East and West would have as their object "détente, entente, and collaboration." Speaking of the status of Europe, he said that France "was not happy about the rigid opposition of the two blocs." Alluding to the status of Germany, he observed that "the settlement which will one day determine the fate of all of Germany and the security of our Continent is a European concern." In the course of his talks on June 22 with the Soviet leaders, he reportedly stated that the United States should participate in the European and German settlement and that the German Democratic Republic was a legal entity, the creation of the Soviet Union.[9] Finally, he suggested that a Franco-Soviet agreement should be the prelude to an agreement entered into by "all the states of Europe."

The joint Franco-Soviet communiqué of June 29 contained the general's proposal that regular consultations should be held, but it could not conceal discord over the German problem. It declared that the two parties exchanged opinions on the subject and that they agreed that the problems of Europe should be examined first of all within a European framework. This laconic way of putting it was explained in the course of the congress of Warsaw Pact nations that convened in Bucharest after de Gaulle's trip to Moscow. According to the closing statement of July 8, a peaceful settlement of the German problem and the security of the European continent depended on "a prior recognition of the existence of two German states." It added that the path leading to reunification "implies the gradual rapprochement of the

[8] Alfred Grosser, *Le Monde*, July 19, 1966.
[9] André Fontaine, *Le Monde*, June 23, 1966.

two sovereign German states." It proposed the convocation of "a general European congress to examine the problems involved in guaranteeing the security of Europe and paving the way for general European co-operation."

Actually, the position of the Warsaw Pact states in 1966 was not very different from that of the Soviet Union as expressed in the memorandum Khrushchev handed Kennedy in 1961; it rested primarily on Western recognition of East Germany.

But the Bucharest statement in no way changed de Gaulle's general views on the status of Europe and Germany. During a visit to Bonn on July 22 he emphasized the connection between the two: "One goes with the other, all of Europe and all of Germany."

Trust and Distrust

By this succinct remark, de Gaulle expressed his fundamental political objectives such as they were in 1966; but he had revealed them only gradually.

The German government, lacking autonomy in foreign policy, concerned about reunification, security, the problem of a unified Europe, was faced with a dilemma: how could it adjust its policy to the increasingly divergent views of the United States, its principal protector, and France, its principal European partner? The solution was to play for time and to postpone the moment of decision.

During the first period of the Fifth Republic, General de Gaulle, involved as he was in the Algerian war, had to compromise with the former "European" political parties of the Fourth Republic, which were strongly represented in the National Assembly. Until 1962, his criticisms of the communitarian conceptions of Europe and the nature of Europe's relations with the United States were expressed in relatively moderate terms. The progress made by the Common Market was considerable.

Thereafter, without losing sight of his long-term objective of a unified Europe, de Gaulle attempted to take the lead, with Germany a strong second, in a Western Europe detached from the United States. In 1962, before and after his trip to Germany, he proclaimed the growing solidarity between the two countries and expressed the hope of promoting "a single and identical Franco-German political policy."

This hope was shattered in 1963. The general, with a docile National Assembly at his disposal after the elections of November 1962, was no longer obliged to deal tactfully with the champions of the Atlantic Alliance or the advocates of a communitarian Europe. He initiated a series of defiant moves aimed at the United States. The German government, obsessed by concern for its security, remained loyal to the idea of Atlantic integration; it parted company with France on the morrow of the signing of the treaty of collaboration. The major issues that separated the two countries were the multilateral force, the Moscow Treaty on the partial nuclear test ban and France's recognition of China.

The hurdle confronting the Franco-German Treaty of Cooperation was the theory of a European Europe. The other issues were resolved before Chancellor Adenauer's retirement in September 1963. His successor, Ludwig Erhard, was less concerned about the French position; the foreign minister, Gerhard Schroeder, made no effort to conceal his policy, which was alignment with the United States and eventual participation in the Alliance's nuclear strategy.

The confidence that de Gaulle expressed in Germany in 1962 changed to distrust in 1964. In an effort to neutralize Germany, he established an entente with the Soviet Union. Perhaps the prospect of reunification, which only Russia could grant, would be stronger than the Germans' obsession with security, which depended upon the United States. The condition laid down by the Soviet Union for Germany's reunification—neutralization— was unacceptable to the Western powers in 1955. De Gaulle himself could not accept it in 1959. In 1965, however, he advocated it in a statement about the European settlement of the German problem, and he urged it on the Soviet Union when he went to Moscow in 1966.

The joint Franco-Soviet communiqué of June 29, 1966, announced the decision of both governments to hold regular consultations on European and other international problems of mutual interest. Franco-Soviet co-operation and Franco-German cooperation coexisted, on paper, in almost identical terms. Was this a substitution or a superimposition?

To raise the question is to emphasize the growing German uncertainties. Always a dynamic nation, Germany had fluctuated in the past between East and West. Now divided, she needed stable partners, in harmony with each other. The quarrels between France and the United States exposed Germany to a dangerous option. Without breaking with France, the Federal Republic chose the United States and became its principal partner in Europe. General de Gaulle tried to establish a Paris-Moscow axis, a new version of an alliance in reverse, in order to counter the Bonn-Washington axis for whose existence he was responsible. "The combination of de Gaulle's abruptness and America's short-sighted reaction to it threatens to bring about what each of the rivals should fear most: a Germany increasingly absorbed in its own unfulfilled national aims and aware of the bargaining position conferred on it by its central position and growing power." In expressing this fear, Kissinger observed that the beneficiaries of Franco-American rivalry will be the nationalists or the quasi-neutralists[10]—or rather the nationalists *and* the quasi-neutralists.

The last statement of de Gaulle's German policy—reunification and neutralization—is the reverse of the Western policy of 1950—integration in a Western democratic Europe allied with the United States.

It runs the risk of upsetting the balance of forces between East and West. The danger is that one day the West Germans, attracted by offers from the Soviet Union, will draw away from American influence and succumb to nationalism in their pursuit of reunification.

[10] Kissinger, *Partnership*, 208.

20

Agricultural Policy and the
Common Market Crises

The Mansholt Plan

IN THE OPINION OF THE FRENCH GOVERNMENT and the Brussels Commission, a common agricultural policy was required to create a customs and economic union—in short, to achieve the Common Market's goals. On January 14, 1962, the Council of Ministers of the Community adopted the first regulations covering the market organization for the principal agricultural products. This done, it was possible to proceed to the second stage. On April 4, 1962, the Six voted a financial regulation creating a European fund to assist agriculture. An agency for collecting levies on imports (substitutes for tariffs), the fund was to supervise all expenditures for implementing the common agricultural policy (compensation for exports, price support for agricultural products, improvement in agricultural structures). The rules for the disbursement of money collected by the fund were to be adopted before July 1, 1965.

In a press conference of January 14, 1963, in which he rejected England's bid to join the Common Market, de Gaulle also formulated what proved to be the best definition of a common agricultural policy: "The system of the Six consists in pooling all the agricultural products of the entire Community, rigorously fixing their prices, prohibiting their subsidization, organizing their consumption among members, and imposing on each of the participants the obligation to assign to the Community any profits accumulated by importing foods instead of consuming the products the Common Market provides."

A common price for all the principal products was indispensable to the success of the Common Market and the progress of multilateral tariff negotiations with the General Agreement on Tariffs and Trade (G.A.T.T.). The United States and the Community were the principal partners in these negotiations. However, differences of opinion persisted between the French, who tended to favor the agricultural self-sufficiency of the Community, combined with some external protection, and the Germans, who were hostile to a lowering of domestic prices and favored storing cheaper foreign produce.

In November 1963 these complications led the Commission's expert in agriculture, Sicco Mansholt, to propose that a single basic price for each species of cereal be adopted for the agricultural season of 1964–1965. The basic price was fixed midway between the highest German and the lowest French prices. From an economic point of view, Mansholt favored a relatively high price for cereals; from a political point of view, his plan tended to strengthen communitarian institutions.

Several times de Gaulle exerted pressure to end the negotiations on a common agricultural policy; he also commented acidly on the Brussels institutions. At his press conference of July 23, 1964, the tenor of his remarks were both pessimistic and threatening. Observing that Germany and France "were not yet in sufficient harmony to devise a common policy," he concluded: "If this state of affairs should persist, it might in the end produce doubt among the French and concern among the Germans; the other four signatories of the Treaty of Rome might mark time and wait, perhaps, for us to break up." The threat became more specific in a communiqué published on October 21, at the end of the meeting of the Council of Ministers: "Without wishing to prejudice further conversations, General de Gaulle, M. Pompidou, and the government have once again emphasized that France will cease to participate in the European Economic Community if the agricultural Common Market is not organized along the prearranged lines." There was no reason, however, for de Gaulle to carry out his threat. On December 15, 1964, the Council of Ministers of the Six came to a general agreement on a series of measures pertaining to the price of cereals; these measures were not very different from those recommended in the Mansholt plan. The Commission was invited to make suggestions for the financing of the common agricultural policy.

The Financing of the Agricultural Policy

The general purport of the proposals adopted by the Commission on March 23, 1965, was conveyed to the European Parliament before the actual measures were submitted for the approval of the Council of Ministers. The measures contained a technical objective and political implications. Technically, they completed the financial regulations of 1962, regulated the joint carrying costs for the duration of the transitional period, and provided for the establishment by July 1, 1967, of a single market for farm produce and manufactured goods. Thereafter, all the expenses of the common agricultural policy, which were shared by the states and the European fund, would be assumed solely by the European fund, which in turn would be subsidized from the budget of the Community. Since the surplus of savings paid into the fund was far from adequate to meet expenses, the Commission proposed to pay the total of all duties collected on manufactured goods into the fund after 1967. The Community would thus have the surplus receipts at its disposal; because of the nature of the surplus, it could not be claimed by the national parliaments. As a matter of compensation, the Commission suggested increasing its powers. The last two proposals were political in nature. Their object was to grant the Community a federal budget and to authorize the Commission to determine the use to which this surplus would be put. President Hallstein, in the hope of furthering communitarian institutions, offered solutions which, viewed objectively, were favorable to France.[1] This tactical error almost spelled the ruin of the institutions.

To be sure, the Commission followed the directives laid down by the Council of Ministers on December 15. But at the opening of the Brussels debate on June 15, it was clear that no state was ready to allocate to the Community the tariffs collected on its manufactured goods. Couve de Murville, president of the Council of Ministers, reversed his prior position by declaring that until 1970 France would not ask for the allotment to the Community of the levies on her agricultural products. Since the Community had no resources of its own, there was no further possibility of strengthening the powers of the Parliament. The French minister insisted that all financial settlements be concluded for the duration of the transitional period, not for one year only as Italy was demanding. By the evening of June 30 he had not obtained satisfaction. The Commission refrained from presenting new proposals, which it usually did when negotiations reached an impasse. Couve de Murville ended the meeting and did not suggest a continuation of discussions beyond the date set, although the Council of Ministers had done so frequently in the past, notably at the end of December 1961 when agricultural problems were being discussed.

A commitment had been made to conclude financial regulations before June 30, 1965. On July 1 the French Council of Ministers published a communiqué deploring the fact that "this commitment, which went back more than three and a half years, has not been kept." It also stated that "new political and economic circumstances arising as a consequence of this final negotiation, had made any agreement on a common financial responsibility impossible." The French Council of Ministers would draw its own

[1] Paul Fabra, *Y a-t-il un Marché Commun?* (Paris: Editions du Seuil, 1965), 90–92.

conclusions. The permanent French representative in the European Community was recalled. French officials would not participate in any further meetings at Brussels.

On July 26 the Commission made a series of new proposals to the other five members of the Council of Ministers. Though they were far more in keeping with the French point of view they were not considered by the French government; the crisis of the Common Market had become political rather than technical in nature.

The Political Crisis of 1965

And indeed, it was in political terms that the general treated the issue in his press conference of September 9, 1965. He gave his own historical account of the European Communities: "The three treaties that established the E.E.C., Euratom and the Common Market, respectively, had been concluded before France's recovery in 1958. They therefore reflected mainly what the other states wanted." He then defined in more categorical terms than in 1962 his own conception of a European union: he compared the "totally unrealistic plan" of a European federation with "the plan of an organized cooperation of states," the only one that was "consonant with what the nations of our Continent really are." He justified the rupture of June 30: "The conjunction of circumstances, whether premeditated or not, of the Brussels Commission's supranational demands, the support of several delegations who declared themselves willing to grant these demands, and finally, the fact that certain of our partners, at the last moment, thought better of what they had been willing to concede earlier—all this made it necessary to end the negotiations." In conclusion, he stated that he had been able "to appraise more clearly the situation in which our nation might have found itself if such and such provision of the Treaty of Rome had been actually applied." He was alluding to two specific provisions: majority rule, which was to be called into play more frequently during the third stage of the transitional period beginning on January 1, 1966; the authority of the Commission, whose proposals had to be adopted exactly as presented by the Council of Ministers, unless amendments were voted unanimously by the Council.

These statements aroused a great deal of feeling in France and in the other states of the Community. On October 26 a meeting of the five members of the Council of Ministers was held in Brussels. France's partners sent an "urgent appeal" asking her to resume her place within the institutions of the Community. They "solemnly reaffirmed the necessity of executing the provisions of the Treaties of Paris and Rome, adhering faithfully to the principles contained therein for the purpose of achieving a gradual merger of national economies, industrial as well as agricultural." At the end of October the French agricultural associations published a white paper in which they stressed that "agriculture had not been the immediate cause of the rupture of negotiations" and professed approval of a common agricultural policy because "the world market does not offer French agriculture outlets and profits equivalent to those one might anticipate from the launching of an agricultural Common Market."[2]

European policy—this was a novelty—became one of the major issues of the presidential election campaign. Concern in economic and especially agricultural circles over the future of the Common Market certainly contributed to de Gaulle's failure to obtain a clear majority in the balloting of December 5.

At a meeting of the Council of Ministers, the Five decided to make some concessions to the French point of view and examine the institutional questions raised by France. The meeting—and this was unusual—was not attended by the members of the Commission. The accord concluded on January 30, 1966, at Luxembourg allowed for disagreements. To be sure, the joint communiqué stipulated that "when . . . very important interests of one or several partners are at stake, the members of the Council will try, within a reasonable period of time, to arrive at unanimous solutions"; but opinions differ on what should be done if there is no total agreement. France reserved the right to create a crisis in order to block any Community decision she might consider contrary to her interest. Her partners were fully aware that in practice, and because of its communitarian spirit, the Council made very slight use of majority rule. It could have been applied on several occasions during the start of the second phase of the transitional stage. But the partners of France reserved the right to invoke it only as a "weapon of deterrence" to facilitate the solution of common problems.

For seven months France refused to attend the meetings of the Council of Ministers. This was illegal: Article 5 of the Treaty of Rome stipulated that member states must make every effort to accomplish the Community's mission by "abstaining from any action that might jeopardize the achievement of the treaty's goals." If France was convinced that her partners had not met their obligations by failing to complete the financial arrangements for agriculture within the period fixed by the time schedule, she could have invoked Article 170 and referred the matter to the Court of Justice.

In violating the letter of the treaty, de Gaulle also did injury to its communitarian spirit. He attempted to eliminate from the Community those elements of integration that were inherent in majority rule and in the powers of the Commission. He was only partially successful, however, because of the pressure of French public opinion and his partners' adherence

[2] *Livre blanc des organisations professionnelles agricoles*, Paris, Oct. 1965, p. 32.

to the principles of the Treaty of Rome. Far from disguising his hostility to these principles, he attempted to discredit them before the Common Market entered the third phase of the transitional period. Since all his indirect methods of discrediting the Treaty of Rome had failed, de Gaulle launched a frontal attack. He had hoped, through his 1962 plan for a Union of States, to subordinate the Commission to the will of the various governments. And he had hoped that the Franco-German Treaty of Cooperation would enable the French position to triumph. When all this failed he openly claimed the right of veto.[3]

The Treaty to Merge the Institutions

The Common Market crisis delayed implementation of a practical reform —the plan to merge the Councils of the three communities and replace by a single Commission the E.E.C. and Euratom Commissions and the High Authority of the European Coal and Steel Community. The idea launched in 1959 by the Action Committee for a United States of Europe, sponsored by the Netherlands in 1961, was not debated by the E.E.C. Council of Ministers until 1963. The merger treaty signed in Brussels on April 8, 1965, made Luxembourg the center of the juridical and financial institutions. Membership in the single Commission was limited to fourteen. Members were to serve for a period of three years. The Council of Ministers supported the principle of a merger of the communities, in other words, of the three European treaties.

As a result of the political crisis of June 30, 1965, only Germany and France ratified the treaty to merge the institutions before the end of the year. Consequently, members of the E.E.C. Commission were still functioning as such when their duties expired on January 8, 1966. In 1966 the other member states ratified the treaty. At a special meeting of the Council of Ministers in Luxembourg on January 30, the Six agreed not to implement the arrangements of April 8, 1965, for ratification of the treaty until the governments had determined the composition of the single Commission. The decision concealed the latent conflict between France and Germany over the renewal of Walter Hallstein's appointment. He was regarded as the principal instigator of the supranational proposals formulated in 1965 for the financing of a common agricultural policy.

The heads of state and governments met in Rome on May 29 and 30, 1967, to celebrate the tenth anniversary of the treaty creating the European Economic Community. At the express wish of General de Gaulle, Walter Hallstein did not speak on that occasion. The only important decision reached at this meeting—which was beclouded by the hostile position the

[3] René Dabernat, *Combat*, Jan. 28, 1966.

general had taken toward England in his press conference of May 16—was to establish, on July 1, a single Commission for the three Communities, under the presidency of Jean Rey.

New Troubles over Euratom and the E.C.S.C.

A unified administration of the three communities seemed highly desirable. The two specialized communities had been in difficulties for several years. They were now in a state of crisis and had neither the political resources nor the economic influence of the Common Market.

At the joint research center of Ispra, Euratom was completing project Orgel—theoretical and technical studies on a new type of uranium reactor. Member states were confronted with the problem of proceeding from research to industrial development, both for project Orgel and their own study projects. But in the domain of nuclear energy the prototype could not be a small scale model and mass production was impossible. Consequently, would it be wiser to limit or to increase the number of these costly prototypes? The decision depended not only on available appropriations but also on the competitive or cooperative nature of the undertaking. In other words, what was needed was a clarification of European industrial policy in regard to nuclear energy. Actually, such a policy was neither defined nor even discussed because no over-all proposal was made by the Commission. Nor was the Commission encouraged by the governments to this effect. By a strange paradox, the United States, whose offer in 1964 to assist with project Orgel had not been followed up, was planning one or several prototypes of this kind. Thus there arose the danger that in a few years the United States would try to sell Europe and the rest of the world licenses for a type of reactor that was first studied by Euratom.

As for the European Coal and Steel Community, it was weakened by the coal crisis of 1959 and paralyzed by the steel crisis of 1966. European industry was seriously challenged by steel industries in Japan and the developing countries. Exports stagnated whereas productive capacity increased. The governments sought national rather than communitarian solutions to the problem, just as they had done in 1959. Such was the spirit of the French plan adopted in July 1966 to assist the steel industry. The German industrialists demanded similar help from their government.

The Economic Decisions of 1966 and of 1968

Negotiations on a common agricultural policy were resumed after the Luxembourg meeting. In sessions held on May 11 and July 24, 1966, three decisions of major importance were reached.

The first had to do with the financing of agricultural exports. The European fund was to take charge of all financial arrangements beginning on July 1, 1967. Half of the money would be provided by levies on agricultural imports and the rest would be made up out of budgetary contributions from the member states. The allotment of these levies established a concrete solidarity of sorts among the Six: the more a country imported agricultural commodities from noncommunitarian states (as did Germany) the more it contributed to the financing of communitarian exports (from France, for example).

The second decision was to fix a common price for all major agricultural commodities other than cereal grains (whose price had been determined in 1964)—milk, beef, sugar, rice, and oils.

The third decision, made possible by the two preceding ones, called for the total elimination by July 1, 1968, of trade restrictions on agricultural products and tariffs on manufactured goods.

All these decisions insured the achievement, well in advance of the time fixed by the Treaty of Rome (eighteen months), of a customs union, made possible by the suppression between the member states of customs duties on manufactured goods, and by the total application of a common tariff on imports from third nations. The decisions also insured the achievement of an economic union in the agricultural sector, made possible by the free circulation of farm commodities within the Community, together with the annual determination of price levels by the Council of Ministers, acting on the advice of the Commission.

An additional decision was reached on May 29, 1968, regarding dairy and meat products. Rejecting a suggestion by Sicco Mansholt to decrease the price of milk in order to limit the expenses entailed by the accumulation of surplus butter, the Council of Ministers instituted a tax on vegetable oil. It also agreed to make some exceptions to the rule of the communitarian administration of expenses for the sale of stocks. Germany and Italy were concerned about the sharp increase in the cost of the common agricultural policy.

But the very future of the customs union was in jeopardy due to the French economic and social crisis of May 1968.

The French Economic and Social Crisis of 1968

Beginning in the university, then spreading to labor and bypassing the instructions of the trade unions, a sweeping movement of contests and claims permeated France. Students occupied the premises of the universities, and shortly thereafter the workers occupied the factories. A general strike ensued which affected more than eight million workers and paralyzed the economy for several weeks, endangering the country's political institutions.

The chief of state was more surprised than anyone else. In a televised speech on December 31, 1967, he had said: "It does not seem possible that we can ever again be plagued by the kind of crises that have caused so much suffering in the past." France, he declared, "will continue to set an example of effectiveness in the conduct of her own affairs."

The origins of the crisis were material and moral: unemployment and a distribution of the national income that was unfavorable to the wage earner, on the one hand; revolt against the yoke of an excessively centralized administration, on the other. Citizens were demanding greater social justice and a larger voice in the decisions of business, education, and the urban community.

Some facts and figures should have alerted the government. For example, between the years 1958 and 1967 a comparison of the hourly wage scale with consumer prices in the Common Market countries showed that the increase in the purchasing power of wage earners during those ten years was only 23 per cent in France in contrast to 38 per cent in Germany.[4]

The government opened negotiations with employers' associations and trade unions, which culminated on May 27 in a substantial increase in wages and social benefits. Similar concessions were subsequently granted to civil servants. All in all, the average nominal increase in wages was 13 per cent in 1968 instead of the usual 6 per cent, which had been the rule during the last two years. How could businessmen assume additional expenses without increasing their prices or dismissing some of their workers, since the price of many products manufactured in France was not competitive?

The regime tottered after a first speech by the chief of state on May 24. He announced a referendum on the "participation" of students and workers in the administration of universities and business enterprises. His radio address of May 30 gave the initiative back to the government. The general announced forthcoming elections and a reshuffling of his cabinet, a reshuffling that eventually consisted merely of exchanging Michel Debré, who became foreign minister, for Maurice Couve de Murville, who was made finance minister.

Everyone wondered whether France would respect the deadline of July 1968 for the launching of the customs union of the Six. In a communiqué of June 26 the government announced that "it had decided to meet in their entirety the commitments it had made within the framework of the European Economic Community and G.A.T.T. regarding the elimination or reduction of tariffs." It took, however, certain precautions: a temporary export subsidy, a four-months' quota for automobile imports, a six-months' quota

---

[4] Office statistique des Communautés européennes, *Dix Ans de Marché Commun en tableaux, 1958–1967* (Brussels, 1968), 81, 85.

for imports of certain steel products, textiles, and electric household appliances. The unilateral nature of the French decision was emphasized on July 5 by Jean Rey, speaking before the European parliament. The Treaty of Rome's provision for mutual aid was not invoked.

The legislative elections of June 23 and 30 gave an absolute majority to the Union pour le Défense de la Republique (U.D.R.), the new name for the Gaullist party. This victory was due in large measure to the fear of a political vacuum and to the firmness shown by Georges Pompidou throughout the entire crisis. Deciding doubtless that the influence of the premier was excessive, de Gaulle replaced him with Couve de Murville on July 12.

On July 17, in stating his general policy, the new premier declared that "the two major dangers against which we must struggle are inflation, on the one hand, and under employment or even unemployment, on the other."

During the initial phase, the government gambled on an expansion of the economy and practiced a generous credit policy, resigning itself to a sizable deficit in the budget. The exchange controls established on May 29 were not applied rigidly and were eliminated on September 6.

Meanwhile, the monetary situation continued to cause concern. As early as the end of July, French currency reserves had decreased by one-third in contrast to the end of April. The outflow of capital, which was considerable in May and June but had decreased during the summer, resumed at an even quicker pace during September and October. A wave of speculation, which strengthened the deutsche mark and weakened the franc, was a reminder of the speculation that took place a year earlier and caused the devaluation of the pound. On November 12 the government increased the discount rate from 5 to 6 per cent. Everyone believed that the conference of the finance ministers of the Group of Ten, which met in Bonn from November 20 to 22, would be followed by the announcement that the franc would be devalued. But on November 24, de Gaulle decided otherwise.

However, the measures taken by France on November 26—increased subsidies for exports, increased rates on the tax on the added value—resulted in a disguised devaluation of the commercial franc, whereas the measures taken a few days earlier by the Germans—subsidies for imports and a tax on all exports—brought about a disguised revaluation of the German commercial mark.

The second phase of the French government's policy consisted in a tightening of credit, a reduction of the budgetary deficit from twelve to six billion francs, the reestablishment and strict application of exchange controls, the extension of price controls. De Gaulle's refusal to devalue the franc called for a certain amount of austerity. Can this policy succeed? Its objectives are ambitious: "to insure the protection of the French currency, reestablish a balance, and pursue without interruption an expansion of the economy," according to the premier's announcement of November 26. These aims can be realized only if both wage earners and investors have confidence in their government.

Common Market Prospects

Is there a Common Market? This is the title of a book by Paul Fabra published in 1965. The author answers the question by saying: "For the present, the Common Market merely constitutes a privileged free-trade area."[5] Is this also true at the close of 1968?

To be sure, the lowering of tariff barriers developed intercommunitarian trade. It more than tripled in nominal value from 1958 to 1967. This largely redounded to the benefit of France, whose volume of foreign trade with the E.E.C. increased from 23.5 per cent in 1958 to 45 per cent in 1967. Germany benefited less, because her manufactured goods are sold throughout the entire world. France, however, reestablished subsidies for exports and quotas for imports on July 1, 1968, at the very moment when the last tariffs between the member states of the Six were eliminated. The customs union still has flaws, particularly because of the disparity between the basis and the rates of the turnover taxes, which results in a discrimination between national and communitarian products. Although the member states decided in February 1967 to adopt a system of taxes on the added value whose rates were to be uniform by 1972, this will be complicated because of France's decision in December 1968 to increase its rates.

The economic union has been achieved for agricultural products. Will this complex and costly structure survive, in view of the fact that agricultural productivity is increasing more rapidly than the demand for food products, in an area that approaches self-sufficiency? Like the coal crisis of 1959, the steel crisis was combatted with nationalist measures—very energetic ones. These measures varied widely precisely because of the strictly nationalist nature of the policies. Efforts to establish a common transportation policy proved only partially successful. The free circulation of labor did not encounter serious difficulties because, during periods of stress, the Community brought in workers from other nations; but progress was slow in gaining for these workers the right to reside permanently in their adopted lands. Steps were taken to free the flow of capital, but they were jeopardized by the reestablishment of currency controls in France. There is no communitarian money market. The Europe of the Six has no multinational industrial

[5] Fabra, *Marché Commun*, 98.

firms because no communitarian legislation for joint stock companies and patents exists. Cooperation in the technological domain is fragmentary.

Monetary cooperation has not met the provisions of the Treaty of Rome, although they are far from being venturesome. It was conspicuously absent at the finance ministers' conference of the Group of Ten in Bonn in November 1968. The disparity between the buying power of the franc and the mark was very plain, but the French and German governments took artificial measures to avert any changes in established par values.

The experience of ten years in the Common Market points up the fallacy of the customs union approach and the economic sector approach if such measures are not founded on a common economic and monetary policy, which in turn presupposes a common political will. The customs union is but a fiction if it is accompanied by considerable monetary disparities and by quotas and exchange controls imposed by one member state.

As early as 1962, General de Gaulle declared that the Economic Community could "neither impose nor maintain itself" unless Western Europe managed to constitute itself politically. But there are increasing differences between France and her partners in the methods of achieving an economic union and also in the goals of foreign policy and defense. To assess all the obstacles to the creation of a common political authority one has but to cite France's refusal in 1965 to adopt the rule of unanimity in the E.E.C., her withdrawal from NATO in 1966, and her second veto of England's entry into the Common Market in 1967. These differences will not soon disappear if we are to judge by General de Gaulle's statement in a press conference on September 9, 1968: "Even though we participate in the Common Market, nonetheless we have never agreed to a so-called 'supra-national' system for the Six, which would submerge France in a nationless entity and would have no policy save that of the overseas protector." As long as France persists in this attitude, the prospects of the Common Market are hardly encouraging.

21

Economic Relations with the

United States

The Kennedy Round

CRITICIZED FOR ITS PRINCIPLES and weakened in its operations, the European Economic Community was nonetheless the tool that gave Western Europe a certain consistency in its competition with the dominant economy of the United States. American superiority was evident in every area: trade, industrial investments, technology, currency. France, at times backed by the Community, at others acting alone, attempted to combat the American hegemony. The cold war she waged against the United States on the economic front paralleled the cold war she waged on the diplomatic front.

The success of tariff reductions within the Common Market led the United States to foster a liberal commercial policy throughout the Western world. Congress gave Kennedy the Trade Expansion Act. This legislation, promulgated on October 11, 1962, empowered the president to reduce the current American tariffs by half, over a five-year period, provided there was reciprocity.

In 1963 a vast multilateral negotiation was begun within the G.A.T.T It was called the "Kennedy Round." The United States and the E.E.C. were the principal parties. The American objectives were to obtain a world-wide reduction of industrial protection and to enlarge the European market for American agricultural products. Throughout the protracted internal negotiations, the position of the Community represented successive compromises between French and German objectives. France was reluctant to lower industrial tariffs whereas Germany advocated their reduction, anticipating an increase in her exports of manufactured goods to the United States. In matters relating to agriculture, Germany hoped to continue importing American wheat at low prices whereas France intended to sell her surplus to her partners. On this point the Commission backed the French because the adoption of a common agricultural policy designed to create de facto solidarity among the member states would strengthen all the communitarian institutions.

The first compromise was reached on November 15, 1964, when the Community held up a list of manufactured goods that were to be given special exemption from tariff reductions. In Germany's opinion, the list was too long, but the common price for cereals, determined on December 15, 1964, was too high to suit France.

The Common Market crisis that began on June 30, 1965, held up internal Community negotiations for several months. As a consequence, multilateral negotiations were also delayed.

A second compromise was arrived at on July 24, 1966. The adoption of common prices for the major agricultural commodities other than cereals enabled the Community to make an offer to the G.A.T.T. General negotiations could now get under way. France had her way in regard to the common agricultural policy. Germany expected compensation in the form of a reduction of tariffs on manufactured goods.

General negotiations were begun immediately. On May 16, 1967, they culminated in a reduction averaging from 35 to 40 per cent on levies for industrial goods, whose total value amounted to forty billion dollars per year. This reduction, which affected between one-third and one-half of the world's trade, gave considerable impetus to commercial relations between wealthy industrialized countries. The division of Europe into two trade areas, the E.E.C. and the E.F.T.A., therefore lost some of its harmfulness and enhanced the possibility of the Free Trade Area members joining one day with the European Economic Community. For the first time the United States showed a willingness to do away with certain obstacles other than tariffs —the administrative practice of the American Selling Price, for example— which had impeded the export of certain European industrial products.

In the large-scale negotiations, the Community made its weight felt. It proved to be a business partner strong enough to hold its own against the United States. It did not permit a splintering of the partnership and, according to Maurice Couve de Murville, it spoke up "like a real European personality."

In the domain of agriculture, the negotiations resulted in only modest gains, and the industrialized nations made only limited concessions to the developing nations. The problem of organizing markets for raw materials was left up in the air.

Tariff reductions were spread out over a five-year period, from 1968 to 1972. On April 9, 1968, because of America's adverse balance of payments, the E.E.C. decided to speed up its tariff reductions while the United States slowed down theirs.

American Investments

The system of international investments enabled anyone holding a new or improved product to produce in the market in which he expected to sell and therefore to refrain from paying tariffs. Throughout the 1950's, American industrial investments were much sought after in Europe, and the French began to fear that foreign capital would be deflected from their market in favor of the British if a wide European free-trade area were created. The launching of the Common Market stimulated a flood of American investments in every nation of the Community. At first, the magnitude of the phenomenon gave rise to a great deal of satisfaction, but eventually it also caused grave concern. This injection of productive capital represented a growth factor, in view of the technological progress that was widely disseminated and the increased competition in the market. It also spelled a growing dependence in sectors where competition existed solely between European branches of American firms—in the electronic computer industry, for example.

The rapid growth of American investments in Europe was in sharp contrast to the relatively slow increase of European investments in the United States and the almost total absence of intra-European investments.

The reasons for America's industrial superiority were both quantitative and qualitative: the size and competitive nature of its domestic market; the size of the firms and the competence with which they were administered; the high profits and the allocation of large proportions of these gains to research and development.

The challenge was such that it called for communitarian solutions. For doctrinaire reasons, France was intent on seeking national solutions. In 1963, using its administrative machinery, the French government began to slow down American investments in France. It thus contravened the Convention concluded with the United States on November 25, 1959, as well as the E.E.C. Code of December 12, 1961, for liberating the flow of capital. In a customs union, however, protectionism can no longer be strictly national: products manufactured in Belgium by a Ford branch whose installation at Strasbourg the French government had not authorized, would circulate freely in France when tariffs were eliminated within the Community. The 1963 policy, somewhat altered in 1965, was completely reversed early in 1966 by Michel Debré, who had become finance minister. This did not prevent General de Gaulle, in his press conferences of May 16 and November 27, 1967, from criticizing the excessive volume of American investments in Europe.

The question was solved, however, by the pressure of economic realities, not by an concerted pressure on the part of Europeans. On January 1, 1968, President Johnson announced that measures to prevent the flight of capital to Western Europe (England, however, was excepted) would be implemented.

Research and the Scientific Industries

Although American superiority was noteworthy in several traditional industries, it was overwhelming in the scientific industries. The research done in scientific industries was financed to a considerable extent by the state because of the close connection of such industries with the weaponry of war. Technological competition and the race in armaments were thus supported by national scientific policies.

Despite systematic efforts on the part of the French government ever since 1958, despite the rapid growth of public expenditures, France in 1962 devoted only 1.5 per cent of her gross national product to research and development, compared to 2.2 per cent in England and 3.1 per cent in the United States. In 1962 France had only 6 researchers per 10,000 inhabitants compared to 11 in England and 23.3 in the United States. In France fewer technicians than engineers were trained each year whereas in other industrialized countries the proportion was two or three technicians for one engineer.[1]

With such feeble means, the French government intended nevertheless to insure the nation's independence in the major scientific industries— nuclear energy, electronic computers, aircraft, and space. We have already noted in dealing with Euratom that the national research program for nuclear power reactors had outstripped the communitarian program.

The computer industry proved a disappointment. In February 1964 the minister of finance refused to authorize General Electric to participate to the extent of 20 per cent in the financing of the Machines Bull Company, but this firm could not compete with I.B.M. He tried at first to find "a purely French solution" to the problem, but failed because of the lack of funds and technical means. In July 1964 he had to authorize a takeover by General Electric of a 50 per cent share in the capital stock of the firm. It was already too late to seek a "European solution," given the position of I.B.M., which controlled 62 per cent of the European market as well as the contracts of its American competitors with British, German, and Italian concerns. The reluctance of the American government, after France's withdrawal from NATO, to authorize the delivery of heavy computers which

[1] "Politique de la science en France," O.C.D.E., 1966. Conclusions quoted from the *L'Observateur de L'O.C.D.E.*, Aug. 1966.

could be used for the French strike force regardless of how they might be initially employed, impelled the French government to work out a "computer plan." The first steps were the merger of the two most effective national enterprises and the appointment of a delegate-general to the computer industry. He would be called upon to supervise, stimulate and distribute subsidies.

Civil aviation paralleled the progress of military aviation in cost and technical performance. The superiority of American aircraft was due to the magnitude of its military market—the industry sold to NATO member states, especially Germany. Also, planes were used far more in the United States than in Europe. The ratio of employment by American industry on the one hand, and Anglo-French industries, on the other, was 2.5 to 1; the volume of business was 8.5 to 1.[2] Therefore the work load of French and British industries was inadequate. The era of the Caravelle was over; in June 1966 Air France ordered Boeing 727's from the United States to replace it. Lord Plowden, appointed by his government to analyze Britain's industrial position, concluded in December 1965 that there was no future for independent national industry. He recommended cooperation with Western Europe. Actually, the French and British did collaborate in constructing a supersonic airplane. The Concorde reached the testing stage for various parts of the plane but the project had to be postponed several times by England because of the growing cost, which was not counterbalanced by orders for the plane from other Western European nations.

The space industry sprang into being when planes carrying thermonuclear bombs were replaced by missiles. The industry, however, also has political and commercial goals. Comsat, a company created in 1963, whose shareholders are for the most part American, will be responsible until 1969 for administering a worldwide system of telecommunication by satellites. The company was established by an international agreement concluded in Washington on August 20, 1964, under the aegis of the United Nations. The satellites are capable of transmitting data, telephonic messages, and televised pictures to all points of the globe. Doubtless the United States will put a "geostationary" satellite in orbit before 1969. It should be able to distribute television locally by means of very inexpensive receiving stations, within the financial means of any small group. Television by satellite will thus become a political tool of major importance, liable to exert a dominant influence by disseminating news and influencing public opinion.[3] It will also be a very valuable tool in advertising products. Since

[2] Christopher Layton, *Transatlantic Investments* (Boulogne-sur-Seine: The Atlantic Institute, 1966), 97.

[3] Jean Delorme, "Une politique de fusées de lancement," *Revue Politique et Parlementaire*, July–Aug. 1966.

telecommunications are regarded as a competitive field, it is very important for the European nations, proceeding either individually or collectively, to manufacture rockets and ultimately enough satellites to produce a complete television program.

Two European intergovernmental organs were created in 1964, one for the launching of satellites (E.L.D.O.—European Launcher Development Organization), the other for space research (E.S.R.O.—European Space Research Organization). These agencies disposed of far less capital than did other agencies devoted to similar goals in the six billion dollar budget of the National Aeronautic and Space Administration (N.A.S.A.) of the United States. After reducing the amount of money allocated to E.L.D.O. in July 1966, the British government decided in April 1968 to put a firm ceiling on its contributions. At this same time, Italy made a similar decision in regard to E.S.R.O. Thus two serious blows were dealt to the first experiments in European cooperation, experiments which failed to arouse sufficient political enthusiasm. There is a danger that Europe will thus give the United States a monopoly in heavy rockets. This would result in abandoning a project to establish a network of telecommunications distinct from the worldwide American technological network.

On November 26, 1965, France succeeded in putting a satellite in orbit with the help of the first French rocket, the "Diamant." In 1967 France was disappointed in the "Coralie," the second stage of a European rocket sponsored by E.L.D.O. She built an artificial satellite, "Symphonie," together with Germany. Apparently France has dropped an ambitious project to set up her own telecommunication network to serve the South American, African, and Middle Eastern countries (Project Safran).

It was assuredly with the medium-term prospect of a direct transmission to private television stations that France concluded an agreement with the Soviet Union on March 22, 1965. The contract was for Russia to adopt French color television, Secam. At a meeting in Oslo in June 1966, most of the Western European states seemed to favor the German-American system, Pal (Belgium and Luxembourg adopted both systems simultaneously), largely out of fear of the political developments that might emerge as a result of the first Franco-Soviet agreement after de Gaulle's trip to Moscow in June 1966.

Europe's Technological Position

The flow of trade and international investments and the impact of the national policies of research point up the technological gap between Western Europe and the United States. So does the flow of technical exchange. In

1961, a comparison of costs to dividends in "know-how," as well as of the number of applications for patents, showed a ratio of 5.6 to 1 in favor of the United States.[4] The lag in Europe was especially marked, and constantly increasing, in the scientific industries.

New products manufactured in the United States differed from those made in Europe not only in quality but also in kind. Competition derived from the temporary monopoly of a product rather than from its price. The strength of an economy soon began to be assessed in terms of its capacity to increase production not only by investments in improved products but also and especially by the amount of research spent on new products. Economic power and growth were therefore determined by research capacity.

Confronted with these new forms of competition, Europe needed to work out new industrial and research policies.

A farsighted industrial policy would be to transform the Community into a real economic union by granting it a corporate legislation and a synchronized fiscal policy and enlarging the market to include England and her powerful multinational concerns. The E.C.S.C. crisis and the absence of any communitarian legislation on corporations and patents showed that the Six were not yet ready in 1968 to adopt a common industrial policy.

An effective research policy would call for a pooling of all findings, a common program, decisions regarding specialization and association on the basis of the resources of each partner; it would call for arranging state orders according to category, and also for including England, whose technological superiority to the Continent in several domains was indisputable. The Euratom crisis, the absence of a European university, France's second veto on England's entry into the Common Market, were proof that the Six were far from ready to embark upon a common research program. To be sure, the ministers in charge of scientific problems retained, at a meeting in Luxembourg on October 31, 1967, six sectors in which technological cooperation on a Common Market scale seemed desirable. But after the rejection of England's request to join the Common Market, the Benelux countries slowed down the implementation of this decision. A common scientific program calls for implementation, both in industry for civilian uses and in the manufacture of armaments—all of which are closely connected. It calls for a mutual trust that transcends technology and which is inconceivable without common objectives in foreign affairs and defense.

As Diomède Catroux has written: "In the absence of a common foreign and defense policy for the duration of a broad technological program, any

[4] C. Freedman and A. Young, *Research and Development Effort* (Paris: Organization for Economic Cooperation and Development, 1965), 53.

attempt at major technological cooperation would be marred by misgivings."[5]

France's scientific policy achieved a certain amount of success, considering the volume of appropriations. But the government's ambition to insure national independence in the principal scientific industries was not realistic in an economy whose industrial production is approximately one-half of that of England and the Federal Republic, and one-tenth of that of the United States.[6]

If Europe is to compete technologically, an economic union that includes England as well as a political union are necessary. The Gaullist conception of Europe is opposed to such a turn of affairs. The warning issued by Jean Monnet in Saarbrücken on January 25, 1968, should be taken seriously: "Unless there is a merger of her resources, in ten years Europe will be an underdeveloped continent."[7]

[5] Diomède Catroux, "Rapport sur l'elargissement de la Communauté européenne et les responsabilités economiques et politiques de l'Europe dans le Monde," *Parlement Européen*, July 1966, Document 93, p. 9.

[6] R. Wagenführ, "Die industrielle Weltproduktion 1950 bis 1964, "Office Statistique des Communautés Européennes, Informations Statistiques, 1965, no. 4, Table 4, p. 11.

[7] *Figaro*, Jan. 26, 1968.

22

Another Veto against England

The Labour Party Rallies to Europe

AFTER JANUARY 1963, when France vetoed England's bid to join the Common Market, Harold Wilson blamed the Conservatives for having negotiated under humiliating conditions. His electoral campaign stressed the new role England would play in the Commonwealth as an alternative to the European role Macmillan had urged upon her.

Upon assuming office in October 1964, Wilson was immediately confronted with a major monetary crisis. England had to borrow three billion dollars from the United States and Europe on a short-term basis in order to protect the pound. This crisis altered Wilson's conception of England's position in the world. He realized that his country would have to choose between dependence on the United States or collaboration as an equal with the nations of Western Europe. He knew that the scientific industries— computers, aeronautics, nuclear research—could be profitable only on a European scale. He assessed the split in the Commonwealth precipitated by the United Nations' decision to invoke economic sanctions against Rhodesia. He was oppressed by the silence he was forced to maintain on the Vietnam war to avoid antagonizing the United States.

"Mr. Wilson's conversion," Anthony Sampson remarked, "was far more surprising than Macmillan's . . . but also more total."[1] 1966 witnessed the first signs of a rapprochement with Europe. One such sign was the appointment of George Brown as foreign secretary. On January 26, 1967, Wilson declared that England must pursue a European policy. Before the

[1] Anthony Sampson, "La Grande Bretagne s'engage vers l'Europe," *Le Monde*, Oct. 20, 1967.

Council of Europe at Strasbourg, he denounced "the enslavement of American industrial society." Accompanied by George Brown, he toured the capitals of the Europe of the Six. His actions were approved by the Confederation of British Industries. By the beginning of 1967, according to the opinion polls, 71 per cent of the British favored England's joining Europe, compared to 40 to 50 per cent in 1961.

On May 2, 1967, Harold Wilson, speaking before the House of Commons, proposed that England should join the European Economic Community. He said that his government "is ready to accept the Treaty of Rome, provided the necessary adjustments for the admission of a new member are made." He realized that "the agricultural policy of the Community is an integral part of the E.E.C." He was convinced, he said, that "Europe has a chance today to take a big step forward toward political unity." After an impressive debate, the government's proposal was adopted on May 10 by an overwhelming majority: 488 to 62.

On May 11 England's request to become a member of the E.E.C. was followed by similar requests from Ireland and Denmark. Norway was soon to emulate the example of its three partners in the European Free Trade Association.

The Quasi-Veto of May 16, 1967

At a press conference on May 16, without prior consultation with France's Common Market partners, General de Gaulle decided to answer the British prime minister. He was to meet his associates on May 29 to commemorate the tenth anniversary of the Treaty of Rome.

He vigorously reiterated the arguments he had advanced in 1963 and added a few others. Referring to economic considerations, he stressed again England's inability to withstand the increase in prices that would result from the application of the common agricultural policy. For the first time he mentioned the monetary problem. England was obliged to curb capital movements because her currency was overvalued. The position of the pound as a reserve currency and the handicap of the sterling balances were incompatible with the "monetary parity and stability" that were essential prerequisites of the Common Market.

Alluding to political considerations, the general again underscored England's special relations with the Commonwealth and the United States. He concluded that England's policies could not be reconciled with those of the Six "unless, in matters of defense, the British reverted to the principle of total self-determination, or unless the Continental countries gave up the idea of forging a European Europe." He said he was disturbed by the requests from other nations of the European Free Trade Association that wished to join the E.E.C. The admission of additional members would radically alter "the inspiration, size, and decisions of the organization which the six constitute today."

At the summit meeting in Rome, in a communiqué dated May 30, General de Gaulle obtained a unanimous agreement not to admit England until the question had been examined by the E.E.C. Council of Ministers.

Despite the quasi-veto of May 16, Wilson accepted the general's invitation to visit him at the Grand Trianon on June 19. The prime minister was received with great pomp but he came away without having obtained a promise to negotiate.

At the Council of the Western European Union, which met at the Hague on July 4, George Brown declared—and this represented an important step forward—that England was ready to accept the common external tariff, whatever it would amount to, after the reductions made by the Kennedy Round had been put into effect.

At the Council of Foreign Ministers of the Six which was held in Brussels on July 10, Maurice Couve de Murville raised another political objection: a broadening of the Common Market might lead the eastern nations to close ranks so that "the relations between the two halves of Europe, which at the moment are improving, may once again present difficulties." Thus, Britain's membership might impede a détente between the two blocs. The French minister persuaded his colleagues to ask the advice of the Brussels Commission. Jean Rey had succeeded Walter Hallstein as its president.

The staggering blow of May 16 was followed by dilatory tactics.

The Advice of the Brussels Commission

According to the Commission's report of September 29 to the Council of Ministers, "the membership of states with ancient and deep-rooted traditions of balance and democracy will be of great value to the Communities from a political point of view." To prevent the increased number of member states from complicating the decision-making process, the Commission suggested that "the institutional regulations governing the treaties should be applied without compromise"—a direct allusion to the application of majority rule which France had tried to postpone. In order to take advantage of this chance to broaden the Community, the Commission wanted the member states to make some real progress in the field of political unity.

The report observed that "the extension of the Common Market to countries that have attained a level of development comparable to that of the Six will facilitate a better division of labor, an expansion of the economy, and an increase in the potentialities of mass production." It assessed precisely the impact of the common agricultural policy on England. The cost of living would increase approximately 3 per cent; and England would be confronted with problems that resulted from her commitment to buy butter from New Zealand and sugar from the Commonwealth.

The observations on economic and financial problems were altogether different in their import. The Commission referred to the chronic difficulties the British economy had encountered in trying to achieve a rate of growth comparable to that of the Six while maintaining at the same time its external balance of payments. The Commission envisaged the possibility of fresh assaults on the pound, primarily because of the current distribution of sterling balances. The Commission doubted England's ability to maintain a 3 per cent growth rate in the forthcoming years. It believed the British economy would benefit from membership in the Common Market only if "measures of adaptation that will make possible a return to permanent equilibrium are adopted quickly enough." Actually, the Commission recommended that the pound be devalued and no longer used as a reserve currency. In this respect, the Commission was of the same opinion as the French government, the difference being that it expressed its views very tactfully, instead of in categorical terms.

Finally, to eradicate the uncertainties that persisted, the Commission advised the states that had requested membership to begin negotiations forthwith and in whatever manner they might deem appropriate.[2]

In a speech on October 5, Pierre Mendès-France suggested that the British candidature should be utilized to organize close monetary co-operation between England and the Six through the creation of a European reserve pool. Europeanization of the pound would open up new markets fort he continental countries. The monetary reserves of the Six could facilitate in part the refunding of the sterling balances.[3] In London, the chancellor of the exchequer, James Callaghan, expressed interest in these suggestions.

Such monetary cooperation, however, did not interest Couve de Murville. He told the Council of Ministers of the Six, at a meeting in Luxembourg on October 24, that England was in no position to assume the obligations of membership in the Common Market. Before negotiating, she would have to reestablish her balance of payments and transform her monetary system.

The Devaluation of the Pound

The British government could have devalued the pound in 1964 and shifted the blame for its decision onto the poor administration of the

[2] Report of the Commission of the Council Concerning the Requests of the United Kingdom, Ireland, Denmark, and Norway to Become Members. Brussels, Sept. 1967, pp. 19, 13, 32, 38, 41, 42, 43, 86.

[3] *Le Monde*, Oct. 7, 1967.

Conservatives. But it did not do so, primarily because of the United States, which considered the pound the dollar's first line of defense. It could have devalued the pound after the 1966 elections, at a time when it was asking the nation to accept a courageous program of deflation. The cabinet was divided. Its deflationary policy did not lead to the restoration of a healthy balance of payments within the prescribed time limits. The two increases in the bank rate—on October 19 and November 9, 1967—did nothing to lessen the pressure on the pound. On November 18 the pound was devalued 14.3 per cent. This was a moderate devaluation and as such was acceptable to both the United States and the member states of the Community. It caused no chain reaction.

On the eve of devaluation, when the Group of Ten met at the International Bank in Basel to discuss lending England another large sum, France demanded strict terms for the loan. On the morrow of devaluation, France agreed to participate in a loan to England through the Monetary Fund. But she was the only member state of the Community that refused to share in a second loan to be granted by the central banks. Finally, at the height of the crisis, France let it be known that on June 1 she had withdrawn from the London gold pool to which the United States and the principal industrialized countries of Western Europe belonged.

It is of course true that France was in no way responsible for the devaluation of the pound, which was caused by financial and psychological factors. But her conduct was certainly not inspired by the spirit of solidarity that generally prevailed among the Western states when one of them was in the throes of a monetary crisis.

General de Gaulle regarded devaluation "as the first step in a movement to break up the sterling zone, on the one hand, and on the other, to terminate the coupling of the dollar with the pound, thereby inaugurating a reform of the international monetary system."[4]

This aspect of Gaullist policy will be discussed in the next chapter.

The Refusal to Negotiate—November 27, 1967

Devaluation would help England to make the necessary adjustments to the common agricultural policy and pave the way for the restoration of her balance of payments. Meanwhile, the British government declared it was ready to discuss the role of the pound as a reserve currency.

In his press conference of November 27, 1967, de Gaulle appeared oblivious to these new developments. On the contrary, he referred to the pre-devaluation report of the Brussels Commission "which demonstrates very clearly that the Common Market is incompatible with England's

[4] René Dabernat, *Combat*, Nov. 24, 1967.

economy in its present state." He reiterated his objections to English agricultural policy, charging that it was incompatible with that of the Community. He also stressed the restriction of capital movement in Britain, contrasting with the monetary freedom within the Six. He spoke of the possibility of a free trade area that would extend throughout Western Europe, or of a European multilateral treaty similar to the Kennedy Round. He added: "But in either case, we would first have to abolish the Community and break up its institutions." France, he said, could not "begin negotiations with the British at this moment because they might lead to the destruction of European unity which France has striven to achieve." At the very most, in order to facilitate matters for England, the French government might agree "to some arrangement ... that would immediately promote trade" between the Six and the four candidates for membership. He concluded: "If Europe is to counteract the vast power of the United States, the ties and regulations of the Community must be strengthened, not weakened."

This pronouncement illustrates the inconsistencies of General de Gaulle's foreign policy. How could the vast power of the United States be counteracted by rejecting England's membership and thereby limiting the geographical expansion of the Community? Or by refraining from applying the institutional regulations governing majority rule? The latter was a fundamental prerequisite for the consolidation of the Community.

The truth is that the general had other plans. It was precisely because England accepted the main economic and monetary conditions laid down by France that de Gaulle vetoed not England's entry into the Community but rather any negotiations prior to her entry. His refusal to negotiate limited the possibility of a debate among the Six on the unspoken political reason for the rejection of Great Britain's candidature: England's presence would change the balance of power within the enlarged Community. France would no longer enjoy the freedom of action which the present situation afforded her. She had been leading in the political game and Germany had been following her lead.

The November 27 veto was a test of Franco-German solidarity. On November 30 Wilson announced that Great Britain had requested entry into the Community and that he would reject any association short of full-fledged membership. The Council of Ministers met in Brussels on December 18 and 19. A crisis seemed inevitable. The communiqué issued by the Six indicated, however, that no rupture had occurred. Agreement was reached on a diagnosis of the situation but opinions differed on what action to take. All the member states believed that the reestablishment of the economic and monetary situation of Great Britain was of major importance, that there had been progress in developing procedures for improving the situation,

but that more time was required. Five of the member states, in addition
to the Commission, felt it was necessary to begin negotiations immediately
in order to make preparations for England's eventual membership. France,
however, "believes that the process of improving the British economy
must be completed before England's request can be reconsidered."

The conciliatory attitude of Germany saved the day. It was due to
General de Gaulle's warning to Chancellor Kiesinger on January 13 and
14, 1967, when the head of the German government paid him a visit in
Paris. Kiesinger had been told that acceptance of England's request would
put an end to Franco-German collaboration and that the unity of Europe
would be jeopardized. In his first speech to the Bundestag, the chancellor
had given priority to cooperation with France.

It was in this spirit that early in 1968 the Federal Republic attempted to
give substance to the "arrangement" to which the general had alluded in
his press conference. Kiesinger used the occasion of his visit to Paris on
February 16 to present the initial draft of a trade agreement. However,
when the foreign ministers of the Six met in Brussels on March 9 and in
Luxembourg on April 5, serious differences persisted between the French
and the Germans on basic questions as well as procedures. After the final
meeting, no further progress was reported toward a trade "agreement."

England Falls Back on Europe

Governmental expenditure abroad were largely responsible for the
difficulties encountered by the pound. A revision of England's foreign
military commitments was inevitable. Great Britain maintained bases and
troops in the Persian Gulf, Malaysia, Singapore, and Hong Kong. Her
navy cruised the Indian and even the Pacific Oceans.

Early in 1967 England decided on the withdrawal of her overseas bases
with the exception of Hong Kong, and also the gradual redeployment of
the troops posted east of Suez. The program was to be completed by 1975.
Immediately after devaluation, the government speeded up the operation,
making 1971 the outside date for completion. Wilson announced this
decision on January 16, 1968. He said: "Our security resides fundamentally
in Europe." The 1968 White Paper on defense provided for a transfer of
navy forces from the Indian Ocean to the Mediterranean. In May 1968
England substantially increased her land and air contribution to the NATO
forces posted in Germany. Thus England's retreat from Asia benefited
Europe.

But her retreat left the United States confronting the Soviet Union in
the Middle East and China in Southeast Asia. British participation in the
Southeast Asia Treaty Organization (SEATO), in CENTO, which united

the pro-Western Middle Eastern states, and in the pact that united England with Australia, New Zealand, and Malaysia, became purely nominal.

Determined to increase her contribution to the defense of Europe, England maintained close technological cooperation with the Continent. Reductions in the 1968 budget did not affect the three Anglo-French projects: the tunnel under the channel, the commercial plane, the Concorde, and the military plane, the Jaguar. They did affect her order for the American army plane, the F 111. On the other hand, in May 1968 England withdrew from the European Launcher Development Organization.

Great Britain's new political objectives were clearly defined in a speech delivered by Lord Chalfont on September 15, 1967: "We hope to exert, from a European base, all the influence we can in world affairs." This goal was more in keeping with England's economic means. In short, Great Britain was seeking in Europe compensation for her empire. When the time comes, she will be an active participant in the construction of Europe.

This was the meaning of the decision to join the Action Committee for a United States of Europe made by the three major British political parties on October 24, 1968 (Jean Monnet was founder and president of the committee). The terms of the Labour Party's letter, which Harold Wilson signed, were significant: "Our party believes that the political, economic, and technological integration of Europe is essential if Europe is to achieve its great potentialities."

The British political parties reached this decision after the new French veto pronounced by de Gaulle in a press conference on September 9, 1968: "Our desire not to risk an Atlantic absorption is one of the reasons why, much to our regret, we have until now postponed Great Britain's entry into the present Community."

23

The Gold War against the eAnglo-Saxons

Changes in the Balance of Payments Situation

DUE TO THEIR TECHNOLOGICAL SUPERIORITY, the United States ran a surplus on its trade and patent balances with Western Europe. This surplus was compensated by the flow of American private direct investment.

Despite an approximate balance in the accounts with Western Europe, the United States' global balance of payments has shown a deficit since 1960. This is due in large measure to gifts and loans to developing countries and to military expenditures abroad. It illustrates the political responsibilities of a world power whose economic condition, at least until 1965, has been sound.

The same is not true of England. In 1960 and again in 1964 she had a deficit in her balance on current accounts as well as the customary deficit in her balance of long-term capital. Her global balance has remained precarious ever since. A low rate of productivity and insufficient domestic investments combine to make Britain's economic position most unsatisfactory.

Unlike the British and the Americans, the Common Market nations have global surpluses. They benefit from the flow of American private investments and accumulate credit balances in their current accounts with non-member states.

For the first time since the war, the two nations with reserve currencies simultaneously show deficits in their balance of payments. This new phenomenon in international monetary relations entails the danger of speculative movements of capital in a liberal system based on the external convertibility of European currencies.

It is in the common interest of industrialized nations with a financial market at their disposal to forestall such capital movements. This was the purpose of the General Agreements to Borrow concluded in Paris on December 15, 1961, between the United States, England, the five Common Market nations (Luxembourg and Belgium together count as one), Sweden, Canada, and Japan. Wilfrid Baumgartner was the prime instigator. States belonging to the Group of Ten granted themselves additional rights to draw from the International Monetary Fund. At the express and justifiable demand of France, the credits were granted to debtor nations in accordance with a special procedure that reserved the decision-making powers to the lending nations, who can lay down certain conditions regarding their use.

Moreover, the Gold Exchange Standard, which had certain advantages when there was a surplus in the American balance of payments and the dollar was in demand, presented certain disadvantages when the dollar supply exceeded the demand. The accumulation of dollars by certain members of the Group of Ten allowed the United States to borrow in large amounts without conditions or reciprocity.

In the annual meetings of the Monetary Fund and among experts, discussion centered on reforms in the international monetary system. Major problems were the need for new liquidities and the means of creating and distributing them. Several times, especially at the Tokyo meeting in September 1964, France criticized the way the Gold Exchange Standard functioned. The Bank of France converted a part of its dollar holdings into gold.

First Skirmishes

In his press conference of February 4, 1965, General de Gaulle advocated a return to the gold standard. He criticized the effects of the Gold Exchange Standard: the willingness of a number of nations to accept dollars in settlement of international surpluses "made it possible for the United States to incur indebtedness abroad with impunity." He believed that this inflationary flood of dollars would incline the United States toward "a growing propensity to invest abroad"; this would lead some countries to "an expropriation of sorts of one or another of their enterprises." He wondered "how far-reaching the difficulties would be if the states which hold dollars should decide sooner or later to convert them into gold." He advocated "the establishment of international exchanges ... on an indisputable monetary basis that does not bear the imprint of any particular country"; and he maintained that "no currency is valid save in direct or indirect, in actual or supposed, relation to gold."

The political objective was to use the dollar to combat the supremacy of the United States. If other central banks, following the example of the Bank of France, converted their dollars into gold, the result could very well be a rush on the declining gold reserves of the United States, a devaluation of the dollar and a serious loss of prestige for the United States.

The theory that the strength of a currency can be measured by the supply of gold held in the central bank is contradicted by the facts. The strength of the dollar rests on the economic and industrial potential of the nation. A dominant economy always leaves its imprint on an international monetary system. Before 1914 the gold standard was a pound sterling standard. The Gold Exchange Standard today is the dollar standard.

If the American policy accommodates itself to the maintenance of global deficits in payments, the European states, the principal holders of dollar balances, will continue to suffer inflationary pressures. If the United States should decide to restore its balance of payments, stop the flow of investments, reduce its imports, and continue its aid to the Third World, a recession would ensue, and Europe would be the principal victim.

The Deterioration of the International Monetary System

The international monetary system has continued to deteriorate ever since de Gaulle's press conference of February 4, 1965, when he took a firm position in favor of the gold standard.

The deficit in the American balance of payments grew as the war in Vietnam was escalated. Expenses for troops and matériel ran high. The American administration had failed to take the necessary budgetary and fiscal measures that might have reduced the pressures at home and consequently the deficit abroad.

The rise in interest rates in the United States made it difficult to protect the pound sterling. Encouraged by the Americans, the British government chose the path of deflation without devaluation. In 1966 efforts were redoubled to achieve deflation. As a consequence, unemployment increased. This was accompanied by a reduction in the balance-of-payments deficit. But the desired goal was not attained.

An overflow of dollars, plus the intrinsic weakness of the pound, aroused anxiety among those who held both reserve currencies. It encouraged the hoarding of gold. For this reason, after 1966 the gold supply ceased to increase in the Western world. America's gold reserves continued to decline and the gold reserves of the Common Market countries continued to increase.

The Monetary Fund and the Group of Ten discussed possible measures to implement a much-needed reform of the international monetary system. Debate centered on the problem of international liquidities, in other words, on the means of payment—gold, currency, or credit—which would enable the authorities of the various countries to settle their accounts. Nations that maintained a chronic deficit, like the United States and England, claimed that the level of international liquidities was inadequate and advocated a substantial expansion of their right to draw from the Monetary Fund. Countries that had a surplus, like the E.E.C. nations, considered the level of liquidities entirely adequate.

The Offensive Strategy of France

The press conference of February 4, 1965, was only a skirmish. General de Gaulle's press conference of May 16, 1967, marked the beginning of a financial offensive against the Anglo-Saxons.

On the morrow of England's request to join the European Economic Community, de Gaulle openly declared that the British currency was over-valued and cast doubt on the ability of the pound to achieve stability. Alluding to the external solidarity which for some time the Six had been made to feel, he attributed it especially to "the pressure exerted by the British and the Americans to induce Europe to accept, at a sacrifice and in order to correct the deficit in their balance of payments, the establishment of an artificial monetary expedient, referred to as new liquidities." Since such an expedient was no longer based on the value of gold, it "would merely add an inexhaustible source of international inflation to that already constituted, under cover of the Gold Exchange Standard, by the arbitrary and excessive release and export of dollars." One month later, France withdrew from the gold pool, although the decision was not made public until November. Created in 1961, the gold pool was an organ of the central banks of the United States, England, Switzerland, and the Common Market countries. It was designed to bolster the $35-an-ounce rate for gold and to meet the demand for nonmonetary gold (stemming from industry and gold hoarders) on the London market. The withdrawal of France increased the American contribution to the pool from 49 to 59 per cent.

Thus, the financial war was waged on three interdependent fronts: the parity of the pound, the possible creation of new liquidities, and gold speculation.

The circumstances that led to the devaluation of the pound have been set forth in the preceding chapter. France did not play a decisive role in this move, which had been delayed too long, but she did not respond generously to England's request for international assistance.

When devaluation of the pound began to appear inevitable, a wave of gold buying commenced. It continued throughout the month of November, mainly at the expense of the American gold reserves.

At his press conference of November 27, 1967, despite the devaluation of the pound, de Gaulle rejected the idea of embarking on any negotiations for England's entry into the Common Market. He also continued his offensive on the financial front. Once again he stressed that, under cover of the Gold Exchange Standard, the dollar was inflated. Again he spoke out against "the abuses" of American investment in Western Europe, the sum total of which, over the last eight years, equalled the accumulated deficit in the American balance of payments—a disputable correlation. In conclusion, he expressed the hope that "the storms presently raging, which are in no way the doing of France, and which have swept away the value of the pound and threaten that of the dollar, will eventually bring about the reestablishment of an international monetary system, the immutability, impartiality, and universality of which constitute the prerogatives of gold."

The Defense Strategy of the United States

Once the pound was devalued, the dollar was in jeopardy. The American government reacted slowly. On January 1, 1968, the president of the United States prescribed a suspension of direct American private investment in Europe, with the exception of England, and urged Congress to enact a tax increase in order to reduce the budgetary deficit. Doubts arose over the efficacy of prohibiting overseas investments and over the chances of achieving a quick improvement in the fiscal situation. In February this caused a second wave of gold buying in the London market which exceeded that of November 1967. The buyers expected a reevaluation of the price of gold in relation to dollars. On March 17 the United States decided to permit the establishment of two different prices for gold. The official rate of $35 per ounce would be maintained for all transactions between the central banks. But the price would be free for non-currency purposes since the gold pool of London had ceased to exist. Thus the free convertibility of the dollar for gold was abolished. The American decision resulted in an embargo on gold, the objective of the United States, unlike that of France, being to decrease the monetary use of gold.

Since France was no longer a member of the gold pool, she was not invited to discuss the matter in Washington on March 17. On Friday, March 15, all the gold markets in Europe—notably the London, Zurich, and Frankfurt markets—were closed. Nonetheless, the Bank of France was officially instructed to keep the Paris market open. The purpose was to point up the disparity between the official and the free-market rate for gold.

Shortly after the embargo on gold, the Group of Ten met in Stockholm to study the proposal of the International Monetary Fund. Earlier, in September 1967, a Fund meeting had been held in Rio de Janeiro, in which a general decision had been reached to establish additional liquidities, referred to as Special Drawing Rights. In Stockholm, the French and the Americans did not see eye to eye. France hoped that the establishment of these new credit provisions would be accompanied by a decrease in the role of the reserve currencies, and especially of the dollar. The United States wanted these new drawing rights to contribute to a demonetization of metal gold by the creation of an international currency of sorts, referred to as "paper gold."

The American point of view prevailed. But France had a clause inserted which enabled any country to refuse to finance a predetermined portion of the Special Drawing Rights. France also managed to obtain a provision stipulating that the E.E.C. could exercise a veto at the Council of the Monetary Fund, provided the vote of the member states was unanimous. Michel Debré, however, would not sign the Stockholm communiqué of March 30, his pretext being that the Group of Ten had refused to discuss a general reform of the monetary system based on a broadening of the role of gold. The unanimity of opinion among the Six on monetary affairs was disrupted at the very moment when the importance of unity was acknowledged and accepted by the United States within the Monetary Fund.

Western Crisis and French Crisis

The pound was devalued, but nobody knew whether it would be able to maintain its current level. The speculation in gold signified a lack of confidence in the purchasing power of the dollar and consequently in its ability to remain the sole reserve currency. Finally, the Gold Exchange Standard ceased to function because, after the embargo, the dollar lost its convertibility with gold. Thus, the deterioration of the monetary system led to a crisis that affected all of the Western world.

The weakened position of the pound and the dollar redounded to the advantage of the mark, not the franc. The circumstances that gave rise to the 1968 French crisis have already been analyzed in Book II, Chapter 20. The crisis entailed grave economic and monetary consequences. Twice the Bank of France was confronted with serious flights of capital: the first time was in May and June, during and immediately following the strikes; the second time, from September to November, after the exchange controls established on May 29 were lifted. At that time a wave of international speculation anticipated a revaluation of the mark and a devaluation of the franc and consequently of the pound.

Under these circumstances, France was obliged to appeal twice to international monetary solidarity, although in recent years she had not set a good example of such solidarity. On July 11, the Bank of France concluded a "swap" agreement for the sum of $1.3 billion with the Federal Reserve Bank of New York and with several central banks in Europe. On November 22, following a meeting in Bonn of finance ministers and directors of centrals banks of the Group of Ten, France received an international loan from her partners of two billion dollars to be used to bolster her currency. The largest loans were made by the United States and the German Federal Republic. On November 24, much to the surprise of the general public, the president of the French Republic announced over the radio that the franc would not be devalued. Somewhat prior to this announcement, the German government had made public its intention not to raise the value of the mark.

Despite these official statements, the disparity between the two main Common Market currencies was patent. The measures taken to slow down German exports and stimulate French exports underscored the factitious nature of trying to maintain actual par values.

French currency reserves, which at the end of April amounted to approximately six billion dollars, decreased 50 per cent by the close of November 1968.

The crisis of the franc in no way solves the dollar problem. Rather, it emphasizes the futility of the gold war de Gaulle waged against the Anglo-Saxons. International currency problems were not mentioned in the press conference of September 9, 1968.

24

The Construction of Europe
and France in 1968

Economic Prosperity and Instability

IN 1968 WESTERN EUROPE was an area of great prosperity. Like the
Americans, and following their example, the Europeans were experiencing affluence. Proof of this lay in the fact that Europe's gross national
product was increasing at a faster rate than that of the United States.

This prosperity rested primarily on the development of trade in industrial
products. It was related to the competitive nature of Western European
production compared to that of its principal rival, the United States; to the
elimination of obstacles to international trade; and to the smooth functioning of the international monetary system, of which the dollar was an essential
component.

It was difficult for European manufactures to gain access to the American
market. Economic relations between Western Europe and the United States,
apart from the ups and downs of circumstance, were marked by a commercial deficit and a deficit in the balance of patents on the European side,
which was offset by the flow of direct American investments in Europe.
The over-all picture reflected the technological superiority of the United
States compared to Europe. This disparity, rather marked in certain of the
traditional industries, was overwhelming in the scientific industries.

Yet the economic vitality of Europe could but gain by the general
freeing of trade, which was characteristic of the Western world, provided,
however, that the European market became unified. As early as 1959 the
signal for a reduction of tariff barriers was given by the Common Market,
soon to be followed by the European Free Trade Association. Thanks to

the successful Kennedy Round negotiations in 1967, the division of Western Europe into two commercial zones was blurred and considerable impetus was given to trade between industrialized countries.

Within Western Europe the Common Market stood out because of its dynamism. The gross national product grew faster here than in the rest of Europe. Intracommunitarian trade more than tripled in nominal value between 1958 and 1967. The E.E.C. exerted a powerful attraction on the member states of the E.F.T.A., each of which requested membership or association. It also attracted certain developing countries that were watching with interest the way the association served the French-speaking Black African republics. Even the Eastern European states were impressed by the success of the enterprise.

Actually, in 1968 when the customs union was established, the Common Market was primarily a zone of preferential trade. The economic union was still fragmentary. It was achieved in the domain of agriculture but at a high cost. Common policies in industry, energy, and technology had hardly been formulated. Putting these policies into effect had to be postponed because of the absence of truly political institutions.

In the present communitarian system, which is more akin to cooperation than to integration, the important economic options of the states influence the evolution of each country. For almost twenty years, Germany and Italy have shown a preference for productive investments in national markets open to international competition. These two countries withstood better than did France the inflationary pressures that began to be felt in Europe after 1962. Their firms generally produced at lower cost and had larger margins of profit to plough back into business than did their French counterparts. The export of machinery and transportation matériel, which is a good indication of a country's capacity to compete internationally, is progressing more rapidly in Germany and Italy than in France. The volume of German exports in this category is triple that of the French, which in turn only slightly exceeds that of the Italians. The impact of the general strike of May 1968 on wages and costs points up the relative weakness of the French economy. When the customs union got under way on July 1, 1968, France was once again forced to fix import quotas. The monetary crisis of November 1968 underscored the overvaluation of the franc compared to the mark.

In 1959 British and German exports were equal in volume; but by 1967 British exports were a third less than Germany's. England's economic growth was slower than that of the Continent. She sacrificed her industry in order to maintain the pound as a reserve currency and as the cement of the Commonwealth. But the break-up of the Commonwealth reduced the advantages that British industry derived from imperial preference without substantially lightening the burdens that weighed on the pound.

The progress made possible by the freeing of trade in the Western world contrasts sharply with the recent deterioration of the international monetary system. To be sure, in 1959 most European currencies had achieved external convertibility and some—the deutsche mark, for example—had achieved total convertibility. Furthermore, the Common Market nations had accumulated a considerable amount of monetary reserves, exceeding in 1967 those of the United States. But since 1964 England has not been able to redress her balance of payments situation, and in 1967 she was obliged to devalue the pound. The deficit in the American balance of payments, which stems from the political responsibilities incumbent on a world power, has grown since 1965 when the war in Vietnam was escalated. The difficulties that plague the two reserve currencies simultaneously stimulated the hoarding of gold to such an extent that early in 1968 the United States was forced to abandon the free convertibility of the dollar into gold. In May 1968 France in turn experienced an outflow of capital and had to resume, until September 1968, foreign exchange controls. The deutsche mark is the strongest of the European currencies but it does not play an international role.

In 1967 the French veto of England's application for membership in the European Economic Community reduced the chances of enlarging the Community to include other nations of Western Europe, and consequently lessened the Continent's ability to exploit fully its potential resources in the domain of industry, technology, and finance.

To be sure, the economic influence of the Common Market is growing in Western Europe just as the economic importance of the German Federal Republic is increasing within the Common Market. But the importance of all of Western Europe, despite its present economic organization and its progress toward affluence, does not seem likely to grow quickly enough in comparison to the United States as long as there are no political institutions capable of promoting true economic and monetary unity.

Political Differences and Uncertainties

The political situation in 1968 was marked by a favorable attitude of public opinion toward a communitarian Europe and by a want of European political and military institutions.

Opinion polls taken in the six Community nations since 1963 have revealed that a very small minority were hostile to the European idea whereas a considerable majority favored integration.

To integrate is gradually to add a new allegiance to one's allegiance to country, to broaden one's civic sentiments to include Europe. The ten years during which the Common Market functioned established among the élite a consensus in favor of the communitarian idea. Employers, farmers, and workers of the six countries had been grouped together in representative associations; together they examined common interests and goals and sought compromise solutions in order to act in unison. The coupling of communes multiplied; it brought together municipal representatives and officials, under the democratic aegis of the European Council of Communes. Meetings between the young people of France and Germany were promoted by the Franco-German Youth Administration.

Although the European Economic Community stimulated the creation of an industrial Europe, and began to create a Europe of workers, it did not lead—although to some this would have seemed a natural evolution— to an extension of its competence from the economic to the political domain. Quite the contrary. The French government tended to create a political organization separate from that of the Community, founded on different principles, and to depreciate the federative provisions contained in the Treaty of Rome. Twice it opposed any extension of the Community, and finally it withdrew from the military organization to which the other E.E.C. nations belonged. In 1960 General de Gaulle suggested to his E.E.C. partners that the solution to political problems could be found in an "organized cooperations of states," with each state retaining its veto power. In 1962 this proposal was rejected by the Netherlands and Belgium. The rupture, which had almost occurred over the question of relations with the Atlantic Alliance, finally came over the issue of England's possible entry into the E.E.C. In 1965 de Gaulle created a crisis in the Common Market over the matter of financing a common agricultural policy. He did so in order to prevent majority rule in the decisions of the Council of Ministers, and to weaken the powers of the Commission. He achieved his ends. In 1963, and again in 1967, against the wishes of all the other member states and the Commission, de Gaulle opposed the entry of England into the E.E.C. In 1966 he decided that France should withdraw from NATO, although his partners retained their membership in it. Until the Soviet Union invaded Czechoslovakia, France's withdrawal from the Atlantic Alliance in 1969 was considered a likely possibility.

A fundamental unity of foreign policy within the framework of the Atlantic Alliance and the possibility of a political federation were implicit in the Treaty of Rome when it was signed. Today they are no longer. In the past ten years a profound divergence of views has persisted between France of the Fifth Republic and the other states of the E.E.C. regarding the principles of a common political organization and the goals of common foreign and defense policies. For this reason, the nucleus of Western Europe, which other European countries were prepared to join, in 1968 still lacks real political and military institutions. The divergence is so serious that no political progress seems possible within the framework of the Six unless new members are admitted. Since new members have been excluded, the impasse is total.

Until now the political influence of France has been both preponderant and negative because of the authority of her leader and the repeated use of her veto power. The influence of England has decreased because of her initial refusal to participate in the construction of a unified Europe and because of the chronic weakness of her currency. The influence of Federal Germany, which for a long time had been curbed by the political and military limitations that were imposed on her, is growing because of her economic importance in the Community and her military participation in the Alliance. The three principal nations of Western Europe do not share a common attitude toward the two super powers, the United States and the Soviet Union.

Europe and the United States

Relations between Western Europe and the United States were determined by a real situation—European dependence. The Europeans could, however, choose between several objectives. Their chances of achieving a given goal would depend partly on American policy toward Europe, partly on the convergence or divergence of the policies of the major nations toward the United States.

Western Europe's dependence was both economic and military. The industrial and technological superiority of the United States was such that the nations of Western Europe, if they do not achieve a true economic union, will have a choice between isolation, which would lead to economic strangulation or free trade, leading to American economic domination. Military superiority stems from the fact that no European state has been able to acquire enough atomic armaments to amass an effective deterrent force against the Soviet Union. The decision that the Americans and the Russians made in 1967 to establish thin anti-ballistic missile networks has rendered the atomic forces of England and France obsolete. The presence of American armed forces in Western Europe, whether nuclear or conventional, gave West Europeans, especially the Germans, a guarantee against Soviet military pressure. It gave East Europeans and Russians a guarantee that West Germany would not acquire nuclear status, a guarantee that was reinforced in 1968 by the nonproliferation treaty. Military and technological dependence were closely linked, in this sense, to Western Europe's weakness in the scientific industries; the political divisions of Europe were one cause of American superiority in the area of defense.

Things being as they were, Western Europe could either resign itself to dependence, attempt to establish a partnership based on equality with the

United States, or it could embark on the road to armed neutrality. The policy of defense would vary according to the option that was chosen. The first alternative, that of an Atlantic Europe, implied acceptance of the fact that the United States alone would possess nuclear weapons and that the president of the United States would have the exclusive right to determine their use. The second meant an associated Europe. It presupposed the creation of a European Defense Community, armed with conventional weapons, and the pooling of French and British deterrent forces that would contribute to a European successor state with political authority and strategic decision-making powers. The third alternative was—according to a phrase coined by de Gaulle—that of a European Europe, which included Eastern Europe and was no longer subservient to an alliance with the United States.

For the past twenty years, America's general policy has been to further the construction of a united Europe. The United States openly supported the E.E.C. and put pressure on England to request membership in it. The American government has nonetheless hesitated on occasion, when faced with the long-range consequences of a policy that might lead to the formation of a powerful political, economic, and military entity in Western Europe. The fear of economic competition played a part in certain provisions of the Trade Expansion Act. The fear of sharing responsibility, not for decisions but for strategic planning, was not overcome until 1967, in spite of the danger of weakening the notion of common interest within a fundamentally unequal alliance. Moreover, the inability of certain Western European countries to create political institutions, together with the French withdrawal from NATO, led certain responsible circles to think that Kennedy's trump card of 1962—Europe as an equal partner—had no future today. The United States might become resigned to the persistent division of the Europeans and to the dependent situation that results from it.

For England, the American alliance is a dogma to which both political parties adhere. A European Europe, a third force, politically separate from the United States, is inconceivable. For a long time, the main concern of the ruling classes was to preserve their priviledged relations with the United States and some cohesion in the Commonwealth. The latter consideration explains why the British request for entry in the E.E.C. in 1961 was made with grave reservations. Around 1966 the Labour Party realized that England would have to choose between economic and monetary dependence on the United States or collaboration, on an equal footing, with the nations of Western Europe within a common organization that was at first economic, and might become political. England's second application for membership reflected the almost unanimous expression of public opinion. The French veto of 1967 in no way changed the British attitude. England accelerated the withdrawal of her bases east of Suez and concentrated her conventional forces as well as her political ambitions on a Europe that in time would become a real power.

The Federal Republic is divided between concern for security, which only the United States can insure, and a desire for reunification, which only the Soviet Union can grant. The government's position is that reunification must not be sought at the expense of security and that it cannot be freely achieved without the support of the West, especially the United States. In West Germany as in England, the American alliance is therefore a dogma professed by the two principal political parties. The German government's relations with the United States are not likely to change unless increased cooperation between the two major powers should lead to an agreement on the status quo of a divided Germany. The communitarian construction of Europe is also a dogma generally accepted to the extent that, for a long time, the need for unity was less urgent than the need for European integration. As a consequence, German public opinion welcomed Kennedy's proposal for an equal partnership between a united Western Europe and the United States. The French government, however, rejecting both European integration and an Atlantic partnership, forced Germany to seek an increasingly difficult conciliation between the principal guarantor of her security and her principal European partner. After Chancellor Erhard assumed office, Germany aligned herself with the United States in all matters directly related to major foreign policy issues and entertained the hope of participating in the multilateral force. Under Chancellor Kiesinger, German foreign policy tended toward a détente with Eastern Europe; Germany reluctantly agreed to the nonproliferation treaty and continue to support the distant idea of a united Europe associated with the United States.

Whereas under the Fourth Republic France had initiated the Atlantic Alliance and the communitarian concept of Europe, under the Fifth she became the embodiment of nationalism, with General de Gaulle working by slow stages toward a reversal of foreign policy. The withdrawal of France from NATO and her "all-azimuths" strategy culminated in neutralism and privileged relations with the Soviet Union. An organized cooperation of states replaced the conception of the Community; the goal of a unified Western Europe was replaced by that of a union of all Europe, including Russia, from the Atlantic to the Urals. Thus, the idea of an Atlantic Europe, or a Europe that was an equal partner of the United States, was discarded in favor of a truly European Europe. But this policy was to be somewhat revised by the Soviet occupation of Czechoslovakia.

In short, England and Germany rallied to the support of Kennedy's "Grand Design," but France opposed it. As long as England, Germany, and France could not agree on foreign policy, Western Europe would have no real influence on world matters.

Europe and the Soviet Union

Dominant in the relations of Western Europe and the Soviet Union was the German problem, which determined the status of all Europe. Would Germany remain divided or achieve unification? If reunification was sincerely desired by the West for the sake of self-determination, what would be the best way to attain it?

Answers to these questions depended first on the attitude of the Soviet Union, and consequently on the relations of the Soviet Union with the United States. Secondly, it depended on the conduct of the principal European states which, by their combined or separate actions, could, to a certain extent, affect the relations between the two leading powers. In these circumstances, France and West Germany were most directly involved. England, as long as she was not a member of the Common Market, could not hold views substantially different from those of the United States.

The division of Germany reflected the relative strength of the Soviet Union and the United States. Fear of the Federal Republic dominated the attitude of the Soviet Union toward Western Europe. The presence of American troops in Western Europe and the existence of the Atlantic Pact gave the Soviet Union a guarantee that West Germany would not act independently, that she would not become a nuclear power. The Soviet Union was therefore entirely satisfied with the partition of Germany and desired to see it perpetuated by the recognition of East Germany. For Russia, reunification entailed a great political danger: Germany's complete gravitation toward the West. Consequently, she demanded in exchange a commensurate compensation: the demilitarization of all Germany and the concomitant withdrawal of the occupying troops. Reunification therefore entailed a great military danger for the United States.

The stakes were high for each of the two leading powers. As long as the cold war has lasted, the German problem has never been thoroughly thrashed out. The détente that followed the settlement of the Cuban affair impelled the two major powers to maintain the status quo. In 1965, when the German attitude was changing, after the formulation of the French conception of reunification (which conflicted with the traditional Western view), and as the prospects for a communitarian Europe were becoming dimmer, the discussion was reopened.

The Western traditional doctrine contained a series of hypotheses. If the Europe of the Six were to be broadened to include England and other nations, if it had strong institutions, especially military ones, then the member states, having integrated their forces, would effectively guarantee their neighbors to the east against unilateral action by any one of them, and would carry greater weight within the Atlantic Alliance. Relations with the Eastern states would improve so that a gradual modification of the status quo would be possible. "The order of priorities remains unchanged: first, build up the European Community and bring Britain into it; then develop an Atlantic partnership between a strong Europe and America; and finally, open the door to the Communist world."[1]

The French doctrine was explained by de Gaulle in his press conference of February 4, 1965. The German problem must be settled "by the combined action of the European peoples," a phrase which, in the mind of its author, included the Soviet Union and excluded the United States. The question of Germany's armaments must be resolved "by an agreement with all her neighbors," that is, by a neutralization that her neighbors would guarantee. And these neighbors would be headed by two utterly unequal powers— the Soviet Union and France. From a practical point of view, de Gaulle wanted to protect France from German ambitions by a Franco-Russian guarantee. Who could fail to see that this "Europe in its entirety," made up of nations jealous of their identity, cut off from the United States, deprived of a common defense and foreign protection, grouped around the demographic and industrial mass of a Germany by assumption reunified and unarmed, would fall under the domination of the Soviet Union? France whose strategic strength did not meet the objective criteria of deterrence, would never be capable of offsetting the power of the Soviet Union. Even if the Soviet Union, obliged to protect itself in the east against the Chinese threat, should decide to risk reunification without an understanding with the United States, it would in its own interest engage in a direct dialogue with Germany.[2] Because of her conventional weapons, Germany would then become the Soviet Union's lieutenant in Europe and its main supplier of engineering products.

As long as the United States and France were more or less in agreement about the institutions of the Atlantic Alliance and of Western Europe, Germany visualized her future from a European rather than a national angle. She could hope that the construction of a united Europe would some day lead to her reunification. The cold war between France and the United States had given Germany—concurrently and paradoxically— ambitions within the Alliance and a desire to explore the possibilities of reunification outside the Alliance.

The withdrawal of France from NATO made the Federal Republic the principal military partner of the United States on the Continent. Having

[1] Christopher Layton, "Europe, Road to Coexistence," *Journal of Common Market Studies*, July 3, 1965, p. 283.

[2] Pierre Hassner, "Le Polycentrisme à l'Est et à l'Ouest," in *Les diplomaties occidentales: unité et contradictions* (Paris: Fondation Nationale des Sciences Politiques, 1966), 38.

given some semblance of satisfaction by proposing the creation of a multilateral force, the United States changed its mind in order to obtain the consent of the Soviet Union to the nonproliferation treaty that was signed in 1968. In 1967, the accession of Germany to the group in NATO responsible for nuclear planning did not prove an obstacle to the agreement with Russia.

During a trip to the Federal Republic in 1962, General de Gaulle sang the praises of the German nation. In 1966 he tried to convince Germany that reunification was possible only in a "Europe in its entirety"—that was the Gaullist conception. He encouraged Chancellor Kiesinger to increase his contacts with the Soviet Union and with Eastern Europe in a spirit that would lead to détente. These efforts were attenuated and the prospects for reunification postponed after the Prague coup.

The conflicting policies of Germany's principal allies give her greater freedom of action in foreign policy today. The coalition government headed by Chancellor Kiesinger is discreet, however, in making use of this freedom. What would happen if the German national party, which since 1966 has made a place for itself in several regional assemblies, should attempt to fill the gap between the economic strength of Germany and her political dependence? Why organize an economic union in the Common Market, why continue to finance French wheat exports if the Community will not be broadened politically to hasten a solution of the German problem? Why not follow the French example and do business tomorrow with the Soviet Union? Germany would certainly carry more weight than France. Since the United States is heavily involved in Vietnam, it might, as de Gaulle has predicted, leave the Europeans to their own quarrels.

Such are the German uncertainties.

The Objectives of a United Europe

Can the European Community, which is still in an embryonic stage, survive the blows which French nationalism has dealt it, and which German nationalism will doubtless deal it tomorrow? A great deal of cooperation and very little integration have recently made Europe prosperous. But this does not assure real technological advances that would guarantee a certain autonomy in the future. The Atlantic Alliance, although badly battered, still insures European security for the moment. But doubts have been expressed about its duration and about the maintenance of American troops in Europe. Political and military institutions capable of shoring up a burgeoning federation do not exist. To survive, Europe must find some goals.

Two factors have inversely affected the work of building a united Europe. The threat of Soviet aggression coalesced Europe in the 1950s

The danger of subversion persists but it no longer plays a catalytic role. The process of decolonization hampered the political will of the two European nations that could have served as federative influences. In the 1950s England and France tried to retain their possessions, or at least to give the impression of still being sovereign overseas. The French empire has been lost in the wake of colonial wars and the Commonwealth has been disintegrated by conflicts of interest and the search for more powerful protectors.

Thus, an obstacle has been removed and a motive attenuated.

In 1968, however, there exist imperious reasons for pursuing the construction of Europe. This vast and difficult enterprise seems to be the answer to three challenges that the Europeans, sided by their education, resources, and sheer numbers, should be able to meet.

The first challenge is that of the status of Germany and of Europe. The détente that is apparent today in the relations between the two Germanies creates a climate conducive to a search for long-range solutions. Such solutions will have to be acceptable to both East and West Germans, to their neighbors, to the United States, and to the Soviet Union. To achieve this, two hazards must be averted: that of German domination of Europe, which would result from the reunification of even a neutral Germany within a divided Europe; and a sudden change in the balance of power that would result from the inclusion of the Soviet Union in a large confederation of "Europe in its entirety." On the other hand, the transformation of the European Economic Community into a political Community, broadened to include England and other states of Western Europe, and concluding, as détente progresses, economic agreements with the Eastern nations of Europe, represents a solution acceptable to the Soviet Union, to whom West Germany integrated into a vast entity would be less dangerous than an independent, nationalist, and dissatisfied German state.[3] Although the invasion of Czechoslovakia in 1968 makes it impossible for the moment, nevertheless, the West must not abandon this objective.

The second challenge is atomic proliferation. The Americans and the Russians have begun to question the value of a global political system founded on the threat of mutual destruction. Jean Laloy has remarked: "A third dimension must be added to the earlier bilateral relationship between adversaries—the danger of utter destruction."[4] The imperfect response to this problem is the nonproliferation treaty signed in 1968. It is imperfect because of China's refusal to sign it and also because several average-sized nations are not far from reaching the technical ability and from mobilizing

[3] Miriam Camps, "Is Europe Obsolete?" *International Affairs*, July 1968.
[4] Jean Laloy, *Entre guerres et paix, 1945–1965* (Paris: Plon, 1966), 234.

the resources to possess, if not a real deterrent force, at least powerful destructive arms. As long as no international deterrent force exists, the best way to prevent international conflicts is to group the small and average-sized nations into larger units. The tendency to form groups, which produces "a certain political order that might be termed intermediary—an order that transcends the states," is an indication of the instinctive reaction of political forms to impending upheavals. This is a step in the direction of world government, which, in view of the dangers to humanity, represents an aspiration of the future, if not yet a political idea. Thanks to the spread of technology and education, and the inevitable changes they bring in our way of life, a trend toward world unity exists today. It can be perceived in our moral values—our attempts to rectify the injustice of unequal distribution of wealth and to minimize the dangers of total destruction.[5] Western Europe, broadened to include England and other nations, unifying its defensive forces and foreign policy, could prevent a unilateral attack by any of its member states and contribute in this way to international peace.

The construction of a united Europe faces a third challenge—that of a confrontation between our great contemporary civilizations. The refusal to align with either of the two rival East and West blocs, a certain differentiation within the two blocs, a cultural revival whose spiritual values have been depreciated because administrative, material, and technical support was lacking—all this compels many old and new states to refrain from sacrificing everything to nationalist ideologies. Rather, they tend to group together, however imperfectly, according to cultural affinities. This is true of the Arab world, Latin America, and Black Africa. Western Europe is the cradle of modern technology. The Americans, and to a certain extent the Russians, today surpass Europe. But during recent centuries, Europe's military and economic conquests have brought it into close contact with nontechnical civilizations. Because of its liberal and scientific traditions, Europe can serve as an excellent link for a fruitful dialogue between different cultures. It can make an effective contribution to the struggle of under-developed countries.[6] Once unified, Europe would be able to organize the peaceful coexistence of regional groups that develop according to types of civilization; it could help to spread federative political institutions that, better than any others, will insure the right of minorities and reconcile unity with diversity.

By taking up these three challenges, aimed at a better organization of the international political system and at the consolidation of peace, a Western Europe in search of the political means to forge its unity will, by these means,

[5] *Ibid.*, 308, 333, 324, 325.

[6] "Pour un dialogue des cultures," *Bulletin du Centre européen de la Culture*, Geneva, Apr. 1962, p. 19.

achieve technological progress and relative power. Earlier we noted the connection between technology and the volume of units of production, the size of the markets and the volume of government orders. The backwardness of closed and stratified European societies is the result of continuing to "suffer progress" instead of meeting it by a "prodigious advance in education,"[7] Europe's long-term prosperity, her relative autonomy in a system of economic inter-dependence, will be determined by her willingness to emerge from isolation.

Ideologies and Strategies in 1968

European ideology, which springs from fear of the Soviet Union, and has been hampered by the process of decolonization, is still uncertain in regard to the general objectives we have outlined. Confronted with nationalist ideologies, Europe had adopted a defensive rather than an offensive position. The change in vocabulary illustrates this change in position. In 1958 the idea of integration clashed with that of association. In 1968 the idea of community clashes with that of national independence.

The French state, personified by its leader, holds high the banner of national independence considered as an end in itself. General de Gaulle, all powerful in France, without his peer in all Europe, heads the movement. The desire for power is contagious, especially when it rests on a solid industrial base. Nationalist ideas are beginning to spread in Germany. The conversion of England to the notion of European unity is still fragile; her entry into the Community is uncertain. As a consequence, none of the principal European nations can or will play a federative role at present. The defense and promotion of the European ideology rests first on a pressure group, the Action Committee for the United States of Europe. This committee comprises the representatives of today's political, liberal, Christian, and Socialist currents in the six states. It rests also in the Brussels Commission—that embryo of European power and symbol of the communitarian ideal. The Action Committee was influential when all six states had parliamentary regimes. It has been much less influential ever since the 1962 elections when the old democratic political parties declined sharply in France. It could play a more active role thanks to the adherence of Britain's three political parties in 1968. The Brussels Commission has the difficult task of convincing the Council of Ministers, which represents the sovereignty of the member states, to accept certain limitations on this sovereignty. As the guardian of the European institutions, the Commission has attempted to establish its authority by taking advantage of the current political situation; it cannot initiate wide-ranging plans. The conflict between the general

[7] Jean-Jacques Servan-Schreiber, *Le défi américain* (Paris: Denöel, 1967), 205, 79.

and the Commission came out into the open in 1963 when England was excluded from the Common Market. The Commission launched an offensive in 1965 but committed a tactical error. The agricultural crisis of the Common Market was followed by a truce that confirmed the decline of the Commission, symbolized by the eviction of Hallstein in 1967. England's entry into the Common Market would put new vitality into the European institutions. The creation of a powerful Europe that will be responsible for its own fate is inconceivable without the simultaneous cooperation of England, France, and West Germany.

Thus, the future of Europe has been compromised apparently when it was on the verge of bearing fruit and when its true goals seemed to emerge clearly. Every revolutionary idea goes through periods of fluctuation. From 1958 to 1968, the Fifth Republic, by exalting national independence, obscured the communitarian spirit that the Fourth Republic had hoped to inspire.

25

Conclusion: The Foreign Policy of the Fifth Republic

The Legacy of the Fourth Republic and the International System

THE FOURTH REPUBLIC was unreservedly part of the Western bloc. It steadily followed the path that led toward the construction of a united Europe. It set an example for other European nations by favoring a reconciliation with Germany.

When the regime fell as a result of congenital internal weakness and the inconsistencies of its foreign policy, it bequeathed to the Fifth Republic a financial crisis, a war of decolonization, and a new instrument for the achievement of economic union between the Six.

The financial and monetary crisis reached such proportions that no one believed France would be able to meet the time schedule for the reduction of tariffs laid down by the Treaty of Rome.

The Algerian war, which followed the war in Indochina, mobilized a large part of the material and moral strength of the nation for the struggle against a rebellion whose purpose was to give independence to an entire people.

The Treaty of Rome, conceived in a communitarian spirit, was a catalogue of declared intentions which could be realized only by the voluntary effort of the member states and the harmonious operation of the institutions the Treaty established. Within these institutions the Commission spoke for the common interest and made proposals to the representatives of the member states, the Council of Ministers.

The political observers in France and abroad asked themselves three questions about the main options of French foreign policy.

465]

The first question: Would General de Gaulle, determined foe of decolonization, advocate of the reconquest of Indochina; critic of Algeria's 1947 status, be willing to deal with the Algerian rebellion, and if so how?

The second question: Would General de Gaulle, the signatory of the Franco-Soviet Pact in 1944, critic of the 1954 "bad protectorate" (his estimate of the North Atlantic Treaty), pursue the policy of close alliance with the Western nations under the guidance of the United States, which Georges Bidault had initiated in 1947?

The third question: Would General de Gaulle, advocate of the dismemberment of Germany long after 1944, determined foe of the communitarian institutions of the Six, seek the gradual constitution of a European federation, the policy begun in 1950 by Robert Schuman?

These questions were raised at a time when the international system was changing as a consequence of the evolution of thermonuclear arms and the political rise of China.

The ballistic revolution that occurred after 1957 multiplied the potency of armaments and contracted the time required to unleash atomic warfare. It influenced the relations between the major nuclear powers and their relations with their respective clients. The United States and the Soviet Union felt a certain solidarity in the face of the danger of destruction and the threat of proliferation. The cold war changed to peaceful coexistence. The two leading powers intended to preserve their right to dispose of nuclear weapons, whereas some of their allies wanted to procure nuclear arms for themselves.

China's atomic ambitions and her interpretation of the Marxist-Leninist doctrine led to friction with the Soviet Union. This conflict, latent in 1958, soon became overt. Although China's power was still in the making, she rose to the ranks of a leading power by virtue of her huge population, her initiation into modern technology, her ambitions in Asia and even in Africa.

The international system, which had been bipolar, now tended to become tripolar.

Such was the situation when de Gaulle, after eleven years of meditation, arrived on the scene and involved France in a great geostrategic game.

The Foreign Policy of One Man

This great game was conceived and carried out by a single individual. To be sure, Charles de Gaulle surrounded himself with valuable collaborators. But they were merely superior agents. He gathered information and advice, but he alone decided.

On June 4, 1958, in Algiers, he told Salan: "I am the minister of Algeria."

The constitution of October 4, 1958, gave the president of the Republic broad powers. He was "the guarantor of national independence, of territorial integrity, of respect for the agreements and treaties of the Community" (Article 5). He appointed the premier and, on the latter's suggestion, the other members of the government (Article 8). He was commander-in-chief of the army (Article 15). He negotiated and ratified treaties (Article 52). However, "peace treaties, commercial treaties, treaties or accords pertaining to the international organization . . . must be approved or ratified by a law" (Article 53).

At the national meeting of the U.N.R. held in Bordeaux on November 13–15, 1959, a few months after the first election of the president of the Republic, Jacques Chaban-Delmas told his audience that "the development of the constitutional role of the chief of state . . . separates two sectors. . . . One might be called the presidential or reserved sector, the other the open and free sector. . . . Actually, the presidential sector includes Algeria, the Community, foreign affairs, defense. The open sector embraces the rest." This public statement, made by the president of the National Assembly, who ranked third in the state, conformed to the facts if not to the law. It was accepted, and Mitterrand explained why: "The political parties kept quiet; they were freed from the burden of Algeria."[1]

In his press conference of September 20, 1962, de Gaulle stated: "The touchstone of our regime is the office of the President of the Republic, designated by the logic and sentiment of Frenchmen to be the chief of state and the country's guide." He then discussed the powers which the constitution conferred on the president, observing that "in the essential areas of foreign policy and national security, he is responsible for direct action." To emphasize the personal nature of the regime, he proposed that the president of the Republic should be elected by a popular referendum. The old political parties were opposed to this. On October 5 a motion of censure was made in the National Assembly; it received 280 votes, which meant that the Pompidou government had only a minority on its side. The constitutional reform was supported on October 28 by 46.44 per cent of all registered voters. The National Assembly was dissolved. The legislative elections of November 18 and 25 sent an "unconditional" majority to the Assembly. The political parties could no longer muster enough strength to offer effective opposition to Charles de Gaulle's foreign policy.

In a press conference of September 9, 1965, de Gaulle expressly claimed all responsibility for the supreme command, planning, and decisions involving the destiny of the nation. He cited the specific areas: "national defense, . . . the Algerian affair, Europe, decolonization, African cooperation,

---

[1] François Mitterrand, *Le Coup d'Etat Permanent* (Paris: Plon, 1964), 101.

our policy toward Germany, the United States, England, Russia, China, Latin America, the East, etc."

Everything was thus made crystal clear: de Gaulle alone would handle foreign policy and it would be *his* policy. He did so cautiously until the referendum in November 1962. After that he grew increasingly daring: he throttled the opposition. Parliament no longer deliberated on the major foreign policy options. It debated academically the consequences of the chief of state's unilateral decisions. The Council of Ministers was informed *a posteriori*. Georges Pompidou acknowledged that only three ministers had prior knowledge of the decision to withdraw from NATO. Going over the heads of the intermediary bodies, de Gaulle announced his decisions to the French people and presented his comments to the press.

The Doctrine

The theoretical premises of Charles de Gaulle's foreign policy were simple and entirely comprehensible to the masses. The general handled dialectics with ease, always with a eye to the contrast between the permanent interests of the state and the transient visions of ideologies.

The major contemporary ideologies (the more or less liberal version of capitalism and the more or less authoritarian version of Marxism-Leninism) merely played a secondary role in the direction of the foreign policy of the leading powers—the United States, the Soviet Union, and China.

The states, on the other hand, the only repositories of decision-making power, the only masters of political action, played a determinant role. The world political scene was composed of states, grouped in ever changing constellations and animated by contrary goals. Their objectives corresponded to abstract notions of strength, power, independence, and glory; they utilized for their own ends both material and moral means. To the category of moral means must be added the ideologies which at times transcended the states, uniting or separating them.

The nation's aim was to acquire power and independence by the combined interplay of force and diplomacy. The spur of political ambition led to a striving for the highest rank in the hierarchy of nations. This ambition was fed by memories of a glorious past. If population, size, acquired wealth, technology did not warrant that an average-size state like France could claim to be a first-rate power, because of her position of independence, France could at least claim to be a great power. This is a broader category; it includes both first- and second-rate nations.

Thus independence, that evidence of power and claim to glory, became an end in itself, a reward for national ambition. Independence did not mean refusal to join alliances; it merely emphasized their precariousness.

Commitments were revocable, the ties would be thin. Cooperation, not integration, the right of veto, not the majority rule, were the key words. Then France would be a nation with free hands. Every possibility would be open to her.

The glorification of the nation-state, indifference to moral law, refusal of solidarity, the philosophy of Hegel, the political ideas of Maurras—all these were part of Charles de Gaulle's doctrine.

This simplified doctrine could serve as a foundation for a variety of diplomatic systems. Thus, for example, de Gaulle might conceivably have attempted to increase the power and rank of France by making her a privileged ally of the United States. But his temperament directed him toward other goals. His resentment toward Americans and Englishmen, nourished during the war and vented in his *Memoirs*, led him to bar the American protectors and their British lackeys from the Europe of his dreams. The desire to play an important personal role in the world impelled him to defy the United States and England even as he removed them from the European scene.

Pivoting on his doctrine, captive of his temperament, this statesman exalted the potentialities of the nation he was guiding; he employed a rigorous method to attain goals that he revealed only when he chose to do so.

The Means

From the time he resumed power, de Gaulle strove to make the best of the foreign policy bequeathed to him by the Fourth Republic. No one knew better than he that the power of a nation depends upon its capacity to exploit the milieu, the resources, and means of collective action.

In 1968, the territories under French suzerainty, with the exception of a few unimportant overseas possessions, consisted of metropolitan France. Because of decolonization, her overseas territories were not a cause of weakness as they had been in 1958. To be sure, France was committed by treaty to defend certain French-speaking African republics, but she no longer had to protect herself from local nationalisms. The end of the war in Algeria freed French foreign policy from a heavy burden. As for the metro-politan area, its strategic importance increased because France was still protected by the Atlantic Alliance, despite her withdrawal from NATO and the adoption of a neutralist policy. Her manpower and natural resources did not change notably between 1958 and 1968. France remained a nation of average size. Doubtless under the Fifth Republic her natural resources did grow, but at a rate that was merely equal or even slightly inferior to that of her direct rivals in continental Europe. Aid to underdeveloped nations, awarded primarily to nations that had replaced the former French Union, constituted a heavier economic burden than that assumed by England or Germany in the same domain.

But it was France's capacity for collective action that changed profoundly. The constitution of 1958, and above all the manner in which it was implemented, substituted a personal regime for government by assembly. Authority was not fragmented. There was but one. Not that the institutions were stable and public spirit strong—the optimum in a democracy—but authority was continuous and opposition was weak—the essence of a dictatorship.

The solid financial and economic foundation that the Fourth Republic had always lacked was quickly acquired under the Fifth, thanks to the excellence of the monetary reform of December 1958. There has been a large surplus in the balance of payments ever since 1959 (only in 1964 was the surplus very small). The flow of foreign investments has been extensive, in spite of the brakes put on certain American investments. France's economic growth was more rapid than England's but slower than that of Germany or Italy. The rate of productive investments, estimated in terms of the gross national product, was lower for France than for her two competitors. Inflationary pressures persisted in a system in which a market economy had not yet been perfected. Within ten years the cost of living rose twice as fast in France as in Germany. In 1958, after devaluation, the franc was obviously undervalued. Such was no longer the case in 1962. The devaluation of the pound in 1967 pointed up the vulnerability of the franc. The freeze of many industrial prices reduced for the immediate future the margin of business profits and jeopardized the future competitive capacity of industry. Industrial employment had been stagnant for several years. Unemployment, measured as a percentage of the active, nonagricultural workers, was the highest in Europe by early 1968. To be sure, a considerable effort had been made in industrial concentration and expansion of scientific research. But research policies were conceived along national rather than communitarian lines and selected for reasons of prestige rather than concern for future profit-earning capacity. The budget continued to support activities that were declining. In 1968, France was relatively under-industrialized compared to her neighbors. But even before the crisis of May 1968, she approached the idea of an E.E.C. customs union with much hesitation. In November 1968, the franc seemed to be overvalued in comparison with the mark.

The Common Market linked the French economy with that of her partners due to the rapid development of intracommunitarian trade and the adoption of a common agricultural policy which provided outlets for French surpluses. Economic union, however, had in nowise been achieved, and industrial and nuclear policies were essentially national. The same was true of the monetary policy.

France's military potential also underwent a profound change. In 1958, she had an army thoroughly trained in subversive warfare. The officer corps had been decimated as a consequence of the revolt of certain of its members during the war in Algeria. France's conventional armed forces had been partially sacrificed to the nuclear strategic force, which became operational in 1963. This nuclear force did not meet the objective criteria of deterrence. It could carry out only a strike-first. There was considerable doubt whether second-generation arms, although costly, would possess different characteristics. The use of nuclear weapons would be determined solely by the French government. Withdrawal from NATO in 1966 underlined the national nature of France's military force.

In short, France in 1968 was geographically compact thanks to decolonization. She possessed an average amount of resources; these were being exploited at a satisfactory but not at an exceptional pace. Thanks to new institutional as well as psychological factors due to the concentration of power, France had a considerable capacity for collective action. This capacity was founded on an economic and monetary basis sounder than that of the past—despite certain signs of vulnerability—and on a highly controversial military basis. The limited resources of a second-rate power were unquestionably augmented under the Fifth Republic, but in such a way as to maximize the freedom of action of the supreme chief of state. The doctrine of independent decision-making transcended the idea of exploiting France's resources to the utmost.

The Method

In order to endow France with the maximum degree of independence and power, de Gaulle centered his political action on a certain number of key principles.

The first of these was unity of action in foreign affairs. De Gaulle always practiced a total strategy that combined the means and goals of diplomacy, the army, and the economy. Refusal to submit to majority rule, full use of the veto power in communitarian organizations and alliances, recourse to nuclear weapons and a firm intention to decide independently how they should be used, liquidation of the war of decolonization, the establishment of a strong currency—all these were so many strategic actions employed by the general to achieve national independence.

The second principle has to do with the essence of strategy which resides in the conflict of wills. De Gaulle adopted General Beaufre's definition of strategy: "the dialectical art of wills using force to resolve their conflict."[2] How can one bend the enemy's will? How can one modify his psychological conduct so that in a situation that is not simply given, but created or exploited to this end, he will accept the conditions one wishes to impose? At this point secondary principles intervene—the primacy of the offensive and the harassment of the enemy, to begin with. In the cold war between the United States and France, de Gaulle constantly took the initiative, alternating between mere pinpricks, like his refusal to participate in the commemorative ceremonies for the Anglo-American landings in Normandy, and important decisions like the restrictions imposed on allied flights over French territory. The gradual evolution of his policies was accompanied by a change of vocabulary. Compelled by the paucity of his means to employ them very sparingly, de Gaulle, that master of rhetoric, made ample use of this boundless resource but always subordinated it to his political action. Algeria was a case in point: evolution within a French framework, self-determination, the most French of solutions, the Algerian Republic, the organic cooperation between the communities, independence. The withdrawal from NATO in 1966 was preceded by a series of steps that stretched from 1959 to 1965 and paved the way for France's disengagement. Rapprochement with the Soviet Union after 1964 was effectuated in rapid stages. Finally, when the domestic situation enabled him to do so, he quickened the pace of his activities and augmented their impact. After the election of a docile majority to the National Assembly in November 1962, England was excluded from the Common Market in January 1963. The decision to withdraw from NATO was proclaimed in February 1966, following the general's reelection to the presidency of the Republic in December 1965. In May 1967 the quasi-veto against England's entry into the E.E.C. was pronounced, soon after the March legislative elections, even though the government had received only a slim majority. A by-product of his fourth principle crops up here, one that has to do with General de Gaulle's gambling instincts: to create a crisis, and to resort to blackmail. "This is the method of crisis, of a test of strength, of double-or-nothing, applied by a man who has total confidence in the superiority of his nerves and who does not allow himself to be awed by his opponent."[3] Thus, in order to oppose the entry of England into the Community, de Gaulle threatened to abolish the institution. The docility of the Federal Republic is surprising, but of course there was the danger that France might decide to recognize the other Germany.

De Gaulle's guiding principle, combined with his secondary principles, would lead him to a scheme of the following type. The general sharply criticized the status quo. He indicated in ambiguous terms a policy which

[2] General Beaufre, *Introduction à la Stratégie* (Paris: Armand Colin, 1963), 16.
[3] André Fontaine, *Le Monde*, June 2, 1968.

would arouse no public concern. He emphasized and spelled out the nature of this orientation by using new formulas that were soon to become slogans. Disseminated by modern communication media, these slogans gradually permeated public opinion. As these slogans little by little won over the public, and as the opposition slowly decreased because of weariness or the fear of creating tensions, he launched additional slogans that pointed the way to new steps in the direction he had chosen. There followed measures for implementing his plans with accomplished fact, ultimatums, or forced negotiation. Examples abound: the three ultimatums on the issue of a common agricultural policy; the negotiations with the United States regarding the evacuation of its bases in France; the negotiations with Germany on the status of French troops stationed there. The concentration of powers in the hands of one man makes possible secrecy, surprise, mobility, and, in the event that resistance is too strong, flexibility. De Gaulle rarely consults his ministers. He is not subject to control by Parliament. He guides public opinion masterfully by means of the air waves.

De Gaulle's third guiding principle was the distinction between short-term and long-term aims, tactics and strategy. If we were to admit, hypothetically, that Gaullist strategy consisted in opposing the two hegemonies and the system of blocs in order to underscore France's independence, then close Franco-German collaboration could only serve to weaken the multilateral relations within institutions like NATO and the E.E.C. which the general considered too restrictive. The 1963 treaty supposedly represented a tactical move. Moreover, bilateral rather than multilateral accords would be conducive to the tactical mobility that was considered indispensable to true freedom of action.

The fourth guiding principle was the recognition of a hierarchy of states. At the top were the five world powers; they were soon to become atomic powers and as such tended to dominate the international scene. At the bottom were the large battalions of underdeveloped nations, all potential clients of the leading powers. Decolonization, together with cooperation, was one way for France to concentrate her strength while preserving or expanding the number of her clients. Between the top and the bottom was the embarrassing German problem. Germany's economy surpassed that of France in importance and dynamism. She had territorial claims and perhaps entertained military ambitions. Since Germany was not to have atomic weapons, it was necessary to discriminate against her and prevent her from rising to the rank of a great power. There is no better indicator of rank and position, of the upgrading and downgrading of alliances, than diplomatic protocol. It was indeed diplomatic protocol that de Gaulle invoked to indicate estrangement (protocol served as an insurmountable obstacle to a meeting between the general and Johnson after John F. Kennedy's assassination), as well as rapprochement (Kosygin, the head of the Soviet government, was welcomed in Paris in December 1966 by 101 cannon salutes, an honor reserved for heads of state).

The choice of principles, the diversity and appropriateness of the means used to implement them, attest the master tactician. Now to be considered are the goals of the strategist.

Over-all Goals

De Gaulle's overriding ambition was to make France an independent nation and a first-rate power.

Independence presupposed the freedom to modify the system of alliances. This must not be achieved at the cost of security. The establishment of a nuclear force protected by the Atlantic Alliance enabled France to disengage herself from the Alliance without risking an immediate threat to her security. The end of the war in Algeria and the decolonization of Black Africa gave France greater freedom of action and her first clients in the international arena.

France would truly become a great power if she played a preponderant role in Europe. But this goal was incompatible with a federated Western Europe and with the system of blocs—the American and Soviet hegemonies.

The vision of an integrated Europe was not to de Gaulle's liking; he rejected it. France would lose her identity within a formless mass. She would not be France. And de Gaulle had a certain image of France; he was himself identified with this image. In a federated Europe, the image would be tarnished and the identity lost. This would happen even if he were offered the presidency of such a federation. For then he would be obliged to submit to the control of a parliament consisting mainly of foreigners. The solution was unacceptable to France and to de Gaulle.

The system of blocs perpetuated both the status quo in Europe and the dual hegemony. In such a system, Western Europe, whether federated or not, would inevitably be subordinated to the United States. France would remain dependent and could never become a first-rate power. The over-all goals of the general led him therefore to reject European integration and to upset the Atlantic Alliance, which held the Western bloc together.

In so doing de Gaulle showed indifference to the ideological conflict between capitalism and Marxism. What did it matter if Marxism—which was becoming middle class—or capitalism—which was increasingly state controlled—should eventually fuse? The important thing was that nationalism—which can adapt itself to either capitalism or Marxism—should triumph over federalism. This was the real antinomy. For France to become truly France, the myth of the Community must be demolished.

The over-all goals were plain. They merely had to be applied to a precise objective: to modify, in the interest of France, for the benefit of her independence and power, the status of Germany and Europe. This objective had two facets, one positive, the other negative: to undo the Yalta settlement; to build "a Europe in its entirety."

These two aspects become clearer if we examine de Gaulle's vision of the world's future. In his opinion, the presence of American troops in Europe was temporary. The struggle against Chinese expansion in Asia and the maintenance of order in Latin America would absorb all the energy of the United States. As for the Soviet Union, which was already becoming a bourgeois nation, it would be forced to liquidate its Asiatic possessions because of China and would become once again a European nation.

To undo the Yalta settlement was to oppose American policy and Kennedy's "Grand Design." This consisted in furthering the unification of Western Europe, which in time would become an equal partner of the United States, defending at America's side respect for individual and collective freedom. From this point of view, a unified Western Europe, like China, would one day have the status of a great power in a system that no longer would be bipolar (the United States and the Soviet Union), but quadripolar.

General de Gaulle denounced American leadership, accusing it of seeking world domination. At the same time he prevented the formation of a partnership in the guise of a European federation. Federalism was derided, the nation-state glorified.

Unlike Kennedy's "Grand Design," de Gaulle's "Vast Enterprise" was not clearly understood. The general enveloped it in mystery, believing this was necessary for its implementation. The mystery was cleared up only piecemeal and at opportune moments. The objectives remained ambiguous during the preparatory stages, but became clearer as they were implemented.

The Pursuit of Goals

For four years the European and North American partners of France suspended judgment on the foreign policy of the Fifth Republic. The economic and financial recovery of France after the monetary reform of December 1958 augured well for the future of communitarian institutions. The general's determination to find a solution to the Algerian problem, even at the cost of great sacrifice, justified the hope that henceforward France would devote herself to her European vocation, as the Fourth Republic had planned to do, taking advantage of British hostility, the disrepute of Germany, and the general confusion. As the federator of Europe, France would not have dominated by coercion. Her industrial potential was plainly inferior to that of England or Germany. France would have prevailed because of her spirit. She would have given the United States of Europe the imprint of a French style through her language and her administration. Between 1959 and 1962 de Gaulle could have chosen a communitarian Europe; he could have given it as much autonomy as the modern world, with its growing economic and military interdependence, would allow.

Actually, the monetary reform and the granting of Algerian independence were, in the general's view, two prerequisites to the attainment of maximum freedom of action in foreign policy. Building the national deterrent force, de Gaulle did everything necessary to create a third prerequisite. Proceeding cautiously, he tried to loosen the bonds that linked France to her partners. He attacked a supranational Europe, which he attempted to replace by a plan, intergovernmental in nature, for a union of nations. He took the first steps toward disengagement from the system of integrated allied forces within NATO.

Although he loudly proclaimed the independence of France—her independence of Europe as well as of the Atlantic Alliance—de Gaulle was nonetheless fully aware of the physical danger that threatened Western Europe from 1958 to 1962, during the second Berlin crisis, to say nothing of the Cuban crisis. He did not hesitate, in both instances, to take a firm stand against the Soviet Union. Of the two hegemonies he believed Russia to be the more dangerous at that time.

1962 brought de Gaulle rewards for all his exertions in French internal affairs. The currency was strong and the economy was expanding. Appropriations were made for the erection of a plant to manufacture enriched uranium for military purposes. The war in Algeria was concluded by the Evian Accords. Finally, through a referendum, the constitution was amended to make possible the election of the president of the Republic by universal suffrage.

The international situation was no less favorable than heretofore for the acceleration of the general's "Vast Enterprise." Pierre Hassner summed up the situation in the following terms: "If French initiative has quickened since 1962, it is because the simultaneous end of the Algerian war and the Berlin crisis, as well as the simultaneous outbreak of the war in Vietnam and the Sino-Soviet schism have combined to give France a freedom of action that is denied the United States, the Soviet Union, and Germany."[4]

Thereupon prudence yielded to audacity. 1963 was the year of defiance. In January de Gaulle rejected the American offer of Polaris missiles which would have subordinated the French deterrent force to the American. Without prior consultation with his partners, the general vetoed England's

[4] Pierre Hassner, "Une France aux Mains Libres," *Preuves*, Feb. 1968.

application for membership in the Common Market. At the same time, he concluded with Germany the kind of treaty of cooperation he had urged on the Six. In July he refused to sign the Moscow accord limiting certain kinds of nuclear tests. In January 1964 he recognized the People's Republic of China.

Then de Gaulle embarked on two complementary strategic operations that were to go on for a period of several years: the cold war against the United States, and the rapprochement with Russia. His aim was to impose his own views regarding the status of Europe and Germany.

These two maneuvers were based on an analysis of the balance of power after the Cuban affair. De Gaulle believed that, as a consequence of the Soviet setback, the threat of a Russian nuclear war against Western Europe no longer seemed real. American domination was far more powerful than Soviet hegemony and had to be combated.

De Gaulle made every effort to downgrade the White House, the dominant world power, just as in earlier days the French monarchy had made every effort to humble the House of Austria, then the dominant European power. The battle was waged on the psychological terrain by denunciation—the words grew sharper and sharper—of the war in Vietnam; on the terrain of alliances by France's withdrawal from NATO in 1966; on the monetary terrain by withdrawal from the gold pool in 1967.

The rapprochement with the Soviet Union was initiated by degrees in 1964, in successive press conferences. In 1965 these efforts were intensified, and they culminated, after the general's trip to Moscow, in the joint Franco-Soviet declaration of June 1966 which constituted a non-aggression pact of sorts between France and Russia.

Since 1966, despite her nominal membership in the Atlantic Alliance France must be considered neutral. The statement issued early in 1968 on France's "all-azimuths" strategy confirms this attitude of armed neutrality. At that time one was justified in wondering whether de Gaulle was planning to withdraw from the Atlantic Alliance or even considering a reversal of alliances. The supposition was based on actions and statements regarding the status of Europe and Germany. It is not a matter of furthering the creation of a neutralist Western Europe following the example of France. For the sake of consistency, such a Europe would have to be politically federated, yet in 1964 de Gaulle refused to consent to majority rule within the E.E.C. Such a Europe would have to include England, yet in 1967 de Gaulle rejected for the second time her request for membership.

How can the partition of Europe be replaced by "a different order, a different balance"? The answer is to be found in the press conference of February 4, 1965, when de Gaulle advocated a European settlement of the German question. Germany was to be reunified and neutralized. The general concluded that a solution to this problem was "the essential, long-term goal of French policy on this Continent." The demand for a Europe of the states, for a Europe independent of the United States (the official definition of a "European Europe"); the inclusion of the Soviet Union in Europe (the only possible interpretation of "Europe from the Atlantic to the Urals"); a European settlement of the German question (with Russia and without the United States)—all these are contradictory proposals unless one assumes a kind of Franco-Soviet condominium over all of Europe. "When the chief of state speaks of Europe from the Atlantic to the Urals, he is expressing his basic and most persistent idea, that is, that Europe must belong to the Europeans—which in his view include the Russians, whether Communist or not," André Fontaine wrote in 1967.[5]

Thus de Gaulle is seeking to reestablish, in fact if not in right, the old reverse alliance, "the beautiful and good alliance." The Franco-Soviet Treaty of 1944 was signed a few weeks after the great powers granted diplomatic recognition to the Provisional Government of the French Republic. The joint Franco-Soviet declaration of 1966 was signed eight years after the general's return to power. The Fifth Republic reversed the foreign policy of the Fourth; during his second reign Charles de Gaulle has pursued the foreign policy he began during his first.

Although the prudence of the first phase of Gaullist diplomacy gave way in 1963 to audacity in the second, by 1967 a real anti-American obsession could be discerned. The most spectacular illustrations of this obsession were the Canadian and Israeli episodes, and the gold war against the Anglo-Saxons. Extremism became apparent, culminating in the refusal to negotiate with England for her entry into the Common Market.

After the Soviet Union's occupation of Czechoslovakia, a rapprochement with the United States seemed likely. Once again, the Russian rather than the American hegemony appeared the more dangerous.

The Balance-Sheet of the Fifth Republic

Ten continuous years of political activity and of concentration of powers in the hands of an exceptionally strong personality, the divisions and weakness of the internal opposition, the passivity of most American and West European statesmen—these were the circumstances that helped de Gaulle to achieve his over-all goals. By the same token, they helped to make France an independent nation and, if not a great power, a greater power.

In the opinion of de Gaulle, the internal prerequisites of freedom of action in foreign policy were a healthy economy, an independent deterrent

[5] André Fontaine, *Le Monde*, July 12, 1967.

force, and release from the constraints imposed by the possession of a colonial empire. Despite grave psychological obstacles, the process of de-colonization ended with the termination of war in Algeria. The monetary reform got off to a good start but industrialization did not attain the pace required by urbanization and an expanding population. For this reason, the vulnerability of the French economy became apparent in 1968. French nuclear weaponry was that of a minor power; the gap between it and the armaments of the major powers kept increasing.

One of the general's specific goals had been achieved: the defeat of a federal-type Western Europe. In ten years the Europe of the Six had suffered an institutional setback and did not extend its membership. Twenty-three years after the German surrender, Western Europe, considered as a totality, had neither political institutions, an army, nor a currency of its own. The advent of a consumers' society did not compensate for this threefold deficiency.

Because Western Europe did not possess the instruments of power, French policy was incapable of achieving the second specific goal that the general had set himself: to limit or counteract the excessive power of the United States.

The third specific goal was a rapprochement between France and the Soviet Union, and the construction of a "Europe from the Atlantic to the Urals." To be sure, of all the Western European nations, France had the closest relations with the Soviet Union. Russia, engaged in a cold war against China and involved in political difficulties with her satellites, tightened her military and political hold over Eastern Europe. For a long time she would apparently be unable to modify the status quo in Western Europe without the approval of the United States.

An analysis of the consequences of the failure (at least temporary) to achieve a federal system for Western Europe, and to initiate the formation of a Europe embracing the Soviet Union will enable us to draw up a balance-sheet of the Fifth Republic's foreign policy.

To begin with, in the psychology of peoples, both Europeans and Americans had "a certain image of France" based on her love of freedom and her dominant role in Western civilization. This image has been tarnished. France's allies feel that she has betrayed the Europe she had hoped to foster as well as the liberal civilization which she represented and which the United States, because of circumstances, defended. The defection of France has been felt in the United States with great bitterness because it had counted on her to serve as the mainspring of European unification and of the Atlantic Alliance. Her defection will affect the relations of the two countries for decades to come. The confidence of Europe in France's guardianship has also been shaken. One must not be deceived by the reserve of Western statesmen; it is dictated by the fear that de Gaulle's answer to their criticisms would unleash a new wave of xenophobia in France.

The purely political consequences of the failure to unify Western Europe are equally serious. The European Economic Community could not progress institutionally as long as the French veto blocked the admission of new member states. Evicted from the Common Market, England had no choice but to place herself more entirely under the protection of the United States. It would be ridiculous to try to build a united Europe without France. As for West Germany, forever torn between her need for security and her hope of reunification, she will have to choose between closer ties with America—England's choice—and a rapprochement with the Soviet Union—France's preference.

The Fourth Republic's foreign policy was aimed precisely at avoiding such a dangerous option. The communitarian approach afforded hope of an eventual solution of the German problem because of the dynamism inherent in the notion of a European federation. The communitarian conception implied a minimum of discrimination against West Germany since she would be entirely integrated into the European political union and the Atlantic Alliance. De Gaulle turned his back on the idea of a federation. He weakened the Alliance. Maintaining that a resurgence of German nationalism was inevitable, he placed power relationships above the bonds of solidarity. Mindful of France's weak position, he sought a solution that discriminated against Germany—her neutralization. The accords of sorts he concluded with the Soviet Union represented a step toward a reversal of alliances, designed to counterbalance West Germany.

Although the example of France was not followed by Germany, French policy unwittingly but effectively served the cause of American economic, technical, military, and political supremacy in Western Europe. American supremacy, however, could not establish political structures without the cooperation of France. Weary of the division that had prevailed in Europe since 1914, the United States might settle for a consolidation of the status quo by concluding an agreement with the Soviet Union. The series of nuclear accords concluded between the two superpowers would serve to facilitate such an entente.

What would happen if the Soviet Union, taking advantage, for example, of the internal dissent in the United States, decided to take the chance of establishing the "Europe from the Atlantic to the Urals" for which de Gaulle has been clamoring? Would France occupy the second place in such a Europe? Should the Soviet Union agree to the general's proposal, it would do so in order, first, to use France as a means of destroying the Atlantic Alliance. Then it would use Germany as an arsenal for supplying Europe with engineering products, even arms. France would soon be relegated to the rank of a third-rate power, a rank that corresponds to her economic position.

But the system that de Gaulle has envisaged, assuming that he sincerely wants the reunification of a neutralized Germany, will not become operative tomorrow. On December 3, 1966, the Soviet Union spokesman, Kosygin, let it be known in Paris that no external force could alter the present division of Germany. Gomulka in 1967, and Ceaucescu in 1968, told de Gaulle the same thing, one in the name of Poland, the other speaking for Rumania. The Russians have no wish to expose themselves to the political danger of a reunified Germany. But they must have been delighted that France had affirmed her freedom of action within the Alliance. The French attitude could have had a disastrous effect at a time when on either side of the border of the two Europes a consensus was emerging in favor of détente. Since the Prague coup, the French attitude has no longer had any significance.

By basing the foreign policy of the medium-sized nation he heads on power relationships rather than on a quest for solidarity, General de Gaulle cannot achieve the goals he is pursuing. His policy only serves to augment the weight of the United States and Germany in the affairs of Western Europe—assuming, of course, that the Federal Republic remains loyal to the West. His attitude will result in a greater role for Germany in a "Europe in its entirety," if she should decide to turn to the East. Thus de Gaulle's policy, while purporting to weaken the United States and encircle Germany, actually reinforces American power and puts Germany in a position to choose sides. But whatever the political constellation might be, the "nation with free hands" will be neither the leader of Europe, the role sought by the Fourth Republic, nor a first-rate power, the goal of the Fifth.

Will France at least benefit from the limited privilege of possessing nuclear armaments? The size of her economy enables her to achieve a considerable destructive capacity, but not a real deterrent force. The French strategic force will be downgraded by the setting up of thin anti-missile missile networks. Perhaps other nations which, like France, refused to sign the nonproliferation treaty (which is sponsored jointly by the United States and the Soviet Union), will one day acquire the rank of minor nuclear powers and insist on autonomous control of their bomb.

The world political system that de Gaulle advocates can be formulated as follows: to each his own bomb, according to his means and independently, with the exception of Germany.

Who can fail to see the dangers of such a system? It combines the maximum of instability, because of the precariousness of alliances, with the maximum of risk, because of nuclear proliferation. Such are, in the atomic age, the consequences of a desire for absolute sovereignty. Yet the nuclear peril, of which the United States and the Soviet Union are completely aware, will compel other states to seek solidarity in regional groupings. These are necessary steps toward a worldwide organization; it is no longer utopian. Under the Fourth Republic, France launched the idea of such a grouping when she spoke of the Community. Under the Fifth, she lost the moral credit she would otherwise have acquired.

Perhaps we can ask ourselves, as J. B. Duroselle does, whether the debunking of certain myths, despite de Gaulle's excesses, has not revealed some fundamental facts about world policy. One may cite, for example, de Gaulle's premonition of China's role in the world; his statement that Europe can maintain its identity only by assuming responsibility for its own defense (and yet in 1952 de Gaulle fought against the European Defense Community, although its advocates advanced the same theory); the proclamation of a need for an entente with the Eastern nations (but this entente became possible only after the Cuban *coup*).[6] In summary, the balance-sheet of de Gaulle's foreign policy shows a debit. The benefits derived from decolonization and cooperation do not in any way compensate for the destruction of a viable international system, based on strong institutions that could have given France a choice position. The attempt to establish a different system, unstable and devoid of strong institutions, can only weaken France's position.

While de Gaulle's finest accomplishment was to have ended the war in Algeria, his worst mistake was to have encouraged German nationalism, which could have been counteracted only by a federated Europe.

The success of de Gaulle's negative influence must be attributed to his single-mindedness and his continuous reign. A flagrant example is the manner in which the general put a stop to all efforts to construct a unified Europe by his systematic use of the veto power. The failure of an undertaking such as the undermining of the dollar—the currency of the dominant industrial power—by a franc with a large gold coverage but founded on a week economy, stems from the disparity between means and ends.

The man whom the director of *Le Monde* described as a "Machiavellian genius," endowed with an "insatiable thirst for power,"[7] has been blinded by a "considerable overestimation of the role and potentialities of France and her leader."[8]

De Gaulle's foreign policy has been termed an aberration. Is it the aberration of the man who imposed it? Is it an historical accident, or an epiphenomenon? Or, on the contrary, is it the collective aberration of all Frenchmen grown blind to their interests and their ideals?

[6] J. B. Duroselle, *Evolution des relations Europe–Etats-Unis* (Paris: Centre international de formation européenne, Dec. 1966).

[7] Sirius, *Le Monde*, Nov. 29, 1967.

[8] Sirius, *Le Monde*, Aug. 2, 1967.

The French and Foreign Policy

Until now the majority of Frenchmen have approved the general's foreign policy. Why?

One explanation is to be found in the national temperament, as it has emerged in modern times. Chateaubriand had this to say about Napoleon: "Daily experience demonstrates that Frenchmen instinctively tend toward power; equality is their only idol. But equality and despotism have secret bonds. The two were the source of Napoleon's strength—in the hearts of Frenchmen, militarily inclined toward power, democratically in love with egalitarianism."[9] The French temperament has not changed. Jean-François Revel observed that France is a "nation in which the leading classes have never rallied to the republic, to the representative institutions, and to the definition of power as a temporary delegation." Thus, Frenchmen offer the world the unusual spectacle of a dictatorship in an era of prosperity. "In part a virtual dictatorship. . . . Self-censorship supplementing repression." The French are the "only literate people who no longer feel the need to understand anything whatsoever about the intentions of those they are asked to elect."[10]

There is also the fact that Frenchmen are steeped in the history of military glory. They forget that the long periods of absolute power—Napoleon I, Napoleon III—ended in disasters that took one or two generations to recover from, that France has never recaptured her former position of power. They cannot accept the inferior economic and military status which is theirs *vis-à-vis* the modern superpowers. On the other hand, they accept lightheartedly the unproductive and dangerous investment in a national deterrent force. The Jean-Moulin Club writes: "The image that France has of herself stems mainly from mythology or psychoanalysis rather than from political science. Nationalism is a reassuring temptation for a frustrated and divided people."[11]

Many Frenchmen envy the success of others, especially that of their protectors. Hostility toward Americans finds an echo in public opinion. General de Gaulle exploits this masterfully. He also knows how to appear before the public as a determined advocate of European construction because he is very mindful of the popularity of this idea. In 1968 the Unesco Clubs and the French Institute of Public Opinion interviewed Frenchmen. Eighty-three per cent of those questioned said they favored the Common Market,

[9] Chateaubriand, *Mémoires d'Outre Tombe* (Paris: Bibliothèque de la Pléiade, 1946), I, 1004.

[10] Jean-François Revel, *En France, La Fin de l'Opposition* (Paris: Juillard, 1965), 30, 47, 60, 127.

[11] Club Jean Moulin, *Pour une politique etrangère de l'Europe* (Paris: Editions du Seuil, 1966), 8.

and 76 per cent thought that a political organization of the Six was desirable.[12]

The knowledge most Frenchmen possess about foreign policy, however, is notoriously inadequate and politicians do not make the most of their opportunities to fill this void in basic education. This was true of the German problem, for example. On the eve of the 1965 presidential election, the magazine *La Nef* published a special issue entitled: "Twelve Politicians Answer Twelve Questions." The third question was: "What do you understand by the phrase 'to forge Europe?'" The sub-questions did not mention Germany. Out of twelve answers, eight were silent on the subject. Only two alluded to Germany incidentally. Guy Mollet and Georges Vedel were the only contributors who went into the problem thoroughly. Mollet said: "Nationalism is contagious and one already hears many Germans speaking of their 'sovereignty' and 'national independence.'" Vedel said: "One cannot separate Germany from the American military protectorate by promising her the French atomic umbrella." Not one of the twelve referred to the general's conception of a European settlement of the German problem, which he explained in his press conference of February 4, 1965.[13] French public opinion was incapable of perceiving the incompatibility of de Gaulle's conception with the principles that underlay the treaties of Paris (1952) and Rome (1957).

However, a small book published in 1963 that had received very little attention contains a scientific analysis of the sibylline formula: "Europe from the Atlantic to the Urals." René Courtin, an ardent Gaullist during the Resistance, a militant Europeanist since the Liberation, sketched the guidelines of what he called "de Gaulle's Grand Design": a Franco-Soviet treaty to reunify Germany; the withdrawal of American troops; the establishment, on either side of the iron curtain, of a vast confederation of sovereign states. He detailed the general's efforts, beginning in 1963, to achieve a rapprochement with the Soviet Union. He observed: "The departure of the American troops, because of France's insistence, would force West Germany to resign herself to a German-Soviet accord." He added: "To force the Americans to evacuate Europe, France might withdraw from NATO and demand the withdrawal of all foreign troops and bases."[14] This prophet was not heeded.

To be sure, even many well-informed Frenchmen do not believe that the Gaullist "Vast Enterprise" may some day lead to a Soviet-German

---

[12] *Communauté Européenne*, No. 118, May 1968, p. 23.

[13] "12 hommes politiques répondent à 12 questions," *La Nef*, Oct. 1965, pp. 152, 186.

[14] René Courtin, *L'Europe de l'Atlantique à l'Oural* (Paris: L'Esprit Nouveau, 1963), 76–90.

rapprochement. Doubtless they prefer not to dwell on such an unpleasant prospect, hoping that the Western world will preserve a modicum of cohesiveness for at least a few more years despite France's neutralism. And they also hope that after General de Gaulle disappears from the political scene no French statesman will be able to pursue the "diplomatic course" that consists of dialectics, tactical maneuvers, the quest for prestige, and insolence; that no statesman will be able to pursue the "economic and budgetary course" that consists in the stagnation of industrial employment and a multiplication of unproductive expenses.

1968 and Foreign Policy

After 1967, the year of excesses, came 1968, the year of truth. Three major events revealed the limitations of the Gaullist foreign policy and somewhat altered its course.

The first event was an internal one. The May crisis, followed by the monetary crisis in November, derailed "the economic and budgetary course." It put a sudden end to the gold war de Gaulle waged against the Anglo-Saxons, because he ran out of ammunition. It underscored the monetary and industrial power of Federal Germany and the corresponding weakness of France.

The second test had to do with the United States. President Johnson's decision to begin talks with the North Vietnamese on March 31 and the unconditional bombing halt on November 1 pointed up the American people's firm desire for peace. One of the basic criticisms de Gaulle had leveled against American foreign policy was no longer valid.

The third event concerned the Soviet Union. The invasion of Czechoslovakia in August demonstrated that the Warsaw Pact was merely a tool of Russian imperialism and that Marxist socialism and freedom were incompatible. It brought home to de Gaulle the strategic advantages Russia had acquired in Eastern Europe and in the Mediterranean.

These events, taken as a whole, signified a weakening of France's position and a change in the European balance of power. It led de Gaulle to revise somewhat his foreign policy, to slow it down and bend the direction of his "diplomatic course."

Twice, in order to protect the franc, France sought recourse in international, and especially American, monetary solidarity. This led to a rapprochement with the United States.

The conception of a Europe from the Atlantic to the Urals, including a Germany reunified but contained by a Franco-Soviet condominium, has lost its plausibility. Quite the contrary is true. The Soviet hegemony now seems more dangerous and the American atomic umbrella more necessary than ever. Although de Gaulle maintains that a détente with the East is a major objective, he has let it be known that France intends to remain in the Atlantic Alliance.

But the general's revision of foreign policy follows a strict nationalist line. De Gaulle has not shed his wolf's clothing. In a press conference on September 9, 1968, he spoke with remarkable frankness and clarity about his aims. He reminded his listeners that ever since 1958 he has tried to put an end to the two-bloc system. He enumerated four occasions that contributed to this purpose: withdrawal from NATO, "which subordinates Europeans to Americans"; disapproval of a supranational system for the Six "which would submerge France in a countryless entity and would have no other policy save that of the American protector"; the rejection of Great Britain's candidacy to the Common Market in order to avoid the risk "of an Atlantic absorption"; a search for political détente and "privileged ties" with the countries of the East.

To be sure, the tone has changed. "Self-satisfaction and the permanent lessons given to others" were no longer suitable because "today the impact of high-flown verbiage will no longer have the same glitter."[15] But the major objectives remain unchanged: opposition to American hegemony; refusal to form a federated Europe; the rebuttal of England.

Like a nineteenth-century statesman, the great political visionary continues to play the card of French nationalism in a Europe of nations.

May the events of 1968 serve to enlighten Frenchmen about the balance of power in the world; may they convince them that there cannot be a global policy for France alone, that the interests of France are to be found in Western Europe, that this Europe will be united or enslaved, and that the internal balance of a united Europe requires the presence of England at the side of Germany and France.[16]

[15] Alfred Grosser, *Le Monde*, June 19, 1968.

[16] Publisher's note: For coverage of French foreign policy until de Gaulle's resignation following the referendum of April 27, 1969, see the author's article "The Last Year of de Gaulle's Foreign Policy" in the July 1, 1969, issue of *International Affairs*, London.

Chronological Resumé,
1944–1968

1944

OCTOBER 23 Allied recognition of the Provisional Government of the French Republic established in Paris since August

DECEMBER 2 De Gaulle's trip to the U.S.S.R. His first meeting with Stalin

DECEMBER 10 The signing of the Franco-Soviet Pact in Moscow

1945

FEBRUARY Yalta Conference

MAY 8 Germany's unconditional surrender

MAY 8 Riots in Sétif and Constantine (Algeria)

MAY 31 Anglo-French conflict over Syria and Lebanon

JUNE 25–28 San Francisco Conference

AUGUST 2 Signing of the Potsdam Accords

AUGUST 14 Unconditional surrender of Japan

1946

MARCH 6 Accord concluded between Sainteny and Ho Chi-minh on the independence of Vietnam

JULY 6 Fontainebleau Conference between the representatives of the French government and Ho Chi-minh

NOVEMBER 23 Bombardment of Haiphong

1947

MARCH   Moscow Conference

MARCH 4   Anglo-French Treaty of Mutual Assistance signed at Dunkirk

MAY 4   Ramadier rid his government of the Communist ministers

JUNE 5   General Marshall's commencement address at Harvard

JUNE 27   U.S.S.R. rejects American aid

SEPTEMBER 20   Vote on the Statute for Algeria

OCTOBER 7   Establishment of the Cominform

1948

FEBRUARY   Communist *coup* in Prague

MARCH 17   Western European Union Treaty signed in Brussels

APRIL 16   Convention for European Economic Cooperation signed in Paris

JUNE 24   Beginning of the Berlin blockade

1949

APRIL 4   North Atlantic Treaty signed in Washington

MAY 12   End of the Berlin blockade

MAY 5   Constitution of the Council of Europe

JULY 14   Explosion of the first Soviet atomic bomb

1950

MARCH   Franco-Saar conventions signed

MAY 9   Schuman's declaration ending Franco-German rivalry

JUNE 25   North Korean army crossed the thirty-eighth parallel

DECEMBER 6   General de Lattre appointed high commissioner and commander-in-chief in Indochina

DECEMBER 23   Signing of a treaty between the United States, France, and the associated states defining the conditions for American aid in Indochina

1951

APRIL 18   Signing of the European Coal and Steel Community Treaty

1952

FEBRUARY   Greece and Turkey join the Atlantic Alliance

MAY 27   European Defense Community Treaty signed in Bonn

1953

MARCH 5   Death of Stalin

JULY 27   Korean armistice signed

AUGUST 20   Sidi Mohammed Ben Youssef, sultan of Morocco, deposed

DECEMBER   Bermuda Conference

1954

APRIL 26   Conference on Indochina held in Geneva

MAY 7   Fall of Dien Bien Phu

JULY 21   Signing of the Geneva Accords on Indochina

AUGUST 19   Meeting of the Six on the E.D.C., in Brussels

AUGUST 30   Rejection of the E.D.C. by the National Assembly

OCTOBER 23   Accords signed in Paris on Germany and Italy's entry into the Western European Union and Germany's entry into NATO

NOVEMBER 1   The beginning of the Algerian insurrection

1955

MAY 3   The new Franco-Saar convention

MAY 5   The German Federal Republic becomes an official member of the North Atlantic Treaty

MAY 7   The U.S.S.R. denounces the Franco-Soviet Pact

MAY 14   Signing of Warsaw Pact

OCTOBER 23   The Saar rejects a European status

NOVEMBER 6   La Celle-Saint-Cloud declaration proclaiming the independence of Morocco

1956

FEBRUARY 6   Guy Mollet visits Algeria

FEBRUARY 25   Communist Party's Twentieth Congress

MARCH 20   Signing of a Franco-Tunisian protocol proclaiming the independence of Tunisia

JUNE 20   National Assembly votes the "Loi Cadre" for the French Black African territories

JULY 26   Nationalization of the Suez canal

OCTOBER 30   Israeli troops invade the Sinai peninsula

NOVEMBER 6   Cease-fire is announced in Egypt

1957

MARCH 25   European Economic Community and Euratom Treaties are signed in Rome

SEPTEMBER   Bamako Congress

489]

1958

FEBRUARY 8 French bombardment of Sakiet Sidi Youssef in Tunisia

MAY 13 Peoples' uprising and military revolt in Algiers

JUNE 3 General de Gaulle is invested as prime minister by the National Assembly

SEPTEMBER 24 French memorandum sent to General Eisenhower and Harold Macmillan on the subject of the Atlantic Alliance.

SEPTEMBER 28 Referendum on the constitution of the Fifth Republic

OCTOBER 21 Guinea announces its independence

DECEMBER 21 De Gaulle is elected president of the Republic and of the Community

1959

MARCH 7 France takes the first steps towards withdrawal from NATO

SEPTEMBER 16 Speech by General de Gaulle on self-determination for Algeria

SEPTEMBER 25 Camp David meeting between Eisenhower and Khrushchev

NOVEMBER 20 The signing of the European Free Trade Association Treaty in Stockholm

1960

FEBRUARY 13 The first French A-bomb is exploded in Raggana

APRIL 2 and 4 Madagascar and Mali become independent

NOVEMBER 14 The Organization for Economic Cooperation and Development replaces the Organization for European Economic Cooperation

DECEMBER Debate and vote in Parliament on the first French military program

1961

JANUARY 8 Referendum on self-determination in Algeria

APRIL 22 The generals' *putsch* in Algeria

JULY 31 Great Britain makes its first request to join the Common Market

1962

MARCH 18 The signing of the Evian Accords between France and the representatives of the Provisional Government of the Algerian Republic

APRIL 8 Referendum of the Evian Accords

JULY 3   The Proclamation of Independence for Algeria

OCTOBER   Cuban crisis

DECEMBER 21   Nassau Accords between Kennedy and Macmillan

JUNE 30   Common Market crisis

JULY 29   Franco-Algerian accord on hydrocarbons

DECEMBER 19   De Gaulle reelected to the presidency of the Republic

1963

JANUARY 14   De Gaulle refuses to agree to the Nassau Accords and rejects England's request to join the Common Market

JANUARY 22   The signing of the Franco-German Treaty of Cooperation

AUGUST 5   The signing of the Moscow Test Ban Treaty

1964

JANUARY 27   France recognizes China

APRIL 27   France takes new steps toward withdrawing troops from the NATO command

OCTOBER 16   China explodes its first A-bomb

1965

APRIL 8   The signing of a treaty in Brussels providing for the merger of the E.C.S.C., Euratom, and E.E.C. institutions

1966

FEBRUARY 1   Luxembourg accords ending the Common Market crisis

FEBRUARY 21   General de Gaulle's press conference in which he announced France's withdrawal from NATO

JUNE 20–29   De Gaulle's trip to Moscow

JULY 24   Conclusion of the accords on a common agricultural policy within the Common Market

DECEMBER   Kosygin's trip to Paris

1967

MAY 16   End of the Kennedy Round negotiations

JUNE 3–8   Six-day war between the Israelis and the Arabs

JUNE 17   China explodes its first H-bomb

JUNE 23–25   Johnson-Kosygin meeting in Glassboro

JULY 24–27   General de Gaulle's trip to Canada

SEPTEMBER 18 MacNamara announces the establishment of a thin A.B.M. network

NOVEMBER 18 Pound sterling is devalued

NOVEMBER 27 De Gaulle refuses to open negotiations for England's entry into the Common Market

1968

MARCH 17 United States witnesses the establishment of two different prices for gold

MARCH 31 Johnson announces the almost total cessation of bombing in North Vietnam

MAY Student revolt and general strike in France

JUNE 23–30 Legislative elections in France

JULY 1 Signing of the non-proliferation treaty

JULY 1 Implementation of the E.E.C.'s Customs Union

AUGUST 21 Russian troops invade Czechoslovaquia

NOVEMBER 20–22 Group of Ten monetary conference in Bonn

Biographical Notes on French Politicians

AURIOL, *Vincent*. 1884–1965. Socialist. Minister of Finance under the Third Republic. President of the Republic, 1947–54.

BIDAULT, *Georges*. 1899——. M.R.P. Minister of Foreign Affairs, 1944–48. Head of the Provisional Government, 1946. Premier, 1949–50. Minister of Foreign Affairs, 1953–54. Exiled from 1962 to 1968.

BLUM, *Léon*. 1872–1950. Socialist. Premier under the Third Republic. Premier, 1946–47.

BOURGÈS-MAUNOURY, *Maurice*. 1914——. Radical. Minister of Finance, 1952. Minister of National Defense, 1956–57. Premier, 1957.

CHABAN-DELMAS, *Jacques*. 1915——. R.P.F. Mayor of Bordeaux since 1947. Minister of National Defense, 1957–58. President of the National Assembly since 1958.

COTY, *René*. 1882–1962. Moderate. Senator. President of the Republic, 1954–58.

COUVE DE MURVILLE, *Maurice*. 1907——. Ambassador to the United States, 1955–56. Ambassador to the Federal Republic of Germany, 1956–58. Minister of Foreign Affairs 1958–68. Prime Minister, 1968.

DEBRÉ, *Michel*. 1912——. R.P.F. Senator, 1948–58. Leader of the Gaullist opposition in the Senate. Minister of Justice, 1958–59. Premier, 1959–62. Minister of Finance, 1966–68. Minister of Foreign Affairs, 1968.

DEFFERRE, *Gaston*. 1910——. Socialist. Mayor of Marseille, 1944–45 and since 1953. Minister of Overseas France, 1956–57.

FAURE, *Edgar*. 1908——. Radical. Premier, 1952. Minister of Finance, 1953–54. Minister of Agriculture, 1966–68. Minister of National Education, 1968.

FAURE, *Maurice*. 1922——. Radical. Secretary of State for Foreign Affairs, 1956–58.

GAILLARD, *Félix*. 1919——. Radical. Minister of Finance, 1957. Premier, 1957–58.

GOUIN, *Félix*. 1884———. Socialist. Head of the Provisional Government, 1946.

HERRIOT, *Edouard*. 1872–1957. Radical. Mayor of Lyon since 1905. Premier under the Third Republic. President of the National Assembly, 1946–51.

LANIEL, *Joseph*. 1889———. Moderate. Premier, 1953–54.

LECANUET, *Jean*. 1920———. M.R.P. Senator since 1959. National President of the M.R.P., 1963–65. Candidate for the President of the Republic, 1965. Mayor of Rouen, 1968.

LETOURNEAU, *Jean*. 1907———. M.R.P. Minister of Overseas France, 1949. Minister of State for the associated states in Indochina, 1950–53.

MAYER, *René*. 1895———. Radical. Premier, 1953. President of the High Authority of the European Coal and Steel Community, 1955–57.

MENDÈS-FRANCE, *Pierre*. 1907———. Radical. Minister of National Economy, 1944–45. Premier and Minister of Foreign Affairs, 1954–55. Minister of State, 1956.

MITTERRAND, *François*. 1916———. Socialist leanings. Minister several times between 1947 and 1957. Leader of the Left opposition since 1958. Candidate for the President of the Republic, 1965. President of the Federation of the Democratic and Socialist Left since 1965.

MOLLET, *Guy*. 1905———. Socialist. Mayor Arras of since 1945. Secretary-General of the Socialist Party (S.F.I.O.—Section Française de l'Internationale Ouvrière) since 1946. Premier, 1956–57.

MONNET, *Jean*. 1888———. Commissioner of the Plan for Modernization and Equipment, 1946–52. President of the High Authority of the European Coal and Steel Community, 1952–55. President of the Action Committee for a United States of Europe since 1955.

PFLIMLIN, *Pierre*. 1907———. M.R.P. Minister of Finance, 1957–58. Premier, 1958. Mayor of Strasbourg since 1959.

PINAY, *Antoine*. 1891———. Moderate. Premier and Minister of Finance, 1952. Minister of Foreign Affairs, 1955–56. Minister of Finance and Economic Affairs, 1958–60.

PLEVEN, *René*. 1901———. Socialist leanings. Minister of Finance, 1945. Premier, 1950–51. Minister of National Defense, 1952–54.

POMPIDOU, *Georges*. 1911———. Principal private secretary to de Gaulle, 1958–59. Premier, 1962–68.

POUJADE, *Pierre*. 1920———. Founder and President of the Union of Defense for Businessmen and Artisans.

QUEUILLE, *Henri*. 1884———. Radical. Several times a minister under the Third Republic. Premier, 1948–49, 1951.

RAMADIER, *Paul*. 1888–1961. Socialist. Premier, 1947. Minister of Finance, 1956–57.

REYNAUD, *Paul*. 1878–1966. Moderate. Premier under the Third Republic.

SCHUMAN, *Robert*. 1886–1963. M.R.P. Minister of Finance, 1947. Premier, 1947–48. Minister of Foreign Affairs, 1948–52.

SOUSTELLE, *Jacques*. 1912——. R.P.F. Governor-General of Algeria, 1955–56. Leader of the Gaullist opposition in the National Assembly, 1957–58. Minister of Information, 1958–59. Exiled since 1962.

Abbreviations

A.L.N.	National Army of Liberation
ANZUS	Treaty between Australia, New Zealand, and the United States
C.E.A.	Commissariat à l'Energie Atomique
C.C.E.	Committee of Coordination and Execution
CENTO	Central Treaty Organization of the Middle East
C.F.A.	Communauté Financière d'Afrique
C.F.P.	Compagnie Française des Pétroles
C.F.T.C.	Confédération Française des Travailleurs Chrétiens
C.G.T.	Confederation Générale du Travail
C.N.R.A.	Conseil National de la Révolution Algérienne
D.E.W.	Distant Early Warning
E.C.S.C.	European Coal and Steel Community
E.D.C.	European Defense Community
E.E.C.	European Economic Community
E.F.T.A.	European Free Trade Association
E.L.D.O.	European Launcher Development Organization
E.P.U.	European Payments Union
E.R.A.P.	Entreprise de Recherches et d'Activités Pétrolières
E.S.R.O.	European Space Research Organization
Euratom	European Atomic Energy Community
F.A.C.	Fund for Assistance and Cooperation
F.A.O.	Food and Agricultural Organization
F.L.N.	National Liberation Front
F.O.	Confédération Force Ouvrière
G.A.T.T.	General Agreement on Tariff and Trade
G.P.R.A.	Provisional Government of the Algerian Republic
I.C.B.M.	Intercontinental ballistic missile
I.R.B.M.	Intermediate-range ballistic missile

M.D.R.M.   Mouvement Démocrate de la Révolution Malgache
M.N.A.   Party of the Algerian People
M.R.P.   Mouvement Républicain Populaire
NADGE   NATO Air Defense Ground Environment
N.A.S.A.   National Aeronautic and Space Administration
NATO   North Atlantic Treaty Organization
O.A.S.   Organization of the Secret Army
O.C.A.M.   Organisation Commune Africaine et Malgache
O.E.C.D.   Organization for Economic Cooperation and Development
O.E.E.C.   Organization for European Economic Cooperation
P.F.A.   Parti de la Fédération Africaine
P.R.A.   Parti du Regroupement Africain
R.D.A.   Rassemblement Démocratique Africain
R.P.F.   Rassemblement du Peuple Français
SEATO   Southeast Asia Treaty Organization
S.F.I.O.   Section Française de l'Internationale Ouvrière
U.D.E.   Union Douanière Équatoriale
U.D.M.A.   Union Démocratique du Manifeste Algéréen
U.D.R.   Union pour la Défense de la République
U.N.R.   Union pour la Nouvelle République
W.E.U.   Western European Union

INDEX OF NAMES

499]

GENERAL INDEX

Action Committee for the United
    States of Europe, 94, 117, 381,
    384, 442, 462
Alaska, 247
Albania, 267, 348
Algeria
  cooperation with France, 232–36,
    238, 239, 240, 241, 242, 330, 333
  statute, 28, 130, 151–52, 162, 165, 169
  war in, 54, 55, 61, 62, 79, 124, 131,
    155–67, 169, 173, 195–216, 217,
    271, 400, 412, 464, 465, 468, 470,
    471, 474, 475, 481
  see also Integration; Sahara
Anzus, 120
Arab League, 149, 186, 230, 231
Armaments
  conventional, 30, 31, 54, 56, 62, 63,
    64, 252, 345, 352, 353
  strategic, 30, 31, 48, 63–64, 245–47,
    256–57, 285–86, 294, 341, 345,
    352, 354, 396
  see also Armaments; National
    deterrent force, French; Nuclear
    strategy
Atlantic Charter, 128
Atlantic Pact. See North Atlantic
    Treaty Organization

Australia, 23, 120, 269, 271, 393, 442
Austria, 16, 77, 357, 369, 373

Bagdad Pact. See CENTO
Ballistic missiles, 48, 50, 55, 62, 277,
    294, 341, 352, 362, 396, 454, 465,
    475. See also Armaments; Nuclear
    strategy
Bamako Congress, 154
Bandung Conference, 155
Baruch Plan, 21
Belgium, 74, 78, 81, 103, 106, 375–76,
    385–88, 444, 452
Benelux, 24, 45, 75, 85, 100, 117, 375,
    400
Berlin
  conference, 38, 42
  first crisis, 25, 29, 73
  second crisis, 259–62, 271, 281, 296,
    321, 351, 387, 402, 403, 475
  status, 21, 35, 58, 123, 326
  see also Germany, West
Bermuda Conference, 143, 144
Beyen Plan, 92
Black Africa. See French-Speaking
    Tropical Africa
Blocs, system of the, 22, 181, 185, 327,
    349, 473, 485